Manufacturing Strategy

Text and Cases

SECOND
EDITION
Manufacturing Strategy

Text and Cases

Terry Hill
London Business School

IRWIN

Burr Ridge, Illinois
Boston, Massachusetts
Sydney, Australia

To
PM, AJ, and JB

This symbol indicates that the paper in this book is made of recycled paper. Its fiber content exceeds the recommended minimum of 50% waste paper fibers as specified by the EPA.

Senior sponsoring editor: Richard T. Hercher, Jr.
Editorial assistant: Gail Centner
Project editor: Lynne Basler
Production manager: Ann Cassady
Art coordinator: Mark Malloy
Art studio: ElectraGraphics, Inc.
Compositor: BookMasters
Typeface: 10/12 Times Roman
Printer: R. R. Donnelley & Sons Company

Library of Congress Cataloging-in-Publication Data

Hill, Terry,
    Manufacturing strategy : text and cases / Terry Hill. — 2nd ed.
       p.   cm.
    Includes bibliographical references and index.
    ISBN 0-256-10666-5
    1. Production management. 2. Strategic planning. I. Title.
  TS155.H46 1993
  658.5—dc20   93–17064

Printed in the United States of America
  2 3 4 5 6 7 8 9 0 DOC 0 9 8 7 6 5 4

Preface

Currently in many industrial companies, strategic developments are predominantly based on corporate marketing decisions at the front end of the debate with manufacturing being forced to react to these at the back end of the process. Since manufacturing managers come late into these discussion, it is difficult for them to successfully influence corporate decisions. All too often, the result is the formulation and later development of strategies which manufacturing is unable to sucessfully support. That is not to say that this happens for lack of trying; the work ethic is strong in the manufacturing culture. However, if the basic link between the manufacturing processes and infrastructure (i.e., manufacturing strategy) and the market is not strategically sound, then—by definition—the business will suffer.

The many reasons why this happens are addressed in this book. Significant among them is that typically the attention of manufacturing managers primarily focuses upon the day-to-day part of their task. It concerns operations detail and is output-oriented, while in strategic terms their role is seen as being reactive.

The purpose of this book is to attempt to raise manufacturing managers' sights and to provide the necessary strategic perspective for the task in hand. It is intended to help them analyze and discuss issues, and to think strategically. Currently, the area of manufacturing strategy is short of concepts, ideas, and language. This further hampers manufacturing managers in sustaining strategic argument. The book goes some way toward correcting this position. It helps provide insights and evaluates manufacturing's corporate contribution through strategic perspectives, rather than just through operational performance. It not only helps manufacturing managers to develop and provide appropriate corporate level inputs, but also enables other executives to recognize and appreciate the strategic perspectives which emanate from manufacturing and which need to be given due consideration within the business debate.

The strategic perspective of manufacturing forms the basis on which the book is written, but the approach places these issues within the rightful context of the corporate whole. Thus, it recognizes that in today's world the majority of companies will be unable to sustain success over a long period of time if their strategy is based upon a single function's view of what is important. The book, therefore, emphasizes the essential requirement to link with those of marketing manufacturing perspectives and other functions in order to determine the best strategies for the business as a whole.

In summary, the book is written as an attempt to:

1. Close the gap between manufacturing and marketing in terms of corporate strategy formulation.

2. Provide a set of principles and concepts which are pragmatic in nature and designed to be applied to each different part of a business.

3. Offer an analytical approach to the development of manufacturing strategy rather than advocate a set of prescriptive solutions. Each business and each part of each business is different. The resolution of strategy through prescription, therefore, is by definition inappropriate. Furthermore, the complexity in manufacturing is such that it encourages companies to take strategic shortcuts. As a consequence, prescriptive approaches seem attractive. The book argues strongly against such approaches. In suggesting a means of developing a manufacturing strategy and raising essential issues throughout, it provides a way of coping with this complexity. The principles and concepts outlined provide a basis for placing operational detail in an essential strategic framework.

Outlined in the book is a basic approach to developing a manufacturing strategy which has been used successfully in many companies throughout the world. It provides a logical, practical, and effective way for manufacturing to interface with marketing in formulating corporate strategy. In so doing, it ensures that the "front-end" debate concerns not just the outward-looking stance of marketing, but the outward-looking stance of the business as a whole. This thereby reduces the number of situations in which marketing-led strategies may be adopted which—in overall terms—will be harmful to the business. It does this by emphasizing the consequences for the total business of different decisions—a technique which is a prerequisite for developing sound strategic direction.

Many executives shy away from discussions of manufacturing because they see it as an area of minute detail. This is because, traditionally, manufacturing is presented in this form. The approach in this book is to group together relevant operational detail into key strategic issues, and to provide an understanding of how these can be applied in companies. The development of a strategic language also provides the opportunity of moving away from what often constitutes current practice—a discussion of operational problems. This is not only an inappropriate manufacturing contribution at the executive level, but also has the effect of dulling the interest of other functions in examining the manufacturing issues involved. Strategic language, on the other hand, helps to orient and maintain the debate at the appropriate level. It stimulates executive interest and enables others to address the complexity by creating a manageable number of manufacturing variables.

The book comprises eleven chapters. Chapter One sets the scene by drawing some important international comparisons at national, industry, and plant levels. The figures embody a growing awareness of the fact that those countries which clearly emphasize the importance of manufacturing's contribution to business success have consistently outperformed other developed countries with a sound industrial tradition.

The core of the book is in the nine central chapters. The headings highlight some key developments within manufacturing strategy. Together they form the substance of the language development as well as the methodologies to be used in its formulation. Chapters Two, Three and Four provide the context and content on the approach to be adopted when developing a manufacturing strategy and details what needs to be undertaken at each step. It includes some illustrations to help with this explanation. Chapter Five deals exclusively with the choice of manufacturing process, the basis for that choice, and the business implications which follow. Chapter Six introduces the concept of product profiling which provides companies with a methodology for testing the current or anticipated future level of fit between the characteristics of their markets and those of their manufacturing processes and infrastructure. Chapters Seven and Eight deal with the concept of focus and the need to assign plants or parts of a plant to a defined set of tasks. The latter provides a detailed methodology statement on how to undertake this development. Chapter Nine is concerned with examining the implications behind make or buy decisions. Companies need to address this strategic one as to where they should position themselves on the process spectrum. Although at first sight these last three chapters appear to concern solely manufacturing process decisions, it is important to recognize that they are also a critical part of infrastructure formulation, since the size and shape of plants are significant factors in what constitutes an appropriate infrastructure, the subject of Chapter Ten. This chapter introduces some important concepts as a way of providing a business with the insights necessary to formulate developments in the wide range of functions within manufacturing. This approach therefore will enable these important, expensive, and time-consuming tasks to be designed in order to support the requirements of a business. It will enable them to be given strategic shape and direction rather than emanating from specialized perspectives.

The final chapter concerns the area of accounting and finance, which is important because it provides some of the essential basic data used in the formulation of strategic decisions. As with Chapter Ten, it is not intended to be a comprehensive statement of the area, but only to represent some production management views of serious shortcomings in this essential information provision. The professional accountant may find the approach provocation; it is intended, however, to be more constructive than that. The issues raised aim to challenge current practice and ideas as a way to stimulate improvement.

Finally, I trust that all who use the book will find it helpful. It is vital that manufacturing take its full part in strategic formulation if industrial companies are to prosper in the face of world competition.

Terry Hill

Acknowledgments

My thanks to the following reviewers who provided valuable advice and commentary on the First Edition. I hope they will be pleased with the Second:

Albert Trostel of University of Saint Thomas
William Newman of Miami University/Ohio
James Danek of California State University/Sacramento
Byron Finch of Miami University/Ohio

I would also like to thank Jay Klompmaker (University of North Carolina) and Bill Morrissey (North Carolina State) for their contribution to research and co-authorship of several important new case studies. Finally, my thanks to Bill Berry who has encouraged and contributed in so many ways. Through his efforts the Faculty Programs have now become an annual event from the early days at Iowa through to this year's program at Ohio State.

Contents

10   Manufacturing Infrastructure Development   185

11   Accounting and Financial Perspectives and Manufacturing Strategy   221

International Comparisons

A new stark reality emerged in the 1980s—the impact of industrial competition. In most industrial nations, the struggle to survive had become, by then, an integral part of each giant company's way of life. To downsize, once anathema to business, had become an acceptable course of action, demanded by necessity or some comprehensive corporate strategic decision. The economic world of the 1980s was very different from that of the 1960s and 1970s. The 1990s are continuing the trend but increasing the pace.

For the most part, however, production decision making in manufacturing industries has not changed to meet these new challenges. In most Western companies, manufacturing management is still subordinate in strategy making to the marketing and finance functions. It continues to concern itself primarily with short-term issues. The argument of this book is that a strategic approach to manufacturing management is essential if companies are going to be able to survive, let alone hold their own or grow by competing effectively in domestic and world markets.

This chapter provides some national and corporate comparisons. It shows how some nations with strong industrial traditions have been outperformed, illustrates the extent of the changes that have taken place, and compares different approaches to the management of manufacturing. The final section focuses on manufacturing strategy, not only to link this chapter to the remainder of the book but also to highlight the increasing awareness of manufacturing as a strategic force at both national and corporate levels.

Manufacturing Output

Trends in a nation's performance within its wealth-creating sectors reflect on its overall prosperity. Since manufacturing is for most countries the most significant activity in this regard, reviewing it provides an insight into a country's general well-being.

TABLE 1-1   **Comparative Manufacturing Output, 1975–1991**
(1975 = 100)

Country	1978	1980	1985	1990	1991
Australia	103	111	110	125	119
Canada	113	114	129	135	128
France	114	118	115	130	128
Germany	113	119	123	142	146
Italy	116	129	126	143	140
Japan	123	143	165	191	193
United Kingdom	103	95	99	112	111
United States	126	126	143	163	160

SOURCE: OECD, *Indicators of Industrial Activity,* 1979, 1985, 1988, and 1992 (3).

Comparative figures on manufacturing output in the 1970s and 1980s reveal the mixed fortunes of major industrial nations. Some countries of manufacturing repute have lost ground particularly in the 1970s, while others (for example, Japan, the United States, and Germany) have maintained sound growth throughout (see Table 1–1).

However, of equal concern to these nations is how well they fared within the increasingly competitive markets they serve. Table 1–2 shows the percentage share gained by selected countries of the export sales of manufactured goods from 1969 to 1980 and from 1980 to 1992, as well as over the whole period. The yearly performances of the different countries vary noticeably, particularly at the extremes. On the whole, though, it reinforces the main message of Table 1–1. Japan again demonstrated its improvement in the manufacturing sector, showing by far the largest improvement in the period reviewed. Germany's strong export position remained fairly constant throughout. The declines in the United Kingdom and United States (the countries that respectively preceded Japan as the world's number-one manufacturing nation) are very marked. And, in between, the steady improvement by a number of West European countries sets an important benchmark.

To complete this initial review, export-import trade ratios are given in Table 1–3 to provide an insight into relative trading performances of main manufacturing nations. Table 1–4 shows the trade balance in 1990 for electronic products for the United States, Canada, and selected Asian countries, some of which are emerging as part of the new wave of competition.

For the United States in particular the overall manufacturing position is worrying. The country has been a net importer of manufactured goods since the late 1960s, although it has shown improvement between the mid-1980s and early 1990s. Most West European countries (with the exception of the United Kingdom) have maintained favorable ratios throughout the 1970s and 1980s, but in all instances the trend has shown a worsening position. Throughout, Japan has maintained a sizable lead, even though it was significantly lower in 1990 than in previous years.

TABLE 1-2   Selected Countries' Exports of Manufactured Goods (percentage share)*

Year	Canada[†]	France	Germany	Italy	Japan	United Kingdom	United States
1969	—	8.2	19.1	7.3	11.2	11.2	19.2
1975	4.3	10.2	20.3	7.4	13.6	9.1	17.7
1980	4.0	10.0	19.9	7.9	14.9	9.7	17.0
1985	6.2	8.5	18.6	7.8	19.7	7.8	16.8
1988	5.1	9.0	19.5	8.2	18.3	8.4	15.3
1989	4.9	8.8	20.4	8.4	17.5	8.2	16.1
1990	4.5	9.7	20.5	8.6	15.8	8.6	15.8
1991	4.4	9.6	19.6	8.4	16.9	8.5	17.0
1992[‡]	4.4	9.7	19.4	8.6	17.4	8.2	17.0
+ (−) % Change,							
1969–80	(7)	22	4	8	33	(13)	(11)
1980–92	10	(3)	(3)	9	17	(15)	—
1969–92	2	18	2	18	55	(27)	(14)

*— = not available.

[†]The 1969 comparisons for Canada are based on 1975 figures.

[‡]1992 figures are based on the fourth quarter of the year.

SOURCE: Central Statistical Office, *Monthly Review of External Trade Statistics* 14 (November 1976); 96 (December 1983); and 201 (October 1992).

TABLE 1-3   Export/Import Ratio for Selected Sectors (1984 and 1990) and Total Manufacturing (1972, 1984, and 1990)*

Country	Aerospace		Electrical/ Electronic Industry		Office Machinery and Computers		Drugs		Total Manufacturing		
	1984	1990	1984	1990	1984	1990	1984	1990	1972	1984	1990
Australia	0.11	0.07	0.07	0.12	0.04	0.09	0.34	0.25	—	0.54	0.46
Canada	0.65	1.25	0.47	0.46	0.40	0.46	0.34	0.25	—	1.01	0.94
France	2.21	1.43	1.12	0.91	0.69	0.59	1.93	1.39	1.10	1.11	0.94
Germany	1.05	0.87	1.45	1.25	0.87	0.66	1.74	1.61	1.53	1.42	1.30
Italy	1.09	1.15	1.19	0.86	0.74	0.82	0.97	0.55	1.31	1.24	1.10
Japan	0.10	0.15	10.55	5.62	5.61	3.96	0.27	0.32	2.82	2.78	1.88
United Kingdom	1.43	1.14	0.73	0.83	0.73	0.84	2.14	1.94	1.09	0.81	0.83
United States	2.98	3.26	0.52	0.69	1.83	0.95	1.70	1.56	0.84	0.63	0.75

*— = not available.

SOURCE: OECD, *Main Science and Technology Indicators,* 1974, 1984, and 1992 (3).

TABLE 1–4   Trade Balance in 1985 and 1992 for Electronic Equipment and Components for Selected Countries ($ millions)*

Country	1985	1992
Australia	(2.6)	(4.3)
Canada	(6.7)	(6.4)
Hong Kong	1.3	2.9
Japan	37.1	60.6
Malaysia	0.7	4.0
Singapore	1.1	7.1
South Korea	2.0	9.0
United States	(14.5)	(19.5)

*Electronic equipment includes electronic data processing, office equipment, controls and instruments, medical, industrial, military, communications, consumer, and telecommunications. Components comprise active, passive, and other.
[†]The trade balance is calculated by subtracting the value of imports from the value of exports. Figures in brackets indicate an unfavorable balance.
Source: 1988 and 1992 *Yearbook of World Electronic Data* (Elseveir, England).

Table 1–4 highlights one of the more recent and important sectors of manufacturing, that of electronics. It shows that some of the emerging industrial nations are effectively competing in export markets with small but improving trade balances in this important sector. The United States, meanwhile, again shows a worsening picture in terms of its competitive position in world markets.

The United States' decline in world industrial markets is there for all to see—loss of market share abroad, increased imports at home. U.S. industry has performed badly for a long time, whatever measure is used.

Against this background of decline, it is interesting to note that successive U.S. administrations have tended to act on the sometimes painful premise that exposure to overseas competition is a necessary ingredient for the development of a strong, domestic manufacturing base. Of deep concern, however, is that manufacturing industry's response to that exposure has been woefully slow. Many firms have complained about "unfair" external competition and focused on domestic rather than overseas competitors. They have adopted inadequate, reactive strategies because they have not appreciated the consequences for manufacturing. Typically, they have filled capacity by chasing orders, increasing variety, and reducing batch sizes, leaving overseas competitors with substantial advantages in the higher-volume segments of their markets. One outcome has been the loss of high-volume markets such as motorcycles, automobiles, trucks, and shipbuilding: the nations that are prospering have often built their wealth base in these sectors.

Many business have failed to recognize, until too late, that the sellers' markets of the 1950s and 1960s have long since passed. They typically became entangled in the period of transition during the 1970s and 1980s. Businesses must now require new strategies that aim to gain and maintain some specific and significant advantages against the most, not the least, powerful competitors.

While the United States in particular was being buffeted by this new competitive surge, some countries seemed to have moved from strength to strength. Of deeper concern still for the United States, the United Kingdom, and other nations with long manufacturing traditions are the facts underlying these trends, especially that of comparative productivity.

Productivity: National Comparisons

A nation's prosperity depends on its comparative productivity. The past two decades of increasing competition have brought this sharply into focus. Although not a precise measure, it affords a way of assessing trends both for the performance of individual countries and their relative positions in appropriate world rankings.

Thus, there are two important dimensions of a productivity slowdown for any nation. The first is the rate of the slowdown itself; the second is the cumulative effect of the slowdown on the comparative level of productivity between a country and its competitors.

When a nation's growth rate lags substantially behind that of other industrialized countries for a protracted period, its standard of living will decline and companies will find themselves at a serious competitive disadvantage. If this condition goes unchecked, recovery will be increasingly difficult to achieve and breaking free from the downward spiral will be a major task. For the first time in its history, the United States is facing the real prospect that its next generation will fail to enjoy a marked improvement in living standards compared with today and may even experience a decline.

Productivity measures the relationship between outputs (in the form of goods and services produced) and inputs (in the form of labor, capital, material, and other resources). Although in practice productivity is not so simple to measure because of the global nature of the figures involved, it does provide an overall review of improvement that lends itself to trend analysis. Two types of productivity measurement are commonly used: labor productivity and total-factor or multifactor productivity. Labor productivity measures output in terms of hours worked or paid for. Total-factor or multifactor productivity not only includes the labor input but also all or some of the plant, equipment, energy, and materials. However, when there is a change in a single-factor productivity ratio, it is important not to attribute the change solely to that one input. Owing to the interrelated nature of the total inputs involved, the change may well be influenced by any or all of the many variables that could contribute to the change. For example, production methods, capital investment, process technology, labor force, managerial performance, capacity utilization, material input/usage rates, capacity scale, and product mix are all potential contributors to productivity

TABLE 1-5   Trends in Output per Hour in Manufacturing for Selected Countries, 1950–1991 (1982 = 100)

Country	1950	1960	1970	1980	1985	1987	1989	1990	1991
Canada	36	52	77	100	120	119	119	120	122
France	20	31	59	91	109	113	128	129	129
Germany*	18	39	67	98	113	112	119	123	125
Italy	17	29	55	96	122	127	135	141	145
Japan	8	19	52	92	112	120	135	144	147
United Kingdom	40	49	71	90	118	130	144	146	150
United States	49	60	79	94	108	117	123	126	128

*Data for Germany relate to the former West Germany.
SOURCE: U.S. Department of Labor, Bureau of Labor Statistics, June 1988 and December 1992.

TABLE 1-6   Output per Worker for Selected Countries 1950–1987 ($ thousands)*

Country	1950	1970	1987	Index 1987 (1970 = 100)
Germany	8.0	21.4	31.6	148
Japan	3.5	15.8	27.6	175
South Korea	—	5.6	13.3	238
United States	23.3	34.5	39.2	114

*Figures are in 1987 dollars. — = not available.
SOURCE: *The Wall Street Journal* (May 1, 1989), p. A1.

improvements. Furthermore, the relative importance of these will vary from nation to nation, industrial sector to industrial sector, company to company, plant to plant, and time period to time period.

Although it may be difficult to get a consensus on the quantitative dimensions of productivity measurement, the qualitative conclusions on the differing levels and trends within nations are clearly shown in Table 1–5. It signals the steady, often significant, growth of some nations throughout the period, a fact reflected in the earlier data on performance.

Table 1–6 shows the slowdown in the U.S. position compared to major competitors, including South Korea, one of the many emerging nations. The U.S. lead is shrinking principally because of the weaker performance of its manufacturing sector. The result is a leveling-off in living standards and a decline in its competitive position.

Productivity: Plant-Level Comparison

In the 1990s, the level of competition in major regions (e.g., North America, Southeast Asia, and Europe) will increase noticeably in many markets. Setting aside argu-

TABLE 1-7   **High-Volume Auto Assembly Plant Productivity, 1989**

	Hours per Vehicle			
Parent Location/Plant Location*	*Best*	*Weighted Average*	*Worst*	*Sample Size*
Japanese-owned plants in Japan	13.2	16.8	25.9	8
Japanese-owned plants in North America	18.8	20.9	25.5	5
U.S.-owned plants in North America	18.6	24.9	30.7	14
U.S.- and Japanese-owned plants in Europe	22.8	35.3	57.6	9
European-owned plants in Europe	22.8	35.5	56.7	13
Plants in newly industrializing countries[†]	25.7	41.0	78.7	11

*The sample includes Chrysler, Ford, and General Motors for the United States; Fiat, PSA, Renault, and Volkswagen for Europe.

[†]These countries include Brazil, Korea, Mexico, and Taiwan.

SOURCE: International Motor Vehicle Program, Massachusetts Institute of Science and Technology (MIT).

ments concerning trade practices, comparative productivity will determine which companies will gain ground and market share.

The auto industry, a core-sector in many countries given the combined size of its assembly activity and supply-chain requirements, is one area in which fierce fighting will take place. With the production capacity available to the top ten auto and truck makers exceeding market sales forecasts, companies will be forced to slim down in search of higher efficiency to compete against new rivals and fresh benchmarks. Tables 1–7 and 1–8 illustrate the task that lies ahead. Of this you can be sure, productivity will be one key factor in the comparative success of companies, and hence nations.

Why Has This Happened?

The reasons why this has happened are many and varied. Some are unsubstantiated opinions, others are supported by fact. Some will be more relevant to some nations, sectors, and companies, and others, less. However, learning from past failures is a step toward determining how to build a more successful competitive future.

Failure to Recognize the Size of the Competitive Challenge

Consciously or otherwise, industry and society at large have failed to recognize the size of the competitive challenge, the impact it was having and would have on our very way of life, and the need to change.

The significant loss of market share in smokestack industries by major industrial nations since 1950 is the most vivid example of those nations' misunderstanding of the size of the competitive challenge. And, the challenge will continue. In the shadow of Japan, there are now many other competitors eager to take a larger share in world manufacturing output. Table 1–9 provides one such example.

TABLE 1–8   **Plant Performance Comparisons, 1987**

Factors	General Motors, Framingham	Toyota, Takaoka	Nummi, Fremont*
Assembly hours per auto	31	16	19
Assembly defects per 100 autos	135	45	45
Assembly space per auto	8.1	4.8	7.0
Average inventory of parts	2 weeks	2 hours	2 days

*Nummi = New United Motor Manufacturing, Inc. It is a joint venture between General Motors and Toyota.
SOURCE: International Motor Vehicle Program, MIT.

TABLE 1–9   **Production of Machine Tools without Parts and Accessories for Selected Countries (Swiss frs millions)**

Country	1985	1988	1990	1990 (1985 = 100)
Belgium	229	303	395	172
Denmark	102	92	118	116
France	1,225	1,157	1,621	132
Germany	7,755	9,614	12,110	156
Italy	2,729	4,086	5,137	188
Japan	13,038	12,706	15,206	117
Korea	439	924	1,186	270
Netherlands	92	97	194	211
Spain	617	1,027	1,410	229
Taiwan	676	1,125	1,307	193
United States	6,465	3,861	4,688	73
United Kingdom	1,780	2,035	2,077	117

SOURCE: CECIMO, *Statistical Overview of the Machine Tool Industry within CECIMO's Countries, 1985– 1990* (1991).

Failure to Appreciate the Impact of Increasing Manufacturing Capacity

World manufacturing capacity up to the mid-1960s was, by and large, less than demand; in this period companies could sell all they could make. With the rebuilding of some industrial nations and the emergence of others, output in both traditional and new industrial nations began to outstrip total demand. The most significant and consistent outcome has been the impact on competition. Overcapacity has contributed to the competitive nature of markets. The results have added to the dynamic nature of

TABLE 1–10 **Gross Domestic Expenditure on R&D as a Percentage of Gross Domestic Product (GDP)**

Country	1981	1985	1989	1990	1991
Australia*	—	1.27	1.23	—	—
Canada	1.23	1.44	1.35	1.38	1.43
France	2.01	2.25	2.34	2.40	—
Germany	2.45	2.72	2.88	2.81	—
Italy	1.01	1.13	1.24	1.35	1.35
Japan	2.32	2.77	2.98	3.07	—
United Kingdom	2.42	2.31	2.27	—	—
United States	2.45	2.93	2.82	2.79	2.75

*1985 and 1989 figures for Australia are for 1986 and 1988 respectively. — = not available.
SOURCE: *OECD, Main Science and Technology Indicators*, 1981–89 and 1991 (2).

current markets both in terms of the form that competition takes and the time scales of change experienced.

Willingness to Invest in Research and Development (R&D)

The pressure to market more and better products has heightened in recent years because of increasing competition and shorter product life cycles. One significant factor to help achieve that is the relative size and trend in research and development investments. Table 1–10 reflects the clear commitment of major manufacturing nations to continue to increase their R&D expenditures. The United States and the United Kingdom, although investing at a level higher than most of the major industrial countries, were the only ones to noticeably reduce the percentage of gross domestic product spent on R&D since the mid-1980s. By 1989, Japan headed the list for the first time.

The final perspective on issues of R&D expenditure is provided by Table 1–11. Many countries with the committed R&D levels of spending shown in Table 1–10 top this up by importing technology at a rate higher than that at which they sell. The United States is the notable exception.

Top Management's Lack of Manufacturing Experience

Top management's lack of experience in manufacturing has further ramifications for a business. Since manufacturing accounts for some 70–80 percent of assets, expenditure, and people, senior executives must fully appreciate all arguments and counterarguments in manufacturing, ensuring that they consider the accompanying wide range of perspectives when making important manufacturing decisions. Once a company has made large investments, rarely does it invest a second time to correct a mistake. There is no such lack of experience in Japan and Germany, where a full and perceptive insight into manufacturing is a prerequisite for top management.

However, the consequences of this knowledge gap do not stop here. As Wickham Skinner observes:

TABLE 1-11   **Technology Balance of Payments (Coverage ratio)***

Country	1984	1985	1986	1987	1988	1989	1990
Australia	0.22	—	0.37	—	—	—	—
Canada	0.85	0.73	0.75	0.98	1.04	0.93	—
France	0.90	0.84	0.83	0.78	0.80	0.83	—
Germany	0.77	0.71	0.82	0.83	0.83	0.78	0.81
Italy	0.29	0.26	0.31	0.38	0.54	0.50	0.58
Japan	0.99	0.80	0.86	0.76	0.79	1.00	0.91
United Kingdom	1.05	1.13	0.95	0.92	0.92	0.96	—
United States	5.52	6.73	6.83	6.65	5.29	5.26	5.78

*Figures greater than 1 show receipts greater than payments. — = not available.
SOURCE: OECD, *Main Science and Technology Indicators*, 1981–87 and 1992 (1).

to many executives, manufacturing and the production function is a necessary nuisance—it soaks up capital in facilities and inventories, it resists changes in products and schedules, its quality is never as good as it should be, and its people are unsophisticated, tedious, detail-oriented, and unexciting. This makes for an unreceptive climate for major innovations in factory technology and contributes to the blind spot syndrome.[1]

And this brings with it many important consequences. One is that senior executives do not perceive the strategic potential of manufacturing. Typically it is seen in its traditional productivity-efficiency mode with the added need to respond to the strategic overtures of marketing and finance. The result is that manufacturing concentrates its effort and attention on the short-term while adopting its classic, reactive posture toward the long-term strategic issues of the business.

The Production Manager's Obsession with Short-Term Performance Issues

Typically, the production manager has, in turn, emphasized short-term issues and tasks. The overriding pressures to meet day-to-day targets and the highly quantifiable nature of the role have led manufacturing executives to focus on the short-term rather than the important long-term issues. Production managers are highly skilled in such short-term tasks as scheduling, maintaining efficiency levels, controls, delivery, and quality, and resolving labor problems.

Skinner rightly believes that:

most factories were not managed very differently in the 1970s than in the 1940s and 1950s. Manufacturing management was dominated by engineering and a technical point of view. This may have been adequate when *production* management issues centered largely on efficiency and productivity and the answers came from industrial engineering and process

---

[1]W. Skinner, "Operations Technology: Blind Spot in Strategic Management," Harvard Business School working paper 83–85 (1983), p. 11.

engineering. But the problems of operations managers in the 1970s had moved far beyond mere physical efficiency.[2]

This trend has continued in line with the fast-changing nature of markets. By the 1990s, the production job has changed from one that concerns maintaining steady-state manufacturing by sound day-to-day husbandry to one that is multidimensional. It is now increasingly concerned with managing greater complexity in product range, product mix, volume changes, process flexibility, inventory, cost and financial controls, and employee awareness because of the more intensive level of domestic and international competition.

This is the nature of the new task. No longer are the key issues solely confined to operational control and fine-tuning the system. The need is for broad, business-oriented manufacturing managers, but companies have produced too few of them. The use of specialists as the way to control our businesses has increasingly led to a reduction in the breadth of a line manager's responsibilities, which has narrowed the experience base. Furthermore, many manufacturing managers, outgunned by specialist argument, have found themselves unable to cope with the variety of demands placed on them. The response by many has been to revert increasingly to their strengths. This has, therefore, reinforced their short-term role and their inherently reactive stance to corporate strategic resolution.

Manufacturing executives do not, on the whole, explain the important, conceptual aspects of manufacturing to others in the organization. Seldom do they evaluate and expose the implications for manufacturing of corporate decisions so that alternatives can be considered and more soundly based decisions can be reached. This is partly because of a lack of developed language to help explain the corporate production issues involved. Lacking, therefore, in strategic dimension, manufacturing has often been forced into piecemeal change, achieving what it can as and when it has been able. The result has been a series of intermittent responses lacking corporate coordination.

Manufacturing Strategy

In the past decade and a half, countries such as Japan, Germany, and Italy, as well as emerging industrial nations such as Korea and Taiwan, have gained the competitive advantage through manufacturing. The Japanese, in particular, have gone for existing markets and provided better goods with few, if any, inherent benefits derived from material and energy resources. The earlier examples serve to illustrate this.

One of the keys to this achievement through manufacturing has been the integration of these functional perspectives into corporate strategy debate; and it is appropriate now to explain what this embodies and how it differs from the conventional approaches to the management of production. In broad terms, there are two important ways in which manufacturing can strengthen a company.

---

[2]W. Skinner, "Operations Technology," p. 6. These views are also confirmed by the author in his book entitled *Production/Operations Management* (Englewood Cliffs, N.J.: Prentice Hall, 1991) pp. 184–87.

The first is to provide manufacturing processes that give the business a distinct advantage in the marketplace. In this way, manufacturing will provide a marketing edge through unique technological developments in its process and manufacturing operations that competitors are unable to match. This is quite rare and examples are hard to find. One such is Pilkington's float-glass process.*

The second is to provide coordinated manufacturing support for the essential ways in which products win orders in the marketplace that is better than such support provided by the manufacturing functions of its competitors. Manufacturing must choose its process and design its infrastructure (for example, controls, procedures, systems, and structures) in ways that help products win orders, and that choice and design must be adaptable to changing business needs. Most companies share access to the same processes, and thus technology is not inherently different. Similarly, the systems, structures, and other elements of infrastructure are universal. What is different is the degree to which manufacturing matches process and infrastructure to those criteria that win orders. In this way, manufacturing constitutes a coordinated response to the business needs that embraces all those aspects of a company for which manufacturing is responsible.

To do this effectively, manufacturing needs to be involved throughout the whole of the corporate strategy debate to explain, in business terms, the implications of corporate marketing proposals and, as a result, be able to influence strategy decisions for the good of the business as a whole. Too often in the past, manufacturing has been too late in this procedure. Corporate executives have tended to assume that competitive strategies are more to do with, and often in fact are one and the same as, marketing initiatives. Implicit, if not explicit, in this view are two important assumptions. The first is that manufacturing's role is to respond to these changes rather than to make inputs into them. The second is that manufacturing has the capability to respond flexibly and positively to these changing demands. The result has been manufacturing's inability to influence decisions, which has led to its seemingly endless complaints about the unrealistic demands placed upon production.

A business must develop a manufacturing strategy not only because of the critical nature of manufacturing within corporate strategy but also because many of the decisions are structural in nature. This means that they are hard to change. If the business does not fully appreciate the issues and consequences, it can be locked into a number of manufacturing decisions that will take years to change. These can range from process investments on the one hand to human resource management practices and controls on the other. Decisions not in line with the needs of the business can contribute significantly to a lack of corporate success. To change them is costly and time-consuming. But even more significant, they will come too late. The development of a corporate policy consisting of a coordinated set of main function inputs will mean that a business would be able to go in one consistent, coherent direction based on a

---

*The development of the float-glass process in the 1950s by Pilkington, a U.K. glass manufacturer, was a remarkable step forward in the technology of float-glass making. The costly grinding and polishing operations in the conventional manufacture of glass were eliminated and the result was plate glass production at a fraction of the cost.

well-argued, well-understood, and well-formed strategy. This is achieved, in part, by moving away from argument, disagreement, misunderstanding, and short-term, parochial moves based on interfunctional perspectives, to the resolution of these differences at the corporate level. Currently, marketing-led strategies leave the aftermath to be resolved by manufacturing, who without adequate, appropriate guidance or discussion and agreement at the corporate level, resolve the issues as best they can largely from their unilateral view of what is best for the business as a whole.

In the majority of cases, manufacturing is simply not geared to a business's corporate objectives. The result is a manufacturing system, good in itself, but not designed to meet company needs. Manufacturing left in the wake of corporate decisions is often at best a neutral force, and even sometimes inadvertently pulls in the opposite direction. Seen as being concerned solely with efficiency, the question of production's strategic contribution is seldom part of the corporate consciousness.

What does all this mean for production managers? One clear consequence is the need to change from a reactive to a proactive stance. The long-term inflexible nature of manufacturing means that the key issues, and there are many of them, involved in process choice and infrastructure development need to be reflected in business decisions, with the business being made aware of the implications for manufacturing of proposed corporate changes. When this is achieved, the strategy decisions that are then taken reflect what is best for the business as a whole. So manufacturing management's attention must increasingly be toward strategy. This does not mean that operations are unimportant. But management must appreciate the impact on business performance of strategy and operations while recognizing that both need to be done well. Top management have, by and large, perceived corporate improvements as coming mainly through broad decisions concerning new markets, takeovers, and the like. However, the building blocks of corporate success are to be found in creating effective, successful businesses where manufacturing supports the market requirements within a well-chosen, well-argued, and well-understood corporate strategy.

Conclusion

The emphasis in successfully managed manufacturing functions is increasingly toward issues of strategy. And there is evidence of a growing and consistent awareness of this fact. For example, the Advisory Council for Applied Research and Development, in its 1983 booklet, *New Opportunities in Manufacturing: The Management of Technology,* specifically recommended that "companies in manufacturing should review the balance of their senior management and ensure that the role of a suitably qualified board member includes responsibility for manufacturing strategy."[3] And a 1990 survey on manufacturing in Europe, Japan, and North America, trying to determine which were

---

[3]Advisory Council for Applied Research and Development, *New Opportunities in Manufacturing: The Management of Technology* (London: HMSO Cabinet Office, October 1983) p. 48.

TABLE 1–12   *Manufacturing Futures Survey, 1990:*
Responses to the Questions Asking for
"the Most Important Improvements in
the Next Two Years"

Country/Region	Rating for the Answer "Linking Manufacturing Strategy to Business Strategy"*
Europe	1
Japan	5
USA	1

*A rating of 1 indicates the highest priority.

the "most important improvement programs in the next two years," showed a high rating for manufacturing strategy across the board (see Table 1–12).[4]

Top management needs to pay a great deal more than lip service to the task of ensuring that manufacturing's input into the strategic debate is comprehensive and that the agreed corporate decisions fully reflect the complex issues involved. Much determination will need to be exercised to ensure that the more superficial approaches to incorporating the wide-ranging aspects of manufacturing into corporate decisions are avoided. The rewards for this are substantial.

Manufacturing executives must begin to think and act in a more strategic manner. In an environment traditionally geared to meeting output targets, the pressure on manufacturing has been to manage reactively and to be operationally efficient rather than strategically effective. It has been more concerned with doing things right (efficiency) than doing the right things (effectiveness). Over the years, this has been seen as the appropriate manufacturing task and contribution. Furthermore, it has given rise to the related assumption that any other posture would imply negative attitudes, with manufacturing appearing to be putting obstacles in the way of achieving key corporate objectives. At times, this puts manufacturing in the vicious circle of corporate demands on manufacturing, manufacturing's best response, a recriminating corporate appraisal of that response, new corporate demands for improved manufacturing performance, and so on. The purpose of this book is to help to avoid the all-too-common corporate approach to manufacturing by providing a set of concepts and approaches that together create a platform from which manufacturing can make a positive contribution to developing powerful competitive strategies. But, manufacturing executives must first accept that they need to manage their own activities strategically, and this is almost as much a change in management attitude as it is an analytical process.

The purpose of thinking and managing strategically is not just to improve operational performance or to defend market share. It is to gain competitive advantage, and it implies an attempt to mobilize manufacturing capability to help to gain this competi-

---

[4]*Manufacturing Futures Survey* (1990), INSEAD, Fontainebleau, France.

tive edge. Kenichi Ohmae, a leading Japanese consultant with McKinsey,[5] suggests that when managers are striving to achieve or maintain a position of relative superiority over competitors, their minds work very differently from when the objective is to make operational improvements against often arbitrarily set, internal objectives.

This chapter has highlighted manufacturing's tendency to emphasize operational efficiency more than competitive advantage. The danger for the business is that manufacturing gets so used to absorbing and responding to demands that reacting becomes the norm. Each crisis is viewed as a temporary situation, which often militates against recognizing the need to review strategies fundamentally. By the time this need becomes obvious, the business is often at a serious competitive disadvantage.

The aims of this book are to help manufacturing reverse its reactive tendencies and change its short-term perspectives; that is, to explain manufacturing from a strategic perspective by identifying the managerial and corporate issues that need to be addressed to establish competitive advantage.

Many traditional manufacturing nations have the capability to turn domestic manufacturing around and to challenge and beat overseas competition in both home and world markets. There are already examples of that turnaround in competitive performance; but the key ingredients include tough, professional management, combining strategic analysis of key issues with the intuitive, creative flair that for so long has been directed primarily toward solving operational problems.

It is imperative that manufacturing managers take the initiative. For some organizations or functions within a business, the *status quo* even suits them. In those same organizations, manufacturing is played off against a forever-changing set of objectives and targets, and it hurts. If manufacturing waits for other corporate initiatives they will not come soon enough. The lack of empathy and understanding by top management toward manufacturing often means that when difficulties arise, the preferred course of action is to get rid of the problem by selling off the business to outsiders. The causes of the problem are seldom addressed. Companies should realize that there are no long-term profits to be made in easy manufacturing tasks—anyone can provide these. It is in the difficult areas where profits are to be made. Furthermore, selling off inherent infrastructure can lead to an inability to compete effectively in future markets. The critical task facing manufacturing managers is to explain the essential nature of manufacturing in business terms, and this must embrace both process technology and infrastructure development.

---

[5]K. Ohmae, *The Mind of the Strategist* (New York: McGraw-Hill, 1982), pp. 36–37.

2 Developing a Manufacturing Strategy—Principles and Concepts

Companies invest in a wide range of functions and capabilities in order to make and sell products at a profit. Consequently, the degree to which a company's functions are aligned to the needs of its markets will significantly affect its overall revenue growth and profit. The size of investment in processes and infrastructure in manufacturing is fundamental to this success. If a company could change its manufacturing investments without incurring such penalties as delay and increased cost, then the strategic decisions within manufacturing would be of little concern or consequence. However, nothing could be further from the truth. The reality is that a lack of fit between these key investments and a company's markets will lead to a business being well wide of the mark. Many executives are still unaware "that what appear to be routine manufacturing decisions frequently come to limit the corporation's strategic options, binding it with facilities, equipment, personnel, basic controls, and policies to a noncompetitive posture, which may take years to turn round."[1]

The compelling reasons to ensure fit are tied to the very nature of manufacturing process and infrastructure investments, which are invariably large and fixed. They are large in terms of the size of the investment ($s) and fixed in that it takes a long time to agree, sanction, and implement these decisions and even longer to agree to change them. Companies having invested inappropriately cannot afford to put things right. The financial implications, systems development, training requirements, and the time to make the changes would leave the company, at best, seriously disadvantaged. To avoid this, companies need to be aware of how well manufacturing can support the marketplace and be conscious of the investments and time dimensions involved in changing current positions into future proposals.

---

[1] W. Skinner, "Manufacturing—Missing Link in Corporate Strategy," *Harvard Business Review,* May–June 1969, p. 13.

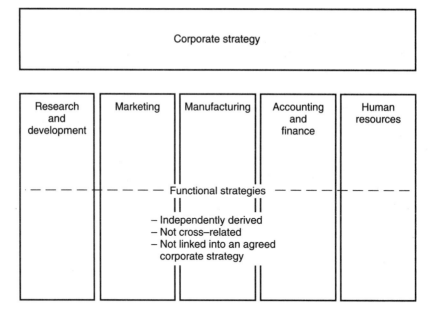

Functional Strategies

In most companies, corporate strategy statements are a compilation of functional strategies and nothing more. They are derived independently both of one another and the corporate whole (see Figure 2–1).

Charged with developing strategies for their own parts of a business, functions such as research and development, marketing, manufacturing, accounting/finance, and human resources prepare such statements independently. The result is a comprehensive list of functional statements that are then put together as the strategy for the corporate whole. However, companywide debate rarely concerns how these fit together or assesses their support of agreed markets. Congruence is assumed and is given credence by the use of broad descriptions of strategy that, instead of providing clarity and the means of testing fit, wash over the debate in generalities.

Through debate and challenge, functional strategies must be developed that support agreed markets with consistency between the various parts of a business. Only in this way can coherent strategies be forged that align all functions to support the business. Thus, corporate strategy is the outcome of functional strategies and can only be achieved by integration across the functional boundaries; corporate strategy, then, is both the binding mechanism for and the end result of this process (see Figure 2–2). Thus, all the functions within a business need to be party to agreeing on the blueprint of corporate strategy. They are then party to the debate and its resolution that facilitates the identification of the individual strategies necessary to support agreed direction and for which each function takes responsibility.

FIGURE 2-2

Integrating functional strategies and forging the corporate strategic outcome

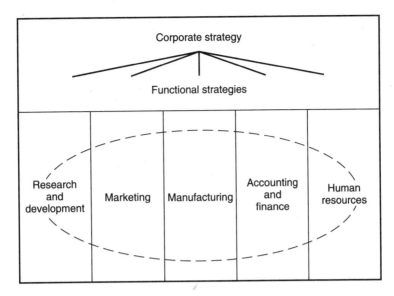

Functional Dominance within Corporate Strategy

In broad terms, the changing world demand/capacity balance has brought with it a change in the fortunes of different functions. Up to the mid-1960s, many industries had enjoyed a capacity/demand relationship that favored manufacturing's position in strategic influence. This, together with postwar growth helped create the dominance of the manufacturing function in many corporations. As the demand/capacity balance began to even out and selling into existing and new markets became more difficult, the power base of corporate influence began to swing away from manufacturing, heralding the rise of marketing. Then by the mid-1970s, the impact of recessions and energy crises had, in turn, opened the door to the influence of accounting and finance. These varying fortunes, however, rarely seemed to be based on what was best for the total good of the business, but more on which functional perspective appeared to provide the key to corporate success or salvation. As a result, those functions out in the cold themselves were left without due corporate influence.

These events reinforced the functional bias within corporate strategy debate explained in the last section. The independent formulation of functional strategies and the failure to cross-relate them has become the order of the day. This failure to debate strategy has led to essential perspectives and contributions of key functions being left out of strategic outcomes.

However, the existence of increasing world competition, overcapacity in many sectors of manufacturing industry, increasing scarcity of key resources, and decreasing product life cycles make it logical for businesses to incorporate all the key functional perspectives when determining policy decisions. Why then, does this not happen? In many organizations, manufacturing adopts or is required to take a reactive stance in corporate deliberations. Yet how can the perspectives of the function that controls such a large slice of the assets, expenditure, and people, thus underpinning the very welfare of a company, be omitted?

Reasons for the Manufacturing's Reactive Role in Corporate Strategy

The importance of manufacturing's contribution to the success of a business is readily acknowledged. The prosperous nations of today owe their success to their wealth-creating sectors, of which manufacturing is a key factor. Why then do manufacturing executives typically adopt a reactive role within strategic debate? Why doesn't this situation improve?

How Production Executives See Their Role

A prime reason why manufacturing's strategic contribution is reactive is that this is how production managers view of their strategic role. They define their role as requiring them to react as well as possible to all that is asked of the production system. They feel they must:

- Exercise skill and experience in effectively coping with the exacting and varying demands placed on manufacturing.
- Reconcile the trade-offs inherent in these demands as best they can.

Thus, rarely do they adequately contribute to the making of corporate decisions, which results in a demand on manufacturing.

They do not explain the different sets of manufacturing implications created by alternative policy decisions and changes in direction. By not contributing at the corporate level, they fail to help the company arrive at decisions that embrace all the important business perspectives.

How Companies See Manufacturing's Strategic Contribution

Companies themselves often reinforce production executives' emphasis on the short-term operational aspects of manufacturing. They too see manufacturing's role as involving the day-to-day operations and signal this orientation through discussion and required contributions.

Companies often reinforce such an orientation by the way in which they develop managers within manufacturing. Many companies typically promote operators to foremen, foremen to managers, and managers to executives, with scant regard for the change in emphasis that needs to take place. They provide little help to make this transition a success. One major company, recognizing the important corporate contribution to be made by its manufacturing executives, instituted a series of tailor-made courses in manufacturing strategy. During the first of these courses, 16 plant managers reflected that as a group their aggregate company service exceeded 300 years, yet the collective training they had received to help them prepare for their manufacturing executive roles was less than 30 days.

The outcome is that the short-term, "minding the store" role is reinforced by corporate expectations. Thus, the accepted and required contribution of manufacturing executives tends to be confined to the day-to-day, and the reactive role in strategy decision making continues to be the reality.[2]

Too Late in the Corporate Debate to Effectively Influence Strategic Outcomes

Manufacturing executives are typically not involved, or do not involve themselves, in corporate strategy decisions until these decisions have started to take shape. Before long, this point of entry into the strategy debate becomes the norm. The result is that manufacturing has less opportunity to contribute and less chance to influence outcomes. As a consequence, production managers always appear to be complaining about the unrealistic demands made of them and the problems that invariably ensue.

Failure to Say "No" when Strategically Appropriate

The "can't say no" syndrome is still the hallmark of the production culture. But this helps no one. Manufacturing executives tend to respond to corporate needs and difficulties without evaluating the consequences or alternatives and then explaining these to others. Any senior executive, including those in manufacturing, must be able to say "no" from a total business perspective and with sound corporate-related arguments. In typical situations, production managers accept the current and future demands placed on the systems and capacities they control, then work to resolve them. In this way, they decide between corporate alternatives, but only from a narrow functional perspective of what appears best for the business. It is essential that this changes. Resolving corporate-related issues in a unilateral way is not the most effective method to resolve the complex alternatives at hand. This resolution needs corporate debate to ensure that the relevant factors and options are taken into account so an appropriate corporate decision can be concluded.

Strategic decisions need to encompass the important trade-offs embodied in alternatives, which have their roots in the process and infrastructure investments associated with manufacturing and are reflected in the high proportion of assets and expenditures under its control.

---

[2] Also, refer to W. Skinner, *Manufacturing—The Formidable Competitive Weapon* (New York: John Wiley & Sons, 1985). The section entitled "Wanted: A New Breed of Manufacturing Manager" provides insights on developments in production management in the period 1980 to 1984 and the changing task to meet, among other things, the strategic role in manufacturing.

Lack of Language to Explain and Concepts to Underpin Manufacturing Strategy

On the whole, production managers do not have a history of explaining their functions clearly and effectively to others in the organization. This is particularly so for manufacturing strategy issues and the production consequences that will arise from the corporate decisions under discussion. On the other hand, marketing and financial executives are able to explain their function in a more straightforward and intelligible manner.[3] By talking about how strategic alternatives will affect the business, they can capture the attention of others in regard to the issues at hand and their strategic outcomes.

However, the reasons for this difference in perspective and presentation are not solely attributable to manufacturing executives themselves. The knowledge base, concepts, and language essential to highlighting corporate relevance and arresting attention have not been developed to the same level within manufacturing as within other key functions. Consequently, shared perspectives within manufacturing, let alone between functions, are not held, which contributes to the lack of interfunctional understanding.

For evidence of this last point, compare the number of books and articles written and postgraduate and postexperience courses provided in the area of manufacturing strategy to those for the other major functions of marketing and accounting/finance. Relatively few contributors address this fundamental area. The result is that manufacturing executives are less able to explain their essential perspectives. Hence, executives from other functions are less attuned to the ideas and perspectives that form the basis for understanding manufacturing's strategic contribution.

Functional Goals versus Manufacturing's Needs

In many organizations, the managers of different functions are measured by their departmental efficiency (an operational perspective) and not overall effectiveness (a business perspective). Furthermore, their career prospects are governed by their performance within the functional value system. As a consequence, managers make trade-offs that are suboptimal for the business as a whole. Typically, the performance of these specialist departments is measured by their own functionally derived goals and perspectives rather than those of line management and hence the requirements of the business itself. Getting adequate and timely resources committed to manufacturing's needs normally proves difficult.

Competing in different value systems, being measured against different performance criteria, and gaining prominence and promotion through different departmental opinions of what constitutes important contributions has gradually fragmented the functions making up a business. It has created a situation where shared perspectives and overlapping views are left to individual accomplishment and endeavor rather than in reponse to clear corporate direction.

---

[3] This argument was put forward in T. J. Hill, "Manufacturing Implications in Determining Corporate Policy," *International Journal of Operations and Production Management* 1, no. 1, p. 4.

FIGURE 2–3

The dichotomy of business views illustrated by the different figures included on typical customer-order paperwork

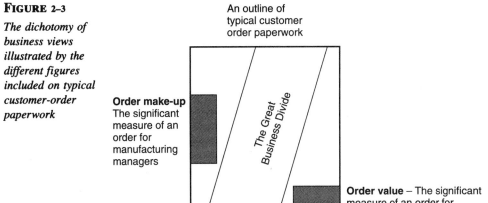

An outline of typical customer order paperwork

Order make-up
The significant measure of an order for manufacturing managers

The Great Business Divide

Order value – The significant measure of an order for accountants and salespersons

SOURCE: T. Hill, *Manufacturing Strategy: The Strategic Management of the Manufacturing Function* (New York: Macmillan, 1993, p. 30 (with permission).

Figure 2–3 illustrates this dichotomy. An accountant or salesperson, when receiving a customer order, will typically look at one figure as being the most significant measure of business relevance—the total value ($s) of the order placed.

Given the same situation, manufacturing managers will look at the order make-up. For them, the business relevance of an order is not its value, but the product mix, volumes, and delivery requirements it embodies. This aspect determines the ease with which an order can be made in terms of the process configurations already laid down and the process lead times involved. It will reflect manufacturing's ability to meet the cost base and delivery schedule of the product(s) ordered, and hence the profit margin and delivery performance that will result.

Where marketing is measured by the level of sales revenue achieved, each dollar of sales in their value system will carry the same weight as any other dollar of sales. Hence, all sales are deemed equal. In reality, all orders are not of the same value to a business. The higher the level of fit between product mix and anticipated volumes and actual sales, the more that target level will normally be met. Product costs based on one level of volumes or process configurations based on a given product mix are rarely, if ever, realigned with incremental volume and mix changes. Even the costing base, which underpins initial forecasts, is rarely, if ever, adjusted each time the market picture alters. A great business divide, therefore, separates the two realities of marketing and manufacturing. The simplistic measure of total sales value disguises those market characteristics so essential to manufacturing's ability to sustain cost and profit-margin structures in a business and other order-winners that create long-term growth.

Length of Tenure

Since the mid-1960s, there has been a growing practice to reduce the length of tenure for job incumbents. Introduced under the umbrella of executive development, it has been seen as a way of broadening perspectives and signaling the company's level of regard for an executive's future within the corporation. However, the significant draw-backs of this trend have largely gone unnoticed. Managerially and strategically it militates against the overall corporate good. It militates against executives' developing the area of responsibility within their control and contributing to the essential long-term strategic requirements of a business. For, without the necessary level of continuity to see through developments and without sufficient understanding of the essential functional perspectives within the strategic debate, executives are discouraged from taking the longer-term corporate perspective. In fact, to start developments in key areas without the time frame to see their completion is arguably irresponsible.

The result is an inclination to maintain the status quo and to meet functional goals above all else. In times of change, neither of these promotes the corporate good. Instead, managers will make decisions that are based on how they will politically affect themselves in the future rather than how they will affect the business's competitive position.

Top Management's View of Strategy

The authors of business plans and corporate marketing reviews look outward from the business. Top executives associate themselves with these activities, seeing them as essential components in the development of corporate strategy. The result is that they give adequate and appropriate attention to the external environment in which the business operates.

Manufacturing plans address stated business needs and are based on the internal dimensions of the processes involved; and top executives are not likely to take part in developing these plans. Typically, executives request and receive a manufacturing strategy statement without becoming involved in its structure, development, or verification. They see manufacturing as not having an external dimension and assume, therefore, that the corporate strategy debate need not embrace these perspectives. Rather, they focus on such manufacturing outcomes of strategic alternatives as capacity and costs.

But, manufacturing plays a vital role in supporting a company's chosen markets. Assessing the investment and time required for such support and which markets to support is fundamental to strategic debate and agreed outcomes. In many companies, however, top management has abdicated the key task in corporate strategy of linking markets and manufacturing or is not even aware that such a linkage should be made.

The Content of Corporate Strategy

The failure of companies to incorporate functional perspectives into their corporate strategy debate stems in part from the approaches to strategy development as advocated by leading researchers and writers in the field. The training of both executives charged with strategy development and specialists who provide relevant support reinforces such failure. This problem is apparent in the content of corporate strategy statements and manifests itself in a number of ways.

Strategy Statements Are General in Nature

Since strategy is general in nature, using all-encompassing statements to express it is deemed appropriate. The result is that expressions of strategy typically use words with more than one meaning. This broadbrush manner assumes that these general perspectives are universal in nature and relevance. But what typifies markets today is difference not similarity. Thus, general statements are inaccurate and misleading. By ignoring the differences within markets, functional strategies become general in nature and driven by their own rather than a business perspective.

General statements may underpin theory, but strategy, like management, is applied. The key to understanding a business is to determine the ways in which it competes in its different segments. And, of this you can be sure, segments will require functional strategies to reflect these differences.

Strategy Debate and Formulation Stops at the Interface

Functional strategies are typically not linked to one another. Most companies require each function to provide a strategic statement but fail to integrate them. The result is that corporate strategies stop at the interface between functions.

This approach is also re-enacted in many large corporations at the next level. Often, multinationals seem unable or unwilling to incorporate individual company statements into a strategy for the whole group. This failure to link, either by default or intent, is a consistent and comprehensive weakness in strategy formulation. The result is that in increasingly dynamic and competitive markets, companies systematically fail to realize their strategic potential and consequently are outperformed.

Furthermore, this apparent lack of need to integrate strategies is paralleled in the literature. A review of books on strategic marketing and corporate strategy will confirm that the link between the marketing-related dimensions of strategy and those of manufacturing is not made. The implication is, therefore, that it is unnecessary. Or, if necessary, its impact is of insufficient consequence to be an integral part of the review process.

Articles and books on marketing strategy were recently reviewed. Of the 1,250 pages covered by the nine articles and three books, less than 1 percent concerned manufacturing. A similar review of ten books in the field of corporate strategy revealed that of the 4,000 pages written, only 2 percent concerned manufacturing. Thus, strategy formulation as advocated and undertaken by leading researchers in the fields of corporate and marketing strategy also stops at the interface. Methodologies are put forward that lead companies into making major decisions and committing a business for many years ahead without requiring essential interface.

The consequences are enormous. First, the risks associated with such approaches in today's markets are substantial. The high level of risk is not a result of the uncertainty of future markets and the unknown moves of competitors but of the process of internal strategy formulation. Second, such approaches consistently result in the failure to create the type of strategic advantage that comes directly from embracing key functional perspectives and arriving at commonly agreed and understood corporate directions.

Whole versus Parts

The underlying rationale for these advocated and adopted methodologies appears to be based on the assumption that corporate improvement can be accomplished by working solely on the corporate whole. Although reshaping the whole is an important facet of strategic resolution, the necessary links to constituent parts and the role of those parts in bringing about agreed directions and change is fundamental. Unless companies forge these links when choosing what is best for business and agreeing on directions to pursue, they are unlikely to arrive at appropriate decisions essential for their growth and prosperity over time.

Typical outcomes

The results of this lack of integration are documents and statements that have the trappings, but not the essence, of corporate debate. With functional strategies independently derived, the nearest they get to integration is that they sit side by side in the same binder. The title "corporate strategy" for most companies is a misnomer. In reality, the strategy is no more than a compilation of functional strategies separated, as in the binder, one from another.

Furthermore, even a department's presentation of its strategy it is not intended to and does not, in fact, spark corporate-based discussion. Those companies that justify this procedure on the grounds that it requires executives to engage in rigorous, functionally oriented debate are not only guilty of false rationalization but also are missing the point. In today's markets, companies that fail to harness the resources of all facets of their business will be seriously disadvantaged. Not only will they miss out, they may well be in danger of missing out altogether.

Developing a Manufacturing Strategy

Companies require a strategy not based solely on marketing, manufacturing, nor any other function, but one that embraces the interface between markets and functions. Thus, what should and must be the link between functional strategies is the markets the business serves or intends to serve. One illustration is the link between marketing and manufacturing. Both functions must have a common understanding and agreement about company markets. Only then can the degree of fit between the proposed marketing strategy and manufacturing's ability to support it be known at the business level and objectively resolved within corporate perspectives and constraints.

For this to take place, relevant internal information explaining the company's manufacturing capabilities needs to be available within a business, as well as the traditional marketing information, which is primarily concerned with the customer and the market opportunities associated with a company's products. It is not sufficient that such information should be available—and often it is not. To be effective, the ownership of its use must be vested in top management. As with other functions, manufacturing strategy is not owned by manufacturing. It requires corporate ownership.

Senior executives need to understand all the strategic inputs in the corporate debate, for without this understanding the resolution between conflicting or nonmatching functional perspectives cannot be fully investigated; hence, individual functions must handle the trade-offs involved.

Typically, top executives inappropriately delegate this task. But, leaving it to others borders on being irresponsible. Developing and agreeing strategy is top management's key task. In fact, it is the one task that cannot be delegated. If it is, top executives will find themselves only able to exercise control over decisions taken in a global, after-the-event way.

Strategic Integration—Linking Manufacturing to Marketing

There is no shortcut to moving forward. There are, however, five basic steps that provide an analytical and objective structure in which the corporate debate and consequent actions can be taken.

Step 1. Define corporate objectives.

Step 2. Determine marketing strategies to meet these objectives.

Step 3. Assess how different products qualify in their respective markets and win orders against competitors.

Step 4. Establish the most appropriate process to manufacture these products (process choice).

Step 5. Provide the manufacturing infrastructure to support production.

These are, in one sense, classic steps in corporate planning. The problem is that most corporate planners treat the first two as interactive with "feedback loops" and the last two as linear and deterministic. While each step has substance in its own right, each has an impact on the others—hence the involved nature of strategy formulation. This is further exacerbated by the inherent complexity of manufacturing and the general failure to take account of the essential interaction between marketing and manufacturing strategies. What is required, therefore, is an approach that recognizes these features and yet provides an ordered and analytical way forward.

The suggested approach to linking manufacturing with corporate marketing decisions is schematically outlined in Table 2–1. It is presented in the form of a framework to help to outline the stages involved. The approach provides the key to stimulating corporate debate about the business in such a way as to enable manufacturing to assess the degree to which it can support products in the marketplace. It has been researched and tested successfully in many industries and business of different sizes.

How It Works

How to use the methodology outlined in Table 2–1 will be covered in two sections of the book. The following sections will overview the basic steps. Chapter 3 will cover the methodology to be followed when undertaking these types of analyses. Specifically,

TABLE 2–1   Framework for Reflecting Manufacturing Strategy Issues in Corporate Decisions (steps involved)*

Corporate Objectives	Marketing Strategy	How Do Products Qualify and Win Orders in the Marketplace?	Manufacturing Strategy	
			Process Choice	Infrastructure

Growth
Survival
Profit
Return on investment
Other financial
  measures
	Product markets and
	  segments
	Range
	Mix
	Volumes
	Standardization versus
	  customization
	Level of innovation
	Leader versus follower
	  alternatives
		Price
		Conformance quality
		Delivery
		  Speed
		  Reliability
		Demand increases
		Color range
		Product range
		Design
		Brand image
		Technical support
		After-sales support
			Choice of alternative
			  processes
			Trade-offs embodied in
			  the process choice
			Role of inventory in
			  the process
			  configuration
			Make or buy
			Capacity
			  Size
			  Timing
			  Location
				Function support
				Manufacturing
				  planning and control
				  systems
				Quality assurance and
				  control
				Manufacturing
				  systems engineering
				Clerical procedures
				Compensation
				  agreements
				Work structuring
				Organizational
				  structure

*Although the steps to be followed are given as finite points in a stated procedure, in reality the process will involve statement and restatement, for several of these aspects will impinge on each other.

- It will provide background for analyzing the cases included in this text by explaining what data are reviewed and why.
- It will give an approach for students to follow if their course requires an in-plant review, or it will help executives undertake reviews of this kind within their own businesses.

The objective of using this framework is to produce a manufacturing strategy for a business (Steps 4 and 5). In all instances this will include a review of existing products plus a review of proposed product introductions. Furthermore, the review will be based on current and future market expectations. This is because manufacturing needs to support a product (i.e., with after-sales service and supply) over the whole and not just a part of its life cycle, and hence the business needs to address this total decision. As product requirements change, so will manufacturing's task. The range of support requirements, therefore, will invariably affect the choice of process (Step 4) and infrastructure (Step 5) considered appropriate for the business over the whole life cycle of each product or product family. Levels of investment will also need to reflect this total support, and the varying degrees of mismatch over the life cycle between the product requirements and manufacturing process and infrastructure capability will need to be understood and agreed. In this way, the business will make conscious decisions at the corporate level. It will exercise its due responsibility for resolving trade-offs between the investment required to reduce the degree of mismatch and the ramifications for the business by allowing the mismatch to go unaltered.

However, to get to Steps 4 and 5 the three earlier steps need to be taken. With some understanding of what is to be achieved in a manufacturing strategy statement, it is now opportune to go through each step in turn and then to explain how the necessary interrelations between these parts come together as a whole to form a corporate strategy for a business.

Step 1—Corporate Objectives. Inputs into corporate strategy need to be linked to the objectives of the business. The essential nature of this link is twofold. First, it provides the basis for establishing clear, strategic direction for the business and demonstrates both the strategic awareness and strategic willingness essential to corporate success. Second, it will define the boundaries and mark the parameters against which the various inputs can be measured and consistency established, thus providing the hallmarks of a coherent corporate plan.

For each company, the objectives will be different in nature and emphasis. They will reflect the nature of the economy, markets, opportunity, and preferences of those involved. The important issues here, however, are that they need to be well thought through, hold logically together, and provide the necessary direction for the business.

Typical measures concern profit in relation to sales and investment, together with targets for both absolute growth and market-share growth. Businesses may also wish to include employee policies and environmental issues as part of their overall sets of objectives.

Step 2—Marketing Strategy. Linked closely to the provision of the agreed corporate objectives, a marketing strategy needs to be developed and will often include the following stages:

1. Market planning and control units need to be established. Their task is to bring together a number of products that have closely related market targets and that often share a common marketing program. This will help to identify a number of manageable units with similar marketing characteristics.

2. The second stage involves a situational analysis of product markets that includes:
   a. Determining current and future volumes.
   b. Defining end-user characteristics.
   c. Assessing patterns of buying behavior.
   d. Examining industry practices and trends.
   e. Identifying key competitors and reviewing the business's relative position.

3. The final stage concerns identifying the target markets and agreeing on objectives for each. This will include both a broad review of how to achieve these and the short-term action plans necessary to achieve the more global objectives involved.

FIGURE 2–4

*How order-winners
link corporate
marketing decisions
with manufacturing
strategy*

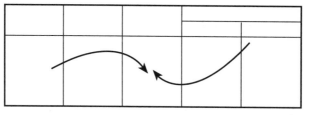

In addition, the company should agree on the level of service support necessary in each market and assess the investments and resources needed to provide these throughout the business.

The outcome of this will be a declaration to the business of the product markets and segments that the strategy proposes and the identification of the range, mix, and volumes involved. Other issues pertinent to the business will include the degree of standardization/customerization involved within each product range, the level of innovation and product development proposed, whether the business should be a leader or follower in each of its markets, and the extent and timing of these strategic initiatives.

Step 3—How Do Products Win Orders in the Marketplace?   Manufacturing's strategic task is to provide, better than the manufacturing functions of competitors, those criteria that enable the products to win orders in the marketplace. As stressed in the footnote to Table 2–1, the debate initiated by this methodology is iterative in nature. This is both appropriate for and fundamental to strategic resolution. Thus, the company as a whole needs to agree on the markets and segments within these markets in which it decides to compete.

In no way can these critical decisions be the responsibility or prerogative of a single function. Typically, however, most companies develop strategy through a marketing perspective (see Steps 1 and 2). Although the marketing debate is preeminent in corporate strategy procedures, the problem is that this is where the debate ends.

As a function, marketing will have an important and essential view. But it is not the only view, and in no way should it be allowed to dominate corporate strategy resolution. Functional dominance, no matter of what origin, is detrimental to today's business needs and must be avoided. An essential perspective of a firm's markets has to come from manufacturing. This perspective is established by determining those order-winners (and qualifiers* as explained later) that manufacturing needs to provide. The procedure is, in reality, to ask the marketing function questions that require manufacturing answers. This step, therefore, is the essential link between corporate marketing proposals and commitments and the manufacturing processes and infrastructure necessary to support them (see Figure 2–4).

However, not only are the relevant order-winners and qualifiers of differing levels of importance in different markets, but the degree of importance will also change over

---

*Suffice here to say that qualifiers get and keep companies in markets but do not win orders.

time. The procedure to be followed and the important issues to be addressed are covered in some detail later in this chapter.

Step 4—Process Choice.   Manufacturing can choose from a number of alternative processes to make the particular products. The key to this choice is volume and the order-winning criteria involved. Each choice, therefore, needs to reflect the current and future trade-offs involved for the various products. The issues embodied in these trade-offs are both extensive and important. Chapter 5, therefore, has been devoted to process choice and will examine in detail the implications embodied in this fundamental decision.

Step 5—Infrastructure.   Manufacturing infrastructure consists of the nonprocess features within production. It emcompasses the procedures, systems, controls, compensation systems, work-structuring alternatives, organizational issues, and so on that are involved in the nonprocess aspects of manufacturing. Chapter 10 discusses and illustrates some of the major areas involved.

   Although the five steps discussed above comprise the elements of manufacturing strategy development, it is not intended here to treat the first two steps in other than a somewhat superficial way—they are dealt with rigorously in other textbooks.[4] The purpose of including them, therefore, is both to demonstrate the integral nature of strategy formulation and to reinforce the interactive nature of the procedures involved. The remaining three steps mentioned above are all dealt with extensively in later chapters. Step 3, which concerns the order-winners and qualifiers of different products, is now discussed in general terms. A more detailed review is provided in Chapter 3.

Order-Winners and Qualifiers

Some order-winning criteria do not fall within the jurisdiction of manufacturing. For example, after-sales support, being the customer supplier, technical liaison capability, brand name, and design leadership are features provided by functions other than manufacturing. It is a corporate decision, therefore, whether or not to allocate resources to provide one or more of these particular features. However, within the mix of order-winners over a product's life cycle, manufacturing-related criteria will normally be the most important.

   The rationale for establishing the order-winners of different products is to improve a company's understanding of its markets. Before outlining the procedure for doing

---

[4] These include D. A. Aaker, *Developing Business Strategies* (New York: John Wiley, 1988); H. I. Ansoff, *Corporate Strategies* (New York: Penguin, 1987); P. J. Below et al., *The Executive Guide to Strategic Planning* (San Francisco: Jossey-Bass, 1987); A. C. Hax and N. S. Mailuf, *Strategic Management: An International Perspective* (Englewood Cliffs, N.J.: Prentice Hall International, 1984); B. Houlden, *Understanding Company Strategy* (Basil Blackwell, 1990); G. Johnson and K. Scholes, *Exploring Corporate Strategy* (Englewood Cliffs, N.J.: Prentice Hall International, 1989); M. E. Porter, *Competitive Strategy* (New York: The Free Press, 1980), and J. Quinn et al., *The Strategy Process* (1988)

this, the following section will describe some important characteristics and issues involved to give essential background and context.

Define the Meaning

To understand a business requires that the discussion is both comprehensive and clear. As mentioned earlier, many companies perceive strategy to be broadly based and are content with arriving at all-embracing but essentially unclear statements. Given that difference rather than similarity characterizes today's markets, a company must understand its markets to achieve adequate and clear outcomes from strategic discussion. A prerequisite is that the dimensions that characterize a company's markets are clearly defined and agreed. Using words that convey more than one meaning will only lead to misunderstanding and an inadequate base on which to establish agreed direction.

Therefore, companies that use descriptions of the success factors in their markets such as *customer service* are ill-served. Customer service can mean any number of things. The key is to agree which dimension of customer service is the important criterion. The reason is simple: without this level of clarity, each executive will walk away from the strategy debate with his or her own idea of which dimension of a particular factor is the most critical to the business. Furthermore, reviewing the importance of the same factor in the different markets served by a company can also embody similar misunderstandings. Most, if not all, companies today are selling products in markets characterized by difference and not similarity, and these essential insights need to be clearly identified as a prerequisite for sound strategy making.

Two words illustrate these points: *quality* and *delivery*. It is essential, for instance, to separate the word *design* from *quality*. Both are related dimensions, but whereas the former concerns creating a product specification, the latter describes the task of meeting the given specification. Although one is the task of the design function, the other is a distinct manufacturing task. The perspectives, however, are interrelated. The issue is that the tasks form part of different functional offerings.

Similarly, take the aspect of *delivery*. Separating the issue of ''on-time'' from that of ''short lead times'' is an essential part of understanding the key dimensions of a market. Describing both under the one word *delivery* will hide essential insights.

Strategy Is Time- and Market-Specific

It is not appropriate to discuss strategy as a set of stereotypes. To do so may simplify the process but will confuse the outputs. To be relevant, therefore, strategy debate needs to be time- and market-specific. Recognizing this will prevent stereotypes from being applied and will help to create and sustain the essential dimension of clarity emphasized earlier.

Definitions of Order-Winners and Qualifiers

The last two sections have emphasized the need to distinguish differences as part of the strategy formulation. To this end, an essential part of manufacturing's task is to recognize and apply the concept of order-winners and qualifiers.

- *Qualifiers* are those criteria that a company must meet for a customer to even consider it as a possible supplier. For example, customers increasingly require suppliers to be registered under the ISO 9000 series. Suppliers, therefore, who are so registered have only achieved the right to bid or be considered. Furthermore, they will need to retain the qualification in order to stay on the short list or be considered as a competitor in a given market. However, providing or attaining these criteria do not win orders.
- *Order-winners* are those criteria that win the order.

Order-Winners versus Qualifiers

The need to identify difference is further underscored by recognizing the essential difference between these two dimensions in a market. To provide qualifiers, companies need only to be as good as competitors; to provide order-winners, they need to be better than competitors. However, qualifiers are not less important than order-winners—they are different. Both are essential if companies are to maintain existing share and grow.

The need to distinguish between those criteria that win orders in the marketplace and those that qualify the product to be there is highlighted in the following example. When Japanese companies entered the color television market, they changed the way in which products won orders from predominantly price to product quality and reliability in service. The relatively low product quality and reliability in service of existing television sets meant that in the changed competitive forces of this market, existing producers were losing orders through quality to the Japanese companies; that is, existing manufacturers were not providing the criteria that qualified them to be in the marketplace. By the early 1980s, manufacturers that lost orders raised product quality so that they were again qualified to be in the market. As a result, the most important order-winning criterion in this market has reverted back to price.

Manufacturing, therefore, must provide the qualifying criteria to get into or stay in the marketplace. But these alone will not win orders. They merely prevent a company from losing orders to its competitors. Once the qualifying criteria have been achieved, manufacturing then has to turn its attention to the ways in which orders are won and ideally to provide these better than anyone else.

Also, if price is not the predominant order-winner, it does not mean that a company can charge what it wishes. Although it needs to recognize that it does not compete on price and therefore should exploit this opportunity, it has to keep its exploitation within sensible bounds. Failure to do so will result in the company losing orders increasingly to those who are more competitively priced. Hence, in this situation a company will have turned a qualifying criterion (i.e., a product highly priced within some limits) into an order-losing criterion where the price has become too high.

Differentiating between Order-Winners and Qualifiers

Having identified and separated order-winners from qualifiers, it is now necessary to distinguish between the importance of one criterion and another. This is done differently for each category:

TABLE 2-2   U.S. Furniture Company: Order-Winners and Qualifiers for Selected Customers in Its Oak Furniture Market*

Criteria	Small Chain			Large Chain		
	1991	*1993*	*1995*	*1991*	*1993*	*1995*
Conformance quality	50	40	35	60	60	60
Price	40	50	55	20	30	30
After-sales service	10	10	10	20	10	10
Delivery reliability	QQ	QQ	QQ	QQ	QQ	QQ
Design	Q	Q	Q	Q	Q	Q
Customer relations	Q	Q	Q	QQ	QQ	QQ

*Q denotes a qualifier; QQ, an order-losing sensitive qualifier.

TABLE 2-3   European Battery Company: Order-Winners and Qualifiers for Selected Markets*

Criteria	*1993*	*1995*	*1997*
Product type 10A			
Design	20	40	40
Conformance quality	20	—	—
Delivery speed	40	30	25
Delivery reliability	QQ	QQ	QQ
Price	20	30	35
Product type B40			
Conformance quality	20	10	10
Delivery speed	20	20	20
Delivery reliability	QQ	QQ	QQ
Price	50	70	70
Technical field support	10	—	—
Product type B500			
Design	50	50	40
Conformance quality	40	30	20
Delivery speed	10	20	30
Delivery reliability	QQ	QQ	QQ
Price	Q	Q	10

*Q denotes a qualifier; QQ, an order-losing sensitive qualifier.

- *Order-winners*—Once order-winners are agreed, appropriate weightings (points out of a hundred) are allocated to each (see Tables 2–2, 2–3, and 2–4).

- *Qualifiers*—Less definition of importance is required for qualifiers. If a company needs to qualify in one market segment on both quality and delivery reliability, then it needs to attain the necessary levels in each. However, some qualifiers will be more critical in terms of a customer's/market's

TABLE 2-4   U.S. Packaging Company: Order-Winners and Qualifiers for Selected Customers*

Criteria	Customer A			Customer B			Customer C		
	1991	*1992*	*1994*	*1991*	*1992*	*1994*	*1991*	*1992*	*1994*
Price	Q	10	25	100	100	100	60	50	40
Conformance quality	30	20	15	QQ	QQ	QQ	QQ	QQ	QQ
Delivery reliability	35	25	20	QQ	QQ	QQ	QQ	QQ	QQ
Delivery speed	—	—	—	—	—	—	40	50	60
Technical/sales support	—	15	25	—	—	—	—	—	—
Customer relations	35	30	25	—	—	—	—	—	—

*Q denotes a qualifier; QQ, an order-losing sensitive qualifier.

requirements, and these are distinguished by labeling them as order-losing sensitive qualifiers (see Tables 2–2, 2–3, and 2–4).

Monitoring Actual/Anticipated Change over Time

Since markets are dynamic, order-winners and qualifiers and/or their associated weightings will change over time. Thus, to monitor this change, relevant criteria and their weightings are agreed over time. The next section details how this is accomplished.

The Procedure for Establishing Order-Winners and Qualifiers

To create the essential interface between marketing and production, a business must understand its markets from the viewpoints of both these functions. Classically, companies often fail to distinguish clearly between the market (business) and marketing (functional) perspectives. This lack of clarity shows itself in several ways. For instance, in many companies the strategy debate typically ends when Steps 1 and 2 of the framework (see Table 2–1) have been accomplished. The assumption is that marketing's view of the market is how the market is. The key nature of Step 3 lies in facilitating the important distinction between the function and the business by asking market-oriented questions requiring manufacturing answers. These questions ask how different products win orders in their respective markets.

In developing a manufacturing strategy, the identification of relevant order-winners for different products is a key step. This helps companies move from what is often a vague understanding of its many markets to a new and essential level of awareness. Too often, companies describe their business as composed of relatively large segments and, in so doing, make the assumption that all products within a segment have similar order-winners because they have similar names, are sold to similar cus-

Figure 2–5

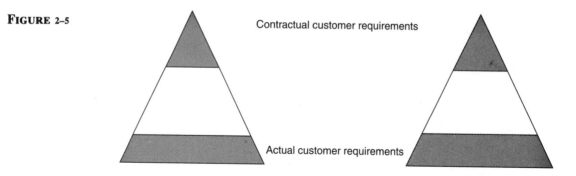

Contractual customer requirements

Actual customer requirements

tomers, or belong to the same segment from the viewpoint of marketing. But products win orders in different ways from one another; they will typically have more than one order-winner, and the order-winners will change over time. Unless the company recognizes these differences, it will not achieve the level of clarity essential to increasing business understanding and on which to base major investment decisions.

The procedure used to gain these insights is as follows:

- Marketing is requested to separate the business into different segments as they perceive them. The procedure, as with other aspects of strategy debate, is iterative in nature. Thus, marketing's separation of the business provides relevant insights and market distinctions for the debate, but they are reconsidered and very often revised as the strategy formulation progresses.

- To focus discussion, marketing chooses sample products and/or customers to represent these market segments. This step serves three purposes. First, it helps to test whether the segments chosen are sufficient to distinguish the market differences that exist. Second, it enables the debate to be oriented toward the particular rather than the general. Third, it allows specific data to be collected and analyses to be completed, which, in turn, provides information giving essential insights into the real nature of the different market segments. As Figure 2.5 illustrates, there is invariably a marked difference between the contractual requirements of customers and the actual requirements of customers. Handled by different people who typically do not interface within their own organizations, the reality of what customers need is invariably different from agreed contracts. Only by checking details can the essential perspectives of reality be identified.

- Marketing is also required to establish two future time periods for each segment. Note that the selected periods may not be the same as they are chosen to reflect the characteristics of each segment.

- The next step is to provide actual and forecast sales volumes for chosen representative products, based on current and future time periods.

- When this information has been gathered, marketing identifies the qualifiers and order-winners relevant to each of the sample products customers chose. Three illustrations are provided in Tables 2–2, 2–3, and 2–4. Weighted percentages for relevant order-winners have to be assessed for both current and relevant future time periods.

- This information now provides the initial input into this part of the strategic debate. In turn, marketing's opinion will be contested both by other functions and by information relating to the issues highlighted by the selection and importance attached to the relevant qualifiers and order-winners. This enables the company to have a clearer and more informed view of what manufacturing must provide to compete effectively in the chosen markets. Only when this is clearly understood can manufacturing strategy be formulated and appropriate decisions made about process and infrastructure investments.

Chapter 4 provides a more detailed review of the methodology to be used in developing a manufacturing strategy and will include a further explanation of the procedure outlined above.

Understanding the Criteria Chosen and Their Relative Weightings

As explained above, marketing is asked to determine the weightings for each relevant criterion. This involves allocating percentage points to each order-winner for both current and future time periods. In this part of the procedure, the discussion concerns not only the individual weights but also the reasons why any changes in emphasis are anticipated in the future.

Where changes do occur, the business must support the full range of criteria together with the changes in emphasis involved. As explained earlier, whereas some of these will be nonproduction features, the major thrust will in fact be from manufacturing. Certainly the provision of any significant changes in emphasis anticipated in the future will typically be manufacturing-based, and the need to reconcile the process and infrastructure investments appropriate to meet the changing requirements will have to be fully discussed, understood, and eventually agreed on by all concerned.

A final word concerns the order-winning criteria put forward by marketing and the percentage weightings proposed. When this procedure is first adopted, there is a danger that marketing will include a host of criteria and often, partly as a result of not distinguishing between their relative importance, spread the percentage points, thus failing to identify the critical order-winning feature(s). Understanding the criteria and weightings selected is necessary to ensure that this situation does not arise. Marketing's clear identification of how orders are won is an essential first step in developing an appropriate corporate manufacturing strategy. As explained earlier, this debate is then fueled by the views of other functions and the collection of relevant data. The company will achieve the necessary level of understanding and essential insights only if such rigorous debate is maintained throughout the strategy-making process.

FIGURE 2–6

*Assessing the
implications for
manufacturing
processes and
infrastructure of
order-winners*

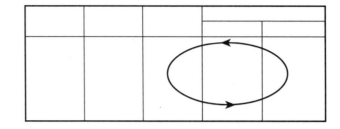

Identifying Qualifiers with the Potential to Become Order-Winners

Part of Step 3 is to identify any qualifying criteria associated with the different sets of products with the potential to become order-winning criteria (for instance, the earlier example of the changed role of quality in the color-television market). Once a company identifies such criteria, it must decide whether to invest in manufacturing to initiate this change. The impact it would have on market share, the time it would take for competitors to catch up, and the investments involved in bringing about this change would be some of the issues to be addressed in this corporate strategy decision.

Identifying Qualifiers That Are Order-Losing Sensitive

The final phase of Step 3 is to identify any qualifying criteria that are order-losing sensitive. Manufacturing must be fully aware of any qualifying criterion that might result in lost orders. Where these are identified, the discussion that follows is aimed at determining the degree of order-losing sensitivity and the degree of risk the business is prepared to accept. The company can make appropriate decisions once it understands the trade-offs between the costs, investment, and sales.

The Outputs of Manufacturing Strategy

Two outputs accrue from the use of this framework.

The First Output.   This concerns a review of the implications for manufacturing processes and infrastructure support of selling products in current and future volumes, as depicted in Figure 2–6. It involves assessing the degree of match between what exists in manufacturing and those processes and infrastructure features needed to provide the order-winning criteria.

This should be done for all future product proposals. So should the essential bi-annual review be designed to pick up any volume or order-winning criteria changes, which may be significant as measured against the relevant base year. In this way, the changes in match and mismatch are monitored, thus detecting incremental marketing changes that have occurred over time and often otherwise go unnoticed. Only by reviewing current and future requirements against the original decisions can the full change be assessed.

FIGURE 2-7

Manufacturing's input into the corporate strategy debate

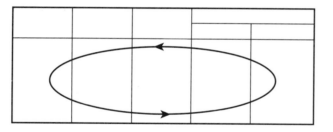

The Second Output.   Once determined, the manufacturing strategy and the necessary investments and time period for change form part of the corporate strategy debate, as illustrated in Figure 2–7.

As a consequence, the company as a whole is now required to review the business in both marketing and manufacturing terms. It changes the style and substance of corporate decisions from functionally based arguments and perspectives to ones that address functional differences by resolving the trade-offs involved at the business level. This corporate resolution therefore leads to an agreed understanding of what are the:

- Business objectives.
- Marketing strategy.
- Manufacturing strategy.

In reality, it will lead to one of five positions based on the degree of fit between the marketing and manufacturing strategic interface:

1. Where the interface is sufficiently close and requires little, if any, adjustment.
2. Where the interface is not sufficiently close, but the corporate decision is not to invest the required time and money to bring it closer to 1 above.
3. Where the interface is not sufficiently close, and the decision is to change the marketing strategy to reduce the mismatch and move toward 1 above.
4. Where the interface is not sufficiently close, and the decision is to allocate the time and investment to enable manufacturing to bring its processes and infrastructure to that required to support the marketing strategy and so move toward 1 above.
5. A combination of alternatives 3 and 4 to move toward the position described in 1.

In situations 3 and 4, the company decides to reposition marketing and manufacturing, respectively, to bring about the position described in 1. In the case of 2, it is essential that the reality of the mismatch is translated into manufacturing targets and budgets to present a manageable, achievable, and hence controllable task. In this way, the inadequacies of manufacturing's performance against budget are separated from the consequences of the corporate strategy decision to accept the mismatch involved. The business is, therefore, able to learn the extent of the consequences resulting from the manufacturing/marketing interface mismatch and use this vital information in its future strategic decisions.

Chapter 4 discusses the outputs described here and provides examples of different strategy applications.

Conclusion

To be effective, strategies must display the following characteristics,[5] which are central to the procedure and the outcomes.

- Congruence of purpose and function—Investments and developments can have a number of rationales, ranging from improving managerial control to increasing efficiency in all parts of the system. But the markets in which a company competes should link functional strategies. Otherwise functions will base strategies on their own perspectives and understanding, which would disrupt the essential gains of coherent direction of the parts and the whole. Congruence of purpose and function, therefore, are essential ingredients of strategy formulation and implementation.

- A focus on key priorities—The coherent direction in which functional strategies need to be formed will lead to an agreement on which developments and investments are the most important for supporting given markets. Priorities for time scales and costs are agreed on, and functions base subsequent actions and activities on these outcomes. This prioritizing mechanism is a key characteristic of effective strategies. It gives essential context, orients actions, keeps the list of tasks small and manageable, focuses attention on what is critical, and promotes coordination and cooperation between the different functions in the core task of being competitive within agreed markets.

- Commitment through understanding—Knowing where the company is going and why is essential if strategies are to be effective. In addition, knowing where and why builds commitment in those involved. An understanding of the rationale underpinning the strategies to be taken and the priorities to be pursued gives essential and appropriate direction in the short-term while providing the basis for strategic rethinking that the future will undoubtedly demand.

- Routine performance measurement—Strategy leads to appropriate direction, the pursuit of priorities, and the essential commitment to see them through. As part of the continuous reappraisal of strategy decisions, performance needs to be monitored on a regular basis. Routine checks are vital in themselves. Adherence to and progress toward agreed strategies is essential for all developments; and close and continuous monitoring of

---

[5] These are based on a presentation by D. Fisher (Ernst and Young) at Princeton, N.J., June 1992.

performance is integral to a strategy's success. Furthermore, strategy is not a once-and-for-all development that remains unaddressed between one review time and the next. Continuous reassessment needs to be undertaken, and the routine measurement of performance is an integral part of this procedure.

Market- or Marketing-led?[6]

Many companies do not keep in sharp focus the critical differences between being market-led and being marketing-led. To substitute the business (market) perspective with a functional (marketing) perspective will invariably lead to distorted strategies and eventually to corporate disadvantage. Checking the characteristic of a strategy based on the perspectives of a single function against those listed above clearly underscores these essential differences.

Unfortunately, in many businesses marketing is becoming increasingly characterized by the perceived role of creating ideas. Generating ideas often becomes an end in itself, with the rigor of testing business fit left to others. Many businesses, however, fail to appreciate that the most significant orders are the ones to which a company says no. For this marks the boundaries of the markets in which it competes, and this defines the context in which manufacturing's strategic response needs to be made.

Manufacturing Strategy

In the past, companies have seen manufacturing's role as being the provider of corporate requests. Corporate-strategy debate has stopped short of discussing the implications of decisions for manufacturing. This has been based on two incorrect assumptions:

1. Within a given technology, manufacturing is able to do everything.
2. Manufacturing's contribution concerns the achievement of efficiency rather than the effective support of market needs.

The result for many companies is that not only have the profit margins they once enjoyed been eroded, but also the base on which to build a sound and prosperous business in the future is no longer available. A company is exposed and vulnerable without the frequent manufacturing strategy checks necessary to evaluate the fit between the business and manufacturing's ability to provide the necessary order-winning criteria of its various products. In times of increased world competition, being left behind can be sudden and fatal. In many cases, averting the end is the only option left. Turning the business around, however, will only be achieved by switching from an operational to a strategic mode, which will require a corporate review of the marketing and manufacturing perspectives and of the financial implications of the proposals.

Manufacturing strategy comprises a series of decisions concerning process and infrastructure investment, which, over time, provide the necessary support for the relevant order-winners and qualifiers of the different market segments of a company. It is

---

[6]See Terry Hill, *The Essence of Operations Management* (Englewood Cliffs, N.J.: Prentice Hall International, 1993), p. 25.

built on keeping the strategic developments relevant to the business; that is, it must reflect those aspects of manufacturing critical to those segments of the firm under review. Identifying the pertinent aspects, and setting aside those that are not, provides for a strategy that is oriented to the market and the simplicity and clarity of direction this affords.

On the other hand, manufacturing strategy is neither

- A list of all aspects typically comprising a manufacturing function and an attempt to develop a strategic statement about each. Differentiating the important from the less important aspects in terms of market needs is a key feature of sound strategy development.
- An exhortation that the strategic perspectives of the manufacturing function should be paramount.

Manufacturing's strategic task is to transform, over time, support for a company's market into an appropriate collection of facilities, structures, controls, procedures, and people. This chapter has provided essential insights into the principles and concepts that underpin this task. The next looks in some depth at order-winners and qualifiers, and the chapter after that at the procedures to follow.

Further Reading

Buffa, E. S. *Meeting the Competitive Challenge: Manufacturing Strategy for U.S. Companies.* Homewood, Ill.: Richard D. Irwin, 1984.

Gunn, T. G. *Manufacturing for Competitive Advantage.* Cambridge, Mass.: Ballinger Publishing Company, 1987.

Mather, H. *Competitive Manufacturing.* Englewood Cliffs, N.J.: Prentice Hall International, 1988.

Samson, D. *Manufacturing and Operations Strategy.* Sydney: Prentice Hall, 1991.

Skinner, W. *Manufacturing in Corporate Strategy.* New York: John Wiley, 1978.

Slack, N. *The Manufacturing Advantage.* London: Mercury Books, 1991.

Voss, C. A. (ed.). *Manufacturing Strategy.* London: Chapman & Hall, 1992.

3 Order-Winners and Qualifiers

The last chapter introduced the concept of order-winners and qualifiers, discussed the rationale behind these perspectives, and outlined the distinguishing characteristics of them. This chapter examines these dimensions more fully, explaining specific criteria in some detail.

The essence of strategy stems from the need for companies to gain a detailed understanding of their current and future markets. Functions are then required to develop strategies based on supporting the characteristics of agreed markets. However, functions should not be reactive within this procedure. On the contrary, they must be proactive in strategic debate, explaining their perspectives so that the rest of the business understands them. This ensures that these perspectives form part of the discussion. Manufacturing strategy, therefore, consists of the strategic tasks manufacturing must accomplish to support the company's order-winners and qualifiers relating directly or indirectly to that function.

Strategic Scenarios and Approaches

As highlighted in Chapter 2, strategic formulation tends to be expressed in general terms. Key reasons include:

- Since strategy implies a broad review, companies also perceive the underlying characteristic of strategic outputs to be broad.
- Companies appear to seek strategies that are uniform in nature. This offers apparent clarity in the form of consistent strategic statements that are easy to express, explain, and address. A desired level of uniformity has inherent attractions no matter what the company's size.

It is not surprising then that typical expressions of corporate strategy include such general terms such as *service, responsiveness,* and *meeting the customer's needs.* In addition, researchers, writers, and advisors have proffered generic statements concerning corporate strategy formulation with expressions such as *low cost, differentiation,* and *critical success factors.* The use of general terms similar to these brings two major drawbacks. First, difference is not brought into focus but is blurred. Second, decisions concerning the nature of the market segments in which a company wishes to compete are not resolved at the strategic level. A company may not recognize that orders for products, often within the same market segment, are won in different ways. This lack of clarity brings conflicting demands on manufacturing, which reinforces that function's reactive tendency and disperses the essential coherence necessary to provide strategic thrust, guidance, and advantage.

Furthermore, this lack of clarity is considered adequate in markets that are increasingly characterized by difference and not similarity. However, ask chief executive officers whether the markets served by the group of companies under their control are similar in nature—the answer would be "no." Ask if the markets served by a typical company are the same—the answer would again be "no." How is it then that companies continue to expect or believe that manufacturing's support (in terms of process and infrastructure investments) for these would be common? If that is not so, then why do companies apply the same manufacturing approaches (often whatever is the latest approach considered appropriate or desirable) to support its different markets not only in one plant but in all its different plants?

The strategic process, therefore, needs to be based on an exact understanding of markets and differences within a market. As highlighted earlier, however, all too often companies debate strategy in general terms and undertake strategy using general courses of action. This invariably and increasingly leads to a lack of fit between functional strategies and corporate markets. Where this happens, companies will find themselves at a serious disadvantage.

Before moving on to how companies need to understand markets, let us review what typically happens to firms in the absence of clear, well-defined strategic debate.

Strategic Vacuum

The absence of a manufacturing strategy within a business typically leads to a strategic vacuum, and into that void continues to be drawn a raft of solutions—panaceas or flavor-of-the-month initiatives.

This type of response is underpinned by a basic logic. Executives recognize that manufacturing, as a significant part of the company, should be making and needs to be making a significant contribution to the overall success of the business. There is, therefore, due pressure on manufacturing to respond to these corporate demands and expectations. Without strategic context, however, manufacturing has traditionally responded by undertaking currently popular solutions. In this way, companies seek to achieve parity in manufacturing by modeling operations on best practice. However, although a solution may be good in itself, its application to the specific problem is often inappropriate. Given manufacturing's reactive nature and the existence of corporate initiatives, it is easy to see why most companies have invested regularly and significantly over the years in responses that by and large, are eventually discarded. The cause of their abandonment is principally the lack of relevance of the solution in the first place.

Understanding Markets

To formulate functional strategies, a company must first clearly understand and agree about the markets in which it wishes to be today and tomorrow. This critical initial step provides the two essential dimensions for the formulation of sound and effective strategies.

1. The in-depth debate about the markets in which a company decides to complete is a prerequisite to strategy formulation. The clear identification is based on a well-articulated understanding of market needs and the implications of these for all functions. It is through this mechanism that functional differences are reconciled with each other and markets and corresponding segments are delineated. Furthermore, since markets are dynamic, strategic debate must be ongoing.
2. With this agreement, functions need to be geared toward meeting the requirements of a firm's current and future markets. Thus, each function's strategic contribution is expressed in terms of priorities, developments, and investments.

The first step, therefore, is to understand markets. To do this adequately, companies need to set aside generic, broad-based statements and seek to identify the level of difference that exists in and the relevant dimensions of each segment in which they wish to compete.

Characteristics of Today's Markets—Difference and Speed of Change

As emphasized in Chapter 2, whereas past markets were characterized by similarity and stability, current markets are characterized by difference and change.

Company approaches to strategic resolution have differed. The range of alternatives is wide, and the variables include formality of approach, type of framework, and extent of the evolutionary nature of the process and outcomes. In evaluating the position to be taken on each dimension of these alternatives, however, companies need to bear in mind that improving outputs is a matter of degree; an alternative approach does not characteristically result in a substantial shift from the company's present position. In most markets it involves incremental improvement and continuous adjustment.

The characteristics of today's markets place a greater need on understanding, and the strategic theme in this book is the need to attain this necessary level of understanding. The last two chapters have outlined a framework for gaining more detailed market insights. A wide range of methodologies has been put forward, specifying approaches that would lead to strategic insights and appropriate answers. However, if any worked, companies would merely need to apply them. The solution is not that easy. To improve, a company needs to continuously and rigorously review its markets.

Unless companies understand their markets better, they will be unable to arrive at successful and workable strategic decisions. Only in this way will they be able to identify the strategic alternatives to meet the needs of their different markets and thus move away from prescriptive approaches and solutions. Researchers and consultants have offered viable solutions but executives have typically failed to understand them and thus have been unable to select what best suits their needs for strategic resolution. They remain impeded by their failure to complete this fundamental task of understanding markets. As with most aspects of management, the essential ingredient in doing a task well is hard work. Understanding today's varied and fast-changing markets is no exception.

Identifying relevant order-winners and qualifiers, and the relative weightings to be attached to them, helps companies to achieve these critical insights. The following sections describe what these criteria are and how they work.

Order-Winners and Qualifiers—Basic Characteristics

This section outlines important background for the discussion of the specific criteria in the next section. A company should keep in mind the following characteristics and issues.

- General statements about markets embody imprecise meanings. As a result, executives take away from corporate strategy discussions their own understandings, which are typically and understandably based on their own functional perspectives. Thus, a prerequisite for sound corporate-strategy development (i.e., agreement by all on what markets the company is and should be in and the characteristics of those markets) is missing.

- Order-winners and qualifiers are both market- and time-specific. Thus, the criteria relating to a market will need different levels of emphasis and will change over time. It follows, therefore, that there can be few general rules.

- When developing order-winners and qualifiers, companies must distinguish the level of importance for individual criteria for each market. To do this, they can weight order-winners by allocating a total of 100 points; for qualifiers, a distinction is made between a qualifier and an order-losing sensitive qualifier, or one that will cause a business to lose customers' orders quickly. Examples of these dimensions were given earlier in Tables 2–2, 2–3, and 2–4, together with supporting text.

- Order-winners and qualifiers and their relative weightings will change over time. To assess these potential changes, a company must weight each criterion for the current period and two future periods. The latter will need to reflect the nature of the market; for example, for a printing company the future time periods may be next year and the year after, but for an aerospace company they would need to be three and seven years, respectively. Again, Tables 2–2, 2–3, and 2–4 illustrate these points.
- In most instances, differences exist between the criteria needed to retain existing customers and those needed to increase market-share or gain prospective customers. These differences will need to be reflected in the relevant order-winners and qualifiers and their respective weightings.
- Similarly, the criteria that relate to winning orders for a primary supplier will differ from those for secondary or other supplier categories. Although customers tend to infer that the criteria are the same, common sense challenges that logic. The large percentage share of demand that typically goes to a primary supplier creates very different contractual demands and opportunities than those for other suppliers. Thus, the way in which secondary or other suppliers win their part of the contract needs to reflect this.
- Not all order-winners and qualifiers are related to manufacturing. However, over time manufacturing-related criteria will often come to the fore—for example, price and reliability of delivery.

Order-Winners and Qualifiers—Specific Dimensions

As mentioned earlier, there is a range of order-winners and qualifiers, and not all of them form part of manufacturing's strategic function. This section, therefore, separates the different categories and reviews typical criteria within each category. As stressed earlier, strategy is market- and time-specific, and therefore, not all order-winners and qualifiers will relate to or be of the same importance to all companies.

Manufacturing-Related and Manufacturing-Specific Criteria

This category concerns those order-winners and qualifiers that are specific to manufacturing and will, where relevant, form part of manufacturing's strategic role.

Price.   In many markets, and particularly in the growth, maturity, and saturation phases of the product life cycle (see Figure 3–1), price becomes an increasingly important order-winning criterion. When this is so, manufacturing's task is to provide the low costs necessary to support the price-sensitivity of the marketplace, thus creating the level of profit margin necessary to support the business investment involved and create opportunity for the future. As in many of the pertinent analyses in manufacturing, highlighting the pockets of significant cost will give direction to the areas where resource allocation should be made and management attention given.

FIGURE 3–1

The generalized product life cycle

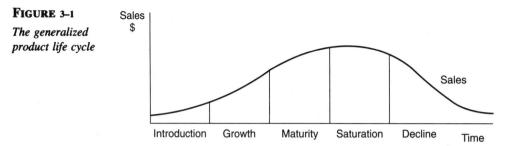

In most manufacturing companies in North America and other developed industrial nations, direct labor is only a small part of the total cost. Materials followed by overheads are usually the two main areas of cost, which should be reflected in the provision of information, allocation of resources, and frequency of review. The likelihood, however, is that they are not.

Since price has been an omnipresent factor in most markets, companies are reticent to consider that it may not be a relevant order-winner. This misunderstanding often stems from the fact that comparisons with alternatives will typically form part of a customer's evaluation of a product. However, for price to be an order-winner, margins must be low. Only in such situations will low-cost manufacturing be a priority. Where margins are high, price is not an order-winner. In these types of market, customers will compare one price to another, not to seek the lowest price but to check that the quoted price is within an acceptable range. Therefore, companies need to recognize the key difference between being price competitive (a qualifier) and competing on price (an order-winner).

The evaluation described here is not unique to the criterion of price. Customers will typically cross-check all relevant criteria. In the case of qualifiers, this is to ensure a ballpark fit, for order-winners, customers will typically be looking for a "better than" performance.

As explained earlier, qualifiers get a company into and maintain it within a market. As such, they do not win orders but are essential prerequisites for a company to be considered as a potential supplier. Where price is a qualifier, a company cannot simply charge whatever it wishes. The company must price the product according to what the market will bear, keeping exploitation within sensible bounds. Failure to do so will result in an increase of orders lost to those who are more price competitive. Hence, in this situation a company will have turned a qualifying criterion (i.e., a product highly priced within acceptable limits) into an order-losing criterion (the price has become too high).

Where price is an order-winner, low (or anticipated low) margins give manufacturing the clear task of reducing costs in order to maintain or improve available margins. Also, when a company decides to reduce price significantly, thus altering its role or its importance as an order-winner, it must similarly change related elements of manufacturing strategy. Companies that elect to alter the role of price would need, therefore, to assess the lead times involved, investment implications, and the cost-reduction potential. Making a strategic decision to reduce price without assessing these factors will invariably lead companies into inappropriate strategies, for the decision to reduce price, although difficult to evaluate, is easy to make. Cost reduction, on the other hand, is easy to evaluate but difficult to achieve.

Cost Reduction.   Many companies do not concentrate their efforts in the area of greatest cost. In many instances, companies direct the most effort toward reducing direct-labor cost. Although an organization must improve productivity at all levels, focusing on the area of greatest cost will tend to yield the best results. Since overheads and materials together typically account for some 85–90 percent of total costs, giving these the pro rata attention they deserve makes sense but often is not done. The traditional emphasis on the control and reduction of direct-labor cost still attracts most of the resources allocated to the overall cost-reduction task. Tradition and experience of what to do still seem to reinforce these practices. (The effect of process lead-time reduction on elements of overhead costs is highlighted in a later section.)

Furthermore, concentrating on one aspect of cost rather than total costs can lead to lost opportunities. For instance, Heinz had undertaken a labor-cost-reduction plan at its Starkist tuna factories in Puerto Rico and American Samoa. With increasing competition from low-labor-cost areas, this policy seemed to make sense. But, a study revealed that the workers were so overworked that each day they were leaving tons of meat still on the bone. Adding workers, slowing down production lines, increasing supervision, and retraining increased costs by $5 million but cut waste by $15 million, thus saving $10 million each year.[1]

Many organizations have undertaken continuous improvement efforts to increase productivity. The key areas for reevaluation, however, are broadly based, reflecting the more significant areas of expense and cost-reduction opportunity. Typical lists include eliminating waste,* product design, quality at source, process redesign, JIT production control systems, set-up reduction, overhead reduction, and the involvement of people.[2]

Experience Curves.   Evidence clearly shows that as experience accumulates, performance improves, and the experience curve is the quantification of this improvement. The basic phenomenon of the experience curve is that the cost of manufacturing a given item falls in a regular and predictable way as the total quantity produced increases. The purpose of this section is to draw attention to this relationship and its role in the formulation of manufacturing strategy. It is helpful to note that while the cost/volume relationship is the pertinent corporate issue, some of the examples will in fact relate price to volume because the information, not being company-derived, uses average industry price as a convenient substitute.

---

[1]R. Henkoff, ''Cost Cutting: How to Do It Right.'' *Fortune* 9 (April 1990), pp. 40–49.

*Sources of waste include doing necessary tasks wrong the first-time (a source related to quality) and doing unnecessary tasks. Estimates of the costs associated with these range from 20–30 percent and 10–20 percent, respectively.

[2]For example, refer to Henkoff (1990) and T. Hill, *Production Operations Management*, 2nd ed., (Hemel Hempstead, UK: Prentice Hall, 1991), pp. 353–56.

The price of a new product almost always declines after its initial introduction and as it becomes more widely accepted and available. However, it is not so commonly recognized that over a wide range of products the cost follows a remarkably consistent decline. The characteristic pattern is that the cost declines (in constant $s) by a consistent percentage each time cumulative unit production is doubled. The effects of learning curves on labor costs have been recognized and reported over the past 40 years beginning with studies on airframe production in the United States prior to the Second World War. However, experience curves are distinctly different from this. The real source of the experience effect is derived from organizational improvement. Although learning by individuals is important, it is only one of many improvements that accrue from experience. Investment in manufacturing processes, changes in production methods, product redesign, and improvements in all functions in the business account for some part of the significant experience-related improvements.

The experience curve is normally drawn by taking each doubling of cumulative unit production and expressing the unit cost or price as a percentage of the cost or price before doubling. So an 80 percent experience curve would mean that the cost or price of the one-hundredth unit of a product is 80 percent that of the fiftieth; of the two-hundredth, 80 percent that of the one-hundredth; and so on. Figures 3–2 and 3–3 show the experience curve for color film and color paper produced by Japanese companies in the period 1965 to 1990.[3] Figure 3–4 also illustrates the basic features of these curves, explained as follows:[4]

1. The horizontal axis measures the cumulative quantity produced on a logarithmic scale. Figure 3–4a and b shows the same information plotted on a linear and logarithmic scale, respectively. The information on Figure 3–4a reveals a smooth curve and the implied regularity of the relationship between unit cost and total volume. However, Figure 3–3b shows the same information plotted on double logarithmic scales. This presentation shows percentage changes as a constant distance, along either axis. The straight line on the log-log scale in Figure 3–4b means that a given percentage change in one factor has resulted in a corresponding percentage change in the other. The nature of that relationship determines the slope of the line that can be read off a log-log grid.

2. Returning to Figures 3–2 and 3–3, the logarithmic scale shows that many doublings of production can be achieved early on, but later vastly larger quantities are needed to double the cumulative unit volumes then involved. This implies, as one would expect, that movement down the experience curve slows with time. Initially, additional growth in annual volumes can

---

[3]Other examples of experience curves include those for the crushed-bone and limestone industry, 1925 to 1971, in the *Boston Consulting Group Perspective* 149, "The Experience Curve Reviewed: V Price Stability"; the Model T Ford, 1909 to 1923, in W. J. Abernathy and K. Wayne, "Limits of the Learning Curve," *Harvard Business Review*, September–October 1974, pp. 109–19; and random access memory (RAM) components, 1976 to 1984, in P. Ghemawat, "Building Strategy on the Experience Curve," *Harvard Business Review,* March–April 1985, pp.143–49.

[4]The computation of an experience curve is clearly detailed in "Experience and Cost: Some Implications for Manufacturing Policy," Harvard Business School paper, 9-675-228 (Revised July, 1975).

FIGURE 3–2

Experience curves for color film produced by Japanese companies, 1965–1990, 1969–1990, and 1976–1990

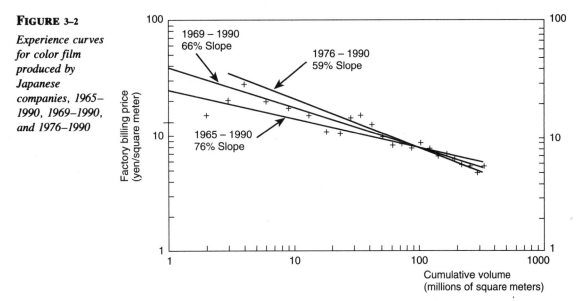

SOURCE: *Photo Electric News* and the *Japanese Economic Journal.*

FIGURE 3–3

Experience curve for color paper produced by Japanese companies, 1965–1990

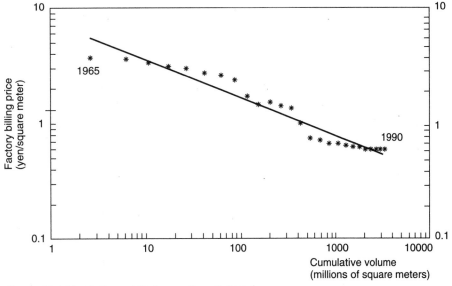

SOURCE: *Photo Electric News* and the *Japanese Economic Journal.*

offset this, but the leveling in demand associated with the mature stage in the product life cycle and the eventual saturation and later decline through technical obsolescence will slow the rate of progress down the curve.

3. The vertical axis of the experience curve is usually cost or price per unit and is also expressed logarithmically. However, the cost or price per unit

FIGURE 3–4

Cost/volume or price/volume relationship expressed on a linear and a log-log scale

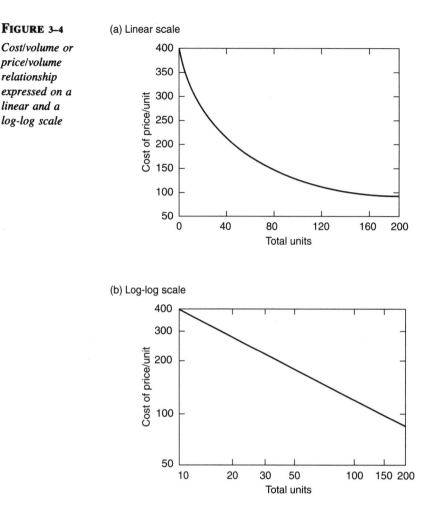

(a) Linear scale

(b) Log-log scale

must be adjusted for inflation to allow comparisons to be drawn over time: Figures 3–2 and 3–3 shows that improvements further down the curve become, in absolute terms, quite small. Thus, as progress is made down the curve, each incremental movement will both take longer and yield less.

The characteristic decline in cost or price per unit was established by the Boston Consulting Group's (BCG) work in the 1960s and early 1970s as between 20 and 30 percent for each doubling of cumulative production. Although the BCG claims that this can go on (in constant $s) without limit and despite the rate of experience growth, in reality this tends not to happen for the reasons expressed earlier.

Furthermore, it is important to stress that the experience curve characteristics are phenomenological in nature. They portray a relationship between cost or price and volume that can, but does not necessarily, exist. Consequently, the BCG concludes that "these observed or inferred reductions in costs as volume increases are not necessarily automatic. They depend crucially on a competent management that seeks ways to force costs down as volume expands. Production costs are most likely to decline under this internal pressure. Yet in the long run the average combined cost of all elements should decline under the pressure for the company to remain as profitable as possible. To this extent the relationship is of normal potential rather than one of certainty.[5]

Many people today advocate different approaches to reducing cost. While some companies strive for dramatic breakthroughs, many are now returning to approaches based on *"Kaizen,"* a Japanese term meaning "continuous improvement." Used by many Japanese companies, the approach has resulted in significant on-going improvements. Consider the subcompact Tercel, the smallest Toyota sold in the United States. The auto contributes modestly at best to profits. Even so, Toyota made the 1992 model faster, roomier, and quieter than its predecessors—it weighs less, achieves equally good mileage (32 mpg on the highway), and remarkably, is similarly priced under $8,000 for a basic four-door sedan. It is $100 cheaper than GM's new Saturn and as much as $1,600 less than other competing models.[6]

Delivery Reliability. On-time delivery (OTD) means the supplying of the products ordered on the agreed due date. It therefore, is a major concern of both the manufacturing and distribution functions. In many businesses, this criterion now constitutes a qualifier; very often, it's an order-losing sensitive qualifier, meaning that if companies continue to miss due dates, customers will increasingly stop considering them as potential suppliers. Thus, unless these firms improve their on-time delivery, they will not get the chance to compete. There is a growing recognition of the importance of delivery reliability as a criterion in most markets. Its change toward being a qualifier is part of that competitive perspective. Increasingly, then, OTD performance is a competitive factor,[7] and its measurement, by customer, sector, and overall is key in most businesses. The need to identify different OTD expectations is a critical step here as with other order-winners and qualifiers.

For the manufacturing function, this involves consideration of capacity, scheduling, and inventory, principally for work-in-process and finished goods. This must be supplemented by regular reviews of those dimensions affecting the company's record on delivery reliability, such as completed line item reviews (product mix made as measured against the production plan) and checks on lead-time performance throughout the total process.

The exactness of the due date can vary from an appointed hour on a given day to delivery of the agreed quantity starting, and finishing, in an agreed week. The level of data collection and the timing and proactive nature of the feedback to customers will

---

[5]*Perspectives in Experience* (Boston: Boston Consulting Group, 1972) p. 12.

[6]A. Taylor III, "Why Toyota Keeps Getting Better and Better and Better," *Fortune,* November 19, 1990, pp. 66–79. Also refer to M. Imai, *Kaizen* (New York: Random House, 1986).

[7]Several authors have stressed the importance of delivery reliability. For example, J. E. Ashton and E. X. Cook, Jr., "Time to Reform Job Shop Manufacturing—Organize Your Factor for Quality and On-Time Delivery," *Harvard Business Review,* March–April 1989, pp. 106–11; and A. Kumar and G. Sharman, "We Love Your Product but Where Is It?" *The McKinsey Quarterly* 1 (1992), pp. 24–44.

need to form part of this decision. As a rule, the more exact the agreed delivery is, the more proactive a supplier should be in the data collection and the more regular the performance summaries and feedback to customers should be.

These data are the source of information about the size of "call-offs" (what a customer actually wants rather than the total quantities expressed in any contract or agreement) and the lead times associated with the delivery. The former concerns the issue of costs and price agreements, the latter leads into the criterion of delivery speed.

Delivery Speed.   A company may win orders through its ability to deliver more quickly than competitors, or to meet the delivery date required when only some or even none of the competition can do so. Products that compete in this way need a manufacturing process that can respond to this requirement. There are two perspectives to the issue of delivery speed. One is where the process lead time, while being shorter than the delivery time required by the customer, is difficult to achieve because the current forward order load (or *order backlog*) on manufacturing capacity plus the process lead time to complete the order is greater than the delivery time required (see Situation 1, Figure 3–5). This is resolved through either a short-term increase in capacity (e.g., overtime working), a rescheduling of existing jobs, or a combination of both.

The other is where the process lead time is greater than the customer delivery requirement (see Situation 2, Figure 3–5). In these situations, manufacturing (for a given process technology) can only meet the customer's delivery requirement by either increasing short-term capacity or holding inventory and thus reducing the process lead time by completing part of manufacturing before the order point and hence in anticipation of winning these types of orders. Schedule changes may facilitate the accomplishment of the task but will not in themselves resolve this type of situation.

FIGURE 3–5

Situations where delivery speed is an order-winning criterion to be provided by manufacturing

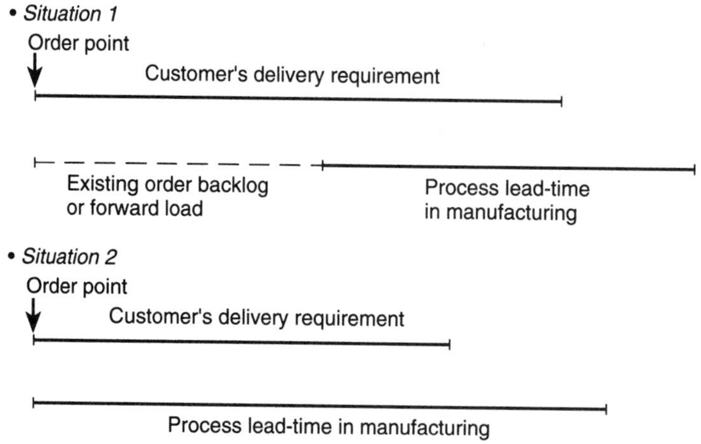

• Situation 1

Order point

Customer's delivery requirement

Existing order backlog or forward load

Process lead-time in manufacturing

• Situation 2

Order point

Customer's delivery requirement

Process lead-time in manufacturing

FIGURE 3-6

Where delivery speed is not an order-winning criterion

Order point

Customer's delivery requirement

Existing order backlog or forward load

Process lead-time in manufacturing

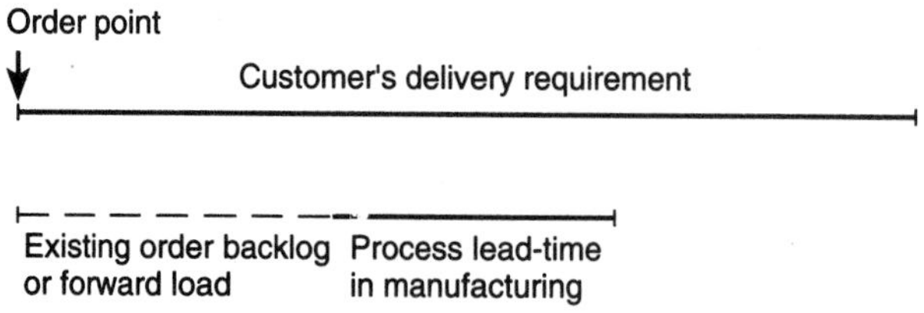

TABLE 3–1   Superfast Producers

Company	Product	Time from Order to Finished Goods (weeks)	
		Old	*New*
GE	Circuit breaker boxes	3.0	0.6
Motorola	Pagers	3.0	0.05
Hewlett-Packard	Electronic test equipment	4.0	1.0
Brunswick	Fishing reels	3.0	1.0

SOURCE: B. Dumaine, "How Managers Can Succeed Through Speed," *Fortune*, February 13, 1989, pp. 5–29 (with permission).

TABLE 3–2   Typical Improvements in Production Flow Times

Example		*Before*	*After*	*Percent Reduction*
Japan				
Washing machines (Matsushita)	Hours	360	2	99
United States				
Motorcycles (Harley-Davidson)		360	3	99
Motor controllers	Days	56	7	88
Electric components		24	1	96
Radar detectors		22	3	86

SOURCE: G. Stalk and T. M. Hout, *Competing against Time: How Time-based Competition Is Reshaping Global Markets* (New York: Free Press, 1990), p. 67 (with permission).

Where process lead time and existing order backlog do not exceed the customer's delivery requirement, delivery speed is not an issue (see Figure 3–6).

With regard to delivery, it is important to distinguish between delivery promise (that is, committing the company to deliver in line with a customer's requirements) and delivery speed. The former can be a commitment in any of the situations described by Figure 3–5, whereas the latter only appertains to situations similar to those given in Figure 3–6.

Increasingly, companies are reducing lead times. Some are endeavoring to shorten them reactively, if not proactively, in line with their perception of their markets or to get a competitive edge. The levels of improvement that can be achieved are incredible, as testified by Tables 3–1 and 3–2.

An organization's response to reducing lead times needs to be corporatewide, and often the lead times associated with before and after manufacturing can be a substantial part of the time it takes from order entry to customer delivery. For example, the time needed for Toyota to schedule a dealer's order is one day, compared to Detroit's five; Milliken, the large U.S. textile manufacture, has been collaborating with General Motors on auto interiors, with Sears on upholstery fabrics, and with Wal-Mart on apparel. Working now as partners rather than separate parts of the operation, Milliken and its customers have been able to reduce, among other things, the lead time required to fill an order by 50 percent.[8]

One principal contributor in this important dimension of reducing lead time, however, is manufacturing. (Note that lead-time reduction in product development is addressed under the section on design covered later in the chapter.) From the moment an order reaches the factory, all elements of lead time need to be reviewed with the aim of reducing each component involved in the total process. To succeed, companies must transform themselves and simply break the paradigms that hold current procedures and norms in place.[9]

Companies can knowingly offer short lead times to customers by holding excess capacity, maintaining low- or zero-order backlogs, or holding inventory at any or all stages in the process. However, in these situations such decisions are not manufacturing-related, as they should emanate from a corporate-based agreement. Furthermore, such circumstances will not constitute a delivery-speed requirement as defined above. Manufacturing's role, however, would be to maintain the various elements on which such decisions are based. A supplier's promise to deliver by an agreed date then leads to the aspect of delivery reliability, which was described in the last section.

With customers typically reducing their own lead times, many companies are finding that the element of delivery speed is becoming an increasing factor in their markets. Consequently, customer lead times are shorter than the combined lead times of material purchase and manufacture (see Figure 3–6). A firm's response to delivery speed, as with all criteria, can be either reactive or proactive. By being reactive, a company will cope with the necessary lead-time reduction as and when it occurs, by some combination of changing priorities, expediting, increasing short-term capacity, or living with some level of failure to deliver on time. By being proactive, a company will reduce its own lead times, thereby obviating delivery speed from being an internal factor while exploiting short lead times in the marketplace. Possible scenarios in which companies may be involved are outlined in Table 3–3. This sets out a series of time-related alternatives, and firms need to determine their current and preferred position by market as the first step to establishing a strategic response. Companies' potential opportunity to reduce lead times will depend on the nature of their markets (for example, whether they sell standard or special products and offer a design-and-manufacturing, or manufacturing-only, capability) and their decisions to hold different levels of raw materials/components, work-in-process and finished-goods inventory. As a company moves (or is able to move) from point 1 to 5 in Table 3–3, overall lead

---

[8]Referred to in J. L. Bower and T. M. Hout, "Fast-Cycle Capability for Competitive Power," *Harvard Business Review*, November–December 1988, pp. 110–18.

[9]Further details and approaches are to be found in G. Stalk and T. M. Hout, *Competing against Time: How Time-based Competition Is Reshaping Global Aspects* (New York: Free Press, 1990); R. W. Schmenner, "The Merit of Making Things Fast," *Sloan Management Review*, Fall 1988, pp. 1–17; and J. D. Blackburn, *Time-based Competition: The Next Battleground in American Manufacturing*, (Homewood, Ill.: Business One Irwin, 1991). Other references include P. Goldsburgh and P. Deane, "Time Is Money," *Management Today*, September 1985, pp. 132–39; and B. Dumaine, "How Managers Can Succeed through Speed," *Fortune*, February 13, 1989, pp. 54–59.

TABLE 3–3   Alternative Responses to Markets and Their Lead-Time Implications

Initial Positions	Length of Lead Times
1. *Design to order*—new product response where companies design and manufacture a product to meet the specific needs of a customer	Long
2. *Engineer to order*—changes to standard products are offered to customers and only made to order. Lead times include the relevant elements of engineering design and all manufacturing	
3. *Make to order*—concerns manufacturing a standard product (any customization is nominal and does not increase total lead times) only on receipt of a customer order or against an agreed schedule or call-off	
4. *Assemble to order*—components and subassemblies have been made to stock. On receipt of an order (or against an agreed schedule or call-off), the required parts are drawn from work-in-process/component inventory and assembled to order	
5. *Make to stock*—finished goods are made ahead of demand in line with sales forecasts. Customers' orders are met from inventory.	Short

*Some customers require companies to make to print (i.e., make a product in line with a given drawing). In such markets, lead times only include raw materials purchase/supply and manufacturing. They do not include design, but some customer-induced redesign during the process will often be involved (as explained on p. 60).

times will reduce. However, as explained above, any repositioning is a corporate decision directly affecting the element of delivery speed. Adjusting its position on this continuum so as to eliminate or reduce the impact of delivery speed would then need to be supported by shortening each element of lead time within the overall process. This would involve a whole range of decisions including capacity, inventory holdings and set-up reduction.

Finally, time-based management has a further, significant advantage. Compared with the more traditional, bureaucratic, or entrepreneurial approaches, it leads to reductions in overhead costs as shown in Figure 3–7.

Quality.   Quality as a competitive criterion has been thrust onto center stage since the late 1970s. Although its importance has been recognized throughout this period, many companies have failed to compete on this dimension. In part this is because the definition of the word *quality* has been broadened to encompass many dimensions. The result has been a lack of understanding and subsequent lack of direction, the hallmark of generic statements that characterize strategy formulation. Table 3–4 lists eight dimensions of strategy and identifies the function(s) that would typically assume prime responsibility for its provision.[10] However in many instances and as recognized here, by separating criteria into "manufacturing-related and manufacturing-specific," "manufacturing-related but not manufacturing specific," and "non-manufacturing-related," there is overlap. Single and joint provision is, therefore, the outcome.

---

[10] These eight dimensions of quality were first listed by D. A. Garvin in "Competing on the Eight Dimensions of Quality," *Harvard Business Review,* November–December 1987, pp. 101–19.

FIGURE 3–7

Overhead costs incurred in time-based management approaches compared with those involved in classic structures

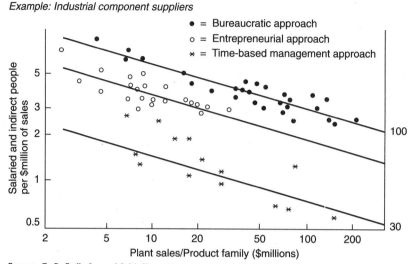

Example: Industrial component suppliers

- ● = Bureaucratic approach
- ○ = Entrepreneurial approach
- ✳ = Time-based management approach

SOURCE: G. S. Stalk, Inr. and J. M. Hout, *Competing against Time: How Time-Based Competition is Reshaping Global Markets* (New York: Free Press, 1990), p. 54 (with permission).

One reason companies do not compete successfully in the quality domain is their failure to clarify which dimension(s) of quality will provide the best results in given markets. Identifying the different dimensions involved is the first step. The next is to agree which, and to what extent each, needs addressing.

In the context of this section, the aspect of quality that concerns manufacturing provision is conformance—making a product to specification. Linked closely to design (which determines the specification itself—see Table 3–4), quality within this definition is a key manufacturing task. Its role in most markets has now been changed from an order-winner to a qualifier.[11] In part this has been brought about by Japanese companies that, as a facet of their competitive thrust in several industrial markets, made products of a high quality. The result has been similar to the color-television example given Chapter 2. Companies, in order to stay in relevant markets, needed to increase their product quality. Having done so, the role of quality then changed from an order-winner to a qualifier. Today, customers expect products to be of a high quality, thus recognizing (at least intuitively) that quality is a given.

One example of the importance of conformance quality within a market is provided by auto vehicles. The growth in Japanese companies' share within the volume and luxury sectors of this market has been outstanding.[12] This is partly due to the continued high levels of quality achieved compared to principal competitors (see Tables 3–5 and 3–6). Link this to their superior productivity performance shown in Tables 1–7 and 1–8 and the reasons for success begin to emerge.

---

[11]C. A. Voss, "Quality in a Manufacturing Strategy," *Total Quality Management*, June 1990, pp. 149–52, elaborates on the role of quality as a qualifier.

[12]Survey, "Executive Cars," *Financial Times*, April 30, 1993, p. II.

TABLE 3–4   The Dimensions of Quality and the Functions Typically Responsible for Their Provision

	Dimensions of Quality	*Functions*
Performance	A product's primary operating characteristics	
Features	Secondary characteristics, the "bells and whistles"	Design
Reliability	The probability of a product malfunctioning within a given period	
Conformance	The degree to which a product is manufactured to the agreed specification	Manufacturing
Durability	A measure of a product's life in terms of both its technical and economic dimensions	Design
Serviceability	The ease of servicing (planned or breakdown) to include the speed and provision of after-sales service	Design and After-sales
Aesthetics	How the final product looks	Design
Perceived quality	How a customer views the product	Marketing and Design

SOURCE: D. A. Garvin, "Competing on the Eight Dimensions of Quality," *Harvard Business Review*, November–December 1987, pp. 101–19.

TABLE 3–5   Auto Assembly Plant Quality—Volume Producers, 1989

	Assembly Defects per 100 Vehicles			
Parent Location/Plant Location	*Best*	*Weighted Average*	*Worst*	*Sample Size*
Japanese-owned plants in Japan	38	52	88	20
Japanese-owned plants in North America	36	55	60	6
US-owned plants in North America	35	78	169	42
European-owned plants in Europe	64	76	124	5
Newly industrializing countries	28	72	191	7

SOURCE: International Motor Vehicle Program, Massachusetts Institute of Technology (1988).

The recent attention attracted by quality-based approaches in management has further highlighted the emphasis on the advantages of completing tasks correctly the first time. This, in part, has been an extension of the improvements in product quality and the significant benefits that have been secured. Much has been written on the approaches that have underpinned this success.[13]

---

[13]Books or articles that specifically address aproaches to quality include R. Caplan, *A Practical Approach to Quality Control* (London: Business Books, 1971); J. M. Juran, *Quality Control Handbook* (Maidenhead: McGraw-Hill, 1974); P. B. Crosby, *Quality Is Free* (Maidenhead: McGraw-Hill 1979); J. M. Juran and F. M. Gryna, *Quality Planning and Analysis* (New York: McGraw-Hill, 1980); W. F. Denning, *Quality, Productivity and Competitive Position* (Cambridge, Mass.: MIT Press, 1982); A. V. Feigenbaum, *Total Quality Control: Engineering and Management*, 3rd ed. (Maidenhead: McGraw-Hill, 1983); G. Taguchi, *Designing Quality into Products and Processes* (Asian Productivity Organization,

---

TABLE 3–6   Auto Assembly Plant Quality—Luxury Vehicles, 1989

| Country/Region | Assembly Defects per 100 Vehicles | | | |
	Best	Weighted Average	Worst	Sample Size
Japan	30	34	35	3
United States	60	65	106	4
Europe	26	77	207	18

SOURCE: International Motor Vehicles Program, MIT.

Demand Increases.   In some markets, a company's ability to respond to increases in demand is an important factor in winning orders. These sales may reflect the high seasonality of customers' requirements or be of a spasmodic or one-off nature. This factor concerns the level of predictability surrounding demand itself as well as others such as product shelf life and the frequency of product modifications in line with market requirements. All will affect manufacturing's response.

Knowing seasonal demand makes it possible to reach agreement between supplier, manufacturer, distributor, and customer about inventory holdings throughout the process, process capacity, and planned increases in labor (e.g., overtime working, additional shifts). With one-off or spot business (e.g., during an influenza epidemic when the demand is for the same product that may have a short shelf life, thus limiting viable inventory levels, or where a product is customer-specified at some point in the process and, therefore, cannot be made ahead of demand, or a significant order for a product over and above agreed call-off quantities or simply an unexpected, sizable order for a given product), holding materials or other forms of capacity, arranging short-term increases in labor capacity (e.g., through overtime), rearranging priorities, or some combination of these will typically be a supplier's response.

The phenomena described here provide another example of the way that a lack of essential clarity can lead to serious levels of corporate misunderstanding. The generalized discussion surrounding these key aspects of a business typically involves words such as *flexibility*.[14] However, the extent to which a company intends to respond to these significant increases in demand is a strategic decision of some magnitude. To allow each function to respond according to its own interpretation invariably leads to major mismatches.

Product Range.   As highlighted earlier, markets are increasingly characterized by difference, not similarity. However, the balance between levels of customization and the volume base for repetitive manufacturing has to be addressed by bringing together the relevant parts of the organization to select from alternatives. That markets are in-

---

1986); F. Price, *Right First Time: Using Quality Control for Profit* (Aldershot: Wildwood House, 1986); and B. G. Dale and J. J. Plunkett (eds.), *Managing Quality* (Hemel Hempstead: Philip Allan, 1991).

[14] The basic misunderstandings surrounding the word *flexibility* are highlighted in T. J. Hill and S. H. Chambers, "Flexibility: A Manufacturing Conundrum," *International Journal of Operations and Production Management, IJOPM* 11, No. 2, (1991) pp. 5–13.

creasingly segmenting is a given. Manufacturing's role is to continue to develop processes that are flexible enough to cope with product-range differences and provide low-cost results. It needs, therefore, to be able to bridge these essential differences in order to retain the volume base so essential to efficient manufacturing.

Thus, where product ranges are widening, process developments need to reflect the broadening nature of the product base and the lower-volume implications that tend to go hand in hand with these trends. The former needs to be recognized at the time when process investments are made. The latter is reflected in reduced set-up times, whether manual or automated (e.g., a numerically controlled facility), so enabling companies to cope with the lower-volume nature of these changes while retaining the necessary levels of cost.

Examples of these trends are seen in the automobile industry. The pressure on automakers at the lower end of the volume scale is to continue to differentiate their products as a way of competing not only with their traditional competitors, but with makers at the higher end of the volume scale as well. BMW's 7 Series offers a marked uplift in customization, more akin to the very low-volume luxury makers such as Rolls Royce and Aston Martin. Handcrafted leather interiors and its "any color" option are examples of this. However, BMW is also aware that Toyota is already planning a production system capable of responding speedily to individual customer requirements. As with all companies, to support increases in product/color-range options successfully, manufacturing needs to develop its processes to provide these in a cost- and time-efficient way. At the moment, BMW's nonstandard color option takes extra time and cost because paint lines have to be cleaned out.[15] A priority in manufacturing is, therefore, to develop a paint-spraying capability to reduce this problem.

Manufacturing-Related but Not Manufacturing-Specific Criteria

Although businesses separate clusters of activities into different functions, in reality they are—and need to form—part of the same whole. Thus, many functions within a company will directly support manufacturing or will undertake tasks that link or directly affect that function's strategic and operational roles.

Design.   The links between design, manufacturing, and markets are the very essence of a business. The way that these interrelate, therefore, is a fundamental, strategic issue. Both design and manufacturing's aim is to provide products according to their technical and business specifications. In addition, these two functions also combine to provide the product developments that come before the ongoing selling/manufacturing activity, which is the commercial substance of companies. Three of the more important dimensions are addressed in this section and have been chosen because they are fundamental to this basic corporate activity.*

---

[15]Reported in J. Griffith, "BMW—Tailoring Its Competitive Challenge", *Financial Times*, October 19, 1990, p. 16.

*The dimensions of quality listed in Table 3–4 that relate to design function provision are addressed in a later section.

Low Cost.   Design is becoming increasingly important in providing essential support for several criteria relevant to today's markets. Products have to be designed with both process characteristics and cost reduction in mind. Thus, design not only concerns functionality, it has a critical impact on product costs. With direct materials typically accounting for some 40–60 percent of the total, the opportunities to reduce costs at source are substantial. In addition, this essential link reinforces the need to meet the design for manufacturing requirements in terms of labor-cost reduction through increased automation and other labor-saving opportunities. For many years, corporate appeals by Western firms to design for manufacture have been more exhortation than accomplishment, a view confirmed by a committee of the National Research Council in the early 1990s.[16] It found the overall quality of engineering design—the process of turning a concept into a finished product, or determining how to make a new toaster, dress, or computer as efficiently as possible—to be poor. Long before a product reaches the store, 70 percent or more of its cost is determined by its design.

Any third-rate engineer can design complexity. In many companies, the emphasis to make it simple is neither part of the designer's makeup nor part of the corporate demands placed on this function. In the 1990s, however, pressure on price will continue to be an important competitive factor in many segments. Thus, design's role in the total corporate response is fundamental in more ways than one.

Product Range.   The increasing level of product diversification has already been recognized as an important factor in today's increasingly competitive markets, and central to this provision is the design function. The pressure on design will vary from market to market, and the interpretation and execution of these is central to a company's ability to remain competitive. The tendency for Western designers to be more interested in functionality than the commercial facets of design is in marked contrast to competitors, particularly the Japanese. As Hiroyuki Yoshida, head of Toyota's design center, reflected, "Whatever the merits of a design, it has to be robust enough to go through our engineering and manufacturing system. The commercial point of design has not been lost. We are in the business to make low-cost high-quality cars for a mass market. We are making cars, not art."[17]

Within this context, as highlighted elsewhere, markets are increasingly segmenting. Design needs to be able to meet these changes and to recognize, certainly in terms of attitude and speed of response, that change is a fundamental characteristic of today's markets and a company's essential support. For example, Honda has had to move from developing its Accord range as a world car (the same model selling into all markets) in the early 1980s to designing two distinct ranges for its home and U.S. markets.

It is now the age of diversification, and those companies unable to keep pace with this growth of diversity will decline. Many companies, therefore, are directing much

---

[16]C. W. Hoover, Jr., cochaired the committee that studied engineering design in the United States. The critical findings were embodied in his article, "U.S. Products Designed to Fail," *Chicago Tribune*, July 6, 1991, p. 15.

[17]Quoted in C. Leadbetter, "Toyota's Conundrum: Creating a Global Car for a Niche Market," *Financial Times*, July 17, 1991, p. 16.

more attention to incorporating the perspectives and preferences of customers into future designs. A classic example of this is provided by Toyota and Mazda. Both have built complexes in Tokyo that incorporate vehicle-design studios in which the visitors are invited to "design" their own cars. Thus, ideas on what constitutes a potential customer's ideal vehicle are included as inputs into future designs.

However, the demand for styling and product features has to be reconciled with other pressures. Environmentally friendly products are not only a growing concern of customers but also high on the agenda of legislative bodies. For example, clean-air legislation in California is at the forefront of changing pressures on vehicle design. Its requirement for minimum percentage sales of low-emission vehicles (LEVs) and ultralow-emission vehicles (ULEVs) has been an added stimulus for improvements on all car and emission standards. Furthermore, the legislation also requires that by 1998, at least 2 percent of all manufacturers' sales will need to be zero-emission vehicles (ZEVs), and this will rise to 10 percent by the year 2003, unless there is a major breakthrough in existing engine technology, companies will have to develop an electric car by the end of this decade.

Most major carmakers have recognized the need to harness design capabilities to meet these environmentally stimulated developments. In 1991, General Motors, Ford, and Chrysler concluded an agreement with the U.S. Government under which a total of $1 billion is to be spent over a period of 12 years to develop advanced battery technology. Similarly, to meet the Los Angeles initiative, the Anglo-Swedish group, Clean Air Transport, won a contract to supply 3,500 electric cars starting at the end of 1992, and Los Angeles City Council, L.A. Water and Power, and Southern California Edison have contributed about one third of the $34m project costs as part of a joint research and development agreement. Production of these vehicles will be relocated to Los Angeles in 1993.[18]

Lead Times.   Reducing lead times within the manufacturing process has already been highlighted as an increasingly important order-winner. Similarly, speed to market with new product designs and developments is becoming a significant competitive factor in today's markets. The increasing priority of speed is based on the recognition that it can simply negate the competition. The results of such improvements, as shown in Table 3–7 and Figure 3–8, speaks for themselves. In addition, companies receive a number of distinct sets of advantages from reducing product design and development lead times, including the following:

1. *Benefits of double gain.* Being first in the market brings advantages of both higher volumes and higher margins—the opportunity for double gain—as explained below:

    a. Product life cycles are extended—if a product is introduced sooner, rarely will it become obsolete sooner. This advantage accrues even more so where customers incur high switching costs. The usual outcome, therefore, of early

---

[18]Insights in the design and development of cars are provided in the *Financial Times* survey, "Car of the Future," May 21, 1991.

TABLE 3-7   Superfast Innovators

Company	Product	Development Time (years)	
		Old	*New*
Honda	Cars	5.0	3.0
AT&T	Telephones	2.0	1.0
Navistar	Trucks	5.0	2.5
Hewlett-Packard	Computer printers	4.5	1.8

SOURCE: B. Dumaine, "How Managers Can Succeed through Speed," *Fortune*. February 13, 1989, pp. 54–59 (with permission).

FIGURE 3-8

Examples of reductions in product-development lead-times

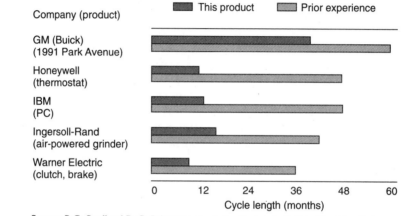

SOURCE: P. G. Small and D. G. Reinertsen, *Developing Products in Half the Time* (New York: Van Norstrand Reinhold, 1991), p. 2. Figure 1–1 (with permission).

product introduction is to gain more customers who, in turn, stay longer (see Figure 3–9).

b. *Increased market share*—The first producer will, in the beginning, command 100 percent market share. Thus, the earlier a product appears, the more likely the prospects of obtaining a large market share. Link this to the previous factor and the impact on total life-cycle volumes is marked.

c. *Higher profit margins*—A company will naturally enjoy a higher level of pricing freedom in the early stages of a product's life cycle. This will, therefore, provide higher margins in the early stages with the opportunity for manufacturing to provide lower costs in light of the volume advantages highlighted above. See Figure 3–10 and also the earlier section on experience curves.

d. *Double gain*—The first three factors combine to give a situation of double gain: companies gain higher sales and also achieve a higher margin on each sale.

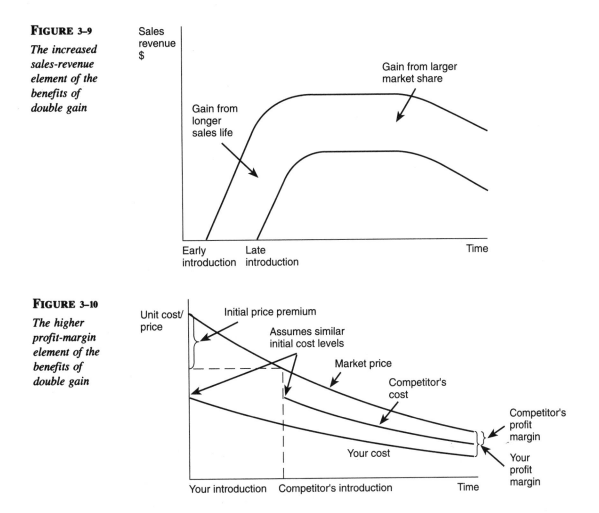

FIGURE 3–9

The increased sales-revenue element of the benefits of double gain

FIGURE 3–10

The higher profit-margin element of the benefits of double gain

2. *Technology, consumer preference, and corporate image.* Reductions in product-development lead times also provide opportunities for companies to sustain technology leadership and corporate image:

   a. *Exploiting technology opportunities*—If an organization can develop products quickly, it is more able to synchronize its product developments with the latest technologies and thus exploit these opportunities fully.

   b. *Matching consumer change*—Short product-development lead times help a business to match market changes, thereby tracking more closely changes in consumer preferences and demands.

   c. *Corporate image*—Developing products more quickly will help a firm to maintain its corporate image of being a progressive front-runner in developments and technology excellence.

3. *Reduction in design costs.* Compressing development lead times also results in a reduction in design costs. This is achieved in part by increased levels of cooperation, which reduces misunderstandings and ensures the incorporation of functional perspectives throughout. In addition, the changed role and contribution of design within the process also leads to less time being spent within the design stages with associated reductions in cost.

Table 3–7 and Figure 3–8 provided examples of what can be achieved, while Figures 3–11, 3–12, and Table 3–8 show how this is accomplished. The position illustrated in Figure 3–11 compares a Japanese and a Western company making the same products, mechanical transmissions. As the figure shows, while the Western company required 30 to 38 months to complete the development and introduction cycles, the Japanese company took 14 to 18 months. A review of Figure 3–11 illustrates the source of this advantage. Although some elements in the process yield a substantial gain, the improvement is more cumulative in nature and emanates from two sources. Steps, at least in part, are completed not sequentially but in parallel, and each step is typically shorter.

A review of Table 3–8 shows similar characteristics to those illustrated in Figure 3–11. It also highlights another important feature—companies within this revision do not just accelerate a stage per se but recognize that it may need to rethink the activities within one phase and its role in the new approach. The "approval" phase in DEC's revised procedures illustrates this outcome.

Table 3–8, which compares development lead times for European, U.S., and Japanese carmakers, provides a more detailed illustration of these sources of lead-time reduction.[19]

This improvement partly stems from the changing values within the different functions involved. Western designers expect to develop products that require little or no modification. As perfection is rarely, if ever, achieved, any necessary changes must be identified in later phases. However, also part of the typical design function's attitudes is a resistance to change since, given the perfection syndrome, a need for change implies failure. The result is long first-phase lead times, which are subsequently further increased because of the inherent resistance to change.

The Japanese alternative is based on a different set of expectations. Knowing that perfection is impossible, designers conclude their proposals much more quickly than their Western counterparts and, ready to accept change, respond to the demands of the modification stages with appropriate expectations and corresponding speed. The result is a significant overall reduction in development lead times.

---

[19]Other examples of product development lead-time reductions are provided in R. H. Hayes, S. C. Wheelwright, and K. B. Clark, *Dynamic Manufacturing: Creating the Learning Organization* (New York: Free Press, 1988); "Time Is Money," *The Economist,* October 8, 1988, pp. 90–95; *Managing Product and Process Development Projects,* pp. 304–39 in J. D. Blackburn (ed.) *Time-based Competition: The Next Battleground in American Manufacturing,* (Homewood, Ill.: Richard D. Irwin, 1991), pp. 121–208; and J. Mortimer and J. Hartley, *Managing in the 90s: Simultaneous Engineering,* (London: Department of Trade and Industry, June 1991).

TABLE 3–8   Average Project Lead Times and Stage Length in Japanese, U.S., and European Carmakers.*

Development Phase	Japanese			United States			European		
	Begin	End	Stage Length	Begin	End	Stage Length	Begin	End	Stage Length
Concept study	42	34	8	62	44	18	62	47	15
Product planning	38	29	9	57	39	18	57	40	17
Advanced engineering	42	27	15	56	29	26	52	39	13
Product engineering	30	6	24	40	12	28	39	16	23
Process engineering	28	6	22	31	6	26	38	8	30
Pilot run	7	3	4	9	3	6	9	3	6
Total	—	—	82	—	—	122	—	—	104

*Data in months before start of production; figures have been rounded. Sample sizes are Japan, 12; United States, 6; and Europe, 10.

SOURCE: B. Clark and T. Fujimoto, "Overlapping Problem-solving in Product Development," in K. Ferdows (ed.), *Managing International Manufacturing* (Amsterdam: Elsevier Science Publishers, BV [North-Holland], 1989).

FIGURE 3–11

Improving response time in new product development (mechanical transmissions)

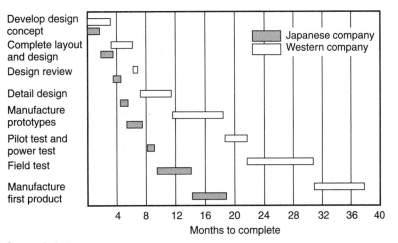

SOURCE: G. Stalk, Jr. and T. M. Hout, *Competing against Time: How Time-based Competition is Reshaping Global Markets* (New York: Free Press, 1990), p. 188, Exhibit 4–1 (with permission).

Distribution.   Distribution's role in quick and reliable delivery has been mentioned earlier. As part of the total process, distribution plays an essential role in delivery.

In addition, the costs of this facet of overall provision have typically been rising both in themselves and as a percentage of the total. Including the costs of storage, warehouse administration, and movement, this element of cost has typically not received the same level of attention as the product itself. Classic examples of this are items that have experienced systematic and significant cost reductions over a number

FIGURE 3–12

*Digital Equipment
Company's
(DEC) reduced
competition time
for a new product
development*

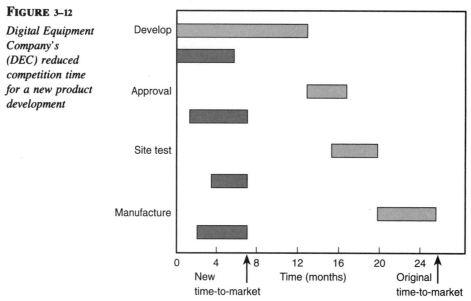

SOURCE: R. Reeve, "Profiting from Teamwork," *Manufacturing Breakthrough,*
January–February 1992, p. 22 (with permission).

of years, such as computers. Highlighting this potential source of cost reduction has
often not received the attention that related activities have.[20]

Nonmanufacturing-Related Criteria

It is not unusual for companies to be in markets whose relevant order-winners are not
directly related to manufacturing. In these types of markets, manufacturing will typically be required to support one or more qualifiers. Some of the more important criteria that frequently characterize markets are now briefly discussed. In all instances,
each function responsible for the criterion reviewed would have the task of providing
and maintaining the required level of support.

Design Leadership.   The role of design and its relationship to competitive issues
such as product-development lead times and product costs have already been discussed. However, one of the design function's principal roles concerns the development of products in terms of features, aesthetics, perceived levels of design in
specification, and reliability (including costs) while in service (see Table 3–4). Furthermore, where frequent design introductions offer a competitive edge, this requirement will be at the forefront of the function's performance priorities. Linked to the
need for shorter product development lead times, this criterion is increasingly emerg-

---

[20]For example, this issue is raised in L. McClean, "Digital Load Gets Lighter," *Financial Times,*
April 23, 1991, p. 12.

ing as a major competitive factor in today's markets. For example, responding to the challenge from Yamaha, Honda almost doubled its range of motorcycle models in less than two years, eliminating Yamaha's short-lived advantage. Liz Claiborne (a designer/manufacturer of separates and sportswear) has introduced two additional apparel seasons to reflect more clearly consumer buying patterns. Seiko has increased its dominant role in the watch market with a highly automated factory capable of producing new models each day. In semiconductors, the competitive factor is largely the speed with which new product technologies can be applied to chips.

The importance of product design has always been recognized. Markets can be dominated by this dimension, and unique design, particularly in the past, has been considered the principal order-winning provision of this function. However, companies are increasingly recognizing the range of contributions that the design function can make in winning orders, the key elements of which have been discussed in earlier sections.

Being an Existing Supplier.   Where a company is an existing supplier, it may continue to win orders in part, or solely, because of this factor. The criterion tends to be relevant to both low volume and spares markets. In the former, manufacturing needs to continue to support the relevant order-winners and qualifiers. In the latter, it needs to recognize the impact that its performance on relevant criteria will have on orders for any new or existing products in the future.

Marketing and Sales.   The marketing and sales functions' principal orientation is toward the marketplace. Its important links to customers and its insights into the characteristics of relevant market segments—including issues of pricing, competitive threats, growth and/or decline of existing segments, and identification of new opportunities—is an essential part of a company's strategic provision.

Brand Name.   Through a variety of activities, including design, advertising, and increasing or maintaining market share, companies seek to establish brand names for their products. Where this has been achieved and maintained, companies will win orders, which is partly due to the image its products have in the markets in which they compete.

Technical Liaison and Support.   In certain markets, customers will seek technical liaison from suppliers during the precontract phase and technical support thereafter. The quality and extent of a supplier's in-house technical capability to support product development, particularly toward its introduction in the early stages of its manufacture, will be an important criterion in these markets.

After-sales Support.   Furthermore, companies may look for ways of differentiating their total product by offering, for instance, a high level of customer support (see Table 3–4. "Serviceability"). One example is BMW. The company has a fleet of 30 cars funded jointly with its dealers and strategically placed throughout the United Kingdom. The purpose is to go to the support of any BMW that has broken down by the roadside. The company will continue to increase this standby fleet until it can sufficiently deal with 80 percent of the breakdowns occuring in all the BMWs in the United Kingdom that can actually be solved at the roadside.

A further example of after-sales support is the motor repairs sector. Compact discs enable a mechanic to call up information on any component or car by typing in the relevant part or the vehicle's chassis number. In repair procedure terms, the mechanic can find out which faults cause which problems and what procedures should be followed. Service sales staff are similarly able to investigate customer details and vehicle records to help in their service-support provision. Companies already using these customer support systems include Volkswagen, BMW, Opel, PSA (Peugeot and Citroen), General Motors, and Toyota.

Benchmarking[21]

The failure of a company to assess and monitor its competitors is at best a mark of corporate complacency and at worst a sign of strategic naivety. For a company, such a monitoring process has two important dimensions.

- A continuous updating of the level and dimensions of competition within its markets.
- Proactivity, seeking to improve its own business performance by learning from other companies about what can be done and how to do things better.

Benchmarking is an approach that was identified and highlighted in the mid-1980s and that many companies believe is essential to help to enhance their competitive position in the 1990s. It does this by redirecting corporate spotlight from assessing internal performance (typically using internal measures) to checking externally how current (albeit improved) performance compares with best practice. In this way it reinforces the clear need to identify market requirements, to differentiate importance, and to establish the levels of performance that need to be achieved within each competitive dimension.

As shown in the earlier section on experience curves, all companies tend to learn and improve through time; but the key question is whether the rate of improvement is adequate to become and/or remain competitive. Benchmarking forces companies to look outward and recognize this external perspective as the appropriate way to iden-

---

[21]Interesting articles on benchmarking include L. S. Pryor, "Benchmarking: A Self-improvement Strategy," *Journal of Business Strategy*, November–December 1989, pp. 28–32; R. Osterhoff et al. "Competitive Benchmarking at Xerox," in M. J. Stahland and G. M. Bounds (eds.), *Competing Globally through Customer Value* (New York: Quorum Books, 1991) pp. 788–98; K. Perowski, "The Benchmarking Bandwagon," *Quality Progress*, January 1991, pp. 190–224; "First Find Your Bench," *The Economist*, May 11, 1991, p. 72; S. Holberton, "Benchmarking—How to Help Yourself to a Competitor's Best Practices," *Financial Times*, June 24, 1991, p. 12; and A. S. Wellbeck et al., "World-Class Manufacturing: Benchmarking World-Class Performance," *The McKinsey Quarterly*, November 1, 1991, pp. 3–24.

tify the levels of performance that need to become their new targets. Furthermore, checking against performance in other businesses (and particularly in unrelated sectors) leads to some distinct advantages:

- It presents the "what" rather than the "how." Thus, companies are presented with targets not solutions, which in turn increases the aspect of ownership. The panacea syndrome mentioned earlier also identifies the inappropriateness of solution-oriented approaches.
- Having targets to aim for helps to create a uniform response from all parts of a business. When goals are common, improvement becomes a shared task.
- It reinforces the executive role, rather than that of support staff as the key element for bringing about sustained performance improvements.
- External, and particularly ex-sector, comparisons are often perceived as being more objectively derived and therefore more readily accepted.
- It opens up new improvement horizons that frequently represent a stepped change in performance. In so doing, it provides the opportunity to leapfrog competitors in selected and relevant dimensions of performance.

Benchmarking is concerned with the search for best practices, whatever their source, in order to achieve superior performance. It therefore involves continuously measuring a company's products, services, and practices against both competitors and the leaders in any business sector. It is, however, not an end in itself but a means to help to achieve superior levels of competitiveness. In this way, it offers an important dimension within the domain of order-winners by ensuring that corporate performance against relevant criteria is measured against externally derived, best-practice norms. Benchmarking, therefore, moves a company from having an inward bias to incorporating external perspectives, which invariably introduces a stepped change in terms of performance. These external antennae help a company to assess what is going on and also to manage itself within its own environment.

Implementing benchmarking starts with determining the key functions within a business that need to be reviewed. When the relevant performance variables to measure these functions have been agreed, then identifying best-in-class performances sets the target. What follows is the task of assessing the action programs to bring corporate performance into line with and then to surpass that achieved by the best-in-class companies.

However, for benchmarking to be successfully implemented, some key elements need to be in place. These include:

- *Rigor.* It is essential that companies ensure that the targets to be achieved are set high enough. Targets, therfore, need to be derived from knowledge and not intuition.
- *Overcoming disbelief.* In the initial phases of this process, companies often need to convince themselves that they can not only do better but can meet the often daunting tasks that benchmarking reviews typically identify.
- *Accountability.* Benchmarking represents an on-going procedure for measuring performance and ensuring improvement. A prerequiste for

this is to instill in everyone the responsibility and authority for identifying, checking, and implementing the changes necessary to achieve this improvement.

- *Culture change.* managers typically spend most of their time on internal issues. Reorienting companies to be externally rather than internally focused is an essential facet on the successful introduction and on-going development of this approach and associated improvement.

Best-in-Class Exemplars

The need for companies to assess themselves against externally derived standards has been stressed throughout this book. Thus, examples need to be identified from a number of different company classifications, including:

- Other parts of the same company—internal benchmarking.*
- Direct competitors.
- Companies in the same industrial sector but not direct competitors.
- Latent competitors.
- Companies outside the industry.

Recognizing the different categories enables a firm to identify a broader range of potential best-in-class sources, thereby improving the quality and representative nature within this critical phase. An example that illustrates the advantages of using best-in-class exemplars is afforded by Figure 3–13. IBM's use of outside-the-industry perspectives helped it to identify its future targets.

Ways to Close the Gap Then Surpass Exemplars

Improving performance is the result of a number of coordinated actions in line with the key functions already identified. The particular improvements will need to reflect the tasks on hand. However, companies must recognize the different levels of achievement that exist:

- *Try harder*—This is a classic approach that, if adopted, implies a failure to recognize the principles underpinning benchmarking.
- *Emulate*—This involves setting achievement targets on a par with competitors and/or best-in-class exemplars.
- *Leapfrog*—This means setting targets higher than existing exemplar norms.
- *Change the rules of the game*—This entails setting the pace in driving the order-winners and qualifiers in relevant markets.

---

*Internal benchmarking is an idea based on identifying the best-in-class within one's own total company in terms of concepts, usefulness, and speed of introduction.

FIGURE 3–13

Benchmarking quality helped IBM identify its best-in-class six-sigma target for 1994*

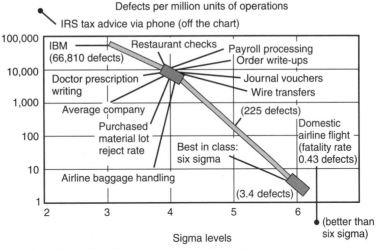

*At the beginning of 1990, IBM admitted its overall defect rate was around three sigma, or 66,810 defects per million operations. By 1994, IBM wants to reach six sigma.

SOURCE: B. C. P. Rayner "Market-driven Quality: IBM Six-sigma Crusade." *Electronic Business,* October 15, 1990, p. 28 (with permission).

TABLE 3–9   **Source and Levels of Targeted Achievement**

	Level of Achievement	
Exemplar	*Emulate*	*Change the Rules of the Game*
Internal benchmarking	80	20
Direct competitors		
Industry sector but not competitor		
Latent competitor		
Outside the industry	20	80

These dimensions constitute target levels of change. The difficulty many companies face at the beginning is in identifying the different levels of achievement. Many find that looking outside helps to more clearly identify levels of higher achievement as shown in Table 3–9.

Competitors Are Moving Targets

Earlier, the need to recognize that order-winners and qualifiers change over time was stressed. This is because markets are dynamic and competitors are moving targets. Companies who set their sights without taking into account these dimensions may find themselves further behind. By failing to identify the rate of improvement of competitors, companies may set themselves targets only to find that the goalposts have moved. The result is that at best they have closed the gap. More typically, however, a company that fails to incorporate the future rate of improvement of its competitors will find itself even further behind and less able to catch up.

Determining Order-Winners and Qualifiers

For companies to gain an understanding of their markets takes time. In fact, strategy debate has a calendar time base that cannot be circumvented. The characteristics of markets and the perspectives of functions must be allowed adequate time, both in their explanation and reception. Going away for a corporate strategy weekend or arranging one-off discussions will lead to generalized statements and little insight.

The strategic facet of order-winners and qualifiers is similarly bound by these characteristics. Seeking to clarify and understand these key insights will take time and requires soundings from different sources.

- *Functional perspectives*—The internal perspectives of the functions that are engaged in the provision of products or that interface with the marketplace hold important insights into customer requirements. Often, however, companies limit this internal review to that of the marketing function. In part, this is based on the historical perception that marketing's view of the market represents the market. Within this context, other functions have failed to assess customers and markets in terms of what they represent from their alternative perspectives. The consequence has been that companies have given undue weight to marketing's view, which has emphasized the need to respond to customer's actual or perceived wishes and demands. Checking the impact on a business has not usually been part of a firm's overall assessment of a market, segment, or customer.

- *Customers' views*—Checking with customers on what they believe they require can invariably lead to a distorted view of reality. Setting aside the aspect of self-interest, customers place orders on suppliers in one system and make demands on supplier's plants in another. Furthermore, customers are unlikely to acknowledge that the business they offer to a supplier is anything other than favorable. Equally, customers often fail to make distinctions concerning different criteria—it is safer to ask for everything at the highest level of provision.

  Most times, those involved in agreeing contracts do not know the critical dimensions of the contracts being discussed. Few have attempted to find out. All present their business in its best light. Thus, to seek the view of customers can only be one part of such an assessment.

- *Actual orders*—The real demands on a supplier are embodied in the characteristics of the individual orders, call-offs, and/or scheduled deliveries placed by customers. Tracing the volumes, lead times, margins, and other relevant aspects of these will bring an essential perspective into evaluating opinion. Many companies, however, fail to analyze the key data that are an inherent by-product of their system and that contain the characteristics of the commercial transactions representing the very nature of their markets.

Conclusion

In today's markets, it is increasingly less likely that companies will have a sustainable, competitive advantage. To compete effectively and continue to be successful, firms need to understand their markets.

However, strategy debate has been and continues to be general in nature. Typical outcomes, therefore, are general descriptions that foster independent responses from functions. But companies that fail to provide coherent strategies will continue to lose out. Unless individual functions are able, and are required, to develop strategies that directly support their markets, these firms will lose substantial and essential advantage.

Distinguishing and weighting order-winners and qualifiers forms a key element of this strategic provision. Without such insights, agreement on what constitutes markets is replaced by individual views grounded in the biases and preferences of different functions. This leads to unsophisticated responses and allows, even encourages, unrelated functional initiatives to be developed.

For manufacturing, investments in both processes and infrastructure are expensive and fixed. Once commitments have been made it is difficult—sometimes impossible—to make changes, certainly within the allowable time frames of current commercial environments. The overall effect on corporate performance is significant. In the short-term it can lead to substantial disparity in performance; in the long-term it can be at the root of overall corporate success or failure.

The Capsizing Effect

The need for companies to be proactively alert stems from the nature of today's markets. Whereas companies in the past could recover from being outperformed and strategically outmaneuvered, this is increasingly less likely. An ever-increasing phenomenon of the current competitive environment is the capsizing effect. Companies find that one day they are confident, secure, and well-directed and the next, capsized and sinking, bottom up. The capsizing effect is often due to a lack of corporate awareness of competitive performance. Not being alert to the dimensions and extent of competitive performance leaves a company vulnerable to significant reversals of fortune and hence irretrievably disadvantaged.

To avoid being competitively outmaneuvered (or sinking altogether), a company must understand its markets with sufficient insight and undertake this task on an ongoing basis. This not only provides understanding of sufficient adequacy on which to base corporate strategic directions but gives the essential inputs from which coordinated and inherent functional strategic outputs are formed.

Hitting Singles versus Home Runs

One essential feature of management that is singularly omitted from its many descriptions is hardwork. Clearly identifying markets, establishing functional strategies to support these, and implementing the outcomes is a demanding role. And, one characteristic essential for completing these necessary parts is persistence. Winning teams build on hitting singles and do not rely on home runs.

Little Is New, Even Less Is Complex

Earlier it was pointed out that any third-rate engineer can design complexity. The same holds true for strategy. Moving from what is complex and uncertain to what is understood and clear is the result of hard work—the same as required of a designer to get from the complex to the simple.

Sound foundations for strategy are built on understanding; and to respond to changing markets, a company must know where it is. In the past, companies have tolerated an inadequate understanding of their markets, with the result that they have been unable to respond and thus lost market share or even lost out all together. Complexity is an inherent feature of most aspects of business and none more so than markets. But it need not be so.

Similarly, nothing is new. The issues and criteria (even the aspect of time) discussed in this chapter are not revolutionary. For example, nearly 70 years ago Henry Ford highlighted the "meaning of time" as an essential and integral competitive factor in all stages of his business from raw materials to distribution.[22] With ore-extraction to sold-product lead times at a little over four days and average shipping times between factory and branches of just over six days, the meaning of time was well-understood and exercised as long ago as the 1920s. What is new is the need to identify markets in terms of what wins orders and then to develop functional strategies to support these. Every long journey begins with a first step—in strategy this first step is understanding your markets.

Further Reading

Hayes, R. H.; S. C. Wheelweight; and K. B. Clark. *Dynamic Manufacturing in Creating the Learning Organization.* New York: Free Press, 1988.

Schonberger, R. J. *Japanese Manufacturing Techniques: Nine Hidden Lessons in Simplicity.* New York: Free Press, 1982.

Schonberger, R. J. *Building a Chain of Customers.* London: Hutchinson Business Books, 1990.

Spendolini, M. J. *The Benchmarking Book.* New York: American Management Association, 1992.

Stahl, M. J. and G. M. Bounds, eds. *Competing Globally through Customer Value.* New York: Quorum Books, 1991.

---

[22]H. Ford, *Today and Tomorrow* (Cambridge, Mass.: Productivity Press, 1988), particularly Chapter 10, "The Meaning of Time."

CHAPTER 4

Developing a Manufacturing Strategy—Methodology

The last two chapters introduced the concepts and principles underpinning the development of a manufacturing strategy. They also discussed the key strategic task of developing a clear understanding of how a company competes.

Functions manage, control, and develop the resources for which they are responsible at both the operational and strategic levels. It is essential that functions do this within the context of how best to support a company's markets. Thus, knowing how a firm competes in relevant markets is a prerequisite for sound strategy development. Without it, functions may pursue good practice but will do so in the dark. That today's markets are different rather than similar is stressed throughout. A basic task, therefore, is to determine what these differences are so that appropriate context and direction can be established and on which functional strategies can be based.

That companies must support their markets is clearly acknowledged. What comprises markets, however, is inadequately established by most companies. Clear understanding of markets is a prerequisite for functional strategy development. A detailed and comprehensive review of a company's markets forms the basis for sound strategy formulation.

Why do companies typically not provide this essential clarification? In part, this is due to their lack of recognition of the form and essential nature of markets. Also, many companies do not know how to undertake such a review.

Checking Markets

To gain the essential understanding of markets requires a detailed review. Only analysis of this depth will yield the insights essential to fulfilling this task. Given that corporate strategy and the functional strategies of which it is comprised are the end result, a company should not have to justify giving adequate time, attention, and resources to undertake the task.

Form and Nature

An introduction to the form and nature of market reviews was provided in Chapter 2, together with the examples given in Tables 2–2 to 2–4. It will help, therefore, to discuss these three different applications to illustrate the form and nature of these outputs.

U.S. Furniture Company.   The example given in Table 2–2 shows the order-winners and qualifiers for two customers in one of this company's markets. As you will guess, the company makes a whole range of products using different types of wood and reflecting different styles. It sells to a number of outlets other than those classified in this table as small chains and large chains; these include, for example, mass merchandisers, moms and pops, large independents, and galleries. The market review, therefore, would need to establish the order-winners and qualifiers for all products in all markets. Very often, products within the same range have similar order-winners and qualifiers, a fact that must be clearly established as part of the analysis. The grouping together with like order-winners and qualifiers is then completed at the next stage. Assumptions on the likeness of segments must be avoided. Approaches based on analysis and verification need to replace the broad-brush overviews that characterize current practice.

What then does the information in Table 2–2 reveal? Without adequate discussion and analysis, companies tend to work on the assumption that particular products (in this case, oak furniture) compete in the same way in different markets. However, Table 2–2 shows that there are marked differences. For large chains, conformance quality is, and will continue to be, the most important order-winner, with price a factor but not a significant one. This contrasts with the way in which oak furniture wins orders in small chains. Here, price and conformance quality were about the same in 1991, but it is anticipated that over time the emphasis will move increasingly toward price. For both types of outlet, delivery reliability and design are essential qualifiers. Customer relations is also a prerequisite, but it is order-losing sensitive for the large chain segment.

European Battery Company.   Table 2–3 illustrates a much wider range of activities. The three product types in the table qualify and win orders very differently from one another. Companies may assume that products of the same type (in this case, batteries) will win orders in a similar way to one another. The price-sensitive nature of product range B is in marked contrast to that of product range C. Similarly, while delivery speed is an order-winner in all three instances, its importance in 1993 for product range A is marked. The role of design also works differently for product types A and C with the latter able to exploit this advantage with price being designated as a qualifier. Finally and once again, delivery reliability as in many markets is an order-losing sensitive qualifier throughout.

U.S. Packaging Company.   This company supplies packaging to a range of customers, three of which are given in Table 2–4. The examples again illustrate how segments can be different from one another. In fact, in this instance, the company wins orders from these customers in very different and sometimes opposing ways. In 1991, price ranged from a qualifier for customer A to being the only order-winner for customer B. Delivery speed, on the other hand, is not a factor for customers A and B but is becoming increasingly so for customer C. And, delivery reliability performs a different though important role with each customer: an order-winner for customer A, and an order-losing sensitive qualifier for customers B and C.

These three examples bring out a number of important points to bear in mind while reading the following sections, which describe the methodology to use when undertaking this work.

1. Markets are characterized by increasing difference. The key to understanding markets, therefore, lies in being able to identify and highlight these differences so as to be able to develop functional responses to support these.

2. Marketing segments markets from the point of view of identifiying differences in customer buying behavior. The examples given as Tables 2–2 to 2–4 illustrate how different order-winners and qualifiers can work within a given marketing segment. Reversing the segmentation process by identifying manufacturing-related differences is, therefore, an essential first step in developing a manufacturing strategy.

3. Order-winners and qualifiers invariably change over time. Hence, strategy is both time- and market-specific, which necessitates identifying differences both today and tomorrow.

4. The process of identifying the order-winners and qualifiers relevant to a company's markets involves all functions as well as appropriate analysis with which to test initial opinions and assumptions. Only by sound, in-depth discussions will the essential characteristics of a company's markets be revealed. In this way, functions are required to explain their perspective and, once agreed, the essential support from manufacturing and other functions (e.g., design and distribution) is clearly identified. This, in turn, will then form the basis on which functional strategies need to be developed, leading to greater coherence within a business and the essential support for agreed markets and customers.

The key to all these points is the in-depth discussion that needs to take place, a style very different from the form and nature of strategic debate in many firms. Only by statement, explanation, analysis, and reexplanation will more accurate and better understood strategic insights be shared by all concerned. Without this, companies will invariably revert to functionally based strategic alternatives, which will typically pull the business in different directions.

Reviewing Relevant Order Winners and Qualifiers

Having reviewed some typical outputs, let us now turn to how discussions are structured and the types of analysis needed to test views and to help distinguish essential differences within a company's chosen markets. To facilitate the strategy debate, it is necessary to start with some stated view of the market as a focal point for discussion.

And, the best place to start is to seek the views of marketing. Marketing should be asked to:

- Segment the market from a marketing point of view and choose products or customers that represent each chosen segment.
- Establish for each segment appropriate future planning horizons that reflect the relevant time scales involved. Normally, this is given as two future time periods similar to the examples in Tables 2–2 to 2–4.
- Select and weight the order-winners and qualifiers for each representative product, customer, or order against the current and future time periods.

Marketing's inputs then form the basis for discussion and are challenged by:

- The opinions of other functions.
- The data collected to test the initial views on how a company wins orders in its markets.

Using the initial views of marketing as the inputs to and focus of debate, other functions express opinions, ask questions, and seek clarification of why segments work the way marketing suggests. The outcomes include an improved understanding between functions and a revised understanding of the markets in which a company competes. This may alter the weightings attributed to particular order-winners and qualifiers or change them altogether.

The more significant inputs into this important debate come from collecting the data and completing the analyses relevant to the markets under review. The purpose of this step is to enable companies to replace opinion with facts. This helps the strategic debate reach sound conclusions based on the needs of the overall business rather than being unduly swayed by the forceful arguments of individual functions. Thus, the discussion also seeks to identify the further analysis necessary to verify the opinions and views expressed as part of a continuous evaluating process. Only in this way can companies move to a level of debate that provides the essential quality and yields the necessary insights on which to make sound strategic decisions.

A review of some of the necessary analyses follows. The principal purpose is to explain the approach and its underlying rationale so as to enable this way of working to be transferred to other areas of analysis and to other companies.

General Issues.   As explained earlier, when a company undertakes the initial review of its markets, it asks marketing to identify products or customers that represent each chosen segment. The analysis is based on these. The assumption underlying the concept of segmentation is that everything that falls within the selected groupings is similar. The purpose of the analysis is to test this perception, not only as a checking mechanism but also to:

- Improve a company's understanding of its markets.
- Allow it to review its markets or parts of them.
- Change its decisions on the relative importance of these parts.

- Form the basis of functional strategies by prioritizing investments and developments.

Thus, the outcomes affect all parts of the business as would be expected. This is illustrated in Figures 2–5 and 2–6.

Manufacturing-Related Analyses.   The key role of analyzing markets in strategic debate has been stressed throughout. As mentioned earlier, however, many companies confine their review of markets to the perspectives held by marketing and consequently limit their analysis to customer surveys, statements on the size and share of current and future markets, competitor analyses, SWOT* reviews, and other classic marketing-oriented approaches.

The purpose of these analyses is to review markets from a manufacturing perspective in terms of the stated order-winners and qualifiers. Thus, the market review moves from an external customer perspective to an internal one that considers what actually happens in the business. This internal review, therefore, supplements the more subjective judgements of customers and externally oriented marketers by adding perspectives based on the reality of the orders placed by customers and the demands these make on the organization to meeting their business specifications. This then allows companies to verify functional views and modify them on the basis of analysis rather than opinion.

Finally, when undertaking this investigation, it is essential that the customer orders and/or contracts reviewed are chosen and verified by the executives involved. Seeking their knowledge of what is representative is essential in order to ensure that the findings are relevant and usable. Once this step is agreed on, the following analyses need to be completed. As you will see, these reflect the principal order-winners and qualifiers which relate to manufacturing. Similar analyses would need to be undertaken to test other criteria, the provision of which is the responsibility of functions other than manufacturing.

Price.   Where price is a criterion, companies need to review the actual costs and margins associated with the orders involved. In many instances, companies use their own form of standard costs as the basis for reviewing margins and making comparisons between one customer or order and another. However, these cost calculations are invariably inaccurate, distorting the decisions based on them. It is essential, therefore, that companies analyze the actual costs incurred in completing the orders under review. Also, in many instances they should increase the order sample being checked to provide a wider basis for comparisons.

The inaccuracies that result from assumptions are thus exposed. For example, Figure 4–1 compares the actual contribution for a representative group of products to the weighting given to price as an order-winner and shows the noticeable inconsistency between these two related factors.

---

*A SWOT analysis determines the strengths, weaknesses, opportunities, and threats relating to a company in its chosen markets.

FIGURE 4–1

A comparison of actual contribution for a group of representative products to the order-winner given to price.

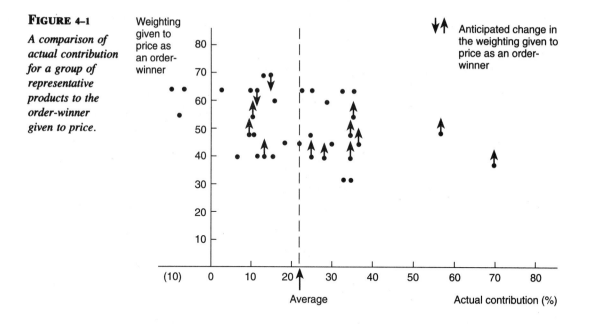

Similarly, Figure 4–2 compares the estimated contribution for a number of representative products to the actual contribution recorded when orders for these products were made on relevant processes.

More accurate cost information provides fresh insights and essential detail on the relative value of different customers or orders. The data given in Figures 4–1 and 4–2 result from summaries of such analyses and give an overview of the differences that typically exist between actual and estimated contributions and between reality and opinions. A company, however, would use the individual data entries. Where necessary, it would complete further analyses to verify different perspectives and trends before reaching a decision.

To improve the quality of the cost data, a company must identify direct costs other than labor and materials wherever possible, for example, delivery charges where a direct delivery service is provided. In addition, it is important to supplement the analysis to give further critical insights where possible. For example, where different orders are processed on the same equipment, and where this is a scarce resource, an additional calculation should be made to identify the contribution earned per machine hour. Contributions as a percentage of the selling price does not give the best insight into the relative value of orders as it assumes that all other nondirect factors involved are of the same relative importance.

Contribution per machine hour, or other scarce resource, relates the contribution earned to the use made by each order of a given process, where, in effect, a company is selling available machine capacity. As illustrated by Table 4–1, the two analyses give very different insights into the worth of these orders. Whereas contribution as a percentage of price gives one rank-order listing, contribution per machine hour gives another.

FIGURE 4–2

Actual versus estimated contribution for a number of representative products.

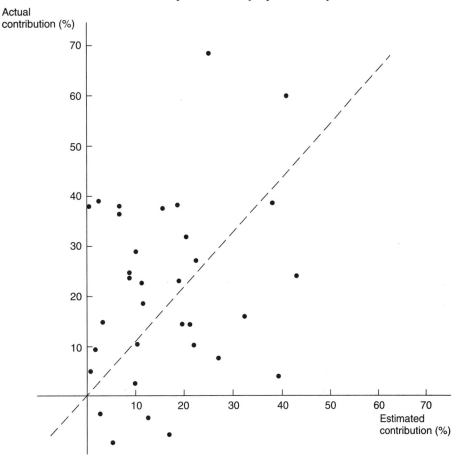

As highlighted previously, the segmentation of markets from a marketing perspective implies that the customers/orders within each segment are similar. From a
marketing perspective this is so; it is the very premise on which the principle of marketing segmentation is built. But, companies lacking other insights extend this similarity concept to other pertinent dimensions of the business, more through a lack of
rigor than an overt statement. Therefore, the key step in manufacturing strategy is to
add those missing dimensions that are relevant to manufacturing. By so doing it
checks how orders are won and the uniform nature of relevant criteria within each
segment. Without this, functional strategies will be pursued that typically are not consistent with how orders are won for different subsegments or customers.

Part of this clarifying process tests perceptions of markets, as shown in Figures 4–1 and 4–2. Table 4–2 goes one step further. In addition to testing initial

TABLE 4-1 **Contribution Percentage and Contribution per Machine Hour Comparisons for Representative Orders***

Order Reference	Price	Direct Costs	Contribution		Machine Hours	Contribution per Machine Hour
631	$ 220	$ 44	$ 176	80%	1.5	$117
205	568	114	454	80	3.9	116
216	1,246	269	977	78	11.2	87
470	244	56	188	77	4.0	47
298	1,960	462	1,496	77	9.3	161
607	3,612	830	2,782	77	13.3	209
512	134	32	102	76	1.5	66
483	4,010	1,004	3,006	75	21.5	140
658	166	42	124	75	0.7	107
313	1,134	306	828	73	5.7	145
284	864	246	618	72	2.1	294
182	724	65	159	71	4.7	14
573	1,066	320	746	70	3.1	240
417	3,345	1,140	2,205	66	7.9	279

*All data are actuals.

TABLE 4-2 **Contribution Percentage of Sales and Contribution per Machine Hour for Representative Orders for Two Segments**

Customer	Actual Contribution*	
	% Sales	Per Machine Hour
Segment 1		
Hulton	41.8	918
Avis Robins	24.6	431
MKC	8.6	288
Clairelle	12.4	152
Aristé	30.7	714
Segment 2		
Pelpac	14.0	243
JRR	8.6	186
Sheuks	16.1	115
Dells	(1.0)	(64)
Avenols	22.3	408

*Customer data is the average for a representative sample of orders.

perspectives, it also checks on the level of consistency within a segment. As the data show, customers within a segment yield markedly different levels of contribution from one another.*

From a marketing point of view, the segments chosen remain valid as they reflect essential marketing differences that are clustered together. From a manufacturing view, however, the segments do not constitute the same level of similarity. These fresh insights challenge the initial views of segment groupings and the level of company awareness of what constitutes above- and below-average business from a contribution-earning point of view. Again, the contribution percentage of sales and contribution per machine hour analyses provide essential and often different insights into this strategic review. Thus, decisions on which market segments, customers, or orders should receive priority in terms of growth, development investment, and support can now be made at a more informed level and on a corporate rather than distinctly functional basis.

The need to collect actual data has been stressed throughout. Shopfloor records are often kept outside the formal system. These records need to be sought, and where they do not exist, a once-off arrangement needs to be made to capture the actual labor, materials, and other direct costs incurred in completing an order or making a given quantity of relevant products. With price known, the calculations are straightforward and the outcomes then form part of the debate on a particular segment or the business as a whole.

Conformance Quality.   Many analyses within companies are completed in a general format. Typical of these is the measurement of conformance quality. However, while its overall effect on costs is relevant, the external dimension of quality is not general but is particular to a customer. Thus, the key dimension here is not average conformance quality level but the actual customer level provided.

Reviewing conformance quality by product, order, or customer yields essential insights. Such analyses will also build into the direct material dimension of costs addressed in the last section.

Delivery Reliability.   As is conformance quality, on-time delivery tends to be measured in aggregate, if at all. Not only does this fail to distinguish the importance of individual customers, it also fails to identify the differing delivery needs of customers.

What constitutes on-time cannot be covered by a simple definition. Customers' needs can range from given hourly slots on a stated day to any day within a given week or even longer period. Others may not want delivery before a given time but will accept delivery any time thereafter, within stated limits.

The task of checking delivery reliability, therefore, must be preceded by defining what constitutes on-time. Measurement of delivery reliability should reflect performance by customer and segment and relate to its perceived role in winning orders. In

---

*Further analyses can also be completed that test the level of consistency within a customer's portfolio of orders.

most companies, delivery reliability will be a qualifier rather than an order-winner, in many, it will be an order-losing sensitive qualifier. Knowing what to measure and its relative importance are as critical as the performance record itself. Where on-time delivery is a relevant criterion, companies should define and measure it as discussed above. Tracking actual orders provides the dimension of reality in the discussion on markets.

Delivery Speed.   The definition of delivery speed was given earlier. Assessing its presence in markets involves comparing the total lead time normally required by all relevant stages of the process—order processing, material/component purchasing, material/component delivery, manufacturing, assembly, packing, and shipping—against the lead time given by the customer—that is, the time between order placement and required delivery.

In some instances, customers will pull forward the required delivery date part way through the process. Companies must identify how such an action affects delivery speed in only part of the process by comparing the remaining elements of lead time to the revised customer lead time.

Many companies have consistently responded to the growing importance of delivery speed in their markets by shortening lead times through actions such as set-up reductions, eliminating delay, and investing in inventory ahead of time. When checking the extent of delivery speed within its markets, a company should note the level of ongoing investment within the business that is a direct result of its response to meeting the demands of this criterion. Such continuing costs should then be set against relevant customers and form part of a compnay's overall evaluation.

Once again, only by checking specific orders and customer requirements can the reality of markets be exposed. This increased understanding provides a more informed view of a business and the reality of how it competes.

Other Criteria.   As discussed in the last chapter, there are many different order-winning and qualifying criteria besides those addressed above. Checks on the extent of their provision and the level of ongoing performance achieved will take, in principle, a form similar to the approaches outlined in more detail for the four criteria addressed here. This is not to imply that some criteria are more important than others. The ones chosen are typically present more often in markets, are related specifically to manufacturing, and provide suitable illustrations of general approaches to follow. Knowing the dimensions to look for and using orders as the basis of analysis will yield the essential insights that companies need to have to succeed in today's competitive environment.

Outcomes of the Market Debate

Checking and debating markets leads to a number of both general and specific outcomes.

General Outcomes.   First, it improves the level of understanding between functions. Functions typically develop strategies independently of one another. While data such as forecast sales and their capacity implications traditionally form part of the forward-looking debate, the nature of markets and the key insights into their differences do not. Thus, shared approaches are not systematically reviewed and agreed.

Second, debate helps bridge the interface between functions at the strategic level. Functional views supplemented by data enable the different dimensions to form the basis for discussion. In this way, essential differences and perspectives are exposed and explored. Set within the context of a company's markets, the debate is moved from views typically expressed from the singular dimension of functions to the corporatewide perspectives essential to arriving at strategic decisions.

Specific Outcomes.   The first specific outcome of market debate is that it modifies initial views of markets. Bringing other perspectives and relevant data to the discussion raises a company's insights into its markets to the desired level of detail that enables key distinctions to be made. This then helps a firm to modify its initial views of the relevant order-winners and qualifiers within each segment. In this way, a company's view of its markets is improved and is also based on shared agreement between functions.

Second, debate forms the basis for developing a manufacturing strategy. The order-winners and qualifiers within a company's markets are the dimensions of a business that manufacturing, as well as all other functions, needs to support. The remainder of the book will address manufacturing-related dimensions and responses. These concern the process and infrastructure-related issues outlined in Table 2–1 as well as issues concerning coping with difference (Chapters 7 and 8) and the links with the perspectives of accounting and finance (Chapter 11).

Relating Manufacturing to Agreed Markets

The last section outlined the way to verify the importance of relevant criteria within chosen markets. The next steps are to test manufacturing's support of these (see Figure 2–5) and also to link manufacturing's strategic response to those of other functions, particularly marketing (see Figure 2–6), through the common denominator of supporting agreed markets.

The data and ongoing discussion result in a clearer and more accurate understanding of a company's markets. Bear in mind that strategy development needs to be an ongoing debate involving continuous tracking of the changing nature of markets. With this essential step completed, the company can establish the strategic role of manufacturing and other functions. Operationalizing strategy is an integral part of the task. With the direction set, manufacturing's task is to prioritize the developments, investments, and measures of performance it will undertake. And, the priorities will be different because the needs of the market segments will be different.

The section that follows highlights further analyses that may reveal important trends or identify relevant issues to be addressed. It also gives a flavor of the tasks that manufacturing would typically undertake to support relevant order-winners and

TABLE 4–3 Annual Quantities per SKU for Four Plants Manufacturing Similar Products

Dimensions	Plant 1	Plant 2	Plant 3	Plant 4
Annual units (in millions)	55.4	128.1	47.6	91.3
Number of SKUs	316	1,642	852	260
Annual units per SKU (in thousands)	175	78	56	351
Number of active compounds	25	72	45	28

qualifiers. However, the nuts and bolts of how to secure these improvements is the province of the production/operations management area, dealt with elsewhere in relevant literature.[1] What a manufacturing strategy provides, therefore, is the priority list that links markets to developments, investments, and tasks and forms the key performance dimensions on which manufacturing should be measured. Strategy statements on their own are of little value—unless they translate into actions and result in continuous improvement, they are without purpose.

Price

What follows is a flavor of the analyses that may be undertaken to check ongoing trends or identify current positions on a number of cost-related dimensions. As explained earlier, these are provided to illustrate the types of analysis designed to give further insights into current or potential problems and to highlight areas for improvement.

Annual Plant Volumes.   At the plant level, distinguishing annual volumes (or annual quantities where items are similar in work content) per product or stock-keeping unit (SKU) enables a check to be made on plant volume orientations. Table 4–3 shows the spread of volumes in four North American plants producing pharmaceutical products. It was part of an analysis to show the broad orientation of the plants at the time of the review. The subsequent realignment of products would require the same analysis for individual SKUs.

Annual Quantities—Volumes per Product.   Many companies fail to assess the degree of incremental change that has taken place in their business over time. Typically, they compare the current year with the one before and in so doing overlook the change

---

[1]For example, T. Hill, *Production/Operations Management* (Hemel Hempstead, U.K.: Prentice Hall International, 1991); L. J. Krajewski and L. P. Ritzman, *Operations Management: Strategy and Analysis* (Reading, Mass.: Addison-Wesley, 1987); R. G. Schroeder, "Operations Management: Decision-Making in the Operations Function" (New York: McGraw-Hill, 1989); and E. E. Adam, Jr. and R. J. Ebert, "Production and Operations Management: Concepts, Models, and Behavior" (Englewood Cliffs, N.J.: Prentice Hall, 1991).

TABLE 4-4 SKUs/Annual Quantity (units in thousands)

Year	Number of SKUs			
	≤250	250–750	750–1,000	1,000+
Current	41	6	6	5
Current minus 3	18	5	3	4
minus 6	8	2	2	4

TABLE 4-5 Actual Contribution per Machine for Different Segments

Segment/Criterion	$ per Machine Hour
Very high volume/price	625
High volume/price	415
Delivery speed	593
Low volume/nonprice*	380

*Orders won predominantly on nonmanufacturing criteria.

over time. One example of this is given in Table 4–4, which shows the changing mix of total annual volumes.

Length of Production Runs. Identifying the length of production runs over time either as an average for different processes, departments, or plants shows relative volumes over time. An analysis of the processes needed to manufacture one of the high demand ($ revenue) products of a U.S. consumer plant revealed that in the previous six years the average production run size (in hours) had fallen to 38 percent of the first full year of production. Checking manufacturing's responding changeover or set-up reductions and inventory holdings then forms a further part of the strategic review.

Contribution per Machine Hour. Relating actual contribution per machine or process hour to other dimensions such as production run lengths (in hours) and units per hour also checks on those dimensions that influence the level of actual contribution earned on a process and within the whole plant. Table 4–5 shows customer-order data identifying contribution per machine hour for four customers representing different segments. In this instance, the analysis provided an unexpected perspective on these segments.

Conformance Quality

Checks on quality levels need to be made that reflect products, orders, customers, and segments. Again, the need to assess how well the specific needs of different parts of

FIGURE 4–3

Correlation between the size (units) of a production run and the net output (units) per hour.

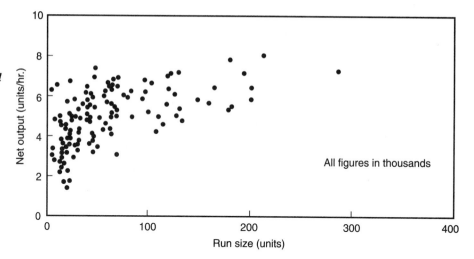

the market are being met is the underlying basis for the review. General reviews provide important perspectives, but specific reviews normally give the essential insights.

One analysis that is important to the price-related dimension as well concerns the correlation between production run lengths/sizes and net output per hour. Figure 4–3 plots these relations for one process, showing higher unit outputs per hour as run sizes increase. However, this also directs attention to why this general, though not unexpected, trend exists and also why there are some distinct exceptions to this relationship. Figure 4–3 shows some low run-size orders achieving high net outputs per hour and vice versa. Investigation as to why will undoubtedly reveal key insights that, in this instance, may relate to quality.

Delivery Reliability

Checks on the relative levels of delivery reliability need to be customer or order related. They must identify any relationships that exist between levels of delivery reliability and, for instance, order size, customer lead times (including schedule changes), process lead times, and material deliveries.

Delivery Speed

Relationships between customer and total lead times are the essence of delivery-speed reviews and also relate to the last section. Other checks that relate, in part, to this dimension include:

- Creating a throughput efficiency index that compares the standard hours involved to make a product with the actual lead times involved from start to finish.
- Measuring changeover/set-up times as a percentage of the total time taken (process time plus set-up time).

Conclusion

The purpose of these checks is to verify various functions' opinions and to move the debate on the essential insights into markets from one based primarily on subjective views to one based primarily on information. The outcomes are twofold:

1. The fresh perspectives and essential insights challenge or verify the views held of segments and customers for each relevant manufacturing-related dimension (e.g., price, conformance quality, delivery reliability, and delivery speed). This will identify the demands of customers and confirm the importance of each dimension's contribution to the business as a whole. Typically, companies over time often replace some 10 percent of existing sales revenue with "better" margin business. The impact on the total is invariably dramatic.

2. Manufacturing's performance is consistently measured against clearly stated requirements of those customers a company has agreed to supply and support. This leads to a priority list of activities relevant to each dimension (e.g., reducing cost, improving conformance quality, reducing total lead times, reducing set-up or changeover times, supporting product range, and so on). In this way, manufacturing's strategic response is set both within the context of the business and within itself.

Corporate Context

Finally, it is essential that the analyses completed for customers/products are set within an overall corporate context. Identifying the relative importance of a customer/product in terms of current and future total corporate profit/contribution levels is essential in arriving at decisions in the best interests of the overall business. Supporting below-average customers today in the belief that they will become above-average customers tomorrow makes good corporate sense.

The following chapters will point the ways forward, offering essential insights into how a company may respond to meet the ever-changing demands of today's dynamic and highly competitive markets. These responses, however, need to be within the context of agreed markets that are clearly understood as to their relevant order-winners and qualifiers.

CHAPTER 5 Process Choice

The way a business decides to make its products is a choice many executives believe to be based on the single dimension of technology. As a consequence, they leave this decision to engineering/process specialists on the assumption that they—the custodians of technological understanding—are best able to draw the fine distinctions that need to be made. The designation of those specialists as the appropriate people to make such decisions creates a situation in which the important manufacturing and business perspectives are at best given inadequate weight, and in many instances omitted altogether.

Manufacturing is not an engineering or technology-related function. It is a business-related function. Whereas products need to be made according to their technical specfications, they also have to be supplied in ways that win orders in the marketplace. This business dimension is the concern of manufacturing. When making decisions, therefore, on in which processes to invest, companies need to satisfy both technical and business perspectives. The former is the concern of engineering; the latter is the concern of manufacturing.

This chapter describes the manufacturing and business implications of process choice; in so doing, it highlights the importance of these issues for making investment decisions. In this way, it helps to broaden the view of manufacturing currently held by senior executives and provides a way of reviewing the manufacturing implications of marketing decisions, hence facilitating the manufacturing input into corporate strategy. This ensures that the necessary marketing/manufacturing interface is made and that the strategies adopted are business rather than functionally led.

Process Choice

When choosing the appropriate way in which to manufacture its products, a business will take the following steps:

1. Decide on how much to buy from outside the company, which in turn determines the make-in task.

2. Identify the appropriate engineering-technology alternatives to complete the tasks embodied in each product. This will concern bringing together the make-in components with the bought-out items to produce the final product specification at agreed levels of quality.

3. Choose between alternative manufacturing approaches to completing the tasks embodied in providing the products involved. This will need to reflect the market in which a product competes and the volumes associated with those sales. The present processes in many existing factories often are not ideal. This issue is dealt with later in the chapter, when the important insights into process choice have been covered.

The choice of process concerns step 3 in this procedure. It will need to embody the decisions made in the other two steps and recognize any constraints imposed by them. However, while these constraints alter the dimensions within the decision (e.g., what is involved), they do not alter its nature. The essence of the choice is linked to the appropriate way to manufacture, given the market and associated volumes involved.

However, having stressed the optimal nature of process choice, there are certain constraints that have an overriding impact on this decision. What these are and how they limit business options will be explained in the next section.

The Manufacturing Function

The principal function of the manufacturing process is to take inputs (materials, labor, and energy) and convert them into products. To complete this, a business usually must choose between different modes of manufacturing. They choose one or, as is often the case, several ways. The fundamental rationale for this decision, however, must be that the chosen process is the one best able to support a company competitively in the marketplace. There are several important perspectives to be taken into account. Each choice of process will bring with it certain implications for a business in terms of response to its markets, manufacturing capabilities and characteristics, level of investment required, unit costs involved, and the type of control and style of management that are appropriate. To help understand these, it is necessary to review the process choices available.

There are five generic types of manufacturing process: project, jobbing, batch, line, and continuous processing. However, in many situations, hybrids have been developed that blur the edges between one process and the next. What these hybrids are, how they relate to the classic types, and what they mean for a business will also be discussed.

Before going on to describe the process choices involved, it is worth noting here that two of them (project and continuous processing) are associated with a particular product type (civil engineering and foods/liquids, respectively), a point addressed later in the chapter. A firm may find that in reality it has little option but to choose the one appropriate process (e.g., oil refining and continuous processing are for all intents and purposes inextricably linked). However, the company must be clearly aware of the precise nature of the business implications involved in the choice it is "forced" to go along with and that the trade-offs associated with these dimensions are fixed.

The Generic Types of Process Choice

Project.   Companies that produce large-scale, one-off (i.e., unique), complex products will normally provide these on a project basis. Examples include products involved in civil engineering contracts and aerospace programs. A project process concerns the provision of a unique product requiring the coordination of large-scale inputs to achieve a customer's requirement. The resource inputs will normally be taken to where the product is to be built, since it is not feasible to move it once completed. All activities, including the necessary support functions, will usually be controlled by a total system for the duration of the project. Resources allocated to the project will be reallocated once their part of the task is complete or at the end of the project.

The selection of project as the appropriate process is based on two features. First, the product is a one-off, customer-specified requirement; second, it is often too large to be moved or simply cannot be moved once completed. The second criterion is such an overwhelming facet of this decision that products of this nature will always be made using the project choice of process. However, businesses will also be concerned with determining how much of the product to make away from site and how best to provide the parts or sections that go into the structures made on site. These will, in turn, often be produced using a different choice of process than project. These decisions need to be based on other criteria, which will become clear in the descriptions of these other choices that follow.

Some confusion arises in the use of the word *project*. It commonly refers to a one-off complex task and/or the managerial style used to control such an event. This needs to be distinguished from its use here, which identifies a distinct process of making a product, the very characteristics of which (e.g., moving resources to and from a site) are detailed above.

Jobbing, Unit, or One-off.   A jobbing process is used to meet the one-off order requirements of customers; for example, purpose-built tooling. The product involved will be of an individual nature. This requires the supplier to interpret the customer's design and specification and apply relatively high-level skills in the conversion process. A large degree of this interpretation will normally be made by skilled employees, whose experience in this type of work is an essential facet of the process. Once the design has been specified, one skilled person—or possibly a small number of them, if the task is time-consuming—is assigned the task and is responsible for deciding how best to complete and carry it out. This may also include a level of responsibility for scheduling, liaison with other functions, and some involvement with arrangements for outside, subcontracted phases, where necessary.

This one-off provision means that the product will not again be required in its exact form, or if it is, the demand will tend to be irregular, with long time periods between orders. For this reason, investment in the manufacturing process (e.g., in jigs, fixtures, and specialist plant) will not normally be warranted.

Jobbing versus Job Shop.   It is worth noting here that confusion often arises around the terms *jobbing* and *job shop*. While the former refers to a choice of process as explained above, the latter is a commercial description of a type of business. For example, a small printing business may often be required to as a job shop or even a jobbing printer. This is intended to convey the nature of the business involved or market served; that is, it describes that the printer undertakes work, typically low-volume in nature, that meets the specific needs of a whole range of customers. However, printing is, in fact, a classic example of a batch process, which is explained in the next section. Thus, from a commercial standpoint, such a firm takes on low-volume orders (hence the term *job*) from its customers and, from a manufacturing perspective, uses a batch process to meet these requirements.

Special versus Customized versus Standard Products.   Finally, it is also important to distinguish between special, customized, and standard products. The word *special* is used to describe the one-off provision referred to earlier in this section—that is, the product will not again be required in its exact form, or if it is, the demand will be irregular, with long time periods between orders. The phrase *standard product* means the opposite—the demand for the product is repeated (or the single customer order is of such a large volume nature) and thus warrants investment.

The word *customized* refers to a product made to a customer's specification. However, the demand for a customized product can be either special (i.e., not repeated) or standard (i.e., repeated). An example of the latter is a container of a particular shape and size, as determined by a customer. Although customized, the demand for such a container (e.g., Coca-Cola or other soft drink products) will be high and of a repeat nature. The appropriate choice of process will, therefore, be determined by volume and not the customized nature of the product.

Furthermore, some businesses are by their very nature the producers of customized products. The earlier example of the printing firm is such a case. Here, products will normally be customized in that the printed material will comprise the logo, name, product, and other details of the customer in question. However, a printer will find a significant level of similarity between the demands placed on manufacturing of the different customer orders. In fact, the differences will be provisioned in the plate containing the specific images and writing and the ink colors and paper size in question. To manufacturing, therefore, the customized jobs are not specials (as defined earlier) but standards. Thus, it will select a process other than jobbing to meet the requirements of the markets it serves. In the printing example, this would be batch, and the rationale for this and what is involved become clear in the next section.

Batch.   A company decides to manufacture using batch processes because it is providing similar items on a repeat basis, usually in larger volumes—quantity × work content—than associated with jobbing.* This type of process, however is chosen to cover a wide range of volumes, as represented in Figure 5–1 by the elongated shape of batch, compared to the other processes. At the low-volume end, the repeat orders will be small and infrequent. In fact, some companies producing very large, one-off

---

*However, companies do manufacture order quantities of one on a batch basis. In this instance, what underlies their process decision is the repeat nature of a product, not the size of an order quantity.

items will adopt a batch rather than a jobbing process for their manufacturing. When this happens, the work content involved will be high in jobbing terms, while the order quantity is for a small number of the same but unique items. At the high-volume end, the order quantities may involve many hours, shifts, or even weeks of work for the same product at one or more stages in its designated manufacturing route.

The batch procedure divides the manufacturing task into a series of appropriate operations, which together will make the products involved. The reason is simply to determine the most effective manufacturing route, so that the low cost requirements of repeat, higher-volume markets can be best achieved. At this stage, suitable jigs and fixtures will be identified to help reduce the processing times involved, the investment in which is justified by the total product output over time.

Each order quantity is manufactured by setting up that step of the process necessary to complete the first operation for a particular product. The whole order quantity is completed at this stage. Then, the next operation in the process is made ready, the total order quantity is completed, and so on, until all the stages required to make a product are completed. Meanwhile, the process used to complete the first operation for the product is then reset to complete an operation for another product, and so on. Thus, capacity at each stage in the process is used and reused to meet the different requirements of different orders.

Examples (in addition to printing mentioned earlier) include molding processes. Here, the mold to produce an item is put into a machine. The order for that component or product is then produced, the mold is taken off, the raw materials may have to be changed, a mold for another product is put into the machine, and so on. Similarly, in metal machining processes, a machine is set to complete the necessary metal cutting operation for a product, and the whole order quantity is processed. When finished, the machine in question is reset to do the required metal cutting work on another item, while the order quantity of the first product goes on to its next stage, which is completed in another part of the process. At times, an order quantity may have more than one stage completed on the same machine. Here the same principle applies, with the process reset to perform the next operation through which the whole order quantity will be passed.

Line.   With further increases in volumes (quantity × work content), investment is made to provide a process dedicated to the needs of a single product or a small range of products. The width of the product range will be determined at the time of the investment. In a line process, products are passed through the same sequence of operations. The standard nature of the products allows for this, hence, changes outside the prescribed range of options (which can be very wide, for example, with motor vehicles) cannot be accommodated on the line itself. The cumulative volume of the product range underpins the investment.

As explained in a later section, it is important to clearly recognize the fundamental differences in what constitutes volume. In a car assembly plant, for instance, customer order quantities are normally small. The eventual owner of a car orders in units of one, which the dealership passes onto the assembly plant as an order for a single car, or cumulates with one or more other orders for single units. In manufacturing terms, however, all orders for single cars are for products that the production process interprets as being the same product. Hence, the order quantity of a car assembly plant comprises the cumulative volume of all orders over a given period. This constitutes the high-volume nature of this business, making line the appropriate process.

Normally, the wider the product range, the higher is the investment required in the process to provide the degree of flexibility necessary to make these products. Where the options provided are very wide and the products involved are costly or bulky, the company is more likely to make them on an order basis only. For example, there will normally be a longer delay when purchasing an automobile (especially if several options are specified)* than say a domestic appliance. The underlying reason is the different degree of product standardization involved. The automobile will be made against a specific customer order, and the domestic appliance to stock.

In summary, in a line process all products (irrespective of the options involved) are perceived to be standard. Thus, the process does not have to be stopped to meet the requirements of the products made on the line. However, in order to accommodate another product in batch (which, for example, may only involve a different color molding), the process has to be stopped and reset.

Continuous Processing. With continuous processing, a basic material is passed through successive stages or operations and refined or processed into one or more products. Petrochemicals is an example. This choice of process is based on two features. The first is very high volume demand; the second is that the materials involved can be moved easily from one part of the process to another; for example, fluids, gases, and foods.

The high-volume nature of the demand justifies the very high investment involved. The processes are designed to run all day and every day with minimum shutdowns, due to the high costs of starting up and closing down. Normally, the product range is quite narrow and often the products offered are purposely restricted in order to enhance volumes of all the products in the range. For example, oil companies have systematically restricted the range of octanes offered and hence increased the volumes of all those grades provided. Another feature in continuous processing is the nature of the materials being processed. Whereas in line there are manual inputs into the manufacture of the products as they pass along, in continuous processing the materials will be transferred automatically from one part of the process to the next, with the process monitoring and self-adjusting flow and quality. The labor tasks in these situations predominantly involve checking the system and typically do not provide manual inputs into the process as they would on a line.

Choices of Processes within a Business. The five generic processes have been described separately because they are discrete choices. However, most businesses will select two or more processes as being appropriate for the products they manufacture, which reflects the different volume requirements of components, subassemblies, and

---

*Whereas this is typically the case in Western motor vehicle plants, Japanese automakers schedule their manufacturing plants on the basis of sales forecasts and make-to-stock rather than order-backlog, make-to-order principles. See pp. 123–24 for a more detailed review.

products. An illustration of this is the use of batch processes to make components and line processes to assemble those components into final products. This occurs because although the quantity required in both operations may be the same (and frequently it is larger in the first, as two or more of the same component are often required for each assembly), the work involved in making a component is much smaller than that in building the final product. The result is that the volume requirements (quantity × work content) for components is insufficient to justify the level of investment for a more dedicated process such as line.

Markets and Product Volumes

As emphasized throughout the preceding sections, the underlying factor in choosing which of the five processes is most appropriate to manufacturing a product is volume (i.e., quantity × work content). The link between the demand for a product and the investment in processes to complete this task is fundamental to this decision. It is important, therefore, to clearly distinguish what is meant by volume.

Though companies express forecast sales in terms of a period (typically a year), manufacturing does not make annual volumes—it makes order quantities. Thus, contracts that agree on period sales, but not the size of actual orders (or call-offs), can be very misleading. On the other hand, manufacturing often cumulates orders from different customers (using order-backlog/forward-load principles), or decides to make products for finished goods inventory to be sold in the future, in order to enhance volume. The choice is restricted by the degree of customization of the product and factors such as current forward load, seasonality of sales, and lead times in supplying customers' requirements. Hence, the horizontal axis in Figure 5–1 concerns order quantities placed on manufacturing. In project and jobbing, products are only made to customer order. In batch, decisions to cumulate demand, or make to inventory, relate to appropriate volumes for the process investments in place and the actual sales-order volume required.

The term *flexibility* is used to describe several different requirements. Two of these relate to volume. One concerns demand increases, and the other alludes to the ability of a process to manufacture low quantities at required levels of cost. In turn, the latter concerns the relationship between set-up and process time. Thus, where a company experiences reducing order volumes but has already invested in a high-volume process designed to manufacture products at fast output speeds, it will need appropriate investment to ensure that it can keep set-up times sufficiently short to maintain this ratio at an acceptable level. Current research work in many manufacturing companies provides numerous illustrations of where annual sales for a product may be similar to those in the past but actual order quantities (or call-offs) have reduced significantly. The link between this section and the previous one is fundamental in terms of process investment.

Technical Specification versus Business Specification

As volumes increase, the justification for investing in processes dedicated to make that product increases. High utilization of plant underpins the investment. Similarly, if

FIGURE 5–1

*Process choice
related to volumes**

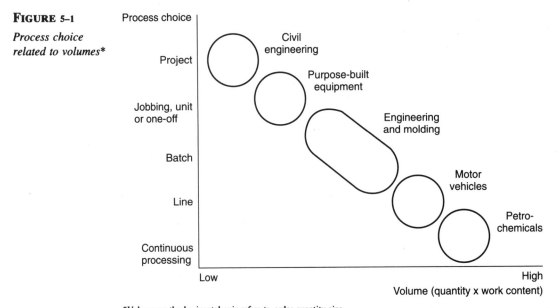

*Volume on the horizontal axis refers to order-quantity size.
SOURCE: T. Hill, *Production/Operations Management*, 2nd ed. (Hemel Hempstead. UK: Prentice Hall
International, 1991), Chapter 4.

processes will not be highly utilized by one product, they need to be chosen so that they are sufficiently flexible to meet the manufacturing needs of other products. Therefore, businesses, when choosing processes, need to distinguish between the technology required to make a product and the way the product is manufactured. On the one hand, the process technology choice concerns the engineering dimension of providing a process that will form, shape, cut, and so forth a product to the size and tolerances required (the technical specification). On the other hand, the manufacturing dimension concerns determining the best way to make a product. This decision needs to be based on volumes and relevant order-winners (the business specification). As volumes rise, the appropriate choice will change, as illustrated in Figure 5–1.

When companies invest in processes, they typically specify the technical requirements. This is recognized as fundamental, and appropriately so. However, they typically fail to specify the business requirement the process investment has to meet. But this requirement is crucial to the success of a business. In the past, manufacturing has failed to develop these critical, strategic arguments and insights. The consequences for many companies have been serious, leading to premature reinvestment of a considerable size, or even the closing down of parts of its business. Leaving the choice of these investments to be made against the single dimension of the technical specification has led to inappropriate decisions, based on the narrow base of technology. Manufacturing's failure to realize that it is the custodian of these decisions has indirectly supported this approach.

The choice of process needs to be understood, not in engineering terms (the technical specification), but in terms of manufacturing constraints and other dimensions of

FIGURE 5-2

The engineering, manufacturing, and business dimension phases involved in process choice

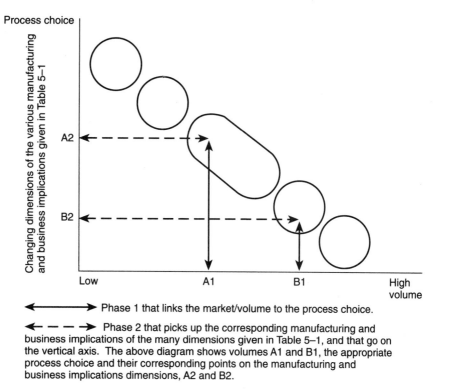

Process choice

Changing dimensions of the various manufacturing and business implications given in Table 5-1

A2

B2

Low   A1   B1   High
                                                                  volume

⟵————⟶ Phase 1 that links the market/volume to the process choice.

⟵ — — ⟶ Phase 2 that picks up the corresponding manufacturing and business implications of the many dimensions given in Table 5–1, and that go on the vertical axis. The above diagram shows volumes A1 and B1, the appropriate process choice and their corresponding points on the manufacturing and business implications dimensions, A2 and B2.

the business specification. Understanding how well a process can support the order-winning criteria of a product, the implications of the process for a company's infrastructure, and other relevant investments is fundamental to this strategic decision. These issues are dealt with in the following section.

Business Implications of Process Choice

It has already been explained that market characteristics (i.e., order-winners and qualifiers) and product volumes are the underlying factors in choosing the appropriate process. In addition, the nature of the product is also a factor in this decision in terms of the two extremes in Figure 5–2, namely, project and continuous processing.

Hence, the procedure used is to first assess the market-volume dimension. This then forms the basis for choosing which process is appropriate to best meet these critical business needs. The engineering dimension provides the initial set of alternatives concerning the ways to meet meet the requirements of the product. However, at this juncture the engineering dimension finishes and the manufacturing and business dimensions start. Phase 1 links the market volumes to the process choice (the manufacturing dimension, which also takes into account the engineering dimension described earlier)—A1 and B1 in Figure 5–2. Phase 2 automatically picks up the corresponding point on each of the various manufacturing and business implications given in Table 5–1; A2 and B2 respectively in Figure 5–2. However, many companies recognize the engineering dimension but not the manufacturing and business dimensions. The engineering proposal currently underpins the major part of process investment decisions, which in turn are based on the forecast market volumes that form part of the corporate marketing strategy. The manufacturing and business implications embodied in a proposal are given scant recognition. But it is these issues that bind manufacturing and regulate its ability to respond to the business needs. Once the investment is made, not only are the processes fixed, but also the whole of the manufacturing infrastructure is fixed. The result is that this decision dictates the extent to which manufacturing can support the needs of the marketplace, the essence of business success.

When Phase 1 in Figure 5–2 is completed, the choice of process is designated. However, at the same time it stipulates the position on the vertical dimensions, which will accrue as a result. Hence, Phase 2 is inextricably tied to Phase 1. Therefore, the decisions in Phase 1 cannot be taken in isolation. The choice has to embrace both Phase 1 and Phase 2. Only in this way will an organization avoid falling into the cyclopean trap from which it will take years to extricate itself. Only in this way will a business take into account the short- and long-term implications that emanate from the decision to manufacture, using one choice of process as opposed to another.

To help explain the business implications of process choice, the perspectives involved have been placed into four categories—products and markets, manufacturing, investment and cost, and infrastructure. Furthermore, the issues for illustration and discussion have been chosen on the basis of their overall business importance. However, there are many other issues equally important to understand, and these have distinct operational rather than strategic overtones.[1]

The critical issue embodied in Table 5–1 is how each perspective reviewed changes between one choice of process and another. Thus, when a company decides to invest in a process, it will at the same time have determined the corresponding point on each dimension within these four categories. It is necessary for companies to understand this and be aware of the trade-offs embodied in that choice.

Table 5–1 contains many generalized statements, which are intended to relate the usual requirements of one type of process to the other four. In almost all cases, there is an arrow drawn between jobbing and line. This is intended to indicate that as a process moves from jobbing to low-volume batch to high-volume batch through to line, the particular characteristic will change from one form to the other. The reason for this approach is to help explain the implications of these choices and examine the consequences that will normally follow.

Companies selling products typically made using the project process will need to make decisions on how much is made away from the site and transported in. Today, for instance, many parts of a civil engineering structure are made off-site by jobbing, batch, or line processes, then brought in as required. Similarly, products with the fluid, semifluid, or gaseous characteristics necessary to avail themselves of continu-

---

[1]Many of these additional issues are illustrated and discussed in T. Hill, *Production/Operation Management*, 2nd ed. (Hemel Hempstead, U.K.: Prentice Hall International, 1991) pp. 61–69.

ous processing may also be made on a batch process basis. Thus, the changing business characteristics displayed in Table 5–1 illustrate the sets of alternatives embodied in these choices as well.

Finally, Table 5–1 has been arranged to illustrate the linked relationship between jobbing, batch, and line choices as opposed to the more distinct process-product relationship existing in project and continuous processing, described earlier. The section that follows adopts this division.

Selected Business Implications

This section further explains the implications of the dimensions provided in Table 5–1. The four categories of products and markets, manufacturing, investment and cost, and infrastructure are explained under each of the process choice headings, helping to link them. Furthermore, to emphasize the separate natures of project and continuous processing and the linked natures of jobbing, batch, and line, the following sections discuss project first, followed by jobbing, batch, and line in one general section, and then continuous processing at the end. Despite their link, jobbing, batch, and line nevertheless differ from each other. Hence, each is discussed in a separate subsection. But since batch often links the change in dimensions between jobbing and line, the latter two processes are dealt with first to help to describe batch within this overall perspective.

Project

Products and Markets.   Companies choosing project processes sell capability. They sell their experience, know-how, and skills to provide for a customer's individual needs. Hence, they are in a market that will require a high level of product change and new product introductions. Its product range will be wide, with low unit-sales volume. It will win orders on aspects such as unique design capability or delivery speed, with price normally acting as a qualifier rather than an order-winner. Through the competitive nature of today's markets, criteria such as quality and on-time delivery have typically changed from being order-winners to qualifiers, as signaled by their presence in all types of market.

Manufacturing.   Oriented toward general purpose equipment, with a specialist plant to meet particular product, design, or structural features, project processes are highly flexible in coping with the low product volumes of the market and design changes that will occur during production. Changes in capacity mix, or in total, can be made incrementally, with the key tasks being on-time completion and meeting the specification as laid down by the customer.

Investment and Cost.   The capital investment in plant and other processes will tend to be low. But there will be some high-cost items, which may be purchased or hired,

TABLE 5–1 Selected Business Implications of Process Choice

Typical Characteristics of Process Choice

Aspects	Project	Jobbing, Unit, or One-Off	Batch	Line	Continuous Processing
Products and Markets					
Type of product	Special/small range of standards	Special	→	Standard	Standard
Product range	Wide	Wide	→	Narrow: standard products	Very narrow: standard products
Customer order size	Small	Small	→	Large	Very large
Level of product change required	High	High	→	Low and within agreed options	None
Rate of new product introductions	High	High	→	Low	Very low
What does the company sell?	Capability	Capability	→	Products	Products
How are orders won?					
Order-winning criteria	Delivery speed/unique design capability	Delivery speed/unique design capability	→	Price	Price
Qualifying criteria	Price/on-time delivery/conformance quality	Price/on-time delivery/conformance quality	On-time delivery/conformance quality	Design/on-time delivery/conformance quality	Design/on-time delivery/conformance quality
Manufacturing					
Nature of the process technology	Oriented toward general purpose	Universal	→	Dedicated	Highly dedicated
Process flexibility	High	High	→	Low	Inflexible
Production volumes	Low	Low	→	High	Very High
Dominant utilization	Mixed	Labor	→	Plant	Plant
Changes in capacity	Incremental	Incremental	→	Stepped change	New facility
Key manufacturing task	To meet specification/delivery schedules	To meet specification/delivery dates	→	Low-cost production	Low-cost production

Investment and Cost					
Level of capital investment	Low/high	Low	↑	High	Very high
Level of inventory					
Components/raw material	As required	As required/low	Often medium	Planned with buffer stocks/low	Planned with buffer stocks
Work-in-process	High*	High*	Very high	Low	Low
Finished goods	Low	Low	↑	High†	High‡
Percent of total costs					
Direct labor	Low	High	↑	Low	Very low
Direct materials	High	Low	↑	High	Very high
Site/plant overheads	Low	Low	↑	High	High
Infrastructure					
Appropriate organizational					
Control	Decentralized/centralized	Decentralized	↑	Centralized	Centralized
Style	Entrepreneurial	Entrepreneurial	↑	Bureaucratic	Bureaucratic
Most important production management perspective	Technology	Technology	↑	Business/people	Technology
Level of specialist support to manufacturing	High	Low	↑	High	Very high

*This would depend on stage payment arrangements.

†However, many businesses here only make against customer schedules or on receipt of a customer order.

‡The finished goods inventory in, for instance, oil refining is stored in the postprocessing stages of distribution and at the point of sale.

depending on their potential usage, availability, costs, and similar factors. Due to the opportunity to schedule materials, the inventory at this stage will be on an as-required basis. Work-in-process levels will be high, but normally much of this will be passed on to the customers by stage payment agreements. In a make-to-order situation, finished goods are small, with immediate delivery on completion. The key cost will normally be materials, and sound purchasing arrangements, work-in-process usage, and control are essential.

Infrastructure. Due to the uncertainties in the process and the need to respond quickly to any customer-derived changes, the organizational control should be decentralized and supported by an entrepreneurial, rather than a bureaucratic, style. In addition, once the business grows, the company must centrally control key items of plant, internal specialist-engineering skills, and other purchased commodities or skills to ensure they are effectively scheduled by project and between projects. The production manager must understand the relevant technology to appreciate and respond to unforeseen difficulties and problems, both technical and nontechnical, and to effectively use the local and centrally based specialist support.

Jobbing

Products and Markets. In essence, a jobbing business sells its capability to manufacture a customer's requirements. It is restricted only by the range of skills of its work force or by its processes. Thus it handles a wide product range, competing on aspects other than price. This does not mean that the business can charge any price it decides. But, if the price is within what is reasonable for the market—and that includes provisions for additional delivery speed or poststart modifications—then price is a qualifier rather than an order-winner.

Manufacturing. As a consequence of the products it provides and markets it serves, the manufacturing process must be flexible. Its major concern is the utilization of its labor skills, with processes being purchased to facilitate the skilled operator to complete the task. Changes in capacity can be achieved incrementally. The order-backlog position, which exists in make-to-order markets, will allow manufacturing to make any foreseen adjustments in capacity ahead of time. The key manufacturing task is to complete the item to specification, on time, since normally this one-off item forms an integral part of some greater business whole, as far as the customer is concerned.

Investment and Cost. Although a lot of the equipment used in jobbing can be very expensive, generally this investment is low, compared to batch and line. In addition, material will tend to be purchased only when an order has been received, with material delivery forming part of the total lead time. Work-in-process inventory will be high with all jobs, on average, being half-finished, while the make-to-order nature of its business means that products are dispatched once completed. There will tend to be few specialist and other support functions, which leads to a relatively lower plant/site overhead cost. These specialist tasks will be largely part of the skilled worker's role, which, together with the high labor content, normally makes this the highest portion of total costs. Material costs will tend to be low; any expensive materials involved will invariably be on a customer-supplied basis.

Infrastructure. Organizational control and style need to be decentralized and entrepreneurial in nature, so as to respond quickly and effectively to meet the inherent flexibility requirements of this market. For this reason, the production executive has to understand the technology involved, as this forms an important part of his contribution to business decisions (e.g., in accepting an order, confirming a delivery quotation, or providing part of the specialist inputs into a business).

Line

Products and Markets. A line process reflects the other end of the spectrum to jobbing. The business sells standard products that, to be successful, are sold on price and are associated with large customer orders. The level of product change is usually prescribed within a list of options; outside this, the product is not normally available. Product design and quality are determined at the outset to meet the perceived needs of the customer, with on-time delivery a qualifier in today's markets.

Manufacturing. To provide low manufacturing costs, the process is dedicated to a predetermined range of products. It is not geared to be flexible outside this range, due to the high costs of change. This provides the opportunity to maintain the necessary quality levels throughout the process. Production volumes need to be high to achieve the level of plant utilization necessary to justify the investment and to underpin the cost structures involved. Output changes are more difficult to arrange, due to the stepped-change nature of capacity alterations.

Investment and Cost. The key to low manufacturing costs is high process investment, which goes hand in hand with line. The volumes involved allow schedules of raw materials and components to be planned with associated buffer stocks to cover the uncertainty of supply. Work-in-process inventory will be low. Although finished goods will tend to be high, many businesses, as part of a decision to keep inventory investment as low as possible, will only make standard products against customer schedules or on receipt of an order. Also, products offering many optional extras (e.g., motor vehicles) will tend to have a policy of only making to a specific order. Hence, even in times of relatively low sales, if the new auto selected includes an unusual set of options and thus is unlikely to have been built in anticipation of an early sale, delivery will be delayed.* Finally, the high areas of cost tend to be in materials, bought-out components, and site/plant overheads, with direct labor a relatively small part of the total.

---

*It is important here to recognize that different approaches are used in the same industry, an example of such is given on pages 123–24.

Infrastructure.   Since the choice of a line process represents a high-volume business, then a more centralized organization, controlled by systems, is more appropriate. On the manufacturing side, the key production executive task concerns the business/people aspects of the job, with specialist support providing the technical know-how for products and processes.

Batch

Products and Markets.   Between jobbing and line, comes batch. This is chosen to cover a very wide range of volumes, as illustrated by the elongated shape depicted in Figures 5–1 and 5–2. Batch links the low/high volume special/standard products and make-to-order/make-to-stock businesses. In most cases, the choice of batch, rather than jobbing, as the appropriate way to manufacture products signals that the production volumes (i.e., quantity $\times$ work content) have increased and are of a repeat nature but insufficient to dedicate processes solely to them, as would be the case in line. Some unique high-volume orders may also be done on a batch basis.

At the low-volume end of batch, the processes are able to cope with a high degree of product change and a high level of new product introductions. Here, the business is oriented toward selling capability, with price starting to become a more important order-winning criterion, due to the volume and repeat nature of the products. At the high-volume end of batch, products have become increasingly standard, order sizes larger, and product change lower, all of which illustrate the shift in product-market characteristics toward line. As mentioned earlier, market pressures have typically changed quality conformance and on-time delivery from order-winners to qualifiers.

Manufacturing.   It can be deduced from the product-market features that batch processes usually have to cope with a wide range of products and production volumes. To handle this task, these processes must be of a general nature, offering a high degree of flexibility. With some items of equipment, the utilization will be low; with others, plant will have been purchased to meet the needs of a product or to offer distinct process advantages (e.g., numerical control [NC] machines, machining centers, and flexible manufacturing systems, each of which will be described in a later section). In these cases, high investment will normally be justified on a usage basis, and the aim will be to utilize the capacity to the fullest.

To help underpin the total process investment, many companies adopt a deliberate policy of increasing the utilization of a plant in three ways:

1. Putting a wide range of products through the same set of processes.
2. Usually manufacturing many of the same products in a single order quantity or batch quantity (hence the name). In this way, the number of set-ups is reduced, which decreases the setting costs and increases effective capacity.
3. Making products wait for processes to become available. This policy, together with the order-quantity decisions above, leads to a work-in-process inventory investment, which, in relation to the size of the business, tends to be very high compared to jobbing and, particularly, line.

Investment and Cost.   To be competitive in markets moving toward the high volume end, a business will increasingly invest in its batch processes to achieve the low manufacturing cost requirement of these markets. As explained earlier, many companies exploit this still further by putting more products through the same processes and, hence, increasing overall utilization. However, the major trade-off associated with this policy is the very high investment in work-in-process inventory. The raw materials, components, and finished goods inventory levels will in turn be associated with the make-to-order or make-to-stock nature of the business. As with all companies in these mid-volume markets, the nearer it is to a make-to-order situation the more the characteristics of that market will prevail, and vice versa. The makeup of total costs is no exception.

Infrastructure.   As the business moves away from the low-volume end of the continuum, centralized controls and a bureaucratic style become more appropriate. The increasing complexity of this growth will change the nature of the specialist functions, with design and production engineering becoming an ever-important support to manufacturing. The production manager's role will be bound up with appreciating and recognizing the critical business issues involved, providing coordination throughout, and spearheading the development of manufacturing systems.

At the low-volume end of batch, the characteristics, though not the same, will in many situations, be more akin to those in jobbing. Therefore, it is important to recognize the extent and trends in these changes and make the necessary adjustments.

Continuous Processing

Markets and Products.   At the other end of the volume spectrum, companies that choose continuous processing will sell a narrow range of standard products in markets where product change and the rate of product introductions are low. The company will sell products rather than capability, and large customer orders will be won principally on price.

Manufacturing.   In a price-sensitive market, the key manufacturing task will be low-cost production. To help keep costs low, the process will be highly dedicated, with the cost structure based on high production volumes, leading to a need to achieve high plant utilization. The fixed nature of capacity also creates restrictions when increases or decreases in output are required, with the decision based on whether or not to build a new facility on the one hand or how often to run the plant (known as *campaigning*) on the other.

Investment and Cost.   The high plant investment and high volume output associated with continuous processing offers the opportunity to keep raw material inventory on a planned usage basis, with built-in buffer stocks to cover uncertainties. Work-in-process will be relatively low in total output, with inventory in finished goods high. This is because of the need to maintain output levels at all times against fluctuating sales patterns. In many cases, however, finished goods are held in the extensive distribution system of a business, and sometimes at its own retail outlets (e.g., gasoline stations).

Owing to the high process investment, direct labor costs are small, with the highest cost usually in materials. Site/plant overheads in this process will be high owing to the need to support the process and handle the high output levels involved.

Infrastructure. The high-volume nature of these businesses lends itself to a centralized, bureaucratic organization control and style. Manufacturing performance is measured against budgets, variance analysis is the order of the day, and investment proposals are centrally monitored. An understanding of the process and product technology is important when running a production unit, together with the ability to coordinate the high level of specialist support provided for manufacturing.

An Overview of Process Choice

To help clarify the issues involved in process choice, an overview of how these alternatives link to one another is now described. The first important fact to stress is that each of the choices embodies a totally different approach to manufacturing a product. Although described in some detail in the chapter, a short explanation of these differences will serve to reinforce this important point.

• *Project.* This is used for one-off products that have to be built on site because it is difficult or impossible to move them once they have been made. Consequently, the resources involved need to be brought to the site and released for reuse elsewhere when they are no longer needed.

• *Jobbing.* This is used for one-off products that can be moved once completed. The responsibility for making the product is normally given to a skilled person, who decides how best to make it and then completes all or most of the operations involved, including checking quality conformance at each stage.

• *Batch.* With an increase in volumes and the repeat nature of products, companies select batch as the effective way to meet the requirements involved. Because the products are repeated, companies can consider investment at each of the manufacturing steps necessary to make them. This includes engineering time to decide how best to make a product, jigs and fixtures to facilitate the completion of certain operations, and equipment purchased with an eye to making these and other products with similar characteristics. However, the volumes involved do not warrant the purchase of dedicated equipment. The operations necessary to complete a product are, therefore, not linked and are said to be decoupled.

• *Line.* When demand is sufficient to justify dedicating equipment solely to making a specified range of products, a line process is normally chosen. The operations necessary to complete a product are linked together so that each product goes from one operation directly to the next and so on. The operations necessary to complete a product in this instance are said to be coupled. The operators involved will physically take part in assembling the products.

FIGURE 5–3

Potential transitions between the different choices of process

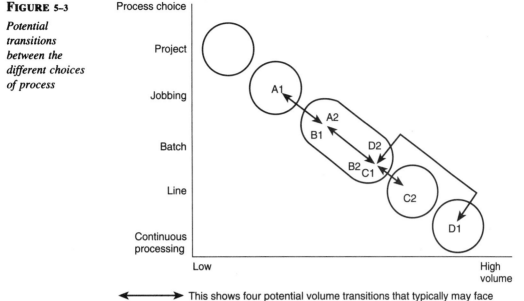

 This shows four potential volume transitions that typically may face a business. The first example shows a move from one off*, low-volume (A1) to repeat order, low-volume demand (A2) for a product or vice versa and the change in manufacturing process that should ideally accompany this movement. Examples B1 to B2, C1 to C2 and D1 to D2 show similar demand changes at different points on the volume scale and requiring similar decisions concerning the realignment of the process choice.

* One-off is a description of uniqueness, not order quantity.

• *Continuous processing.* When the demand for a product is such that the volume required necessitates a process being used all day and every day, further investment is justified. The equipment in this instance is designed to automatically transfer the product from one stage to the next, check the quality within the process, and make adjustments where necessary. The investment associated with this is warranted by the volumes involved.

To emphasize these distinctions, Figure 5–3 shows the gap between the five choices outlined. It also makes the point that whereas there will sometimes be a transition from jobbing to low-volume batch, from low-volume to high-volume batch, from high-volume batch to line, or from high-volume batch to continuous processing, the same will not apply between project and jobbing or from line to continuous processing. Similarly, when volumes reduce toward the end of a product's life cycle, the reverse movement may take place, but again it would only go as illustrated in Figure 5–3.

Transition in these instances refers to the possibility that a business may, as volumes increase or decrease, change its choice of manufacturing accordingly. However, project and continuous processing are prescribed by the nature of the product itself and the volumes involved. In this way, businesses with these characteristics are precluded from considering any other process in a transitional movement, as described here and shown in Figure 5–3. Those products that lend themselves to being produced using continuous processing (e.g., fluids, gases,and foods), are often produced on a batch basis, where the production volumes involved are not adequate to justify the high investment associated with continuous processing.

When product volumes increase or decrease, companies should ideally realign their choice of process as appropriate to the new levels of volumes. However, many companies find themselves unable, or unwilling, to commit the fresh investment necessary to complete this realignment, especially where the volume movement is downward.

Hybrid Processes

As mentioned earlier, many companies have developed hybrid processes to better enable them to support the characteristics of their markets. Some comprise a mix of two of the five generic processes; others are developments within an existing process type, often based on the use of numerical control (NC) machines. Some of the more important hybrid developments are now explained, and to help position these in relation to the generic processes, they are included together in Figure 5–4. However, the list includes some (e.g., machining centers) that have been generally applied and are provided as standard items* from a supplier's catalog.

Finally, as with all hybrids, there is a root stock. Thus, although each hybrid format will comprise a mix of two process types, it will still be classified as belonging to one or the other. This phenomenon is highlighted by the headings of "batch-related" and "line-related" in the sections that follow. These hybrids have batch and line roots, respectively. What happens is that they alter some of the trade-offs described in Table 4–1. Some will improve and some will worsen. What a company seeks is an overall set of trade-offs that are better for the business as a whole than those provided by the current process(es).

Batch-Related Hybrids

Numerical Control (NC) Machines. An NC system[2] is a process that automatically performs the required operations according to a detailed set of coded instructions. Since mathematical information is the base used, the system is called numerical control. The first applications were to metal cutting processes such as milling, boring, turning, grinding, and sawing, but in recent years the range of NC applications in-

---

*In reality, some customization may be offered, but the substance of this equipment is standard.

[2]More advanced NC systems were introduced in the late 1960s in the form of computer numerical control (CNC), which replaced the hard-wired control unit of the NC system with a stored program using a dedicated minicomputer. Hence, the memory storage rather than paper-tape input makes the process more reliable and more flexible in program changes. Direct numerical control (DNC) systems consist of a number of NC and/or CNC equipment connected to a centralized computer. The centralized source of information provided by DNC helps in the control of manufacturing. Flexible manufacturing systems (FMS) combine the DNC principle together with the other features described in a later section.

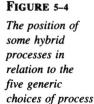

FIGURE 5–4

The position of some hybrid processes in relation to the five generic choices of process

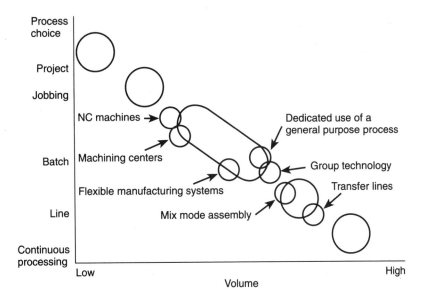

cludes tube bending, shearing, and different forms of cutting. The operation of machine tools is from numerical data stored on paper or magnetic tapes, tabulating cards, computer storage, or direct information. Compared with conventional equipment, NC machines offer increased accuracy, consistency, and flexibility, even with the need to meet very complex manufacturing requirements. Thus, design changes and modifications require only a change in instruction, nothing more.

In reality, an NC machine is a development of a batch process; it is also low volume in nature. It is batch because the machine stops at the end of one process and is reset for a new job or new program being loaded. It is low volume because the set-up times are short, hence providing an acceptable ratio between set-up times and the length of the run before the next set-up. The position of NC machines on Figure 5–4 illustrates this.

However, the trade-off against conventional plant operations is the increased investment associated with NC processes. In addition, the introduction of the new technology and associated changes can create problems for the operators, setter, and supervisor in terms of their roles, the level of specialist support, and skill requirements.

Machining Center.   Machining centers, which first appeared in the late 1950s, combine NC operations previously provided by different machines into one machining center. With tool changing automatically controlled by instructions on the tape, and carousels holding up to 150 tools and more, the underlying rationale for this development is to maximize the combination of operations completed at a single location.

A machining center typically embraces several metal cutting facilities (for example, milling, boring, and drilling), which are applied to a given piece of work in a predetermined sequence reflected in the NC program. The relevant range of tools is stored in a magazine. The appropriate tool is then selected and the particular operation completed. The hybrid nature of this process is that several operations are completed before the item of work is removed. Thus, a machining center completes many operations in sequence, without removing the items from the process. This reflects aspects of line within what is, in reality, still a batch process (i.e., the process stops and resets itself not only between operations but between one item and the next).

In this way, a machining center changes the pattern of work-in-process inventory associated with the generic process that could be adopted as an alternative, namely batch. Just as in line, a part now goes through a number of operations in sequence and thus changes the process design from functional to product layout. However, in most companies, the pre- and postmachining operations are performed on another process choice (e.g., batch). This use of a combination of processes would change the relevant point on the dimensions shown in Table 5–1. Machining centers, as do all NC-based processes, increase flexibility (e.g., reduced set-ups and the resulting ability to meet the low-volume requirements of products) in relation to an alternative non-NC process, due to the nature and level of the capital investment involved. This is reflected in Figure 5–4.

Thus, machining centers are a hybrid between batch and line; as a consequence, the position on some trade-offs (see Table 5–1) changes. For instance, work-in-process inventory within the machining center will decrease compared to completing the same operations at individual and unconnected workstations. Similarly, the relative level of investment will increase. As you will note, both these changes are more toward a line process. However, as explained earlier regarding hybrids, the root process is still batch.

Flexible Manufacturing Systems.   Whereas a machining center is best suited to low volumes, a flexible manufacturing system (FMS) is appropriate to mid-volume requirements, as shown in Figure 5–4. This too is designed to complete a given number of operations on an item before it leaves the system. However, rather than the item being contained in a single center, in an FMS the workpiece is transferred from one process to the next automatically. Besides volume differences, the physical dimensions of the items to be machined are typically much larger than those completed by machining centers.

Flexible manufacturing systems are a combination of standard and special numerical control (NC) machines, automated materials handling, and computer control in the form of direct numerical control (DNC)[3] for the purposes of extending the benefits of NC to mid-volume manufacturing situations.[4] Whereas NC equipment and particularly machining centers accommodate relatively low-volume demand, much less attention has been given to improving manufacturing's approach to mid-volume, mid-variety products, although this accounts for a large part of the products that would fall into the batch range of volumes.

---

[3]See footnote 2.

[4]P. R. Haas, "Flexible Manufacturing Systems—A Solution for the Mid-Volume, Mid-Variety Parts Manufacturer," SME Technical Conference, Detroit, April 1973; and J. J. Hughes et al., "Flexible Manufacturing Systems for Improved Mid-Volume Productivity," *Proceedings of the Third Annual AIEE Systems Engineering Conference*, November 1975.

FMSs are designed around families of parts. The increased volumes associated with the range of products justify the investment; this combined with the inherent flexibility of the NC equipment creates the rationale for using FMSs in this mid-volume segment of demand. Classic families of products are:

1. By assembly: Grouping parts together that would be required to make a single assembly (e.g., an engine). The system would be designed to allow the user to order against an assembly requirement, rather than scheduling order quantities for each part through an appropriate series of functionally laid-out processes.

2. By type: Categorizing parts by type for a range of similar products. This would relieve higher volume production processes of the low- to mid-volume part numbers and thus reduce the number of changeovers involved. This aggregate family demand justifies the capital investment, with the inherent flexibility within the FMS allowing a relatively wide range of products to be considered and facilitating the balancing and rebalancing of the work load as product mix and volumes change.

3. By size and similar operations: The specification of the FMS in this situation reflects the physical size of the parts and the particular operations that need to be completed. Again, the flexibility within the system extends the range of work with which it can cope and allows high utilization owing to its ability to handle product mix and volume changes.

A typical series of events in processing a part in FMS (see Figure 5–5) is as follows:

- A DNC system directs a cart carrying an empty fixture to a load station and also advises the loader which part is to be loaded.
- On completion, the loader signals that it is ready; the computer directs the part to the first operation, selecting, if available, the lowest backlog potential.
- The part is automatically unloaded, the appropriate NC program selected, and the work completed.
- This procedure will be followed until the part is finished, whence it goes to the unloading area and out of the system.

The hybrid nature of FMS is based on logic similar to that described for machining centers, that is, maximizing the combination of operations completed at a single location. The additional capital investment will bring with it both lower cost and lower work-in-process inventory advantages, trade-offs more akin to line. However, the root process is still batch.

Group Technology.   The first three hybrid processes concerned the use of NC equipment as the basis for the process change. However, alternative hybrid processes can be adopted that use conventional or non-NC equipment. Three are described here. The first is a batch-line hybrid known as group technology.

The underlying difference between the choice of batch and line processes is one of associated volumes. Group technology gains for batch processes some of the

FIGURE 5–5

An example of a 15-station random FMS provided as a 3-stage installation

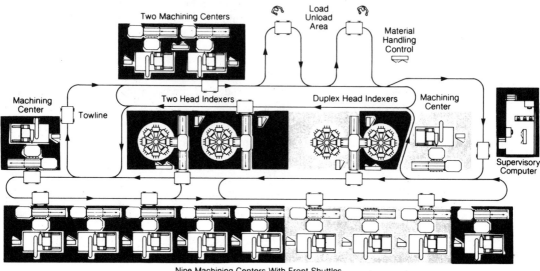

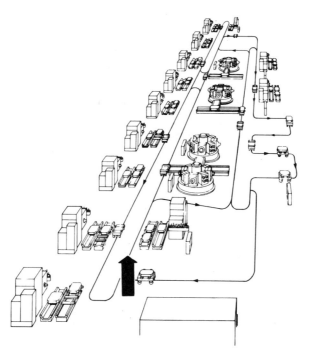

SOURCE: Kearney & Trecker Corporation, *KT's World of Advanced Manufacturing Technology*, 2nd ed. (1983) (with permission).

FIGURE 5-6

Group layout and the transition from a functional (batch) to line (product) layout

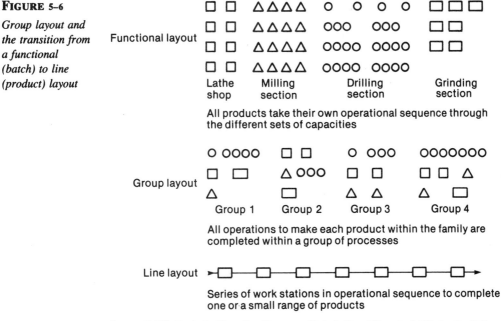

Functional layout

Lathe shop   Milling section   Drilling section   Grinding section

All products take their own operational sequence through the different sets of capacities

Group layout

Group 1   Group 2   Group 3   Group 4

All operations to make each product within the family are completed within a group of processes

Line layout

Series of work stations in operational sequence to complete one or a small range of products

SOURCE: T. Hill, *Production/Operations Management* 2nd ed. (Hemel Hempstead, UK: Prentice Hall International, 1991) p. 141 (with permission).

advantages inherent in high-volume line situations. It does this by changing the process or functional layout associated with batch manufacturing into the product layout associated with line (see Figure 5–6).

The approach involves separating out those processes that do not lend themselves to the application of group technology because of such factors as the level of investment and health considerations (e.g., noise or process waste/fumes). The next step is to group together families of like products. The criteria for this selection are similar to those outlined for FMS. However, note that the process flexibility inherent in group technology applications is not of the same order as in FMS.

The third step is to determine the process configuration necessary to manufacture each product family involved and to lay out the cell or line to reflect the required manufacturing routings. The final stage is to complete a tooling analysis within each family, with a twofold aim. The first is to group together those parts within the family that can use the same tooling. This forms the basis for scheduling to reduce setting time. The second is to include this feature as part of the design prerequisites for future products.[5]

As diagramed in Figure 5–4, group technology moves a business's volumes toward the high end. In so doing, group technology changes the process on many of the

[5]A fuller explanation is given in T. Hill, *Production/Operations Management* 2nd ed. (Hemel Hempstead, U.K.: Prentice Hall, 1991) pp. 140–45; also refer to G. A. B. Edwards, *Readings in Group Technology* (Machinery Publishing Company Ltd., 1971), and J. L. Burbidge, *The Introduction of Group Technology* (Portsmouth, N.H.: Heinemann Educational Books, Inc., 1975).

Table 5–1 dimensions from batch to line. Most important, it creates an inherently less flexible process in that to reuse any spare capacity brought about by a decrease in product family volumes will not be easy, or even possible, without moving the location of the plant; a form of process investment. The key advantages to be gained from group technology include reduced lead times and lower work-in-process inventory. There is also a series of advantages associated with any form of small-scale manufacturing unit. A detailed review of these issues is provided elsewhere.[6]

Linked Batch.   As with most of the developments discussed in this section, linked batch is a hybrid of batch and line. However, linked batch does not need to encompass a large number of processes, which is more typical in the examples given earlier. In some instances, only two or three sequential processes may be linked; in others, for example, food packing, the whole of the process may be linked. Whereas in the other examples the investment decisions are typically made as part of a complete process review, linked batch is undertaken on a more piecemeal or evolutionary basis. That is, where only two or three processes are linked, decisions are typically piecemeal in nature; linking the whole set of processes is quite often the result of changing volumes over time and adaptive use of existing capacity to meet the process requirements of other products. The sequential processes, though physically laid out in line (i.e., one operation follows another), are run as a batch process (i.e., when product change is required, all the linked operations have to be stopped and reset to accommodate this change). Irrespective of the length of the set-up changes, the fact that the process has to be stopped makes it a batch process.

Dedicated Use of General Purpose Equipment.   Where the volume of a specific part is sufficient, manufacturing can justify the allocation of a process to its sole use. This dedication is not in the plant itself but in the use of a general purpose process. Thus, the potential flexibility and other characteristics illustrated in Table 5–1 of a general purpose process are retained, and they will be reclaimed when volumes reduce. Characteristically, then, the process is not altered. Hence, the process is still batch and, therefore, general purpose in nature. What becomes dedicated is the use of the process, which reflects the volume requirements for the product in question.

Thus, the hybrid stems from a change in use (as explained earlier) to reflect the high-volume demand for a product and not a physical change to the process itself. It remains a batch process, even though during the period in which its use is dedicated to the manufacture of a given product it may (e.g., for color changes) or may not be reset.

Line-Related Hybrids

Just as the last section discussed developments and hybrids rooted in batch processes, this section reviews hybrids related to line.

Mix Mode Assembly Lines.   A line process that can cope with a broad range of products without stopping is known as a mix mode assembly line. In reality, compa-

---

[6]Ibid.

nies determine the product range for all line processes when they make the process investment. However, the term *mix mode* has been used to reflect processes in which companies have made systematic and purposeful investments to increase the product range involved. Typically, this entails programming the line to make small quantities of different products in a predetermined sequence.

The origins of a mix mode assembly line are twofold. On the one hand, a reduction in demand for existing products releases capacity, which a company may wish to reuse. This, in turn, can lead to the adaptation of an existing line process to accommodate other products. On the other, a mix mode assembly line may be developed to handle the operations necessary to complete a number of products currently completed in other ways (e.g., using linked-batch processes). What makes the root here a line process is that it does not have to be stopped and reset to accommodate the next product.

Mix mode assembly lines are designed to cope with a range of products in any scheduled combination. This is achieved by the use of computer-controlled flow lines that schedule work according to the overall production requirements and the short-term work loads at the various stations. The increased range of products that can be accommodated justifies the investment necessary to achieve a higher level of this aspect of flexibility. In this way, a mix mode assembly line is an alternative process to batch that could be used to meet the required level of volume of the products in question.

As can be deduced from this explanation, a mix mode assembly line is not technically a hybrid, in that the characteristics of another process have not been combined with those of line. Instead, it is a line process that can accommodate the requirements of a wider range of products than can typically be made on a classic line process. It has been included here to illustrate how process investment can change certain relevant trade-offs in a business.

Transfer Lines.   The last hybrid process to be discussed is transfer lines. Where the volume demand for products is very high, further investment is justified. Transfer line is a hybrid between line and continuous processing. However, its root process is still line because it can be stopped without major cost. The position of transfer lines on Figure 5–4 illustrates the features of this process. The high demand justifies investment designed to reduce the manual inputs associated with a line process and to move more toward a process that automatically transfers a part from one station to the next, positions it, completes the task, and checks the quality. Furthermore, deviations from the specified tolerances will be registered, and automatic tooling adjustments and replacements will often be part of the procedure. To achieve this, the process is numerically controlled in part or in full, which provides the systems control afforded, in part at least, by the operator in the line process.

Review of the Use of Numerical Control (NC) in Hybrid Processes

Whereas linked batch, group technology, and the dedicated use of a general purpose process are derived from alternative uses of conventional, non-NC processes, the

FIGURE 5–7

Hybrid NC process choice related to volume

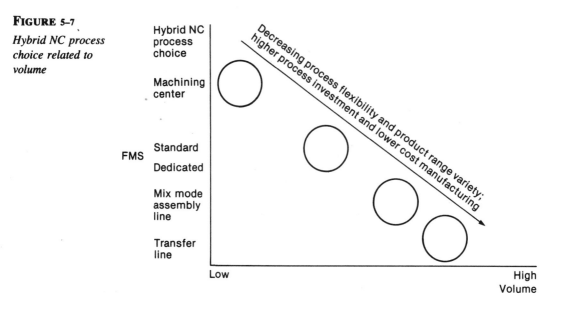

other 4 hybrid processes are based on the concept of numerical control in one form or another.*

The last section explained, and Figure 5–4 illustrated, that the basis for the choice between one NC hybrid process and another is volume. As with the choices between the five generic processes outlined in Table 5–1, the implications for these choices have to be understood and taken into account at the time of their selection (see Figure 5–7). The NC base of these processes brings with it a level of flexibility that is far greater than that inherent with non-NC alternatives. This means, therefore, that the process is more able to cope with a wider range of products and to handle product mix changes over time. However, dedication in these alternatives starts to be introduced when processes are brought together to meet the needs of a given range/family of products. In order to thereafter reuse these, further and often substantial investment will have to be made to relocate, adapt, or change existing processes and their configuration to meet the needs of other products. This change is illustrated by the gap between

---

*NC refers to the operation of machine tools from numerical data stored on paper or magnetic tape, punched cards, computer storage, or direct information. The development of machining centers results from the concepts of NC. In a machining center, a range of operations provided using a carousel with up to 150 tools or more (i.e., embodied in the center) from which the program will select as required, with some taking place simultaneously as required. Consequently, a machining center is not only able to cope with a wide range of product requirements; it can also be scheduled to complete one-offs in any sequence desired. More advanced NC systems include computer numerical control (CNC) systems using a dedicated minicomputer to perform NC functions and direct numerical control (DNC), which refers to a system having a computer controlling more than one machine tool. A DNC system includes both the hardware and software required to drive more than one NC machine simultaneously. To do this, DNC uses a computer, which may be a minicomputer, several microcomputers linked together, a minicomputer linked to a large computer, or a large computer on its own.

TABLE 5–2   Time Taken in Two Parts of the Process by Different Automakers

Process Part	Time Taken (days)	
	Detroit	Toyota
Scheduling a dealer's order	5	1
Lead time to make the product	5	2

SOURCE: J. L. Bower and T. M. Hout, "Fast-cycle Capability for Competitive Power," *Harvard Business Review,* November–December 1988, pp. 110–18.

machining centers and FMS. As the choice moves to the other end of the spectrum, the implications of dedication will begin to take hold.

Figure 5–7 illustrates the rationalized use of NC-based processes as they relate to volume. As with the generic processes described earlier, while volume is the basis for choice, two other equally important dimensions must be a part of this decision. The first is the changes in volume expected over time. The second is the host of implications to the business that must be understood and taken into account when arriving at this decision. Some of these are shown in Figure 5–7, but Table 5–1 provides a more complete list.[7]

Corporate Manufacturing Responses to Similar Markets

Different approaches are used in the same industry. Companies making similar products may choose similar processes yet manage the total manufacturing task in significantly different ways. Thus, process choice as shown in Table 2–1 is only one part of manufacturing's strategic response. As the example in Table 5–2 illustrates, manufacturing's strategic contribution to achieving competitive advantage must reflect the mix of all its parts.

As explained earlier, Japanese automakers schedule their plants in accordance with sales forecasts and work on make-to-stock rather than on order-backlog, make-to-order principles. Furthermore, given little order backlog, these companies are now offering to make and deliver an auto to a customer's specification in a much shorter time.

As stressed throughout, coherence between the many elements involved results in an integrated strategy. By raising the auto specification, a company keeps options low and thereby reduces customer choice. This in turn leads to fewer schedule adjustments. In many instances, the automobile specified may be already planned or even in stock. Similarly, reducing lead times in all parts of the process is a significant factor (see Table 5–2) in helping to achieve this difference. Thus, recognizing the order-winners

---

[7]A fuller range, including operational issues, is provided in T. Hill, *Production/Operations Management,* 2nd ed. (Hemel Hempstead, UK: Prentice Hall, 1991), pp. 61–69.

and qualifiers in relevant markets becomes the focus of activity and facilitates coherent functional support for key criteria.

Technology Strategy

Advances in computer control have brought fresh opportunities for the United States and other Western manufacturers. The potential for innovation in manufacturing is greater now than it has ever been. Advanced manufacturing technologies (AMT) have provided a viable option to sourcing manufactured components and products from other parts of the world. There is no doubt about the potential, and recent reports indicate an expected boom period, with "some sectors, such as robotics and computer-aided design, growing at over 30 percent a year. By 1990, the entire AMT industry was expected to have annual sales of more than $30 billion."[8]

The approach to the use of technology and ensuring the suitability of its application creates the most concern. Tripping over engineering white elephants in the past should make companies understandably wary, not of technology improvements themselves, but of approaches that lead to sizable investments in inappropriate technologies. However, the preoccupation with the search for panaceas may well lead companies to duplicate yesterday's mistakes. Indeed, the case for a technology strategy in itself should sound warning bells. Articles advocating technology-strategy links abound. These articles concern, for the most part, descriptions of the technologies and illustrations of specific applications and resulting improvements. But they fail to explain how to select technological investments that best support a business. Without this conceptual base, companies are unable to make assessments and draw distinctions. As a result, they have to fall back on hunch, or support the judgment of specialists, who are devotees of technological innovation and advantage, rather than business-oriented executives trying to ensure fit with the market and viewing process investment in a supportive role.

To some extent, the emerging call for companies to develop technology strategies has its roots in recent process innovations and computer applications in manufacturing. Historically, the clear link between manufacturing and the marketplace, which developed in the growth years following the Second World War, led to a well-understood manufacturing strategy that was appropriately reflected in the activities and developments within the process, production, and industrial engineering functions. Not only was the status of engineering clearly reinforced, but it also evolved that engineers were perceived to be the custodians of determining appropriate process and relevant elements of infrastructure investments.

This postwar role also led to, or reinforced, the low status of manufacturing management, with the attendant difficulties discussed in Chapter 2. These role character-

---

[8]I. Rodger, "Pressure to Innovate," in "Manufacturing Automation," *Financial Times (London) Survey,* February 5, 1985, p. 17.

istics in manufacturing were established in relations with other specialist functions, with similar consequences, some of which are discussed in later chapters on process positioning, infrastructure, and accounting.

Flexibility—A Strategic Cop-Out?

For many businesses, past investments in dedicated processes have proved inappropriate for current markets. New investment requirements have been brought about, in part, by pressures of competition. But the response has often been to purchase new equipment with sufficient flexibility for a wide range of products and to cope with low order-quantity requirements. However, decisions that are not based on assessments of the marketplace and evaluations of alternatives are tantamount to strategic cop-outs! "If in doubt, resolve the doubt" has become "if in doubt, buy flexibility."

One company, after witnessing an overall decline in volumes throughout the parent group, committed itself to the purchase of flexible processes to cope with an environment of change. An analysis of processes, product life cycles, and order-winners clearly showed that the purchase, in part, of dedicated plant would best meet these requirements. This eliminated a $0.25 million investment on unnecessary flexibility. As another illustration, three companies, each manufacturing in different segments of engineering, were using expensive NC machines primarily on high-volume products. Discussions revealed failures in the companies to separate comparisons of process capability of holding tight tolerances (current versus early 1970s technology) and the business needs of the process (low cost based on high volumes).

Technology Push versus Pull Strategies

Process investments can be based on either technology push or pull strategies. In a push strategy, the rationale for process investments comes from technology-based arguments; pull strategies reflect technology investments based on defined market needs. It is critical that companies with push strategies see arguments concerning the corporate potential to sell the spin-offs from the proposed technology investments as being only *part* of the evaluation. They must be sure to evaluate such investments on their own merits also.

Manufacturing Strategy and Technological Opportunities

Current process innovations present an important opportunity for companies to compete effectively in worldwide business. However, committing scarce resources to investments based primarily on the perspectives of specialists, or in search of a panacea to update and realign manufacturing, presents enormous and unnecessary risks. It is essential that technology alternatives form part of manufacturing strategy developments, as discussed in this and the previous chapter. A business must link investments with a well-argued understanding of its markets if it is to avoid inappropriate major capital expenditure.

Conclusion

Assessing the level of mismatch between its current processes and current business, determining the adjustment it must or is able to achieve, and making the appropriate choice of process for future products are difficult and critical production management tasks—difficult, in that the decision is complex; critical, in that the process investment will be substantial, and changes will be expensive and time-consuming to implement.

The Nature of Markets and Manufacturing

One of the core problems facing companies is that markets are inherently dynamic and manufacturing is inherently fixed. Markets are continually changing in response to internal initiatives and external pressures, while manufacturing remains fixed in terms of the trade-offs embodied in its investments. Thus, whereas market change is an inherent outcome of time, manufacturing will not change unless a conscious decision is made and additional investment is committed. A company that fails to make these commitments will have a manufacturing function less able to support its markets.

Manufacturing's Strategic Response

Typically, companies have responded to the need to choose manufacturing processes by leaning solely on the engineering/technology dimension. But, an engineering solution is not what is required. The engineering input concerns providing alternative technological options that will enable the product to be manufactured. However, the choice of process concerns how manufacturing is then completed. This will involve the product/market, investment/cost, and infrastructure, besides the manufacturing dimensions, all of which have been examined in this chapter.

Engineering prescriptions, technology solutions seeking problems, or the belief that panaceas are on hand have been instrumental, in part, for the uncompetitive position in which many North American manufacturing companies currently find themselves. Couple this with a marketing-led strategy in some business that has over-reached itself, or the more universal impact of incremental marketing changes that, over time, have altered business without companies recognizing the strategic consequences involved, and the result has been the erosion of large, traditional markets by our competitors. Other companies, persuaded by the apparent desirability of new markets or the short-term solution to get out of tough manufacturing industries, have also left the way clear in these high-volume, established markets. However, there is no long-term future in easy manufacturing tasks. The short run may appear attractive, but tomorrow matters.

Successful manufacturing nations have been systematically picking off many existing U.S. and other industrial nations' markets by a combined marketing/manufacturing strategy, thus creating, at the expense of its competitors, a sound industrial base essential to a nation's long-term prosperity and growth. The Japanese have, in fact, built their manufacturing base on traditional smokestack industries.

Further Reading

Blois, K. J., "Market Concentration—Challenge to Corporate Planning." *Long Range Planning* 13 (August 1980), pp. 56–62.

Bolwijn, P. T.; J. Boorsma; Q. H. van Breukelen; S. Brinkman; and T. Kumpe. *Flexible Manufacturing: Integrating Technical and Social Innovations.* Amsterdam: Elsevier Science Publishers B.V., 1986.

Burbridge, J. L. "The Simplification of Material Flow Systems." *International Journal of Production Research* 20 (1982), pp. 339–47.

Dale, R. G.; J. L. Burbidge; and M. J. Cottam. "Planning the Introduction of Group Technology." *International Journal of Operations and Production Management* 4, pp. 34–37.

Financial Times Survey. "Manufacturing Automation." February 5, 1985, pp. 17–22.

Goldhar, J. D. "Some Summary Thoughts—Manufacturing, Technology and Corporate Strategy." Presented at the Society of Manufacturing Engineers, Manufacturing Productivity Solutions 1982 Conference, Detroit, November 14–17, 1982.

Goldhar, J. D, and M. Jelinck. "Plan for Economies of Scope." *Harvard Business Review,* November–December 1983, pp. 143–48.

Harvard Business School. "Types of Production Process and Their Characteristics," 8–678–071 (revised 1978).

Hayes, R. W., and S. C. Wheelwright. "The Technology of Manufacturing Processes." In *Restoring Our Competitive Edge—Competing through Manufacturing.* New York: John Wiley & Sons, 1984.

Hyer, N. L., and U. Wemmerlov. "Group Technology and Productivity." *Harvard Business Review,* July–August 1984, pp. 140–49.

Leonard, R.,and K. Rathmill. "The Group Technology Myths." *Management Today,* January 1977, pp. 66–69.

Linder, J. O. "Flexible Production Organization—A Discussion of Efficiency." Paper, Department of Industrial Management, Chalmers University of Technology, Göteborg, Sweden.

Malpas, R. "The Plant after Next." *Harvard Business Review,* July–August 1983, pp. 122–30.

Miller, S. S. "Making Your Plant Manager's Job Manageable." *Harvard Business Review,* January–February 1983, pp. 69–74.

Schmenner, R. W. *Production Operations Management—Concepts and Situations.* Chicago: Science Research Associates USA, 1981.

Zelenovie, D. M. "Flexibility—A Condition for Effective Production Systems." *International Journal of Production Research* 20, no. 3 (1980), pp. 319–37.

Product Profiling

A company needs to have a comprehensive understanding of how well manufacturing can support its business as alternative processes are chosen. The size of and time scales involved in these process investments create issues that must be addressed in the corporate strategy debate. Chapter 5 discussed the implications of process choice, provided insights, and consequently, outlined some of the blocks on which to build manufacturing's strategic dimension. Assessing how well existing processes fit an organization's current market requirements and making appropriate choices of process to meet future needs are critical manufacturing responsibilities, owing to the high investment associated with the outcomes of these decisions.

When companies buy processes, however, they often fail to appreciate the business trade-offs embodied in those investments. Product profiling enables a company to test the current or anticipated level of fit between the characteristics of its market(s) and the characteristics of its existing or proposed processes and infrastructure investments (the components of manufacturing strategy—see Table 2–1). The purpose of this assessment is twofold. First, it provides a way to evaluate and, where necessary, improve the degree of fit between the way in which a company wins orders in its markets and manufacturing's ability to support these criteria (i.e., manufacturing's strategic response). Second, it helps a company move away from classic strategy building characterized by functional perspectives separately agreed, without adequate attempts to test the fit or reconcile different opinions of what is best for the business as a whole.

In many instances though, companies will be unable or unwilling to take the necessary steps to provide the degree of fit desired because of the level of investment, executive energy, and time scales involved. However, sound strategy is not a case of having every facet correctly in place. It concerns improving the level of consciousness a company brings to bear on its corporate decisions. Living with existing mismatches or allowing the level fit to deteriorate can be strategically sound if a company is aware of its position and makes these choices knowingly. Reality can constrain strategic decisions. In such circumstances, product profiling will help increase corporate awareness and allow a conscious choice between alternatives. In the past, many companies have not aspired to this level of strategic alertness.

The Need to Expand Manufacturing Strategy's Language Base

Manufacturing has had difficulty expressing important perspectives in a manner that provides for corporate debate and discussion. Unless it can do this, other business functions will find difficulty in embracing the issues on hand and, in turn, being party to their resolution. Intuition, experience, and gut-feeling must give way to business-related concepts and explanations. This is not to imply that the former are of little value. On the contrary, they form an integral part of sound management practice. However, at the strategic level they must be explained in a way that other executives can understand, so allowing them to become part of the on-going corporate debate and strategic outcomes. In fact, one of the key tests for the usefulness of management theory is whether or not it crystallizes the intuitive insights of experienced executives. In this way, it contributes to the essential intellectual nature of the management debate— intellectual not in the sense of theory but reflecting the complex and applied nature of the management task.

Each business will require its own approach and resolution. The examples described in the following sections met the specific needs of those businesses to which they relate. They should not be considered universally applicable. The conceptual base on which these analyses rest, however, can be transferred and used to prepare similar analyses that will yield their own profiles.

Product Profiling

Inconsistency between the market and manufacturing process capability to support the business specification of its products, can be induced by changes in the market or process investments, or a combination of the two. In all instances, the mismatch results from the fact that while manufacturing investments are inherently large and fixed (once a company has purchased them, it will have to live with them for better or for worse for many years), markets are inherently dynamic. In addition, corporate marketing decisions can often be relatively transient should a business so decide. The inherently changing nature of markets and a company's ability to alter marketing perspectives to allow for change and repositioning are in opposition to manufacturing decisions that bind a business for years ahead. A company must reconcile this, which requires strategic awareness, recognition, and action.

Product profiling is a way to ascertain the level of fit between the choices of process that have been or are proposed to be made and the order-winning criteria of the product(s) under review. The sections that follow describe situations and, to some extent, different levels of the same problem.

Levels of Application

Product profiling can be undertaken at either the level of the company or process. Company-based applications provide an overview of the degree of fit between all or significant parts of a business and existing manufacturing facilities or its proposed manufacturing investments and developments. Process-based applications provide a check of the fit between the products that the equipment under review is to provide.

Procedure

The procedure used in product profiling is outlined below. This details the basic steps to follow, but the essential direction of the analysis needs to reflect the match/mismatch issues within the whole or parts of a business. Remember, the purpose of profiling is to draw a picture to help identify the current or potential problem, hence allowing discussion of and agreement on what steps should be taken to improve the company's strategic position.

1. Select relevant aspects of products/markets, manufacturing, investment/cost, and infrastructure as outlined in Table 5–1. This choice must meet two overriding requirements.
   a. The criteria selected must relate to the issues on hand and reflect the strategic dimensions of relevant markets. Thus, dimensions other than those given in Table 5–1 will often be selected, as the examples that follow illustrate.
   b. The number of criteria selected must be kept small enough to allow the picture illustrating the issues to show through. Choosing too large a list will blur the essential clarity required and detract from the facilitating role that this approach plays within strategic formulation.
2. Display the trade-offs of process choice that would be typical for each criterion chosen in 1 above. This provides the backdrop against which the product or products can be profiled.
3. The purpose of profiling is to provide comparison. The next step then is to profile the products, product groups, or companies involved. This is done by positioning the selected product(s), group(s) of products, or companies on each criterion selected. Remember, this is a comparative technique; therefore, you are looking to show the relationship of one product to another, compare a company today with what it was (or would be) in a selected earlier (or later) period, or review one business with another. The purpose is to test the correlation between market requirements and manufacturing's current or proposed response to their provision. Thus, the profiling (i.e., the position on each chosen dimension where what is being reviewed is placed) is to display a comparative picture and not become an issue of exactness.
4. The resulting profile illustrates the degree of consistency between the characteristics of the market(s) and the relative provision of the processes

and infrastructure within manufacturing. The more consistency that exists, the straighter the profile will be. Inconsistencies between the market and manufacturing's inherent ability to meet these needs will result in a dogleg-shaped profile.

Remember throughout that the purpose of a profile is to display the issues relevant to a business and enable a company to review the degree of alignment that exists. This pictorial representation of those dimensions relevant to a business allows the executives responsible for strategic decisions to recognize the issues, their origins, and the corrective action to take.

The examples that follow illustrate the points above and afford the opportunity to discuss particular applications.

Company-Based Profiles

Inducing Mismatch with Process Investments

As emphasized in the last chapter, all process choices include fixed business trade-offs that can be changed only by further investment or development. Thus, a company's investment in a process embodying trade-offs inconsistent with part or all of its markets induces mismatches between process and market unless the company changes its markets. These would correspond to the relative size and importance of the process(es) involved and the associated level of reinvestment.

A company producing a range of cartons, for example, decided to invest $6 million in part of its processes, which was core to a range of its products accounting for some 30 percent of total sales revenue. Based on the current level of activity, the investment would have been payed back in 5.5 years. However, to meet the parent group's return-on-investment, four-year norms, the company needed to increase the output of these products by some 50 percent.

For some time, the company's marketing strategy had been to position itself in the higher-quality end of all its markets. However, to gain the larger volumes necessary to justify this process investment, the company had to go for business won on price. Soon, the company had almost 15 percent of its total business with distinct low-cost needs, while having to meet the schedule-change needs of a further 30 percent. The consequences were significant and the ramifications substantial. Within a short space of time, the process investment had introduced manufacturing conflict in a large part of its total business.

Product profiling can draw attention to the sort of mismatches involved here, by graphically representing key marketing and manufacturing differences that the single set of processes had to accommodate (see Figure 6–1).

In the example given above, the $6 million process investment was, in terms of its point on the jobbing-batch-line continuum in Figure 6–1, consistent with its existing processes and chosen to support its existing business. However, the additional price-

FIGURE 6–1

A product profile illustrating mismatch between the market and manufacturing induced by process investment

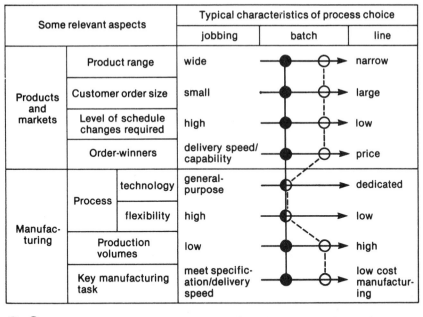

● ◐   Position of existing products on each of the chosen dimensions and resulting profile ———

○ ◐   Position of new products on each of the chosen dimensions and the resulting profile – – – –

sensitive business required different process and infrastructure support. The straight-line and dogleg relationships in the figure reflect this.

Applying the Same Manufacturing Strategy to Two Different Markets

The first example concerned the impact of a process investment on the fit between a company's market and its manufacturing capability. Without a well-developed manufacturing strategy, the company was unconsciously driven by other functional (in this instance, finance) norms and arguments into an inappropriate major investment. Failure to recognize that investment decisions need to be based on strategy, and not functional perspectives and prerequisites, is a common contributor to poor corporate performance.

However, an equally important source of inappropriate investment decisions is the assumption that to meet different corporate requirements a similar manufacturing strategy approach can be applied. Typically, this happens where specialists' views form the basis of initiatives, rather than a manufacturing strategy formulated to the requirements of individual markets. Again, product profiling can provide a graphic description of the resulting mismatch and help explain these differences.

Faced with a decline in markets and profits, a company undertook a major internal review of its two manufacturing plants. To provide orientation for its business, it

FIGURE 6–2

A product profile illustrating the level of match and mismatch between two plants and their respective markets induced by applying the same manufacturing strategy to both plants

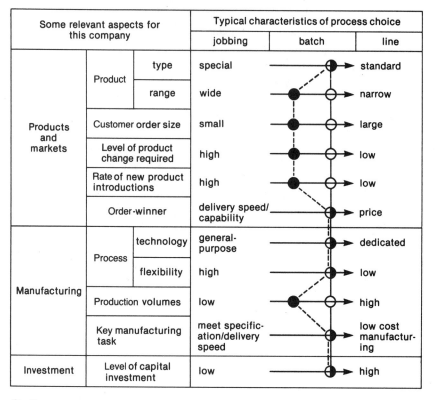

Some relevant aspects for this company			Typical characteristics of process choice		
			jobbing	batch	line
Products and markets	Product	type	special		standard
		range	wide		narrow
	Customer order size		small		large
	Level of product change required		high		low
	Rate of new product introductions		high		low
	Order-winner		delivery speed/ capability		price
Manufacturing	Process	technology	general-purpose		dedicated
		flexibility	high		low
	Production volumes		low		high
	Key manufacturing task		meet specific-ation/delivery speed		low cost manufactur-ing
Investment	Level of capital investment		low		high

○ ◑ Position of Plant A on each of the chosen dimensions and the resulting profile ———

● ◑ Position of Plant B on each of the chosen dimensions and the resulting profile — — —

This figure reflects the consistency of products and processes for Plant A, and the inconsistencies for Plant B reflected by a straight line and dog leg shape, respectively.

decided to manufacture different products at each of its two sites; each plant, then, manufactured distinct products and associated volumes. Four or five years later, the number of product types handled by Plant B was eight times as many as Plant A, and, as one would expect, product volume changes were reflected in this decision. While in Plant A, average volumes for individual product rose by 60 percent, in Plant B they decreased by 40 percent. In addition, to redress the decline in profits the company also embarked on major manufacturing investments at each plant, involving identical process investments and infrastructure changes. Figure 6–2 illustrates how these changes fitted Plant A's markets, while they led to a significant mismatch for Plant B.

The procedure followed is similar to the one outlined in the previous section. Again, the first step is to describe, in conceptual terms, the characteristics of product/ markets, manufacturing, investment/cost, and infrastructure features pertinent to the

FIGURE 6–3

*The level of
inconsistency on
all points of the
dimensions on the
vertical axis*

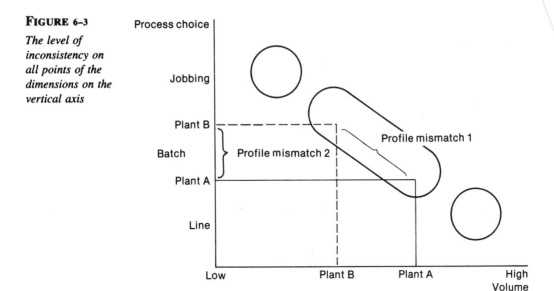

business. The dimensions selected for these two plants are detailed in Figure 6–2. First, the characteristics that reflect the change between jobbing, batch, and line need to be described. Thus, the product range associated with jobbing is wide, and becomes increasingly narrow as it moves through to line. Whereas, customer order size is small in jobbing, and becomes increasingly larger as it moves through to line and so on. These dimensions represent the classic characteristics of the trade-offs embodied in process choice. Plant A's profile shows a straight-line relationship between the products and markets and the manufacturing and infrastructure provision. However, Plant B's profile shows a dogleg due to the difference in markets, compared to the similar process and infrastructure investments made in each of the two plants.

Based on Figure 6–2, Figure 6–3 provides a further illustration and additional insights into the extent of the mismatch brought about by applying the same manufacturing strategy to Plants A and B described here. Whereas Plant A had appropriate process investments in line with its product volumes, Plant B did not (referred to as "Profile mismatch 1" on Figure 6–3). As a consequence, whereas Plant A was appropriately positioned on each dimension on the vertical axis (see Figure 6–2 and Figure 6–3), again Plant B was not (referred to as "Profile Mismatch 2" on Figure 6–3).

Incremental Marketing Decisions Resulting in a Mismatch.   For many companies, changes in market needs happen over time, and these incremental changes are more typically the source of mismatches in a business. Product profiling provides an important way of describing these changes and their overall impact on a company.

As highlighted earlier, while markets are inherently dynamic, manufacturing is inherently fixed. This is not, however, a result of attitudes or preferences—markets will simply change over time whether or not a company so desires, whereas the manufacturing investments will stay as they are unless deliberately changed by development or further investment.

Product profiling is a way of mapping the fit between the requirements of current markets and the characteristics of existing processes. The key to identifying these differences lies in the recognition that while the needs of the market may have changed, the characteristics of the manufacturing process and infrastructure investments will not. These, as emphasized in Chapter 5, will remain fixed, unless there is further, appropriate investment.

To illustrate, a company had experienced a decline in sales in the period 1981 to 1987. To maintain profit levels, the company's marketing strategy in this period had been to offer more products. Consequently, the product range widened while the customer order size reduced and the number of production schedule changes increased. To explain the significant problems that then existed, it is necessary to compare the current year with the year the process and infrastructure investments were made. This is because a company invests in processes to reflect the characteristics of its markets, as perceived at that time (in this example, 7 years ago). As can be seen here, 7 years ago (as with Plant A in the last sample), there is a match between the products/markets, manufacturing process, and infrastructure. However, the incremental marketing changes in this seven-year period had had the cumulative effect of moving leftward this company's position on several of the relevant product/market dimensions. The order-winning criteria had remained the same, and without the required process/infrastructure investment and change, manufacturing had increasingly been less able to cope effectively. The implications for manufacturing of the incremental marketing changes in these years are revealed when drawing the equivalent profile for the current year. Again, the profile mismatch illustrates that manufacturing had become increasingly less able to support the changing marketing trends, which the dogleg profile illustrates (see Figure 6–4). A diagram similar to Figure 6–3 could be drawn to represent Figure 6–4, as was provided for Figure 6–2.

Reallocation of Products Due to Downsizing

Companies faced with a reduction in overall demand often decide to downsize total manufacturing capacity as a way of meeting future profit expectations. This decision involves the reallocation of products from one plant to another, thereby enabling one to downsize or close while improving current machine utilization in the other. Debates of this kind are based on two checks:

- A technical specification fit between the products to be made and the process.
- The financial implications of the different decisions.

Often, however, companies fail to check whether the business specifications of the products to be transferred match the process. There have been many illustrations of this source of mismatch in the late 1980s and into the 1990s. The resulting profile is similar to that in Figure 6–4 but is due to stepped rather than incremental changes. It results from the failure to recognize that different units of capacity, though meeting similar technical specifications, do not have the same business specifications.

Some relevant aspects for			Typical characteristics of process choice		
			jobbing	batch	line
Products and markets	Product range		wide		narrow
	Order size		small		large
	Frequency of changes	product	high		low
		schedule	high		low
	Order-winners		delivery speed/ capability		price
Manufacturing	Process technology		general-purpose		dedicated
	production volumes		low		high
	Ability to cope with change	product	easy		difficult
		schedule	easy		difficult
	Set-ups	number	many		few
		expense	inexpensive		expensive
Organizational	Control		decentralized		centralized
	Style		entrepreneurial/ informal		easy

○ ◑ 1981 company position on each of the chosen aspects and the resulting profile_____

● ◑ 1987 company position on each of the chosen resulting profile_ _ _ _ _

The current year profile illustrates the dogleg shape, which reflects the inconsistencies between the high-volume batch processes and infrastructure purchased 7 years ago, and the current market position.

Internal Sourcing Decisions Based on Unit Costs

Often within a group of companies the same product will be manufactured in two or more locations. Executives with profit responsibility for a region will understandably look to sourcing costs as a major factor in profit performance. Where two or more plants make the same product, differences in unit price will attract some sister companies within the group to place their business with the least cost company. In the early 1990s, a North American multinational was under pressure to maintain its record of profit performance; the various parts of the business were required to match or even improve their own performance. The result was that executives switched their internal source of products on the basis of lowest unit cost as an important way of maintaining or improving their own individual profit performance. Within a short time, however, the least-cost plant found that it could no longer maintain its previous cost levels. Attracting volumes of differing (often low) levels and other market requirements led to its best plant grossly underperforming. A product profile showed why, with reasons similar to those described in the last two examples, although with different origins.

Process-Based Profiles

Company-based profiles help reflect changes at the corporate level and identify the varying degrees of match or mismatch that exist or will exist if market needs and characteristics are not reflected in manufacturing. Process-based profiles provide similar insights but concern the review of a single process (or group of similar processes) in relation to the products produced on it (them). There can be more than one process-based profile completed within a single plant.

A prime reason why mismatches develop is that as demand for a product(s) changes, capacity is released. The typical result is that companies will allocate other products to that process on the basis of a technical specification check but not a business specification check. These may be either derivations of products already made in that process or new products. In both instances, the product range widens, overall individual order quantities decrease, and the process stops and starts more often.

The outcome is that the process will increasingly be required to support the business specification of two or more products that have different order-winners or other market characteristics than one another. Profiles based on a format similar to those given earlier will help explain this to a business so that decisions are changed or expectations realigned.

A U.S.-based pharmaceutical company located the manufacture of a major new product in its Kansas City plant. The initial sales of this product justified forecasts, and following this initial success the company introduced product variants to maximize total sales revenue. These variants took the form of dosage, package size, and labels/leaflets in several languages. Sales continued to grow, and the company purchased further packaging equipment, similar to the existing processes, to meet increased capacity requirements. Variants continued and so did total sales. Though not competing on price (brand name was an important factor for this product in winning orders), margins deteriorated. Furthermore, as competing products entered the market and price levels were revised, overall profit levels fell short of expectations.

The profile in Figure 6–5 helps explain why. A mismatch between marketing and manufacturing resulted from engineering and manufacturing's orientation shifting away from exploiting the potential cost advantages associated with volumes toward that of product introductions necessitated by the variations strategy. The process investment and manufacturing orientation were misaligned with the needs of the market and the profit potential associated with reducing costs. Consequently profit margins were short of the level necessary to support the high R&D expenditure essential to secure future growth and market penetration in pharmaceutical markets.

FIGURE 6–5

*A profile of the
product variants
packed on a
number of similar
packaging lines*

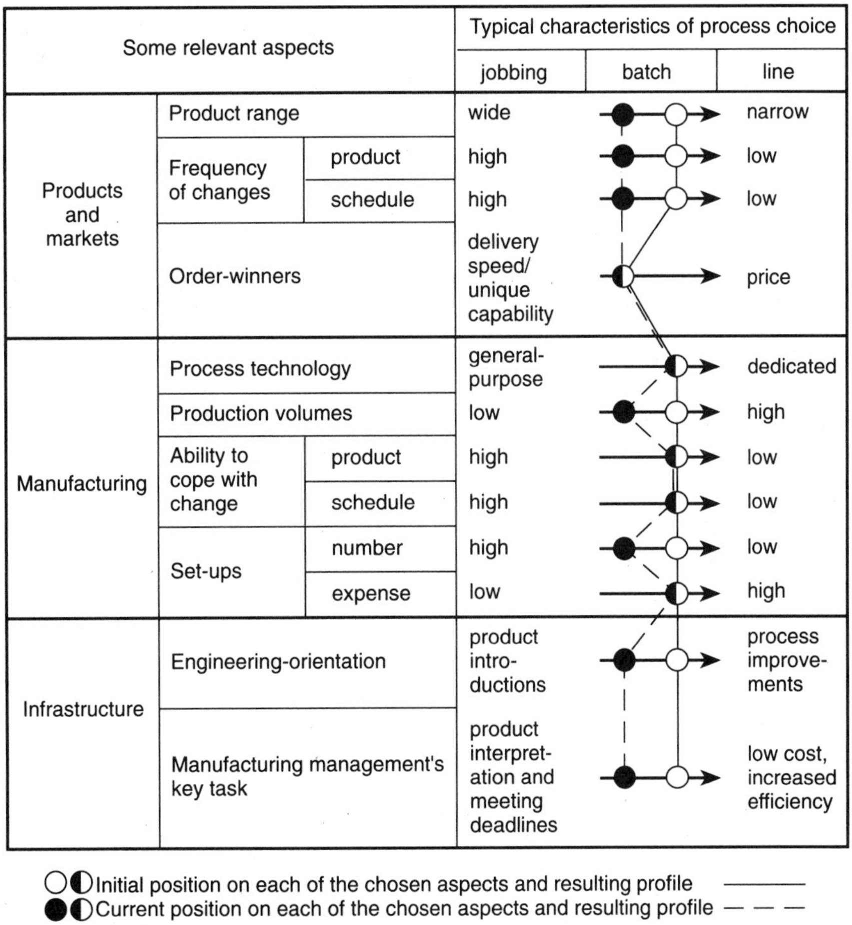

Some relevant aspects			Typical characteristics of process choice		
			jobbing	batch	line
Products and markets	Product range		wide		narrow
	Frequency of changes	product	high		low
		schedule	high		low
	Order-winners		delivery speed/ unique capability		price
Manufacturing	Process technology		general-purpose		dedicated
	Production volumes		low		high
	Ability to cope with change	product	high		low
		schedule	high		low
	Set-ups	number	high		low
		expense	low		high
Infrastructure	Engineering-orientation		product intro-ductions		process improve-ments
	Manufacturing management's key task		product interpret-ation and meeting deadlines		low cost, increased efficiency

○◐ Initial position on each of the chosen aspects and resulting profile   ———
●◐ Current position on each of the chosen aspects and resulting profile — — —

Using Product Profiling

The examples given in the previous sections illustrate the role product profiling may play in helping a company to check its existing product and process choice relationship and allow, where relevant, comparisons to be made between similar applications, or to measure trends over time. However, the reviews given were based on hindsight, not on the forward-looking characteristics of strategy. When a company is able to illustrate current positions and future alternatives, it can discuss alternatives and determine which strategic direction best meets the needs of the business. In this role, product profiling helps companies determine the business perspectives of manufacturing.

However, companies that are, for whatever reason, experiencing a mismatch between their current market needs and existing manufacturing processes and infrastructure face a number of alternative choices. These are,

1. Live with the mismatch.
2. Redress the profile mismatch by altering the marketing strategy.
3. Redress the profile mismatch by investing in and changing manufacturing and its infrastructure.
4. A combination of 2 and 3.

Alternative 1 affords companies the opportunity to consciously make a decision on the trade-offs involved. This may be the correct strategic choice. It does bring a company's expectations more in line with reality, makes it aware of the real costs of being in different markets, changes the measures of performance by distinguishing between those based on business-related decisions and those based on functional achievement, and raises the level of corporate consciousness about the overall consequences of maintaining product profile status quo or the decision to improve or widen any *mismatch* that may exist. Furthermore, future decisions concerning new products are now more able to incorporate these essential perspectives; such decisions reconcile the diverse functional perspectives under the mantle of what is best for the business overall.

Alternatives 2 and 3 concern ways of straightening existing—or consciously avoiding the widening of existing or creating of new—mismatches. These decisions may be taken independently or in unison. Alternative 2 involves influencing corporate policy through changes or modifications to existing or proposed marketing strategies. In this way, the implications for manufacturing of marketing decisions are addressed and included as an integral part of the corporate strategy debate. Thus, manufacturing is able to move from the reactive stance it currently takes to a proactive mode, so essential to sound policy decisions.

Alternative 3 involves a company's decision to invest in the processes and infrastructure of its business, to either enable manufacturing to become more effective in its provision of the order-winning criteria and support in the marketplace for existing products, or to establish the required level of support for future products. As does Alternative 2, it enables manufacturing to switch from a reactive to a proactive response to corporate marketing decisions. Thus, by receiving pertinent inputs at the strategic level, the business becomes more aware of the implications involved and is able to arrive at strategic options based on the relevant and comprehensive inputs necessary to make sound judgments at the strategic level.

Conclusion

The reasons companies fail to incorporate the manufacturing perspectives into the strategy debate are many. For one, manufacturing is traditionally presented as a technical or engineering-related function. This not only creates barriers to discussion, it also misrepresents the key perspectives a company needs to address. A major thrust within manufacturing strategy is to reorient its contribution from a technical/engineering to a business perspective. This not only opens the debate by providing meaningful insights, it also introduces those manufacturing perspectives that can contribute to the success of a business. In this way, it helps create the link with other functions by using the common denominator of the market to create interest in and highlight the relevance to other functions. The results are business-based discussions leading to essential strategic outcomes.

Product profiling is one such development. By translating process investments into business issues, companies are able to assess the fit between these major resources and the markets they are required to support. In addition, being able to explain trends, mismatches, and options in picture form enhances the power of the illustration and increases its role in corporate understanding and debate. It leads to sound strategy developments by enabling functions to explain themselves in corporate terms and provides a language to enhance essential discussion and agreement.

Focused Manufacturing— Principles and Concepts

Manufacturing is inherently a complex task, and managing this complexity is a key corporate role. The complexity involved, however, does not emanate from the nature of the individual tasks that the job comprises. In all but highly technical, special product market segments, it is not difficult to cope with the technology of the product or process. In most situations, the process technology and wherewithal to make the product involved have been purchased from outside, with appropriate engineering and technical know-how provided inside to support the manufacturing requirement and underpin any necessary development. In a similar way, product design and the associated technology falls under the auspices of the customer and/or design function. Hence, neither process nor product technologies are generally difficult to understand or manage from the viewpoint of the manufacturing function.

The complexity in manufacturing stems from the number of aspects and issues involved in the task, the interrelated nature of these, and the level of fit between the manufacturing strategy task and the internal process capability and infrastructure.

In all instances, the level of complexity is derived largely from, or can be controlled by, the corporate strategy decisions made within the business itself. However, whereas past research has identified the number and interrelated nature of the tasks and issues involved as being a fundamental characteristic of complexity (the small-is-beautiful syndrome[1]), the fit between the manufacturing strategy task, the internal process capability, and infrastructure has only recently received close attention. These latter issues come under the heading of "focused manufacturing."

---

[1]Brought to prominence in E. F. Schumacher's book, *Small Is Beautiful: Economics as if People Mattered* (New York: Harper & Row, 1975).

Focused Manufacturing

Focused manufacturing concerns linking an organization's manufacturing facilities to the appropriate competitive factors of its business(es), with the aim of enabling that company to gain greater control of its competitive position. One of the most difficult tasks in managing manufacturing is responding to the different market demands made on the facilities. This is due to the wide and often diverse nature of these demands and the level of complexity generated in the corresponding parts of the manufacturing function, including suppliers. Many companies are now finding that focusing the demands to which individual facilities must respond can markedly reduce the level of complexity involved in managing those operations. This results in an improved overall performance.

When explaining focus, the words *narrow* or *narrowing* are often used. For example, Skinner, who was the first to expound the benefits of focused plants, argues that "a factory that focuses on a narrow product mix for a particular market niche will outperform the conventional plant, which attempts a broader mission."[2] However, taken at face value, this argument can be misleading. Many companies do not have the "narrow product mix" alternative referred to here. The issue of focus, therefore, is more accurately explained in Skinner's fuller definitions, which formed part of his fourfold view for effecting basic changes in the management of manufacturing. Two of these were:

> Learning to focus each plant on a limited, concise, manageable set of product, technologies, volumes, and markets
>
> Learning to structure basic manufacturing policies and supporting services so that they focus on one explicit manufacturing task, instead of on many inconsistent, conflicting, implicit tasks.[3]

The emphasis here is on a limited and consistent set of tasks, which will often be far from the layman's definition of narrow. So, to avoid confusion and the implication of a simplistic resolution of the infinitely complex reality of business, the dimension of narrow should be omitted. It is the homogeneity of tasks and the repetition and experience involved in completing these that form the basis of focused manufacturing. Thus, focusing the demands placed on manufacturing will enable resources, efforts, and attention to be concentrated on a defined and homogeneous set of activities, allowing management to prioritize the key tasks necessary to achieve a better performance. In most plants, however, a meaningful level of plant focus is rarely understood, let alone achieved. There are several factors that have contributed to this position over the last 15 to 20 years.

Principle of Economies of Scale in Markets Characterized by Difference

For many years it has been (and still is) argued that the principle of economies of scale is a sound and appropriate way of organizing and managing businesses. As an under-

---

[2]W. Skinner, "The Focused Factory," *Harvard Business Review*, May–June 1974, pp. 113–21.
[3]Ibid., p. 114.

lying approach, it is highly attractive. However, for most organizations today this approach no longer works well. The advantages that can accrue from applying economies of scale are no longer being realized because the markets and the necessary corporate response to and support for them have changed. While markets in the past were characterized by similarity, today's markets are characterized by difference.

Economics of scale are most appropriate for and best applied to high-volume, steady-state markets (i.e., where similarity is the hallmark). However, for most companies these conditions no longer reflect the nature of their businesses.[4] For many, these prerequisites are far from their own realities. In fact, if anything, the opposite applies. Their markets are low-volume and dynamic in nature (i.e., where difference is the hallmark).

The key reasons why the conditions have changed are discussed below.

Marketing

Marketing-led strategies are usually based on principles of growth through extending the product range. Invariably, new products (even those requiring new technologies) are manufactured, partly at least, on existing processes, and almost always within the same infrastructure. The logic for this is based on the principle of the economies derived from using existing plant capacity where possible and being supported by the existing overhead structure. Over time, the incremental nature of these marketing changes will invariably alter the manufacturing task. The result is complexity, confusion, and worst of all a production organization that, because it is spun out in all directions by a kind of centrifugal force, lacks focus and a doable manufacturing task.[5] When asked to provide the different order-winning criteria for a range of products, a factory must make a series of compromises.

Increases in Plant Size

Faced with a shortage of capacity, companies find the attractions of on-site expansion irresistible. The tangible arguments of cost and overhead advantages, plus the provision of a better hedge against future uncertainty, provide the basis against which companies measure the alternatives. They rarely take into account the costs of the associated uplift in complexity and the bureaucracy that develops as factories try to cope. These changes are further hidden or disguised by their piecemeal or incremental nature. Schmenner concludes that:

> Big plants usually have formidable bureaucratic structures. Relationships inevitably become formal, and the worker is separated from the top executives by many layers of management. All too often, managers are shuffling the paperwork that formal systems

---

[4]The need for differentiated strategies is also identified in Schroeder, Anderson, and Cleveland, "The Content of Manufacturing Strategy: An Empirical Study," *Journal of Operations Management* 6, no. 3 (1988), pp. 405–16; and A. Roth, "Differentiated Manufacturing Strategies for Competitive Advantage: An Empirical Investigation" (Research Report Series, School of Management, Boston University, 1987).

[5]Skinner, "The Focused Factory," p. 118.

have spawned. . . . Although there has to be some formality in plant operations, too much can wipe out the many informal procedures that keep plants nimble and able to adapt to change.[6]

Manufacturing

To aggravate the situation of compromise described in the last section, manufacturing in these circumstances will rarely have a definition of its task. It will be required to perform on every yardstick, with these often changing from one day to the next, depending on the pressures from within and outside the business. The result is that manufacturing, without an agreed strategy, will respond as best it can, independently deciding on the best corporate compromises or trade-offs involved. Invariably the result is reduced plant performance.

Plant Utilization

Embodied in these scale principles is the argument concerning the high utilization of plant. As capacity is released due to a falloff in demand for a product(s), companies typically reutilize the spare capacity by introducing new products. In most companies, the justification for purchasing new processes or equipment will usually be partly based on total volumes. Companies by planning to use existing process capacity to complete some or all of the operations for new products will more easily meet this investment hurdle. However, when evaluating the suitability of processes for a product, companies invariably only check that technical specifications are met. They rarely check the consistency of the business requirement (i.e., manufacturing task) for each of the new products involved. Furthermore, this check is necessary not just for current requirements; it must be made over time as products go through their life cycles and relevant order-winners correspondingly change.

Specialists as the Basis for Controlling a Business

Management perceives the use of specialists as the appropriate way to control a business. "These professionals, quite naturally, seek to maximize their contributions and justify their positions. They have conventional views of success in each of their particular fields. Of course, these objectives are generally in conflict."[7] Furthermore, the essential link between the activities of specialists and the major functions of a business requires close cooperation and understanding. Too often, that is not present. The failure of companies to clearly define the focus of their business exacerbates this problem. Without this direction, there is insufficiently shared understanding of what is required. Thus, support systems, controls, information provision, and other features of infrastructure are not developed in line with the appropriate and agreed corporate needs. Trade-offs are not made, therefore, against the shared understanding of the business.

---

[6]W. Schmenner, "Every Factory Has a Life Cycle," *Harvard Business Review,* March–April 1983, p. 123.

[7]Skinner, "The Focused Factory," p. 45.

FIGURE 7–1

In pursuit of panacea—which three-letter acronym next?

SOURCE: With permission, Operations Institute, Johnson & Johnson.

They are assessed on the fragmented and uncoordinated views and advice of specialists, and based on what seems best at the time, rather than on an agreed strategic appreciation of competitive performance.

Looking for Panaceas

Emanating somewhat from the last point is the approach by many businesses to seek resolution to problems through panaceas. The search for which of the many three-letter acronyms is the key to success has become the strategic pastime of many firms (see Figure 7–1). Most companies can recall their own redundant solutions. The latest example of a long line in manufacturing is exhorting businesses to adopt the best of the Japanese system as a matter of course rather than one effective way of meeting a defined need. Although in themselves such developments can substantially contribute to business success, they need to be derived from strategic discussion and in line with appropriate focus.

There are two prerequisites to achieving this potential, both of which relevant Japanese companies have met. First, developments in manufacturing, as well as other functions, need to fit the market needs of a business. Japanese companies undertook developments in response to requirements placed on their manufacturing functions to improve given activities recognized as critical to the overall success of the business. The result was the just-in-time, total quality management, and other concepts and approaches.

The second prerequisite concerns time. To undertake, develop, and fit major initiatives into existing structures requires adequate time. After all, it took those Japanese companies some 30 years to perfect their ideas and to adapt these approaches carefully to the needs of their business. Characteristically, Western companies expect and even demand their implementation and successful adoption to be achieved overnight. The rushed nature of this approach results in inappropriate applications and unrealistic expectations.

The panacea approach will at best only distract management from the essential resolution of its strategic direction; at worst it will imply that there is no longer any need to be concerned—all is in hand.

Trade-Offs in Focused Manufacturing

The choice of focused manufacturing implies trade-offs. In arriving at this decision, companies must distinguish between the gains associated with size reduction and manageable units and those that accrue from the approach adopted toward achieving focused manufacturing. A reduction in size may well go hand in hand with the decision to focus; however, companies must differentiate the advantages resulting from any decision to reduce size and those unique to each choice.

Downsizing versus Focused Plants

It is important to separate the concepts of downsizing (i.e., reducing the size of plants) and focusing. Focusing manufacturing businesses will invariably lead to reduction in plant sizes. There are, however, advantages and disadvantages to these reductions. Smaller plants will bring such advantages as the potential for improved communication, greater orientation toward a well-understood and agreed set of business objectives, simpler and more appropriate forms of control and managerial style, higher levels of employee participation and motivation, shorter process lead times, lower work-in-process inventory, reduced complexity of the production-control task, and a more accurate assessment of financial performance. On the other hand, smaller plants run contrary to the concept of economies of scale and may well lead to the need to increase or duplicate certain processes or parts of the infrastructure such as procedures and specialist capabilities.

Since these advantages and disadvantages result directly from the change in size itself, companies must base their choice of approach on the characteristics of each alternative. There are three approaches to focusing facilities. The characteristics of each are listed in Table 7–1 and summarized below.

Alternative Approaches to Focused Manufacturing

Based on Products/Markets.   This orients relevant parts of the manufacturing facilities toward a particular customer or generic group of products, a basis for focus that reflects the breakdown of actual or forecast sales typically used by companies. Typifying a marketing perspective, such a focus often mirrors this function's view of the business.

Based on Processes.   This groups together products that are made with similar processes. The principal rationale is to gain advantages such as concentrated expertise

TABLE 7-1   Characteristics of Alternative Approaches to Focusing Facilities

Characteristics	Alternative Approaches		
	Products/Markets	*Processes*	*Order-Winners**
Orientation—basis	Product/market name	Process	Manufacturing task
—rationale	Marketing's view of the market	Plant utilization	Order-winners to be provided by manufacturing
—principal functional stimulus	Marketing	Engineering	Manufacturing
Minimum duplication of plant involved		✔	
Range of volumes produced			
Widest	✔	✔	
Narrowest			✔
Conflicting order-winners to be provided	✔	✔	
Products stay in the same unit for all or most of their life cycle	✔	✔	
Greatest potential for orienting and evaluating appropriate levels of infrastructure within the units			✔

*Often related to volume.

and improved utilization of manufacturing processes. It accomplishes this by identifying like products on the basis of their process requirements.

Companies that make repeat or standard products with insufficient volume to go to line (a common situation) will choose batch as the appropriate process. This enables spare capacity to be utilized and reutilized by any product requiring an operation(s) to be completed by the process in question. The approach to focus described here is based on a similar rationale. Products needing the same process will go into the same manufacturing unit, thereby avoiding the potential duplication of investment. However, when plants are broken down into two or more focused units, no matter what the basis for achieving this, the process capacities allocated to the smaller units will never be as fully utilized as they are when using a batch process. The latter arranges processes on a functional basis (i.e., all equipment providing similar technical capabilities to be put into the same geographical area and managed as a whole unit). This arrangement facilitated the utilization and reutilization of process capability.

Breaking plants down on the basis of processes enables a company to minimize plant duplication, as shown in Table 7–1. This principle is known as group technology, which was identified as a hybrid process in Chapter 5.

Based on Order-Winners.   This approach allocates products to a particular unit on the basis of different order-winners and qualifiers that manufacturing needs to provide. By focusing parts of a manufacturing unit, this approach creates conditions where the task (i.e., what manufacturing has to do well to support the particular order-winners and qualifiers) is consistent. Often this orientation is paralleled by differences in volume levels, but this is not always the case. As shown in Table 7–1, breaking down plants into two or more units provides the best conditions for creating a consistent and coherent set of manufacturing requirements, tasks, and priorities.

In reality, many businesses are best served by adopting a combination of approaches when focusing plants, as explained more fully in the next chapter. Of primary concern to a company is how to achieve focus. To give this its due weight, the next chapter has been devoted to explaining the steps involved in detail. It gives examples of different applications to help illustrate how the outcomes reflect the realities of different plants. Meanwhile, the sections that follow continue to examine the principles on which focus is based.

Plant-within-a-Plant Configuration

As stressed throughout, one important trade-off, implicit if not explicit, in focused manufacturing is that of plant size versus the economies of organizational scale. Although the ideal would be plants individually focused to the needs of markets and arranged on the basis of the alternatives given in Table 7–1, this is often not practical on two counts. First, many companies own existing sites, with sizable investments in the bricks and mortar, utilities, plant, offices, and other facilities. Second, as businesses change, there is a real danger that the manufacturing complexity associated with lack of focus could gradually permeate some of the plants. Where rearrangement is constrained by the size of initial plants, their geographical location and the distribution difficulties involved, process and infrastructure support considerations, and the like, the flexibility of overall size (i.e., the larger the factory, the greater the permutations available) can often be to a company's advantage. However, although this second aspect may not be a major issue for many companies, the first is.

The way to provide focus in these situations (as implied in the earlier example of the supplier to the vehicles markets) is to adopt a plant-within-a-plant (PWP) configuration. This involves physically dividing sites (even to the point of using partitions, different entrances, and other facilities), thus providing a ''separate'' plant within which manufacturing is focused to the needs of different parts of its total business. This reduces units to a more manageable task, attracting the advantages of both focus and smaller size.

Although the trade-off for these distinct and often critical gains is the apparent loss of economies of organization size, PWP provides the opportunity to review overheads in line with each focused manufacturing plant. These judgments are much easier to make, owing to the improved clarity between business needs, direction, and overhead requirements. The amorphous mass takes on shape, which in turn allows each

part of the business to reflect its needs in terms of overhead provision. The total b̲ ̲ ̲ ̲-
ness can then assess the relative contribution of each part to its overall success.

Focused manufacturing creates a structure in which each plant or PWP has its own
facilities where it can concentrate on every element of the manufacturing task. Each
part of the facility comprises its own processes and infrastructure, which are developed in line with each task. This not only provides significant gains in sustaining,
qualifying, and meeting the order-winning criteria; it also decreases the likelihood of
the agreed focus being undermined, which is known as *focus regression.*

Focus and the Product Life Cycle

An earlier section examined the three principal approaches to focusing manufacturing,
summarized in Table 7–1. However, where possible companies should seek to focus
plants on the basis of providing manufacturing with a consistent task (i.e., supporting
similar order-winners). Splitting on the basis of products/markets or process typically
results in the creation of a smaller version of the larger whole. Since downsizing will
always result in the advantages of being smaller, the key is to gain, as much as possible, the many other advantages available, some of which were given in Table 7–1.

As mentioned earlier, separating plants on the basis of order-winners and qualifiers will often be paralleled by differences in volume levels. The link between volume
and order-winning criteria as presented in Table 5–1 was clearly established and explained. An illustration of this concerns the nature of the product life cycle and the
changes in volume and order-winning criteria that take place over time.

Over a number of years, a telecommunications switchgear company had moved
from Product A to Products B and C, with Product D to be introduced in the near
future. These changes reflected product technology developments that moved from
mechanical (Product A) to electromechanical to finally electronic (Product D).

All four products basically performed the same task for the customer—more sophisticated, but the same task. As is often the case, there was a considerable overlap
between the life of one product and that of another. As a result, there was a need to
manufacture more than one range at a time, plus spares for each range. The spares
service was part of the company's commitment to the past, as well as demonstrating
to its current customers that they would be provided for in the future. In order, therefore, to establish the whole of the manufacturing task, the company had to review the
whole of the corporate marketing requirements, as this would provide a true picture of
the issues involved. A review of these products appears in Table 7–2.

Product A, based on a mechanical technology, was no longer sold as part of a new
contract. Sales were restricted to spares or replacement equipment for existing instal-
lations. The processes required to make this product were specific to this range, as the
other three products were based on electronic product technology and required different processes. Products C and D reflected the rapid advance in microtechnology.

The company, while maintaining the process capability unique to meeting the
spare parts and replacement equipment sales of Product A, currently produced both

TABLE 7–2   Changes over Time in Production Volume and the Main Manufacturing Task for Current and Future Products

	Product			
Aspect	A	B	C	D
Production volumes				
Current	Low spares volumes	Large	Low	—
In two to three years	Low—little change	Decreasing	Increasing	Low
Manufacturing task based on agreed order-winners and qualifiers				
Current	Delivery speed	Cost reduction	Quality/delivery reliability	—
In two to three years	Delivery speed	Cost reduction	Cost reduction	Quality/delivery reliability

Products B and C on the same processes. With Product D already being earmarked as the next stage in the product development, the question facing manufacturing was, Which processes were appropriate to meet both the technical and market requirements of the three products based on similar technology? The decision concerned the principle of *process and product focus.*[*][8] This concept helps a company look at its present and future product decisions for manufacturing, by considering what type of focus would best suit the corporate market needs. Being *process focused*[†] means that the manufacturing facility is designed on a general purpose basis and is thus able to meet the needs of a relatively wide range of volumes. These requirements would typically include product development, low volumes, intermittent, uncertain demand patterns, and delivery speed. When a plant is *product focused,* it is designed to meet the needs of what is often (compared with a process-focused plant) a relatively narrow range of products, normally with high volumes and/or similar process requirements. Such a plant is, therefore, specialized in order to meet the low-cost requirements of what would typically be a price-sensitive market.

The manufacturing strategy adopted by this company for its electronic products had been based on the provision of a general purpose production process. It was man-

---

[*]These different types are broad descriptions of approaches to focus. Though they do not always provide an appropriate strategic fit between the market and manufacturing, they are sound, generalizable explanations. They provide a useful insight into the key differences that exist for many products throughout their life cycles.

[8]Product and process-focused plants are examined in R. H. Hayes and R. W. Schmenner, "How Should You Organize Manufacturing?" *Harvard Business Review,* January–February 1978, pp. 105–18; and R. J. Mayer and K. U. Agarwal, "Manufacturing Strategy: Key to Industrial Productivity," *Outlook,* Fall–Winter, 1980, pp. 16–21.

[†]The first edition of this book used the phases *product* and *process focus* in the opposite way to their use here. This earlier decision was made to be consistent with early writers in the field. However, finding that practitioners were confused by a use of terms that appeared to be the wrong way round, I have altered the terminology accordingly.

FIGURE 7–2

Orientation of a particular manufacturing facility

Process focus (general purpose facility)   Product focus (facilities dedicated to products)

ufacturing Products B and C and intended to manufacture Product D in this way. This decision had been taken to meet three main objectives:

1. To handle known product development with an existing facility and so avoid the need to plan for new facilities at each stage.
2. To minimize total product costs for all items, accepting that this may not be possible for individual products.
3. To be better able to handle volume fluctuations due to variable demand patterns from major customers.

However, by the very nature of general purpose processes, each product will be assumed to have similar order-winners and hence, a similar manufacturing task will be appropriate. In this situation, these processes would be suboptimal in meeting the cost-reduction requirements of Product B and later those of Product C.

A facility to provide the existing and future market requirements would need to encompass the characteristics of both a process- and product-focused plant as described earlier. To provide these in one process will always lead to compromise. However, where this trade-off is between the key order-winning criteria of different products, the company must make alternative provisions for focused manufacturing.

This distinction is shown in Figure 7–2 by a product focus/process focus continuum.[9] Establishing where a production facility stands on this spectrum and in which direction it is evolving will allow a firm to review where it is and where it should be in terms of manufacturing's support of its markets. In this way, it provides one of the essential inputs into the corporate strategy debate by highlighting the degree of match between the marketing and manufacturing strategies. It brings the company's attention to any current levels of difficulty and the possible ways to provide what is best for the business as a whole.

In developing its manufacturing strategy, the company in the example became aware of the type of focused manufacturing appropriate to its products as they went through their life cycles (illustrated in Figure 7–3).

In the early stages of growth, manufacturing will be faced with less predictable sales volumes, product and process modifications, customer orientation, and varying levels of delivery speed. The provision of these will usually best be met by the capability and flexibility characteristics inherent in process focus. In the period of maturity,

---

[9]The company example described in this section and Figure 7–1 was first detailed in T. J. Hill and R. M. G. Duke-Woolley, "Progression or Regression in Facilities Focus," *Strategic Management Journal* 4 no. 2 (1983), pp. 109–21.

FIGURE 7-3

A typical product life cycle and its relationship to focus

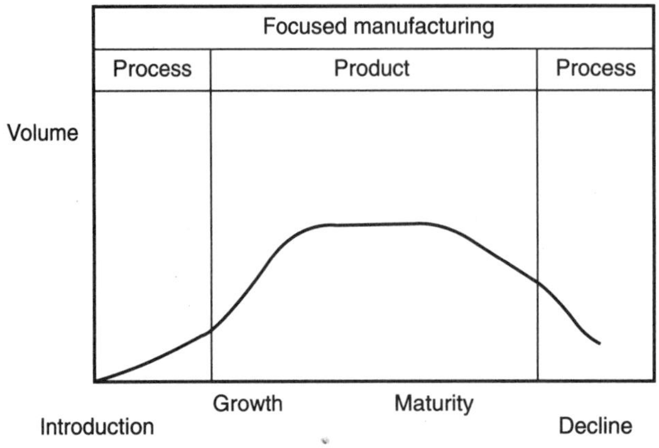

when the high-volume sales and the product technology have been fixed, attention is totally directed toward processes, with low-cost manufacturing becoming predominant (i.e., product focus). Finally, in the period of product decline, the manufacturing requirement will revert back to being a process-focused facility due to the change in volumes and order-winning criteria.

A look back at Table 5–1 and relevant discussion will not only further illustrate these differences but also help to underpin the underlying rationale for focus. Companies will continue to find themselves needing to support different markets, and their position will be one of continuous change. Manufacturing's effective support of these differences is a key factor in overall corporate success.

Progression or Regression in Focused Manufacturing[10]

By definition, a single manufacturing process cannot provide the aspects of process and product focus at the same time. The recognition of the critical trade-offs to support the corporate marketing requirements is an essential component of a sound manufacturing strategy. In practice, however, every facility faces some variety in the corporate marketing requirements for its products. A company must be aware of these fluctuations in variety and evaluate the consequences of these changes. The increase in product variety within the company described earlier and the associated differences required by these products over time led to an increased diffusion between products and processes. This, in turn, led to movement away from its preferred focus, known as *focus regression*. On the other hand, to become increasingly competitive a facility needs to take appropriate steps to achieve greater movement toward its preferred focus, known as *focus progression*. This would require the company described earlier to align Products B and C and later Product D to their appropriate focus. For,

---

[10]This concept was first introduced in Hill and Duke-Woolley, "Progression or Regression, p. 118.

only in this way could the key task be addressed by manufacturing for the different products at the respective stages in their life cycles.

Conclusion

Achieving and maintaining focused manufacturing needs to be an overt corporate activity. Focus does not occur naturally—in fact, there are normally forces at work that militate against it. These forces, as detailed below, need to be recognized so action may be consciously taken to ensure that improved focus is not inhibited through corporate neglect or traditional views of what is best for the business.

• *Marketing* often stimulates the desire to create and maintain a broad product line. This is, and has been for some time, an integral part of marketing's strategy. Thus it has become a felt need, with overtones of image, and frequently constitutes an important measure of the function's own performance.

• *Sales* holds the understandable view that it is easier to sell a broader line. This is reinforced by commission schemes for salespeople, normally based on total sales value ($s). It implies that sales of all products are of equal value to the business and fails to recognize the need to differentiate one product sale from the next. This function will also argue that a review of total competition reveals a wide variety of features on offer, affording wider selection for the customer. It follows that as customers' preferences vary, a wide range better meets the total diverse needs. This may well be true some of the time, but it does not usually hold true all the time. Often customers' preferences are based on unsubstantiated or nontechnical rationales. In these circumstances, it is much harder to sell a product that meets customers' actual as opposed to perceived needs. Finally, in businesses experiencing seasonal or cyclical demand, there is often a strong argument to increase variety to help smooth out such patterns.

• *Manufacturing* also inhibits focus for reasons such as being bound by past union agreements on work practices, high investment costs associated with the purchase/ movement of processes, and the risk of uncertain benefits.

• *Accounting and finance* similarly stimulate forces that work against focus. These include capital restrictions and rationing, the overriding emphasis on short-term earnings, and the prevalence of cost information, which distorts reality by failing to provide data that allow sensitive insights to be gained.

• *Corporate* forces also limit the steps taken, because of a general resistance to including the manufacturing perspective in the corporate strategy development and a reluctance to increase the interaction between marketing and manufacturing. The trend stems largely from divisions between specialists and executives within management and the predominance, at different times, of a single function in formulating strategy. The background and perspectives brought to strategy discussions by key managers, therefore, have been too narrowly based. This leads to corporate imbalance, in the first instance, and insufficient breadth in the second, on which to base appropriate revisions. The changed economic circumstances from the late 1970s through the 1980s has forced companies to arrive at strategy decisions based on what is best for the business as a whole. This change has been brought about by the increased level of corporate consciousness within the business. Strategies developed out of a single functional perspective, which were then superficially overlaid by particular perspectives as and when they arose, are rapidly being replaced by genuine corporate debate. However, until that happens, corporate forces will drive out focus and other manufacturing strategy arguments, placing these functional perspectives in their customary reactive position.

Supporting Markets Characterized by Difference

Failure to challenge how well existing concepts apply to the current and future needs of a business is at the root of today's problems for many companies. By continuing to use concepts and approaches developed for markets, the characteristics of which are very different from the needs of today and tomorrow, companies are finding increasing difficulty in competing effectively. With manufacturing measured on every yardstick and corporations failing to address the size and relevance of its enormous overhead expense, the process of determining appropriate strategic direction (and its effective pursuit) is inadequately managed.

However, substituting one approach for another is not the answer. Making better use of large key resources is the aim. With markets characterized by difference rather than similarity, it is essential that firms learn to effectively compete in market segments that are different to one another.[11] Markets based on different order-winners will present conflicting requirements for manufacturing to support only if facilities (processes and infrastructure) are not organized to meet these differences. Focus is an appropriate response to the increasing levels of difference that characterize today's markets. Thus, focused approaches make more sense and lead to substantial improvements on every significant corporate dimension. Being able to fashion manufacturing facilities and supporting activities to the particular needs of various markets enables companies to compete effectively. Approaches based on reducing or eliminating diversity within corporate portfolios as a strategy in itself are unsound. Advocates of these policies are not only turning their backs on today's reality but also on opportunities. Competing in diverse markets is not in itself strategically unsound. What makes such a business mix unsound is the failure to recognize and reflect the very differences that exist. Being competitive and successful in different types of markets is a prerequisite for a company today, and the concept of focus offers principles by which to achieve this.

Ways Forward—Halting the Drift into Unfocused Manufacturing

The development of a manufacturing strategy, as outlined in Chapter 2, provides one overriding advantage: It offers a meaningful and realistic way for manufacturing to

---

[11]See Schroeder et al. (1988), Roth (1987), and D. A. Garvin, "Quality on the Line," *Harvard Business Review* 1 (1983), pp. 65–75.

communicate with the rest of the business. By doing this, it provides the base on which to build, creating a positive move to halt the drift into unfocused manufacturing.

The first step is to concentrate management attention and effort onto the core business areas. As a company adjusts to marketplace changes, then product lines, customer characteristics, customer preferences, and order-winning criteria all change. There must be a reference point from which, or around which, to build the corporate strategy. This reference is the existing core of the business, in which a company has a clear competitive advantage. Concentration by production and marketing on the core business is essential. However, there are several aspects, general and specific, that need to be addressed.

Overall, it is important to use the opportunity created by the strategic development procedure to redress some of the general inhibitors detailed earlier. The development of an appropriate manufacturing strategy will, in itself, induce a corporate strategy, which embodies the marketing and manufacturing perspective. In so doing, it will get both these functions to pull in the same corporate direction, by matching production and marketing with the corporate need and measuring the achievement of both against the same corporate yardsticks. Similarly, capital budgeting needs to be couched within the long-term corporate plan and each expenditure measured in terms of the agreed focus. Revisions need also to be made in the accounting system, in order to provide data more relevant to these decisions and the necessary information on which to base them and monitor future performance.

Now it is time to consider the tasks essential to achieving focused manufacturing. The fundamental purpose behind focus is to establish a plant mission, based on the development of an appropriate manufacturing strategy. In many instances, it will result in a split of processes and infrastructure of existing facilities and the establishment of plant-within-a-plant configurations. When these steps are taken principally to refocus existing plants, manufacturing must establish and agree on an optimum plant size. This will restrict the task to what is meaningful and manageable and limit the future potential for focus regression. But this is not enough. Manufacturing's task is to ensure that focus progression becomes an integral part of their strategic task. This is facilitated in two ways: The managerial consciousness of the importance and strategic strength derived through focus, and an annual program to give direction to ensure its achievement.

CHAPTER 8

Focus—Methodology

The principles and concepts underpinning focus were outlined in the last chapter. We now turn our attention to the steps to take when developing focused plants.

As stressed throughout, today's markets are characterized by difference not similarity. The task facing manufacturing, therefore, is how to cope with the marked levels of difference that typically exist in a firm's markets. Increasingly, manufacturing is turning toward the design and development of focused plants or plant-within-a-plant configurations. However, before discussing the steps to achieve focus, we should consider the origins of existing plant structures, how they are currently arranged, and the reasons for these decisions.

Origins of Existing Plants

Driven by the concepts of economies of scale and control through specialists, resulting manufacturing plants are typically large, with process layouts based on functional similarity and centralized infrastructures. The outcomes are similar to that in Figure 8–1. Processes are often shared to facilitate higher levels of equipment utilization, and the firm's organization combines line/executive functions with appropriate specialists undertaking advisory and support roles. The rationale supporting economies of scale arguments has been discussed earlier. The concept of focus challenges the relevance of the manufacturing application of these principles in support of today's markets.

Moving to Focused Plants

The last chapter explained the concept of focus and the alternative approaches to achieve it. The idea is to arrange manufacturing in such a way as to create a consistent task within each focused unit. The steps to take in focusing existing

FIGURE 8-1

Typical layout of existing plants based on economies of scale principles (not to scale)

Support functions

Goods receiving

Manufacturing facilities typically
laid out by process similarity

Shipping

Support functions

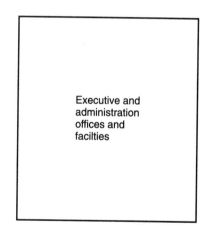

Executive and
administration
offices and
facilties

manufacturing facilities are detailed below. However, before discussing the methodology, it is important to bear in mind the following:

1. Focus should not be seen as the preferred dogma on which to base
   manufacturing arrangements. Replacing one dogma with another will lead to
   inappropriate investments or future situations of misalignment through
   neglect or lack of knowing what to do and how to do it.

2. In reality, companies will typically use two or more approaches when
   focusing plants. Some developments will combine economies of scale
   principles with those of focus. Others will use a combination of the
   approaches to focus explained in the last chapter, namely products/markets,

processes, and order-winners/volumes. Since combinations often yield the best overall results, companies must be pragmatic rather than dogmatic.

3. Very often, companies will not be able to arrive at appropriate focused approaches for all parts of a business. When applying chosen approaches, companies may find that they are left with parts of the whole with which they can do little. Though requiring improvement, it can be difficult if not impossible to develop these remnants within the concept of focus, because of insufficient similarity within the markets and the manufacturing task.

4. The principle of applying focus is to improve on what currently exists. Focusing parts of a business not only leads to gains within these parts but also simplifies that which remains unchanged, thus facilitating developments throughout.

5. The final point is one of approach. It is often best to rearrange a business parts at a time, enlarging the scope of change one phase at a time. Choosing areas where the rationale is clearest helps to reduce the size of the task, maintain acceptable time scales, improve the rate of success, and allow everyone to learn.

The underlying theme when focusing a business must be pragmatism. Thus, if one approach to focus does not bring improvement in a particular situation, that facet should not be applied. In most businesses, combinations of approaches will secure the best level of overall improvement. However, a company needs to determine the desired extent of change to achieve what is best overall and be wary of the inertia and resistance to change that exist in most organizations. Furthermore, the process of change needs to be ongoing. As markets will continually change, manufacturing's response will need to reflect these fresh demands. In the past, many companies have failed to question existing approaches in part because of the fundamental logic of the current approach but also because there has not been a viable, well-argued, and well-articulated alternative. Focus provides one such challenge.

Steps toward Focused Plants

This section outlines the steps to be followed when applying the concept of focus. As with most responses, it is iterative in nature and needs adequate time to work through the issues involved and the alternative outcomes under review.

Process Review

The first task is to review the existing manufacturing processes to identify any that are too expensive to duplicate.* Examples of these will differ from one business or

---

*In some instances, there may be other factors, for example, space constraints. But often these also constitute cost-related reasons for not duplicating existing capabilities.

industry to the next. It may be a particular process such as heat treatment or cleaning/coating/finishing facilities; or it could be the whole of a process requirement to make particular products. This technical sweep, therefore, identifies the realistic constraints in moving from economies of scale to focus as a basis for plant configurations. Those processes that should not be duplicated will retain their batch-process, economies-of-scale features.

In some companies, products may well be tied to given processes. Any rearrangement, therefore, of the different manufacturing tasks involved would lead directly to process duplication, with potentially high additional investment. Upstream processes will often fall in this category. Downstream processes (e.g., packing) are normally less likely to be affected by this constraint because of the lower levels of investment typically involved.

Identifying Manufacturing Order-Winners and Qualifiers

The next step is to identify the manufacturing-related order-winners and qualifiers. These will form the basis for determining any rearrangement of manufacturing, given the constraints identified in the process review.

These criteria need to be carefully evaluated, then matched to the relevant plant focus. Failure to do this will often lead to an inappropriate choice and to a lack of understanding of the rationale on which to base future decisions in line with ever-changing market needs. Throughout, the principle is to create (within the constraints of reality and what is best for the business) a coherent set of tasks for manufacturing within each plant configuration. The manufacturing task needs to be based on a set of similar order-winners and qualifiers wherever possible. Once the focus split is agreed, considerations of hardware (processes) and software (infrastructure) can proceed again.

Process Rearrangement

Process rearrangement is then completed. Processes are allocated and physically moved to the agreed units in line with product requirements regarding capability and capacity. Those not to be duplicated will, as explained earlier, retain their batch-process features, still based on economies of scale. In this way, companies need to arrive at pragmatic decisions that best suit the business overall. Some processes are too expensive to duplicate, given the level of utilization that would result. These would need to still be managed, organized, and controlled on a batch-process basis to serve the varying needs of the business.

Infrastructure Rearrangement

The final stage concerns reviewing the infrastructure requirements of the different manufacturing units. The selection, while reflecting the market needs of each manufacturing unit, must be tempered by sensible constraints and principles. These are addressed in Chapter 10, which concerns the development of manufacturing infrastructure.

In this stage, companies reshape existing overheads by allocating relevant support/specialist functions (in terms of both capability and capacity) to each focused unit. This enables support to orient its activities to the particular needs of each different part of the business. To this end, the overhead resources must actually be physically allocated (i.e., relevant staff must be located at the site) not merely nominally designated.

At the same time as reshaping existing overheads, companies also need to work up from the bottom of the organization. This means determining what elements of work would best constitute the shopfloor task. By working from both ends, companies can challenge existing paradigms and approaches, which will result in fresh insights into how best to reshape the "soft side" of manufacturing's response.

The issues of infrastructure and the job of work are dealt with in more detail in Chapter 10. Suffice it to say that the first step in this stage is to identify those aspects of a support function's tasks that are truly specialist in nature and those that are candidates for being completed elsewhere. This then enables a company to consider who would best complete the latter, what would be their appropriate reporting structures, and where they should be geographically situated.

The importance of this part of an organization's review is twofold.

- Overheads are typically a very large part of an organization's total resource provision. Thus, orienting this to support the needs of its various markets will be a significant factor in the level of corporate success.
- Whereas process reallocations are constrained by issues such as investment, the opportunity to reshape and reposition overheads is not as restricted by such factors. Therefore, this aspect of strategic review will often provide more opportunities to make the sizable gains brought about through focus.

In reality, companies often decide that a combination of these approaches best suits their needs because the duplication of investments alters the trade-offs under review. Thus, certain advantages need to be foregone for the sake of the business overall. Similarly, companies ideally could argue for green-field provision as the ideal response to the market differences at the root of these proposals. However, companies' existing sites are usually an overpowering factor in the eventual decision. Approaches to meet these different realities include plant-within-plant configurations, a concept dealt with in the last chapter.

The following examples will illustrate some of the issues raised so far:

> A major supplier of components and products to the private, commercial, and off-highway home and export vehicle markets was reviewing one of its principal manufacturing facilities. The company's attempts to cope with product range increases, volume changes, and the growing original equipment (OE)/spares mix resulted in accumulated complexity. Its
>
> *continued*

factory was difficult to manage, had high work-in-process investment, and was increasingly unable to meet customers' delivery needs or earn a satisfactory level of return on its investment.

To reduce the manufacturing task to a manageable size, it decided to create several units based on a product/market split. These units, the company argued, would best reflect customers' needs while reducing work-in-process investment requirements. To test the validity of the approach, the company initially took the smallest manufacturing unit within the product/market split and, as convenient, relocated its processes and infrastructure within an unused part of the existing site. The first review highlighted a series of gains, which, as analysis showed, resulted from the manageability of the small size. A more testing analysis, however, showed that the order-winning criteria for different parts of this and the other product/market units were not being addressed any more specifically than before the reorganization. The company had merely created smaller versions of the larger whole, which, in fact, mirrored the problems of the bigger manufacturing units, except those associated with plant size. The high and low volumes linked to OE and spares demand, respectively, called for different order-winning criteria. The appropriate split here would have been to separate units by volume, which would have created the necessary link between the manufacturing task and the market. The gains owing to small size would automatically follow.

A large European electronics manufacturer was facing the decision on where to site its thick-film facility. It had two manufacturing units in geographically separate sites, but it needed to double its overall capacity in the near future to meet the anticipated growth in thick-film application. The alternatives were either to spread the increase over both sites or to reexamine its process needs and reflect these in the plant selection. On reviewing this problem, the company recognized two issues as fundamental to the choice. The first concerned the widening quality demands of products; the second, the extent to which each location could attract an adequate level of engineering and development infrastructure support. Through discussions of the effects of these implications, the company saw that in this instance the exacting product specifications, low volumes, development activities, and necessary high caliber of engineering and specialist support came together to form a coherent set of process and infrastructure requirements. The demands on the process and support staff for the low product specification and high volumes required a different set of processes and infrastructure. With this now clearly established and the availability and likelihood of attracting sufficient engineering and specialist staff at each location identified, the choices fell into place. In addition,

continued

by keeping the process capabilities separate for the two groups of products the problems of establishing, identifying, and maintaining the quality requirements for items with very different levels of product specification were considerably reduced. Therefore, choosing the plant focus on the basis of process split enabled the company to recognize, appreciate, and take account of the key practical constraints involved. These were reflected in the focused manufacturing decision, thus aligning the plant to the different market segments.

A large food company had grown from its beginnings at the same manufacturing site. Over the years, it had developed an organizational structure designed to realize the benefits of having selected a site that was sufficiently large to contain expansion and well-placed to access the local labor pool and relevant distribution channels.

Like many companies, although enjoying good profits and steady growth in real sales, it continually questioned its cost base and the appropriateness of its organizational setup. Therefore, it decided to move away from its traditional and well-established style of centralized support functions and apply the concept of focus. In process terms, it found that the technical requirements of groups of products meant that these could only be made on certain processes. Therefore, this prevented any opportunity to cross-link different products by markets or order-winners. Furthermore, it could not justify duplicating plant because of the equipment, buildings, and space costs involved. However, the company reviewed its products' order-winners and adjusted current arrangements to create a consistent manufacturing task within its market segments. In this way, therefore, the marketing/manufacturing interface (see Table 2–1) led to improved business fit primarily through realigning markets rather than changes in manufacturing.

However, the real gains came when the company reviewed its infrastructure. It recognized that the centralized specialist and other overhead functions were not aware of the distinct differences within its markets nor, consequently, of the different manufacturing tasks required. A review of information provision and supporting activities and priorities revealed a marked inconsistency between what was needed and what was provided. By reallocating specialist and other staff, where appropriate, to the separate manufacturing units, the company tailored support to the particular needs of each part of the business. This led to significant reductions in overheads caused by unnecessary duplication of procedures and systems and unwanted provision of support staff. Such gains could not have been achieved with the inadequate direction provided by the company's traditional centralized approach.

Conclusion

Focused plants, whether individual units or plant-within-a-plant configurations, offer to many companies real improvements sufficient to justify the investments involved. The increasing levels of difference within today's markets are exposing the inappropriateness of yesterday's approaches in the form of reduced competitiveness and loss of market share. Firms are increasingly questioning the approaches taken in the past while searching for sensible developments that will bring more appropriate manufacturing responses and improved support for the differing sets of market needs.

Introducing focus is one alternative, with the best outcomes often resulting from a mixed approach based on fit and realism. But companies must understand the relevance of focus as a way forward before introducing it. Moreover, the rate of its introduction needs to be tempered by what can be achieved and the challenges these ideas bring.

Many companies need to review their manufacturing provision with some urgency. Splitting out those parts of a business which more readily lend themselves to focus is the place to start. However, avoiding the dogmatic use of these approaches is essential in order to gain the substantial and lasting benefits which can accrue. But, the dynamics of markets will necessitate continuous review and revision in order to avoid the drift into focus regression inherent in organizations.

CHAPTER 9
Make or Buy?

An important facet of a company's manufacturing strategy concerns the question of whether to make or buy—the issue of process positioning. This consists of the width of a firm's internal span of process, the degree and direction of vertical integration alternatives, and its links and relationships at either end of the process spectrum with suppliers, distributors, and customers. The make-or-buy decision, therefore, has major ramifications within the business itself. As an integral part of corporate strategy, it can be crucial to survival. However, the investment involved in earlier integration moves or decisions to buy rather than make parts of products, often justified on the short-term rationale of profit return,[1] can restrict a company's ability to change direction in the future.

Reasons for Choosing Alternative Strategic Positions

Although in theory every item can be made or bought, in reality the choice is far more restricted. Few businesses, however, when taking stock, find that their current position has been arrived at as part of some strategically based set of arguments over time. There are a number of reasons behind companies' decisions on process position, some of which are now outlined. They have been chosen to reflect important factors and to illustrate the different levels of corporate awareness involved.

Core Elements of the Business

Most companies choose to keep in-house those processes that represent the core elements of their business. For instance, a company that manufactures its own finished

---

[1]R. H. Hayes and J. Abernathy, "Managing Our Way to Economic Decline," *Harvard Business Review,* July–August 1980, pp. 67–77.

items will invariably retain the assembly-onward end of the production process. The reasons include the wish to retain immediate control of product identity, design security, final product quality, and the ultimate link with its customers.

Strategic Considerations

Ideally, make or buy decisions are chosen in response to the strategic requirements of the business. This decision will include a manufacturing strategy input concerning aspects such as lower cost and improved control. It will also take into account nonmanufacturing arguments concerning the marketplace and the competitive conditions in which a business operates.

Span of Process and Product Technology

Often, a significant increase in product technology can lead to a corresponding decrease in the internal span of process. This arises where a company applies technology changes to its existing products, or on the introduction of new or similar products within its range. Without the in-house process capability to meet all of the new and more complex product technology requirements, a company must buy the technology in the form of components. Normally, this narrowing takes place in the earlier stages of the process where the new technology developments are the most radical; the later processes are kept in-house because the technology associated with them is more in line with existing manufacturing expertise and closer to the final product itself. Figure 9–1 provides an example of this in the strategy adopted by the telecommunications company referred to in Chapter 7 (Table 7–2). When the company only produced Product A, it had developed the in-house processes necessary to complete most of the manufacturing involved. However, the advent of Product B, and later Product C, heralded a distinct technology change from mechanical (Product A) to electromechanical (Product B) and electronic (Product C). Not having the manufacturing process capability to provide these new requirements, the company brought them in from outside in the form of components. The narrowing of the internal span of processes that resulted is shown in Figure 9–1.

In these situations, the decision on when and by how much to widen the span of process, after the initial narrowing, is a significant strategic issue; in practice, it is often treated as an operational decision. As another example, consider the case of hand-held calculator manufacturers. Bowmar, one-time market leader, failed to successfully integrate backward into integrated circuit production and eventually withdrew from the business, while Texas Instruments (TI) successfully integrated forward into calculators and took over market leadership. One major reason for TI eventually displacing Bowmar was that its comparative process position gave it more opportunity to reduce costs and exploit the potential experience curve gains. And that is what it did. Bowmar, restricted to assembly cost gains, was limited by its suppliers' price reductions for a large part of its costs. TI, on the other hand, had no such limitations. In a related example, *Business Week* provided a survey within the calculator market.[2]

---

[2]"Why They're Integrating into Integrated Circuits," *Business Week,* September 28, 1974, p. 55.

FIGURE 9-1

The reduction in span of process with increases in the technology of the product (not to scale)

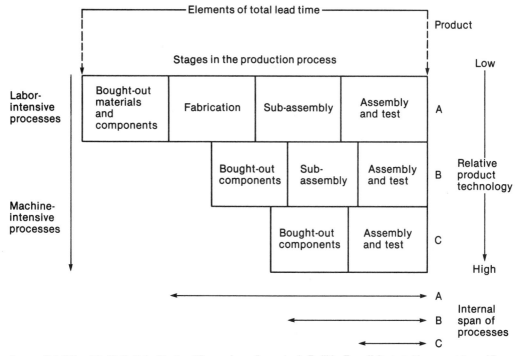

SOURCE: T. J. Hill and R. M. G. Duke-Woolley, "Progression or Regression in Facilities Focus," *Strategic Management Journal* 7 (1983), pp. 109–21 (with permission).

Part of this concerned the stated strategy of Commodore at that time; one that was to change within a couple of years. It quotes Commodore's president arguing that backward integration was neither necessary nor desirable. To retain the ability to get into and out of a technology, and as when necessary, was considered by Commodore to be well worth the higher component costs associated with this strategy. However, in 1976, Commodore's purchase of MOS Technology, an ailing manufacturer of calculator chips, "is sometimes credited with Commodore's later success in small computers."[3]

Product Volumes

Companies faced with the different tasks involved with manufacturing high and low volumes can adopt a plant-within-a-plant alternative, as reviewed in Chapter 7. A company may also consider buying out those products with a low-volume demand, for instance, which would, in turn, normally lead to a narrowing of the internal span of process. An example of this decision involved a manufacturer of engine parts for

[3]R. H. Hayes and S. C. Wheelwright, *Restoring Our Competitive Edge: Competing through Manufacturing* (New York: John Wiley & Sons, 1984), p. 219.

agricultural and diesel trucks. When the low-volume spares demand was reached in a product's life cycle, the company increasingly subcontracted component manufacturing where the machining processes involved were only used on operations for components for that product or products with similar low volumes. In that way, it reduced its span of processes and kept the manufacturing task within agreed bounds.

Yesterday's Strategies

It is not unusual for companies' process positions to result directly, at least in part, from yesterday's strategic decisions. Reduction in product life cycles, changes in product and process technology development, and an acceleration in worldwide competition over the past 20 years have all contributed to companies taking their eye off the ball. Unless periodic revision is made of this important strategic area, the impact on costs and manufacturing complexity will go unnoticed until a radical overhaul is necessitated. The damage meanwhile, especially in times of accelerating change, can be irreparable.

Shedding Difficult Manufacturing Tasks

Over recent years in the United States and Canada, companies have tended to shed difficult manufacturing tasks by subcontracting or divestment. Many companies approach this decision with an eye more on the difficulties embodied in the task rather than on the strategic consequences of the make-or-buy decision they are about to take. Short-term gains, taken on their own, look most attractive. However, the accompanying loss of skill, essential manufacturing know-how, and infrastructure may limit a company's ability to respond in the future. A maxim to bear in mind is, "if the manufacturing task is easy, then any company can do it." The key to manufacturing success is to resolve the difficult manufacturing issues, for this is where high profits are to be made.

Some companies have, in the ongoing evaluation of these decisions, omitted related costs and investments, thus distorting the picture. One large company established an off-shore manufacturing capability to avail itself of the low costs inherent in that decision. In its subsequent assessment of that investment, however, the company failed to recognize that the established costing and financial procedures did not allocate appropriate costs and inventory holdings to the off-shore site. Consequently, all rework costs and in-transit inventory were charged against the home-based plant. The distorted figures reinforced this, leading to similar decisions in the future. However, when the accounting rules were changed, future options became less attractive.

Thus, this type of decision often gives inadequate weight to important strategic issues. Issues concerning surrendering the ownership of costs and quality and the need for an appropriate infrastructure base from which to launch changes in direction are ignored and thus lost as future options. Proponents of such strategies typically have the superficial understanding of business development associated with the analysis of figures, rather than a grasp of reality.

Issues Involved in Changing Make-or-Buy Decisions

While in the past, changes in make-or-buy decisions have principally been associated with the widening of a company's initial span of process, more recently many businesses have considered reducing process spans. Faced with a decline in demand and the associated reduction in capacity requirements, companies have, possibly for the first time in their recent histories, been confronted with the necessity to decrease parts of their span of processes, and often on many major business fronts.

When repositioning whether for growth or contraction, a business must fully assess the issues involved. In particular, a business must determine whether or not the real costs and investments in process and infrastructure are achievable. Additional sizable investments are often incurred after the event, which, although not included in the original decision, form an integral part of securing the benefits of the original undertaking. In the same way, cost and investment reductions assumed to accrue from divestment may not be achieved when anticipated, and sometimes not at all. An illustration that typifies this concerns the support functions within a firm's overhead structure. Often, the extent of overhead support necessary to effectively sustain the new process investment and/or growth into new products in understated, while the anticipated reduction in overheads, associated with a narrowing of a firm's internal span of process, is generally overestimated.

It is also necessary to separate the issues involved in these decisions between those that essentially support strategy and those that do not. To ensure that span-of-process decisions are consistent with key corporate objectives (or if not, are recognized as not being consistent) is an important management task. Decisions can all too often be taken without this appropriate level of clarity. This differentiation of issues provides the opportunity to review these critical manufacturing decisions, in the light of relevant corporate strategy considerations, by allowing comparisons between options to be made on the basis of appropriate information. Separating the strategic arguments into their functional derivatives will add further clarity to the corporate understanding of the basis on which these important manufacturing decisions need to be addressed.

Particular issues will differ from one case to another, and the level of importance of issues will vary. Some of the more important advantages and disadvantages are listed here. How effectively a business is able to achieve the mix of benefits and risks involved, yet offset costs wherever possible, depends on a functionally capable and alert management team and the level of understanding and agreement they have reached on the strategic issues involved.

Costs and Investments

One of the fundamental sets of trade-offs involved in span-of-process decisions concerns costs and investments.[4] The level of investment will determine the width of process internal to the business and in so doing will have a direct bearing on the levels

---

[4]For example, refer to C. Batchelor's review of the gains secured through subcontracting and reported in his article "Lower Overheads and Increased Productivity," *Financial Times*, April 23, 1991, p. 14.

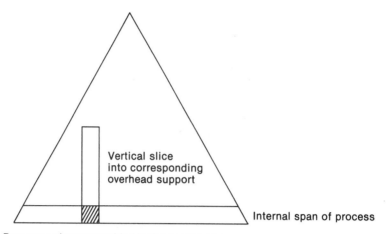

FIGURE 9–2

Corresponding overhead support to the process under review (which will form part of the corporate decision on process narrowing—known as vertical slicing)

of cost involved. The principal areas of cost associated with span-of-process decisions are:

- Transaction costs concerned with the buying, selling, and physical handling of materials throughout the relevant processes.
- The costs associated with improving the coordination between the supply, production, and distribution activities.
- The costs associated with combining similar overhead activities. Companies can do this when they widen their span of process. However, centralization of activities makes it difficult to achieve the apparent overhead gains when internal span of process is narrowed. In these situations, companies must assess whether or not the *vertical slicing* into those overheads attributable to a proposed reduction in span is in fact achievable (see Figure 9–2).
- The investment in hardware, controls, procedures, and other relevant infrastructure requirements. Although the tangible costs of plant and equipment are readily identified and agreed to in principle, the costs resulting from changes in the less tangible areas are not as apparent nor as easily quantified. In turn, decisions on them are subject to judgment and require close examination. Invariably, these areas of projected costs are cut on the assumption, or based on the argument, that the existing infrastructure can or will have to cope.

In situations of process widening, many companies neither clearly identify all the investment and associated requirements involved nor hold a shared view of the strategic relevance of the proposed span-of-process changes. Invariably in these circumstances, sufficient allowances will not have been provided, or the necessary allocations will be squeezed out of the proposals as a result of the apparent conscientiousness of those involved. The outcome will be an underestimation of the investment needs in the short-term, which will normally result in a number of further investments in the future. The final tally will sometimes be well in excess of that on which the initial strategic decision was based.

Two further important ramifications of widening the internal span of process concern a company's ability to adopt different options. First, the capital used up in these moves prevents its use elsewhere. Second, the implied commitment to a market and the product and process technologies and life cycles involved can be highly risky. The inherent inflexibility accumulated in these strategies may result in a sluggish response to change, high levels of unplanned capital expenditure, and often sizable write-offs.

Strategic Considerations

Although decisions on process repositioning usually embody their own set of specific strategic considerations, there are some important general considerations that help form the basis for strategic action.

- *High entry barriers.* In industries where a wide span of process brings with it a set of distinct advantages, increasing the internal span will raise the financial and managerial resources required to enter and compete effectively with existing businesses. Established companies may, therefore, raise the stakes, thus discouraging new entrants.
- *Supply assurance.* The supply of critical materials may well be of such importance to a company that this gain alone will be the basis for the investment involved. However, as with all forms of backward integration, the issue of whether or not a company aims to keep the supply capacity solely in balance with its internal needs raises its own set of advantages and disadvantages.
- *Secured outlets.* In the same way as supply can be assured by integrating backward, securing outlets can result from integrating forward. Additional advantages also accrue with this move from improved feedback that leads to the position of being more aware of demand changes and provides the opportunity to increase the accuracy of forecasts.

The Managerial Task

Changes in span of process will invariably lead to a change in the total management task within the business. These come under three broad headings:
- *The level of complexity.* One important consequence that invariably comes from a widening of process span is the increase in complexity and the hidden costs associated with these incremental uplifts. The associations of synergy are probably more apparent in the level of complexity than elsewhere. Here, one and one really are greater than two.
- *The question of balance.* When companies increase their span of process they face the questions of the trade-offs involved between whether or not to keep the supply or outlet in balance with the rest of the business. A large group of manufacturing companies, deciding on a policy of expansion, asked the individual companies involved to put forward proposals relevant to their own business. One such company, a cable

maker, proposed integrating backward into wire drawing. To limit the investment involved, it purchased a local site and installed capacity roughly in line with its own needs. With the high price of copper, neither part of the business wanted high material inventory. As a consequence, the production runs on which the drawn-wire cost structure had been based, and which sustained the investment rationale, could not be maintained. This was because of the program changes necessary to meet cable sales and the low-inventory planned for in the overall investment. Since one part of the business was not adequately decoupled from the next, even shorter runs and overtime working in the wire-drawing plant could not prevent cable delivery dates being missed. Eventually, the company had to reexamine issues of capacity balance and decoupling inventory levels.

• *The manufacturing task.* Span-of-process changes bring corresponding changes in the manufacturing management task. The cable-making/wire-drawing example had one further important rider. The management team assumed that their knowledge of cable making together with existing internal organizational and control systems would be sufficient to anticipate likely difficulties and to cope with any that were unforeseen in the processes involved in drawing wire. They underestimated the change in the manufacturing management task, which partly contributed to the wire-drawing unit's failure to break even in the first 20 months let alone meet the projected return on investment.

The traditional argument for ownership has been based, at least in part, on the economies of large scale. In the last two or three decades, this argument has been a major thrust within existing accounting perspectives. Based on inadequate analysis of what the new reality would bring, the economies-of-large-scale rationale has often been the principal distorting factor in these critical decisions. In many companies, the impact has been further disguised by the buildup of complexity associated with incremental process widening. In most situations, it is not the technology considerations but the control and other infrastructure features of the manufacturing task that are affected.

Levels of Vertical Integration

The previous sections introduced some of the important perspectives, issues, and context concerning make or buy decisions. The following sections address alternative strategies. This first section concerns dimensions of vertical integration, what is entailed and the benefits and disadvantages involved. The next main section flags up a growing problem for many industrialized nations: the hollowing of the manufacturing sector. The final section discusses a company's alternatives to widening the span of processes. These sections offer a mix of the advantages associated with the approaches discussed in the two previous sections.

Dimensions Involved

The principal dimensions of vertical integration are the breadth and level of activity and the form it takes. *Breadth* addresses decisions on which of the principal activities a firm decides to perform in-house. This involves functions such as design, manufacturing, and distribution. Closely linked to this is the decision on the amount, or *level*, of each activity to be undertaken in-house and how much will, therefore, be subcontracted. Finally, the *form* concerns the level and type of ownership, trading partnership arrangements, and other issues that are addressed in the following sections.

Benefits of Vertical Integration

All make-or-buy decisions bring a mix of internal and external benefits and costs. In particular, decisions on vertical integration offer a company a number of inherent competitive advantages that are linked to increased knowledge of markets and technology, improved control over its environment, and increased opportunity to support the characteristics of its markets. These include:

• *Improved market and technological intelligence.* This increases ability to forecast accurately trends concerning key aspects of a business from demand patterns to cost changes. Furthermore, it provides guarantees for supplies and markets, which in turn strengthens a firm against known and opportunistic competitors in given markets.

• *More readily available technological innovations and options.* This leads to greater coherence and transfer within the total organization; that is, the sharing of technology initiatives and opportunities by collaboration. In addition, it enables companies to transfer experience, thereby increasing the level of knowledge of events and so reducing some areas of uncertainty.

• *Increased control over relevant aspects of a firm's environment.* These opportunities can take the form of backward integration to reduce dependency of supplies and forward integration to help to gain market penetration or acceptance. Instances of the latter range from overcoming strong entry (even monopoly) barriers, to gaining acceptance of new products. With regard to the former, St. Gobain, a French glassmaker, purchased the U.K.-based glass processor and merchant, Solaglass, in 1990 as one way of entering the U.K. glass market, which at the time was dominated by Pilkington Glass. The advent of both aluminum and rayon provide examples of the way vertical integration facilitated the acceptance of the use of these new materials as substitutes in existing markets.

• *The provision of low-cost opportunities.* This is accomplished by generating internal demand and thereby contributing to the high-volume requirement for low-cost manufacturing. One example of this is the semiconductor market. Destined by the year 2000 to exceed $100 billion in sales, Japanese companies such as Fujitsu, Hitachi, Mitsubishi, NEC, and Toshiba have progressively outcompeted their U.S. rivals partly through the high level of integration that characterizes their businesses. Semiconductors were invented in the 1950s, and since then three decades of accelerating growth produced by 1990 a worldwide industry of $56 billion, more than double what it was in the mid-1980s. However, the highly integrated Japanese semiconductor manufacturers are able to make their products at increasingly lower costs than their competitors throughout the rest of the world. A substantial part of this is the result of the high-volume base created by internal, corporate demand. Japanese giant *zaibatsus* make semiconductors along with everything else from robots to cars and satellites. The result is that Japan currently has 50 percent of the world semiconductor market, with the United States at 37 percent and Western Europe at 11 percent.

• *The differentiation of products.* This can occur in all aspects of production from product customization to the availability and use of alternative new materials as a way of meeting a product's technical, cost, and other requirements.

Costs of Vertical Integration

The degree of success of vertical integration depends on how well it has been thought through and fits the needs of the enlarged business. In instances in which it has not been thought through, rationalization tends to replace strategic rationale. In addition, vertical integration is based on the assumption that the potential benefits are tangible and achievable rather than illusory. In some instances, companies may integrate because the opportunity to do so was available and timely. Those that fail to separate the action itself from the rationale underpinning that action may unknowingly incur significant disadvantages.

Level of Integration[5]

The final dimension concerns the level of integration a firm chooses to undertake. At the extreme, firms may decide on a *fully integrated strategy,* where all their requirements for a given material, product, or service are bought internally. In these instances, the supplying units are usually fully owned subsidiaries. This alternative works best where:

1. The level of price competition does not require companies to pursue the lowest cost alternatives to compete effectively in a market.
2. The advantages derived from accessibility to scarce resources outweigh other factors.
3. Capacity increases are not stepped in nature, which can create investment obstacles in terms of changing demand and associated volumes.

The more usual level of integration is referred to as a *taper-integrated strategy.*[6] With this, firms rely on outsiders to provide a portion of their requirements, which enables the integrated facilities to use capacity to the full by alternating the make-or-buy decision to advantage. However, such strategies, especially when exercised to the full, incur a number of disadvantages:

1. Alternating the make-or-buy decision to advantage militates against developing good customer/supplier relations. In the long run it may alienate suppliers, as such strategies often do not provide them with adequate lead times to enable resources to be switched, capacity to be reduced, or alternative sales to be secured.

---

[5]K. R. Harrigan, *Strategies for Vertical Integration* (Lexington, Mass.: Lexington Books, 1983) also addresses these issues.

[6]Harrigan, chap. 2, discusses these alternatives and offers frameworks to help in their selection.

TABLE 9-1 Trends in Component Sourcing for U.S. Manufacturers

| | Percent of U.S. Manufacturers | | | |
| | 1988 | | 2000 | |
Levels of Outsourcing	Actual	Cumulative	Estimated	Cumulative
Percent components outsourced				
81–100	8	8	9	9
61–80	8	16	14	23
41–60	14	30	20	43
21–40	23	53	25	68
1–20	36	89	25	93
None	11	100	7	100
Percent components made outside the United States				
81–100	1	1	4	4
61–80	2	3	5	9
41–60	7	10	15	24
21–40	14	24	25	49
1–20	42	66	34	83
None	34	100	17	100

SOURCE: Department of Trade and Industry Report, "Manufacturing into the Late 1900s" (PA Consulting Group, HMSO, 1989), p. 46.

2. By definition a taper-integrated strategy implies splitting volumes and reduces those conditions that maximize low-cost opportunities.

3. Alert suppliers may charge a price premium where volumes are low and subject to fluctuations.

The forms of integration discussed in this section entail at least some degree of internal provision. However, there are several alternatives to integrated strategies, as explained in a later section.

The Hollow Corporation

There is an increasing recognition of and growing concern about a phenomenon referred to as the *hollow corporation*.[7] Where companies have considered the question of how manufacturing should best be organized to meet the dynamics of their markets, many have shied away from addressing and incorporating the manufacturing dimension within the debate concerning the appropriate short- and long-term strategy for a business. The attraction of low-cost manufacturing opportunities in the Far East,

[7]See, for example, a special report entitled "The Hollow Corporation," *Business Week*, March 3, 1986, pp. 56–76.

Eastern Europe, and Mexico has lured many U.S. manufacturers to subcontract substantial parts of their existing processes without due regard for, adequate understanding of, and sufficient in-depth debate about the long-term implications of these critical and often irreversible decisions. Table 9–1 illustrates this continuing trend. The simplistic rationale of problem avoidance has such siren-like qualities as to make the decision difficult to argue against.

However, as mentioned in the previous section, the long-term consequences of these decisions to companies and to nations has neither been fully recognized nor adequately assessed. Such decisions bring the instant rewards of solution and profit. For many organizations, moving offshore becomes a last resort to offset sizable structural disadvantages. The alternative is to become competitive in the relevant dimensions such as design, price, quality, and delivery performance. But usually the impact of this short-term thinking has not been fully assessed. To the nation as a whole there is increasing dependency on imports, compounded by a loss of technological know-how and ownership, which will invariably lead to being driven out of business altogether.

Companies pursuing this rationale rarely do so as a way of buying time to enable them to regroup strategically. For most it is a comprehensive solution in its own right, with an apparent disregard for the long-term implications and inherent constraints imposed on future strategic options.

Furthermore, the ripple effect means that for every $1 of imports there is a further substantial loss to a nation's economy as a whole.[8] In addition, as time goes on these offshore plants will draw the service jobs that surround manufacturing. And at a company level, the effects are similar. Once skills have been transferred out, that know-how will eventually be lost within that company.

---

[8]The ripple effect concerns the real cost of imports to an economy. For each $1 billion of foreign-made consumables it was estimated that the total cost to the U.S. economy was $1.43 billion on top of $1 billion imports themselves, as reported in the following table.

Area of Cost of the Economy	*$ Millions*
Imported automobiles	1,000
Other vehicles engaged in hauling raw materials and finished products	200
Steel and fabricated metal parts	184
Machine tools	98
Rubber and plastics	67
Nonferrous metals	46
Chemicals	40
Other manufacturing	343
Wholesale and retail margins, transportation, warehousing, and utilities	348
Mining	47
Finances and insurance	39
Plant construction	16
Total	$2,428

SOURCE: Data Resources Inc., *Business Week*, March 1988, p. 61.

At the extreme, the postindustrial company could be vertically disaggregated, relying on other companies for manufacturing and many essential business functions.[9] They become industrial, corporate shells. And, there are strong forces pushing companies this way. In the short-term, these decisions offer fixed asset freedom and dynamic networking, both arguably suited to meeting the characteristics of today's markets. Such arrangements allow companies to respond quickly to exploit new markets and new technologies. The organizations become more agile, flexible, and responsive. Typically, firms need less capital, carry lower overhead costs, and can better tap into outside technology. In essence, they are more entrepreneurial.

The outcome of this is that manufacturing companies of a new kind are evolving—those that do little manufacturing. They import components and assemble them or import the products themselves and sell them. The result is a hollowing of once-powerful manufacturing companies. Following a strategy of this kind, companies become trapped in a position where their ability to compete is increasingly undermined by their own and their competitors' actions. Unchecked, this will invariably lead to the abandonment of their status as strong industrial companies and the retardation of their capacity for innovation and productivity improvement. The erosion of a nation's wealth-creating activity is the aggregate effect of these policies, which in the end, reduces the standard of living enjoyed by its people.

However, the full impact of the disaggregation philosophy on the welfare of corporations and nations is only now being realized. Many firms are finding themselves hamstrung. They are increasingly exposed to competition from suppliers yet have less security of supply and control of production; they lose design and manufacturing expertise, which forms the essential springboard from which to launch their strategic response. Furthermore, once taking this strategic option, it is difficult to alter course. Strategic options become increasingly restricted and future positions reinforce original rationale, subsequent logic, and chosen outcomes. To rebuild alternatives has infrastructure and time dimensions that are unappreciated and consequently unaddressed.

Alternatives to Widening Internal Span of Process

The discussion so far has implied that the choices companies must make also involve an ownership or nonownership option. Either a company invests in the process through ownership or it buys out its requirements from suppliers. Many companies perceive that in certain situations they have only two viable options, or Hobson's choice.[10] To them being reliant on suppliers is not a feasible alternative.

However, where greater control is necessary, companies should seriously consider alternatives to widening the internal span of process. In assessing whether or not the decision should be by investment, companies must separate strategic from tactical

---

[9]*Business Week*, March 1986, pp. 63–66 introduces the notion of postindustrial corporations that could subcontract everything from manufacturing to invoicing customers.

[10]Thomas Hobson, a Cambridge carrier, had a policy of letting out his horses in rotation, without allowing his customers to choose among them. Hence, they had to take or leave the one on offer.

issues and trace the strategic arguments to their functional source. Only in this way will a business be able to clearly establish whether or not a decision has to be through investment ownership.

The alternatives are based on an appropriately high degree of liaison between those involved. Some involve legal agreements or arrangements of some kind. Others attempt to exploit opportunities with links that are beneficial to all concerned.

Joint Ventures

Companies often have to exploit opportunities, particularly in areas such as applied technology and research. Where companies have similar needs and both can benefit from joining together, a joint venture is a sensible alternative.

Joint ventures are separate entities sponsored by two or more actively involved firms. Because joint ventures draw on the strengths of their owners, they have the potential to tap the synergy inherent in such a relationship and the improved competitive abilities that should accrue. Since the late 1970s, joint ventures have increased substantially. In 1983 alone, the number of cooperative strategies announced in industries such as communications systems and services exceeded the sum of all previous U.S. ventures in those sectors.[11]

This trend has continued, and domestic joint ventures have become an important way of improving the strengths and reducing the weaknesses of cooperating businesses. Businesses willing to undertake strategies involving a high degree of commitment and cooperation can exploit opportunities from which they previously would have been debarred, due to investment or lead-time barriers.

Joint ventures should not be seen as a convenient means of hiding weaknesses. If used prudently, such ventures can create internal strengths. They can be resource-aggregating and resource-sharing mechanisms, allowing sponsoring firms to concentrate resources where they possess the greatest strengths.[12] Box 9–1 provides a comprehensive list of reasons for forming joint ventures and is classified into internal, competitive, and strategic uses.

Joint ventures, therefore, not only share investment but, often more important, provide direction and make possible fresh opportunities.

Identifying the areas in which to focus attention, with the knowledge that the developments will have a commercial outlet, can give substance to this decision. Reducing risk in this way while also limiting the investments required to bring the activity to fruition is an ideal solution. By providing this mix, a joint venture is a sensible alternative to the owner/nonowner options.

Nonequity-Based Collaboration

Companies unwilling or unable to cope with joint venture arrangements can resort to an appropriate form of nonequity-based collaboration to meet their needs. These

---

[11]K. R. Harrigan, "Managing Joint Ventures—Part I," *Management Review,* February 1987, p. 24.
[12]Ibid., p. 28.

Box 9–1

Motivations for Forming a Joint Venture

A. Internal uses.
 1. Share costs and risks (reduce uncertainty).
 2. Obtain resources where there is no market.
 3. Obtain financing to supplement firm's debt capacity.
 4. Share outputs of large, underutilized plants.
  a. Avoid wasteful duplication of facilities.
  b. Utilize by-products and processes.
  c. Share brands and distribution channels, widen product lines, and so forth.
 5. Intelligence: Obtain a window on new technologies and customers.
  a. Improve information exchange.
  b. Improve technological and personnel interactions.
 6. Create innovative managerial practices.
  a. Strive for superior management systems.
  b. Improve communications among small business units.
 7. Retain entrepreneurial employees.

B. Competitive uses: Strengthen current strategic positions.
 1. Influence industry structure's evolution.
  a. Pioneer development of new industries.
  b. Reduce competitive volatility.
  c. Rationalize mature industries.
 2. Preempt competitors (first-mover advantages).
  a. Gain rapid access to better customers.
  b. Expand capacity or vertical integration.
  c. Acquire advantageous terms and resources.
  d. Form coalition with best partners.
 3. Respond defensively to the blurring of industry boundaries and globalization.
  a. Ease political tensions (overcome trade barriers).
  b. Gain access to global networks.
 4. Create more effective competitors.
  a. Develop hybrids possessing owners' strengths.
  b. Have fewer, more efficient firms.
  c. Buffer dissimilar partners.

C. Strategic uses: Augment strategic position.
 1. Create and exploit synergies.
 2. Perform technology or skills transfer.
 3. Diversity.
  a. Rationalize (or divest) investment.
  b. Leverage owners' skills for new uses.

mechanisms provide the means of establishing cooperative working arrangements, which need a long-term base if the collaboration is to yield meaningful and useful results. Such arrangements include:

- Research and development consortia to enhance innovation and the exploitation of results.
- Cross-marketing agreements to provide opportunities, such as utilizing by-products, widening product lines, and sharing distribution channels.
- Cross-production agreements to avoid facilities duplication, provide vertical integration opportunities, and transfer technology know-how.
- Joint purchasing activities to enhance buying power in terms of price gains and increased supplier allegiance.

Long-Term Contracts

Where technologies have already been established, many companies prefer to arrange long-term contracts with suppliers. For both parties, such an agreement provides added predictability and increased assurance, which helps when establishing long-term plans. The key trade-offs here are between flexibility, in volume commitment and sourcing, and the classic set of gains, which have to do with price and delivery. In this way, a customer can enhance the commitment of suppliers to meeting its needs and requirements, while providing increased stability for the supplier itself.

Customer-Vendor Relations

Traditionally, U.S. companies have restricted themselves to an owner or nonowner position. Furthermore, the prevailing attitude toward suppliers has been to exercise the more extreme positions within the two alternatives. At the nonowner end, companies choose to exercise the arms-length, free market philosophy toward their suppliers. The consequence is that customer/supplier relationships are based on short-term agreements, which are invariably multisourced. In this way, added leverage is gained by playing one supplier against another as part of the drive to achieve better terms, especially concerning price.

This perceived need, especially by larger companies, *to control their own destiny* by ownership or retaining the power over supplies through multiple sourcing characterizes the current view of how best to manage these relationships. Many companies employ the "you need us more than we need you" principle to threaten their suppliers. Typical of this is the approach displayed by the motor manufacturers toward the automotive component industry. Ford's review of the Japanese threat, referred to in Chapter 1, illustrates the classic position. Faced with the realities of tough foreign competition, Ford's message to its suppliers, through a series of presentations, was to show them what they had to achieve in order to make Ford, and hence their own businesses, viable. The one aspect not mentioned is a most critical ingredient to Japanese companies' success: the customer/supplier relationships engendered by the Japanese motor manufacturer.[13]

---

[13]An extensive review of this approach is provided in the NEDC Report, *The Experience of Nissan Suppliers: Lessons for the United Kingdom Engineering Industry,* May 1991. This approach not only

TABLE 9–2   **The Role of Customer/Supplier Relations in a Company's Competitive Stance**

Country of Origin	*Base of Competitive Analysis*		
United States/Western Europe	Carmaker	versus	Carmaker
Japan	Carmaker and its suppliers	versus	Carmaker and its suppliers

Which alternative is best depends on the particular company's conception of what constitutes the business. American and West European truck and automobile companies consider the competition to be between carmakers; while the Japanese realize that it is a carmaker and its suppliers versus another carmaker and its suppliers (see Table 9–2).

Significantly outperformed, many companies are highlighting areas where comparative supplier performance is low. But it appears that they often fail to differentiate between symptoms and causes, or to appreciate that these results emanate from a comprehensive approach in which all parts are needed to make a successful whole.

These approaches, however, are in many ways much more difficult to manage than those based on the relatively simple premise of power or legal agreement. Ownership, open-market strategies, or contractual arrangements all provide a power base for the customer. Losing their power base presents a much more demanding task. However, Japanese companies tend to view their key suppliers as partners in a joint venture. While not based on a legal agreement, it is constituted on the shared understanding that it is a long-term relationship, to the benefit of both parties. Furthermore, it is not limited to a prescribed set of issues, as is often the case in joint ventures and invariably so in long-term contractual arrangements. For this to work, three important conditions must exist.

1. Both organizations must have a shared understanding of the long-term nature of what constitutes a mutually beneficial relationship. This does not, however, imply that the customer/supplier relationships are not rigorous. The essential characteristic of this liaison is that their fortunes are interlinked. The Japanese capture the essence of this with the term *codestiny*. But to make this happen requires two other important conditions.

2. As customers and suppliers are interlinked, and as such form part of the same business, they must each achieve the level and nature of the commitments involved. At the operational end of the business, the supplier must meet quality, delivery, and price in line with the customer's agreed needs. Similarly, the customer must fulfill the scheduling, payment, and volume agreements on which the suppliers have based their commitment.

3. Finally, companies must recognize that not only is the quality of purchased materials and components rooted in the processes of their suppliers, but so is the basis

characterizes the Japanese motor industry (also refer to J. Griffiths, "How Toyota Filters Its Component Suppliers," *Financial Times,* April 10, 1991, p. 11) but also other Japanese industries as well. Also refer to C. Batchelor, "Supplying the Japanese—Painstaking Assessment of Product Quality—A Close but Informal Relationship," *Financial Times,* May 21, 1991, p. 12.

for cost reduction. Many U.S. manufacturing companies design components without understanding the process capabilities of their suppliers. To trade with a supplier yet not systematically discuss how best to make changes for the common business good of both parties is difficult to explain away. An example comparing two approaches serves to highlight the differences involved. The procedure by which U.S. truck and automobile companies will typically incorporate changes to components or assemblies is time-consuming (normally several years) and provides little incentive to suppliers. However, the Boston Consulting Group's report on the British motorcycle industry exemplified a basic difference when it summarized the approach adopted by a Japanese producer:

> In 1974, Honda informed some parts suppliers that it did not want a parts' price increase for the next five years. Honda is now currently working closely with the suppliers to help them to rationalize and modify parts design. Honda is also suggesting new production methods and technology to the suppliers.[14]

The essential difference in approach springs from how organizations encourage and facilitate their suppliers to help satisfy their own requirements and strengthen their own competitive positions. Typically, the gains passed on to a supplier by the customer as a result of the supplier taking the initiative to reduce overall costs are disproportionately small to the effort involved. This is due to the leverage exercised by customers in the supplier/customer relationship. Furthermore, in such instances, the contribution to keeping costs low comes principally from suppliers. Honda, on the other hand, widened its contribution base to reducing costs from a supplier-only position to one that included its own contributions plus the joint contributions rising from the customer-supplier relationship it had forged with a more equitable sharing of the gains secured. The increase in cost-reduction opportunities and the motivation to secure these was marked. And this was some 20 years ago.

Just-in-Time Production

Although dealt with more extensively in the next chapter, the just-in-time (JIT) production concept is an essential facet of some Japanese managements' drive for manufacturing and productivity improvement. JIT is based on a simple principle. The idea is for all materials to be active in the process at all times, thereby avoiding cost without appropriate benefit. The concept is neatly summarized by Schonberger as the aim to "produce and deliver finished goods just in time to be sold, subassemblies just in time to be assembled into finished goods, fabricated parts just in time to go into subassemblies, and purchased materials just in time to be transformed into fabricated parts."[15] However, for this to work efficiently requires effective cooperation and coordination between the various parts of the process. Where these are not owned, only

---

[14]"Strategic Alternatives for the British Motorcycle Industry." A report prepared for the Secretary of State for Industry by the Boston Consulting Group (HMSO, July 1977), p. 34.

[15]R. J. Schonberger, *Japanese Manufacturing Techniques: Nine Hidden Lessons in Simplicity* (New York: Free Press, 1982), p. 16.

sound supplier/customer relations will enable this to work. But the gains are considerable. Toyota can point to an inventory turnover of 70 times on purchased parts and work in process and 16 times if finished goods inventory is included.[16]

Conclusion

Companies must carefully assess the different factors that motivate them to change their span of process. In the past, and carried on the winds of growth, many companies repositioned their point on the process span as a matter of course. Believing that they could manufacture anything, many companies decided to widen their process spans without an adequate understanding of strategic fit and the tactical consequences involved. Companies must complete similar strategic and tactical analyses when deciding whether or not to narrow their process spans in times of market retraction, being careful to avoid the lure of short-term improvements without considering the long-term and strategic outcomes.

In making its decision, a company needs to assess the true extent of the process and infrastructure investments to be made. In this way, it will be able to consider the benefits to be gained from the proposed repositioning, while clearly taking into account the trade-offs involved in the alternatives. Besides the strategic issues involved, span-of-process repositioning will enmesh a firm in a series of organizational issues that will require a careful reappraisal of its infrastructure. The extent of make or buy changes will establish the level of infrastructure change involved.

The key manufacturing issues are related to the size and nature of the manufacturing activity. Many U.S. industrial firms are faced with increased problems in manufacturing control. Most spend money to solve the control problem. Few start with the appropriate step of deciding what should or should not be made in-house as an integral part of manufacturing strategy. Determining the size of the manufacturing task, therefore, is the necessary first step. This needs to be completed before investing in the manufacturing infrastructure, to ensure that the time and money spent is necessary and appropriate to the key manufacturing tasks involved.

Further Reading

Armour, T. J., and D. J. Teece. "Vertical Integration and Technological Innovation." *Review of Economics and Statistics* 62, (August 1982), pp. 470–74.

Arrow, K. J. "Vertical Integration and Communications." *Bell Journal of Economics* 6 (Spring 1975), pp. 173–82.

Bailey, P., and D. Farmer. *Purchasing—Principles and Management*. 5th ed. Pitman, 1986.

---

[16]Taken from G. O'Donnell, "How Australian Industry Points the Way on Kanban," *Production Engineer*, July–August 1984, pp. 19–20.

Blois, K. J. "Vertical Quasi-integration." *Journal of Industrial Economics,* July 1972, pp. 253–72.

Buzzell, R. D. "Is Vertical Integration Profitable?" *Harvard Business Review,* January–February 1983, pp. 92–102. Offers an analysis based on the profit impact of market strategies (PIMS) data to assess a number of relationships including vertical integration and profitability; vertical integration, investment intensity, and return on investments; and vertical integration, relative market share, and profitability.

Cavinato, J. L. *Purchasing and Materials Management.* St. Paul, Minn.: West Publishing Company, 1984.

Cherry, J. V. "Vendor's Viewpoint: Quality, Response, Delivery." *Quality Progress* 17, no. 11 (November 1988), pp. 40–42.

Dempsey, W. A. "Vendor Selection and the Buying Process." *Industrial Marketing Management* 17 (1978), pp. 257–67.

Ford, H. *Today and Tomorrow.* Productivity Press, 1988.

Gale, B. T. "Can More Capital Buy Higher Productivity?" *Harvard Business Review,* July–August 1980, pp. 78–90.

Harrigan, K. R. *Managing for Joint Venture Success.* Lexington, Mass.: Lexington Books, 1986.

Kraljic, P. "Purchasing Must Become Supply Management." *Harvard Business Review,* September–October 1983, pp. 109–17.

Petit, R. E. "Vendor Evaluation Made Simple." *Quality Progress* 17, no. 3 (March 1984), pp. 19–22.

Porter, M. E. *Competitive Analysis.* New York: Free Press, 1980. Chapter 14 provides an extensive discussion of the potential benefits and limitations of vertical integration.

Schonberger, R. J. *Building a Chain of Customers.* Hutchinson Business Books, 1990.

Schmalensee, R. "A Note on the Theory of Vertical Integration." *Journal of Political Economy,* March–April 1973, pp. 442–29.

Williamson, O. E. "The Vertical Integration of Production: Market Failure Considerations." *American Economic Review* 61 (May 1971), pp. 112–23.

CHAPTER 10 Manufacturing Infrastructure Development

The need for a business to resolve the issues of process choice in line with the manufacturing strategy requirement has been paramount in the book so far. To reiterate, companies must clearly understand which manufacturing processes can best meet the needs of the marketplace, or how well existing processes provide the order-winners for products in different segments. However, the task facing manufacturing is not simply to choose the process and necessary hardware. Once this has been analyzed and the trade-offs reconciled, the emphasis shifts. It must now ensure that the structure and composition of the component parts, or functions, that provide the necessary systems and communications within a company are also developed in line with the manufacturing strategy requirement. Process choice concerns the features of hardware, the tangible ways in which the products are manufactured. But the task is more than this. The supporting structures, controls, procedures, and other systems within manufacturing are equally necessary for successful, competitive manufacturing performance.

These structures, controls, procedures, and other systems are collectively known as the *manufacturing infrastructure*. It comprises the inner structure of manufacturing, and necessarily includes the attitudes, experience, and skills of the people involved. Together, they form the basis of the manufacturing organization, charged with the task of providing the necessary support to the areas of responsibility involved.

As illustrated in Table 2–1 manufacturing strategy comprises both processes and infrastructure. Getting one in line with market needs and not the other will lead to inconsistencies similar to the levels of mismatch illustrated in Chapter 6. Thus, aligning process characteristics with market needs is insufficient in itself. The impact of infrastructure investments on sound manufacturing strategy provision is as critical as process choice and, in some companies, more so.

Infrastructure developments are characterized by their high level of investment and their fixed nature. These decisions, therefore, are as binding as their hardware counterparts and must be made with the same clear link to the needs of a company's markets. If not, problems will arise identical to those already highlighted for process

FIGURE 10-1

*The inexorable link
of components of
manufacturing
strategy with each
other and with the
business needs*

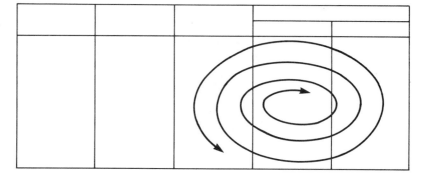

decisions. Company executives will respond with genuine concern to requests for additional investment and time to undertake the redevelopment or reorientation of systems or other facets of infrastructure. Furthermore, companies need to parallel continuing market changes with appropriate development in manufacturing. The inherently fixed nature of manufacturing infrastructure is often coupled with an inertia for change stemming in part from corporate reviewing procedures built on functional goals and perspectives. Often, those responsible for the realignment of the essential components of manufacturing infrastructure are unaware of or unable to respond to the growing need to make the necessary and appropriate changes. One underlying message in Peters and Waterman's *In Search of Excellence* is that success depends on awareness.[1] Building the infrastructure on a manufacturing strategy base does just this. It gives appropriate direction and allows a choice between alternative sets of trade-offs to be made. The company then has a shared awareness of what is required in manufacturing if it is to support the current and future needs of the business in the best way. And the necessity of linking manufacturing to the marketplace through its process hardware and organizational software is established. Thus, the components of manufacturing strategy must be inexorably linked to give them coherence and synergistic purpose (see Figure 6–1).

The infrastructure, therefore, represents part of the complexity inherent in manufacturing. To develop an appropriate infrastructure to support manufacturing effectively, a company must understand this. This involves two important dimensions. The first concerns the way the company is structured internally and why it has evolved that way. The second involves recognizing the key perspectives to be taken into account when developing the important areas of infrastructure.

By themselves, most elements of infrastructure do not require the same level of investment nor do they have the same impact on manufacturing's strategic role as does process choice; but taken collectively they do. Together, their importance in providing the strategic support for the business cannot be overstressed. Similarly, the difficulties

---

[1]T. J. Peters and R. H. Waterman, Jr., *In Search of Excellence: Lessons from America's Best-Run Companies* (New York: Harper & Row, 1982).

experienced through the interaction of inappropriate systems and the costs involved in effecting major changes can be of the same magnitude as those decisions involving manufacturing hardware. Transforming over time the support for the marketplace into an appropriate collection of facilities, structures, controls, procedures and people comprises the manufacturing strategy task. As Hayes and Wheelwright conclude:

> it is this pattern of structural [*process*] and infrastructural decisions that constitutes the "manufacturing strategy" of a business unit. More formally, a manufacturing strategy consists of a sequence of decisions that, over time, enables a business unit to achieve a desired manufacturing structure [*process choice*], infrastructure, and set of specific capabilities.[2]

In relation to corporate strategy, they recognize that "the primary function of a manufacturing strategy is to guide the business in putting together the set of manufacturing capabilities that will enable it to pursue its chosen competitive strategy over the long term."[3]

Manufacturing Infrastructure Issues

Manufacturing infrastructure comprises a complex set of interacting factors. Western companies have traditionally coped with this by breaking their infrastructures into appropriate sets of responsibilities or functions and deploying people to provide the necessary support. To work effectively this requires a high degree of coordination linked to manufacturing's strategic tasks. However, the reality does not bear out the theory. Typically, these parts or functions are managed separately and come together primarily at the tactical or operational interface. Developments within the infrastructure are given the level of detailed attention they require at the points of application. It is at these levels where meaningful, in-depth discussion takes place, no doubt stimulated by the real need to make the particular area of infrastructure development work effectively. However, the merits of the individual parts and how they fit together are rarely encompassed by any strategic overview. For this reason, piecemeal developments, propounded in the main by specialists, lead to an uncoordinated approach to infrastructure design.

It is essential that the basic parts of the organizational framework reinforce and support the manufacturing task. This enables the company to get away from functionally based perspectives of what is appropriate and important. The only way to achieve this is to orient discussion on the requirements of the business; that is, to replace functional argument by the corporate resolution between alternatives and to replace unilaterally stimulated argument of what is best for the business by corporate-based

---

[2]R. H. Hayes and S. C. Wheelwright, *Restoring Our Competitive Edge: Competing through Manufacturing* (John Wiley & Sons, Inc., 1984), p. 32.

[3]Ibid., p. 33.

argument of the same. This then provides a base on which to develop a comprehensive, coordinated, and directed infrastructure to meet the firm's current and future needs. It not only enables a company to get its orientation right, but it also enables it to avoid being saddled with functions that are no longer required or are inappropriately weighted when related to the business needs. Changing the *status quo* is difficult, unless the firm knows why and how it wants or has to change. Only then is it able to move from subjectively based to objectively based analyses and decisions. This requires a very clear statement of what constitutes the manufacturing task—the manufacturing strategy appropriate to the company. Once functional managers understand and appreciate this, a company can reshuffle the *status quo*. It is then in a position to avoid situations where vested interests argue for the retention or growth in capabilities/ capacities for their own sake rather than for their relative contribution to the current and future success of the business.

Questions stemming from these views concern why functions hold on to their current level of size and why they argue for their own retention and growth. In many instances, they do so because it is the best perspective they have. Only when a business orients functions toward the outside (i.e., what the market requires) can it provide the opportunity for alternatives to be measured against corporate-related criteria. The provision of a common, relevant base enables functional arguments to be put into perspective. It shifts the evaluation of proposals from the use of subjective to objective criteria. It gives appropriate direction to which all infrastructure development must aspire, while also providing the detailed checklists against which developments can be evaluated. In this way, these costly developments will meet manufacturing strategy requirements rather than functional or specialist perspectives. Furthermore, by looking outward and forward, developments will be made with a knowing eye on future competition and thus become more likely to incorporate the manufacturing needs of tomorrow.

If the functions charged with making effective infrastructure provision are not given strategic direction, there is the real possibility that specialist support functions will pursue their own points of view, a problem many businesses experience today. Firms need the functional and specialist capabilities to make sense of the complexity. Without these inputs, they cannot reach the level of effectiveness necessary to meet today's competitive pressures. The difference between an infrastructure based on a number of specialist views and one coordinated to meet the needs of a business by an appropriate strategy is significant for most firms and critical for many.

The review and incremental development of infrastructure within the strategic context of manufacturing is equally important—it concerns altering the balance or changing the focus of development so that it is in line with the manufacturing task, and hence forms an integral part of manufacturing strategy. A firm's ability to backtrack on its decisions is also important at times. This activity, however, is often thwarted by the difficulties presented by specialists who are typically highly analytical people capable of arguing their case with great clarity and strength and protecting their own views and areas of responsibility in a vacuum. The existence of a manufacturing strategy provides the parameters for analysis and debate to either reconcile arguments or views or redirect development work.

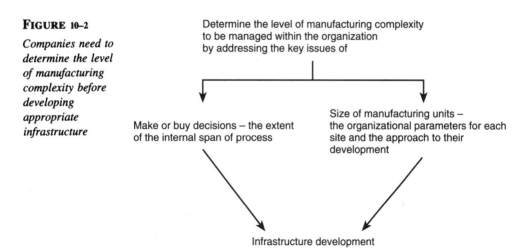

Infrastructure Development

Strategy comprises the development and declaration of a shared view of business direction. But unless a business regularly updates its strategy in response to market change, it will not notice diversions from it, and individual interpretations of strategy, rather than the strategy statement itself, will become fact. In both instances, fragmentation will occur and the necessary cohesion will diminish.

The successful development of infrastructure requires care. Many companies have adopted a piecemeal approach by resolving one facet at a time, as often stimulated by the apparent need of the moment as by a carefully selected priority. Picking off one area makes sense as a way of coping with the complexity involved. However, many organizations even in these situations do not undertake sufficient analyses before determining the area for development. This preliminary analysis need not become a complex debate; Figure 10–2 points to the essential issues—the need to determine the make or buy decision and define the size of the manufacturing units. Thus, rather than investing money, time, and effort in resolving the current complexity, a company should define the level of complexity it wishes to handle. Only then is it able to decide how best to manage the chosen level, and only then is it able to develop the infrastructure appropriate to its needs. For once a company understands its manufacturing task and the organizational makeup involved (its *organizational profile*), the direction and content of any infrastructure development will become clear and comprehensible.

Many companies in the past have pursued the economies of large scale without fully evaluating the net gains involved (see Chapter 7 on focus). A classic approach to achieving these apparent gains has sometimes been to centralize at corporate and plant levels. This had led to centralized functions being created throughout the organization. Primary counterarguments concern the increased complexity involved in large organizations and the difficulties of reshaping them in times of change. In many instances, the anticipated gains of centralized functions have proved to be an organizational El Dorado.

The chapter so far has emphasized the importance of appropriately developing manufacturing infrastructure and its significant contribution to providing the necessary manufacturing support to the marketplace. However, before discussing some of the key areas of infrastructure design, it will be worthwhile to highlight practical, but general considerations.

1. It is most important to determine and agree on the important areas of infrastructure within manufacturing. A discretionary approach to change is essential to ensure that scarce development resources are used in those areas that will yield the best returns. The approach to change must reflect those areas that will have the most strategic impact, a point emanating from the concept of the 80/20 rule.[4]

2. As with process choice, it is necessary to establish and then choose between sets of trade-offs that go hand in hand with each decision. The criteria, however, against which to measure the trade-offs must be concerned with manufacturing's strategic role.

3. The essence of sound infrastructure design is that it must respond to the dynamics of reality. Although some areas will require major change, much of the necessary change can be achieved incrementally. Once drawing this distinction, the company must regularly review areas of manufacturing infrastructure to effect the necessary developments, including the simplification and even withdrawal of controls, systems, and procedures. It is most important, on the other hand, to avoid major change wherever possible. In many cases, the need for major change reflects the degree of mismatch between requirement and provision that has developed incrementally over time within the relevant area of infrastructure. Often, sizable and lengthy disruptions are required to put things right.

4. Linked to the issue of avoiding situations of stepped change is the decision of what constitutes the job of work and what is the role of specialists within an organization. Although addressed later in the chapter, it is important to emphasize here that continuous development is easier to bring about where the responsibility for identifying and implementing improvements is locally based. Employee involvement creates conditions where changes are brought about by incremental developments. On the other hand, control through specialists can result in the need for changes being undetected or unattended. In these circumstances, the requirements for change will often be set aside, and when eventually addressed, developments and tasks involved tend to be large.

Important Infrastructure Issues

A company that fails to develop its infrastructure, as part of its response to meeting the needs of its marketplace, is likely to experience two linked consequences.

---

[4]The 80/20 rule reflects the implied relationship between two sets of data or consequences. In this instance, it illustrates that 80 percent of the total strategic benefit to be gained from infrastructure development will arise from 20 percent of the areas of application. The use of the figures 80 and 20, however, is illustrative of the relationship implied in the selected phenomenon and not intended to be definitive.

1. The business position may worsen because, among other things, the systems and controls will fail to give executives accurate and timely indicators to help them to manage the business and initiate the necessary developments.

2. The key components of infrastructure necessary to help reshape or rebuild the business may not be in place when they are most necessary and most urgently required.

The approach to developing the separate parts of a manufacturing company's infrastructure involves two integrated steps. The first is determining the marketplace or competitive requirements; that is, each aspect of infrastructure must be built around the way products win orders. The controls, systems, procedures, attitudes, and skills involved will then be oriented toward those manufacturing tasks pertinent to the order-winning criteria of different products. The second is ensuring that the necessary level of coherence and coordination exists in the various but related parts of manufacturing infrastructure. In this way all the software pulls in the same, appropriate direction and the company releases the synergy inherent in this substantial investment. In addition, those involved feel the consequential facilitating and motivating benefits of coherent direction. It was not easy to select which infrastructure issues from the many that could warrant attention to discuss here. Although the relevance and importance were factors in this decision, more than a small slice of subjective opinion was involved. Relevance, however, may not be so important here because it will change between businesses; thus, the discussion that follows is primarily meant to explain the principles of infrastructure design and development rather than to make a comprehensive statement on manufacturing infrastructure.

The rest of the chapter concerns a number of organizational issues and some of the key areas of operational control. The other important aspects of infrastructure, not covered here, will need to be similarly developed, using the same elements and procedures described in the following sections.

Organizational Issues

The development investment and running costs required to maintain the support functions within a manufacturing business are high. The rationale for this high cost provision is based, in part, on providing adequate and appropriate support to make manufacturing more effective and efficient. It is essential to ensure that this is achieved. Most organizations, however, have treated the approach to developing relevant support for manufacturing as an operational and not as a strategic issue. Consequently the approach of many businesses to critical aspects of organizational design has not been based on the necessity to support manufacturing's strategic role. Some of the consequences of this are now discussed.

Role of Specialists

Most manufacturing firms in the United States make extensive use of specialists in running a business. The approach adopted by companies in the past has been to create functions comprising specialist staff to supply expert advice, guidance, and activity in various relevant areas. The intention has been to provide the major line functions with the necessary help. In the past three or four decades, this trend toward the employment of specialists has been growing in manufacturing and other sectors of the economy.

In light of increasing world competition, companies must reassess the extent of use of specialists and the appropriateness of its direction. Before discussing alternatives to the typical pattern of specialist provision currently used in most firms, it would be helpful to review some of the ways in which this concept of control has tended to evolve as a method of examining the current position, while providing some possible insights into the ways forward. The emphasis throughout will be toward the manufacturing function, although the points raised and suggestions made may well prove pertinent in other line areas.

Specialists and Economies of Scale

The rationale underpinning the concept of control by specialists is to bring together staff to provide the capability, support, and development deemed necessary to help line functions meet the needs of a business. This involves the principle of economies of scale, addressed in Chapter 7 on focus. Furthermore, the placement of these groups has traditionally been on a functional basis, and eventually, though not always initially, they have been positioned in a reporting structure that has been outside the main line functions.

Consequently many companies adopting this concept of control experience several major difficulties. Some of the reasons such control is not highly effective include:

• *The question of ownership.* The lack of detailed understanding shared by line and staff functions of the important perspectives of each other is legendary. To redress this in the past few years, words such as *user-orientated, user-sensitive,* and *user-friendly* have become part of the standard approach in an attempt to overcome the inherent difficulties created by this organizational arrangement. However, attitudes and detailed insights take time to change.

• *Role clarity.* The roles and relationships shared by line and staff functions within the common decision procedures in which they are involved has resulted in certain instances, in a large measure of misunderstanding and criticism, leading even to acrimony and derision. This is due, in part, to the people themselves, the different salaries, reporting, and working structures involved, the implied criticism of the specialist's activity, the high level of failures, apparent lack of interest or time allocation by specialists in the postimplementation period, and the relative inexperience of specialists both in organizational and personal terms, which leads to a failure to appreciate that the only hard task in management is managing. However, the perceived roles of the line and support functions within the whole of these areas of development or day-to-day support procedures are too often not clarified either at the organization or operational levels.

Line managers invariably see the specialist function as a means of improving an area of operational weakness. As busy executives, and not owning, in organizational terms, the time or control of the specialists involved, line managers often take a reactive role in the key periods of the development program. But it is these managers who must make the final decision for the development to be effective. Hence, such decisions are often delayed until later when the problems invariably arise. The results are far from effective.

   • *Organizational relevance.* The principle of control through specialists and economies of scale is appropriate in high-volume and stable markets. The 1980s saw markets increasingly moving away from those characteristics, a trend continued in the 1990s. Companies, therefore, need to reconsider this basic tenet. It does not, however, mean that they should swing to the opposite end of the continuum. They need to avoid the 0–100 management[5] response that has characterized many changes in the past. There are points on any continuum besides 0 and 100 (i.e., where a company is now and the point that represents the very opposite set of characteristics). It does mean though that companies need to reconsider appropriate organizational responses to meet the changing and different needs of current and future markets. In most, simply distinguishing those tasks that are clearly specialist in nature from those that are operational will start the process of reconsidering what tasks should go where.

Functional Silos

In many organizations, the specialists' role and area of responsibility has grown. However, this growth has been determined more on the basis of perceived organizational neatness than on making best use of the specialists' contribution to meet the needs of the business. Typically, as illustrated in Figure 10–3, areas of responsibility, once within the province of the line functions, have been drawn into the authority sphere of specialists (Phase 1). Classically, an independent reporting structure then evolves (Phase 2). The result is that key sets of responsibilities that need to be integrated into the line activities are separated, and the inherent difficulties associated with this structure when trying to redress the lack of necessary integration are now apparent in many companies. Functional silos have evolved in which individual goals and objectives tend to have higher priority for resource allocation than does the support of line activities.

Control from a Distance

An invariable consequence of this approach is that companies evolve into organizations with too many people and too much control over manufacturing by financial analyses and reporting systems developed without adequately reflecting the business itself. This has been brought about, in part, by the belief that effective management can be maintained at a distance, using controls, systems, and feedback developed by specialists. Often the hands-off controls being used have not reflected key trends,

---

[5]This expression, 0–100 management was developed to highlight the pendulum-like response to problems or disadvantages that typifies organizational action. On the other hand, companies need to reposition themselves on a gradual and continuous basis while clearly recognizing that the diverse nature of markets will require diverse response.

FIGURE 10–3

Typical phase in the evolution of specialist functions in an organization

Phase 1
with the introduction of specialist functions, sets of similar responsibilities are organizationally realigned.

Phase 2
Over time, the specialist functions develop their own 'independent' reporting structures.

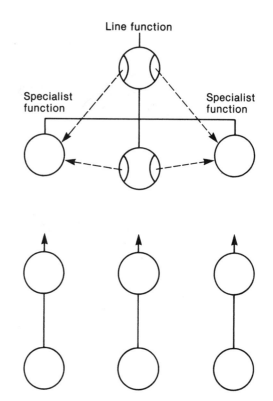

while those responsible for exercising and monitoring control have lacked the necessary knowledge of the business under review to detect changes and to ask penetrating questions at the opportune time. At best, this has contributed to the decline in performance; at worst it could accelerate this decline by emphasizing, for instance, short-term performance improvements at the expense of medium- and long-term strategic requirements. While this way of reviewing performance gathered momentum in the 1970s and 1980s, companies are now reassessing the practice. The practice was stimulated and given credence by the predominant role of specialists, but companies are reconsidering the value of leaning too heavily, sometimes solely, on the views and contributions of these functions.

Reward Systems

Companies need to reflect the relative importance and contribution of executives to a business by the level of remuneration and opportunity for advancement provided. Attracting able people into key jobs, therefore, needs to correspond to the organization's reward system. Many companies, unfortunately, have failed to correlate executives' salaries with the direct effect those individuals have on the success of the business. What has unduly influenced salary structures and the opportunity for promotion are factors such as apparent scarcity, assumed contribution, and market rates for salaries.

Consequently all too often companies have offered higher salaries to those whose influence falls in the 20 percent of the 80/20 rule. Thus, the more-able people have been attracted away from those line functions that affect the 80 percent of what constitutes business success.

Too Many Layers

One outcome of the extensive use of specialists is organizations with too many layers. At the head office, corporate staff can turn into an expensive bureaucracy. At plant level, divisional staffs, built up by middle management as they get promoted, are retained by their successors. Steward of McKinsey & Co. claims that "ever since the 1960s, when we started to believe that a professional manager can manage everything, we've been on the wrong track." The random rotation of managers, based upon this belief, led to "the new managers, unfamiliar with the businesses they were expected to run, [hiring] staff to advise them. When they moved on, a new manager repeated the cycle. . . . The problem was compounded when companies started going international.[6] Economies of large scale have also contributed to this problem. "Along with bigness comes complexity. . . . And, most big companies respond to complexity in kind, by designing complex systems and structures. They then hire more staff to keep track of all this complexity."[7]

The results are reviewed in Figure 10–4, which illustrates the changes in layers of management that have taken place from the 1900s through to those anticipated by the year 2000.

The way forward has been to reduce the layers and cut out the fat. The response at DuPont's Maitland plant (Ontario, Canada) is typical. During the 1980s, it reduced the number of layers in organizational hierarchy from 11 to 6 (see Figure 10–5) and shed 700 employees, many of them highly paid middle managers. As in most organizations, it was not that these employees were not doing a good job; but their roles slowed down procedures and constituted tasks that did not add value. Before the cut, a production manager at the Maitland plant supervised 90 workers through 6 foremen; today he as a staff of 40 and no foremen. Similarly, if workers needed a new tool the decision to purchase came from higher up. Today they order it directly from the supplier. In addition, customers now telephone the plant directly about orders, speeding up the procedure that previously would have gone through DuPont's Toronto head office and four layers of bureaucracy. The result is that everyone benefits from this kind of flexibility.[8]

The way forward for many companies is increasingly clear. The question to be answered is, Which is the best approach to take? For many companies, the classic response has been to implement across-the-board reductions. Having cut the work force and dispensed with the frills, companies would request managers to reduce all round

---

[6]"A New Target: Reducing Staff and Levels." *Business Week*. December 21, 1981, pp. 38–41.

[7]Peters and Waterman. *In Search of Excellence*, p. 306.

[8]A detailed review of the changes at DuPont's Maitland plant is given in D. Stoffman's "Less Is More," *Report on Business Magazine*. June 1988, pp. 90–101.

FIGURE 10–4

*The number of
levels within
a typical
organization at
different times*

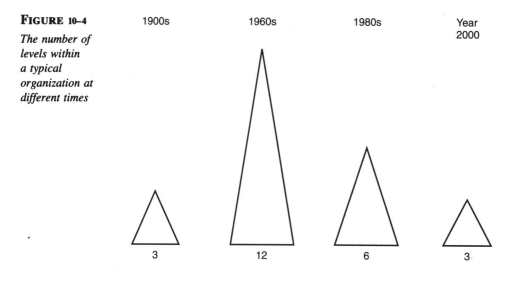

Number of levels

by an appropriate percentage. But these haphazard cuts left most corporate or central staff intact, the divisional ratios between managers and work force rising, and organizations more sluggish and less profitable.

This approach smacks of the specialists' view of an organization: To make the bottom line come right, just change the figures. This assumes that the existing structure will be appropriate in a reduced form. However, many businesses are realizing that the one thing they must not do is to take an axe to the job. Reshaping an organization requires careful surgery with reductions in line with the business. It needs to start with the business and build up from the bottom as well as down from the top. Many organizations in the past have only built top-down, without an assessment of the contribution of each part to the business as a whole. This has merely added to the layers. Reshaping an organization needs to take into account the role of functions, establish the responsibility for decisions and boundaries of authority, and agree the appropriate level and reporting structure between the line and support functions involved. It helps to clarify that the line functions will in many instances always make the important decisions due to the authority/responsibility link that must exist. Also, support functions will in many instances provide a clerical/administrative backup filtering service or front position. For example, in recruitment their role is advisory and usually, quite rightly, consists only of drawing up a short list. In industrial relations negotiations, the specialist provides a first negotiating line to allow those with prime responsibility to take any necessary fall-back position.

The business-related approach, therefore, enables a company to develop its organization in line with its needs and it also provides the opportunity to change the perception of roles at all levels in the organization from top to bottom. Finally, not only is this procedure based on the business, but it also blocks off any functional or personal escape routes that tend to be prevalent in many companies.

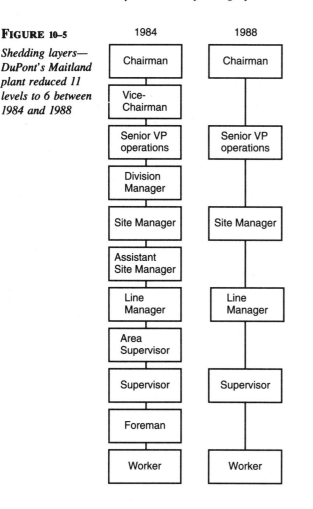

Operational Effects of Structural Decisions

A significant consequence of the decision to extensively use specialists within a business is the effects it has at the operational level. One important issue concerns role definitions on the shopfloor and other similar jobs throughout an organization.

The Operator's Job

The concept of an operator's job as perceived in most Western manufacturing companies is that of a "doing" task (e.g., operating a machine or assembling a product). For this reason, when there are no appropriate doing or making tasks to be completed, the dilemma facing the shopfloor supervisor is between recording a labor excess and completing work not required in the current period (i.e., creating inventory). This problem is made even worse by process investment. Management reduces the job skills and the work involved when they invest in plant and equipment. In order to redress the

FIGURE 10–6

*The separation of
the three facets
of work and the
gap between them
created by the
organizational
structure*

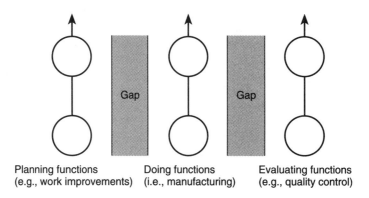

Planning functions   Doing functions   Evaluating functions
(e.g., work improvements)   (i.e., manufacturing)   (e.g., quality control)

reducing job interest and to capitalize on the opportunity to use the time released in an effective way, it is first necessary to change the concept of work.

The premise on which this change should be built revolves around the fact that work, in effect, consists of not only the doing task, but also the tasks of planning and evaluating.[9] In many companies, however, work has been separated into these three components, with each part completed by a different function. The rationale for this is a by-product of the use of specialists and the development of support functions within an organization. Figure 10–6, therefore, is an extension of Phase 2 in Figure 10–3. It illustrates a typical structure, the separation of important activities at the operator level, and the inherent gap created by the structure between these three intrinsic parts of work. This has resulted from the development of organizational structures using specialists and functional reporting procedures. It has led to a situation where the inherent contribution of operators to work-improvement activities has been lost and the essential link between the responsibility for manufacturing and quality has been served.

Strategy-Based Alternatives

For many companies, the organizational structure consisting of line and support functions is proving less than effective. Structures designed for stable, high-volume markets increasingly fail to meet the needs of today's markets, which are characterized by low volumes and instability set in an environment of increasing competition, worldwide overcapacity, and dynamic markets.

Any evaluation of structures and detailed roles, however, needs to ask: Will it meet the requirements of the business? The suggested areas of change that follow are intended to reflect more accurately existing responsibility structures or are designed to facilitate an appropriate and relevant contribution by people throughout the organiza-

---

[9]This and some of the other concepts discussed here are taken from a set of well-developed work-structuring principles that have been presented in various unpublished papers, 1979–81, by P. C. Schumacher, Schumacher Projects, Godstone, Surrey, UK.

tion. If firms are to compete effectively in world markets, their structures need to be both dynamic and designed to tap the relative potential of all their employees.

Functional Teamwork

Companies need to reconsider the currently held view of line and support functions. The alternative is to build specialist functions back into the line with them reporting within that authority/responsibility structure. The principal consequences of this would be:

- Changing the reporting structures removes the problem of the line management/specialist interface not working.
- It clarifies the current role of specialists into those areas which (a) are primarily within the scope of the specialism—for example, quality assurance, the development of robotics within productivity improvement, and production planning, and (b) should be under the auspices of the line management function—for example, quality control, internal efficiency activities, and production control, respectively.

This would enable an organization to build its structure around sets of coherent, interrelated activities rather than, as at present, around activities with similar names. It would not *per se* lead to reductions in people—although invariably it does—and in fact, would sometimes lead to increases of staff in certain functions. Although pushing decision-making activity from the center to the plant and from specialists into the line may not change staffing levels, it would dramatically change the relevance of activities undertaken and assignment priorities established. The benefit, for instance, for manufacturing managers to have the opportunity to generate cost analyses in line with their own perspectives and requirements and in line with their contribution to corporate decisions has to be seen to be believed.

The process is one of reshaping overheads. To be successful, it will need to challenge fundamentally current structures, attitudes, and expectations. Organizations that are functionally driven and controlled through specialisms are top-heavy and unresponsive. They fail to capitalize fully on the abilities of their people and the time availability created by investment. This reconsideration is based on the rationale of continuous improvement. The result is that not only do organizations become more cost-efficient, they also become more effective. The following sections address related issues.

Structure of Work

As implied by the comments on what constitutes work, organizations need to build aspects of planning and evaluating back into the doing task. Enhanced by the *functional teamwork* concept described above, and as part of the rationalization of work and relative contributions by different employees. Figure 10–7 suggests how parts of those planning and evaluating activities, presently completed by support functions, should be reassigned to those currently responsible for the doing tasks. In this way, not

FIGURE 10–7

*Incorporating the
doing tasks with
appropriate
planning and
evaluating steps*

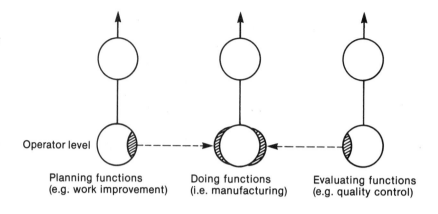

FIGURE 10–7

Incorporating the doing tasks with appropriate planning and evaluating steps

Operator level

Planning functions
(e.g. work improvement)

Doing functions
(i.e. manufacturing)

Evaluating functions
(e.g. quality control)

only does such an action lend support to the arguments put forward in the last section, but it also provides a tangible common-sense illustration of the effect this can have. These actions facilitate the materialization of productivity-bearing improvements and, at the same time, create greater job interest for all concerned.

It releases specialists from nonspecialist work and gives operators work that involves the three important dimensions that make up meaningful tasks by broadening their responsibilities and allowing them both to plan and to evaluate the work they carry out.[10] Although these changes bring small returns in themselves, the cumulative effect can be enormous and the contribution made to providing manufacturing's strategic contribution, significant.

Examples from DuPont's Maitland Plant illustrate this. Under the previous system, a customer's quality complaint was handled by head office. Now the operator who made the product goes to see the customer and decides how to correct the problem. Problems are cleared up more quickly and customers are happier. At the other end of the spectrum, "staring at a bank of computers is not a stimulating way to spend a 12-hour shift. To make [an operator's] job more interesting and more useful to the company, [operators] are trained—in their off hours and at overtime rates—in computer technology. [They then become] responsible for maintaining computers in the plant's control room and for helping to develop expert systems."[11]

A different perspective that reinforces this issue concerns payments systems used for operators. Typical systems pay the job not the person and are based on analyses and evaluations. Such approaches reinforce inflexibility and create barriers to change. An alternative to these is a skill-based system. This is built on the concept that individuals should be paid for their skills, a perspective that allows for and encourages change similar to that depicted in Figure 10–7.[12]

---

[10]A key feature of quality circles (dealt with later in this chapter) is that those involved not only implement their ideas but also evaluate the gains they yield.

[11]Stoffman, "Less Is More," pp. 97–98.

[12]See E. E. Lawler III and G. E. Ledford Jr., "Skill-based Pay: A Concept That's Catching On," *Management Review,* February 1987, pp. 46–51.

Cascading Overheads

Linked to both the structure of work and the role of specialists within an organization is the cascading of overheads. Companies should seek to push work as far down the organization as possible. Coupled (as is the concept of work structuring dealt with in the last section) to an investment by the firm in the training of the individuals involved, the systematic cascading of overheads will help increase the level of flexibility required, allow any spare time created as a by-product of process investments to be usefully absorbed, and provide those involved with a more meaningful task.

This involves changing the levels at which decisions are made and allowing people to decide on how best to complete tasks once they have been given the relevant parameters and information.

Quality Circles or Productivity Improvement Groups

As part of the organizational changes advocated here, the introduction of quality circles or productivity improvement groups needs careful consideration. The necessary care in evaluating their role and contribution, however, has not always been exercised by those Western companies that have adopted them. In many instances, they have been perceived as panaceas and as such have been evaluated and implemented at an operational level and not as part of a strategic organizational change to draw out the continuous improvement potential of the shopfloor.

This essential difference in the way that quality circles are perceived goes some way to explaining the overall rating attributed to this activity as reported in the 1990 *Manufacturing Futures Survey.* Table 10–1 reports the level of payoff over the two-year period from 1988 to 1989 for three regions.

The concept of quality circles emanates from Japanese business practice. The name derives from the fact that quality was Japan's initial major manufacturing problem after the Second World War; hence, some organizations have changed the name to productivity improvement groups. Quality circles illustrate the impact of participation on the productivity increases that can be achieved in all aspects of performance. They systematically involve workers in the improvement of quality, productivity, and similar operations activities. This form of worker involvement in Japan has been

TABLE 10–1   Relative Payoff from Quality-Circles Activity, by Region

Region	Relative Payoff from Quality-Circles Activity (1988–9)
Europe	23
Japan	3
United States	12

growing rapidly. Figure 10–8 shows a steady increase in the number of circles and their membership in Japan in the period from 1965 to 1991.[13]

By the late 1970s, many other countries in the world were adopting this approach. It was recognized as a way of providing the systematic involvement of the workforce, and the returns on the investment of training given and time spent were impressive and numerous. Many reviews of the adoption of quality circles are available.[14] However, the distinction has not been drawn in many firms between a major organizational change adopted as an operational response and one adopted as part of a strategy-led response to improving the effectiveness of manufacturing. This has led some reviewers to conclude that "in many U.S. organizations . . . quality circles are already in the adoption–disappointment–discontinuation cycle that has been characteristic of many other managerial fads."[15]

The failure of US manufacturing companies to recognize the value of the shop-floor contribution is widespread. The use of quality circles or productivity improvement groups is an aid to redressing this imbalance and "tapping what is probably our most underdeveloped asset—the gold in the mind of our workers."[16] For this to be effective, the company needs to be genuinely committed to the principle of continuous improvement and to accept seriously that this can only be achieved by participative management. The structures then need to be developed to make the *principle* work in *practice* and then to support its development throughout while not interfering with the nature of that development. In this way, companies are able to start tapping into their collective wisdom. The change is a strategic one. It accepts that there are significant benefits to be derived from detailed operational improvements, that implementing improvements quickly and effectively must be on a participative basis, and that people, as a group, have the ability to evaluate each others' ideas and develop them.

---

[13]These figures are provided in a year-by-year review of the adoption of quality circles within Japanese business—*Forman Quality Control,* 256 (1984), p. 59.

[14]Other references to the adoption and outcomes of quality circles include "Why Does Britain Want Quality Circles?" *Production Engineer.* February 1980, pp. 45–46; three articles published in S. M. Lee and G. Schwendiman (eds.), *Management by Japanese Systems* (New York: Praeger Publishers, 1982) Part II, Quality Circles, pp. 65–118: Hill. *Production/Operations Management* (Hemel Hempstead, UK: Prentice Hall, 1991), pp. 374–77; R. J. Schonberger, *Japanese Manufacturing Techniques: Nine Hidden Lessons in Simplicity,* ch. 8 "Quality Circles, Work Improvement and Specialization, pp. 181–98; M. Robson, *Quality Circles in Action* (Gower, Aldershot, UK: 1984); D. H. Hutchins, *Quality Circles Handbook* (Pitman, London: 1985); I. A. Temple and B. G. Dale, *White Collar Quality Circles in UK Manufacturing Industry: A Study,* Occasional Paper Series, no. 8510. Department of Management Sciences (UMIST, 1985); E. E. Lawler and W. A. Mohrmann, "Quality Circles: After the Fad," *Harvard Business Review,* January–February 1985, pp. 65–67; and B. G. Dale and J. Lees. *The Development of Quality Circle Programmes* (Manpower Services Commission, London: 1986). In addition, J. R. Arbose in his editorial "Quality Control Circles: The West Adopts a Japanese Concept," *International Management,* December 1980, pp. 31–39, provides a wide-ranging list of savings achieved from applications in various countries, a checklist for starting up and K. Ishikawa's list of the eight tools of problem analysis in which group leaders need to be trained.

[15]R. Wood, F. Hull, and K. Azumi, "Evaluating Quality Circles: The American Application," *California Management Review,* 26, no. 1 (Fall 1983), pp. 37–53.

[16]Arbose, "Quality Control Circles," p. 31.

FIGURE 10–8

The growth of quality circle membership in Japan between 1965 and 1991

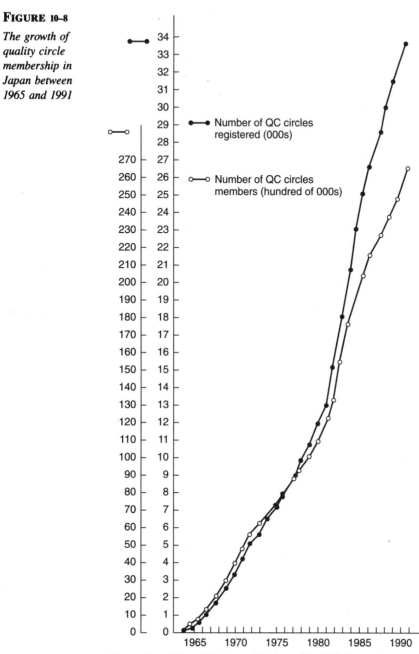

SOURCE: Japan Union of Scientists and Engineers (May 1992). Personal communication.

Participative management is not a soft style. It is both demanding and results oriented. The difference is embodied in the changed views of work and relative contribution of those involved. Functions, and groups of people who are high potential contributors, need to be clearly identified. Similarly, other functions and groups need to be placed in their relative positions on the continuum depicting business needs. Fulfilling potential or eliminating low contributors will bring noticeable improvements.

Operational Control

Infrastructure development is a wide-ranging area, and the aspects addressed in this chapter are not meant to provide either a comprehensive or even a representative coverage. They have been chosen because they constitute some of the important aspects of manufacturing infrastructure. Also, their treatment is intended to offer guidelines on how to develop other areas within the manufacturing strategy of the company. In this section, therefore, only three facets of operational control are covered. The first, quality, has been selected because of its important role as either a qualifying or order-winning criterion. The second, inventory control, was chosen because often it is the biggest single asset in a manufacturing company's balance sheet. The final aspect, control of manufacturing, has been addressed because of its role in delivery performance, which concerns other important qualifying or order-winning criteria. In addition, the conclusion of the chapter discusses a payment system development chosen because of its inherent role in the motivation of people to achieve the relevant performance criteria to be provided by manufacturing and as an example of how all facets within infrastructure need to develop within a strategic overview.

Control of Quality[17]

In many instances quality conformance is a qualifying criterion in manufacturing strategy terms and its impact on market share is more dramatic than probably any other single factor.

In many sectors, Japanese companies have systematically increased the level of product quality to such an extent that they have fundamentally changed customers' expectations not only in these markets but as a general rule. Initially challenging existing norms where quality conformance was a qualifier, they made and sold products with a markedly lower level of defects. The results were dramatic. Suddenly, unable to meet the distinctive higher-quality levels, companies found that they were no longer qualifying to compete in their traditional markets. Loss of market share followed. To regain a place on customer's short lists, companies were required to reconsider their basic approach to quality provision and to take on board the markedly higher expectations of their customers. Today, quality is now a qualifier in many markets. Thus, failure to meet existing quality expectations or to track future improvements will lead to an order-losing scenario and attendant consequences.

---

[17]The dimension of quality referred to here is conformance.

TABLE 10-2   Responsibility for Quality Control and the Type of Process

Process	Task	Responsibility for Quality
Project and jobbing	The task and quality are normally integrated in the skills of the person	Usually vested largely in the performance of the task or provision of the service; that is, the person responsible for this part of the process plus supervisory support
Batch and line	Work has been deskilled to reduce, among other things, labor costs; inspection and later quality control introduced	Theoretically vested in the person providing the task, with supervisory, quality control, and inspection support; in reality, the quality control and inspection functions are primarily responsible
Continuous processing	Quality is determined by the process and, therefore, reintegrates quality into the task	Usually an integral part of the process design; the facilities to monitor quality are usually controlled by the person responsible for other aspects of the task

SOURCE: T. Hill, *Production/Operations Management*, 2nd ed. (Hemel Hempstead, UK: Prentice Hall, 1991, p. 370).

In the past, companies often did not recognize the possible strategic consequences of separating the total responsibility for quality conformance from the person responsible for completing the task. In project and jobbing this division has rarely, if ever, been introduced. In continuous processing, quality checks have been built into the process, thus retaining the link between the doing and evaluating task within the process itself. However, in batch and line, the responsibility for completing the task and achieving the required levels of quality, while argued to be one and the same, are really two separate responsibilities (see Table 10–2).

Obviously, the most appropriate time to check conformance to specification is when the item is made. However, under the systems still often used in batch and line processes, work is checked after its production. Either the length of time between production and quality inspection or when quality checks are taken will have a direct bearing on a company's ability to minimize the repercussions of below-quality work.

This raises two important issues concerning quality that need to be agreed at the corporate level and then form part of manufacturing's response to the business need:

1. A *reactive or proactive approach to quality.* The first issue is to determine whether to adopt a reactive or proactive approach to quality. In the former, the emphasis is toward detection, with the objective of preventing faulty work being passed on to subsequent processes. This will minimize the costs involved in rectification, scrap, returned products, and nonrepeat business.

A proactive approach emphasizes prevention rather than detection. It requires allocating resources to make products right the first time, more of the time. This is achieved by reviewing the quality of design and conformance to identify the factors affecting these two features. Quality control is then designed around this analysis.

2. *The responsibility for quality.* The responsibility for quality concerns two separate issues. The first concerns defining the departmental responsibilities throughout the process; the second, the responsibility for measurement.

TABLE 10–3   **Baldrige Award (points allocation by category)**

Category	Points
Information and analysis	60
Strategic–quality analysis	90
Leadership	100
Human-resource utilization	150
Quality assurance of products and services	150
Quality results	150
Customer satisfaction	300
Total	1,000

In recent years, the distinction between quality assurance and quality control has become more marked. Quality assurance is the function charged with the task of developing the quality structure, and the responsibilities and activities within that structure, together with establishing procedures to ensure the organization meets the agreed quality levels for its products. Quality control is that aspect of quality assurance that concerns the practical means of securing product quality, as set out in the specification. The separation of roles between the people completing the work and those given specific responsibility for checking the quality achieved, albeit as a backup activity, has been in force for a number of decades. This separation has been further emphasized by the reporting systems that have developed in many organizations (see Figures 10–3 and 10–6).

To facilitate manufacturing's task, an infrastructure change has to be implemented. Quality control needs to revert to the set of activities for which manufacturing is responsible, while the quality checks need to form part of the operator's role.

The importance of this essential change is gaining widespread recognition, as illustrated by the points allocated to this orientation within the Baldrige Award[18] (see Table 10–3). However, the extent to which Western companies have incorporated these fundamental changes in their pursuit of quality improvements is not as extensive as generally assumed. Although commitment to quality improvement from top management is high, Baldrige examiners report that applicants "have been surprised to find they come up short at the other end of the organizational chart. Many companies with high-profile reputations for quality have been told to do more to empower their employees as well as their upper ranks."[19]

However, the importance of achieving high product quality is being clearly recognized. Respondents in Europe and the United States placed product quality as their

---

[18]The Malcolm Baldrige National Quality Award is a U.S. Government industry venture but supported solely by the industry-funded Baldrige Award Foundation. Started in 1988, the program entails assessment against the criteria given in Table 10–3.

[19]P. Burrows, "Five Lessons You Learn from (Baldrige) Award Entrants," *Electronic Business*, October 15, 1990, pp. 22–24.

number-one competitive priority over the following five years, clearly signaling an overall recognition of this issue.[20] At the corporate level, companies clearly illustrate the importance they attach to achieving major improvements in quality. IBM, for instance, admitted at the beginning of 1990 that its overall defect rate was around three sigma, or 66,810 defects per million operations. By 1994, IBM wants to reach six sigma, or 3.4 defects per million operations.[21]

The gains are considerable, not only in costs but also in customer relations and job interest. However, it will not happen overnight. Traditions die hard, and the investment in training needs to be clearly recognized. However, with the responsibility for good quality work now back where it belongs, companies can also move from the reactive approach that they invariably adopt, and almost dictated by the existing departmental and on-line responsibilities for quality, to the proactive approach necessary to ensure that manufacturing will be able to provide the quality requirements demanded by current and future markets.[22]

Control of Inventory

In most manufacturing companies, inventory is usually substantial, whereas, the methods used to control it are typically casual. They lack the level of sophistication and insight appropriate for an item that stands at some 30–40 percent of most companies' total assets. While decisions to use funds for plant and equipment, for instance, are normally carefully monitored, the relative effort and attention given to the control of inventory is generally too little and too late. Increases in inventory happen, and concern to exercise due control over this sizable asset comes after the event. This is because inventory control is based on a number of operational activities without the strategic overview of control warranted by an investment of this size.

There are two general characteristics about inventory that illustrate, above all, the level of business disinterest in its control and the underlying perspectives on which existing controls are built. First, many companies take complete physical counts of

---

[20]Interestingly, Japanese respondents in the same Manufacturing Features survey placed product quality as their number-four competitive priority. They are apparently now looking to other priorities to give them a competitive edge.

[21]B. C. P. Rayner, "Market-driven Quality: IBM's Six Sigma Crusade," *Electronics Business*, October 15, 1990, pp. 26–30.

[22]There are many references to the advantages to be gained and examples of the results of such decisions. These include J. M. Juran, "Product Quality—A Prescription for the West," *Management Review*, June 1981, pp. 9–20; Schonberger, *Japanese Manufacturing Techniques*, pp. 47–82 and 181–98; D. A. Garvin, "Quality on the Line," *Harvard Business Review*, September–October 1983, pp. 65–75; C. Lorenz, "A Shocking Indictment of American Mediocrity," *Financial Times*, October 17, 1983; T. Kona, *Strategy and Structure of Japanese Enterprises* (New York: Macmillan, 1984), pp. 194–196.; M. Imai, *Kaizen: The Key to Japanese Competitive Success* (New York: Random House, 1986), ch. 3; T. G. Gunn, *Manufacturing for Competitive Advantage: Being a World Class Manufacturer* (Cambridge, Mass: Ballinger, 1987); J. P. Alston, *The American Sumurai* (Berlin: Walter de Gruyter, 1989); B. G. Dale and J. J. Plunkett, *Managing Quality* (Hemel Hempstead: Philip Alan, 1990); N. Slack, *The Manufacturing Advantage* (London: Mercury, 1991); and M. J. Stahl and G. M. Bounds (eds.), *Competing Globally through Customer Value* (New York: Quorum Books, 1991).

stock on as few occasions as possible, often as little as twice a year to coincide with the financial accounting periods. Furthermore, as the date for stock taking approaches, companies commonly create an unrepresentative picture of inventory inside the business by holding off purchases at the front end and moving existing inventory inside the business itself. The rationale for this is to reduce the inventory holding *per se* and so record a more favorable position in relevant financial statements. This also reduces the size of the clerical task involved. Manufacturing companies look on these tasks as a chore rather than an opportunity to collect valuable data essential to the control of what is often the biggest single asset on their balance sheets.

Second, inventory breakdowns are normally expressed in terms of the stage the material has reached in the process: namely, raw materials/components, work in process, and finished goods. This choice, however, is made solely to facilitate the evaluation of inventory as an input into the profit-and-loss account and balance sheet. Thus, the outcome of this data-collection exercise is viewed primarily as a provision of information to the accounts function and not as an important opportunity to create the basis for controlling this large asset.

The purpose of having inventory is to provide a set of advantages that reflect a business' needs. Depending on what constitutes the needs in the marketplace and the agreed manufacturing requirements within the business, the size and spread of inventory will differ. Effective control is based on an understanding of why inventory is held where it is and what functions it provides. Currently, however, many companies attempt to control inventory by global, across-the-board mandates over short time periods. This approach neither reflects real control nor time dimensions.

Causal Analysis as a Basis for Inventory Control.   There are two broad categories of inventory: corporate and mainstream. Corporate is the type of inventory that does not provide a manufacturing function (often accounting for some 20 to 25 percent of the total holding).[23]

The types of corporate inventory are numerous and reflect the nature of the manufacturing company involved. Typical, of these are:

- Sales inventory to support customer agreements.
- Sales inventory owing to actual sales being lower than forecast.
- Marketing inventory to meet a product launch.
- Purchasing inventory incurred to achieve quantity discounts.
- Corporate safety stocks caused by uncertainty of supply (e.g., possible national or international strikes).
- Slow-moving inventory under various related subheadings.

The control of corporate inventory requires information on the stock by cause. Thus, once recognizing the inventory category and separating this into its appropriate type, the company can set targets in line with the business needs (and this obviously may not

---

[23]See Hill, *Production/Operations Management*, pp. 263–66, for a more detailed discussion on the types of corporate inventory and their control.

always be a reduction), charge responsibility for inventory control to the appropriate function, and monitor it. A company is then able to understand the return it receives for its investment, decide on the value for money associated with that holding, and use this information as part of its overall review of functions, customers, policies, and the like.

The function of mainstream inventory is to facilitate the manufacturing process at all stages. However, in order to exercise meaningful and effective control, the company must understand the types of inventory within this category and classify the relevant holding accordingly.

Three important aspects are involved in this:

1. *The dependent/independent demand principle.* When the rate of issue for an item does not directly relate to the use of any other item, it should be treated as an independent pattern of demand. Examples include finished goods and factored items. Conversely, items with demand linked to the use of other items are said to have a dependent demand pattern. For example, components and subassemblies. This distinction enables companies to recognize that whereas the demand for independent items will have to be arrived at through forecasting or similar techniques, the demand for dependent items can be calculated.

2. *The functions provided by mainstream inventory.* Holding mainstream inventory provides a number of distinct functions within manufacturing. These causes need to be distinguished, and inventory data collected accordingly. The functions are:

- *Decoupling inventory.* Separating one process from the next allows them to work independently and decouples otherwise dependent parts of the total operation. Decoupling inventory concerns materials waiting for processes so that each process can be most efficiently used. It is not found in jobbing, line, or continuous processing because the person and process, respectively, move the inventory from one operation to the next on a continuous basis. It is, however, at the very essence of batch manufacturing.

- *Cycle inventory.* This relates to the decision to manufacture a quantity of products (sometimes referred to as a lot or batch size) that reflects criteria such as set-up to production-run length, customer order size, and call-off patterns. The rationale for cycle inventory is to reduce set-up costs and to help maximize the use of process capacity by increasing production-run lengths.

- *Pipeline inventory.* This is the inventory needed to be held when companies decide to subcontract one or more processes to an outside supplier at some time during the total process lead time. All the inventory associated with this decision is classed as pipeline.

- *Capacity-related inventory.* One way to cope with anticipated sales is to plan production in line with sales forecasts. This, however, often leads to a situation of peak-capacity requirements involving overtime, recruitment of additional labor, and the holding of spare process capacity. Another way is to plan some sort of level production program, stockpiling inventories in the low-sales periods for selling in the high-sales periods. This is known as capacity-related inventory and concerns transferring work from one time period to the next in the form of inventory. It provides one way of stabilizing production capacity in an environment of fluctuating sales levels.

- *Buffer inventory.* This concerns the problem that average demand, by definition, varies around the average. In order to cope with this, companies hold higher levels of inventory to reflect this variation. Buffer inventory's function, therefore, is to help to protect the process core against the unpredictable variations in demand levels or supply availability. The higher the service level or the lower the level of stockout risk set up by a business, the greater the quantities of buffer inventory required. A decision to hold inventory in excess of this requirement, however, should be classed as safety stock and fall within a corporate inventory provision.

In undertaking this control task, an agreed area of the business is selected for analysis—it is not necessary to review the whole business. The purpose of the analysis concerns identifying where large blocks of inventory occur and not with assessing the whole of the inventory holding and the level of exactness called for in an annual stocktake, the results of which go into published accounts. Inventory is then identified by position in the process and by its function. If a parcel of inventory provides more than one function (e.g., those of cycle and decoupling), then an arbitrary split is made and the dual function recorded. As before, the data outcomes concern magnitude not exactness. Any large amounts of inventory are then further analyzed and systematically reduced.

The key to inventory reduction, therefore, concerns removing inventory that is not adding value. It eliminates the unnecessary and arrives at a level sufficient to support current systems and corporate commitments and decisions. To do this, companies need to identify the reasons why excess inventory has been generated, change the rules and procedures to stop this recurring, and use up existing inventory while preventing inflows of inventory except those that are necessary.

Many companies, however, compare current inventory levels with those proposed using alternative manufacturing planning and control systems. By doing this they compare current inadequate control with best-practice control of proposed alternatives. But companies should first reduce inventory levels to necessary norms and then decide whether or not the reduction benefits accruing from alternative proposals are sufficient to justify the investments and changes involved. In this way, decisions are made on a like-for-like basis, thus enabling companies to identify the real sources of improvement.[24]

3. *The 80/20 rule.* A review of inventory based on a Pareto analysis[25] will almost certainly reveal that some 20 percent of the items will account for about 80 percent of the value. Using this as the basis for an ABC classification allows a company to exercise tight control over the relatively few items that are high in value. However, on the low-value items, excess buffer inventory holdings allow the controls to be simple and the records to be minimal.

---

[24]Ibid., pp. 261–62, for further details on this point.

[25]A Pareto analysis orders the data from highest down to lowest. The list provided then helps to show the 80/20 relationship that exists between the data being reviewed.

Based on these three perspectives of inventory, the control exercised can now reflect the important, the large, and the relevant. Once a business knows why and how much inventory is being held it can divert attention, effort, and the level of control accordingly. Two examples to illustrate this approach will help to amplify the issues involved.

1. A company involved in manufacturing low-volume, standard products had 24 percent of its total assets tied up in work in process despite using a sophisticated scheduling system. The products involved represented hundreds of standard labor hours over many processes, including assembly, and were subject to schedule changes by customers. An analysis of its work in process revealed levels of decoupling inventory that were a distinct overprovision of this function. The 80/20 rule typically prevailed. As response to customers' schedule changes was considered to be part of manufacturing's task, the company took several decisions concerning its high inventory holding.

An ABC analysis on work in process by product enabled it to cut back on cycle inventory and to shorten the process lead time for high-value components and subassemblies deliberately. In the future, high-value parts were made strictly in line with a customer's orders and were accelerated through the various processes by giving them priority. Low-value components and subassemblies were made in excess of requirements and scheduled into the process well in advance of delivery needs. In this way, the advantages of cycle inventory were achieved for many items but at least-inventory investment. Similarly, they were now scheduled to "meander" through the processes in a controlled way while offering efficiency opportunities without incurring correspondingly high inventory investment.

2. A plant that was part of a large group of companies received an across-the-board corporate directive to reduce inventory by 15 to 20 percent in a given time period. The plant involved manufactured optional features for vehicles. However, to make a sale, the customer required short delivery response to minimize the off-the-road time for any vehicle. To provide this distinct order-winning criterion, the products had been designed to have a high proportion of standard parts and subassemblies to gain some economies of scale and to maximize coverage of the wide range of products involved, while minimizing inventory holdings. Manufacturing, to meet this short lead time, needed to hold all parts in stock so as to reduce the overall process lead time and to allow itself the time to respond to the market. Only when inventory's role within the manufacturing strategy was explained was the corporate directive rescinded.

Finally, when reviewing inventory holdings it is important to look at Table 5–1. It illustrates how the implications for inventory holdings of raw materials/components, work in process and finished goods would differ with each choice of process. As a starting point the trade-offs involved between inventory investment, plant utilization, efficiency, and other operational factors need also to be taken into account when reviewing the fundamental decisions addressed in Chapter 5. However, this in no way precludes a company from changing the mix in trade-offs that surround inventory investment. The description of just-in-time production systems given later provides an alternative approach to managing processes. In so doing it picks up a fresh set of trade-offs for manufacturing and the business, which, on the plus side, include a sharp reduction in inventory levels. It is essential, therefore, that the manufacturing strategy debate concerning process choice and the role of inventory in this configuration (see Table 5–1) explains and amplifies the implications for the business and the critical nature of the trade-offs involved.

Control of Manufacturing[26]

Many firms see manufacturing investment and agreements on markets to be independent sets of decisions. Few appreciate the need to link the two. The result, which has been a theme throughout the book, is that firms have made and continue to make large investments in process and manufacturing infrastructure without setting them within a strategic context. However, the high cost and fixed nature of manufacturing investments and their key role in helping to secure the short- and long-term prosperity of a business make this doubly risky.

No Strategy, Poor Systems.   One such area that illustrates the general problem outlined above is that of manufacturing planning and control (MPC) systems. As a large infrastructure investment and as a critical function in the management of manufacturing this provides a classic example of the panacea-driven approach that has characterized past decisions in the manufacturing function. Material requirements planning (MRP), just-in-time (JIT), and optimized production technology (OPT) are recent illustrations. Bought more for their apparent benefits than business fit, it is not surprising that previous research reported that 63 percent of the MRP applications studied[27] cost as much as $5 million, yet failed to realize their full benefits.

A medium-sized U.S. furniture company made high-volume standard products using simple process technologies, with few operations and little work-in-process inventory. To support short customer lead times there were high levels of finished goods inventory. The company controlled manufacturing using central scheduling and manual shopfloor controls supported by visual checking and verbal communications between departments. To improve equipment utilization, productivity, and order tracking on the shopfloor, the company installed a computer-based shopfloor control system with automated order-tracking, queue-control, and capacity-planned features costing about $0.75 million. In business terms, the principal area for improvement was an increased level of sales support by fulfilling customer orders more quickly while keeping the finished-goods inventory under control. The key to achieving this would have been to improve the master production-scheduling function to better reflect actual sales in plant schedules, so avoiding imbalances in finished-goods inventory characterized by shortages and excess stockholdings. The investment in the shopfloor control system was not only unnecessary but resulted in added paperwork, with a corresponding increase in overheads. It also diverted key supervisory effort from other areas.

Responding to the technology developments in the telecommunications field, a European company moved from electromechanical to electronic-based products. While

---

[26]This section is based on W. L. Berry and T. J. Hill, "Linking Systems to Strategy," *International Journal of Operations and Production Management* 12, no. 10 (1992), pp. 3–15.

[27]R. G. Schroder, "Material Requirements Planning: A Study of Implementation and Practice," American Production and Inventory Control Society, Falls Church, Va., 1981.

TABLE 10–4   Linking Manufacturing Strategy to the Design of the Master Production Schedule

Strategic Variables			Master Scheduling Approach*		
			MTO	ATO	MTS
Markets	Product	Type	Special	———>	Standard
		Range	Wide	———>	Predetermined and narrow
	Individual product volume per period		Low	———>	High
	Delivery	Speed	Difficult	———>	Easy
		Reliability	Difficult	———>	Easy
Manufacturing	Process choice		Jobbing/low volume batch	———>	High-volume batch/line
	Managing changes in sales and mix		Through order backlog	Through WIP or FG inventory	Through FG inventory
	Meeting delivery speed requirement		Through rescheduling requirements	Reduces process lead time	Eliminates process lead time

*MTO = make-to-order   MTS = make-to-stock   FG = finished goods
ATO = assemble-to-order   WIP = work-in-process

components for the old products were made in-house, using a range of batch processes and final assembly lines, the company purchased the new product technology in the form of components.

Beset with several dimensions of manufacturing change, the company retained its previous MRP system as a tested and proven device. However, in doing so it overlooked the critical shift in manufacturing. Whereas the old products required the emphasis to be placed on the control of a broad range of complex, internal processes and the inherent work-in-process inventory, the key control issues for the new products were vendor-scheduling and component-inventory management. Retaining the previous MRP system led to a failure to switch resources to vendor-scheduling and to highlight component as opposed to work-in-process holding as the key area of inventory control. As a result, pressure was placed in the wrong areas, shortages increased, and the control system was unable to cope with the new demands.

A U.K. aerospace company manufacturing a wide range of products at all stages in their life-cycles invested in a comprehensive, standard computer-based MRP system to meet all its requirements. The complexity of the data, training needs, and system running and support requirements were reflected in the costs involved—$8 million over a two-and-a-half-year period plus high running costs. A postinstallation review highlighted that although the system met the needs of original equipment products, it did not meet the needs of the spares business. It was estimated that 60 percent of the original data base investment was not necessary. Instead, the planning and control needs of the spares business could have been better provided, at significantly less

TABLE 10–5   Linking Manufacturing Strategy to the Design of the Material Planning Approach

Strategic Variables			Material Planning Approach	
			Time-Phased	Rate-based
Markets	Product	Type	Special	Standard
		Range	Wide	Narrow
	Individual product volume per period		Low	High
	Ability to cope with changes in product mix within a period		High potential	Limited
	Delivery	Schedule changes	Difficult	Easy
		Speed	Through scheduling excess capacity	Through inventory
Manufacturing	Process choice*		Batch	Line
	Source of cost reduction	Overhead	No	Yes
		Inventory	No	Yes

*In jobbing, shopfloor control is handled by the operator.

cost, by simplified master scheduling, materials planning, and shopfloor controls; there was no need for the order-tracking, queue-control, and priority-despatching features essential to the OEM part of the business.

From Panaceas to Policy

The examples given in the last section show how firms may invest in planning and control systems that, though sound in themselves, do not fit the needs of the business. The outcome not only results in unnecessary expenditure but also leads firms to assume that this aspect of manufacturing has been resolved.

The way for companies to improve the fit of these investments to the needs of the business is to link markets to processes and to MPC systems. This not only requires clear understanding of markets and the subsequent link to manufacturing but also of the way that MPC systems differ in themselves and the key characteristics they embody.

The market debate has been a consistent theme, and the steps involved have been highlighted earlier. With this complete, companies next have to link markets through manufacturing strategy to the design of the master production schedule (MPS). The conceptual base for explaining differences and appropriate responses is given in Table 10–4. This shows how companies need to select the base type of MPS to reflect the characteristics of their markets while similarly matching other aspects of manufacturing on relevant dimensions. In this way, companies develop coordinated responses in line with market needs to improve the level of support within manufacturing.

In the same way, firms must review the other facets of planning and control systems to identify and develop relevant parts of the MPC system. Table 10–5 identifies

TABLE 10-6   Linking Manufacturing Strategy to the Design of the Shopfloor Control System

Strategic Variables			Shopfloor Control Approach	
			Push Type	Pull Type
Markets	Product	Type	Special	Standard
		Range	Wide	Narrow
	Individual product volume per period		Low	High
	Accommodating demand versatility	Total volume	Easy/Incremental	Difficult/stepped
		Product mix	High	Low
	Delivery	Speed	Achieved by schedule change	Achieved through finished goods inventory
		Schedule changes	More difficult	Less difficult
Manufacturing	Process choice*		Jobbing/low-volume batch	High-volume batch/line
	Source of cost reduction	Overheads	Low	High
		Inventory	Low	High
	Changeover cost		High	Low
	Control of manufacturing	Key feature	Order status	Flow of materials
		Basis	Person/system*	System
		Ease of task	Complex	Easy

*In jobbing, shopfloor control is handled by the operator.

the market and the manufacturing implications in terms of the design of materials planning approach. It helps to explain why time-phased or rate-based approaches are appropriate given the different market characteristics manufacturing needs to support. In addition, it shows appropriate processes while identifying the orientation of selected key tasks in manufacturing. Finally, Table 10–6 links these to the design of the shopfloor control system and illustrates the rationale for alternative control approaches. Once again, it shows how alternative shopfloor control approaches line up with different market features and also provides a link to key manufacturing responses and tasks.

Thus, Tables 10–4 to 10–6 provide an overview of MPC systems and illustrate the way in which market differences require different MPC-system responses. They help to show how the elements of alternative systems are consistent within themselves and how the development of appropriate responses needs to be accomplished within all facets of this major aspect of manufacturing infrastructure provision. Companies who fail to make these essential links will invest in systems that are inappropriate for the markets in which they compete and hinder manufacturing's ability to meet customer needs.

TABLE 10–7 The Relevant Manufacturing Tasks and MPC System Investments of Two Companies Serving Different Markets*

Company	Market Characteristics	Order-Winners and Qualifiers	Manufacturing: Task	Manufacturing: Features	Manufacturing Strategy: Master Production Scheduling	Manufacturing Strategy: Material Planning	Manufacturing Strategy: Shopfloor Control

Company A	• Customized products
	• Wide product range
	• Low volume per product
	• Make-to-order
	• Initial versus repeat orders
	• Future order call-offs
		• Design capability
		• Delivery speed
		• Delivery reliability (Q Q)
		• Quality (Q)
		• Price (Q)
			• To reduce process leadtime
			• Manufacture to engineering specifications and quality standards
			• To achieve delivery reliability
				• Batch manufacturing
				• Long process routings
				• High precision work
				• Accommodate delivery and design changes
				• Labor cost equals 60 percent
				• Control of actual costs
				• Process and product uncertainties
					• Make-to-order/assemble-to-order
					  +Customer orders
					  +Anticipated orders
					  +Forecast orders
					• Used for rough cut capacity planning due to long lead-time impact on delivery
					• Customer order promising
						• Time-phased material planning
						• Material is particular to customer orders
						• High obsolescence risk
						• Extra materials needed for scrapped items
						• Trade-off: shorter lead time versus raw material inventory
							• Push system
							• Priority of scheduling of shop orders
							• System supported by dispatching and production controller personnel
							• Capacity requirements planning by work center
							• Order tracking and status information

Manufacturing Strategy

Company	Market Characteristics	Order-Winners and Qualifiers	Manufacturing		Manufacturing Planning and Control System		
			Task	Features	Master Production Scheduling	Material Planning	Shopfloor Control
Company B	• Narrow product range • Standard products • High-volume per product • Seasonal demand • Sales from finished goods inventory at distributors • Introduction of new products • Changing product mix	• Price • Delivery speed (through finished goods inventory in distribution divisions) • Quality (Q) • Delivery reliability (Q) • Base design and (Q) peripheral design changes	• To provide a low-cost manufacturing support capability • To support the marketing activity with high delivery speed through finished goods inventory	• High-volume batch and line production process • Short set-up times; Small batch sizes • Low-cost manufacturing • Low labor cost • High material cost • Inventory reduction (raw material, components, and WIP) • Overhead reduction (low MPC costs)	• Make-to-stock • Manufacture to forecast • Level production • Three-month frozen planning horizon • Manufacture to replenish distribution inventories	• Rate-based material planning	• Pull system • Kanban containers • JIT flow of material • Low raw material, component, and WIP inventory

*Q denotes a qualifier, a capability required in order for the company to enter and remain in its market; QQ denotes an order-losing sensitive qualifier, a capability that is not supported leads to a rapid loss of business.

Why Don't Panaceas Work?

Solutions presuppose that market requirements and corporate characteristics are the same. But today, nothing is further from the truth. Markets are not characterized by similarity but by difference. Therefore, linking elements of manufacturing strategy to markets is fundamental. A sound manufacturing strategy is one where decisions and investments in processes and infrastructure are consistent with a company's markets. Table 10–7 provides an illustration of two companies competing in different markets. It shows the link between their markets and relevant order-winners and qualifiers, the corresponding manufacturing tasks, and the supporting processes and manufacturing planning and control systems.

It starts by showing the key differences in the markets served by the two companies. Tracing across from these market characteristics to the manufacturing responses shows clear differences in the latter while illustrating how each set of responses is consistent with the market needs of each company.

This is how the task of manufacturing—in all facets of its support for the varied needs of markets—needs to be fulfilled. Without the critical step of linking clear market definition to an understanding of the conceptual phase of manufacturing process and infrastructure options, the relevant and consistent choices will not be made, and the panacea-driven approaches will be perpetuated.

Conclusion

The JIT production system within Toyota has all the classic hallmarks of strategic infrastructure development. It works well because Toyota has demonstrated that it understands the need to reconcile the three major phases in its business—the before phase (its suppliers), the owned phase (its own processes), and the forward phase (the sale of cars through its networks). It works because Toyota has managed its forward phase in such a way that it freezes schedules, thus demanding or requiring little change in its own or its suppliers' processes. In this way, it has cushioned its manufacturing core from the instability of the marketplace, thus preventing it from being exposed. The stability so created means that Toyota is able to demand exact deliveries, so much a feature of the JIT production system. In this way, it has earned this favored position and can and does, therefore, demand these benefits from supplies, thus forcing the inventory forward and out of the system, rather than the other way round.

Many Western car companies do not appreciate these essential links. They show due sensitivity in the forward phase because they must generate goodwill and motivate their distributors to sell more cars. In the before phase, the converse happens. They believe here that threatening suppliers will bring best results. And this is a very telling difference.

Providing a clear manufacturing strategy for the business enables those responsible for infrastructure development to work from a common base, in a common direction, to meet a common requirement. Historical, personal, and in some instances almost esoteric views fall by the wayside to be replaced by a strategic underpinning of infrastructure. This provides relevance by meeting the needs of the business and continuity by ensuring that the long-term requirements are an integral part of current thinking and decisions. Without a strategy-based approach these wide multifunctional areas are open to personal judgments, prone to fixed ideas, and swayed by arguments based on what specialists can readily provide rather than the inputs necessary to meet the dimensions of manufacturing. The interactive nature of the dynamics within manufacturing, not being the responsibility of any one specialist or support function, is not at the forefront of the argument or application. The responsibility for this is clearly and wholly manufacturing's. Thus, underpinning these with a clear and well-argued manufacturing strategy will provide the direction and mechanism for common evaluation.

On an entirely practical basis, the development and introduction of a payment system illustrates how any facet of infrastructure can and needs to be designed to support a company's competitive strategy, and not to be in keeping with the efficiency oriented perception of manufacturing's strategic role.

A medium-sized manufacturing company wished to replace its existing payment scheme for hourly-paid employees, which had fallen into disrepute. The initial proposals centered on a classic productivity-based scheme, involving individual bonus-related earnings. When it recognized the need to develop this in the context of a manufacturing strategy, the company postponed work on the scheme until the necessary, earlier work was completed. Three order-winning qualifying criteria were highlighted—delivery speed, delivery reliability, and price. With these now forming the basis of the manufacturing task, the scheme that was eventually developed reflected these criteria. Delivery performance now accounts for half the potential performance earnings, while the other half is for improvements in productivity. Furthermore, to encourage a broader view of work, the payments were made twice a year on factory-wide achievement related to attendance time.

The shape and emphasis now more accurately reflected the needs of the business and encouraged an important part of manufacturing's contribution by the way it was designed.

The Last Word: "Why the West Will Lose"

On the need to challenge the way in which U.S. companies organize themselves and to consider the definitions of role, responsibility, authority, specialists, and all the other facets of organizations, the last word belongs to Mr. Konosuke Matsushita. The difference in views is stark, and the challenge to rethink existing approaches is clearly stated. One thing is certain—to be successful in the future, companies will need to be adaptive and effectively use all the resources within the business.

We are going to win and the industrial West is going to lose: there is nothing much you can do about it, because the reasons for your failure are within yourselves.

Your firms are built on the Taylor model; even worse, so are your heads. With your bosses doing the thinking, while the workers wield the screwdrivers, you are convinced deep down that this is the right way to run a business.

For you, the essence of management is getting the ideas out of the heads of the bosses into the hands of labor.

We are beyond the Taylor model: business, we know, is now so complex and difficult, the survival of firms so hazardous in an environment increasingly unpredictable, competitive, and fraught with danger, that their continued existence depends on the day-to-day mobilization of every ounce of intelligence.

For us, the core of management is precisely this art of mobilizing and pulling together the intellectual resources of all employees in the service of the firm. Because we have measured better than you the scope of the new technological and economic challenges, we know that the intelligence of a handful of technocrats, however brilliant and smart they may be, is no longer enough for a real chance of success.

Only by drawing on the combined brain power of all its employees can a firm face up to the turbulence and constraints of today's environment.

This is why our large companies give their employees three to four times more training than yours; this is why they foster within the firm such intensive exchange and communication; this is why they seek constantly everybody's suggestions and why they demand from the educational system increasing numbers of graduates as well as bright and well-educated generalists, because these people are the lifeblood of industry.

Your "socially-minded bosses," often full of good intentions, believe their duty is to protect the people in their firms. We, on the other hand, are realists and consider it our duty to get our own people to defend their firms, which will pay them back a hundredfold for their dedication. By doing this, we end up by being more "social" than you.

SOURCE: K. Matsushita. "Why the West Will Lose: Extracts from Remarks Made by Mr. Konosuke Matsushita of the Matsushita Electric Industrial Company, Japan to a Group of Western Managers," *Industrial Participation.* Spring 1985, p. 8.

CHAPTER 11

Accounting and Financial Perspectives and Manufacturing Strategy

Two common denominators are used in manufacturing businesses as the basis for control and performance measurement. The first is the time base on which manufacturing principally works. Product mix and volumes, capacity, efficiency, utilization, and productivity are all normally measured by time. The second common denominator is that of money. At the corporate level, forecast activity levels, performance measures, levels of investment, and similar activities use the money base. The importance of getting the correct links between the time-based and money-based measures is self-evident. Correct not only in terms of being accurate, but also in reflecting the key perspectives associated with the business itself.

The money-based denominator issues addressed in this chapter are controlled by what, in many companies, is frequently one of the least developed functions: accounting and finance. Based on approaches established when business activities were very different, this area has not really faced up to resolving many of the important changes in business with appropriate developments. This chapter highlights a number of areas that need to be addressed from the point of view of both manufacturing and overall strategy. It will link the areas of manufacturing and corporate strategy with accounting and finance and illustrate some of the key issues that need to be developed and the essential direction these improvements need to take. In addition, it will show the ways in which manufacturing strategy will influence and, in some cases, facilitate some of these changes, while also drawing attention to the essential nature of manufacturing's needs and the accounting and financial information provision.

The purpose of this chapter is to make a number of critical observations about the impact on manufacturing of finance and accounting practices. The observations are made from a manufacturing executive's perspective; hence, they may well be provocative when examined by the professional accountant. If this causes debate between manufacturing and finance executives, the purpose of this chapter is achieved. Solutions to the issues addressed must be worked out in the context of a particular company's corporate and manufacturing strategies. Since the financial systems in a

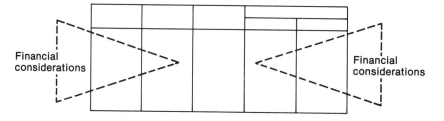

business can, and do, have a major impact on manufacturing's ability to develop and maintain effective competitive strategies, one essential objective of the finance function must be to give manufacturing the ability to measure and assess its performance accurately in relation to major competitors and the competitive value of investment proposals. The chapter deals with two broad areas of interaction between finance and manufacturing: first, the effect on manufacturing strategy of investment appraisal methods; second, how management accounting systems critically affect the control and performance measurement of manufacturing operations.

Investment Decisions

The approach to developing a manufacturing strategy was explained in some detail in earlier chapters. One important consideration highlighted in those explanations was the level of alternative investments associated with different decisions (see Figure 11–1). Many organizations, bounded by cash limitations, need to commit their scarce resources wisely. However, the criteria for assessing the level or nature of this critical corporate decision have rarely been arrived at with the care and in-depth analysis that is warranted. In many companies, investment decisions initially chosen or stimulated by corporate competitive requirements are finally evaluated solely by accounting measures and methods of appraisal. The effect of these financial measures on both strategy and the consequent investment decisions is illustrated by the framework introduced in Chapter 2. Accounting methods of investment appraisal are generally based on one important premise—the relative return on capital associated with each investment proposal under review. With capital investment in limited supply and capital rationing a widespread consequence, the argument to invest predominantly on the basis of return is not only built into the appraisal system itself, but invariably is reinforced by the discussion and argument that will take place. In this way, the figures will unwittingly support investment return as the predominant or even exclusive measure on which to assess these key corporate strategy decisions.

The consequences of this undue weighting have been felt by many companies, and the ramifications within manufacturing industry have been widespread. The necessity to question this view of investment decisions has stimulated a series of well-argued articles and papers, which illustrate the simplistic nature of the accounting perspective and challenge its unevaluated application. As early as 1974, Dean declared that "because of our obsessive concentration in short-term gains and profits, U.S. technology is stalemated.''[1] Hayes and Abernathy's 1980 article said it all in the title, ''Managing Our Way to Economic Decline,''[2] and again with Garvin, Hayes captured the essence of the issues in the article ''Managing as if Tomorrow Mattered''[3] in which they make, among other things, a concerted challenge on current accounting approaches to investment appraisal. They provide a detailed argument to support their view that companies have increasingly turned to sophisticated, analytical techniques to evaluate investment proposals. The long-term result has been that many of the managers involved have ''unintentionally jeopardized their companies' future.'' As Hayes and Gavin conclude, ''investment decisions that discount the future may result in high present values, but bleak tomorrows.''

Since then, the basic criticisms have been taken on by others, particularly from the accounting profession. Of these, Kaplan well illustrates these growing concerns, as clearly shown in the title of his book with Johnson, *Relevance Lost: The Rise and Fall of Management Accounting*[4] and again with Cooper in the two articles, ''How Cost Accounting Distorts Product Costs''[5] and ''Measure Costs Right: Make the Right Decision.''[6]

The Need for a Strategic View of Investments

When evaluating investments, companies need to make a strategy-based review. What constitutes a sound investment needs to be measured by its contribution to the agreed corporate strategy, and not by how well it meets the criteria laid down by a set of accounting rules and evaluations. In one of several critiques of current management accounting, Simmonds observes that,

> the emphasis . . . accounting and finance have placed on return on investment over the years has subtly transmuted into a widely- and deeply-held belief that return comes from the investments themselves. . . . The truth is much different. Sustained profit comes from the competitive market position. New production investment to expand sales must imply a change in competitive position, and it is this change that should be the focus of the investment review. Without it, the calculations must be a nonsense.[7]

---

[1] R. C. Dean, Jr. ''The Temporal Mismatch—Innovation's Pace versus Management's Time Horizon,'' *Research Management*, May 1974, pp. 12–15.

[2] R. H. Hayes and J. Abernathy, ''Managing Our Way to Economic Decline,'' *Harvard Business Review*, July–August 1980, pp. 66–77.

[3] R. H. Hayes and D. A. Garvin, ''Managing as if Tomorrow Mattered,'' *Harvard Business Review*, May–June 1982, pp. 71–79.

[4] H. T. Johnson and R. S. Kaplan, *Relevance Lost: The Rise and Fall of Management Accounting* (Boston: Harvard Business School Press, 1987) includes important insights into accounting systems, for example, Chapter 8. ''The 1980s: The Obsolescence of Management Accounting Systems.''

[5] R. Cooper and R. S. Kaplan, ''How Cost Accounting Distorts Product Costs,'' *Management Accounting*, April 1985, pp. 20–27.

[6] R. Cooper and R. S. Kaplan, ''Measure Costs Right: Make the Right Decisions,'' *Harvard Business Review*, September–October 1988, pp. 96–103.

[7] K. Simmonds, ''Strategic Management Accounting,'' in R. Crowe (ed.), *Handbook of Management Accounting*, 2nd ed. (Aldershot: Gower Publishing, 1988), pp. 25–48.

This sleight of hand has been detected by all too few companies. Consequently, the key factor by which investment proposals have been assessed has increasingly swung away from strategy considerations toward levels of investment return *per se.* Return must be defined in terms of improved long-term competitiveness rather than just short-term measures.

Changing the basis of investment appraisal is both complex and fraught with difficulties. It is one of those issues in which manufacturing executives have traditionally felt relatively weak, those who control the cash are professionally very strong. The debate has therefore been one-sided, with manufacturing the casualty by default. The arguments that investments must provide a quick payback are financially, and emotionally, attractive. They tend, however, to oversimplify the investment issues at stake and fail to drive executives toward determining and analyzing those fundamental criteria that constitute the components of competitive strategy.

A short section on investment can only begin to open up the debate from the manufacturing perspective by providing some guidelines that manufacturing can use to raise key questions. The hope is that finance executives will also use them to develop their own appreciation of the strategic issues involved in manufacturing investment decisions. Nine key contentions are made, each of which is expanded to give substance, but none can be claimed to be comprehensively examined. They are:

1. Investment decisions must be based on order-winning criteria.
2. Financial control systems need to be developed to meet the needs of the investment evaluation process.
3. Investments are not separate decisions but need to be considered as part of a corporate whole.
4. There can be only one given reason to substantiate an investment proposal.
5. Excessive use of return on investment (ROI) distorts strategy building.
6. Government grants are not necessarily golden handshakes.
7. Linking investment to product life cycles reduces risks.
8. Manufacturing must test the process implications of product life cycle forecasts.
9. Investment decisions must quantify infrastructure requirements.

Investment Decisions Must Be Based on Order-Winning Criteria

The impact of investment policy and appraisal methods on manufacturing strategy's contribution to the competitiveness of a business is clearly significant. If high hurdle rates are imposed, capital investment will invariably decrease. In times of capital rationing, the argument put forward in support of high return-on-investment thresholds is that they motivate a company to cream off the more attractive investment proposals and hence use available funds for the best opportunities. But this line of argument fails to assess the relevance of investment proposals in the context of an agreed corporate strategy. The result, at best, is hit-and-miss alignment of essential investments with manufacturing's strategic contribution; at worst, the investments essential for manufacturing to provide its contribution to market objectives are not even made.

For instance, delays in appropriate investment would lead to costs not declining as expected. Hence, achieved experience curve gains would fall off and if the delay itself and extent of the investment requirement were large, loss of market share would eventually follow.[8]

Manufacturing strategy arguments for process investment to meet order-winning criteria, other than price and the associated low-cost manufacturing task, come up against the difficulties of accounting and finance-based rationale. Proposals, for instance, to invest in processes that increase production flexibility when customer response and delivery speed are the key order-winning criteria will be difficult to prepare in an appraisal system where return on investment is paramount. Similar forces will also work against facilities focus, irrespective of the importance of its role within manufacturing's support of the business needs. As explained in Chapter 7, focus will invariably lead to process duplication. However, investment appraisal systems often fail to incorporate as part of the evaluation procedure the need to orient facilities to better meet the order-winning criteria of markets. This, by implication, gives undue weight to return on investment or capacity utilization and will militate against focus in manufacturing.

Other accounting and financial perspectives will also work against the pursuit of focus in manufacturing. This function's desire and argument to manage earnings and cash flows by smoothing cyclical business swings carries substantial weight. However, focused manufacturing requires greater interaction between manufacturing and sales/marketing which leads to a higher level of shared dependence between these two prime parts of business. This argues against smoothing, with the dynamics of sustaining and improving market share growing in significance and carrying more weight than the smoothing argument of accounting and finance.[9]

Investments such as computer-aided design (CAD) provide an example of the limitations in the accounting approach to investment appraisal. CAD is usually evaluated on the cost savings attributed to its introduction. However, a significant gain associated with this investment is the speed of response to customer changes, particularly in a make-to-order business. Often companies do not recognize this increased competitiveness as part of corporate strategy. So, the contribution that CAD can make in corporate strategy support will neither be evaluated as part of the investment appraisal nor systematically developed and exploited at all stages in the business.

In a reflective mood, Drucker pinpoints a belief in their own accounting figures as one of the common mistakes made by companies, which always leads to trouble.

---

[8]Several authors highlight these types of consequences including Boston Consulting Group, "The Experience Curve—Reviewed: II History;" S. Rose, "The Secrets of Japan's Export Prowess," *Fortune,* January 30, 1978, pp. 56–62; and Simmonds, "Strategic Management Accounting."

[9]This argument also forms part of S. C. Wheelwright's research paper no. 517, "Facilities Focus: A Study of Concepts and Practices Related to Its Definition, Evaluation, Significance, and Application in Manufacturing Firms," Graduate School of Business, Stanford University, December 12, 1979, p. 55.

The conventions are very inadequate, inappropriate. . . . It gives [companies] the wrong information. They don't know what the real savings are. . . . Cost accounting gives you information on the cost of doing, but not on the cost of not doing—which is increasingly the bigger cost. Quality and downtime are neither of them in the model.[10]

In developing a sound understanding of their need to compete effectively in different market segments, companies will recognize the importance of relevant order-winners. With these established and reflected in the evaluation of manufacturing performance, companies can assess their importance and take them into account when judging appropriate investments. Until then, companies will continue to use apparently "hard" data as the predominant, or even sole, arbitrator. Thus, in developing manufacturing strategy companies must recognize the role of order-winners in the evaluation procedure and ensure that they reflect the business and not accounting conventions.

An assessment of current and future markets in terms of order-winning criteria is essential in a company's investment proposal procedure, especially when investments are based on a forecast sales increase. This will be a review of the way that both the existing and proposed capacity support relevant order-winners. In particular, it should identify levels of match or mismatch with an eye toward changing the way the company will win current and future orders.

Financial Control Systems Must Meet the Needs of the Investment Evaluation Process

Financial control systems tend to be designed to meet the needs of accountants; consequently, they are usually structured around a network of expense codes/account numbers, clinically constructed to facilitate electronic processing and the consolidation of final accounts and budget reports. From the accountant's viewpoint, this is a reasonable way of handling what is often complex analysis. The result, however, is that business transactions are then analyzed on the basis of the account codes available and thus often squeezed through a straitjacket of top-down apportionment to provide accountants with a view of expenditure and its relationship to business activity.

Taking such an approach, many financial control systems seek to trace actual expenditure to points of authorization and compare it to planned expenditure. The authorization provides the link on which to establish explanation and the formulation of corrective action. As highlighted in the last section, these evaluation procedures create major problems for a manufacturing company seeking to update its technology in response to order-winning criteria. The order-winning criteria may be one of two types:

- Product oriented; for example, quality conformance, lowest cost supply, or modular construction.
- Process oriented: for example, lead time, quantity ordered, or adaptability to product range or customer order size.

---

[10]G. Foster, "Drucker on the Record," *Management Today,* September 1987, pp. 58–59 and 110.

TABLE 11–1   Typical Financial Control System Provision versus Investment Evaluation Requirement

Dimension	Financial Control System Provision	Investment Evaluation Process Requirement
Direction	Backward • Examine expected historical trading performance	Forward • Project future performance
Orientation	Internal • Examine and report on current business performance	External • Evaluate current and future markets and competitors
Time scale	Short-term • Review performance monthly	Long-term • Examine expected performance over a given period
Expenditure base	Revenue expenditure • Trace performance on the evaluation of revenue	Capital expenditure • Evaluate investment in facilities to incorporate risk
Control base	Return on investment • Assess return in respect of the net capital employed	Cash-flow control • Relate expected cash flows to initial cash outlays

Existing financial control systems tend not to provide management with a realistic basis for analysis against these criteria. In fact, in some instances, existing systems are misleading.

Table 11–1 provides a summary of some of the key differences between traditional financial analysis (geared to a steady state, low-variety, high-volume, and slowly changing business environment) and the approaches to analysis required by the highly competitive nature of today's business environment.

Investments Decisions—Not Separate but Part of a Corporate Whole

Companies with more than one site, particularly multinationals, need to review investments within the context of total corporate markets and total manufacturing provision. In the past, investments have tended to be taken as a series of separate decisions. At best, companies have identified process overlaps, but usually they have not reviewed corporate marketing and manufacturing strategies for the whole business. The result is that the link between current and proposed investments has not been forged. The outcomes of this include excess capacity, uncoordinated strategic responses, conflict, and a failure to capitalize on corporate size and worldwide presence. One executive reflected on his company's failure to include separate decisions as part of a corporate whole: "the outcome is that whereas the group has companies everywhere [global reach] it does not compete on a global basis." Part of the problem—and one of the outcomes—for this company was that investments, being reviewed as separate decisions, did not require the corporate whole to be part of the essential context for these decisions. Overcapacity was rampant.

Given the increasingly competitive nature of global markets, companies need to move toward total reviews of their many businesses in order to assess within and between geographical regions. Only in this way can manufacturing's response be continuously reshaped. This will not only improve the fit between existing capacity, capabilities, and chosen markets, it will also provide an overall view of existing manufacturing capabilities for current and future markets, the necessary investments, and the appropriate location of these within the total business.

There Can Be Only One Reason to Substantiate an Investment Proposal

Investment appraisals submitted for review will typically include an extensive list of arguments and reasons for supporting a particular proposal. In many companies, the appraisal procedure has developed into an art form. Not only are the numbers massaged, but also the rationale underpinning the investment typically encompasses a long list of arguments in the belief that the cumulative weight of these will win the day. Consequently, the essential clarity that should pervade these critical proposals is neither recognized as being essential nor required in the evaluating decision procedure.

This results in two major disadvantages:

1. *Stated reasons do not always reflect reality.* In many instances, proposals reflect corporate norms and expectations that are recognized to be prerequisitesfor consideration let alone success. As Table 11–2 shows,[11] key decisions are often taken for undisclosed reasons and essential control of investments and agreement on their underlying support for a business is obviated.

2. *The essential argument needed to distill investment issues and insights is not considered necessary.* If investment proposals do not require a distinction to be drawn between prime and other reasons, the essential argument needed to distill the key issues is not an inherent part of these procedures. Hence, the rigor necessary for sound strategic argument is typically not undertaken. Furthermore, with the passage of time the real reasons for investments are lost and postinvestment evaluations, if undertaken at all, are set against wrong strategic dimensions. The outcome is that "before" and "after" evaluations are typically not recognized as key steps in investment proposal procedures.

Companies, therefore, should adopt the maxim that there can be only one given reason to substantiate an investment proposal. The logic may appear at first to be simplistic, but the rationale is sound. If one reason alone cannot support an investment, the substance and focus of the arguments need to be questioned. While such a procedure does not disallow listing secondary reasons, it will force strategic debate and clarify the essential rationale underpinning these key decisions.

---

[11]S. Parkinson, T. J. Hill, and G. Walker, "Diagnosing Customer and Competitor Influences on Manufacturing Strategy," in F. Bradley (ed.), *Marketing Thought around the World,* Proceedings of the 20th Annual Conference of the European Marketing Academy, Dublin, May 1991, pp. 741–55.

TABLE 11-2   Documented and Perceived Reasons for All Investments over a Two-and-a-Half Year Period—U.K. Manufacturing Company

Purchase Reasons	Documented	Perceived
Cost reduction	50*	19†
Update/introduce new technology	37	55
Increase throughput/productivity	37	17
Increase capacity	37	27
Part of a reorganization	28	34
Improve quality	25	16
Process dedication requirement	25	21
Reduce changeover times	21	—
Improve product flexibility	20	—
New process/existing technology	18	1
Reduce supervisory costs	16	12
Purchase of available machine	15	17
Improve material control	10	—
Reduce lead times	6	—
Process modernization	5	22
Automate process	4	—

*To be read: In 50 percent of the cases cost reduction was documented as a reason for investment.
†To be read: In 19 percent of the cases, cost reduction was perceived to be a reason for investment. Perceived reasons were attained sometimes after investment had been made.

Excessive Use of ROI Distorts Strategy Building

North American companies, highly sensitive to the shareholders' view of short-term declines in profits, have become all the more prone to adopting a short payback posture. Furthermore, in times of low-profit performance, the pressure invariably increases to effect short-term recovery programs as a way of demonstrating improvement and management action. In turn, the argument to set high thresholds can win the day when inadequate strategic direction and agreement have been reached, or when the real need for investment has not been identified. Like drowning men clutching at straws, companies are attracted by the promise of higher returns. But investments in manufacturing processes and infrastructure taken out of their strategic context can commit a company for years ahead in an inappropriate direction. Although procedures require potential benefits to be clearly explained before investments are made, few companies rigorously assess the actual level of benefits achieved to determine the extent to which reality measured up to the proposals and to identify why any significant disparities arise. A U.K. survey in the early 1990s verified this practice. It found that while 96 percent of respondents reported a requirement to demonstrate quantifiable future benefits from capital investment, only 58 percent validated these after the fact.[12] While hindsight is not a substitute for foresight, such assessments provide a

---

[12]R. Davies, C. Downes, and R. Sweeting, "*U.K. Survey of Cost Management Techniques and Practices, 1990/91*" (Price Waterhouse, 1991), p. 11.

review of the effectiveness of these critical decisions. These analyses not only identify the actual level of return but also enable a company to measure the extent to which past investments have supported its corporate strategic requirements.

The approach to investment appraisal in Japan and West Germany has a different basis. When they invest they are often prepared to sacrifice the short-term for longer-term profits that accrue from market share and increased volumes. In this way, they demonstrate two important differences in approach. First, they avoid the delusion that in an imprecise environment, numbers are precise and thereby reliable; that is, they understand that the use of numbers does not reduce risk. Second, they accept that to run a successful business, risks must be taken.

Ohmae summarizes the clear difference in approach between Western and Japanese businessmen. Discussing the investments made by two Japanese companies, he concludes that "in neither case . . . is any attention given to return on investment (ROI) or payback period, let alone to discounted cash flow. In both, the dominant investment criterion is whether the new business is good for the corporation as a whole."[13] Ohmae illustrates these differences by posing the following questions:

> How many contemporary U.S. corporations relying on ROI yardsticks would have embarked on the development of a business that required a twenty-year incubation period, as did Nippon Electric Company with its computer and semiconductor businesses? . . . Would Honda have so obstinately persisted in using its motorbike profits to bring its clean-engine vehicle to market if it were a corporation that measured the ROI of each product line and made its decisions accordingly? In fact, would any manufacturers be entering the four-wheel vehicle market in today's environment if ROI were the investment criterion?[14]

In many companies, a by-product of the emphasis on ROI in the corporate evaluation of investments has been an increasing tendency to view these proposals as a series of one-off, unrelated events, and not, as they invariably are, characterized by strategic sequence. Only when companies review investment decisions in the light of their corporate strategies, and in turn their marketing and manufacturing strategies, will the essential cohesion be established. Until this happens, companies will be in danger of investing in ways that will not give them the necessary synergistic gains of strategic coherence. An example of what happens is provided by a company involved in the manufacture of office equipment and supplies. Over the years, the company had added on capacity in a piecemeal way. It eventually had seven manufacturing units in the same road, only two of which were interconnected. On paper, buying new sites as they were required made a better return on investment than resiting the business. However, the costs of handling and transport between units added complexity and overhead duplication. The position was only assessed when a new chief executive called a halt to the proposal to add another part to the "rabbit warren."

---

[13]K. Ohmae, "Japan: From Stereotypes to Specifics," *The McKinsey Quarterly,* Spring 1982, pp. 2–33.

[14]Ibid., p. 3.

Government Grants Are Not Necessarily Golden Handshakes

With disproportionately high unemployment rates in parts of many Western countries and the impact of declining primary and secondary sectors of the economy, most governments have, understandably, pursued a policy of trying to attract manufacturing and other activities to these areas to redress the regional imbalance. In a similar way, they have persuaded organizations to take on ailing companies or parts of companies to avert significant instances of primary and secondary redundancy. In addition, at plant level, governments have attempted to stimulate or support investment in manufacturing companies to help increase their competitiveness in world markets. In each instance, the carrot has been a generous system of grants and other awards. Many companies, attracted by the size of the handouts and the cash and return-on-investment gains they represent, have decided to take up the offer and relocate or establish all or parts of their business in one of a number of distressed areas, take on a relatively large piece of manufacturing capacity at one go, or invest in state-of-the-art equipment to improve their manufacturing process capability. Companies that have not established clear strategic parameters and have evaluated proposals largely in terms of return or cash injection have all too often rued the decision. They are often bound by a minimum period of residence, by the relative size of the investments involved, or by the desire to save face, at least in the short-term or while the custodians of the decision still have responsibility for the business concerned. Examples are numerous.

One carpet company integrated vertically into yarn production instead of continuing its policy of buying from a number of yarn suppliers. The mill selected was in a remote area and some 100 miles away from the parent company's carpet plants. Besides all the difficulties associated with recruitment at all levels in the mill and the distances involved in what was a linked process, the company incurred one additional and fundamental problem. The decision to split the processes into yarn and carpet manufacturing was made on the basis that it was a natural break in the processes involved. However, the company had established its niche in the quality end of the markets. Separating the business at the natural break between the sets of processes involved had satisfied the investment-oriented arguments. But, at the same time, the essential quality-control link had been broken between yarn spinning and carpet manufacture, both of which were now a corporate responsibility. Thus, a manufacturing split based on processes had ignored the essential qualifying criterion of producing high-quality carpets. The quick feedback and opportunity for close liaison were not easy to exploit. In the early months, top management was preoccupied with justifying the investment from both parts of the total business. Reality, however, proved more difficult to handle than the order lines implied in the integration proposals.

In another example, a medium-sized company decided to establish a subcontract machining facility. The company abandoned its first choice of the industrial site for one some 25 miles away. The carrot offered was that the latter had a development classification attracting a high level of grant and expenditure exemptions. This alternative proved significantly more attractive to the executives, banks, and other financial institutions, who all developed a fixation on the impact it made on ROI, profit, and cash flows. However, when the order-winning criterion of delivery speed was imposed into the debate, these accrued financial advantages paled in significance. Without the sales, the calculations had no foundation.

Finally, a large manufacturing company that had great difficulty in achieving adequate profit margins was persuaded to absorb part of another group of companies. The cash injection offered as part of the governmental proposal to avert job losses swung the balance. The difficulties of absorbing such a large addition to manufacturing capacity, matching systems, controls, and other parts of the infrastructure, besides the production processes involved, added to the company's already difficult task. The rationalization that ensued cast serious questions on the fit between the decision and the strategic needs and direction of the existing business.

Linking Investment to Product Life Cycles Reduces Risk

Many companies entering markets for existing replacement or new products make decisions on process investment. These must reflect the forecast demands for those items at the various stages in their life cycles. As explained in Chapter 5, most products do not move from jobbing to batch to line levels of volume over the life cycle. In fact, this rarely happens. Companies assess the market or base their forecast volume requirements with customers. They then have to plan their investments in accordance with the relevant volume parameters established by these procedures. It does not make sense for them to invest at one level of volume, then reinvest in response to subsequent market growth. The difficulty inherent in these decisions is the judgmental nature of predicting the future. Where a high level of certainty exists, there is less difficulty in matching the process investment to eventual product volumes. However, in areas of uncertainty, and given the characteristic ways of appraising investments and evaluating the various alternatives, companies invariably place themselves in a yes/no situation. Long delivery times for equipment further aggravated this position. Commitments have to be made months, sometimes years, in advance of the scheduled launch. An alternative to this can be considered in many situations.

Figure 11–2 shows a projected life cycle for a product. At 1, process investment decisions would have to be made and purchase orders raised, in order for the plant to

FIGURE 11–2

Alternative approaches to investment decisions

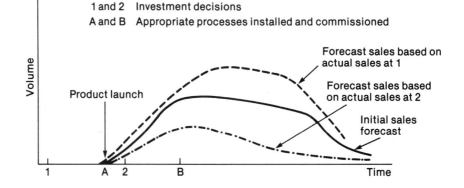

1 and 2   Investment decisions
A and B   Appropriate processes installed and commissioned

Forecast sales based on actual sales at 1

Forecast sales based on actual sales at 2

Initial sales forecast

Product launch

Volume

1   A   2   B   Time

be installed and commissioned to meet the intended product launch at A. The alternative approach is to delay the process investment decision until 2, allowing sales forecasts to be amended in line with the actual sales to date. The trade-off embodied by adopting this second approach is that the process choice would be more in line with the requirement. In this example, the new forecasts could be higher, lower, or somewhat near the same as the original forecast. Hence, the eventual investments would be more in keeping with the actual sales levels. To do this, yet minimize investment, would require that existing processes could cope with the manufacturing task to point B. The company would, thereby, not be able to meet the level of manufacturing costs necessary to yield adequate margins. In this way, the trade-offs between loss of profits in the period between A and B and the risk of inappropriate investments being made would have to be assessed.

Manufacturing Must Test the Process Implications of Product Life-Cycle Forecasts

In many instances, investment proposals rarely cover each main phase of a product's life cycle. Yet, manufacturing's task is to produce the product over each phase of this cycle and respond to the consequent variations in volumes. Returning to Chapter 7 on focus, the importance of distinguishing between product and process focus (see Figure 7–2) brings with it the need to provide alternative sets of processes. However, not only does the production engineering function classically ignore the change in the manufacturing task toward the end of a product's life cycle, but also the potential process investment requirements associated with this change are ignored. Hence, many companies must retain a high-volume plant to meet low-volume requirements. Faced with this mismatch, manufacturing does the best it can. Unfortunately, many businesses do not recognize the need to look at the alternative approaches. What happens is that manufacturing unilaterally chooses the solution that makes sense in the light of the production difficulties, constraints, and performance measures, within a company. However, the fit of the solution can then to be changed in circumstances where the trade-offs involved have come under corporate scrutiny (for example, the inventory holding associated with making order quantities in excess of sales call-offs or requirements). Given that the order-winning criteria associated with the volumes involved at these stages in a product's life cycle are invariably different (see Figure 11–3), the process choice appropriate to these stages should be realigned if manufacturing is to be able to provide the essential criteria at each stage of a product's life cycle. Thus, the investment proposal needs to include the processes necessary to manufacture effectively (in line with the varying needs of the market) throughout each stage.

The viability of a proposed product introduction should be over the whole of its life cycle and so include the investments necessary to cope with the same time period. This does not happen. Companies often assume that the process installed for the high-volume phase is the only requirement. Where existing processes can cope effectively with the change in volumes, the costs involved with this transfer (often quite high) also need to be recognized in the initial stages and included as part of the corporate assessment.

FIGURE 11–3

Product life cycles, order-winning criteria, and process investment interact

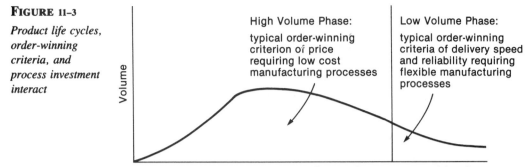

High Volume Phase:

typical order-winning criterion of price requiring low cost manufacturing processes

Low Volume Phase:

typical order-winning criteria of delivery speed and reliability requiring flexible manufacturing processes

Volume

Process investment considerations

Investment Decisions Must Quantify Working Capital and Infrastructure Requirements

Many investment decisions are distorted in two ways. On the one hand, they ignore intangible, difficult-to-evaluate reductions or benefits, which accrue from the investments.[15] On the other, they underestimate the working capital needs associated with each proposal and often ignore altogether the infrastructure costs involved. The tangible nature of the investments associated with the equipment, plant, and support services involved in a process have led to a clear identification of the costs involved. However, many areas of investment directly associated with the capital expenditure being proposed have been overlooked or ignored in the past and, in many instances, are understated or assumed to be unnecessary at present. Only in the last 10 years have companies required a statement of the additional inventory necessitated by the process proposals under consideration. The drive by most companies to reduce inventory since the early 1980s has been an important stimulus for this change. Even so, many proposals understate inventory. This is because those involved in the preparation of a capital expenditure proposal are invariably not responsible for inventory levels within manufacturing. This leads to a significant underestimation of the levels actually needed to sustain manufacturing.

The effect on the infrastructure requirements that will emanate from particular manufacturing process investments is often either underestimated or not evaluated when expenditure proposals are prepared. Often, those who prepare the proposals are not the people responsible for either the control of manufacturing or the achievement of required levels of performance. Thus, an oversimplified review of infrastructure requirements is made. Consequently, companies do not recognize any increase in complexity and they assume that existing systems, controls, and structures are not only adequate but also appropriate. The incremental nature of such assumptions leads to a deterioration in a company's ability to control and assess its manufacturing function and the eventual overhaul of one or more parts of its infrastructure. The costs associated with such developments can be high. For example, one company estimated

---

[15]Davies et al., *U.K. Survey,* p. 11, confirmed this point. Although 96 percent of respondents were required to demonstrate quantifiable future benefits, only 55 percent regarded intangible benefits as playing an important role in the justification process.

that to install a revised manufacturing control system in a typical plant cost upward of $500,000.

When a company is starting with a green-field site on which to make a single product, its investment decisions will usually take full account of the need for services, systems, and controls for the major aspects of infrastructure. However, most companies are more complex and are generally investing in existing plants or introducing products to be made in already up-and-running processes. Usually, investment considerations when introducing a product are more akin to the following examples:

1. The decision to enter a market will require an investment in all the processes necessary to manufacture the product in question. While similar to the green-field site example referred to above, the product in this instance will be assumed to use existing site services, support systems, and overheads. However, this assumption belies reality. It ignores the increase in complexity and corresponding demand placed on the nonprocess aspects of manufacturing that go hand in hand with the decision and the resulting deterioration of the effectiveness of existing systems and structures.

2. Most product introductions generally use parts of the existing manufacturing processes. This compounds the problem. There will be an increase both in inventory and in the complexity brought on by the shared use of existing processes and infrastructure and the interplay between them.

Operating Controls and Information

To assess its current performance, a company needs control information that reflects the key areas of its manufacturing task. Although there is a lot of information collected and recorded, many companies fail to clearly separate the difference between records and control.[16] Furthermore, "the development of the marketing orientation [in many companies] has led to an increase in the amount of market-based information available to management. In contrast, the paucity and limited availability of relevant internal information is striking."[17] One key problem area is that of management accounting. Although money is used as the common denominator to assess current and future corporate performance, this function is often lacking in relevance and sensitivity toward changing circumstances.

The Simplistic Nature of Accounting Information

The accounting information provided in most companies can be characterized in a number of ways (also refer to Table 11–1). First, it is historically based. Although this

---

[16]T. J. Hill and D. J. Woodcock, "Dimensions of Control," *Production Management and Control,* 10, no. 2 (March–April 1982), pp. 16–20.

[17]K. J. Blois, "The Manufacturing/Marketing Orientation and Its Information Needs," *European Journal of Marketing* 14 (June 15, 19), pp. 354–64.

is an inherent part of cost information, accountants, and thus the business, do not consider it to be of paramount importance in producing information that is relevant and close to reality. Second, invariably the information provided is primarily focused on management accounting relating to the business as a whole rather than the management control of manufacturing. This leads to the inadequate provision of critical information by which management can assess performances and make future decisions.

In broad terms, accountants primarily work on the basis of norms. They choose averages to simplify the measurement task. The procedure then is to compare each part of the business to a norm. However, the global nature of these comparisons hides the key to control. Failing to go back to the information from which the average has been drawn obscures the level of performance achieved. An average is a compilation of many parts, but it is important to be able to assess the level of performance within each. The argument put forward in defense of the averaging approach is that to collect and update data for all parts would be very time-consuming and expensive. Therefore, it is necessary to simplify the procedures and tasks involved to make some sense of reality and to be able to report within an acceptable time scale.

Reality, however, is complex. The controls need to reflect and measure reality. The accountants' approach is to simplify reality by simplifying the controls used. In this way, they are able to account for all the parts yet cope administratively with the task; that is, they meet the obligation of "accounting for everything in a systematic way." However, the basis for control in companies needs to reflect the complex business issues and not the tasks required by company law. Hence, the controls need to reflect the size and importance of the area concerned—detailed controls for the significant areas and simple, broadbrush controls for the insignificant areas.

Several general examples will serve to illustrate these points:

- Most companies use total sales revenue as an indicator of successful performance. Invariably this leads to a situation where the contribution of individual products is not rigorously examined. In profit-and-loss account terms, the top line becomes the measure of sales performance, and the bottom line, the measure of manufacturing performance. What fails to be clearly distinguished is that the two performances are inextricably linked. This consequently reinforces the argument by marketing of the need to retain all products. The simple measure of the marketing performance fails to distinguish the relative contribution of each product. Hence the conclusion that all sales are equally good business.
- It is usual for manufacturing's task to be based on a proposed or forecast level of volumes. Invariably the volumes experienced differ from period to period, and over time. However, rarely are costings provided for the different volume levels. It is essential to establish costings for the varying levels of through-put. In this way, the costings appropriate to the volume levels experienced will be used. This will then allow a company to assess a period's performance in a more exact way and to establish the reasons for the level of achievement or lack of achievement recorded.

TABLE 11-3   Some Accounting Approaches, Depending on the Type of Process

	Type of Process	
Aspect	*General Purpose*	*Dedicated*
Overhead		
Recovery	Process or product oriented	Blanket rate per standard hour
Control	Complex control: needs to assess the impact of product mix and volume changes, alternative routings, and other similar factors	Simple variance control, derived from comparing actual to standard unit volumes
Costs		
Setups	Direct to product	Overhead rate based on machine utilization
Process scrap	Specific to the process or product	Blanket allowance
Quality	Direct to product	Overhead rate established
Tooling	Direct to product	Overhead rate established
Maintenance	Direct to process	Overhead rate established
Basis for pricing	Product cost basis	Contribution basis
Development of accounting procedures and controls	Bottom up	Top down

SOURCE: Based on ideas developed by Clive Turner Associates, "Tall Trees," Barkers Lane, Wythall, West Midlands, United Kingdom B47 6BS.

- Accounting systems should reflect the type of processes being used. As shown in Table 11–3, the treatment of costs, pricing, and the development of accounting procedures and controls will vary. The costing structure and performance reporting system needs to take account of these differences in order to distinguish between the provision of sensitive cost information and the measurement of performance.

- Plant decisions constitute a large business risk because of the size of the investment, the forecast sales basis for that decision, and the flexibility/process cost trade-offs involved and their relationship to the market. However, the accounting policy on depreciation reinforces this risk when it is classified in relation to the type of plant rather than the life of the product for which the plant is to be purchased. Typically, the plant is depreciated by rule-of-thumb accounting classifications. For instance, one large manufacturing company used the rules in Table 11–4, which were based on historical usage and precedents.

    The gains accrued from having common accounting procedures belied the simplistic nature of this policy. Consequently, this sizable asset becomes detached from its essential business orientation in order to accommodate the administrative requirements of the accounting function and policies involved.

TABLE 11–4   **Rules-of-Thumb Accounting Practices**

Item of Plant	Typical Length of Depreciation in All Parts of the Company (in years)
Tool room equipment	25
Presses	20
Automatic lathes	15
Numerically controlled machines	10
Machining centers	5
Test	
Dedicated	5
General purpose	10

The Need for Accounting System Development

Demands for accounting system developments are not new. Criticisms leveled at existing approaches have become both increasingly vocal and broader-based. So far these overtures have resulted in little progress other than some tinkering at the edges. Some argue that the concerted pressure for these improvements has increased because of growing competition and loss of market share.[18] In part this is so. But the real reason is not one of blame.[19] To be able to assess options and alternative strategies, companies need insights, and in the competitive climate of the 1990s, the pressure to make significant and speedy strategic responses has never been greater. However, accounting systems, even in their recording mode, do not provide information that helps the decision process. It is neither relevant nor timely. A far more fundamental question concerns accountants' perception of the role of accounting systems. Past history clearly marks them, at best, as being reactive. Hence their bean-counter/record-keeper image. What is needed is an executive response, proactively developing systems that fulfill the needs of the decision-making processes necessary to meet the demands of today's markets and competitive threats.

Revisions are being made. A U.K. survey in 1991 reported that in the previous five years "significant revisions to cost-management systems were cited by 68 percent of respondents." However, the survey also reported that many of these revisions "were 'traditional' rather than 'new' accounting techniques and practices."[20] The implication drawn by the authors of the report was that "introducing advanced cost-techniques and practices may not be the best costing improvement for many businesses." The concern is that developing basic systems will not give a company the insights it requires. For if traditional practices provided what was needed, then the essential criticism leveled against these systems would not be widespread and growing.

---

[18]For instance, refer to W. L. Ferrara, "More Questions than Answers: Is the Management Accounting System as Hopeless as the Critics Say?" *Management Accounting,* October 1990, pp. 48–52.

[19]Ibid., p. 48.

[20]*U.K. Survey,* Davies et al., p. 16.

In their attempts to improve the competitive nature of their performance, many North American companies are paying greater attention to a whole range of improvements in quality, processes, inventory holdings, and work force policies. All are essential measures to effect this change. Not only is the level and urgency of response high, but the approaches have challenged and are challenging the very basis of previous practice. The same cannot be said of accounting.

For example, in markets characterized by difference not similarly and by a rapid rate of change "most companies still use the same cost-accounting and management-control systems that were developed decades ago for a competitive environment drastically different from that of today."[21] When trying to assess the level of contribution provided by each product as a prerequisite for judging what steps to take, many companies find that the accounting information provided fails to differentiate between them. While everyone knows that higher volumes decrease costs and product proliferation increases them, rarely are these essential trade-offs differentiated within accounting procedures. Classically, the core activities generate the substantial parts of a business. However, companies need appropriate information to assess sensibly the trade-offs associated with product breadth and focus. Noncore products are characteristically marginal in their contribution to a firm.

> Far worse than this, they may create added cost, which will be hidden by an average allocation to all products and customers. As a consequence, the essential core business may be deemphasized or overpriced, while the marginal extensions of the product line and customers served may be underpriced or overemphasized in their importance. This may be true even though a real competitive advantage exists in the core business while there is no comparable advantage in the extension coverage.[22]

The impact on business competitiveness can be significant.

Working on the Left Side of the Decimal Point

Information used in companies is not accurate. Plus or minus 10 percent is the rule of thumb used by many. Accounting information is no exception. That these "analyses are rarely, if ever, exact [and] all they can do is give a 'feel' for the financial dimensions of various activities and opportunities" is a realistic view.[23]

The typical presentation of accounting information is a giveaway. Figures to one or two decimal points give a spurious level of data accuracy. All that the system has provided is the refining of inaccurate data, and accounting functions rarely remind those using the data that it is not as accurate as it may appear.

Working only on the left side of the decimal point brings significant advantages even using existing systems. The information is easier to use, its role in the decision-making process is reinforced, and the need to understand the issues and to ensure that all relevant perspectives are considered is highlighted.

---

[21]R. S. Kaplan, "Yesterday's Accounting Undermines Production," *Harvard Business Review,* July–August 1984, pp. 95–102.

[22]Boston Consulting Group Perspective no. 219. *"Specialization or the Full Product Line,"* 1979.

[23]Ferrara "More Questions than Answers," p. 52.

Assessing Current Performance

Companies control their businesses using different procedures in different time periods. At different periods, a company will have a strategic plan (usually agreed the previous year), budgets based on the strategic plan, and revised budgets reflecting current events and levels of activity.

However, many companies then compare actual performance with the budget as the principal way of reviewing overall corporate performance.[24] But this comparison will not provide insights into performance. The company's revised plans are what need to be set against actual performance. This will, therefore, enable actual performance to be set against the actual plan. Budget changes that result from adjustments to strategic plans need to be reviewed separately in order to assess the planning procedure, the reasons for change, and the impact of revisions on corporate expectations.

Allocate, Not Absorb Overheads

The accounting practice that leads to this situation is the application of the allocation and absorption approaches to overheads. In most manufacturing companies, overheads are between 25 and 50 percent of total costs[25] and are usually increasing both in themselves and in terms of their relative size.[26] Yet all too often the bulk of these are absorbed. A review of one manufacturing company revealed that some 80 percent of total overheads were absorbed. As these costs accounted for over 40 percent of the total, the implications were alarming. Overhead costs are predominantly absorbed because it involves less administrative work and system maintenance than alternatives. Many accountants abuse this principle still further, by using one overhead absorption rate for several parts of the business involved, and often absorbing on a single basis rather than the number necessary to reflect the business and improve the relevance of the information provided. One company within a group of manufacturing companies had seven

---

[24]Davies et al., *U.K. Survey,* p. 11, reported that budget versus actual was employed by 98 percent of respondents as a performance measure. However, only 35 percent utilized flexible budgeting procedures.

[25]A fact confirmed in the 1991 U.K. survey, which reported that for 51 percent of all respondents, overheads represented 26 percent or more of total costs. See Davies et al.

[26]The increasing size of overheads was clearly shown in the comparison of cost structures between 1960 and 1986, given below:

	Percent of Total	
Element of Costs	*1960*	*1986*
Direct labor	22	15
Direct materials	56	53
Overheads	22	32
Total	100	100

SOURCE: "Management Accounting in Advanced Manufacturing Environments Survey," *Computer-Aided Manufacturing International* (CAM-I) January 1988. Also, C. Berlinger and J. Brimson, *Cost Management in Today's Advanced Manufacturing: The CAM-I Conceptual Design* (Boston: Harvard Business School Press, 1988) quoted an earlier survey in the United States by the National Association of Accountants showing similar cost trends.

sites, with uses ranging from holding and distributing raw materials through spares, low-volume manufacturing, and high-volume manufacturing to distribution of finished goods. Overheads for all seven sites were pooled and were then absorbed at one common rate for each site based on the single factor of direct labor hours. Faced with declining profits, the group executive turned to the basic performance evaluation of each site. The answers told them very little.[27]

A business needs more sensitive information at all times. The only meaningful way to account for this sizable set of costs is to reflect reality. It not only needs to have each site accounted for separately but also to have the distinction drawn between products within a site. It is essential, therefore, for accounting functions to adopt the policy of allocating overheads wherever possible.[28] As a general rule, a minimum target of allocating 80 percent of total overheads should be the initial aim. The consequences would be that then only a relatively small portion of total costs would need to be spread on an absorption basis.

Information that provides more accurate insights is a prerequisite for making sound management decisions. This is particularly so regarding:

1. *Products.* Decisions concerning pricing and the impact on margins, sales, and growth potential are at the very core of commercial activity and will significantly influence the financial performance of a company.

2. *Opportunities for cost reduction.* When the sources and extent of costs are more clearly identified, the opportunity to reduce costs is improved. This opportunity is particularly enhanced by developments in activity-based costing addressed in the next section.

Activity-Based Costing

Activity-based costing (ABC) identifies costs on an activity rather than functional base. Many companies currently use the latter approach, which directly leads to the need to disperse these groups of cost using some allocation/absorption procedure. Identifying costs on the basis of activity eliminates the need for a two-stage procedure.

Thus in ABC, activities/transactions are the focus of the costing system, as it is they, not products, that cause costs to be incurred. While products consume direct materials and direct labor, activities consume overhead resources with products currently consuming activities. Thus, ABC is particularly concerned with understanding the cost of activities and their relationship to products/services. The approach taken is as follows:

---

[27]Kaplan, "Yesterday's Accounting," p. 96, provides another example of what, all too often, is a common situation.

[28]Overhead allocation involves the allocation, apportionment, or allotment of overhead costs to the appropriate cost center or cost unit. Overhead absorption is achieved by dividing the costs involved on a suitable basis (e.g., standard labor hours, direct clocked hours, direct labor costs, material costs, or floor space) and then spreading them on a *pro rata* basis in line with the common factor that has been chosen.

- Identify the major activities.
- Determine the underlying factors that cause the activity to occur—known as *cost-drivers*.
- Create cost-pools to collect activity costs that have the same cost-driver. The major activities (see above) must therefore constitute a homogeneous set of tasks and costs such that cost variations in any pool can be explained by a single cause.
- Attribute the costs of the activities gathered with each cost-pool to the products/sources based on cost-drivers (i.e., how much of the activity has been used by the product/service in question).

In this way, ABC is a more sophisticated absorption/allocation system resulting in a more accurate identification of costs. There are two important but distinct uses of the information provided by ABC—product decisions and opportunities to reduce costs.

Product-related decisions.   Analysis of the cost structure of overhead activities enables a full review of products/services, customers, markets, and profitability. It is used, therefore, to support key decisions about

- Product pricing.
- Growth, decline, renegotiation, or exiting from market segments, customers, and/or products.

Reducing or Reshaping Nonvalue Activities.   Once a company's key activities have been agreed, ABC identifies non–value-added activities. It assesses whether both types of activity are necessary in part or at all and whether each is efficiently provided. It thus ensures that the cost of non–value-added activities is visible and so enables management to review the size and shape of overhead costs as part of its operational decision-making process.

However, whereas companies investing in ABC always use the new information in product-related decisions, many do not use it to review non–value-added activity.[29] In fact, any organization that has not systematically reduced overhead costs as a direct result of ABC has failed to use this approach in the true sense of the word. Unfortunately, many businesses still fall into this category and thereby miss many of the real opportunities for overall improvement. A survey in 1991, in fact, revealed that while 32 percent of respondents had ABC in place, only 11 percent were using cost-drivers as performance measures.[30]

---

[29]The Davies et al., *U.K. survey*, p. 12–13, revealed that whereas 90 percent of respondents used costs as an important factor in establishing prices, only 30 percent "attempted to allocate indirect/nonmanufacturing costs to products on a cause and effect basis."

[30]Ibid., p. 15.

Focused Manufacturing Helps to Identify Overhead Costs

The concern that the accounting functions have failed to develop systems that would improve key insights into product costs and non–value-added activities has been expressed earlier. The last two sections have addressed key perspectives and reviewed recent developments to meet these criticisms.

A significant reason why the accounting functions have been unable to provide adequate costing-system developments has been that the problem has become too complex to be handled by a single solution. However, unless companies find ways of driving out costs and arriving at sound product decisions, they will have problems in competing effectively in today's tough market conditions.

Adopting the manufacturing strategy principles of focus and plant-within-plant configurations (see Chapter 7) will also facilitate the provision of more accurate cost information. These approaches enable a company to identify more easily the overheads associated with each part of manufacturing and to assess the contribution provided by each part to the whole business. This change brings with it a shift from the principle of accounting for overheads on a functional basis to that of a dedicated overhead allocation. Thus, instead of summarizing the costs involved in providing a support function as a total for that function, it accounts for those overheads that are dedicated to or are directly associated with a part of manufacturing. Not only does this now enable a company to assess more clearly the contribution of its different parts, but in times of change it will enable a company to take out or increase the vertical slice of overheads associated with that part of the process under review. Thus, it allows change to take place in a more orderly and sensible way. It aligns accounting decisions with manufacturing strategy needs and avoids accentuating the already wide gap between the support needs of manufacturing activities and the perceived role of support functions. When overhead costs are clearly identified with a particular sector of manufacturing, the level and nature of support can be agreed to meet the current needs of that sector and to reflect any changes identified in the future.

A further refinement to these changes involves making any functional overhead into a business unit. This moves a business away from the position where an accountant or accounting procedure arbitrarily spreads the unallocated overhead to make the books balance to a position where each part of the business declares a budget for the amount it intends to purchase from each overhead function. The gains are obvious.

Beware, however, of two possible developments.

1. The counterargument put forward by accountants that these changes are difficult to accomplish and lack a high degree of accuracy. These changes will, in fact, enhance the relevance and accuracy of this information in the light of the business needs.

2. Attaining accuracy as an end in itself. The corporate gain is providing information to help prioritize product decisions and cost-reduction activities.

Create Business-Related Financial Information

The key role of business-related financial information has been highlighted in the sections concerning cost-system developments. As an essential input into developing both a marketing and manufacturing strategy, accounting information is rarely designed specifically to provided analyses that would form an integral part of the formulation of either function's strategic statement. Examples of key marketing information in addition to those specifically mentioned earlier include:

- *Customer sales and profitability.* An assessment of both the sales and total costs associated with selling to and support for major customers enables a company to establish the true worth of these relationships.
- *Market share and profitability.* Identifying the value of sales in each market, its relative size, associated costs to promote and support relevant activities, and the level of profitability for each market segment are essential inputs into formulating a marketing plan.

For the manufacturing side of the business, information that is rarely provided by existing accounting systems but that would offer invaluable insights in the strategy formulation includes:

- Cost estimates of manufacturing at varying levels of throughput.
- Capacity analyses identifying any bottleneck or limiting factor in the manufacture of each product (known as *analysis of contribution by limiting factor*). This enables companies to assess proposals to increase capacity and to decide how best to allocate existing capacity in the meantime (see Chapter 4).
- Cost estimates for supplying items outside the normal product range.

Finally, the need to separate out those costs incurred by manufacturing but not induced by manufacturing decisions is seldom reflected in the control statements provided by the accounting system. Excess manufacturing costs incurred as a result of a change in schedule to meet a sales or customer request, for instance, are usually not shown under their own separate headings (e.g., manufacturing excess cost due to customer schedule change).

Provide Performance-Related Financial Information

The final area of development concerns the provision of accurate performance-related information. As the measurement of actual performance needs to be set against targets that reflect reality, so levels of performance within a business will differ from one part to another. Not all products can be expected to achieve the same performance standards during each and every year of their lives. Therefore, why should products in different stages of their life cycles be forced to meet the same minimum standard each year? For this to be appropriate would require an unbalanced portfolio made up solely of products all in the same stage of their life cycles.

Once performance expectations have been resolved, the next issue concerns the level of expected activity. Budgets, by definition, are out of date by the time they are completed. It is necessary, therefore, to review the budget figure by using the latest information. In this way, the basis for establishing and assessing levels of performance is changed from a budget to a latest-estimate basis. One clear example of this is the use of flexible budgeting, which changes the cost base in line with actual volumes and alters the basis for related cost information (e.g., overhead absorption either by traditional or ABC systems).

The last illustration concerns the distortions businesses experience as a result of the way in which they calculate inventory values. In many situations, inventory desensitizes cost information by becoming a cost buffer. Most accounting systems assume that costs are held in the value of work in process as calculated in the system. Often, accumulated cost excesses are discovered when the inventory is physically counted at the end-of-period stock taking and then recorded as an inventory or stock-taking loss. Since many firms physically count inventory only twice a year, control or responsibility is not easy to establish.

Conclusion

The growing criticism of existing accounting systems and investment appraisal procedures is more than justified. The accounting profession in the Untied States and many other Western countries has come to be responsible for providing financial information. Unfortunately, accounts have generally been reactive in responding to the changing needs of business and have spent too much of their time keeping records rather than providing information for, and partaking in, the control and development of the business. The description of bean-counter sits well.

Two general misconceptions have contributed to this:

- Management concerns developing not just maintaining existing procedures.
- Like other functions, accountancy has failed to recognize that its role is subservient to that of the business. Its prime task is to respond to and meet the needs of a business. The *raison d'être* of a function exists through the business. Functions do not exist in their own right. Evaluating a function's contribution, therefore, needs to be set within this frame.

The potential contribution of accounting and finance functions is significant. The key insights and overall executive role it can bring to a business are considerable. However, to realize this level of effectiveness, companies must recognize changes in need and respond to them in a appropriate manner. This chapter has posed several issues that companies must address. Of these, three dimensions need to be at the forefront of accounting provision.

Markets Are Changing

The traditional perspective of productivity and evaluation of investment decisions needs to be modified in line with the needs of the business, reflecting how these needs are secured. The principle that should drive today's businesses is based on keeping existing customers and winning new ones, not lowering labor costs. Cutting lead times, boosting quality, improving delivery reliability, reducing inventories, and supporting product range are factors that top the list in these endeavors. Accounting systems and financial reviews need to reflect this.

Businesses Are Characterized by Difference, Not Similarity

Difference not similarity characterizes today's businesses. Rules and procedures need to embrace this. Levels of control, therefore, should be established to ensure that the more difficult and complex a proposal, the less formal and bureaucratic the approach. Investment proposals for relatively small sums are well served by laid-out procedures and predetermined hurdles. Major investments on the other hand, are ill served by such approaches. Yet usually one set of rules applies, as characterized the bureaucratic belief that the essence of control has its root in well-defined procedures.

However, major investments need approaches that are the very opposite of current developments and executive behavior. The maxim should be that the larger the investment, the more informal the approach and the lack of definition within the procedures used. Thus, major investments should be led by strategy and subject to open debate, ideally involving nonexecutive contributions to enhance neutrality. Putting forward functional proposals in line with agreed and structured procedures discourages strategic debate, stifles discussion, and encourages rationalization—the very opposite of what is required to handle these complex and fundamental strategic decisions.

Linking Process Investment Decisions and the Evaluation of Control Systems

In many companies, the link between process investment decisions and the need to provide supporting control systems is not appreciated. Decisions about processes are not only tangible, but they are also taken at a different phase in the decision sequence (see Table 11–5). On the other hand, the sizable investments associated with manufacturing process decisions of working capital and infrastructure are often obscured for exactly the opposite reasons—they are less tangible and occur in the operating phase of the installation.

Furthermore, when a process investment is installed on the shopfloor, a distinct accounting change takes place. At the preoperation stage highlighted in Table 11–5, a process is singularly evaluated in great detail as part of the investment appraisal system and is cash-flow oriented. However, once installed this same process will no longer be treated as an individual item in accounting control terms. Instead, it will be controlled by a number of broadbrush accounting systems based on profit. It will become just part of a functionally based set of assets and costs comprising a range of investments that differ in usage, degree of dedication to the manufacture of specific products, age, and support-system requirements. The change in accounting treatment highlights the contrasts involved and the necessary high level of control in the preoperation phase compared with the lack of sensitivity in the global controls once the asset is being used.

TABLE 11-5   The Three Phases in an Investment Program

Phase	Time Scale	Features of the Investment	Tangible Nature	Features of Evaluation and Control
1.	Preoperation	Fixed assets in the form of plant, equipment, and associated installation costs	High	Constitutes taking one investment in isolation. Traditional investment appraisal techniques used, which are *cash-flow* oriented
2.	Operating	Supporting working capital in the form of inventory		The investment now becomes an integral part of the business summary. It reverts to revenue accounts that measure *profit* to investment as the basis of control
3.	Operating	The service and support overheads necessary to provide an appropriate level of infrastructure	Low	or assessment. Control of individual investments now relatively loose—rarely have postaudits.

Source: Based on ideas developed by Clive Turner Associates.

Ways Forward

What then are the ways forward? They involve changes at two levels in the organization. At the top, many executives have perceived their role in accounting and finance in a different form. Often they become involved in, or even spearhead, activities designed to generate earnings by financial transactions. This has the major drawback of diverting management effort and interest away from the business core. They become more distant from the prime profit-generating activities of a manufacturing business. They start to control from a distance. Without the understanding of each firm's strategies, they feel unable to contribute to the essential developments that must be made in the tough competitive climate of manufacturing. They feel exposed and become less able to evaluate the necessary long-term alternatives. As a consequence, they increasingly exert pressure by short-term measures and assessments. Lower down the organization, plant executives being measured by the short-term success of the business often respond by adopting similar opportunistic patterns of behavior such as reducing expenditure or withholding investments to increase profits and improve cash flow in the short-term. Similarly, groups of companies often monitor investments centrally and against a common set of criteria. However, they leave the postinstallation assessment to be taken at plant level. Seen as part of their role, the group executives' action reinforces the predominant role of financial measures when assessing investments and weakens the key responsibility link between the investment decision and its future evaluation. The need to decentralize these responsibilities could not be more strongly argued.

The way forward is through the emergence of strategy-based decisions and controls. Accounting and manufacturing need to determine together the investment criteria and day-to-day accounting-control provision that should be adopted. Not only will this orient manufacturing toward its key tasks, it will also provide information that is both relevant and current. This growing awareness of the need for strategic management accounting needs to be accelerated if companies are to be able to make sound manufacturing and other strategy decisions.[31] It is most necessary, therefore, that firms stem the apparent drift away from their manufacturing focus.

Perhaps a final lesson for West European companies is that "in Japan, perpetuation of the enterprise, not profit, is the driving force. As Toshiba's Okano puts it: The company is forever."[32] Although in no way implying that this should be adopted as the corporate-value system, it highlights one essential difference. Strategy is the driving force; survival and success will only be achieved through a strategic orientation, and this must become the pattern by which companies both give direction and assess current and future performance.

---

[31]Simmonds, "Strategic Management Accounting."
[32]Ohmae, "Japan: From Stereotypes to Specifics," p. 7.

CASE 1
ANONKE APPAREL COMPANY, LIMITED

"Our change in marketing strategy has been very successful! Sales are growing rapidly, but profits have been less than expected during the past year," observed Mr. Mana, the managing director at Anonke Apparel, in his annual budget review. "Our sales to U.S. and European companies, such as Zeus and Leland, which sell through mass merchandisers have all shown major increases and, in fact, have exceeded our budgeted targets. However, the fact that we have not met our profit objectives is quite surprising considering the major investments in advanced process technology that we have made recently to improve labor productivity and reduce costs in our pattern making and cutting operations."

Mr. Mana also noted recent problems with deliveries to some key customers.

Phoenix, Gorgio, and Fountainblean are putting pressure on us for much quicker delivery while other customers have complained about late deliveries. Zeus, for example, is currently pressing for 150-day deliveries, and a two-week delivery window during their peak selling seasons in April through September. In the future, we believe that customers will be pressing for 60 to 120 day deliveries. In fact, we are now negotiating with a new customer that wants delivery 45–60 days after fabric receipt. Perhaps we should be considering changes in our production planning and scheduling system to support these changes in delivery requirements.

Background

Anonke Apparel was established 12 years ago in Bangkok as a garment manufacturing company, wholly owned and managed by Thai businesspeople, one of whom is the managing director, Mr. Mana. At that time the company had five employees and produced children's wear, which was sold through Bangkok department stores. Now the company produces entirely for export. Five years ago Anonke built a four-story plant on 7,000 square meters of land to house its 800 employees and its operations with a monthly production capacity of 50,000 garments. Exhibit 1 shows a picture of these facilities.

The company's sales have shown substantial growth. A second building was completed during the past year, doubling the plant floor space, which houses the firm's current work force of 1,500 employees. Exhibit 2 provides an organization chart indicating the firm's three main functions: marketing, finance, and production. Exhibit 3 shows financial results for the past five years.

Marketing

As shown in Exhibit 4, Anonke's sales are primarily made to European and U.S. customers with a growing proportion in Asia. Import quotas are a dominant characteristic for U.S. and European markets. From Exhibit 4 it can be seen that approximately 95 percent of the company's sales are made to countries having import quotas. Therefore, sales growth can only occur in

EXHIBIT 1 Company Building and Products

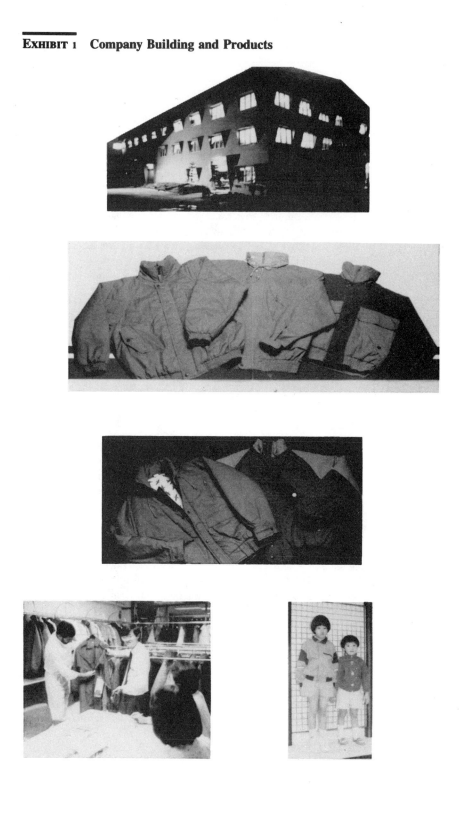

EXHIBIT 2   Organization Chart

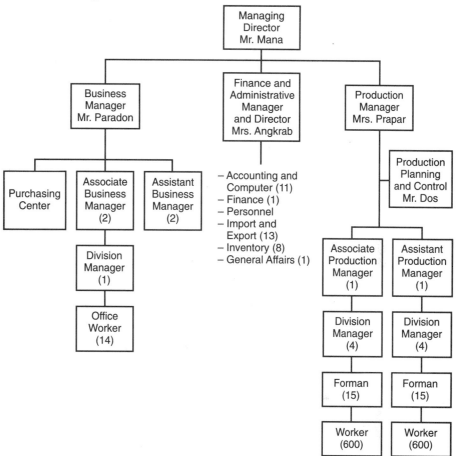

Note: The figures show number of staff in each section

those countries where Anonke is not yet selling to its quota limit or where quota limits are being increased.

Quotas are based on specific products. For example, in Europe, quotas are placed on all types of jackets, skiwear, parkas, jogging suits, pants, shorts, and blouses. However, there is no quota on raincoats. To export to a quota market, a company must get quota approval from the Thailand government's Foreign Trade Department. The quota limits sometimes change because of trade negotiations and political events.

There are two types of quota. Performance quotas are awarded according to the export history of a company. Central pool quotas result from companies unable to sell up to their quota limit, or from trade negotiations.

Quotas are increased for one of two reasons. First, countries typically provide for a small annual increase, e.g., 3–5 percent to account for normal market growth. Second, occasionally the governments of Thailand and the importing country engage in trade negotiations which result in substantial increases in quota limits. For example, Thailand and the United States

---

EXHIBIT 3 Profit and Loss Statement ($000)

	YEAR Y − 5	YEAR Y − 4	YEAR Y − 3	YEAR Y − 2	YEAR Y − 1
Income					
Revenue	$1,376	$5,522	$10,412	$14,846	$15,730
Other	78	120	315	813	1,033
Total	1,454	5,642	10,727	15,663	16,763
Expenses					
Cost of goods sold	1,190	4,949	7,508	13,053	14,188
Sales and administration	172	476	2,850	1,316	1,636
Interest	57	182	308	710	828
Total	1,419	5,607	10,666	15,078	16,652
Profit before tax	35	35	61	585	111
Current assets					
Cash	92	91	60	23	482
Accounts receivable	233	922	740	1,893	1,079
Inventory	116	1,510	1,099	2,990	1,868
Others	73	232	772	848	417
Total	514	2,755	2,671	5,754	3,846
Fixed assets	401	1,551	2,419	3,100	3,308
Total assets	915	4,306	5,090	8,855	7,154
Liabilities					
Current liabilities	285	2,732	3,638	6,003	4,908
Accounts payable	204	550	729	1,321	597
Others	253	351	238	573	452
Total	742	3,633	4,605	7,897	5,957
Long-term liability	60	446	0	61	299
Owners' equity	131	220	440	440	440
Retained earnings	(18)	7	45	457	458
Total liabilities	915	4,306	5,090	8,855	7,154

NOTES: All case exhibit financial information is expressed in dollars rather than bhat, which is the local currency.
Y = current year.

recently reached agreement to significantly increase U.S. quotas for apparel. When such an increase occurs manufacturers rush to increase their sales to the importing country so that future annual increases are made from their newly expanded sales base.

Failure of a firm to sell its entire quota to an importing country in any one year results in loss of quota. But the loss is triple the actual sales gap. For example, if a company shipped 90 percent of its quota in one year, in succeeding years its quota would become 70 percent of its original quota. These lost sales units are then put into the central pool to be allocated to other manufacturers.

Customers.   Anonke's products are found in department stores, boutiques, specialty stores, mail order catalogs, and wholesaler clubs. They are bought by clothing companies, importers, buying offices, and, in some cases, the outlets themselves. Anonke's customers not only differ by distribution channel, but they also display significant differences in their buying behaviors, as shown in Exhibit 5.

EXHIBIT 4   Sales by Country

Country	Year Y Sales Value	Percent	Year Y − 1 Sales Value	Percent	Quota Country	Sales Growth Year Y/Y − 1
United States	$3,954,160	19	$3,731,415	23	Yes	1.06
France	3,713,282	18	3,427,603	21	Yes	1.08
Italy	3,077,531	15	2,938,637	18	Yes	1.05
West Germany	4,310,049	21	2,236,853	14	Yes	1.93
United Kingdom	1,494,363	7	1,132,203	7	Yes	1.32
Netherlands	1,235,637	6	505,094	3	Yes	2.45
Benelux	25,806	0	500,345	3	Yes	0.05
Denmark	41,291	0	361,781	2	Yes	0.11
Canada	174,096	1	310,281	2	Yes	0.56
Switzerland	149,493	1	243,952	2		0.61
Austria	261,669	1	175,729	1	Yes	1.49
Belgium	793,887	4	118,834	1	Yes	6.68
Ireland	90,096	0	106,784	1	Yes	0.84
Spain	208,211	1	73,159	0	Yes	2.85
Japan	192,262	1	59,837	0		3.21
Hungary	46,706	0	32,942	0		1.42
United Arab Emirates	35,955	0	30,946	0		1.16
Mexico	87,293	0	12,630	0		6.91
Turkey	7,777	0	8,714	0		0.89
Hong Kong	32,329	0	1,637	0		19.75
Sweden	55,826	0	1,207	0	Yes	46.26
Australia	21,353	0				
Netherlands Antilles	2,887	0				
Czechoslovakia	42,393	0				
Finland	22,860	0			Yes	
Greece	29,764	0			Yes	
Lebanon	41,345	0				
Norway	18,703	0				
Panama	11,419	0				
Peru	5,065	0				
Poland	32,687	0				
Portugal	40,073	0			Yes	
Singapore	16,573	0				
Taiwan	16,450	0				

NOTE: Y = current year.

Buying Pattern A1.   One group of customers (referred to as buying pattern A1), of which Zeus, Leland, and Phoenix are examples, have widely recognized brands. Because of their relatively higher retail prices, these customers can afford to advertise and heavily promote their products. Some of these customers have the additional benefit of substantially advertised and widely known brand names from their footwear lines. These brands rival some consumer products such as Coke, Colgate, and Gillette in terms of customer awareness.

In meetings with Anonke's salespeople, these customers' designers bring a whole collection of (sometimes as many as 50) styles. Because of their familiarity with textile manufacture, the

---

EXHIBIT 5   Buying Patterns

A1	A2	B
Zeus (DMSB)	Ibrahim (B)	Jean Valjean (S)
Toddlers (DMS)	Gorgio (S)	Bach (W)
Leland (DMS)	Monmouth (S)	Iberian (F)
Eurotech (DMS)	Pierre Duree (B)	Naomi (D)
Phoenix (DMS)	Sumata (DS)	Larouche (M)
	Peppi (DMS)	Mulder (D)
	Candida (DS)	Fountainbleau (M)
	Italia (DS)	Daisy Wraps (DMS)
		Niebuhr (DMS)
		Conti (DS)
		Etyia (DS)
		Apres (DMS)

NOTE: D = department store; M = mail order; S = specialty store;
B = boutique; and W = wholesale club.

---

designer typically specifies the fabric, color, and the fabric supplier. Anonke submits a sample produced from the designer sketches for each style, which are subsequently altered and revised. The designer specifications for this group of customers are very exacting and reflect the customer's substantial knowledge of the garment manufacturing process.

Product specifications, price, and delivery are agreed upon with the customer, including the supplier and the price to be paid for the fabric. Although the customer provides a forecast of sales, the actual order quantity depends on the level of sales at retail. Each month a buy is made for delivery four months hence.

Buying Pattern A2.   Customers exhibiting this buying pattern are very similar to A1 customers except that they base their buying decisions more on the product features that Anonke is able to provide. For example, Anonke is able to embroider, offer special zippers, and incorporate special pocket designs into its garments.

These customers also tend to be smaller than A1 customers and have significantly smaller advertising budgets. They typically promote and advertise their products only in their own countries. Although they may have well-known brands locally, they are less known outside their own domestic markets. These customers also typically own their own retail outlets.

Buying Pattern B.   These customers have no designers. Some B customers submit a small number of samples (10 to 20), and Anonke selects those of interest. Other customers select styles from Anonke's showroom. Once the styles have been selected, Anonke suggests and buys the fabric they will use in the garment's manufacture and quotes a price on the spot. Five months delivery is typical in this market.

Another group of B customers buys directly from Anonke's inventory of finished goods. This inventory consists of product made from excess fabric, quality seconds, and products for which other customers have refused to accept shipment because of late delivery.

Exhibit 6 shows current year company sales, price, margin, cost, productivity, and order data for each of these buying pattern types. These data were derived from a representative sample of customer orders, which are shown in Exhibit 7.

EXHIBIT 6   Market Segments by Buying Pattern Type

	A1	A2	B
Last year sales			
$000,000	8.6	3.0	4.1
Percent of total	55	19	26
Sales growth			
last three years (%)	278	157	146
Price ($/pc.)	12.90	25.16	9.47
Contribution ($/pc.)	3.07	7.20	2.76
Contribution ($/hr.)	1.47	1.89	1.88
Direct material ($/pc.)	8.14	15.41	5.56
Direct labor ($/pc.)	1.69	2.55	1.15
Direct material % of price	63	61	59
Productivity (pc./hr.)	0.41	0.26	0.68
Production lot size			
Hours	28,250	13,299	11,743
Pieces	12,541	3,490	7,974
Average quoted lead time (days)	171	159	166
Average actual lead time (days)	199	174	187
Average order lateness (days)	28	15	21

Market Segments.   Customers place orders with Anonke for a variety of reasons. Some customers use traditional criteria such as price, delivery speed, quality, and delivery reliability (see Exhibit 8). Other criteria used include Anonke's ability to produce a wide range of order sizes (referred to as production flexibility in Exhibit 8). The ability to offer certain special product features (such as a variety of pocket designs, embroidering, and unusual fabric combinations), close sales relationships, familiarity with specific country markets, and a long-standing partner relationship in producing a particular collection of garments are other criteria. Exhibit 9 shows current year company sales, price, margin, cost, productivity, and other data for each market segment.

Products.   Anonke's product lines include a wide range of high-quality men's, women's, and children's wear. Winter and summer-weight jackets, raincoats, blouses, shorts, sport jacket and pants combinations, jogging suits, parkas, and skiwear are all produced by Anonke. Jackets are produced from a standard woven fabric. Prices range from under $5 to over $40, with $15–20 being most typical. Adding to the complexity of the manufacturing task is the wide variety of fabrics for both the outer body and the lining of the garments.

Garment industry products can also be classified as either classic or casual wear. Classic garments tend to emphasize the use of high-quality, expensive fabrics. These garments are not high fashion, but are formal wear that tend to have long product life cycles. Casual garments, Anonke's primary range, tend to focus on the quality of workmanship. These garments are more informal and their designs tend to include a wide variety of colors.

Management captures the overall difficulty of the manufacturing task required to produce a particular garment with the use of a numerical scale, ranging from 1 to 6 (with 1 being the most difficult and 6 being the easiest to manufacture). Jackets are often some of the most difficult

EXHIBIT 7 Representative Sample of Customer Orders

Item Description	Product Difficulty Code	Price per Piece ($)	Direct Material $/Piece	Direct Labor $/Piece	Percent Contribution Margin	Contribution Margin/Piece	Dollar Contribution Margin/Hour	Productivity (pieces/hr)	Production Order Size (in pieces)	Date Order Received	Date Order Promised	Date Order Shipped
Lady's jacket	1	$25.91	$15.59	$3.39	26.75%	$6.93	$1.60	0.231	1,058	03/22	08/20	09/10
Children's jacket	1	23.34	9.27	2.61	49.10	11.46	2.78	0.243	850	10/18	02/28**	03/07**
Lady's jacket	1	30.58	15.08	2.52	42.45	12.98	3.17	0.244	1,344	02/26	07/30	09/20
Men's jacket	1	28.82	16.86	2.79	31.79	9.16	2.13	0.233	2,424	03/29	08/30	09/18
Boy's shorts	5	2.09	1.61	0.35	6.32	0.13	0.75	5.722	117,733	05/14	10/15	10/15
Men's jacket	3	18.01	11.70	1.75	25.29	4.55	1.31	0.289	3,204	04/08	10/30	10/30
Men's ski wear	1	35.75	18.13	5.21	34.71	12.41	1.63	0.132	2,992	10/08	03/30**	03/30**
Men's shorts	6	4.46	2.32	0.75	31.11	1.39	0.00	n.a.	30,950	05/15	01/30**	01/01**
Men's jacket	3	19.73	9.27	1.51	45.37	8.95	3.62	0.404	2,845	12/25	05/15**	05/18**
Stadium jacket	2	25.25	16.72	2.82	22.61	5.71	1.44	0.252	5,216	07/15	02/28**	03/24**
Lady's raincoat	4	20.00	11.95	1.66	31.96	6.39	2.36	0.369	4,025	04/29	10/15	10/26
Men's jacket	3,5	31.30	19.21	2.46	30.76	9.63	2.77	0.288	11,971	06/24	10/31	12/13
Women's pant	5	6.27	3.93	0.86	23.68	1.49	0.00	n.a.	4,514	05/15	09/30	09/30
Men's jogging suit	3,5	11.83	6.56	2.30	25.12	2.97	1.04	0.351	28,518	05/03	02/15**	02/29**
Jacket	3	13.92	6.88	2.52	32.49	4.52	2.00	0.441	5,405	05/25	10/30	11/30
Lady's jacket	1	15.96	7.95	2.41	35.08	5.60	1.23	0.219	1,400	11/17	03/15**	03/30**
Jacket and pants	3,5	20.86	17.07	3.12	3.16	0.66	1.63	1.373	7,590	05/15	09/15	10/16
Women's jacket	3	11.75	7.49	1.55	23.05	2.71	1.13	0.416	5,712	06/01	10/30	10/30
Men's jacket	2,5	22.88	10.62	1.72	46.11	10.55	2.88	0.273	3,350	10/01	03/10**	03/14**
Men's jacket	3	9.45	6.79	1.20	15.48	1.46	0.77	0.528	48,190	02/12	08/01	01/15**
Jacket and pants	2,5	44.62	32.78	4.15	17.23	7.69	1.88	0.244	2,605	12/07	04/30**	06/30**
Lady's jacket	1	17.25	8.49	3.21	32.14	5.54	1.49	0.269	1,500	04/30	08/30	08/30
Men's jacket	1	25.85	16.93	3.06	22.68	5.86	1.23	0.210	1,714	01/10	07/01	08/04

Men's jacket	2	21.12	10.82	2.22	38.23	8.07	2.37	0.293	6,044	05/04	10/15	12/07
Men's jacket	1	27.56	20.33	3.74	12.65	3.49	1.02	0.291	5,190	08/06	12/28	12/28
Men's jacket	2	20.13	10.69	1.20	40.93	8.24	3.52	0.428	2,850	11/10	04/15**	08/04**
Men's jacket	1	30.36	18.02	3.59	28.84	8.76	1.39	0.158	8,246	02/10	08/26	09/14
Lady's jacket	2	21.01	11.31	2.21	35.65	7.49	2.12	0.282	1,500	01/15	05/30	09/26
Men's raincoat	1	22.99	12.75	1.99	35.89	8.25	2.50	0.303	1,833	05/04	10/15	11/15
Men's jacket	2	29.04	19.72	1.96	25.34	7.36	2.45	0.333	3,945	06/17	11/30	12/28
Men's jacket	1	27.78	16.68	2.87	29.62	8.23	1.82	0.221	3,464	12/18	06/30**	07/19**
Men's jacket	1	36.30	19.91	14.44	5.36	1.95	0.12	0.060	1,470	02/12	07/15	07/20
Men's jacket	2	18.81	9.49	1.44	41.87	7.88	3.68	0.468	4,016	06/06	12/15	12/20
Men's jacket	1	33.39	24.56	3.53	15.85	5.29	0.98	0.185	2,352	01/29	08/18	08/18
Men's jacket	1	25.25	15.02	2.75	29.63	7.48	1.81	0.242	3,002	08/06	12/28	12/28
Children's jacket	3	14.76	7.11	1.60	41.06	6.06	3.33	0.550	4,017	06/27	11/15	11/30
Women's jacket	1	23.08	13.06	3.23	29.41	6.79	1.31	0.193	1,364	06/26	11/30	12/16
Men's jacket	1	32.23	22.04	2.84	22.80	7.35	1.63	0.222	2,930	12/17	05/31**	06/19**
Women's jacket	1	23.88	13.15	4.06	27.96	6.68	0.97	0.145	1,216	12/17	06/30**	07/08**
Men's raincoat	4	41.75	21.89	3.60	38.95	16.26	2.99	0.184	2,171	01/29	08/31	09/02
Men's jacket	1	28.88	18.08	2.30	29.41	8.49	2.30	0.271	2,400	01/29	06/30	08/25
Blouse	3	17.16	9.52	2.22	31.60	5.42	1.92	0.354	5,000	01/19	05/30	05/30
Men's jacket	2	20.32	10.00	2.46	38.66	7.85	5.07	0.645	2,671	06/26	12/01	12/30
Men's coat	4	26.33	15.10	2.23	34.17	9.00	2.36	0.262	879	02/18	07/30	07/30
Men's jacket	1	24.86	15.05	2.83	28.10	6.99	1.56	0.223	2,970	04/20	11/30	12/04
Men's parka	1	24.26	12.67	2.27	38.41	9.32	2.62	0.281	3,964	02/05	05/31	06/08
Men's jacket	2	26.57	11.72	2.75	45.55	12.10	3.14	0.259	3,710	02/16	07/30	09/12
Men's jacket	1	26.29	14.75	2.82	33.18	8.72	1.95	0.224	1,000	02/06	07/30	07/30
Coat	4	22.98	14.69	1.74	28.53	6.56	2.45	0.374	6,031	02/06	07/30	07/30
Men's coat	4	30.02	18.83	2.78	28.00	8.40	1.88	0.223	1,098	02/18	07/30	07/30
Men's jacket	2	21.01	11.84	2.15	33.46	7.03	2.09	0.298	3,524	10/06	01/15**	01/15**
Men's jacket	3	15.29	9.00	1.68	30.14	4.61	1.86	0.405	9,781	07/25	12/30	12/30
Coat	4	28.72	17.52	2.31	30.95	8.89	2.47	0.278	7,530	02/06	07/30	07/30

EXHIBIT 8   Market Segments by Order-Winning Criteria

Buying Pattern	Brand Type	Home Office Location	Sample Sales	Segment	Manufacturing					
					Production Flexibility	Quality	Delivery Speed	Delivery Reliability	Price	Capacity Uplift
A2	L	France	Sample	Few	Q/Q	Q/Q	Q/10	0/10	Q/Q	
A2	L	France		competitors	Q	Q	Q		Q	
B	L	Spain				Q/Q	0/15	0/15	40/10	
B	L	United States		Price					70/70	
B	N	Italy				Q/Q	10/10	20/20	30/30	
A1	N	United States			10/10		10/20	15/15	25/25	
A1	L	United States			10/10		10/15	15/15	30/35	
B	N	Switzerland		Large	20/20		20/20	20/20	20/30	
B	L	France		volume	20/20		20/20	20/20	20/25	
A1	N	West Germany	Sample		10/10		10/20	15/15	15/15	
A1	N	West Germany			10/10		10/20	15/15	20/20	
A1	N	West Germany			10/10		10/20	15/15	25/25	
A1	N	United States	Sample		10/10		10/20	15/15	15/15	
B	L	West Germany			20/20			20/20	20/30	
A2	N	Netherlands			20/20			20/20	20/20	
B	O	West Germany			10/10			20/20	10/10	
B	L	France			10/10	Q/Q		20/20	10/20	
B	L	Netherlands		Product	30/0			20/0	20/0	
A1	N	France		features	10/10			20/20	10/10	
B	L	West Germany			10/0	Q/Q	10/20	20/20	20/30	
A2	L	Italy	Sample		10/10	20/15	10/10			
A2	L	Japan			20/20		0/20	20/20	20/10	
B	N	West Germany			20/20	Q/Q	10/10	20/20	Q/Q	
A2	L	France	Sample	Delivery	Q/Q	Q/Q	Q/20	Q/10	Q/10	10/0
A2	L	Italy	Sample	reliability	10/10			20/20		
B	L	Italy			10/10			20/20		
A2	L	Italy			10/10			20/20		

For xx/yy, xx = current year and yy = three years hence will be phased out. Percentage is occuring within a customer's management. Superior workmanship or fabric material. Longstanding sales relationship. Purchased because is was produced in a particular country. Superior knowledge of local market. Reliable quote where competitors do not. n: Long term customer relationship in producing a given collection. Important to change suppliers because design detail confidentiality is desired. (N) or Local (L)

products to manufacture and raincoats are among the least difficult. Exhibit 7 shows garments, which are illustrative of these levels of difficulty.

Competitors.   The firm faces competition from companies located in Thailand as well as global competition from Hong Kong, Taiwan, Singapore, Korea, China, Japan, and Eastern Europe. Its main competitors in Thailand are shown in Exhibit 10. These competitors differ depending on the type of product manufactured. The J. E. Garment Company is the principal competitor in terms of raincoats and long coats. There are three main competitors in men's, women's, and children's jackets: Thai Masa, Far East Woven, and Autraya Garment. In terms of

Product Features	Nonmanufacturing						Order-Winning Criteria Group
	Sales Relationship	Country of Origin	Market Familiarity	Have Quota	Partnership (Collection)	Few (Competitors)	
20/20	Q/Q		20/10		25/35	35/15	1
20/20	Q/Q		10/10		35/35	35/35	1
20/20	10/10		10/10	20/20			2
		10/10		20/20			2
10/10	10/10			20/20			2
15/15	10/10			10/0	5/5		3
15/15	10/10			10/0			3
10/10				10/0			3
10/10	0/5			10/0			3
20/20	10/10			10/0	10/10		3
20/20	10/10			10/0	5/5		3
15/15	10/10			10/0	5/5		3
20/20	10/10			10/0	10/10		3
30/30					10/0		4
30/30					10/10		4
30/30	20/10			10/0	0/20		4
30/30	10/10			20/10			4
	20/0				10/0		4
30/30	20/20				10/10		4
20/20	10/10				10/0		4
30/20	0/20			10/0	20/25		4
10/10	20/20		10/0				4
30/30					20/20		4
20/20	Q/Q	Q/Q	20/10		50/30		5
20/20	20/20				30/30		5
20/20	20/20				30/30		5
20/20	20/20				30/30		5

sportswear, the Thai Hong Kong Garment Company and the Best Wear Company are the main competitors. New competition is expected from companies located in Indonesia and Malaysia.

Manufacturing

The same basic production process is used for all of the garments produced by Anonke. This process has five main steps: pattern making, cloth cutting, subassembly, final assembly, and finishing and packing. These steps are indicated in the flow diagram shown in Exhibit 11. Exhibit 12 shows the physical layout of the production process in the original four story building.

Pattern Making.   The pattern-making operation begins with either a product sample or product specification sheets. A paper pattern is made for each component part of the garment. Next,

EXHIBIT 9   Market Segments by Manufacturing Order-Winning Criteria

	Few Competitors	Price	Large Volume	Product Features	Delivery Reliability
Last year sales					
$000,000	0.60	0.50	8.90	3.50	2.20
Percent	4	3	57	22	14
Sales growth					
last three years (%)	−5	−44	272	245	132
Price ($/PC)	27.17	3.80	13.05	25.11	22.96
Contribution ($/pc.)	10.62	0.72	3.14	7.27	7.53
Contribution ($/hr.)	2.54	1.38	1.48	1.77	2.28
Direct material ($/pc.)	13.73	2.54	8.24	14.95	13.27
Direct labor ($/pc.)	2.82	0.54	1.67	2.89	2.16
Direct material % of price	51	67	63	60	58
Productivity (pc./hr.)	0.24	1.95	0.40	0.24	0.30
Production lot size					
Hours	4,531	16,197	26,138	12,853	13,366
Pieces	1,084	31,588	11,592	3,132	4,049
Average quoted lead time (days)	146	172	170	164	161
Average actual lead time (days)	173	176	197	190	166
Average order lateness (days)	27	4	27	26	5

a computer wand is moved around the perimeter of each paper pattern and the exact dimensions of a piece are transmitted to a computer representation of that piece. The computer pictures of the pattern parts are then placed on a template of the cloth as it would be on the cutting table. An operator moves the part patterns around to minimize the trim loss at the cutting table operations. A paper sheet is then printed out showing the exact location of each garment part on the cutting table. This sheet is checked for accuracy and sent to the cutting table department. Exhibit 13 shows a picture of each step in the pattern-making operation.

Cloth Cutting.   The company has eight automatic cutting machines, of which seven are used for cutting garment parts, and one is used for cutting padding materials. Each machine can cut 3,500 parts per eight hour day for garments and 500 for padding units. Layers of cloth are placed on the cutting table and the paper pattern template is placed on top of the cloth. Next, a plastic sheet is placed over the paper pattern and a vacuum is drawn, compressing the layers of cloth. The cutting operator uses a cutting machine to cut out the individual parts. Each garment part is numbered for identification purposes. These parts are then separated by style, size, and color and combined into a single lot before the order is sent to the sewing section. Exhibit 14 shows pictures of the automated cloth-cutting operation and also the manual cloth-cutting operation both used in the company.

Subassembly.   A subassembly area with 10–15 employees is located next to each final assembly line. Complicated features such as pockets and embroider subassemblies are made in this area in order to simplify the operations on the final assembly line. Exhibit 15 shows pictures of the typical operations in a subassembly line.

EXHIBIT 10 Direct Competitors

Company	Sales ($000,000)	Number of Sewing Machines	Production Percentage							Quality	Notes
			Coats	Shirts	Blue Jeans	Jackets	Suit Coats	Sport	Other		
J. E. Garment	$100	3,000	30	30	20	20				M/H	Mass production/Large lot size
Thai Europe Fashion	48	1,900				15	85			M/H	Mass production/Large lot size
Siam Garment	40	1,500		65		25		10		M/H	Mass production/Large lot size
Thai Masa	38	1,200		30		60		10		M	Mass production/Large lot size
Far East Woven	26	1,200				100				M	Mass production/Large lot size
Autnaya Garment	23	1,100				40	40		20	M/H	Mass production/Large lot size
Thai Hong Kong Garment	16	900						100		M/H	Mass production/Large lot size
Anonke Garment	15	900		10		50		40		M/H	Mass production and production flexibility
Best Wear	10	800				30		70		M	Mass production/Large lot size
Bangkok Garment	10	400		65					35	M/H	Mass production/Large lot size

NOTE: M = medium-quality level produced; M/H = medium- or high-quality produced.

SOURCE: Interview.

EXHIBIT 11   Production Process

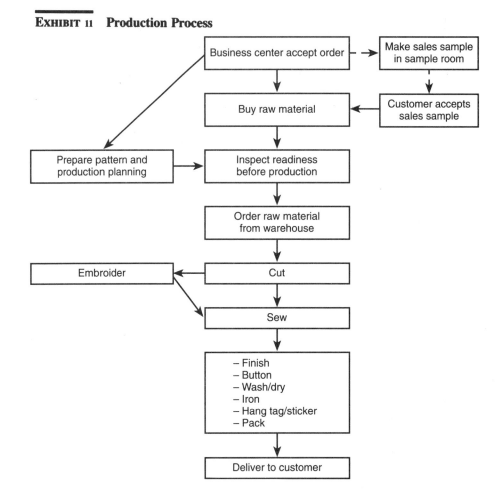

Final Assembly.   The company has 22 sewing lines, each line having 35–40 operators. In total, all 22 sewing lines produce 3,500–4,500 garments per day depending on the garment type and level of difficulty. Exhibit 16 shows pictures of typical operations on a final assembly line.

Finishing and Packing.   The finished products are sent from final assembly to the finishing and packing department. This section has 150 people. They attach buttons, wash, iron, hang, tag, and pack the garments. Forty of these employees perform the quality control function. They inspect each process in the finishing department. Pictures of these process steps are shown in Exhibit 17.

Production Planning.   After the business department accepts a customer order, the material requirements are computed and sent to the purchasing department. It normally takes 10 to 15 days between the receipt of an order and the placement of purchase orders for materials. The purchasing lead time for standard fabric types provided by Thailand suppliers is 10 days.

EXHIBIT 12 Plant Layout for the Original Building

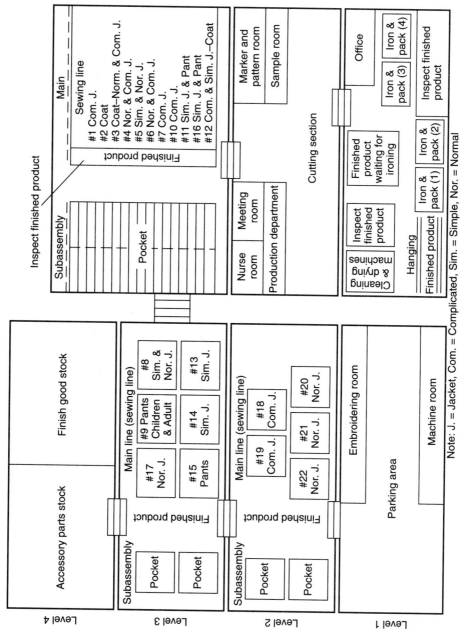

Note: J. = Jacket, Com. = Complicated, Sim. = Simple, Nor. = Normal

EXHIBIT 13   Pattern Making

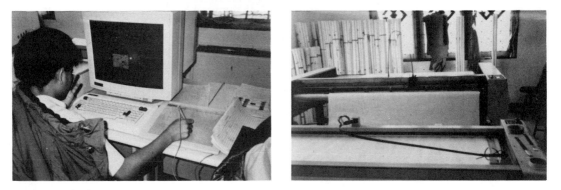

However, 40–60 days are required if special fabrics are ordered abroad. At the same time, the pattern for the garment is produced by the pattern making department.

Five days prior to the start of production, the production staff checks the readiness of the pattern and the availability of raw materials, manpower, and machines. Next, cloth is issued from stock to the cutting department and garment processing is started. It normally takes 45–60 days for garment production. Exhibit 7 provides a representative sample of customer orders, indicating the overall supplier and production lead times experienced by the company. A representative sample of customer orders showing a further breakdown of the overall manufacturing lead time by process stage is shown in Exhibit 18. Exhibits 19 and 20 give capacity information typically considered in scheduling orders on the different plant operations.

Planning the manufacturing operations is especially difficult because of the seasonal nature of the garment market. Exhibit 21 shows the degree of variation in sales and shipments over the course of a year. The summer and fall is the peak season. This is made even more difficult because it is the rainy season in Thailand and some of the employees, especially those from the northeast, return to their provinces to help the family grow rice during this period. A sales peak also sometimes occurs in December because many garment manufacturing companies increase their production levels at this time to ensure using all their export quota.

Labor Costs.   To motivate their employees to produce high quality products, Anonke pays the work force on a daily wage basis. The daily wage depends on the skill and experience of the

EXHIBIT 14   Cloth Cutting

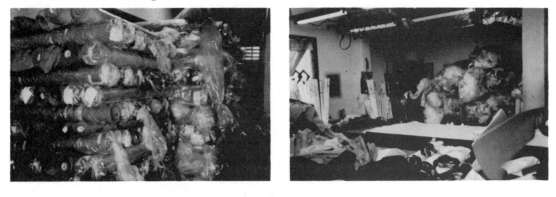

employee. New unskilled employees make $3.60–4.20 per day. Those with one year of experience make $4.75–5.00 per day, and highly skilled people with more than three years experience make $5.20–5.80 per day. These rates do not include overtime. The company provides classroom training at a location in the newly constructed plant to provide their employees with basic sewing skills. This creates flexible employees who can adjust easily to different garment styles and different garment processing operations.

Recent Marketing Initiatives

Last year the marketing strategy of the company was reviewed and several changes were made "in order to achieve the company's sales growth and profitability objectives," explained Mr. Paradon, the marketing director.

Customer Mix.   The firm's marketing strategy was adjusted to target large U.S. customers like Zeus and Leland in order to capture as large a portion as possible of the new quota limits made available by the recent Thailand/U.S. government negotiations. Customers like these are particularly attractive because they place large orders and require shipment throughout the year.

European Sales.   During the past year Mr. Paradon has also emphasized sales to European customers. This was done because of this market's higher prices and more stringent quality

EXHIBIT 15   Subassembly

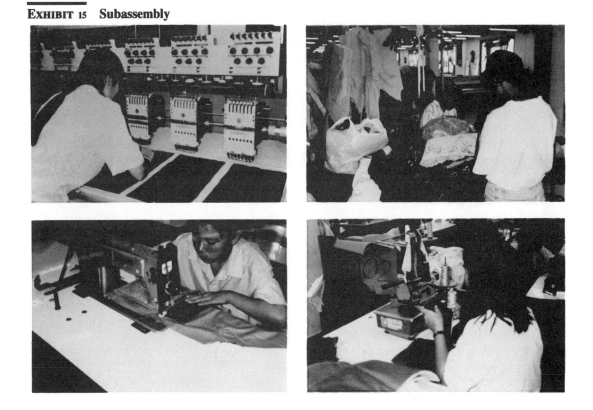

requirements. Higher quality requirements restrict competition, while some European countries (e.g., Benelux) have fewer quota restrictions.

Jacket Production.   In the past the company has produced a relatively wide range of products. Last year's were made up of 10 percent shirts, 50 percent jackets, and 40 percent sportswear. This year the projected sales mix is 10 percent raincoats, 50 percent jackets, and 40 percent sportswear. The company has adopted this strategy for several reasons, including the fact that there is limited competition in these products since they are more difficult to manufacture. Furthermore, there are important economies of scale from limiting the product range, and there are higher prices and margins for these products. The effect of this product policy is to focus the company's efforts on products that enable the company to develop a specialized manufacturing skill involving a high level of workmanship.

Recent Manufacturing Initiatives

During the past few years several investments were made by Mr. Mana in the manufacturing process.

Pattern Making.   Two years ago Anonke invested in computer technology to produce garment patterns with computer-aided design equipment. This equipment, shown earlier in Exhibit

EXHIBIT 16   Final Assembly

13, enables the company to achieve much higher material yields, thereby reducing costs. It also enables the firm to improve the quality of patterns and the time associated with pattern making.

Cloth Cutting.   Three months ago Anonke invested $300,000 in an automated cloth-cutting line. This line includes eight cloth-cutting stations controlled by a microcomputer. Computer information from the pattern-making operation is used to program this machine. As a result, the company has been able to reduce the number of cloth-cutting operators from 100 to 35. In addition the new machine produces more accurate parts, creating a higher material yield and improved product quality. Exhibit 14, shown earlier, includes pictures of this line, which is located in the new plant completed last year.

Special Purpose Sewing Machines.   The company has replaced some of the general purpose sewing machines with special purpose machines that are dedicated to particular sewing operations, such as embroidery, trimming, and hemming. These machines enable the operators to achieve higher productivity and permit higher-quality workmanship and product quality.

Flexible Sewing Lines.   The sewing lines at Anonke are designed differently than those in other garment manufacturing companies. At Anonke many of the complicated operations, such as making pockets, have been removed from the final assembly line and placed into a subassembly area. This has the effect of simplifying the operation of the production line, enabling a

EXHIBIT 17   Finishing and Packing

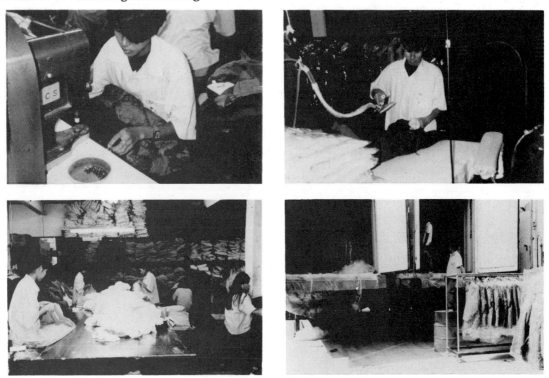

major reduction in the changeover time in switching from one order to another. Also, this decision enables the sewing operators to achieve a higher productivity level and requires less learning time in moving from one order to the next.

In addition, the company has recently consolidated all of the purchasing functions into one staff position and has assigned an individual with this responsibility. This was done to improve supplier coordination concerning fabric lead times and delivery dates and to provide additional sourcing activities in order to reduce material costs.

Manufacturing Strategy

"Our flexible production strategy has enabled us to gain a significant competitive advantage," observed Mr. Mana. "Most of our competitors have longer production lines and do not use the subassembly approach that we have adopted. As a result, their changeover times are higher. In order to achieve high productivity and low manufacturing costs, these companies must have significantly longer production runs. We are able to accept much smaller orders for products having customized designs and are thus able to target specialized market niches."

EXHIBIT 18 **Representative Sample of Customer-Order Lead Times**

Customer/Style	Quantity	Date Order Accepted	Date Material Ordered	Date Material Received	Date Manufacturing Started	Promised Delivery	Actual Shipping Date
Gorgio							
Day	4,000	22/04	20/06	30/08	04/09	30/11	30/11
Sasa	4,000	22/04	20/06	30/08	15/09	30/11	30/11
Mini	4,000	18/10	18/02*	30/03*	22/04*	30/05*	08/06*
Fox	4,000	18/10	04/02*	30/03*	22/04*	30/05*	08/06*
Ultimate	4,000	22/04	12/07	30/08	23/11	30/11	20/12
Naomi							
XX2	1,500	06/12	10/12	10/03*	16/04	30/04*	01/05*
XX1	4,500	06/12	10/12	10/03*	12/05*	15/06*	15/06*
XX8	1,800	19/04	15/05	30/09	26/10	15/11	15/11
XX2	3,650	13/10	05/12	25/03	06/04*	30/04*	01/05*
XX1	2,320	13/10	05/12	25/03*	26/06*	15/07*	15/07*
Ibrahim							
6620	4,500	21/01	27/02	30/03	17/05	20/06	20/06
6842	3,600	21/01	27/02	30/03	16/06	10/07	07/07
5930	1,060	19/02	27/02	30/03	10/07	30/07	23/07
4142	1,694	24/03	26/03	15/05	19/07	30/07	01/08
1480	345	28/02	27/02	30/03	12/07	30/07	23/07
Phoenix							
XY-22	3,500	22/07	01/08	30/08	10/10	30/10	08/11
Sultan	3,400	08/08	24/08	30/09	25/11	31/12	30/12
Dover	11,200	02/01	10/01	25/02	03/04	30/04	14/05
Ascot	7,800	02/01	20/01	05/03	05/04	15/05	27/05
Peppi							
Squire	5,050	05/08	25/08	30/09	13/11	28/12	28/12
Duke	2,980	05/08	25/08	30/09	02/12	28/12	28/12
Tower	3,040	06/02	03/03	15/04	24/05	27/06	26/06
Peak	4,140	06/02	03/03	30/04	21/06	24/07	30/07
Ginger	1,230	06/02	03/03	30/04	25/06	12/07	11/07

NOTE: xx/yy = day/month.

*Following year.

EXHIBIT 19 **Production Process Capacities**

Process	Number of Machine Centers, Groups, Tables	Number of Workers	Production Rate (per day)
1. Pattern	6–8 tables	6–8	4 styles
2. Marker by			
Machine center	2 machine centers	5	2 or 3 styles
Hand	2 machine centers	10	6 styles
3. Cutting	8 tables/4 groups/ 7–8 machine centers	80	4,000 pieces
4. Sew (22 line)	30–35 machine centers per line	35–40 persons per line	3,500–4,500 pieces
5. Packing	4 groups	150	6,000 pieces
6. Inspection	3 tables	30–40	3,500–4,000 pieces

EXHIBIT 20   Sewing Line Capacity

Sewing Line	Type of Product	Skill Level	Production Rate	Number of Employees	Number of Machine Centers
1	Coats and complicated jackets	4,1	200	40	33
2	Coats	4	200–250	34	34
3	Coats and normal and complicated jackets	4	150–200	38	35
		1,2	150		
4	Normal and complicated jackets	1,2	200–300	31	36
5	Simple and normal jackets	2,3	150–200	34	38
6	Normal and complicated jackets	2,3	150–200	38	35
7	Complicated jackets	1	150–200	33	31
8	Simple and normal jackets	2,3	250–300	37	31
9	Pants				25
	Children pants	5	1,000	30	
	Adult pants		400–500		
10	Complicated jackets	1	175–225	31	32
11	Jackets and pants			33	31
	Pants	5	500		
	Simple jackets	3	250		
12	Coats and jackets			29	29
	Coats	4	150–200		
	Jackets				
	Complicated	1	150–175		
	Simple	3	200–250		
13	Simple jackets	3	250–300	39	35
14	Simple jackets	3	250–300	39	35
15	Pants	5	500–800	29	28
16	Jackets and pants			34	31
	Pants	5	500–800		
	Jackets	3	250–300		
17	Normal jackets	2	200–250	38	29
18	Complicated jackets	1	150–200	41	40
19	Complicated jackets	1	200	35	37
20	Complicated jackets	1	150–200	38	34
21	Normal jackets	3	200	37	34
22	Normal jackets	3	250–300	40	34

EXHIBIT 21 Monthly Sales (000 units) for Last Year

Customer	Total	January	February	March	April	May	June	July	August	September	October	November	December
Zeus	300.3	25.4	23.2	15.3	50.8	22.0	31.6	12.14	11.9	10.2	8.7	45.5	43.0
Leland	28.0					.01	.01				4.1	23.7	
Eurotech	32.9											14.3	18.6
Daisy Wraps	99.1										60.0		39.1
Toddlers	2.1					2.1							
Ibrahim	23.0	0.2					4.3		3.2	14.6	0.7		
Gorgio	40.4	0.1				4.0	NA			NA	NA	NA	
Pierre Duree	1.0									1.0			
Naomi	21.7					6.1	3.5			4.3		1.8	6.0
Fountainbleau	25.8				3.8	7.6					8.0	6.5	
Larouche	12.6		1.5	3.2		2.8	5.1						
Peppi	14.5	1.5							3.0	2.9			7.1
Candida	38.7	2.3					5.2	10.3	9.1	4.9			7.0
Italia	14.1								5.7	6.7	1.7		
Conti	6.1							3.0		3.1			
Etyia	41.7	4.8					1.3	7.9	7.6	10.4			9.7
Phoenix	215.9	0.1	.07	4.6	7.4	22.2	24.9	22.7	1.3	8.2	23.5	41.8	59.0
Jean Valjean	14.2						3.3	3.9		2.2		4.7	
Bach	49.7	3.6					4.1	20.2	6.1	0.9		2.9	12.0
Niebuhr	10.6							2.7	7.9				
Aprés	28.0						3.5	8.2	6.4	6.7	3.3		
Monmouth	17.9					2.3	9.3	2.4					3.9
Mulder	6.9								6.9				
Iberian	7.3							4.9		2.4			
Sumata	7.3						.04			2.9	4.4		
Total sales of the company	1,305	48.3	26	78	71.1	79	120	114.5	87	115.5	140	165.2	26

NOTE: Some orders from 25 main customers are missing.

Case 2
Aztec Holdings, Inc.

"Our review of actual sales during the last nine months indicates no improvement compared with our results over the past several years," concluded Roger Whinston, the general manager of Aztec Holdings.

> Although we are meeting our profit objectives, we are not meeting our forecast uplift in sales and actually appear to be losing market share. To achieve sales growth in our markets, we recognize the need to achieve a major reduction in our delivery lead times. This will help differentiate our products from those of our competitors.
>
> However, our lack of sales growth is very surprising considering the recent investments we have made to install just-in-time manufacturing methods in the plant. It is clear that JIT has provided a major reduction in production lead times and work-in-process inventory and that this should have helped us improve our customer service in terms of delivery speed and reliability. However, we have needed to work substantial overtime hours in order to improve our delivery lead times in a period when the utilization of our factory is only running at 70-80 percent.

Background

Aztec Holdings manufactures industrial batteries for a wide range of applications. The company is a wholly owned subsidiary of Pittston Industries, a U.S.-based conglomerate with diverse businesses in the health care, computer, automation, and transportation industries. Both the company headquarters and the manufacturing facilities are located in Cleveland, Ohio, and serve the U.S., Canadian, and Mexican markets.

Marketing

"The last two decades have seen a noticeable increase in the number of applications for which motive power batteries have been used. We anticipate that the growing concern for the environment will see this trend continue," explained Roger Whinston. "Currently, we recognize a number of segments which reflect a wide range of applications. Our statistics indicate that the world market for industrial batteries breaks down into Europe (44%), North America (32%), Japan (11%), and the rest (13%)."

Batteries for industrial applications contain a number of cells. While the sales of industrial batteries are normally referred to in terms of batteries, manufacturing quantities are expressed in terms of cells. Industrial batteries for all applications except access platforms require about the same average number of cells per battery. Access platform applications have a larger number of cells per battery.

The North American market served by Aztec can be segmented in terms of original equipment manufacturers (OEM) and replacement sales, and by the type of battery application. Aztec sells both OEM and replacement batteries in the following major areas of application: materials

This case study was written by Professors W. L. Berry (Ohio State University) and T. J. Hill (London Business School). It is intended for class discussion and not as an illustration of good or bad management. © Professor W. L. Berry or AMD Publishing (U.K.). Inquiries in the U.S.A. to Zip Publishing, 1634 N. High Street, Columbus, Ohio 43201.

EXHIBIT 1   Sales Analysis

Market Segment	Percent Total Sales	Percent Sales (cells)	Percent Sales by Type within Segment (cells)	Percent Sales by Type within Segment (sales $)
Materials handling	60%	65%		
OEM			38%	27%
Replacement			62	73
Wheelchairs	12	7		
OEM			70	70
Replacement			30	30
Cleaning equipment	9	5		
OEM			57	42
Replacement			43	58
Golf carts	11	12		
OEM			24	18
Replacement			76	82
Access platforms	8	11		
OEM			26	22
Replacement			74	78
Total	100	100		

handling equipment, wheelchairs, industrial cleaning equipment, golf carts, and access platforms. A breakdown of Aztec's sales in terms of these market segments is shown in Exhibit 1.

Aztec's sale of industrial batteries in these market segments varies substantially over the course of the year. Exhibit 2 presents monthly sales data during the past year expressed in terms of cells. It shows both the sales made directly from the plant and the sales made from the firm's field warehouses.

Materials Handling Equipment.   The sale of industrial batteries for materials handling equipment represents the largest segment for Aztec in terms of sales revenue dollars (60%) and total cells (65%). The split between OEM and replacement sales in terms of revenue (dollars) and cells is given in Exhibit 1.

The OEM market segment includes manufacturers of materials handling equipment. Some of these companies specialize in particular materials handling applications such as vehicles designed for narrow aisle applications in warehouses. Other manufacturers offer materials handling equipment for vehicle applications such as for manufacturing plants, the logging industry, and cargo handling. As is the case for all the market segments served by Aztec, the company offers both batteries of standard and special design to equipment manufacturers.

Because of the major inroads into the North American market made by Japanese materials handling equipment manufacturers, the battery price in the OEM market is much more sensitive than in the relevant replacement market. The order size for OEM customers is relatively large, and a failure on delivery reliability can result in a loss of business. These customers place schedules that specify, for 90 percent of their requirements, delivery within 14 days with the remaining 10 percent for delivery in 15 days or more.

The replacement market includes industrial and government customers who have purchased equipment and have experienced a battery failure. When a lift truck goes down the customer needs close support in order to return the vehicle to service. This requires fast delivery of the

EXHIBIT 2   Sales Seasonality

Month	Plant Sales (units)	Ratio to Monthly Sales Average	Field Warehouse Sales (units)	Ratio to Monthly Sales Average
January	12,605	.75	15,177	1.09
February	12,996	.77	18,057	1.30
March	19,135	1.14	17,516	1.26
April	18,993	1.14	12,782	.92
May	18,930	1.13	13,163	.95
June	19,807	1.18	15,613	1.12
July	19,735	1.18	13,233	.95
August	14,271	.85	9,530	.69
September	16,952	1.01	14,650	1.05
October	19,436	1.16	11,825	.85
November	15,268	.91	11,696	.84
December	12,818	.77	13,311	.95
Monthly average	16,728		13,879	

NOTE: Plant sales are exclusive of field warehouse sales.

replacement battery. In fact, 60 percent need battery replacements in seven days or less. Another 30 percent require delivery in up to two weeks, and the remainder within 30 days.

Wheelchairs.   The sale of industrial batteries for wheelchairs is a relatively small portion of Aztec's sales in terms of sales revenue dollars (12%) and total cells (7%). Within this segment, OEM sales represent 70 percent of the sales dollars and 29 percent of the cells. Likewise, the sales of replacement units within this segment represent 30 percent of the sales dollars and 71 percent of the cells. The split between OEM and replacement sales in terms of revenue dollars and cells is given in Exhibit 1.

The OEM market segment includes nine U.S. companies that manufacture wheelchairs of standard design. Although these chairs are sold with a wide variety of customer-selected options and features, the batteries are relatively standard in design and their features vary only with the size of the wheelchair. In addition, there are numerous small companies that sell wheelchairs that are custom built to the patient's specifications on a local basis. Recently, several Swiss and German companies have entered the North American market.

In this market segment the superior battery design gives the company an edge over its competitors, and price is not normally a major factor in winning these orders. However, delivery reliability is critical, and a failure to deliver on schedule can result in a loss of business. Seventy percent of the orders for OEM units are placed specifying delivery within 14 days of the placement date. The remaining 30 percent is for delivery in 15 days or more.

The customers in the replacement market segment include a wide variety of medical equipment distributors, hospitals, pharmacies, and health care units that sell wheelchairs to patients. These firms provide a number of services to their customers, including both the sale and rental of wheelchairs, a medicare and insurance filing service, the repair and servicing of the unit, and a variety of other related equipment and accessories.

Because the unit cost of a battery is significant, they are not typically stocked by replacement market customers. Therefore, it is important to provide a quick response when a battery failure occurs. Orders for replacement batteries are invariably required within seven days. Waiting more than seven days would not be accepted by customers who would go elsewhere.

Industrial Cleaning Equipment. The sale of batteries for industrial cleaning equipment is also a small part of Aztec's sales in terms of sales revenue dollars (9%) and total cells (5%). Within this segment, OEM sales represent 42 percent of the sales dollars and 57 percent of the cells with the balance made up by replacement units (see Exhibit 1).

The OEM market segment includes manufacturers of industrial cleaning equipment. These companies typically manufacture units for a broad range of industrial, government, and service sector applications. While their product includes a range of standard models, the customer has a wide range of optional features and accessories to select from in buying a unit for a particular application. One of these options is the engine type, which may use gasoline, LP gas, or electric as the fuel source.

Because of heavy overseas competition in the North American market, price and delivery speed are major factors in the purchase of this type of equipment. Many of the industrial cleaning equipment manufacturers have been looking to their suppliers for JIT support in the manufacturing process. As a result, 70 percent of the units are required within 7 days of the schedule placement date and the remainder within 14 days. Furthermore, a failure on delivery reliability can result in a loss of business.

The replacement market includes manufacturing companies, municipal units, and private cleaning services contractors. A failure of the battery is costly to these companies because of the resulting equipment downtime and the need to maintain the cleaning schedules of their customers. Therefore, there is an overriding need for quick delivery support with seven days as the maximum delivery lead time from placement of an order.

Golf Carts. The sale of batteries for golf carts is a relatively small portion of Aztec's sales in terms of sales revenue dollars (11%) and total cells (12%). Within this segment, OEM sales represent 18 percent of the sales dollars and 24 percent of the cells with replacement units making up the balance (see Exhibit 1).

The OEM market includes several major companies that specialize in the manufacture of golf carts and a number of local companies that represent a very small share of this market. Although golf carts can be purchased with a variety of options and special features, the batteries are of a standard design with relatively few battery models. While some of the carts use a gasoline engine, about 75 percent of the market requires an electric drive, and this percentage is increasing.

The entry of overseas competition from both Asia and Eastern Europe in the golf cart market has resulted in a high level of price sensitivity for these batteries. The customer order sizes are relatively large and are affected by the seasonal nature of this business. The golf cart manufacturers expect short delivery cycles—70 percent of the units are scheduled to be delivered within 14 days of the call-off date with the remainder in up to one month.

The customers in the replacement market include distributors selling equipment for golf and other sports, golf courses, and private individuals. Since these customers do not stock replacement batteries, relatively short delivery times are required, particularly in the summer. From the date of order placement, 60 percent of the units sold require delivery within 7 days, 30 percent looking for up to 14 days, and the remainder require delivery within one month.

Access Platforms. The sale of batteries for access batteries accounts for 8 percent of sales revenue dollars and 11 percent of total cells. The OEM and replacement split is given in Exhibit 1.

The OEM market includes four major manufacturers that specialize in the design and manufacture of access platforms. Because of the governmental requirement for the certification of this product to industrial safety standards, these manufacturers tend to provide a small number of standard models, which can be outfitted with a number of different optional accessories. However, a relatively large range of battery sizes and capabilities are required because of important differences in size and weight in access platform applications. Although one of the major access platform manufacturers in the world is located in Europe, overseas competition in U.S. markets has been limited. One explanation for this has to do with the requirement for governmental certification of new products.

The sale of batteries to manufacturers of access platform equipment involves working with a customer's engineering design group as well as its purchasing department. The battery design for these units is relatively straightforward, and price is often an important factor in getting the order. Because batteries for this type of equipment are very expensive, customers schedule their requirements with very short lead times. From the date of the order placement, 70 percent of customer sales are scheduled for delivery within 7 days, and the remainder for delivery within 14 days. A failure to meet the required delivery date can result in the loss of this business.

There are a wide variety of customers in the replacement market, including companies such as commercial construction contractors, electric power companies, manufacturing plants, and municipal government units. Price is not normally an important factor in the replacement market. However, because of equipment downtime caused by battery failure and the resulting problems in meeting customer schedules, the length of the delivery lead time is an important issue in this segment. Seventy percent of customer sales are looking for delivery within 7 days, and the remainder for delivery within 14 days. Delivery performance against promised dates is an important but not a critical factor in this segment.

Sample customer orders that are representative of these market segments are shown in Exhibits 3 and 4. These data reflect the customer order sizes and Aztec's delivery performance in each of the segments.

Manufacturing

Industrial batteries are manufactured using relatively few components. A battery consists of one or more cells that are assembled into an outer container. Each cell includes a lid, a container, a number of positive and negative grid plates, a variety of electrical connectors and fittings, and fluid. The industrial battery product line at Aztec includes approximately 500 items that are manufactured on a make-to-stock basis.

Manufacturing Process.   The battery cases, cell lids, containers, electrical hardware, and fittings are purchased from suppliers. However, the positive and negative grids are manufactured by Aztec, which involves the processing of lead. The manufacturing process used consists of four main steps as shown in Exhibit 5.

The first step involves grid manufacturing. The negative and positive grids are produced to stock using grid casting machines located in separate manufacturing departments. Next, a coating is pasted on the surface of the grids in different manufacturing departments for the positive and negative grids, and they are stocked in finished form. Subsequently, pickling and humid-setting operations are performed on the grids. They are then dried in a baking operation and placed into inventory.

The second and third steps in the manufacturing process are plate processing and cell assembly. These are organized into high- and low-volume production units. The high-volume units produce approximately 100 cell types, and the low-volume units manufacture about 400 differ-

EXHIBIT 3   Customer-Order Sample

Market Segment	Customer	Product	Actual Order Quantity	Date Order Placed	Order Reference Number
Materials handling					
OEM	Austin	XX143	18	26/2	121
OEM	Standard	DQ156	36	12/5	803
OEM	Logan	CD103	24	37/4	568
OEM	Austin	WP222	24	02/1	234
Replacement	National	DQ102	12	13/3	141
Replacement	Hornes	WQ431	50	21/1	956
Replacement	Bexler	XX120	10	42/5	501
Replacement	Scotio	WE563	12	24/2	172
Wheelchair					
OEM	McKiney	QQ300	20	11/3	630
OEM	Jones	EW345	5	24/1	931
OEM	Wexler	WE213	10	36/2	719
Replacement	Amer-Hos.	ER908	24	39/1	677
Replacement	St. Mary	QQ203	6	33/4	498
Replacement	Ford	CC781	80	41/4	222
Cleaning					
Replacement	Ace	AW213	6	48/4	403
Replacement	Downtown	AW233	2	31/5	772
Golf cart					
OEM	Player	WT112	12	43/2	861
OEM	Nicholas	WW455	96	09/1	384
Access platform					
OEM	Modern	TR563	24	36/4	555
OEM	Downeys	TR234	45	05/3	916
OEM	Speedy	RW231	46	45/1	119

NOTES: 1. These orders are representative of those promised by the company. The company works on a five-day-per-week basis.
2. xx/yy = week number/day.

ent cells. Plate processing involves the production of a subassembly of positive and negative grids to meet the specifications for a particular battery cell. After plate processing, both the completed plates and a wide variety of purchased parts are stocked prior to the cell assembly operation.

In cell assembly, the plate subassemblies, electrical connectors, and fittings are assembled, placed in a plastic container, and the lid is sealed. Afterwards, the cells are charged and transferred to either finished goods inventory or the battery assembly operation.

The final step in the manufacturing process is battery assembly. Only 25 percent of Aztec's sales require this step. Normally, the cells are shipped to the firm's field warehouses or to customer locations where they are assembled into a battery case.

Just-in-Time Manufacturing. During the past two years, Aztec has made a major investment in introducing just-in-time methods into the manufacturing process. Investment in new equipment and a new process layout has enabled major improvements in processing methods to

---

EXHIBIT 4 Customer-Order Delivery Promise Data

Order Reference Number	Promised Delivery Date	Actual Delivery Date
121	34/3	37/4
803	17/2	17/1
568	44/4	43/1
234	03/4	04/5
141	14/5	14/2
956	23/1	22/5
501	49/1	50/3
172	29/1	25/1
630	13/4	13/1
931	26/5	27/4
719	39/1	39/5
677	40/3	40/4
498	39/1	37/4
222	42/4	42/2
403	50/2	50/2
772	31/5	32/3
861	47/4	48/3
384	12/1	12/1
555	37/4	37/3
916	05/3	06/2
119	45/1	45/5

NOTES: 1. These orders are representative of those promised by the company. The company works on a five-day-per-week basis.

2. xx/yy = week number/day.

---

be made, including substantial reductions in changeover times, and important reductions in work-in-process inventory and manufacturing lead times.

Three parts of the process are now operated on a just-in-time basis: grid manufacturing, high-volume plate processing, and high-volume cell assembly. As a result, the high-volume cell assembly unit is able to produce cells in small lots, and components such as plates and grids are produced as required using Kanban methods. Furthermore, the vendors for high-volume connectors and fittings, containers, and lids supply Aztec on a just-in-time basis with daily deliveries.

Because of the wide range of products and components required, the low-volume products are still produced on a make-to-order basis. This means that production is scheduled on a batch basis in the low-volume cell assembly unit and the low-volume plate assembly unit. Since there is a relatively small range of positive and negative grids in grid casting, both the low-volume and high-volume grids are manufactured on a just-in-time basis.

Manufacturing Lead Times. The production lead time for both the high- and low-volume cell assembly units is one day for cell assembly and 3–4 days for cell charging. However, one week is normally allowed in scheduling each of these operations. Also, one week is normally

EXHIBIT 5   Battery Manufacturing Process

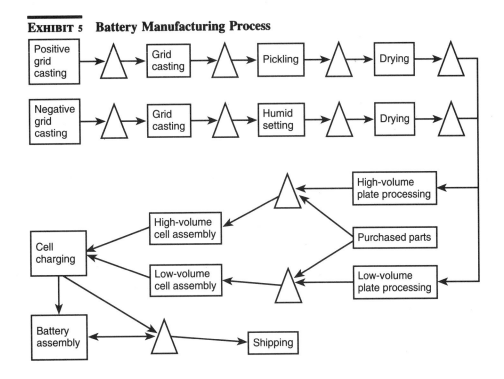

allowed for plate processing, and one week for the combined operations of grid casting, pasting, pickling/humid setting, and drying. Those orders involving the assembly of cells into a battery case require a further manufacturing lead time of three days.

All purchased parts, except the plastic cell containers, are stocked by Aztec. Because of the cost and variety of height dimensions of containers, bulk orders for these items are placed on suppliers with high-volume containers supplied on a JIT basis by the suppliers. This means that daily deliveries are made by suppliers against a schedule delivery issued one week in advance.

Low-volume containers are scheduled on a make-to-order basis and require between three and eight weeks of purchasing lead time. Since the containers involve relatively few width and depth (base) dimensions and material specifications, a standard-sized container is, on occasions, cut to the required height by Aztec at an extra cost in order to fill a low-volume order requiring immediate shipment.

Tight control is maintained over the inventory of the lead used by Aztec in the manufacturing of the grids and plates. Since lead represents 45 percent of the manufacturing cost of a battery, both the supplier delivery times and the inventory of lead is carefully monitored by the company.

Manufacturing Planning and Control

Aztec's manufacturing planning and control system can be characterized by the inputs and outputs shown in Exhibit 6. Sales orders are received both at the field warehouses and at the company headquarters in Cleveland. The sales administration staff enters the sales orders, indicating the required customer delivery date, using the satellite terminals of the computer-

EXHIBIT 6   Aztec Manufacturing Planning and Control System

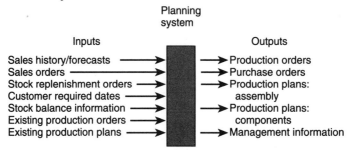

based sales order processing system. If inventory is available, sales administration allocates product to the sales order and goods are picked, dispatched, and invoiced to the customer. If inventory is not available, the following guidelines are observed in making customer delivery promises:

a. Ex-stock deliveries can be quoted for 3–5 days delivery, depending mainly on the transport lead time.

b. Products that are currently in the charging area can be quoted for a 10-day delivery, depending on their status in charging.

c. Products for which components are available can be quoted for delivery in approximately two weeks.

d. Products that require the ordering of components would require two weeks plus the material lead time involved.

Each warehouse carries an agreed level of finished goods inventory, which reflects the local sales history patterns and trends. The field warehouse stock is replenished from the central warehouse at the Cleveland plant, which holds inventory in accordance with the company's overall sales history patterns. Daily computer reports advise the head office sales administration when the field warehouse stocks require replenishment, and they issue stock replenishment orders to transfer inventory from Cleveland.

Each week sales administration reviews the past 4 months sales history and the 12-month sales average in order to facilitate material procurement. This data is shown in Exhibit 7 for seven representative products. Computer generated reports indicating outstanding sales and stock replenishment orders (Exhibit 8), stock balances (Exhibit 7), and production orders for end products (their master production schedule is shown in Exhibit 9) are used in this procedure.

On a weekly basis, sales administration meets with the assembly manager and the production planning and control manager to finalize the master production schedule for the week after next. The portion of the master production schedule (MPS) covering the next six weeks for the representative products is shown in Exhibit 9. Minor revisions to next week's master production schedule are also made, taking into account any new and urgent sales orders. In order to accommodate these short notice changes, component stocks include a "buffer stock" level.

A computer-based materials requirements planning (MRP) system is used to support manufacturing planning and control. The production planning and control department issues production orders for end products (their master production schedule) in line with the forecast supplied by sales administration. The MRP system is then run against these production

EXHIBIT 7   Sales History Data

Product Reference Number	Previous Four Months Sales				Last 12 Months Sales Average	Current Finished Goods Inventory
	November	December	January	February		
MTW55	198	0	29	2	230	71
MTS24	362	304	382	552	625	49
MTQ50	1,290	1,222	1,561	1,733	1,235	5
MTQ14	219	185	241	631	303	11
MTX21	139	356	239	438	317	32
MTV10	36	372	50	90	184	24
MTV42	76	0	24	26	22	0

NOTE: The current finished goods inventory is that which is on hand at the beginning of the first shift on Monday morning of week 26 after production and shipments in week 25 have been accounted for—see Exhibits 8 and 9.

EXHIBIT 8   Customer-Order Backlog

Product Reference Number	Known Delivery Requirements					
	Week 26	Week 27	Week 28	Week 29	Week 30	Week 31
MTW55						
MTS24	509					
MTQ50	742					
MTQ14	192					
MTX21						1728
MTV10				108		
MTV42						

EXHIBIT 9   Master Production Schedule—Cell Assembly

Product Reference Number	Week 26	Week 27	Week 28	Week 29	Week 30	Week 31
MTW55	50	50	100		100	100
MTS24		150	300	300	300	300
MTQ50		900		900		900
MTQ14	800		500		600	
MTX21	84	42	84	84	84	84
MTV10	56	56	56	56	56	56
MTV42			36	72		72

Exhibit 10   Production Performance against Master Production Schedule (MPS)

Product Reference Number	Week 25, MPS	Week 25, Actual
MTW55		
MTS24	350	314
MTT42	150	137
MTQ16	200	201
MTC41		87
MTW36	100	104
MTQ50	900	897
MTQ14		602
MTX30	42	
MTX21	42	42
MTV61	310	213
MTT28	210	204
MTQ47	105	315
MTW16	112	172
MTV10		56
MTV42		
MTV81	28	
Total	2,549	3,344

Percent actual to MPS: 131%

NOTE: This data is a representative sample of the plant results for week 25.

Exhibit 11   Container Stock Cycle Count Results

Type/Part Number	Description	On-Hand Computer	Inventory Actual	Balance Difference	Percent Difference
High-volume					
667	Container	326	306	−20	−6
128	Container	436	492	56	13
424	Container	332	320	−12	−4
832	Container	1,426	1,374	−52	−4
527	Container	716	668	−48	−7
Total		3,236	3,160	−76	−2
Low-volume					
221	Container	128	159	31	24
382	Container	12	0	−12	−100
112	Container	156	154	−2	−1
968	Container	84	84	0	0
421	Container	251	235	−16	−6
Total		631	632	1	0
Grand total		3,867	3,792	−75	−2

orders, taking into account existing inventory and purchase-order information for low-volume components.

Manufactured components are planned and controlled in different ways depending on their setup and lead times. Items with short setup and lead times (such as tubular positive plates and small parts) are controlled using a Kanban style pull system driven by assembly usage. Items with relatively long setup and lead times are controlled by the production planning department. In this case, weekly schedules are issued to each manufacturing department, which take into account future assembly plans and existing inventory balances.

Two types of capacity planning reports are prepared by the production planning and control manager. One on a quarterly basis indicates the estimated production rate (i.e., the number of cells per week) for the six different production groupings of tubular, flat plate, rail, BX, DX, and RX. The second report is issued weekly and indicates the percent of plant and manpower utilized during the previous week. Neither of these reports translates the MPS (i.e., the number of units of each cell product item to be produced in each week over the coming six weeks) into capacity requirements for the individual manufacturing processes.

The actual assembly and component production is reviewed daily to check progress against the schedule. The overall assembly performance is reviewed weekly at a sales/production meeting held each Monday when "panics" are identified and order priorities are established. An example of manufacturing performance against the production plan is shown in Exhibit 10 for a sample of representative products. Because of the critical role played by on-hand inventory balances in Aztec's MRP system, Exhibit 11 shows the results of a recent cycle count for several representative cell container items. Although not shown, similar results should be expected for the cell finished goods inventory.

CASE 3
CLIFTON INDUSTRIES

No doubt, you are all aware that we have today received confirmation of the acceptance for what is our first contract with a second U.S. customer. The North American market is large, and breaking into it has been difficult. But, hopefully, this success will help to turn more of our tenders into orders [see Exhibit 1]. It also represents putting into place the second half of our revised marketing strategy. With two major U.S. customers on board we can begin to feel we are getting ourselves established in this market. Our initial entry into electronic products was the first part of our recent marketing decisions and here too we anticipate more orders in the future. [See Exhibit 2.]

Keith Mills, the managing director of Clifton Industries, was commenting upon aspects of marketing strategy at a board meeting in the early part of 1987, as part of a review of corporate strategic direction.

Background

Clifton Industries Ltd. is part of Berbeck Industries Group Plc, a large European-based conglomerate involved in a diverse range of industries including machine equipment, electronics, civil engineering, oil-refining, chemicals, and domestic appliances, besides aerospace. Berbeck Industries Group is a decentralized organization, apart from major capital investments, which have to be sanctioned at group level. Thus Clifton Industries, as with other companies in the group, determines its own corporate strategy, which is presented to the group's board of directors each year. To all intents and purposes, it runs as an independent business with few group-based support services (see Exhibit 3).

Clifton Industries is one of several companies in the Berbeck Group involved in supplying a whole range of products to aircraft manufacturers. Although this range is wide, there also exists a considerable overlap in terms of process capability, labor skills, and manufacturing infrastructure (e.g., design, process engineering, and other support functions) between companies within the group. Clinton Industries is, relative to other aerospace parts of the group, small in terms of sales revenue (£s). Other related companies, with as much as four to five times the annual sales, have similar manufacturing capabilities, but are clearly and consciously kept apart one from another in terms of products manufactured (see Exhibit 4).

To foster this segment of its total business, Berbeck Industries has for some time now had a main board director with executive responsibility for its aerospace companies. In the last 10 years, the group has taken over three U.S. aerospace companies, as much to gain firsthand knowledge of how to enter North American markets as for anything else. In this and in other ways, the aerospace companies have built up a very close understanding of current and future world markets in related products.

A feature of the aerospace business is that it is able (to a considerable extent) to assess its future load. Original equipment (OE)[1] commitments are known and changes in sales levels are

---

[1]Original equipment (OE) contracts refer to sales of products, which form part of the construction of new aircraft. Spares orders are for products that replace original equipment, following a specified number of flying hours or due to wear and tear.

This case study was written by Professor T. J. Hill (London Business School) and S. H. Chambers (University of Warwick) © AMD Publishing (U.K.). It is intended for class discussion and not as an illustration of good or bad management.

Exhibit 1   Summary of Contracts Received and Tenders Submitted for Electromechanical Products in North American Markets

Product		Actual and Projected Annual Sales Revenue (£m)										Average Selling Price per Unit (£s)
Reference	Type	1986	1987	1988	1989	1990	1991	1992	1993	1994	1995	
C 14612	Cu	0.42	0.63	0.63	0.25	0.15	—	—	—	—	—	515
C 14625	Cu	0.03	0.10	0.30	0.60	0.80	0.80	0.80	0.60	0.60	0.20	285
T 4289	M	—	—	0.11	0.11	0.12	0.12	0.11	0.06	—	—	312
T 4315	Cu	—	0.20	0.25	0.25	0.30	0.25	0.20	0.10	0.05	—	800
T 4332	M	—	0.07	0.10	0.12	0.14	0.12	0.10	0.07	0.07	0.07	460
T 4376	Cu	—	—	—	0.45	0.50	0.50	0.50	0.20	—	—	1,250
T 4387	Cu	—	—	0.13	0.16	0.25	0.25	0.30	0.30	0.10	—	850
T 4401	M	—	0.13	0.40	0.50	0.70	0.80	0.90	0.70	0.50	0.20	290

NOTES: 1. Cu = customer-specified design; M = modular design; T = tender; and C = contract

2. All prices have been adjusted by estimated inflation and are based on 1986 figures.

3. The modular design philosophy was based on the need to achieve low costs in price-sensitive markets, such as North America.

4. For explanations of "tender," "contract," and "projected annual sales revenue," see the notes at the foot of Exhibit 2.

EXHIBIT 2 Summary of Contracts Received, Tenders Submitted, and Inquiries Received to Date for Electronic-Based Products

Stage	Product Reference	Market	Projected Annual Sales Revenue (£m)							Average Selling Price per Unit (£)
			1987	1988	1989	1990	1991	1992	1993	
C	14586	U.K.—Military	0.30	0	1.10	1.20	0.70	0.50	0.10	2,550
E	262	U.K.—Civil	—	—	0.50	0.50	0.50	0.50	—	1,000
E	283	Europe—Civil	—	—	—	0.75	0.80	0.90	1.00	1,650
T	5160	U.K.—Military	—	—	1.25	2.50	2.70	3.00	1.50	425
T	5200	U.K.—Military	—	—	—	0.10	0.10	0.10	0.10	320
E	305	Europe—Military	—	—	0.60	0.20	0.40	0.45	—	670
E	327	U.S.—Civil	—	—	—	2.50	6.00	8.50	6.00	1,800
T	5360	U.K.—Military	—	0.15	0.15	0.25	0.35	0.35	0.25	500
T	5380	U.K.—Civil	—	—	—	—	0.05	0.10	0.15	175

NOTES: 1. C = contract received; E = enquiry; and T = tender.

2. All prices shown have been adjusted by estimated inflation and based on 1986 figures.

3. **Enquiries:** Company representatives regularly visit current and prospective customers and are consulted about the possible use of products for new applications and on new aircraft currently at the design concept stage. These consultations lead to informal enquiries for which guide prices need to be provided. The probability of any of these enquiries being later formalized into request for formal tenders is about one in four.

4. **Tenders:** When projects are approved for detailed design expenditure, product specifications and tender documents are sent out by the aircraft manufacturer. Suppliers are required to quote prices and terms, which form a tender document, which is considered to be an offer and hence legally binding.

5. **Contracts:** The chosen supplier is awarded contracts based on the tender. These are legally binding, and may contain penalty clauses for late delivery. A contract will often comprise more than one product.

6. **Timing:** Tenders are submitted up to three years (sometimes even four years) ahead of the first delivery schedule. On receipt of a contract, a company would be involved in design and premanufacturing work, which may take up to 60 percent of the total lead-time between the award of the contract and the first delivery.

7. **Projected annual sales revenue:** These figures are based on schedule deliveries in the appropriate year. Deliveries comprise manufactured items.

EXHIBIT 3   Clifton Industries Organization Chart, January 1, 1987

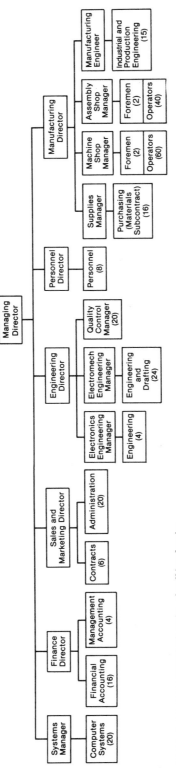

NOTES: ( ) indicates authorized number of staff in a function.

There are currently two vacancies in the electronics engineering provision. Of the two engineers in position, one has just joined the company.

Of the 24 engineering and drafting staff in electromechanical section, 16 are engineers (of whom two work on a subcontract basis).

EXHIBIT 4 The Companies Comprising the Aircraft Components Division of Berbeck Industries Group PLC

Company	Year	Clifton Industries	Blackdown Aerotech	Aviation Brakes	Berbeck Aircraft Components	Midland Aerospace
Product range		Small electro-mechanical controls, switches, and relays	Electromechanical actuators for aircraft services	Specialized braking systems	General precision electromechanical, hydraulic, and mechanical components	Major engine and flight control mechanisms, electromechanical, mechanical, and hydraulic
Approximate number of employees (1986)		255	350	440	680	845
Actual Sales Revenue (millions)						
Regular contract O.E.	86	5.9	12.4	17.0	30.1	37.2
	89	7.3	14.2	20.4	28.7	41.5
	91	9.8	18.7	22.2	26.5	49.5
Spares, repairs, inter-mittent O.E.	86	5.3	6.9	7.8	12.5	18.6
	89	4.0	7.5	8.6	14.5	20.5
	91	2.9	8.7	9.8	17.8	20.5
Total	86	11.2	19.3	24.8	42.6	55.8
	89	11.3	21.7	29.0	43.2	62.0
	91	12.7	27.4	32.0	44.3	70.0

NOTES: 1. All sales revenue forecasts have been adjusted for inflation, and are based on 1986 values.
2. Revenue figures for 1989 and 1991 are current forecasts.

EXHIBIT 5   Relative Levels of Forecast Sales Revenue by Categories

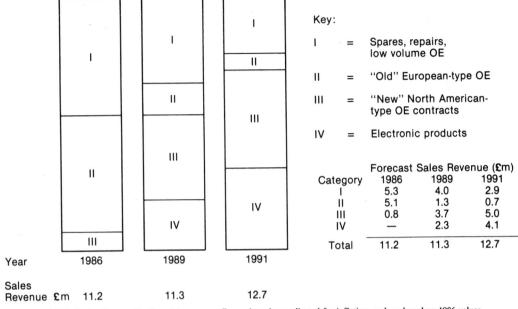

Key:

I   =   Spares, repairs, low volume OE

II   =   "Old" European-type OE

III =   "New" North American-type OE contracts

IV   =   Electronic products

Category	Forecast Sales Revenue (£m)		
	1986	1989	1991
I	5.3	4.0	2.9
II	5.1	1.3	0.7
III	0.8	3.7	5.0
IV	—	2.3	4.1
Total	11.2	11.3	12.7

Year	1986	1989	1991
Sales Revenue £m	11.2	11.3	12.7

SOURCE: 1986 Marketing Strategy Review. Sales revenue figures have been adjusted for inflation, and are based on 1986 values.

usually signaled some time ahead. Forecast sales (£s) for spares are based on past OE sales and historical trends. In September 1986, Keith Mills was appointed managing director of Clifton Industries. His predecessor, who had been with the company for many years, was near retirement age. It seemed opportune for someone new to take on the task of determining the company's future and the anticipated changes that would need to be brought about. The directive to Keith Mills, who came from another aerospace company within the group, was to maintain the current performance of the company and secure its long-term future. Clifton Industries had performed well in financial terms, but the fall off in future sales of existing products was a major concern for the group. A key feature of Keith Mills's assessment would include a review of the marketing strategy changes put forward in 1985, concerning North American markets and electronic products. The overall decline in existing OE contracts was identified in 1986, as implied by the change in forecast sales mix given in Exhibit 5.

Marketing

Up to the mid-1980s, all major contracts had been with European aircraft manufacturers. As illustrated in Exhibit 6, products scheduled for future deliveries have a wide range of volumes and are at different stages in their product life cycles.

In 1984, it became apparent that the company would experience a major shortfall in its future order book, due to an overall decline in European sales. "We had to assess alternatives and determine in which markets we would most likely be successful in getting orders," explained James Normann, the sales and marketing director. He continued,

EXHIBIT 6 Sample of Representative Products from the OE Order Book, as of December 31, 1986

		Contract Details			
Product Reference	Total Standard Hours per Unit	First Year Produced	Last Year with Regular Schedules (actual or anticipated)	Planned Production (units) in 1987	Comments
A 380	7.0	1972	1983	4	Single order for Brazil
A 436	11.8	1980	1988	100	
L 187	12.6	1982	1993	130	
A 399	1.3	1976	1987	35	Electrical lead assembly
L 190	7.9	1984	1996	510	
A 458	5.8	1985	1997	480	Product design not yet final
J 99	8.9	1983	1991	98	
A 446	18.0	1983	1991	107	
A 391	24.2	1975	1988	375	
A 396	12.2	1975	1988	229	
A 440	26.4	1981	1989	40	
J 41	20.0	1965	1978	20	Irregular schedules
J 72	19.5	1970	1984	23	Airline order
L 192	25.5	1984	1996	8	
A 438	9.6	1980	1989	40	
L 158	14.7	1976	1988	23	
L 198	6.7	1987	1995	103	
A 456	7.2	1985	1996	460	
L 153	29.2	1969	1987	69	
S 26	1.5	1974	1988	200 ⎫	Small products originally
S 42	1.3	1980	1989	1,350 ⎬	purchased in batches
S 43	1.9	1980	1989	100 ⎪	of 2500
S 32	1.5	1978	1989	1,200 ⎭	
A 300	9.4	1968	1982	40	
A 175	13.3	1960	1973	4	

NOTE: Once the main scheduled contracts have been completed, there is invariably a legal requirement to provide units, spares, and repairs, until there are four or less aircraft in use throughout the world. Experience indicates that this period is for at least 25 years.

A review of world markets revealed two areas, both of which undoubtedly appeared to be segments, which were large and displaying growth potential. The first was to supply products of a type similar to our current electromechanical designs to North American aircraft manufacturers [see Exhibit 7, which gives estimated costs of the first three contracts for U.S. customers]. The second was to design and manufacture electronic products for Europe and North America. However, time was pressing. Although marketing highlighted the sales fall-offs in 1984, and in early 1985 proposed a strategy to compensate for this loss by entering these two new markets, the decision by the business took time. This was due to the stepped nature of the change—we had, as a company, been linked to European manufacturers for the whole of our existence—and the fact that it had to be reviewed by the group as a whole. In the meantime, the lead time between contracts being signed and initial deliveries got increasingly shorter. With the shortfall in sales getting closer, the need to make decisions started to become critical.

EXHIBIT 7   Estimated Costs for the First Three Electromechanical (OE) Contracts for U.S. Customers

		Estimates per Unit		
		Purchases (£s)		
Product Reference	*Labor Standard Hours*	*Material*	*Components*	*Subcontract Work/Processes*
A 463 (M)	4.8	4	94	25
L 195 (M)	16.4	15	66	40
J 105	14.0	1	56	1

NOTES: M indicates modular design.
Further detail is given on these products in Exhibit 9.

James Normann then went on to explain the characteristics of existing and new markets. The North American market ($s) is up to 10 times greater than its European equivalent. However, it is significantly more competitive. The U.S. market is already served by four large companies, all U.S.-based, with sound experience and highly competitive. Normann summarized the differences as follows:

> Even when we become established, the North American market will be price-sensitive. All U.S. aircraft manufacturers allocate most contracts on a dual-sourced basis. Even so, the annual quantities involved are normally much greater than typical European contracts, and the volume provides for low-cost manufacturing. However, European agreements have usually been single-sourced, and although the volumes tend to be smaller, the agreed prices have provided very satisfactory margins, with spares orders offering even greater opportunities, due to the price uplifts we can command. With North American contracts, the pressure on price will undoubtedly be present even in the later stages of a life cycle as alternative supplies will always be available. The first contracts completed in 1986 also required shorter lead times than European equivalents, particularly in terms of first deliveries after the contract had been placed. With dual sourcing, delivering on time is now even more important, as failure would directly affect our supplier rating, and hence future sales.

On the aspect of electronic products, James Normann explained the strategic importance of entering these markets:

> Electronic applications are already replacing electromechanical equivalents, and this trend is going to increase in the future. There are not many European suppliers who have an electronics capability—in terms of design through to manufacture. Our decision to go into electronics was almost preordained. Product technology developments are with us, and we have to see the opportunities and recognize the need to get into this changing and developing business. Part of the marketing strategy has been to embody the opportunity/threat perspective in its decisions. Initially, it is proving most rewarding.

He continued to explain that margins on electronic products were similar to existing OE contracts. "The important aspect at this stage, however, is to ensure that we deliver the contract schedules on time," James Normann emphasized. "There are not many suppliers with whom we are competing, so successful contracts will reinforce our position as a viable source of these products."

Information on these and existing OE and spares markets is provided in Exhibits 8 and 9.

Exhibit 8

Summary of Recent Market Analysis, Conducted by the Group for Each of the Operating Companies of the Aircraft Components Division

1. U.K./European Airframe and Engine Manufacturers' OE Requirements
   a. Civil contracts
      - Recent growth is expected to level off.
      - Intensive competition from North American aircraft manufacturers will result in reducing market prices. This is beginning to lead to some price-cutting at the component supplies level.
      - Delivery reliability is becoming increasingly important, and penalty clauses are included in certain contracts.
   b. Military contracts
      - Most orders for the largest European collaborative project are nearly completed, and no more OE work is anticipated after 1988. Other European projects are significantly smaller, but are generally won on the technical merit of the product.
      - The next generation of European military aircraft is being designed and large-scale manufacture is expected in about 1992. A move away from electromechanical to electronic systems is anticipated, but the extent of this change is not yet clear but will take place over a number of years.

2. Spares and repairs
      - The demand for spares and repairs is expected to decline by about 8 percent per annum over the next six years.
      - The customers (airlines and air forces) can only obtain spares from the OE suppliers. Prices and margins are high. Delivery is generally required within 30 days of order, and this is usually achieved by holding inventory. Frequent failure to deliver on time may result in serious complaints to the airframe manufacturer, which may affect negotiations for new OE contracts.

3. North American ("new") electromechanical business
      - Many North American contracts are typically ten times the volume of the largest United Kingdom or European equivalents.
      - In each area of component supply, tenders will be usually submitted by three or four major U.S. companies. There is intensive competition for contracts, price is always the most important order-winning criterion, and dual or multi-sourced contracts are normally awarded. Lead times are typically half those experienced in Europe, and large penalties for late delivery are required.

Exhibit 8
(concluded)

European suppliers have not been seriously considered until recently, but may now be asked to tender, which would intensify price competition among the North American suppliers.

4. Electronics
   - The concept of electronics being used to control all aircraft systems is gaining acceptance, and is being widely assessed.
   - The market is potentially very large, with apparent high margins at least in the early stages. Orders at this time are won on the technical merit of the products, rather than on price.

Manufacturing

The existing processes within manufacturing comprise batch manufacturing to make components, which go to assembly for building into the required products. The process demands of aircraft components and subsequent assemblies require high skill levels, with continuous investment in new and replacement processes, in order to provide the necessary capability to meet the exacting and critical demands of aircraft products. Assembly consists of relatively simple jigs and fixtures, with from one to four assemblers involved in the final build of each product.

The range of processes and labor skills within the company are suitable to manufacture almost any product made within the group. In fact, over the last few years, Clifton Industries has taken on the spares manufacture of products, the OE contracts for which were provided by other aerospace companies within the group. This, together with its own spares requirement, has been met by extending its manufacturing capability to handle low-volume products.

The company's decision to move into North American and electronic markets has brought about some necessary changes within design and manufacturing. The first of these concerns the concept of modular-designed products. Exhibit 10 provides some of the rationale and background to the introduction of modular designs. "The key to being able to gain the opportunities for low-cost manufacturing depends on achieving the volume potential envisaged in the original proposals. There is no doubt that the North American markets are significantly larger than our current OE sales levels and this, it appears, should translate into volumes," explained Mike Harris, manufacturing director.

"The products are similar to their European equivalents in terms of work content. It is the increase in unit quantity which will provide the volume uplift," he continued. "In anticipation of the need to relook at manufacturing, we commissioned a report from our manufacturing systems engineering group, which is centrally based within Berbeck Industries." They reviewed the business, and Exhibit 11 summarizes their findings. "We have held back on implementation until Keith Mills was able to understand the business and contribute to this sizeable investment decision. It is to be discussed in the near future, once the corporate marketing review has been completed. The systems engineers were very convincing in their arguments, and group interest on the outcome of these proposals is most noticeable."

EXHIBIT 9   Analysis of Actual Costs Incurred for a Representative Sample of Electromechanical OE Products

Category Reference	Description	Product Unit Reference Number	Typical Unit Selling Price (£)	1986 Annual Sales (units)	Current Actual Labor Standard Hours/Unit	Actual Purchases (£ per unit)		
						Material	Components	Subcontract Work/Processes
I	Low-volume OE	A 286	2,102	6	22.3	12	120	84
		A 376X	1,023	20	14.3	10	38	14
		A 420	810	3	6.4	1	20	5
		L 150Y	1,920	15	32.4	32	67	32
		L 160	2,040	27	52.8	33	197	45
		J 64	650	25	7.8	6	70	10
II	"Old" type OE	A 385	1,545	155	12.1	4	57	15
		L 185X	836	360	29.6	22	92	15
		J 96	380	440	9.5	8	139	32
III	"New" type OE	A 463	250	120	10.4	4	132	31
		L 195	450	180	24.9	16	158	56
		J 105	318	260	14.9	1	58	1

NOTES:
1. The 1986 average direct labor pay rate was £5.10 per hour, including fringe benefits.
2. Products listed in Categories I and II were produced in 1986, and are typical of contracts for "old" products.
3. Category II products are mature, medium/high-volume products.
4. Products listed in Category III are considered typical of the "new" North American business. The products listed here are a representative sample from initial U.S. contracts.
5. Category III Products A 463 and L 195 are both of modular design.
6. The Category III products are, in the light of subsequent contract information, considered to be representative in terms of selling price relative to labor and material content, and of annual unit sales.

· **Exhibit 10**

The Modular Concept for Electromechanical Engineering Design

Based on a 1980 analysis of the 80 most frequently ordered, existing product types, the chief engineer considered that, in theory, these could be superceded by a new range consisting of only eight standard modules, thereby significantly reducing manufacturing variety and increasing cumulative volumes.

It was recognized that:

- Considerable engineering work would be required to develop the new modular products. Consequently, a budget of £300,000 spread over four years was agreed. Design work would be done by existing engineers.

- No existing orders could be converted to the new range. The modular products were, therefore, to be used in tenders for new applications requiring delivery from 1985 onward.

- Most contracts would require minor adaption to the modules to meet specific customer requirements for shape, weight, performance, and fit. It was recognized that, in some instances, modular products would, therefore, be overdesigned in terms of their proposed application.

- The very advantages of this initiative would be gained by the potential reduction of manufacturing complexity, the higher component volumes resulting from the reduced range, and the larger bought-out and sub-contract volumes. It was argued that these would offer the potential to reduce manufacturing costs, thus enabling the company to tender successfully in price-sensitive (specifically North American) markets.

Harris continued:

With regard to electronic products, we are finding it difficult to recruit appropriate engineers to enable us to meet all aspects of these new, and very different type of products. Delays through the personnel procedures did not help initially, and we now find that there is a scarcity of suitably qualified people. The agreed establishment of five staff members (including the manager) is to meet the first phase of our entry into these markets. This represents a major engineering change both in terms of design and process engineering, as well as placing very different demands on manufacturing. Although arrangements have been made to source most of the electronic subassemblies from specialized suppliers, manufacturing obviously retains overall responsibility, including final assembly and test. Later, it is our intention to reconsider how much of the total process is completed internally. We have our first military contract with deliveries due to commence in May 1987. That's only a few months off, but the product designs are not yet finalized, and the majority of the process engineering work is thus delayed. As you can imagine, we have much to do in manufacturing, and the pressure is on from the rest of the business about whether or not we can pull back the time lost and deliver to program.

Exhibit 11

Summary of Manufacturing Systems Engineering's Report, June 1986

The report was asked to advise on how manufacturing should best approach the task of producing the wide range of old and new electromechanical products. A separate review of electronic product manufacture had just begun. The report recommended:

1. Splitting manufacturing into four units with profit center accountability:
   - Component manufacturing.
   - Subassembly and assembly for "new electromechanical products."
   - Subassembly and assembly for all other electromechanical products.
   - Experimental and preproduction unit, comprising machining and assembly.

2. The major investment and attention should be in a high-volume assembly area to be located in a part of the factory currently used for storage. A layout was devised comprising four subassembly and three assembly cells, based on work-flow analysis, and using the principle of bringing together products which required similar subassembly and assembly processes. This would require an investment of approximately £500,000. The benefits were assessed as being:
   - Reduction in average assembly time from 23 days to 7 days, giving a £63,000 work-in-process inventory reduction.
   - Increased manufacturing efficiency, resulting in annual savings in direct labor of £45,000.
   - Annual indirect labor costs reduced by £95,000.

3. The analysis was based on the following 1989 forecast production of units.

Type	Number of Units per Year	Average Standard Hours/Unit
New (North American)	12,000	7.4
Old	2,500	17.3

   No assessment of the split between machining and assembly standard hours was made, but was assumed to be similar to the mix experienced in the past. The number of contracts or schedules was not available.

4. The rationale for the detailed analysis and redesign of the assembly facility was as follows:

Exhibit 11
(concluded)

- New products were anticipated to have a relatively higher bought-out content, thus gradually reducing the content of machined work.
- The performance of assembly directly affects customer satisfaction in respect of delivery reliability and conformance quality.
- It was easy to classify products as either "old" or "new" business.
- There were fewer manufacturing routes in assembly than in machining. It was thus only possible in the time available to complete a production flow analysis for assembly.
- In assembly, there are many consecutive operations on the same workcenter, making a cellular solution appropriate and readily applicable.

On the spares and repairs aspects of the business, Mike explained that unfortunately these often are neglected, due to other, more important priorities:

Sharing the same machining processes and assembly facilities, spares tend to get fitted in wherever we can. Sales complain about our performance, although they admit it is tolerated by our customers [see Exhibit 12]. If, however, there is an urgent requirement, we will give it the necessary attention, even though it does disrupt our main production effort. As with all the other companies involved in this business, we get good margins on these orders (the price for spares is up to three or four times that agreed for the equivalent OE unit, with repairs yielding even higher margins), which compensates for the inefficiencies in manufacturing associated with very low volumes and the infrequent nature of the orders. There is no doubt about it, we could get more business if we proved better suppliers. Certainly, we lose repair contracts to specialists in this work and also the airlines' own repair facilities because we are unable to meet the delivery dates required. How much we are losing we don't known. The problem is, however, that it is difficult to justify manufacturing these orders when OE contracts need to be given priority. With these latter contracts, we need to meet delivery schedules, and our record has to be, and is, correspondingly better than for spares and repairs [see Exhibit 13].

Mike Harris then went on to explain that the business had recognized the increasing production control problems, especially given the complexity of individual products and the widening range. This control issue, however, was common to all the aerospace companies within the group, and the problem had, therefore, been addressed and resolved on a global basis. The solution was to introduce a materials requirement planning (MRP) system to cover the loading, sequencing, and scheduling of all OE, spares, and repairs. The decision to implement a common MRP system had been taken, and Clifton Industries had begun this task in the early 1980s. "It has been up and working for some time now, and we are looking to it to help improve the delivery performance in all aspects of our business," commented Phil Bradshaw, the systems manager.

Complex problems are difficult to resolve, and the computer and other resources needed to tackle this important aspect of manufacturing have been considerable [see Exhibits 3 and 14]. Give the company its due, it has been prepared to face reality and resource these needs accordingly. This has, however, been helped by the group MRP initiative and subsequent provision of resources and investment

EXHIBIT 12   **Spares and Repairs: A Representative Sample of Orders Completed during 1986**

	Works Order		Actual		Date (week number) Delivery		
	Number	Invoiced Value (£s)	Direct Labor (total hours)	Materials (£s)	Customer Order	Required	Actual
Civil Repairs							
	04	1,465	10	103	3	8	9
	20	772	6	26	10	14	18
	32	3,353	22	440	11	16	18
	64	16,995	142	1,250	15	20	20
	69	6,325	46	60	22	28	29
CR86	75	1,698	18	6	26	30	36
	81	475	4	25	31	35	48
	87	3,680	32	140	39	44	43
	94	2,307	17	88	42	47	48
	98	297	2	7	44	48	52
Military Repairs							
	06	2,334	27	120	4	18	16
	14	6,605	62	740	8	21	24
	28	19,871	260	25	10	22	25
	33	3,705	47	20	16	30	27
	41	6,462	70	540	16	28	22
MR86	64	26,030	310	2,650	21	36	34
	78	1,165	10	250	30	42	47
	81	9,907	120	1,760	36	46	50
	84	527	5	15	39	50	51
	94	3,335	40	125	40	52	51
Civil Spares							
	74	360	3	25	4	8	13
	156	1,630	16	210	9	13	16
	208	2,565	19	375	11	19	19
	311	457	4	160	16	20	22
	392	152	1	48	21	26	38
CS86	450	506	4	125	25	29	32
	521	1,403	14	256	28	40	44
	630	260	2	125	34	38	38
	727	732	7	70	36	40	44
	786	326	2	46	39	43	49

NOTES: 1. The agreed basis for charging repair work differs from customer to customer.

2. Repair orders range from those requiring simple adjustment and the retesting of single units, to the complete rebuilding of several units, necessitating the replacement of most moving parts.

3. "Actual direct labor hours" include the following activities: dismantle, component manufacture (as required), assembly, and test.

4. Civil spares, which are classified as fast-moving, are items held in finishing goods inventory to be delivered (in compliance with international agreements) within one month of the order being placed. The details of orders shown here are for those items not classified as "fast-moving."

5. Military spares are only made to air force orders, with typical order lead times of 6–12 months. In most instances, the national air force holds finished goods inventory of spares, and lead times are calculated to allow adequate time to manufacture the items required.

EXHIBIT 13   Delivery Performance on a Representative Sample of Recent Electromechanical (OE) Contracts

	Delivery by Product Category (units)							
	Contract Placed June 84				Contract Placed May 84		Contract Placed July 84	
	A 176 (I)		A 410 (II)		J 80 (II)		L 100 (III)	
Date	Required	Actual	Required	Actual	Required	Actual	Required	Actual
1984								
November							3	
December								2
1985								
January					14			
February					8	4	3	
March			18		24	4		
April			18			18		
May	5		24		26	14	6	4
June	5		29		24	18		
July		7	10	21		8	6	
August	5		12	10		16		
September			12	20		10	6	6
October	5	6	12	48				
November	5	2	12	25		4	6	9
December			12	15			6	
1986								
January	5	3	11	28				15
February			10	11				
March		3	11	39				
April		2	10	10				
May			11					
June		7	10	5				
July			10	5				
August			10	5				
September								
October								
November								
December								

support. We have had the basic system installed now for 18 months, although the new product introductions will bring another large updating requirement, and no doubt will delay the necessary developments and improvements we need to make. However, we realize the task is very important and are responding to these justifiable demands for associated manufacturing improvements.

Corporate Decision on Future Markets

"The falloff in sales is real. The only question confronting us is how to resolve the problem. The marketing initiative has a lot going for it. The basic logic is sound in terms of growth and future potential. Also, the question is: What would be a realistic alternative? We have begun to

EXHIBIT 14   Trends in Average Costs (£s) per Standard Hour 1980 to 1986

Year	Average Cost (£) per Standard Hour		
	Direct Labor	Overhead	Total
1980	4.44	12.80	17.24
1981	4.90	14.40	18.98
1982	5.18	19.20	24.38
1983	5.60	22.06	27.66
1984	6.10	24.18	30.28
1985	6.44	25.63	32.07
1986	6.88	28.14	35.02

NOTES: 1. Direct labor cost includes all fringe benefits paid by the company. It also reflects the level of effective performance achieved in production and is, therefore, higher than the pay rate given in Note 1, Exhibit 9.

2. "Overhead" includes indirect labor, salaries, and all other company overheads, including divisional charges.

make inroads into these markets, and that is another point in favor of continuing with this initiative. Like all decisions of this nature, it is large and will commit us for years to come, so we must make sure it is the appropriate course of action," were Keith Mills concluding comments. "I must ensure that the direction we take is appropriate in terms of fit and timing. The suggested changes take us into distinctly different segments and markets. While the direction may be indisputable, the timing may be in question. We have a lot of work to do, the change in direction is radical, and time is short!"

CASE 4
CONTROL ELECTRONICS INC.

"It certainly appears that Don's proposal will meet the board's capital investment criteria, and thus continue our successful policy of obtaining the very best available equipment for assembling and testing our products," concluded Ted Jackson (vice president of manufacturing).

> I'm sure that we can now make a sound application for the purchase of the automated radial component inserter so, if all goes to plan, you could be supervising its installation six months from now. We'll get together again next week to go over the details, so I can finalize our application, and have it ready for next month's board meeting. In the meantime, I will discuss the proposal with Brad Young, as he may see additional advantages from a marketing perspective. These days, customers certainly like to see "state of the art" equipment as part of their suppliers' processes.

Ted Jackson felt a certain satisfaction in being able to be so positive when summing up the weekly manufacturing meeting. Recent meetings had seemed devoid of any new ideas, and nearly all the latest plant developments had been stimulated by external/market forces, in particular the introduction of the new surface-mounted technology (SMT) processes. The proposed purchase of a radial component inserter would mechanize part of an otherwise labor-intensive element of assembly and should ensure improved quality in that part of the task. The production engineering manager, Don Poluski, was also pleased. For too long, he had been unable to specify suitable equipment to mechanize many of the remaining manual tasks. But, equipment was now available for a significant part of these remaining tasks and showed a good payback period. The only outstanding question seemed to be whether there would be an allocation of a further $130,000 to the company when an apparent shortage of capital existed within the group. To succeed, the supporting case would certainly have to be sound and consistent with the company's accepted strategy of keeping up with appropriate technology development, as one way of helping to reduce corporate dependence on skilled labor. Don decided to go back to his summary of the data on radial component insertion (Exhibit 1) in order to check the payback period calculations for himself.

After the meeting, Ted went to see Brad Young, the marketing manager, about the proposal. "I cannot see that it will make much difference from a marketing or sales perspective," said Brad. "The customers will not see a change in quality, as faulty assemblies are currently detected at the testing stage, and reworked as necessary. And you are not suggesting that the automation will reduce our prices, are you? My only concern is that you should remain responsive to urgent requirements for additional delivery quantities and schedule changes. At present, that is one of our greatest strengths—a factor supported by your successful breakdown of manufacturing into small, self-contained groups. Many of our customers simply cannot accept late deliveries, as keeping their high-volume production lines running is critical for them in the short term, and crucial for us in the long. As for customers liking the image of new technology, that is true, and we are not short on that score. Finally, I hope you will not require too much of the design engineers' time on the project, as they are already overloaded with new product development work."

This case study was written by Professor T. J. Hill (London Business School) and S. H. Chambers (University of Warwick) It is intended for class discussion and not as an example of good or bad management. © AMD Publishing (U.K.).

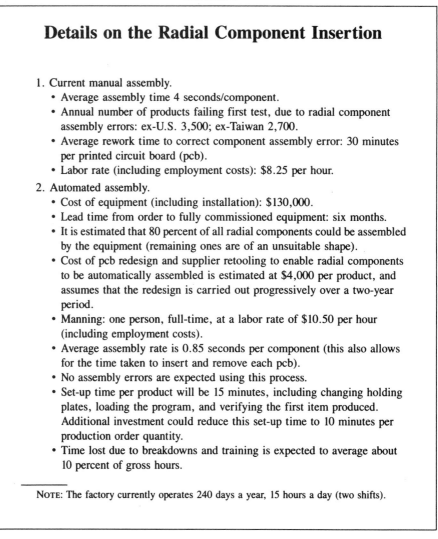

Exhibit 1

Details on the Radial Component Insertion

1. Current manual assembly.
   - Average assembly time 4 seconds/component.
   - Annual number of products failing first test, due to radial component assembly errors: ex-U.S. 3,500; ex-Taiwan 2,700.
   - Average rework time to correct component assembly error: 30 minutes per printed circuit board (pcb).
   - Labor rate (including employment costs): $8.25 per hour.
2. Automated assembly.
   - Cost of equipment (including installation): $130,000.
   - Lead time from order to fully commissioned equipment: six months.
   - It is estimated that 80 percent of all radial components could be assembled by the equipment (remaining ones are of an unsuitable shape).
   - Cost of pcb redesign and supplier retooling to enable radial components to be automatically assembled is estimated at $4,000 per product, and assumes that the redesign is carried out progressively over a two-year period.
   - Manning: one person, full-time, at a labor rate of $10.50 per hour (including employment costs).
   - Average assembly rate is 0.85 seconds per component (this also allows for the time taken to insert and remove each pcb).
   - No assembly errors are expected using this process.
   - Set-up time per product will be 15 minutes, including changing holding plates, loading the program, and verifying the first item produced. Additional investment could reduce this set-up time to 10 minutes per production order quantity.
   - Time lost due to breakdowns and training is expected to average about 10 percent of gross hours.

NOTE: The factory currently operates 240 days a year, 15 hours a day (two shifts).

Ted left with mixed feelings on how appropriate the proposed automation would be, and to what extent the customer would benefit from the investment. On returning to his office, he selected the file "Order-Winning Criteria" (Exhibit 2), which had been prepared as part of the recent annual strategic review, and sat down to consider the position once more.

Company Background

Control Electronics (CE) is a subsidiary of a large U.S. conglomerate, Stellex Industries Inc, involved in the manufacture of specialized engineering components for the defense, domestic

EXHIBIT 2 Order-Winning Criteria for Representative Products

		Order-Winning Criteria Weightings							
Product	*Year*	*Price*	*Delivery Speed*	*Delivery Reliability*	*Quality*	*Existing Supplier*	*Product Design*	*Ability to Modify Design*	*Anticipated Weekly Quantity (units)*
Group A									
4DA	86	90	0	QQ	10				2,250
	88	80	10		10				150
	90	80	10		10				120
16DA	86	30		QQ	Q	0	70		750
	88	70		QQ	Q	30	0		3,200
	90	70			Q	30	0		50
Group B									
5EA	86		40			60			150
	88		30			70			130
	90		30			70			100
12EA	86		Q	20	30	0	40	10	1,050
	88		Q	20	20	20	30	10	900
	90		30	0	10	60	0	0	200
14EA	86		Q	10	10	0	60	20	20
	88		Q	10	10	60	20	0	40
	90			0	10	90	0	0	5
Group C									
5VA	86	60	20	QQ		20			4,500
	88	70	20	QQ		10			3,500
	90	0	20	Q		80			1,000
Group D									
2MV/C	86	0			QQ	0	80	20	100
	88	50			QQ	50	0	0	300
	90	0			QQ	100	0	0	10
8MV	86	30	20	QQ	30	0	20		250
	88	50	10	QQ	20	20	0		300
	90	60	0	QQ	20	20	0		200
Group E									
6FN	86		30	Q		70			150
	88		30	Q		70			100
	90		30	Q		70			100
2EA	86	50	0		20	30			1,130
	88	0	40	Q	0	60			200
	90	0	30	Q	0	70			150

NOTE: Q denotes a qualifier and QQ an order-losing sensitive qualifier.

appliance (white goods), and automotive markets, although some general subcontract work is carried out.

CE was formed in 1981 to bring together, on one specialized site, the manufacture of electronic circuit board assemblies. During the late 70s, it had become apparent that requirements for electronics were growing significantly in all the industries served by Stellex Industries, and each subsidiary had developed suitable electronic products to meet its own customers' needs. Much of the manufacture and assembly of the circuit boards had been subcontracted, but in the case of the domestic appliance division, a large, well-equipped facility had been set up, which then became the basis of the new company, Control Electronics. It was decided from the outset that CE would deal directly with all its customers, whether internal or external. The success of the new venture became rapidly apparent—growth averaged over 20 percent per annum, with return on investment rising to 34 percent in 1985 to 1986, which made it one of the best performers in the group.

Not all the other subsidiaries were doing so well, largely as a result of extended difficulties in the automotive components market. This had left the group in a vulnerable position, and capital spending was severely restricted, with the acceptable payback period now at four years or less. Within these constraints, CE had managed to obtain most of its capital needs for assembly and test equipment. Stellex Industries had recognized the potential for the high growth and large margins inherent in many new markets for electronics, and had seen that this growth potential could only be sustained through significant levels of automation, as this would help to overcome skilled labor shortages and provide the consistent quality and lower cost requirements of these markets. The same approach had been applied in other, more traditional, subsidiaries within the group, resulting in significant investment in CAD/CAM and CNC machines.[1]

In addition to its excellent manufacturing facilities, CE also had a very large product development department, which already had a sound reputation for product innovation and design responsiveness. In the 1980s, many of CE's customers were finding the need to modify the design of their products, at a very late stage in their development, often to respond to their own competitors' latest innovations and promotions. Even when a design had been finalized and tested, it might be changed during early production runs in response to other technical changes in the original equipment (OE). Ted Jackson had recently discussed this point with the board. "We are increasingly having to avoid purchasing some major components, or manufacturing some products in quantities greater than about one week's demand, as there seems to be an increasing probability that the design will be changed in some way at short notice. And it's our own design and marketing departments that seem to be major contributors to these changes. They are positively encouraging and assisting the customers to overcome problems by product redesigns. It certainly doesn't help manufacturing to get costs down. At the same time, we are having to cope with an ever-increasing level of new product introductions, as some of our old, high-volume products appear to be on the way out." Exhibit 3 gives details of all products currently manufactured by CE.

Marketing   Much of the rapid growth, which had been achieved since the formation of CE, could only be attributed to the company's available capacity at times when market demand was expanding rapidly. The main role of sales had been to maintain sound customer contacts and collect the technical details for new applications. Meanwhile, the design and development department had been expanded and now offered a design service that was considered to be one of the best in the industry.

---

[1]CAD/CAM is the abbreviation for computer-aided design/computer-aided manufacture, while CNC refers to computer numerical control.

EXHIBIT 3   Information on All Products Manufactured in 1986

Product Reference	Year of OE Production 19— First	Year of OE Production 19— Last	Stage in Product Life Cycle (late 1986)	1986 Average Weekly Output (units)	Standard Minutes per Unit	Material and Bought-out Costs ($ per unit)	Selling Price ($/unit)	Number of Radial Components
Group A: Domestic-Appliances								
4DA(T)	78	87	LM	2,250	8.3	$ 47.96	$ 56.44	16
6DA(T)	82	88	M	1,125	2.9	24.84	27.70	12
8DA	83	87	LM	1,800	27.8	35.52	46.62	20
9DA(T)	83	87	LM	1,500	5.9	28.00	32.04	21
11DA(T)	84	87/8	LM	2,250	3.9	19.72	22.36	18
12DA(T)	84	89	M	1,500	4.4	29.00	46.62	23
13DA	85	89	M	750	16.7	25.66	43.80	28
14DA	86	89	M	750	16.7	29.00	50.62	26
16DA(S)	86	88	G	750	16.7	29.32	81.40	8
Group B: Engineering Applications								
5EA	80	85	S	150	104.3	142.60	477.16	18
7EA	81	85	S	120	134.3	278.62	375.40	23
9EA	83	86	S	30	124.4	262.44	694.74	14
10EA	83	88	M	60	35.3	136.68	423.54	22
12EA	85	89	M	1,050	25.6	69.64	179.94	13
13EA(S)	86	89	G	20	31.5	111.20	378.40	7
14EA(S)	86	88	G	20	31.5	91.50	356.16	5
17EA(S)	86	90	I	70	64.2	132.82	678.18	11
Group C: Vehicles								
5VA	79	89/90	LM	4,500	13.4	18.72	30.54	14
18VA	80	89/90	LM	4,500	17.3	56.76	75.72	8
Group D: Military Applications (vehicles and equipment)								
2MV/C	86	89	I	100	68.3	96.28	222.00	24
3MV	84	87	LM/D	150	39.0	54.70	175.92	14
5MV	85	88	G	50	91.1	377.34	634.18	25
8MV	86	90	G	250	21.2	6.66	19.44	8
Group E: Sundry and Low-Volume Products (including pilot line for new products)								
3DA	73	90	M	140	6.3	10.92	20.04	3.
6FN	74	84	S	150	53.1	32.08	71.46	12
16GM	75	83	S	150	37.4	5.80	19.62	21
2EA	75	86/7	D	1,130	4.7	1.60	5.52	4
4EA	77	88	LM	75	17.3	5.28	28.20	0
9FN	78	88	LM	75	42.5	50.44	115.30	10
10TM	79	84	S	15	12.5	5.34	47.70	4

NOTES: 1. (T) indicates PCB components assembled in Taiwan, and supplied to CE for further processing and testing.

2. (S) indicates the use of surface-mounted technology in these products.

3. Last year of OE production is either actual, if 1986 and before, or forecast, if for 1987 onward. When OE production has ceased, there is a spares requirement for a minimum of 10 years. OE refers to supplies to customers, who are currently making original equipment (e.g., new automobiles or military vehicles), as opposed to spares supply.

EXHIBIT 3 *(concluded)*

---

4. 1986 weekly output figures are based on 52 weeks per year.
5. The data in the column "Standard Minutes per Unit" include all operations at CE, including test.
6. In the "Sundry and Low-Volume Products" group, no products are made on a regular basis. Order requirements are cumulated and products are rarely made more than twice in a given week. Due to the infrequent nature of this work, the operators often have to work from drawings.
7. The abbreviations used in the column, "Stage in the Product Life Cycle" mean:

I	Introduction	S	Saturation
G	Growth	LM	Late mature
M	Maturity	D	Decline

By 1985, it became apparent that this approach to marketing was endangering the future development of the business. In each market, strong competitors were evolving, often specializing in a narrow range of products and frequently undercutting CE prices on high-demand items. In addition, many of the older, standard products seemed to be declining in volume and were expected to cease to be OE[2] items within a few years. For these reasons, Brad Young had been appointed, in early 1986, to introduce professional marketing skills into the business. His early visits to major customers quickly highlighted a widespread awareness of the increasing advantages provided by surface-mounted technology (SMT) products for some specialized applications. The technical manager and some of the senior salesmen had also identified this need, and a combined report, in the summer of 1986, led to the simultaneous development of a few SMT products for certain customers and the purchase of the sophisticated equipment needed to attach SMT components to circuit boards. In this way, CE had differentiated itself from the smaller, specialized competitors, who would have found difficulty in justifying the purchase of an expensive plant for a limited range of products.

In 1987, Brad reviewed the markets and prepared a marketing strategy, which is summarized in Exhibit 4.

Manufacturing

All electronic and mechanical components are purchased from wholesalers and manufacturers worldwide. Printed circuit boards (pcbs) are purchased from specialist manufacturers in the United States.

Manufacturing involves the assembly (insertion or attachment) of the appropriate electronic components and terminals onto pcbs, an automated soldering operation (flow soldering), manual assembly of sundry components, (for example, spacers) touch-up,[3] first testing, encasement into metal or plastic boxes, and final testing. Products failing either tests are reworked by hand and retested.

There are three types of components (axial components, integrated circuits, and radial components) used in the manufacture of the company's products, as shown in Exhibit 5. Typical conventional products contain hundreds of different axial components, all of which are inserted into production order quantities of pcbs by automatic computer-controlled equipment (sequencer, autoinserter, and verifier) located on a functional basis in a central process area. CE is well equipped for these operations, and existing plant is being updated to improve output rates

---

[2]See Note 3 on Exhibit 3 for an explanation of OE.

[3]Touch-up refers to a visual inspection and manual rectification of any unsatisfactory soldered joints.

Exhibit 4

Summary of Current and Future Marketing Strategy

1. Domestic Appliances Market

Although CE was founded on the basis of its success in this segment, severe pressure from competition has resulted in a low (8 percent) and decreasing market share and severe price competition from a large number of small, specialized suppliers. Due to an increasing level of appliance imports, a further decline in market volume over the next five years is forecast. The marketing policy is to continue to serve the requirements of our two remaining customers and maintain a low cost base through the assembly of high-volume products in Taiwan. The company would be prepared to withdraw from supplying either customer if competitive pressures cause further erosion of margin. The potential for SMT products will be explored.

2. Engineering Applications

This major market includes manufacturers of control mechanisms, machine tools, and robotics, principally in the United States and Canada. This is CE's largest and most profitable segment. Because of the complexity of designs and service requirements, there is only limited competition, mostly from similar businesses in the United States. CE is a technical leader in the field, and this advantage will be exploited by a major marketing and selling effort, which should result in an overall 20 percent growth in volume per year into the 1990s. New products will be of conventional and SMT types, whichever is appropriate to each application.

3. Vehicle Applications

Current sales are to only one customer, and unit volumes are high, but declining by about 10 percent per year. This business is only maintained by keeping prices at just below those quoted by competitors, and there seems to be little scope for developing high-volume products for other customers in this field. This is because vehicle manufacturers either have their own electronics-manufacturing subsidiaries or have developed satisfactory relationships with several other low-cost producers. CE's policy is to continue to serve this account reliably, but to be prepared for the end of the product's OE life by around 1990. The company would offer its development skills for any replacement product, which will tend to be SMT-based.

Exhibit 4
(concluded)

---

4. Military Applications (vehicles and equipment)

This market is the most diverse in terms of product size and value. Although CE only entered the market in 1983, the company has developed excellent relationships with various manufacturers of military equipment, and is seen as a high-quality producer. In some particularly critical applications, CE is one of only two suppliers qualified to produce and test to the high quality standards demanded. Three of the current products are increasing in volume, resulting in growth of around 25 percent per year. However, it is anticipated that this rate of growth will only be for a few years, then it will level off. The marketing effort will then be applied to ensure further growth, particularly for SMT products.

5. Product Support

The company will continue to supply spare units as required to all existing customers. As many OE product applications are expected to terminate over the next few years, growth in spares is expected to be significant.

6. Other Markets

No other new markets are to be pursued in the five-year plan.

NOTE: The phrase *original equipment manufacturer* (*OEM*) refers to a customer who makes the final product (e.g., automobile or military vehicle). Similarly, *original equipment* (*OE*) refers to the end product involved.

---

and to increase capacity. See Exhibit 6 for details of some of the processes employed and Exhibit 7, which illustrates different stages of a typical product.

All other components (radials, integrated circuits, and mechanical components, such as terminals) are assembled by hand. The electronic components can sometimes be mixed or positioned incorrectly on a complex pcb. For this reason, these operations are aided, where possible, by computer-controlled equipment (known as manuserts), which present the assembler with the correct components and define the assembly positions with an indicator light.

Manufacturing is divided into seven sections; four product-related groups (A to D), one low-volume product group (E) (see Exhibit 3), and two process areas (axial components insertion and flow soldering). Each product group is responsible for the assembly and testing of a specific range of products defined by market application (e.g., domestic appliances). The two process areas comprise general purpose equipment used to perform insertion and soldering operations on almost all products. All manufacturing groups currently operate on two 7.5 hour shifts per day, over five days. Groups A, B, and D use general purpose equipment, such as manuserts. These permit the rapid setups (less than five minutes) necessary to cope with the wide product

EXHIBIT 5   Typical Components Used in the Company's Products

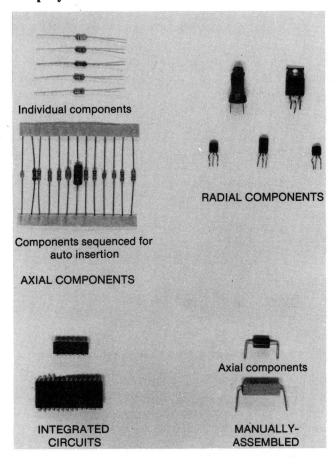

range involved, and require only moderate levels of skill, allowing the manufacturing function to use a mix of full- and part-time personnel. However, skilled employees are needed to use the complex testing equipment, and are also required to operate the axial components insertion and flow soldering equipment. Group C is equipped with two production lines. Operatives are generally trained to do only a limited range of tasks, using dedicated equipment.

Each group is headed by a group manager, supported by his own team of supervisors, production engineers, industrial engineers, planners, and quality controllers. All use tight quality control systems, incorporating statistical process control methods, which fully involve the operatives.

Groups B and D have been used for the development of the just-in-time (JIT) planning approach, based on Kanban boxes. The maximum batch size is currently one day's demand. This has successfully reduced work-in-process and finished goods inventory levels to less than three days' requirements, and each product type scheduled for delivery is made on a daily basis. This control method leaves little margin for error, but there have been few occasions in the last six

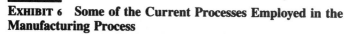

EXHIBIT 6   Some of the Current Processes Employed in the Manufacturing Process

EXHIBIT 6a—Auto insertion

EXHIBIT 6b—Flow soldering

EXHIBIT 6c—Assembly area

EXHIBIT 6d—Testing procedures

EXHIBIT 7   Three Different Views of a Typical Product

EXHIBIT 7a—Reverse side of a pcb

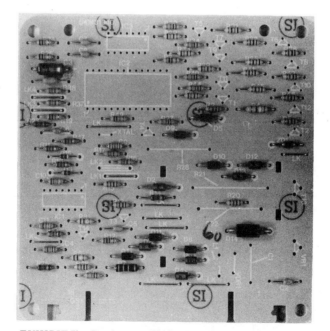

EXHIBIT 7b—Partly assembled pcb

EXHIBIT 7c—Pcb after assembly

months when delivery delays have caused serious problems. Groups A, C, and E are still controlled by a traditional MRP-driven "push" system.

Five of the Group A products, with relatively stable scheduled demand, are assembled at a subsidiary in Taiwan, but are flow soldered, tested, and encased at CE. A recent accountant's report confirmed that this remained the lowest cost method for these products and, in addition, assembly capacity at CE would be inadequate to handle these products. Other conventional products from this group were being considered for potential transfer to Taiwan.

Some new products are designed for surface-mounted technology (SMT) applications. This method has several advantages over conventional products, including:

- Improved in-service reliability.
- A more compact and smaller product.
- Improved component reliability and consistency, resulting in lower levels of rework.
- Circuits can be designed and manufactured by CAD/CAM, allowing quicker response to market needs.

While much of the manufacturing of SMT products involves new, specialized assembly equipment, these products still retain radial and mechanical parts, which must be assembled elsewhere by hand or automated equipment.

As explained earlier, there are two manufacturing areas located centrally within CE on a functional basis. These are for axial component insertion and flow soldering. All conventional (i.e., non-SMT) products for manufacturing groups A to D are processed in order quantities of an agreed size by the axial component insertion equipment and, similarly, SMT products by the automated SMT equipment. Both sets of automated processes are complex, capital intensive, and manned by high-calibre, skilled technicians. Setups are very short, usually less than five minutes.

All conventional and SMT products are flow soldered after final assembly. This equipment is expensive and requires a high level of maintenance. Operators need to be methodical in their approach, although high levels of technical knowledge are not necessary.

The five manufacturing groups (A to E) use these two processes by transporting to the appropriate area the product quantities being manufactured. These products are then scheduled in line with the priorities and work loads that exist at the time. When the order quantity is processed (usually within two to three hours) it is returned to the appropriate group for subsequent operations to be completed.

Group E was established to handle low-volume products (at the beginning or end of their life cycles). It employs highly skilled operators, able to work from drawings without the use of assembly aids (e.g., manuserts). Most products are routed through the autoinsertion facility, but all go through flow soldering.

Manufacturing Strategy

"It is important for us to pursue a positive technology strategy, especially with the fast pace of development which characterizes the electronics industry," were Ted Jackson's concluding remarks. "There is no doubt that our past process investment decisions have provided part of the basis for the company's continued growth and success. Our technology strategy has served us well in the past, and the automated radial component inserter will not only build on, but will help extend this in the future. Only in this way will the company keep ahead in what is recognized as being a highly competitive market."

CASE 5
FRANKLIN, SINGLETON AND COTTON

"Now that we have had the opportunity to gain sufficient understanding of this new part of our business, it is opportune to address the several areas of potential improvements we have already identified," remarked Dave Cullis, managing director of the Franklin, Singleton and Cotton (FSC) plant. He was referring to the fact that FSC had only recently been taken over by the Brannan Group and that he had assumed overall executive responsibility for this plant as well as his other executive commitments elsewhere in the group. He continued by identifying one of these opportunities as being

> . . . the solvent-free lamination process and the potential market opportunities that exist. As the only solvent-free process we have in Europe then we anticipate that we should now be able to compete in those segments of our overall market that require solvent-free adhesion by building on our existing business and seeking further opportunities that this alternative technology offers. Early next month we will meet to review these particular issues. This will give us a chance to consider the analysis work completed so far and to identify, and ideally provide, any other information that will help us in deciding what best to do with the additional capacity we have in this part of our business.

David Cullis was addressing the board of directors at Franklin, Singleton and Cotton (FSC) about six months after the takeover.

Background

FSC is now a wholly owned subsidiary of the Brannan Group, an Irish-based conglomerate comprising textiles and paper as well as packaging. Located on the outskirts of Leeds in the north of England, FSC supplies a range of U.K. companies with growing export sales to most EC countries.

Marketing

FSC supplies flexible packaging to a range of customers whose own end products include snacks, beverages, confectionery, food (including frozen foods, meat, poultry, and dairy products), and a range of nonfood products (see Exhibit 1). The packaging specification reflects the needs of each customer and can be any combination of printed or unprinted and laminated or unlaminated.[1]

When taking over FSC, the Brannan Group not only wished to increase its market share in related segments but also recognized the opportunity of supplying new customers. In addition, the process configuration within the FSC plant matched the mix within the group as a whole, thus giving more flexibility in terms of meeting the needs of all its customers.

---

[1]Laminated film is where two or more films are put together either before or after printing. The purpose of laminates is to improve certain properties in the packaging (e.g., as an air/moisture barrier to improve the shelf-life of a product) and thereby enhance these in terms of its end use, or to protect the print or gloss levels of the base film.

This case study was written by Professor T. J. Hill (London Business School), it is intended for class discussion and not as an example of good or bad management. © AMD Publishing (U.K.).

Exhibit 1   Representative Sample of Laminated Orders in the First Three Months of the Current Year

| Job Number | Sector | Technical Requirements | | | Sales Value (£s) |
		Flexographic	Gravure	Lamination	
G937	Food			✔	6,110
G982	Confectionery		✔	✔	13,612
G991	Food			✔	14,142
H022	Confectionery		✔	✔	18,281
H098	Confectionery	✔		✔	5,128
H110	Snacks	✔		✔	10,410
H114	Food	✔		✔	16,865
H120	Food	✔		✔	6,451
H155	Confectionery	✔		✔	3,916
H157	Food	✔		✔	7,241
H222	Snacks		✔	✔	7,162
H253	Nonfood	✔		✔	6,924
H261	Food			✔	8,816
H334	Food	✔		✔	4,612
H340	Food			✔	10,339
H357	Beverage	✔		✔	15,718
H364	Confectionery		✔	✔	6,408
H389	Nonfood	✔		✔	4,413
H402	Beverage		✔	✔	17,916
H424	Food	✔		✔	9,778
H450	Confectionery			✔	2,794
H486	Food	✔		✔	4,693
H522	Beverage		✔	✔	26,710
H553	Snacks	✔		✔	23,862
H554	Food	✔		✔	18,222
H618	Snacks		✔	✔	5,974

Manufacturing

When the design art work has been agreed with a customer (and in many instances, the order will be for a repeat design), then either cylinders or plates will be prepared (see Exhibit 2). The orders are then scheduled into manufacturing in line with agreed specifications and delivery dates.

As shown in Exhibit 3, orders can go through a number of routes depending on which printing process is required and whether or not the product is to be laminated. Lamination can either be on the printed or unprinted side of the film. Whereas the former would have to be completed after printing (the route shown in Exhibit 3), the latter would usually be laminated first then printed afterwards in order to minimize potential losses in the process. In addition, some products do not require printing but do require lamination.

Lamination.   The laminator at FSC uses solvent-free adhesion and, as shown in Exhibit 3, is a separate process to that of printing. The alternative (and the one which is the most frequent arrangement in the Brannan Group) is known as in-line lamination, where a product is printed and laminated as part of a sequential set of processes.

Exhibit 2

An Overview of the Manufacturing Process

All orders require a technical specification to be agreed in terms of the materials to be used and the printing required.

- Film specification—this concerns details of the materials to be used to form the packaging itself.
- Artwork—where printing is required, the designs, narrative, and colors will need to be agreed by the customer. Negatives are produced from the artwork, and these form the basis for making cylinders or plates.
- Gravure process—using copper-coated cylinders onto which designs are etched, gravure is more suited to products that would not undergo design changes and hence would attract large, cumulative volumes over many orders and often long time periods. Gravure cylinders are expensive to produce compared with flexographic plates and hence lend themselves to more stable designs.
- Flexographic processes—using plates as the format for transferring designs, flexographic (often called flexo) processes are best suited to shorter runs and products where packaging design changes are more frequently required.
- Lamination—the packaging for certain products is enhanced by putting together two or more films or substrates, which enhances the packaging by improving given characteristics to increase shelf life. Lamination can be completed before or after printing and is also provided on unprinted film using adhesives, the basis of which can be solvents, aqueous (comprising a much reduced level of solvents), or solvent-free.
- Finishing—these processes slit 'parent' or 'mill' rolls into individual coils ready for loading onto customers' packaging lines.

Both the printing and laminating processes are reel-to-reel formats in that the film is fed into the machine in reel form and then re-reeled at the other end of the machine after being printed or laminated. Exhibit 4 gives details of a representative range of orders that were processed through the laminator in the first three months of this year.

"Currently, the demand for products to be laminated only requires a single shift to be worked, with overtime as necessary. A working week comprises 37.5 hours with overtime working when required either to finish a job or meet a delivery date," explained Brian Sutcliffe, the manufacturing director. "The takeover by the Brannan Group has given us a real opportunity to increase our sales of packaging where solvent-free lamination is a requirement of the customer. In addition, there is also the possibility of transferring work within the group in order to make best sense of the increased capability."

"The volumes processed through the lamination machine vary from one week to the next (see Exhibit 1), which reflects the number of jobs (there were 65 jobs completed in the first

EXHIBIT 3   Manufacturing Processes: Typical Product Flow

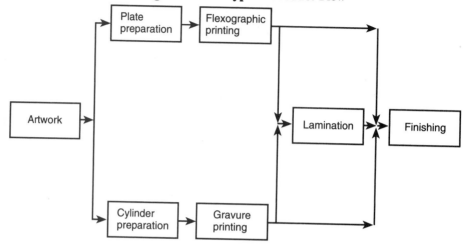

Note: In addition to the product flow above, products may be:
Laminated first and then printed
Laminated and not printed
In both instances, the product would go through the appropriate process sequence.

three months of this year) and the complexity of the lamination.'' Some details of the lamination department are given in Exhibits 5 and 6.

Future Opportunities

''The solvent-free capability of FSC's laminator appears to provide a significant opportunity to grow sales in this segment, especially given the spare capacity available,'' reflected Dave Cullis.

> As the rest of the plant already works on a 24-hour basis over five days, then additional overhead costs will be relatively small and the infrastructure is in place. Certainly one of our main initiatives now is to review the current orders within FSC to identify those on which we can build while looking at the larger customer base within the Brannan Group to identify opportunities for future growth.
>
> The initial analysis of laminated orders completed at FSC shows that all of them could be completed at one or more of the other U.K. plants. A similar review is now being completed of the orders completed at the other plants, and then we need to get down to identify orders that could be sensibly switched and other segments or opportunities with this wider customer base. A technical review [Exhibit 7] is the first step towards this—the order analysis is on the way and should be available soon.

EXHIBIT 4   Representative Sample of Orders in the First Three Months of the Current Year

Job Number	Direct Costs (£s)	Lamination Machine Hours
G937	4,753	5.0
G982	8,379	18.4
G991	2,895	23.0
H022	13,825	24.6
H098	4,475	4.8
H110	9,333	3.0
H114	11,882	15.3
H120	4,773	4.0
H155	3,452	9.5
H157	6,298	4.0
H222	7,101	3.1
H253	6,281	6.3
H261	6,396	4.8
H334	4,648	3.1
H340	7,510	12.3
H357	11,797	10.2
H364	6,197	3.3
H389	4,622	3.8
H402	12,583	13.4
H424	8,302	4.4
H450	1,860	3.3
H486	3,295	3.9
H522	20,782	13.0
H553	20,077	14.5
H554	14,020	10.5
H618	2,402	3.1

NOTE: Direct costs included the direct labor and direct materials cost for both printing (where applicable) and laminating.

EXHIBIT 5   **Output (meters) in the First 13 Weeks of the Current Year**

Week	Output (meters)	Actual Setup Time (hours)
1	44,700	2.3
2	179,440	10.1
3	227,550	6.4
4	224,650	5.9
5	149,150	11.2
6	120,650	10.8
7	244,300	4.7
8	179,120	10.3
9	195,610	14.6
10	145,900	9.5
11	163,050	11.2
12	240,050	5.4
13	50,500	10.6

NOTE: Weekly output depends, in part, on the length of the working week, which will be affected by national holiday closures. These occurred in weeks 1 and 13.

Printers are highly skilled workers whose payrates reflect a high level of skill and effectiveness of working.

EXHIBIT 6   **Some Data on the Lamination Department in the First Three Months of This Year**

Total hours worked in the period	528
Normal hours per week	37.5
Overtime hours in the period	63
Number of jobs completed	65
Standard setup time (minutes/job)	55
Standard throughput speed (meters/hour)	9,000

NOTE: There were three national holidays in the period, and these days are not included in this total.

Exhibit 7

Technical Review of Alternate Laminating Processes

- Currently, there are three alternative processes by which film can be laminated:
    a. solvent-free—as the name suggests, this is free of solvents.
    b. aqueous—low solvent base.
    c. solvent-based—high solvent base.
- Although the adhesive material costs are similar for each process, b and c both require drying facilities with attendent energy costs.
- Running speeds vary, depending on the process and the particular item of plant. Within the Brannon Group, the relevant running speeds are:
    a. solvent-free—100–200 meters/minute.
    b. aqueous—50–100 meters/minute.
    c. solvent-based—50–120 meters/minute.

For b and c, drying restricts relevant throughput speeds.

As with most manufacturing processes, the length of the production run also has a direct bearing on the throughput speeds achieved.

CASE 6
HOFFMANN TOBACCO

Curt Muller sat back. He had just finished analyzing last month's performance summary for the two manufacturing units, a review that confirmed the significant disparity between their results. After discussions, initiatives, and promises, the Norwich plant's performance was still well short of target. In addition, this was in marked contrast to the Edinburgh plant, which seemed to go from strength to strength. And, the reasons for this difference were not at all apparent. In fact, the similarity of investments and approaches undertaken at each site made comparisons easier to make and contrasts easier to conclude. The problem was to identify the fundamental nature of this difference, which was marked in itself and difficult to understand given the circumstances involved.

Background

Hoffmann Tobacco was a wholly owned subsidiary of Teison Industries Inc. a North American holding company with interests in papermaking, printing, and textiles, besides the tobacco industry. With its head office based in Virginia, the Teison Group had subsidiaries throughout North America, Europe, and Australasia. Hoffmann Tobacco (HT) had two manufacturing plants within the United Kingdom (besides others in continental Europe) that produced cigarettes for both domestic and overseas markets. It was recognized that while imported cigarettes would have some appeal in overseas markets, they would inevitably lose out to other brands (particularly local products) on the basis of price. In addition, a climate of reducing demand for cigarettes in the United Kingdom and other traditional markets added to the pressure for HT to offer a wider range of products and also to reduce costs wherever possible.

Marketing

Due to the growing recognition of the harmful effects of smoking on a person's health, the level of cigarette sales in many countries had fallen appreciably. The tobacco industry had, therefore, been forced to rethink its strategy in order to adjust for the loss of sales revenue and profit that had resulted.

In addition, the move from shorts to king-size cigarettes, the introduction of cut-price cigarettes from R. J. Reynolds, Philip Morris, manufacturers in Germany, and own brand labels (e.g., Victoria Wine and Spa Grocers) added to the pressures for additional investment to meet new brand requirements and essential reductions in cost.

HT's marketing strategy was to increase market share at home (in an attempt to maintain current sales revenue in what was recognized to be a declining market) while increasing exports abroad. The principal target areas for growth in export sales were the Middle East, West Africa, and the European duty free segments.

In broad terms, HT's marketing strategy had four principal features:

This case study was written by Professor T. J. Hill (London Business School). It is intended for class discussion and not as an example of good or bad management. © AMD Publishing (U.K.).

- **Advertising**—to target those segments of the market in which people currently smoked and for whom smoking had some appeal, while emphasizing those features of the product that gave the most actual or perceived benefit.
- **Product quality**—to ensure that the product was manufactured and presented at the highest level of quality in terms of tobacco blend, feel and look of the cigarette itself, and packaging as a way of maintaining its position.
- **Price**—the decline in sales had resulted in surplus manufacturing capacity within the U.K. cigarette industry as a whole, which, together with the low-priced European cigarette imports mentioned earlier, had placed significant emphasis on the need for cost reduction. In addition, export sales had similar pressures on price due to the nature of these markets and the low-priced alternatives manufactured domestically in each of the countries or regions in question.
- **Product range**—in response to the fact that while cigarettes were bought for many reasons, one of those clearly identified was image. Although this was in part related to product quality, the need to offer a wide range of products was a most important way of increasing both HT's share of the U.K. market and sales in current and future export markets.

One further feature of the U.K. market also emphasized many of the changes taking place. The continued growth in sales to multiple retailers (e.g., Tesco and Sainsbury) at the expense of the small retail outlet meant an increasing squeeze on prices similar to that which these retailers had successfully applied to food and other products in the past. This factor further emphasized the need to reduce costs in order for HT to remain competitive within its markets.

In overall terms, HT has fared much better that most of its competitors. Imperial Tobacco, Rothmans, and BAT had all been forced to reduce capacity. Imperial had closed sites in Bristol, Nottingham, and Glasgow, with a loss of 1,700 jobs; Rothmans had shut its Basildon plant, with 1,200 job losses; and BAT had closed its Liverpool unit, with its associated 1,800 jobs. During this period, HT had been able to increase market share of U.K. cigarette sales while increasing exports in both existing and new areas. However, much of this had been due to having the best brands in the market. In addition, overall corporate performance had been enhanced by sales of cigars and tobacco for pipe and roll-your-own sales.

Manufacturing

One part of the total response to declining cigarette sales and increasing competition had been a productivity improvement drive in the key manufacturing areas. In this context, the company and the Tobacco Workers Union (TWU) agreed a whole series of changes that needed both worker cooperation and substantial capital investment. The aim of the program was to help the company survive in a competitive market while maintaining real corporate earnings, especially in future years. The changes were a combination of restructuring, process investments, and changes in working methods and manning levels.

Restructuring.   In the context of declining sales for cigarettes, the need to improve the links between the marketing and production functions was well appreciated. The previous structure had formalized the separation of these two parts of the business and was recognized to be an important source of liaison, communication, and coordination problems.

In order to improve these important links within the business, a policy decision was taken to allocate those products to be made at each plant in such a way as to achieve greater product

EXHIBIT 1 **Volume of Production by Brand Type at Each Factory over the Three-Year Transition Period**

Factory Location	Brand Type	Percent Product by Volume Each Year		
		1	*2*	*3*
Edinburgh	Virginia Mild			
	United Kingdom	33	47	61
	Europe duty free	10	21	32
	Hoffmann Special	20	14	7
	Hoffmann Special (plain)	25	15	—
	Other brands	12	3	—
	Total	100	100	100
Norwich	Virginia Mild			
	United Kingdom	35	17	10
	Europe duty free	18	10	—
	Hoffmann Special 10s	15	18	19
	Hoffmann Special	16	15	17
	Hoffmann Special 50s	3	4	3
	Gold Tip	6	10	14
	Hoffmann Mild	—	3	3
	Hoffmann Special (plain)	—	9	16
	Mild Leaf	—	3	4
	Other brands	7	11	14
	Total	100	100	100

NOTES: 1. Europe duty free is packed in both 200s and 300s.
2. The "other brands" category at Edinburgh totaled six brand types in year 1. This category at Norwich totaled 6 brand types in year 1 and 17 brand types by year 3.
3. The Hoffmann Mild brand is produced as both a plain and tipped cigarette.
4. Year 3 is the current year to which the case study relates.

identity within the business as a whole. This orientation also needed to reflect the capacity requirements at each plant and was undertaken over a period of three years, as shown in Exhibit 1. Completed last year, it was agreed by all the principal functions concerned to have brought a significant improvement to the working relations, particularly between the marketing and production functions.

Process Investment. Multifunctional task forces were established in both plants to undertake a review of the manufacturing and distribution activities. Their broad terms of reference were to recommend the best process mix, manning levels, and working practices to achieve the required production levels with associated lower costs. Considerable work was undertaken to identify the technical suitability of available processes that incorporated the latest designs and controls and offered significant improvements in terms of throughput speeds.

The principal investment proposals concerned the secondary stage[1] of the manufacturing process, which involved the making and packing of the cigarettes themselves. The throughput speeds of cigarette-making and packing machines had increased considerably since the late

---

[1]The primary stage was concerned with preparation and blending, which were completed prior to the secondary stages (see Exhibit 2).

1960s. The new generation of Protos could now run at making speeds of 8,000 cigarettes per minute (cpm) compared to the current Molins makers, which worked at speeds of 5,000 cpm. In addition, the Molins HLP4 and the GD packers gave corresponding uplifts in throughput speeds. Finally, the proposals also called for the introduction of a number of conveyor/reservoir systems with elevator arrangements that were designed to link a maker and packer together. With reservoir capacity giving storage space in excess of 50,000 cigarettes, the system comprised an automatically controlled conveyor that linked the two parts of the process together (see Exhibit 2, which gives a brief description of the cigarette-making process). As cigarette makers have much higher throughput speeds than packers, then the basic concept of linking one maker to one packer can be extended by additional conveyors enabling the linking together of machines of different speeds in order to achieve desired levels of matching and the resulting improved use of capital investments overall.

The process investments centered around the provision of two major savings:

- High-speed makers and packers that would reduce the number of machines required for a given production volume and hence reduce the direct operator, indirect support, and overhead requirement throughout.

- Secondary process investments to allow further reductions in direct and indirect employees by mechanizing certain tasks and reducing the manning levels involved in taking part-finished products from one process stage to the next.

Exhibit 3 summarizes the present product-mix characteristics at both plants, while Exhibits 4 and 5 list the current secondary equipment in use at Edinburgh and Norwich, the advantages to be gained, and the anticipated reduction in costs.

Current Position

By involving the employees and trade union representatives at an early stage and continuing this high level of involvement throughout, the necessary reorganization and manpower reductions that had ensued were completed without any signs of animosity or disagreement from those involved. The overt and genuine wish to involve those concerned in the rationale for the proposed changes was built on many years of increasing openness displayed within the company. The result was that the relatively complex sets of arrangements were duly completed on time and the expected reductions in factory-based staff (totaling in excess of 500) were achieved.

However, although the planned labor reduction had been accomplished within the set time scales, the anticipated profit improvements had only been achieved at the Edinburgh plant. Given the similarity of investments made and the gains in labor cost reductions that accrued, it was difficult, at least from a distance, to understand the success of one application and the relative failure of the other.

Brent Murdoch (plant manager, Norwich) was currently completing an in-depth review of the reasons behind this underperformance. He explained

Over the last three years the market has changed. Customer lead times are now much shorter, and as many of our products are now customized at least in terms of packing, then there is increased pressure on meeting agreed delivery dates. This is particularly so in export markets and the lower-volume end of our business, which we tend to support. We estimate that ideally we need between three and five weeks to meet a delivery, depending upon the degree of customization involved. As higher-volume items are normally met from finished goods inventory, then the total lead times estimated above[2] are for customized products, including larger-volume orders of an infrequent nature from some less-developed

---

[2]The lead times of three to five weeks quoted here comprise material lead time plus process lead time.

Exhibit 2

An Overview of the Cigarette-Making Process

Growing the Tobacco Leaf

Tobacco plants are grown in five main areas of the world—Asia, North America, Europe, South America, and Africa. There are three principal varieties of tobacco—Virginia, Burley, and Oriental, which are harvested differently. With both Virginia and Oriental plants, the leaves are picked selectively, starting from the bottom upward. This allows each leaf to ripen fully on the plant. The Burley plant, however, is harvested as a whole so leaves higher on the plant have less ripening time than the lower leaves. Cigarette companies take a mix of different tobaccos and blend them to meet their own product specifications in line with particular market segments. HT's recipes can use over 50 different grades of leaf, from all varieties of tobacco, to formulate a single blend, and leaves from up to three different crop years will be be blended to even out any variabilities in flavor.

Primary Processing

When the blender believes the tobacco samples are ready for processing, the matured crop is brought into a cigarette-making plant (such as the Edinburgh and Norwich plants discussed in this case study). The primary processes comprise a number of steps. The dried and compressed leaves are first conditioned (to make them pliable) by steam moisturizing, then mixed in appropriate blend proportions in a long, blending bin. The blended leaves (or lamina) then go to a compressing chamber, where they are sliced into finely cut tobacco and dried once more. The tobacco leaf stem is separately processed, blended in a similar manner to but cut more finely than the leaf. After drying, lamina and stem are then blended together in precise quantities. Flavoring (e.g., menthol) may be added at this point in the process. The cut tobacco is now ready.

Secondary Processing

The cut tobacco, paper, filters, tipping paper, and packaging are all controlled by very advanced production systems. Correct amounts of tobacco blend pass into the machines through airlocks and are combined and spread onto moving belts. The tobacco is sucked into a continuous rod, meets the paper, and is sealed into shape and printed with the repeated blend name in line with the desired length of the eventual cigarette. Electronic weighing heads ensure that every cigarette contains its precise weight of tobacco. The continuous length is then cut into individual lengths, two of which are then joined to a double length filter and fused together with tipping paper for a fraction of a second. Cutters then halve the filter, and pairs of cigarettes are conveyed to the end of the line, with faulty cigarettes being eliminated by automotive scanners. Here they are loaded onto trolleys for taking to the

Exhibit 2
(concluded)

An Overview of the Cigarette-Making Process

packing area (see Figure 1). It is this transfer to the packing units that part of the new investments at Edinburgh and Norwich are designed to overcome. With these changes, cigarettes are conveyed directly to the packing units through the reservoir arrangement described in the case study narrative. The figure provides an outline of the process for cigarette making. The link to packing machines would be made at the end of the process shown in this outline diagram.

As some 85 percent of all cigarettes made are filter tip, then the filter-making process is an integral part of the second processing unit. The material is processed from a bulk feed to achieve specified filter consistency. The long tube of filter is then cut into rods equal to the requirement for two cigarettes in line with particular specifications. These are then transferred to the cigarette maker as shown in Figure 1 and fused to the cigarettes as described earlier.

The final stage is packing, where cigarettes are automatically packed, foil-wrapped, and cartoned for delivery.

countries. At our last review, about 65 percent of all orders received were for delivery in less than five weeks, while almost 35 percent were for less than three weeks. But, this pattern is increasingly common through businesses and certainly is mirrored in our Edinburgh plant. In addition, whereas our overall sales (both in terms of revenue [£s] and number of cigarettes sold) has slightly increased, since the decision to orient different products to the two plants the order size for our products has, if anything, declined. About half the orders received are for 100,000 cigarettes or less, with over 75 percent for up to 500,000. Although many of these are for our higher-volume products and are, therefore, cumulated within the production scheduling system, there are also those products that experience a more intermittent pattern of demand as you would anticipate with lower-volume products. Certainly this mix of work embodies a wider range and spread of volumes than before and particularly compared to Edinburgh. However, overall the planned investments are achieving the desired labor cost reductions we anticipated. It has been a long haul, but through good working relationships we have negotiated the necessary changes and implemented them in line with the plan. On the new eqipment itself we have experienced some problems [see Exhibit 6], which we are in the process of investigating. Certainly, however, the new high-speed makers and packers have made a sizable impact on our capacity needs (and subsequent manning levels), and the concept of linking makers with packers has reduced the work-in-process inventory and associated labor support in a most dramatic fashion. All that's left is to get Norwich's performance up to plan and on a par with that being achieved in Edinburgh.

FIGURE 1

The layout for a typical new generation cigarette maker

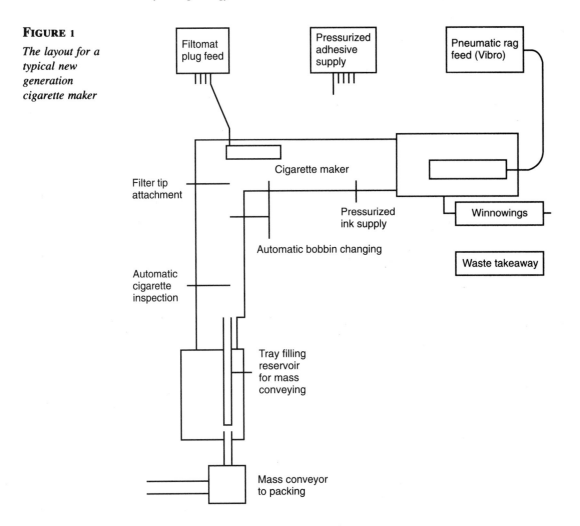

Exhibit 3

Overview of Current Blends, Brands, Packing Sizes, and Product Codes at Each Factory Location

HT's current range of products reflects its need to increase the number of cigarette types as part of its competitive response in both home and export markets. In the normal way, a product code was allocated wherever there was a difference in blend, brand, length of cigarette, or packing specification from one requirement to another. Thus, export orders often required packing and insert changes, the number of cigarettes per pack would differ to facilitate the use of slot machines (see Note 1), and different packs are used to meet the perceived needs of customers. Below is a summary of the differences currently required at each plant.

Number of Specifications Used in a Typical Month	*Edinburgh*	*Norwich*
Average		
Blends	3	12
Brands	3	25
Product codes	65	560
Number of Different Packings per Cigarette Size (in mm)		
70	—	4
80	—	2
84	1	5
95	—	2
100	—	2

NOTES: 1. Slot machines refer to the coin-operated dispensing machines increasingly used in clubs, restaurants, airports, and other public places. Customers serve themselves through inserting the appropriate amount of cash required.

2. The different packings used included hinged lid, shell and slide, soft cup, box, and drum.

EXHIBIT 4   Principal Secondary Equipment at the Edinburgh and Norwich Plants before and after the Capital Investments Had Taken Place

Equipment Category	Edinburgh		Norwich	
	Before	*After*	*Before*	*After*
Filter rod makers	6	6	6	6
Free-standing plain				
Makers	2	—	4	6
Packers	2	—	4	6
Free-standing filter				
Makers	30	8	34	7
Packers	40	10	42	8
Linked makers and packers—filter	—	15	—	20

NOTES: 1. Filter rod makers are the machines used to make the filter tips (see Exhibit 2).

2. The equipment for making and packing plain (or nonfilter tip) cigarettes that was originally sited in the Edinburgh plant was transferred to Norwich when these products were also resited.

3. The investments involved to meet these changes (new equipment, reorganizations, and compensation payments) totaled over £40 million for both plants. About 80 percent of this was spent on new equipment and the reorganization of existing equipment (including linking the making and packing processes) both within and between the two plants.

Exhibit 5

Rationale Supporting the Capital Investments Summarized in Exhibit 4 and the Resulting Reductions in Labor

The rationale supporting the capital investments in both plants was principally as follows.

The linking of a maker and packer required a conveyor and reservoir facility which provided an automatic feeding system from one process to the next. Previously (and currently with free standing equipment) indirect labour was used to transport cigarettes from the makers to the packers. This would necessitate the movement of cigarettes loaded onto trolleys often from one floor to another and usually involving lengthy distances.

In order to decouple the maker from the packer the total holding of made cigarettes in a conveyor and reservoir system was in excess of 50,000. Thus, this afforded the two processes a practical level of independence within the linked system.

The advantages offered concerned a significant reduction in indirect labour together with small (but significant in terms of actual costs) savings on direct materials, particularly tobacco and is explained in more detail below.

The principal gains which accrued from these changes were:

1. Direct labor cost reduction—The introduction of higher-speed makers and packers, together with the increased efficiency of the new equipment,* resulted in a reduction in direct labor requirements.
2. Direct material cost reduction—The new equipment and concept of linked processes resulted in a reduction in material loss/waste from lower levels of rejects and damaged product in the process.
3. Indirect labor reduction—The linked process concept reduced the need for indirect support in several ways, including movement of product, storage, administrative support, and maintenance/technical support for the equipment.

The expected results of these improvements were a 20 percent reduction in factory-related staff and an anticipated 1 percent reduction in material costs. Over 90 percent of this planned labor reduction was achieved by the introduction of linked processes in the two plants.

---

*Efficiency in this context refers to actual output achieved compared to the expressed or standard output and came from reduced downtime and the greater level of attainment of expected throughput rates.

EXHIBIT 6   Downtime Analysis Experienced on the Linked Processes at the Norwich Plant

Reasons for Stoppage	Downtime as a Percent of Total Observations
Making Machine	
Related directly to linked process	
Conveyor/reservoir fault	2.1
Reservoir full	3.3
Need to empty reservoir on a changeover/end of a shift	9.4
Other	3.8
Total	18.6
Unrelated to linked process	
Maker fault	14.2
Other	2.5
Total	16.7
Total for the making machine	35.3
Packing machine	
Related directly to linked process	
Conveyor/reservoir fault	2.7
Reservoir empty/waiting on a changeover/start of a shift	12.9
Other	2.1
Total	17.7
Unrelated to linked process	
Packer fault	16.1
Other	2.8
Total	18.9
Total for the packing machine	36.6

NOTE: The conveyor/reservoir faults given for both the makers and packers are independent of each other, as they are related to the feed into and out of the reservoir.

CASE 7
HONEYWELL PACE

Until January 1982, Bob Naylor, factory manager of Honeywell's High Technology Unit (HTU) in Newhouse, Scotland, had been concerned with ensuring firm orders for his products so that he could manufacture in the high-volume stable quantities for which his plant was designed. During two years of steady growth, he had succeeded in persuading Honeywell's Process Automation Center Europe (PACE) in Brussels, the only outlet for HTU's products, to place firm orders six months before production, and had permitted only a 20 percent variation on orders placed for the second quarter and no variance for the first quarter.

But when in January 1982 he became the first operations manager of PACE, reporting to its director, John Dickens, Naylor saw the issue from a different perspective. One of his first tasks had been to review PACE's 1982 inventory plan. Controller[1] usage, as shown in Exhibit 1, had grown steadily since 1978, and he knew from an earlier meeting, held in October 1981 to plan HTU's production schedule, that PACE had expected demand to rise to 2,500 units in 1982. Before becoming operations manager of PACE, he had laid plans to increase controller production at HTU from 35 to 50 units per week.

However, the decline in world commodity prices and demand had suddenly begun to affect investment levels in PACE's customer industries, and expected orders had failed to materialize. The January business forecast revised annual projections downward to 2,120 controllers, but checks with sales subsidiaries made Naylor suspect that even this figure was optimistic, and he settled for a revised plan of 2,000 units. The February forecast reduced expected usage yet again to 1,700 units. Because, at this point, Naylor had already accumulated an excess inventory of 380 controllers, more than enough to meet his total needs for three months, he realized that drastic action was called for. He telephoned Jack Fraser, HTU's new factory manager. "Get ready to close and take a vacation," he warned, only half joking. "I won't be needing any more deliveries for three months." A few hours later, he received a telephone call from Peter Williams, president of Honeywell Europe, who insisted that HTU could not close, and that Naylor would have to accept deliveries from HTU.

Quite apart from the immediate problem, Naylor wondered how he could prevent similar problems from occurring in the future. He determined that one of his first tasks as operations manager at PACE would be to establish a better system for inventory planning and control.

History of Honeywell

In 1906, Mark C. Honeywell founded the Honeywell Heating Specialities Company in Wabash, Indiana, to build water-heating equipment. Through a series of mergers and acquisitions, the company developed expertise in manufacturing automatic temperature controls for industrial processes and later for heating regulation in office buildings. Prewar experimental work in electronics led to the development of the first successful electronic autopilot in 1941, which was used on U.S. bombers in World War II.

---

[1]Controllers, manufactured at HTU, were a major component of the process control system by PACE, the TDC 2000.

Certain names and figures in this case are disguised. This case was prepared by Professors K. Ferdows (INSEAD) and C. Spray. © 1985 (with permission).

EXHIBIT 1   PACE Controller Usage

Year	Usage (*units*)
1978	537
1979	1,106
1980	1,479
1981	1,791

After the war, Honeywell continued to expand its control system operations, developing domestic, commercial, industrial, and military applications. Much of the expansion was overseas, including the establishment of the Belgian subsidiary in 1946, and the first factory in Newhouse, Scotland, which was opened in 1950. Sales grew rapidly in the postwar period from $13.5 million in 1946, to exceed $100 million for the first time in 1950, and $1 billion by 1957.

At the same time, Honeywell developed interests in the new data processing industry, purchasing Raytheon's interests in Datamatic Corporation in 1957 and merging with General Electric's computer division in 1970. In 1971, Honeywell reorganized into two large worldwide operating units. Control Systems and Information Systems. By 1982, Honeywell earned net profits of $273 million on worldwide sales of $5.49 billion and employed 100,000 people.

Over the years, Honeywell Control Systems divided into five groups, each specializing in products for different markets: Commercial Buildings, Residential Components, Industrial Products, Aerospace, and Defense. A sixth group, International Operations, controlled overseas operations for the product groups, and was divided into four large geographic segments—Europe, Far East and Australia, Latin America, and Canada (see Exhibit 2). Within the Industrial Products Group (IPG) were several divisions, including the largest, the Process Control Division (PCD), which manufactured a range of 2,400 instruments to measure and control industrial process variables (see Exhibit 2).

In 1975, PCD launched a product that represented a new approach to industrial process control systems, the TDC 2000. A first attempt to offer industrial users a complete package of control instruments organized into a coherent system, it consisted of instruments to measure process variables such as flow, pressure, and temperature that were linked to "controller" units. The systems could contain several controllers, each of which measured up to eight variables, and presented information about them in a digestible form to operators. In most cases, the system also regulated automatically the processes it measured. Because complete reliability was essential to users for whom even a brief breakdown could mean serious safety hazards and costly production losses, all systems contained backup units to take over if any part of the system failed.

Because the number and combination of variables that users wished to measure differed considerably, until the launch of TDC 2000 the users or their contractors had designed their own systems, based on the range of components offered by Honeywell and other competitors.

Design of a highly reliable low-cost system, flexible enough to meet the very different needs of users in a wide range of industries, had required five years of intensive research and development effort. The final product consisted of a hundred or so different modules that could be mass-produced as standard items, from which Honeywell systems engineers could select, in consultation with customers, to design a custom-built system that met the customer's exact requirements.

The PCD recognized that module production and system assembly required very different skills, and decided from the outset to keep the two steps of the manufacturing process com-

Exhibit 2   Honeywell Organization Chart, 1982

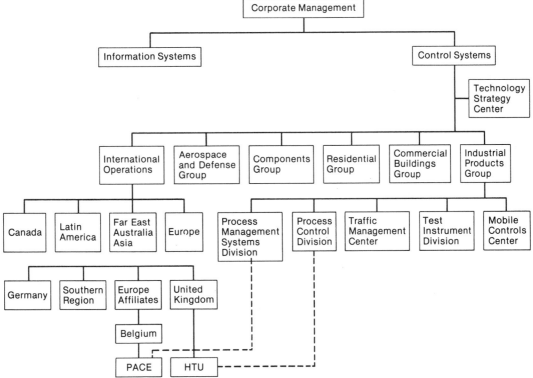

pletely separate. Units to manufacture standard modules were established in existing CD factories at PCD's Fort Washington headquarters and in Phoenix. A few low-volume models were also made at the Kamata/Isehara plant in Japan, but no module was made in more than one location.

Because systems design and assembly of modules required close contact and cooperation with customers, a network of five systems centers was established from the outset near the main user markets. A headquarters center was opened in Phoenix, a second U.S. center was in Fort Washington, and overseas centers were located in Canada, Australia, Japan, and Europe. Each center served its local market only, ordering the modules it required from PCD factories. In 1979 a separate Process Management Systems Division (PMSD) was formed to control the systems centers worldwide (see Exhibit 3 for details of the PCD and PMSD factory networks). While overseas manufacturing and sales were managed by the International Operations Division, PCD and PMSD retained control of key areas such as future product research and development and determined the international transfer prices at which PCD sold standard modules to PMSD.

TCD 2000 found an immediate market among the large petroleum and petrochemical companies in refining and distilling plants throughout the world, which accounted for half its sales. Other users were producers of major processed commodities, such as steel, sugar, cement, wood pulp/paper, and electricity (for a profile of major European purchasers see Exhibit 4).

EXHIBIT 3   PCD/PMSD Factory Network, 1982

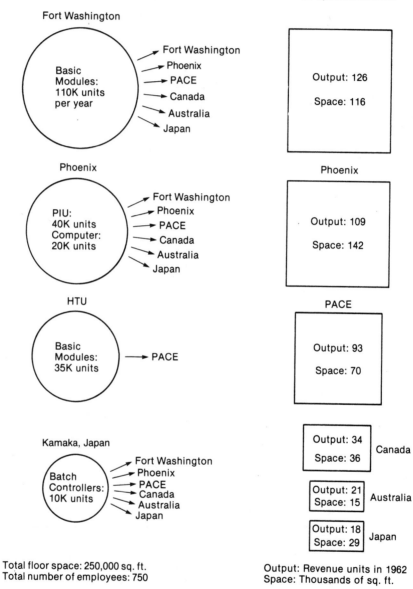

PCD Standard Product Factories

PMSD Systems Centers

Fort Washington

Basic Modules: 110K units per year
→ Fort Washington
→ Phoenix
→ PACE
→ Canada
→ Australia
→ Japan

Output: 126

Space: 116

Phoenix

PIU: 40K units
Computer: 20K units
→ Fort Washington
→ Phoenix
→ PACE
→ Canada
→ Australia
→ Japan

Phoenix

Output: 109

Space: 142

HTU

Basic Modules: 35K units → PACE

PACE

Output: 93

Space: 70

Kamaka, Japan

Batch Controllers: 10K units
→ Fort Washington
→ Phoenix
→ PACE
→ Canada
→ Australia
→ Japan

Output: 34
Space: 36   Canada

Output: 21
Space: 15   Australia

Output: 18
Space: 29   Japan

Total floor space: 250,000 sq. ft.
Total number of employees: 750

Output: Revenue units in 1962
Space: Thousands of sq. ft.

Total number of employees: 850

EXHIBIT 4 PACE Multinational Accounts for TDC 2000

	Projects	Loops
Company A	9	1,152
Company B	3	800
Company C	7	1,936
Company D	7	618
Company E	5	448
Company F	7	902
Company G	34	3,876
Company H	15	2,430
Company I	64	13,202
Company J	31	3,440
Company K	5	228
Company L	4	608
Company M	6	2,904
Company N	22	1,742
Company O	8	380
Company P	18	3,600
Company Q	65	4,024
Company R	23	3,804
Company S	10	2,030
Company T	28	3,214

NOTE: These are very large multinational companies such as BASF, Dow, Mobil, BP, Shell, Union Carbide, Exxon, Alcoa, Dupont, and ICI.

Half the sales were for new plants. The system accounted for only a fraction of plant cost—a $500 million plant would require typically a system costing $1 million. Other sales were to replace existing instrumentation because it was obsolete or installation could be justified on the basis of cost reduction through process optimization. In later years, a further important source of sales was existing TDC 2000 users, who wished to expand their system.

When Honeywell launched TDC 2000 in 1975, it had defined a new product market, which its ability to demonstrate a track record for reliability and a strong international customer base made it difficult for other companies to enter. When competition did arrive in the early 1980s, it was accompanied by a sudden decline in investment levels in the process industries, and both these factors contributed to lower order levels during 1982. Nevertheless, TDC 2000 still accounted for about 40 percent of world sales. There were two or three international competitors and a few national competitors in each of the major Organization for Economic Cooperation and Development countries that normally enjoyed an advantage in bidding for their government contracts. A new generation of TDC 2000s development, which involved the introduction of higher-order computer controls for total plant management, was due in 1983 to 1984 and was expected to strengthen Honeywell's technical leadership of the market.

TDC 2000 in Europe

In 1975, John Dickens, formerly head of Systems Development Engineering at Honeywell's U.K. subsidiary, was given responsibility for establishing the European Systems Center for design and assembly of TDC 2000. The Process Automation Center Europe (PACE) was established in Belgium in vacant office and factory space within Honeywell Europe's headquarters on the outskirts of Brussels.

Company documents defined PACE's basic charter as follows:

> It is a prime objective of Honeywell to supply digital control systems of high quality in cost effective configurations and with delivery lead time to meet customer schedules. PACE is a central source for such systems and the activities which relate to them, including: presales support, technical consultation, system design, project management, assembly, test, and commissioning/service back-up. It was founded to provide the efficiency of a single high-volume operation, concentrated direct lines of communication with the factory sources and management, and a central pool of product and application knowledge.

Dickens believed that PACE had a twofold role:

> For logistic reasons, PACE acts as a coordination center between the 16 European sales subsidiaries. Since most of our customers are multinational in size and scope, it is important that there is coordination on design standards and pricing.
>
> There are also considerable economic advantages from having a centralized organization. For example, by having only one central Guest Center where the system can be demonstrated to potential customers there is a substantial reduction in investment required in demonstration systems.
>
> Additionally, by centralizing the systems design and engineering function, we can maintain specialized expertise that could neither be developed nor justified economically on a country by country basis.

Between 1975 and 1980, sales of TDC 2000 in Europe grew rapidly from a few thousand dollars to over $100 million (see Exhibit 5). Throughout most of this period of steady growth, PACE successfully achieved both sales and profit targets while meeting customer delivery schedules for more than 95 percent of orders. This required a constant expansion of PACE's manufacturing floor space and personnel. After renting additional space locally, PACE finally moved into its own permanent offices and factory adjacent to the Honeywell Europe headquarters in mid-1982.

Growth of PACE was matched by the other systems centers, and by 1978 the PCD recognized that the level of expected future worldwide sales could not be met by the production of modules from the existing PCD plants.

In considering how to increase production, PCD reviewed its original policy of making each module in only one location, which it felt made TDC 2000 particularly vulnerable to sudden stoppages in one of the plants: Shortages of a single module could delay shipment of an entire system. In particular, there was concern that any labor unrest in the United States could affect assembly operations in Europe. The PCD therefore decided to establish a special plant in Europe to provide a duplicate source for PACE of the main modules, thereby reducing its dependence on the U.S. factories. The new factory would supply none of the other assembly centers because it was feared that this would be seen by the U.S. plant unions as a threat to their continued existence.

Newhouse in Scotland was chosen as the most appropriate site for the factory, called the High Technology Unit (HTU) to distinguish it from other local firms using older electronic technologies. Honeywell's own plant at Newhouse had been established in 1950 to manufacture analog instruments and pen recorders, but the market for them had declined by 1978 as they neared the end of their life cycles. Numbering 7,000 at its peak, the work force had fallen to 1,500 and further reductions were planned. Although HTU was able to use the administrative services (personnel, finance, et cetera) of the main factory, HTU required different manufacturing skills and was therefore able to include only a few existing Honeywell employees in its 100-strong work force.

EXHIBIT 5   PACE Growth, 1975–1982—(A) Systems Shipment per Year, (B) Installed Base, Cumulative, (C) Production Space Evolution

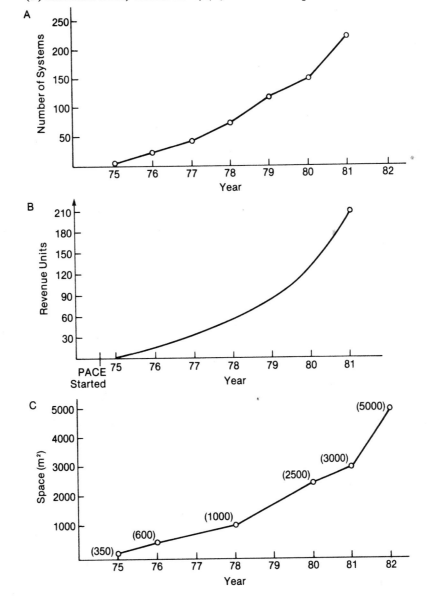

Bob Naylor, formerly a production manager in Burroughs' U.K. subsidiary, was recruited as factory manager of HTU, reporting to Honeywell's Scottish factories manager based at Newhouse. He established HTU from scratch in an unused 26,000 square-foot building adjacent to the main factory, and began by manufacturing TDC 2000 modules that had the highest volume usage, gradually duplicating more of the products previously made only in the United States. When HTU reached capacity it was intended to supply about 80 percent of PACE's long-term needs. In this way, HTU would be protected from variations in PACE's demand, which would be met from other PCD plants, so that it could manufacture in high-volume stable quantities. In most cases, HTU used similar or identical production machinery and techniques to those used in the United States, and its performance was judged against cost standards set for the U.S. factories. Because HTU's transfer prices to PACE were the same as those fixed for the U.S. factories, matching U.S. cost standards was essential for profitable operations.

About 60 percent of HTU's total costs were for raw materials, half of which were purchased locally and the rest from other Honeywell divisions or from Honeywell-approved vendors. Lead times varied considerably, but could be up to 3 months for circuit boards and 12 months for integrated circuits.

These constraints meant that HTU had to plan its production schedules a year to 18 months in advance and could not respond quickly to sudden increases or decreases in demand from PACE. Therefore, Naylor insisted on firm orders six months in advance from PACE. The HTU held no finished goods inventory, shipping all modules to PACE as soon as they were completed and invoicing PACE for them on the dispatch date.

Organization of Honeywell Europe

Honeywell Europe was split into four geographic regions—West Germany, United Kingdom, European Affiliates, and Southern Region—each with approximately equal sales (see Exhibit 6). The latter two divisions were further subdivided by country. Each country was a separate profit center, responsible for both local selling activity and manufacturing operations, and its performance was evaluated on the basis of its success in maximizing sales and profits and minimizing factory costs.

PACE reported directly to the managing director of the Belgian subsidiary; HTU reported to the manager of Honeywell's Scottish factories, who in turn reported to the chairman of Honeywell U.K. The structure of the 16-country selling organizations varied according to their size, but TDC 2000 sales were normally a responsibility of an Industrial Products Group (IPG) sales manager, to whom several salespersons reported, some of whom would be TDC 2000 specialists.

Honeywell Europe also had vice presidents of finance and administration, of technology and operations, and of marketing, and a director of employee relations, to whom PACE and HTU reported in a matrix structure, drawing on the services and specialist expertise they provided. The functional vice presidents provided important links between countries, coordinating aspects of strategy and policy between them and resolving intercountry disputes. They were the only formal link between PACE and HTU below the president of European operations.

PACE in 1982

In 1980 sudden sales growth had for the first time led to problems in meeting delivery dates, with inventory shortages causing delays in 25 percent of deliveries. To resolve the problem and to prepare for expected continuing expansion in sales, Dickens decided to recruit an operations manager. Bob Naylor, with his intimate knowledge of HTU's operations, was considered an

EXHIBIT 6   Honeywell Europe Organization

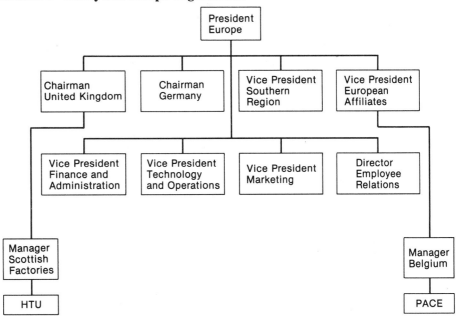

ideal person to manage the important relationship with HTU, and Dickens recruited him to fulfill the new role. After working closely with PACE during 1981, he finally moved to Brussels
in January 1982.

After Naylor's arrival, Dickens restructured PACE as shown in Exhibit 7. Besides an important support staff providing technical, financial, and administrative services, the organization was designed to focus on three key areas: management of individual projects, management
of day-to-day operations, and strategic planning of future development.

Project Management.   Serge Dupont was responsible for systems engineering. Reporting to
him were four project managers, each of whom was in charge of a team of four or five engineers.
The project manager was assigned to a project at an early stage, often before the order was
confirmed, and he was responsible for all stages in coordination with the appropriate department (see Exhibit 8 for details of a typical project flow through PACE). During early discussions
with a potential purchaser, the project manager and PACE team in general provided technical
support and coordination with the sales subsidiary, particularly where projects were for multinational companies, were large (e.g., over $750,000), had new or complex process applica-
tions, or had intrinsic safety requirements.

With advice from PACE, the sales subsidiary then prepared a final job quotation that included a general system specification, a price, and a delivery date. At this point, the project
manager reserved the bulk materials required for assembly and a slot in the production schedule.
As soon as the order became firm, the project manager issued a project plan and a project milestone schedule (see Exhibit 9) specifying the freeze dates by which customers had to approve
progressively more detailed aspects of the system's design. The systems engineers then designed the detailed system layout, confirmed the materials requirements, and prepared detailed
drawings for use by the production department during assembly.

EXHIBIT 7   PACE Partial Organization Chart, 1982

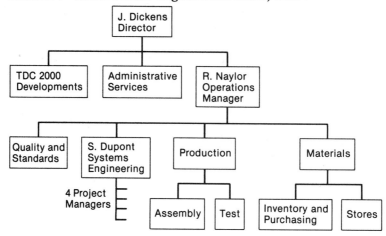

In the production, 17 assembly workers with general fitting skills were managed by a foreman, who assigned specific orders to small teams that completed all phases of the assembly operations. The system was thoroughly tested at PACE before shipment to the subsidiary and delivery to the customer. Customer acceptance was either at the PACE test station or when installation at the customer's plant was completed. A project took from three to nine months to complete, according to size, and the customer was billed progressively via the country sales subsidiary, as costs were incurred.

Operations.   While project managers coordinated the progress of individual projects through production, Naylor oversaw overall operations and worked on the development of standards and systems for all stages of the design, assembly, and testing procedure. Commenting on his role, Naylor said:

> I'm a great believer in having adequate data, then analyzing it to extract useful information. This is not only for my sake, but for the benefit of those reporting to me as well. As I often explain to them, they need good data as much as I do. Without it, they cannot justify their actions and the productivity of their departments.
>
> At the same time, computer printouts are no substitute for practical knowledge of the job. For example, I insist that my schedulers know not only part numbers, but the function of the part as well. This means that if one part is out of stock they can make sensible suggestions to the systems engineers about possible substitutes.

He believed that it was important to instill these attitudes in all his subordinates. With these attitudes, he wished to establish formal performance standards to introduce what he described as "the disciplines of a real factory." In 1982 he was considering which were the key parameters he should set out to measure.

Strategic Planning.   Naylor's arrival allowed Dickens to devote more of his time to the longer-term planning of PACE's development, leaving day-to-day operating concerns to Naylor. In particular, he was able to coordinate future sales strategy with the country subsidiaries and work on the development of TDC 2000.

EXHIBIT 8   Project Flow through PACE

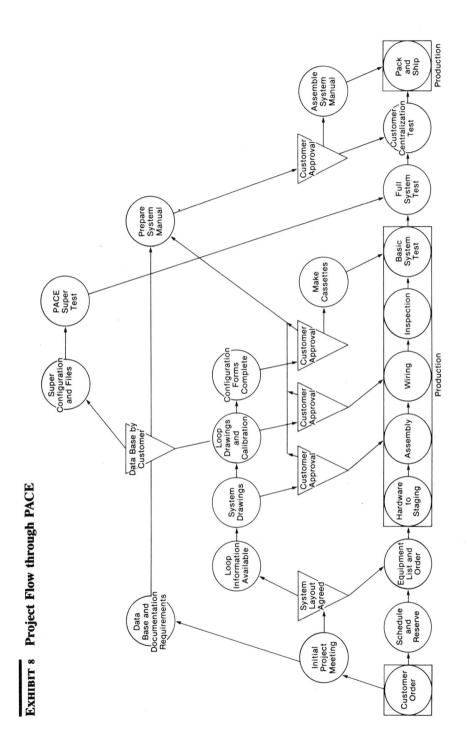

EXHIBIT 9   Project Milestone Schedule

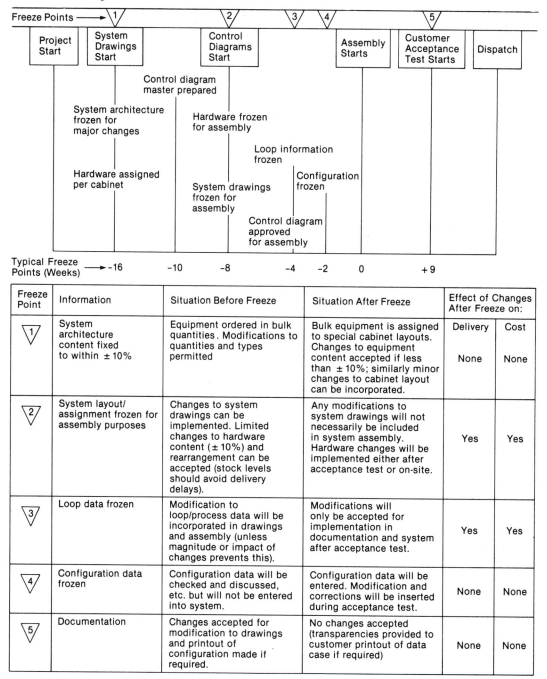

Freeze Point	Information	Situation Before Freeze	Situation After Freeze	Effect of Changes After Freeze on:	
				Delivery	Cost
1	System architecture content fixed to within ± 10%	Equipment ordered in bulk quantities. Modifications to quantities and types permitted	Bulk equipment is assigned to special cabinet layouts. Changes to equipment content accepted if less than ± 10%; similarly minor changes to cabinet layout can be incorporated.	None	None
2	System layout/assignment frozen for assembly purposes	Changes to system drawings can be implemented. Limited changes to hardware content (± 10%) and rearrangement can be accepted (stock levels should avoid delivery delays).	Any modifications to system drawings will not necessarily be included in system assembly. Hardware changes will be implemented either after acceptance test or on-site.	Yes	Yes
3	Loop data frozen	Modification to loop/process data will be incorporated in drawings and assembly (unless magnitude or impact of changes prevents this).	Modifications will only be accepted for implementation in documentation and system after acceptance test.	Yes	Yes
4	Configuration data frozen	Configuration data will be checked and discussed, etc. but will not be entered into system.	Configuration data will be entered. Modification and corrections will be inserted during acceptance test.	None	None
5	Documentation	Changes accepted for modification to drawings and printout of configuration made if required.	No changes accepted (transparencies provided to customer printout of data case if required)	None	None

Recently, Dickens was appointed to represent Europe on the Industrial Products Group Worldwide Manufacturing Council, which meets two or three times a year to consider the future management of PMSD and PCD factories and products throughout the world, and he was also a member of the Worldwide Systems Centers Council, which considered operating issues and future strategy for the PMSD system centers. Because of the complexity of Honeywell's formal reporting structure, these were valuable opportunities to discuss important issues for PACE and to coordinate the activities of system centers worldwide.

Dickens also spent much of his time developing PACE's formal strategic and operational plans, which in 1982 it presented separately from the Belgian subsidiary to the European Board. The two-stage cycle began in April with a strategic review. Dickens reviewed PACE's past strategy and presented his view of PACE's future mission and his proposed methods for achieving goals in specific areas. The plan was discussed, amended, and approved by July. The approved strategy provided the basis for developing an operational plan that defined detailed financial objectives for the following year. The plan was first presented in mid-September and discussed during the next six weeks before final acceptance.

Solving the Inventory Problem

Naylor felt that inadequate forecasting was at the root of PACE's inventory problems. "One of the difficulties," he explained, "is that we have long lead times in this business, but we can only see a few months ahead."

The forecasting unit at Honeywell's European headquarters at that time provided predictions of overall dollar sales revenue for the year ahead, divided into quarters. It based its forecasts on overall economic variables such as capital spending levels in PACE's customer industries. Recently these forecasts had failed to foresee the downturn in sales. Naylor decided to supplement this overall business view with his own review of expected sales levels at each of the subsidiaries. To compile these forecasts Dickens recruited Veronique Meister, who had worked for Honeywell Europe for 12 years and knew well the people working in the sales subsidiaries.

Veronique Meister made monthly telephone calls to all 16 sales subsidiaries to review all likely orders for the forthcoming year with sales managers, asking them to assign a booking date, and a probability that the job would be booked. Using her own knowledge and judgment to assess the accuracy of their predictions, she included in her forecast any order she thought had a more than 60 percent probability of being placed. The forecasts provided aggregate data concerning value of sales at customer prices, which Naylor converted into controller usage because these were a main determinant of system cost. In 1982 Naylor estimated that one controller was used per $22,000 of sales. By analyzing past data, Naylor had developed a simple computer model that gave him an average usage of each module per 1,000 controllers. Thus he could convert sales data into an expected usage of each standard module per month.

In this way, Naylor managed to tap the large amount of hard information available in the sales subsidiaries and use it to adjust his assembly schedule, which he planned by the week for the six months ahead. Because the schedule for the first quarter was based substantially on actual orders, it usually required little change, but demand for the rest of the year was less certain and Naylor found the forecasts helpful to develop rough assembly plans that he changed as the booking picture developed. Naylor also used the forecasts to develop his inventory plan, which he discussed monthly with Jack Fraser, HTU's manager, who used PACE's inventory plan to plan his production schedule and materials ordering.

Materials ordering for HTU was a more complex process because each module contained several thousand components, some of which had to be ordered up to a year in advance. These lead times were a major constraint on HTU's flexibility. HTU used a computerized MRP schedule to produce data for component requirements.

Business forecasts indicated that sales would show no improvement until the end of 1983. While PACE was flexible enough to withstand the slump in sales reasonably well, the consequences were more serious for HTU, which was preparing plans to move to a four-day work week in 1983 and was concerned that if short-time working continued it would lose its highly trained work force to new factories that were opening nearby, leaving it unable to meet the upturn in demand predicted for 1984.

By the end of 1982, despite substantially improved forecasting methods, PACE had not been able to resolve its inventory problems. The substantial cost of holding unused modules, running to several years' supply of some low-usage models, had depressed PACE's profits in 1982. Both Dickens and Naylor had become convinced that the problem would not be resolved until HTU shared with PACE responsibility for meeting inventory holding costs. Accordingly, they requested a meeting of senior Honeywell Europe staff so that they could make recommendations for changes in the formal relationship between PACE and HTU. Shortly before Christmas 1982, they met to discuss how they would present their case.

CASE 8
HQ INJECTION MOLDING COMPANY

"If we are to adhere to product launch schedules, we must try every mold on receipt, then bring in the mold maker to modify it as required, regardless of whether we can then go ahead and produce initial launch quantities," said George Brett, the manufacturing director. "If we leave mold testing until we are ready for a production run there is a risk that the need for substantial mold modification will cause us to miss launch dates."

HQ Injection Molding had been a major components supplier to the domestic appliance industry prior to its acquisition by one of its customers. It also, at the time, had its own range of homeware products, and supplied components to other industries. Some 10 years ago, the group was restructured and notice was given that the group requirements on the company would be phased out over the following two years. At that time, the parent company accounted for over 50 percent of existing capacity (Exhibit 1 shows the makeup of machine sizes).

This was not the only problem. The company's homeware range also faced competition from small firms who were able to compete effectively in this sector of the market.

"The consumer saw our homeware products as plastic first and homeware second," said George Brown, the current managing director. "The traditional image of plastic as a cheap and transient material dominated, and we competed in the marketplace on price, rather than on the basis of our products. We had to rethink how we were to compete." The company evolved a marketing strategy to design, manufacture, and sell ranges of high-quality products. This would enable it to compete in a different sector of the market where price was not the dominant order-winning criterion. Over the years, the company designed several ranges of new products and the mold introductions associated with this are summarized as Exhibit 2.

Manufacturing

A brief outline of the process is shown as Exhibit 3. Starting with the raw materials, a molded product is produced. Certain subsequent operations (such as removing the sprue—i.e., excess plastic from the mold passageways—by hand, knife, or drill, checking the quality of the molding, and first packing operations) are all completed at the machine. The products are then transported in containers to the work-in-process stores. From there, they are withdrawn as required by the assembly department, who complete any subassembly operations (e.g., gluing or welding components), assembly (e.g, fit lids to bases and attach labels), and finally pack into inner and outer cartons, prior to transportation to the finished goods warehouse. With many of the products from the original product ranges the assembly and packing was completed during the molding process, as the work content was relatively small due to the bulk style of packaging involved.

Raw Materials

The advent of the new range of products brought with it a significant increase in raw materials types and colors. In order to support the new product concept, more expensive materials were

This case was prepared by Professor T. J. Hill (London Business School). It is intended for class discussion and not as an illustration of good or bad management. © AMD Publishing (U.K.).

Exhibit 1

Details of Injection Molding Machines

Below are details of the number of machines available in each machine group defined by the company.

| | Number of Machines | | |
| | Current Year Minus | | |
Machine Group	8	1	New
1	29	1	—
2	15	11	5
3	5	8	6
4	2	2	1
Total	51	22	12

Details of the "new" machines in each group are:

| | Year of Purchase/New Machines | | | | | | | |
| | Current Year Minus | | | | | | | |
Machine Group	7	6	5	4	3	2	1	Total
2	—	—	—	—	3	2	—	5
3	2	1	1	1	—	1	—	6
4	—	—	—	—	—	—	1	1

A typical machine is given in some detail below.

| | Features of an Average Machine | | |
Machine Group	Cost (£000s)	Shot Weight (ozs)	Locking Pressure (tons)
1	116	10	200
2	276	45	450
3	333	60	600
4	360	150	600

NOTE: Cost includes the purchase price of the machine and installation costs at current year prices.

EXHIBIT 2   Summary of the Molds Introduced or Planned in the Last Seven Years

| | Current Year Minus | | | | | | | |
Product Type Range	7	6	5	4	3	2	1	Current Year
A	—	—	1	5	—	—	—	—
B	—	4	1	1	4	4	2	—
C	19	8	10	8	3	1	—	—
D	4	20	—	6	1	2	12	—
E	4	19	—	26	9	14	15	30
F	—	—	—	—	—	2	—	—

NOTES: 1. Product range types A and B belong to the original (prechange) designs, while C to F were of the revised (postchange) designs. Further details are given in Exhibit 5, under the column headed "Product Range."

2. The number of molds indicates the number of different products within each range. However, in many instances, one mold will have two or more impressions on it, so that in every molding cycle one, two, or more products would be made depending on the number of impressions on that mold.

3. The dimensional sizes of old and new products vary across the different product ranges but, in overall terms, tend to be similar.

EXHIBIT 3   An Outline of the Manufacturing and Assembly Process

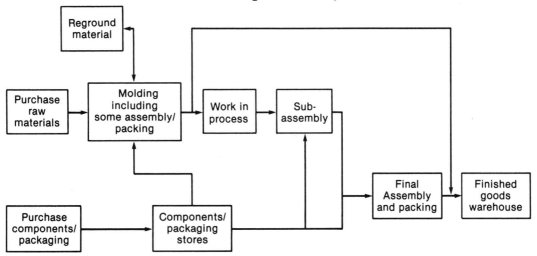

NOTE: All products do not go through each stage of the manufacturing and assembly process.

introduced and the color range was widened. Also the old products had tended to be molded where close color matching was not required and material specification was less critical. Moreover, the new products were clustered around a "matching" range of products as a strategy to enhance sales, with the purchaser having bought one item for the home being more likely to buy another item of the set when next purchasing. This meant that it was necessary to maintain color matches over a long period of time.

Toolroom

Nine skilled men (including three apprentices) work days, while one skilled man provides a breakdown service for the mold shop covering the period 22.00 to 07.00 hours. About 15–20 percent of their time is spent on new molds and the remainder on modification and repair.

Design

Over the years, design had expanded to become a separate function with a manager and four staff. Their job was to liaise with customers (often large department stores), agree on design detail, then complete the drawings. The manager of the toolroom then undertook to make or subcontract the molds and get them into production. The toolroom always had one draftsperson, who dealt with mold modifications.

Technical Services

Earlier, the technical support to the mold shop had been provided by John Burton, currently the technical manager. John had extensive knowledge of injection molding and had provided specialist help on the shopfloor. The work varied and included:

1. Contributing to the design of a mold at the start of the mold-making process.
2. Getting new molds to a production state, and establishing the settings and adjustments to be made in all future runs.
3. Fine tuning a mold at the start of its production run (very important in terms of productivity).
4. Helping to determine the necessary modifications to a mold.

Before the switch in product concept, John would spend most of his day on task 3, but increasingly, due to the new product strategy, John and his staff of three technicians spend the majority of their time on the other three tasks.

> Until six or seven years ago, we concentrated on thinning product wall thickness and reducing cycle times because, particularly with the long production runs associated with the old-type products, this kept the cost down. The mold was made as cheaply as possible, and we used black plastic where we could so that we could use reground plastic of mixed colors. And, of course, we would use contrasting colors for lids and bases, to avoid the need to color match.
>
> The new products changed this. We increased wall thickness to give products greater rigidity and substance, color match became critical, lids and bases were the same color, quality took precedence over cycle times, packaging became far more important, and quality became the order of the day. The repercussions of this on the shopfloor were considerable. A new team had to be trained and premolding treatment of material became necessary to achieve the necessary color and quality standards.
>
> Many existing machines were old and often unable to meet or maintain the new product specifications. Until new machines could be justified, sanctioned, and installed, many preliminary operations

were necessary to overcome the inadequacies of the old machines. As an estimate, only some 25 percent of the machines were originally up to the new technical specifications required, due to wear and tear.

On the technical side, our existing fitters had to be retrained to set up molds with complicated water circuits, heating subsystems, temperature controls, and complex core-pull and ejection systems. A new class of staff, the technician, became necessary. Recruitment from outside proved fruitless, and our best setters took on this role, with the best operators replacing them as setters.

The proposed range of molds appears bigger and more sophisticated. Machine setting is now more difficult, and the machine adjustment controls are inadequate for the fine level of tuning required. When several new ranges are introduced within a short period, everyone is under pressure. The new machines due this year will have microprocessor control with the setup reductions it brings, justifying the 15 percent increase in capital cost. Although we expect this margin to decrease over the next year or two, persuading top management that this additional expenditure is necessary as standard policy is a different matter. These three new machines will be groups 2, 3, and 4, with locking pressures of 400, 600, and 600 respectively.

Maintenance

According to Phil Stokes, the maintenance manager, "many of the old machines weren't up to the quality specifications required by the change of product mix. For this reason, new machines were bought and the worst of the old machines sold. Now, besides the high-volume, low-margin products, we also make low-volume products. Our revenue and profits have both increased. For my department, this has meant fewer machines and fewer problems." Exhibit 4 gives the financial information for the company for the last seven years.

Mold Shop

"We are now in a totally different manufacturing situation than we were previously," was George Brett's opening comment when discussing the present situation. At the beginning of the changeover, he explained, there were many technical difficulties that had not been foreseen. These ranged from the inadequacies of many old machines to do the job, through to the molding properties of the new materials. He recalled how jobs had often to be allocated to a larger machine in order to achieve the required product specification (i.e., the increased locking pressure provided was needed to keep the mold closed during machine cycle, hence avoiding "flashing"). Also, the great difficulties experienced with color matching, especially in the "bright, modern" colors now being used.

> We even had to rethink our mold design, in some cases, from one which minimized the cycle time by injecting in the center of the mold (i.e., the shortest distance for the material to flow) to injecting so as to minimize the sprue mark, which lengthens the time cycle[1] and complicates the molding process. Since then, we have overcome these initial difficulties and many more besides. But, in doing so, it has resulted in a lot of pressure, effort, and cost. At times we can have seven or eight of the machines working on new products, which effectively means no production, and a complete loss of productive standard hours from some 30 percent of our capacity. The problems of trying to complete the tasks of a development unit and a production unit under the same roof, and calling on the same capacities and skills, are enormous. The pressure of achieving deadlines, particularly when little or no slack time has

---

[1]Cycle time is the length of time it takes for the machine to close the mold, inject the material, initial cooling, open the mold, and present the molded part for the operator to remove from the mold. In many instances, a mold is so designed as to complete this last operation on a part or wholly automatic basis.

EXHIBIT 4   Some Financial Management Information for the Last Seven Years (year ended December 31—all figures in £000s)

	Current Year Minus						
	7	6	5	4	3	2	1
Fixed assets							
Plant	561	552	399	420	612	838	980
Molds	102	130	170	180	320	584	620
	663	682	569	600	932	1,422	1,600
Current assets							
Inventory	262	532	1,029	1,259	1,559	2,243	2,567
Debtors	483	798	842	817	1,321	963	1,373
	745	1,330	1,871	2,076	2,880	3,206	3,940
Current liabilities							
Creditors	626	532	628	1,134	1,774	1,744	1,765
Overdraft	2	480	412	42	38	284	575
	628	1,012	1,040	1,176	1,812	2,028	2,340
Working capital	117	318	831	900	1,068	1,178	1,600
Net assets employed	780	1,000	1,400	1,500	2,000	2,600	3,200
Financed by							
Share capital	50	50	50	50	50	50	50
Retained profit	280	420	530	570	830	1,760	2,660
	330	470	580	620	880	1,810	2,710
Group indebtedness	450	530	820	880	1,120	790	490
Net capital employed	780	1,000	1,400	1,500	2,000	2,600	3,200
Net sales	2,552	2,872	4,212	4,466	5,810	5,394	8,021
Net profit before tax	146	185	274	362	564	708	1,050

NOTES: 1. Working capital = current assets − current liabilities.
2. Net assets employed = fixed assets + working capital.
3. Any difference between the net profit for any year and the increase of retained profits is due to a transfer of profit to the group.

been allowed in the plan (the design/customer agreement phase always absorbs whatever slack there is), requires all our attention so that normal production has to look after itself.

As shown in Exhibit 1, the available production capacity had shifted toward larger machines, sometimes in actual numbers, but markedly as a percentage of the total capacity available. To keep molding costs down moved the argument toward multi-impression molds, whereby every cycle produced a "shot" with each of the impressions in the formed state (e.g., two lids or two bodies, or two lids and two bodies, and so on). Of course, multi-impression molds always become much larger and much more sophisticated. These, in turn, require larger machines and accounted, in part, for the drift away from the earlier mix of machines. In addition, mold changes and setups take longer, and details of a representative sample of products throughout the current range is given as Exhibit 5. Besides the cost advantages inherent in multipurpose molding, particularly with high-volume production runs, another advantage gained is that it facilitates the molding of a product that has more than one component and where color matching is essential.

Part of the production management's job was to consider ways of reducing costs throughout the process wherever possible. Some of these suggestions come from marketing pressure in addition to the continuous flow of ideas from manufacturing itself, with the aid of support services such as work study, toolroom, and design. Exhibit 6 gives cost breakdowns for some representative products from across the current ranges.

Assembly

The assembly department undertakes subassembly, final assembly, and packing, and is located away from the mold shop in a 50,000-square-foot warehouse, which also contains work in process and some of the finished goods inventory. The work of this department has increased with the need for packing and presentation that accompanied the new products. At the other extreme, any assembly or packing of the industrial products is mainly carried out at the machine. There are, at present, some 17 assembly benches and three subassembly locations, with 27 full-time and 16 part-time packers, and an indirect staff of three.

Finished Goods Warehouse

Although the product quantities have decreased since the early 1970s, the requirement for warehousing is considerably higher. Reasons for this include:

1. Subcontract industrial work for the group was molded on a contract basis and shipped daily to the various companies.
2. The traditional homewares and industrial products were (and still are) packed several together, inside a box or polyethylene bag.
3. Components required to assemble the new ranges of products are greater.
4. The emphasis on quality means that components have to be stacked with greater care.
5. The new products are packed individually in inner boxes, increasing the space requirement at the finished-goods stage.

Work-in-process and finished goods warehousing capacity has been increased significantly, as shown in Exhibit 7.

Production Control

"The new range of products presents a set of production control problems, which are different from those of the old products," said Geoff Sissons, the production controller. "The number of components and the assembly and packing requirement have increased the complexity of the process." Exhibit 5 illustrates this.

In addition, the uncertainty inherent in the mold-testing process, the procedure for agreeing packaging, and the launch dates have added factors, which made planning and control far more difficult.

EXHIBIT 5 Production, Sales, and Inventory Details on Several Products

Product[1]	Machine Group	Number of Impressions[2]	Colors	Number of Components[3]	When Last Molded Months Ago	Color Changes
(A) General Homewares—Original Product Concept						
1132 Tray	2	2	1	3	27	1
2225 Bowl[6]	2	1	8	2	1	3
1138 Bucket[6]	3	1	8	2	6	3
1386 Jug	2	1	1	3	2	1
1263 Tray[6]	2	1	8	5	5	4
2687 Tidy	3	1	2	4	1	2
2241 Bin	3	2	6	7	1	5
2366 Bin	3	1	1	2	—	1
1393 Box	2	2	2	2	1	1
1267 Tub	3	1	1	1	5	1
8282 Bowl[7]	3	4	6	3	2	6
(B) Industrial Moldings—Original Product Concept						
6900 Board	2	1	2	1	8	2
6908 Basin	4	2	1	2	2	1
6074 Lid	2	1	1	2	3	1
6010 Tray	4	2	1	—	50	1
6085 Knob	1	2	5	1	16	2
6990 Frame	3	1	1	4	2	1
6491 Cap	1	6	1	1	6	1
6209 Case	2	1	1	5	4	1
8860 Tray[8]	4	1	12	1	—	1
8009 Case	3	2	2	1	8	2
8010 Tray	3	1	2	1	4	1
(C) General Homewares—Revised Product Concept						
3910 Container	3	1	10	5	1	3
3941 Rollholder	2	1	3	8	10	3
3995 Container	3	1	10	5	30	4
6115 No. 4	3	4	6	5	14	5
6110 No. 9	2	1	9	4	20	1
6246 No. 28	4	2	12	4	1	5
6151 Jug	2	1	4	3	20	3
6313 Box	1	1	4	6	30	1
6332 Rack	4	1	6	3	3	3
6846 Shelf	4	2	2	9	4	2
6463 Clock	3	1	4	10	14	3

Production Run (hours)		Production Runs Last 12 Months	Hours to Change[13]		Annual Sales (units)	Finished Goods[14]		Outstanding Orders	
Last[4]	Average[6]		Mold	Color		Units	Colors	Units	Colors
1700	1700	—	2(½)	—	20,686	67,159	1	—	—
192	248	6	2(1)	2	159,120	33,769	8	—	—
138	138	1	3(1½)	2	13,236	5,829	5	—	—
190	147	3	3(1)	—	44,237	34,618	1	—	—
70	120	4	2½(1)	1½	48,162	15,050	8	—	—
124	82	7	7(3)	2	50,400	8,280	2	—	—
103	100	4	13(5)	2	47,646	3,642	5	195	1
156	120	6	7(1)	1	11,779	—	—	288	1
190	83	6	2½(1)	1½	22,405	3,987	2	—	—
44	44	1	2½(1½)	1½	13,465	734	1	—	—
220	250	2	10(4)	2	57,840	480	6	—	—
144	144	1	1(—)	½	6,735	—	—	—	—
62	62	1	22(10)	—	—	—	—	—	—
45	45	1	3(1)	—	—	—	—	—	—
106	106	—	3(1)	—	—	—	—	—	—
125	125	—	2(½)	½	—	—	—	—	—
163	163	1	24(10)	—	—	—	—	—	—
110	511	6	2½(1)	—	533,318	—	—	48,703	1
95	83	7	7(3)	—	65,159	1,152	1	—	—
2400	371	10	9(3)	½	159,489	4,804	6	19,835	1
60	54	1	11(5)	½	5,443	3,650	2	—	—
90	36	2	11(5)	½	2,741	717	1	—	—
134	87	9	4(2)	3	35,238	520	2	7,917	3
55	55	1	13(3)	3	3,312	610	2	432	1
77	77	—	3½(2)	1½	157	108	2	—	—
20	20	—	9(1)	6	13,814	28,225	6	—	—
24	24	—	3(1)	2	1,242	6,660	8	—	—
81	39	9	7(3)	4	14,472	6,485	12	—	—
102	102	—	9(2)	2	3,284	1,035	2	209	2
24	24	—	3½(2)	2	405	6,294	3	—	—
106	106	1	10(4)	3	18,453	2,489	5	—	—
42	92	2	8(4)	2	10,598	2,003	2	—	—
78	78	—	2½(1)	1½	6,393	1,749	4	—	—

EXHIBIT 5 *(concluded)*

Product[1]	Machine Group	Number of Impressions[2]	Colors	Number of Components[3]	When Last Molded Months Ago	Color Changes
(D) Bathroom Ranges—Revised Product Concept						
5426 Holder	3	2	10	7	—	2
5229 Dish	4	2	9	6	—	2
5624 Holder[9]	2	1	10	8	—	3
5315 Dish[9]	2	1	5	7	—	3
6213 Hook	2	2	10	6	17	2
6420 Mirror	4	2	11	9	1	1
6428 Holder	1	2	13	5	1	2
6606 Beaker	3	4	5	6	1	2
6397 Caddy	3	1	4	8	1	2
6309 Mirror	4	1	4	8	1	3
(E) Kitchen Ranges—Revised Product Concept						
4141 Bowl	4	2	4	4	2	2
8284 Large sieve[10]	3	2	4	7	1	3
4150 Small sieve[10]	2	2	4	7	1	3
4151 Large spoon[11]	3	2	4	4	3	4
4156 Small spoon[11]	3	2	4	4	3	4
4161 Scraper[11]	4	4	4	4	3	4
4159 Jug	2	1	4	4	3	3
4219 Cutter[12]	2	8	4	4	3	4
8424 Mold[12]	2	8	4	4	2	3
4213 Holder	2	1	4	6	5	3
General—Revised Product Concept						
2849 Hanger	3	12	6	3	—	5
6049 Bracelet	2	4	6	2	22	4

NOTES: 1. In the case of several of these products there is more than one molding involved (e.g, a body and a lid)—here the principal molding (e.g., the body) has been analyzed as representative.

2. If a product involves only one molding, but there is (say) two or four impressions on the relevant mold, this means that such molds have been designed to make the product concerned in (say) multiples of two or four, each time the molding cycle is completed (the exception to this is given in Note 11).

3. Number of component refers to the number of different components used in assembling a product. The components will usually be purchased, and typically are metal fittings and other nonplastic parts.

4. If no production runs in the last 12 months, the last order has been taken as average.

5. Average production run has been taken over the last 12 months (see 4 above).

6. The color range of these products was increased from 3 to 8 as part of extending the "revised product concept" to products of the "original concept."

7. This product was in fact packed in assorted colors and held in finished stock as such.

Production Run (hours)		Production Runs Last 12 Months	Hours to Change[13]		Annual Sales (units)	Finished Goods[14]		Outstanding Orders	
Last[4]	Average[6]		Mold	Color		Units	Colors	Units	Colors
67	155	14	4(2)	2	119,367	—	—	12,816	8
45	110	7	4(2)	2	40,819	966	4	4,196	4
40	40	1	14(2)	2	—	3,240	3	3,240	3
20	20	1	14(2)	2	—	1,080	3	1,050	3
47	47	—	4(2)	1½	2,018	12,725	8	—	—
39	39	5	5(2)	1½	11,768	15,283	7	—	—
35	35	5	2½(1)	1	16,913	21,392	10	—	—
33	50	3	5(2)	1½	24,244	18,785	4	3,000	1
95	34	3	8(4)	1½	10,752	11,167	4	—	—
43	32	4	4(2)	1½	9,720	3,994	3	1,500	1
60	80	8	3(1)	1½	58,850	12,280	4	—	—
100	35	8 }	3(1) }	1½	39,638	96	1	8,222	3
100	63	8 }	}		35,450	233	1	1,607	2
367	117	4 }			74,020	49,017	3	—	—
367	140	4 }	6(3) }	1½	98,828	4,961	2	608	1
367	144	4 }			119,765	26,666	3	—	—
143	72	7	9(4)	1½	54,022	4,764	4	—	—
90	47	5	4(2)	1½	162,492	188,261	4	—	—
108	26	6	5(2)	1½	122,472	95,994	4	—	—
142	36	6	4(1)	1½	19,128	34,178	4	—	—
183	50	9	11(3)	2	540,615	58,333	6	—	—
74	74	—	2(1)	1	—	—	—	—	—

NOTES:
8. The range of colors for this item was due to the fact that customers tended to prefer their own color for reasons of brand image, recognition, etc.

9. New product range—outstanding orders represent initial launch.

10. Both these products are on the same mold.

11. These three products are on the same mold.

12. Impressions are of different shapes—two sets of shapes × 4 impressions.

13. Hours to change a mold includes changing the mold, then the time taken to get the mold working to production and quality requirements, which is shown in brackets. For example, Tray 1132 2(½) means 2 hours to change the mold and get it working into production and quality requirements. Of this 2 hours, the adjustment process to get it working to production and quality requirements after the mold change takes ½ hour.

14. The colors in stock are not the same as those required for outstanding orders.

15. The products shown here are considered to be representative of both their own and the total product range.

EXHIBIT 6   Cost Details Of Representative Products

					Cost Details (pence per 12)				
Product Details		Raw Materials	Labor		Packaging and Components	Mold Depreciation	Overheads		Total
Range	Item		Molding	Assembly			Molding	General	
A	2225 Bowl	254	35	—	38	25	179	148	679
A	2687 Tidy	409	56	—	78	40	303	242	1128
A	2366 Bin	2103	142	—	272	160	787	957	4421
A	8282 Bowl	44	6	8	11	4	32	25	130
B	6491 Cap	9	—	—	1	1	15	8	34
B	8860 Tray	1621	88	—	668	116	491	695	3679
B	8009 Case	1093	73	—	515	83	406	496	2666
C	6246 No. 28	1799	110	103	435	280	609	839	4175
C	6846 Shelf	457	79	106	764	108	438	324	2276
D	5426 Holder	288	105	69	311	100	508	300	1681
D	5624 Holder	163	92	88	272	77	440	232	1364
D	6420 Mirror	1942	139	334	2469	317	773	951	6925
D	6428 Mirror	578	165	78	786	173	812	518	3110
D	6606 Beaker	237	91	73	298	82	411	246	1438
E	8284 L sieve	250	48	49	409	20	112	61	949
E	8424 Mold	21	6	10	17	6	29	19	108
F	2849 Hanger	54	4	8	18	4	21	25	134

NOTES: 1. Raw material costs are normally adjusted twice a year.

2. Molding and assembly labor costs are based on calculated standard times.

3. Mold depreciation is a fixed percent of the first stage costs, which comprises raw materials, molding overheads, mold depreciation, and molding labor.

4. Molding overheads are based on the machine size cost below:

Group	1	2	3	4
Molding overhead allocation (£ p)	19.48	22.95	24.60	24.60

If a product is to be molded on a machine in Group 1, then the molding overhead allocation will be based on £19.48 and so on. These allocations include indirect molding labor, production staff, development, factory, utilities, plant depreciation, blocks, dies, and plant repairs.

5. General overheads are calculated as a fixed percentage of first stage cost.

6. The product ranges abbreviations A to F are explained in the notes to Exhibit 5.

7. "Pence"—one penny = one hundredth of a £.

Then, the marketing department often requires additional colors in order to increase sales in existing markets or break into new markets. [An example of such a request is shown as Exhibit 8.] These short runs and special colors often have target dates which necessitate fitting them in at all stages of the process at the expense of normal production runs. It is difficult to balance these two sets of priorities.

Marketing

The marketing department is split into product areas and subdivided into home and export. Each subdivision has a sales manager who reports to Mark Williams, the marketing director. Mark, who has been with the company for 12 months, confirmed that the change in product direction had enabled the company to compete successfully in a new sector of the market. "Before I joined, the company had already achieved recognition as a front runner in this section, manufacturing high-quality, well-designed products. Frankly, this was one of the reasons I took the job."

EXHIBIT 7   Changes in Components/Packing, Work-in-Process, and Finished Goods Warehousing over the Last Seven Years

Warehousing	Current Year Minus	Size (square feet)	Distance (miles)	1979 Total (square feet)
Components/packing	7	5,000	—	
	4	5,000	—	10,000
Work-in-process	7	9,000	—	
	3	9,000	—	18,000
Finished goods	7	27,000	—	
	6	10,000	20	
	4	40,000	1	
	3	(10,000)	20	
	1	20,000	3	87,000

NOTE: Last year the rented cost of warehousing was about £5.00 per square foot. All the above is rented at an average of about £4.00 per square foot. Three years ago the 10,000 square foot finished goods warehouse previously taken on was sold.

EXHIBIT 8   Production Details for Marketing Samples in New Colors

Product	Color Requests (units)					Actual Time Taken per Product (minutes)		Allowed Molding Standard Time per Product (minutes)
	Beige	Brown	Blue	Green	Total	Molding	Color Change	
4012 Dish	24	42	24	42	132	405	65	156
4013 Holder	20	42	24	42	128	550	100	152
4014 Beaker	24	42	24	42	132	480	60	111
4018 Holder	24	42	24	42	132	260	60	129
4019 Holder	24	42	24	42	132	670	110	132
4020 Sticks	40	42	30	42	154	270	60	137
4021 Ring	60	60	36	36	192	390	95	200
4023 Rack	20	36	20	24	100	1140	220	175
4028 Rail	24	42	24	42	132	445	60	139
4029 Frame	24	42	26	42	134	530	120	137
Total	284	432	256	396	1368	5120	950	1468

NOTES: 1. Color change time is the total time taken to change from one color to another in this production run. It is in addition to the actual molding time given here.

2. "Actual time taken per product" is the actual number of standard minutes taken to mold the quantity of the product in question. "Allowed molding standard time per product," on the other hand, is the number of standard minutes calculated to be necessary to mold the quantity of the product in question.

Exhibit 9

Technical Note

Multi-impression Molds

An important design decision to be made concerns the number of impressions to be built into a mold. A single impression would mean that with every shot only one molding is produced. With multi-impression molding, then two or more products (depending upon the number of impressions) are made with every shot, thus giving a significant decrease in molding time to complete an order quantity. This could be a lid or base of the same product, two lids and two bases of the same product, two or more identical products (e.g., a tray), or two or more products that are not identical (e.g., a set of spoons to be sold as a set), or two or more different products to be sold as different products in the marketplace.

- Normally the number of impressions are even-numbered to retain balance in the mold.
- The capital cost of a two-impression mold is more than twice the cost of a single-impression mold of the same item due to the increased complexity of the mold design.
- The more impressions per mold then the larger the mold size (i.e., physical dimensions) and the longer time it takes to set up and color change.

Molding Machine

With wear and tear over time, molding machines increasingly find it more difficult to achieve the upper limits of their specification. One common problem is that when the raw material is injected into the mold under pressure, then the machine is less and less able to exert the locking pressure necessary to keep the two halves of a mold together. It if does not, then flashing (thin pieces of material on the edge of the molding) will become apparent. If flashing does appear with a low-quality item it can be trimmed off; with a high-quality item, this would normally make it a reject.

Molding

A mold can go onto any machine, providing that the machine is physically large enough (i.e., to take the physical dimensions of a mold), has the shot weight to fill the mold and hence produce a complete molding, and has the locking pressure to keep the two halves of the mold closed during the machining cycle.

Hence, the division of molding machines into four groups reflects the fact that machines are in a range of "sizes" (i.e., physical dimensions, such as the opening

---

Exhibit 9
(continued)

---

to take the mold, shot weight, and locking pressure). Molds, therefore, are loaded according to the appropriate machine size. There is little opportunity to sensibly transfer one mold to another machine group.

Finally, the size of a mold is primarily a factor of the dimensional size of the product (e.g., height and diameter). Similarly, the molding cycle time (i.e., how long it takes a machine to inject material into the cavity of the mold) is a factor of product size, the wall thickness of a product, and, to a much lesser extent, the condition of the machine (i.e., the effects of wear and tear).

As Mark continued to explain, the markets for the two products the company currently manufactured and sold were very different.

Sales of the old product are normally negotiated on a large volume contract, with call-offs to meet the agreed customer deliveries. In the new markets, retail outlets hold our ranges, but the mix of products and colors means that we often need to be able to supply orders within a few days. While this is not always possible, we have a good reputation from our customers for the level of support we provide. For, as they emphasize, if the exact product wanted by their customers is not available at the required time, then often the sale is lost as they spend their money on something else altogether.

Mark explained that he had continued to push this policy and had been instrumental in bringing out several new ranges since joining the company. The latest was due to be launched quite soon, with another due out early this year. "This redirection has also had a few spinoffs in the older homeware range, where we have redesigned some packaging, and increased and improved the color range."

Corporate Policy

"We have come a long way since those days of change," said Graham Brown, managing director.

My predecessor had the foresight to rethink corporate policy when the group restructuring created the substantial excess molding capacity. For the past two years, I have reinforced this sound strategy. The marked increase in sales is anticipated to continue, and home and export sales support this forecast. The lower-volume products have allowed us to gradually decrease our overall molding capacity. It is now important that we use this capacity efficiently and, in making the budgets for the coming year, we have taken account of the anticipated nonproductive demands on the manufacturing facilities. But although these new product launches make large demands on the system, they are our future life blood. We must keep costs down, and so look at all areas of costs. Our decision to go toward multi-impression molds is one way of staying competitive [see Exhibit 9]. Our recent and future product ranges reflect this perspective.

CASE 9
KAWASAKI USA

History of Kawasaki Heavy Industries (KHI) and the Lincoln, Nebraska, Plant

At their Akashi Works in Japan, KHI's motorcycle division builds about 500,000 motorcycles per year, of which 90 percent are exported. In 1975 KHI established a plant in Lincoln, Nebraska, to improve the product line and response offered the North American market. In the United States, KHI is organized as Kawasaki Motors Corporation, USA. At its headquarters in Santa Ana, California, are located research and development, marketing, sales, and distribution. A distribution center is also located with the plant in Lincoln.

Several factors were thought to be important in selling motorcycles, including product quality, product performance, price, and the cosmetics of the product design (styling). Many customers are in the 18 to 25 year old age range and want products that are inexpensive and "fast." Kawasaki is effective in designing and introducing new models quickly, with many models having only a three-month product life.

In addition to motorcycles, the Lincoln plant produces snowmobiles and jet ski products. Engines for the snowmobiles and jet skis come from Akashi, but over 50 percent of the other parts come from American suppliers. Both products require fabrication of miscellaneous parts and extensive body preparation prior to assembly (see Exhibits 1 through 4).

Motorcycle production consists of assembly with fabrication of frames, gas tanks, and miscellaneous parts. Most engineering originated and new models started production in Akashi. One year after introduction, the tooling for models popular in America was shipped to Lincoln for follow-on production.

Kawasaki hired American managers to run the Lincoln plant by basically American methods, but with goals and standards set by the Japanese as follows:

- Quality of production.
- Productivity (including the budget).
- Employee relations.

Everything did not go well. Snowmobiles and jet skis started in low-volume batch operations, which the Americans understood. However, the Japanese wanted to produce all products by the fast-flow repetitive production techniques used in Japan. More than language and culture prevented the Americans and Japanese from clearly understanding each other. They were simultaneously attempting two different approaches to managing the plant.

They had difficulty getting the right part to the right place at the right time. Inventory was randomly assigned to bin locations in the stores areas, and there was excess inventory. Parts might be on hand, but could not be found. Defect and rework rates were high. The quality of finished units was acceptable, but correcting errors was expensive.

Prepared by Robert W. Hall, Indiana University. Reprinted with permission, the American Production and Inventory Control Society, Inc., *Kawasaki USA*, 1982.

This case is written for instructional use only and does not represent a criticism of the management practices of Kawasaki Motors Corporation, U.S.A., or of Kawasaki Heavy Industries, Limited, Japan.

Exhibit 1

Plant and Products Kawasaki USA

Plant:	Approximately 220,000 square feet
	450 production employees
	Primarily a one-shift operation
	Mostly an assembly operation
	Fabrication and painting of:
	Gas tanks—the most "cosmetic" component of a motorcycle
	Bike frames and miscellaneous parts
	All other parts are purchased, or come from Kawasaki-Japan
Products (units):	Motorcycles, 10 models:
	Street bikes, approximately 70–90 percent Japanese parts
	Dirt bikes, approximately 50 percent Japanese parts
	KLT (three-wheel) bikes, approximately 50 percent Japanese parts
	Snowmobiles: 6 models, approximately 30 percent Japanese parts
	Jet skis: 1 model, approximately 30 percent Japanese parts
Volume:	Seasonal demand, i.e., the demand rate varies from 220 units/day
	in the spring to 40 units/day in the fall
	About 75,000 total units for 1981
	Each model has a bill of materials with no options
	There are 100 different single level bills of material
	Approximately 6–700 part numbers per finished unit
	Approximately 10,000 total part numbers in the system
	About 2,500 active part numbers

Getting the Confidence of the Work Force

Butt recognized that solution of the problems required management to work directly with the plant floor work force. His first goal was to gain enough confidence from the workers to make this possible. Under Butt's leadership the management adopted the following objectives:

Get the right part to the right place at the right time. Put parts only where they are needed. Attain an uninterrupted flow of production, which requires:

- Reducing setup times.
- Reducing lot sizes and inventory levels.
- Joining as many subassembly operations as possible to final assembly.
- Doing it right the first time (improving quality).

The managers leading this program had to work directly with the floor personnel and adopt the basic concepts of the Japanese Kanban system for getting the right part to the right place just in time for it to be used. This implies no inventory and no mistakes.

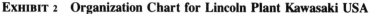

EXHIBIT 2   Organization Chart for Lincoln Plant Kawasaki USA

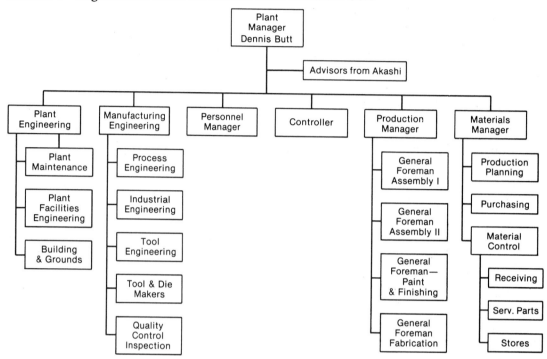

EXHIBIT 3   Layout Sketch Kawasaki USA Lincoln Plant

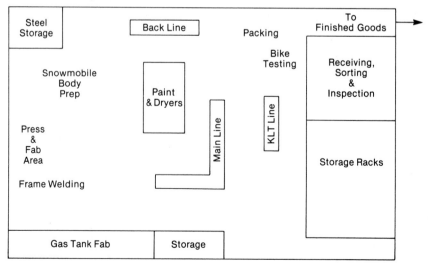

EXHIBIT 4   Physical Material Flows Kawasaki—Akashi, Japan, and Lincoln, Nebraska

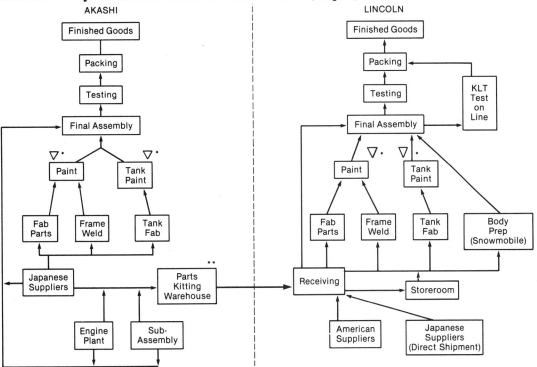

*Both Lincoln and Akashi keep a planned parts bank at this point. However, Lincoln keeps proportionately more: one or two day's on hand at Lincoln, but less that half a day at Akashi.

**The Akashi Works supplies many parts to Lincoln, all packed in lot sizes of 200 (or submultiples) ready to take directly to the lines at Lincoln. Parts from American suppliers are inspected, counted, and repacked in 200s to take to the lines.

Some of the managers had always had proven results from "hard-nosed methods" and found it difficult to change. Almost all the managers were convinced that a materials requirement planning (MRP) system was the solution and found it difficult to change their materials philosophy.

However, the problems at Lincoln were so serious that they needed a faster resolution than MRP promised. Dennis Butt estimated that full development of the MRP system would have required a million dollars and an unknown number of years.

At the same time, the Kawasaki Akashi Works in Japan had just finished four years of Kanban development. The pilot project had been in their motorcycle plants, and results were so successful that Kawasaki Heavy Industries decided to implement Kanban in all plants. A delegation from Akashi visited Lincoln to persuade the American management of the merits of Kanban.

Dennis Butt needed little persuading. He knew that MRP implementation would be complex and time-consuming and that Lincoln needed a quick turnaround. The other managers had more difficulty accepting the merits of Kanban, but reluctantly abandoned the MRP project $300,000 into its development.

Inventory Management

To reduce inventory, assembly lot sizes were set at 200, approximately one day's production on the main motorcycle line. The Akashi Works began shipping all large parts for each model in kits of 200 ready for movement directly to the assembly line. In that way, it was also easier to keep all the parts for a model run together. Parts received from American suppliers were inspected, counted, and repacked in 200s, ready for the lines.

To get parts to the right place, floor locations were specified for each part. Pick lists for each model run were generated by computer from the line schedules. Material handlers used them to get the right parts to the designated locations in time for each model run.

EXHIBIT 5   Inventory Control System—Kawasaki USA

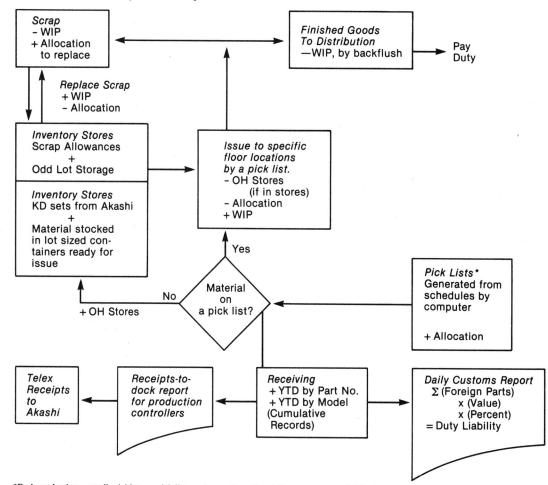

*Each production controller initiates a pick list run two or three days before parts are needed by the schedule. Pick lists are done by computer explosion of the bill of material combined with floor use locations (routings). The pick list generates allocations against inventory.

EXHIBIT 6   Kawasaki Motors Corp. USA Lincoln Pick List Allocation

05/27/81
09:37:24
PAGE 0001

ASSY P/N: 82KZ440 F08L   QTY = 200

ASSY DESC: CLUTCH CABLE   WORK STATION: 82KM400 F08L   LOT = BOB J.

LINE NBR	ITEM NUMBER	ITEM DESCRIPTION	QTY NEEDED	UNIT ISS.	BIN —LOCATION—	NOTES	QTY ALLOCATED	QTY PICKED
0001	540111072	CLUTCH CABLE	200		EMPTY		0	( )
					55K3—			
					55K4—			

END-OF-REPORT

This practice began on the main motorcycle line, and at first the operators and foremen were dubious. They anticipated that keeping the lots of parts intact would be bothersome. However, they soon found the extra trouble to be worth it because the practice reduced errors and expediting, the first major step in getting the right part to the right place at the right time.

In the Lincoln inventory system shown in Exhibits 5 and 6, the generation of pick lists is a key feature, but the Japanese advisors could not understand why they were needed. In Akashi, material handlers are expected to know the parts needed without such a list, but at Lincoln there is difficulty getting the same person to pick the parts for the same area each day.

The Kawasaki inventory system at Lincoln was very similar to a bulk issue system used by many American repetitive manufacturers. Issues from the storeroom decreased the on-hand balance and increased the work-in-process balance. However, the issues to the plant floor all went to a specific location, and the fixed lot sizes improved work-in-process accuracy. Sometimes parts went directly from the receiving dock to the line and Kawasaki wanted to do that with all parts.

Cycling counting had been initiated but not fully developed. The official inventory was taken by an annual count. Cycle counters checked samples of items selected at random from inventory. If the on-hand balance was within $\pm \frac{1}{2}$ percent, the record was considered accurate. On that basis, motorcycle parts were considered to be 90–95 percent accurate and snowmobile parts about 70 percent accurate.

Much of the improvement in inventory accuracy came from the issue of standard lots to designated floor locations. The odd lots with nonstandard counts were kept in stores, and the decreased level of inventory helped keep straight what was on hand. Using space released from stores, the Lincoln plant could expand production without extending its walls.

Balancing Operations for Straight Flow Production

To reduce the buffer stocks between operations, the rates of production of all operations needed to be balanced. By May 1981 several subassembly operations had been tied directly to the final assembly lines, saving space and inventory. However, the fabrication rates of frames and gas tanks proved more difficult to equate with final assembly rates. The welding rates of the KLT frames were matched with assembly, but the frames for the larger models were not.

Weld rates on all frames do not match assembly rates. It takes extra inventory to buffer the problems of tank preparation from assembly. The Lincoln plant had hoped to have some Kanban cards in circulation between final assembly and these areas by June 1981, but the problems proved more difficult than supposed. A true "pull system" cannot be implemented without solving them.

Production Planning System

Exhibit 7 outlines the production planning system of the Lincoln plant. The planning system contains several elements of the MRP system that has been in development. The final assembly schedule serves as the master production schedule (Exhibit 8). From this, other plans are derived by exploding the schedules manually. An example of this is the frame welding schedule in Exhibit 9. Note that the daily rate of frame welding is well below the rate of frame use in assembly, so the buildup of buffer inventory must be time offset from the requirements of the assembly schedule.

A manual explosion is also used to develop purchasing requirements. Each production planner develops purchase release schedules from the final assembly schedules and the fabrication schedules. These schedules go to purchasing to be built into the blanket purchase agreement or to use as revisions to previous delivery schedules.

It was unnecessary to explode requirements at Lincoln for the parts shipped from Akashi. The final assembly schedule was sent to Akashi, and the requirements to be shipped were exploded in Japan. Therefore the planning bill of materials for most of the materials planning in Lincoln included only non-Akashi parts.

Since the volume of the Lincoln plant was comparatively small, Akashi would treat parts orders from Lincoln as any other customer. Lincoln provided Akashi with schedules in advance, and it would ship the parts as long as deviation from the schedule was not substantial. The real shipping requirements were established by cabling the assembly schedule for Lincoln to Akashi six weeks ahead of time. No special link had been developed between the Lincoln master schedule and the Akashi master schedule.

Sales of all products were seasonal. By building inventory ahead of the selling seasons, Kawasaki leveled the production schedules of the Lincoln plant. All finished units transferred immediately to distribution, and the plant had no further responsibility for them. Without detailed records, plant personnel estimated finished motorcycle inventories at 18–20 days in May 1981.

The final assembly schedule (master schedule) was nearly level each day in units made and in total work load. Only the KLT 250 assembly schedule was identical every day because of the high volume involved. The main motorcycle assembly line schedule averaged 200 motorcycles each day except where a model change was scheduled.

The lot size of 200 was common to all motorcycles, whether assembled on the main line or not. For example, lot sizes for the KLT were 200, although the line was scheduled for 60 per day.

The lot size for most snowmobile and jet ski parts was also 200. The planning for uniform lot sizes on those products has just begun, but the schedule planning was complicated since weather was a great factor in the sales for these products. One consequence was that it was necessary to rework many unsold snowmobiles in stock to refit them as current models. The prospects of a level schedule in assembling snowmobiles therefore seemed difficult to assure. Motorcycle demand was more predictable so the early effort to reduce setup times and balance operations rates concentrated on these products.

The schedule was adjusted in line with the actual production in the Lincoln plant. According to foremen, if the daily assembly schedule were met early in the day, the lines continued to work until the close of the shift. If unfavorable events put them behind schedule, they would try to catch up as quickly as possible, sometimes by working overtime. Low sales in early 1981 meant

Exhibit 7

Planning System of the Lincoln Plant Kawasaki USA (as of May 1981)

Sales Forecast

- By models in monthly buckets.
- One-year horizon.
- Three-month replanning cycle.

Sales Plan

- A set of requirements by model on the finished goods warehouse at Lincoln, which is supplied by the Lincoln plant. To get this, the forecast is "adjusted" by Akashi.
- One-year horizon.
- Three-month replanning cycle.
- Closest three months are firm.
- The requirements of the Lincoln plant are based on this.
- Plan is approved by the plant manager, Akashi Sales, and Kawasaki USA Sales in Los Angeles.

Production Plan

- The basis of the plant budget.
- 18-month horizon for capacity projection purposes. The last three to six months are based on an in-plant forecast.
- Three-month replanning cycle.
- Three months are frozen by the agreement on the sales plan.
- Six weeks are absolutely fixed by the shipping lead time from Akashi.

Daily Production Schedule

- This is a final assembly schedule by days. It serves as the master production schedule.
- The planning horizon is one year, but only the earliest four to five months are given planning attention in detail.
- A major replanning cycle occurs every three months corresponding to the planning cycle of the sales plan and production plan.
- A minor replanning cycle occurs weekly.
- Three months are frozen by the sales plan and also by the planning horizon at Akashi from which parts are shipped.
- Six to seven weeks are frozen unchangeably because of agreement with the Akashi Parts Kitting Warehouse on the sequence of kits to be shipped.

Exhibit 7
(*concluded*)

Fabrication Schedules

- These are developed by manually exploding and offsetting the schedules from the daily production schedule (final assembly schedule).
- Because fabrication rates are not yet balanced with assembly rates, it is necessary to build frame and gas tank buffer stocks ahead of final assembly. This results in a buildup and drawdown of inventory.
- One or two day's inventory ahead of final assembly is usually necessary.
- Parts kits from Akashi are ordered on the basis of the daily production schedule. The kit explosion is done in Akashi.
- Parts from other suppliers are ordered on the basis of a manual explosion of the daily production schedule and the fabrication schedules.
- Each production planner is responsible for the manual explosions of the model schedules for which he/she is responsible and for seeing that materials are on order.
- Major replanning cycle each three months. Minor replanning cycle weekly.

Planning Data

- There are three bills of material:
  1. Engineering bill of material.
  2. Manufacturing bill of material—Used for backflush of WIP based on the count of complete units transferred to the distribution warehouse.
  3. Assembly or "pick list" bill—This is the list of parts needed for final assembly.
- Capacity planning is done manually on the basis of historical standards. They keep a record of hours by part number in fabrication and of assembly hours by model.
- Records of buffer inventories on the floor are based on production counts at the following points:
  1. After frame welding.
  2. After fuel tank painting.
  3. After assembly (transfers to distribution).
- Engineering changes are coded by the production planner responsible. On the engineering bill the code is as follows:
  *Part being phased out.
  **Part being phased in.
- Most changes are timed to occur with the beginning of a specific lot and the following data is coded on the manufacturing bill:
  1. Effective date.
  2. Run out quantities of the phased out part.
  3. Serial number of the unit on which the change will be effective. (Just starting.)

EXHIBIT 8 Daily Production Schedule

Date 3/26/81

Production Week	#5			#1			#2		#3		#4		Total
Day	6/1	6/5	6/8	6/2	9/5	6/8	6/22	6/26		6/24	6/30		

Model

(3 Wheel Bike)

Model														Total
T250 Order #														
T250 Qty	60 60 60 60			60 60 60 60			60 60 60 60		60 60 60 60		60 60			1320
T200 Order # / Qty														
1250 Order # / Qty														
400 Order # / Qty														
M400 Order #														
M400 Qty		140	220 40		220 180		100 100							1000
500 Order #														
500 Qty	160 220 220 20			40 160	60		220 120							1440

(Main Line Schedule)

Model														Total
J650 Order #														
J650 Qty	60 140			40 220 140			100	100						800
650A Order #														
650A Qty	220 180			220 180			100 210							710
700 Order #														
700 Qty							50 100 50							200
00 Order # / Qty														
M400 Order # / Qty														

(Snowmobile, Back Line)

Model														Total
M600 Order #														
M600 Qty	15 25 35 35		35 35 35 35	35 35 35 35		35 35 35 35				30 30				695
00 Order # / Qty														

371

Exhibit 9   Frame Welding Schedule KJ 650

	4-27	28	29	30	5-1
Planned Build					
Balance on Hand					
Release					
Lot #/Balance Pts					
Order #					

	5-4	5	6	7	8
Planned Build					
Balance on Hand					
Release					
Lot #/Balance Pts					
Order #					

	5-11	12	13	14	15
Planned Build					
Balance on Hand					
Release					
Lot #/Balance Pts					
Order #					

	5-18	19	20	21	22
Planned Build					
Balance on Hand				45	75
Release			20	25	30
Lot #/Balance Pts		225	205	200	150 →
Order #	55 AWO6 →				

	5-25	26	27	28	29
Planned Build					
Balance on Hand		110	161	219	277
Release		35	51	58	58
Lot #/Balance Pts		115	6A 200	46 →	
Order #	55 AWO6 →				

	6-1	2	3	4	5
Planned Build					
Balance on Hand		335	393	457	509	567
Release		58	58	58	58
Lot #/Balance Pts		90	234	174	116	58
Order #	55 AWO6 →				

	6-8	9	10	11	12
Planned Build	20	150	30		
Balance on Hand	605	455	425	425	425
Release	58				
Lot #/Balance Pts					
Order #	55 AWO6 →				

	6-15	16	17	18	19
Planned Build			40	220	40
Balance on Hand	425	425	405	243	161
Release		20	58	58	
Lot #/Balance Pts		200	180	122	64 →
Order #	55 AWO6 →				

	6-22	23	24	25	26
Planned Build					100
Balance on Hand	219	277	335	343	351
Release	58	58	58	58	
Lot #/Balance Pts	206	148	90	32	174 →
Order #	55 AWO7 →				

	6-29	30	7-1	2	3
Planned Build	100				
Balance on Hand	309	367	425	425	
Release	58	58			
Lot #/Balance Pts	116	58	–	–	–
Order #	55 AWO7 →				

	7-6	7	8	9	10
Planned Build					
Balance on Hand	425	425	425	425	425
Release					
Lot #/Balance Pts					
Order #	55 AWO7 →				

	7-13	14	15	16	17
Planned Build					
Balance on Hand	425	425	425	425	425
Release					
Lot #/Balance Pts					
Order #	55 AWO7 →				

	7-20	21	22	23	24
Planned Build	50	220	130		
Balance on Hand	375	155	25	25	25
Release	200				
Lot #/Balance Pts					
Order #	55 AWO7 →				

	7-27	28	29	30	31
Planned Build					
Balance on Hand	83	141	199	225	225
Release	58	58	26		
Lot #/Balance Pts	142	84	26		
Order #	55 AWO7 →				

	8-3	4	5	6	7
Planned Build	160	40			
Balance on Hand	65	25	25	25	25
Release					
Lot #/Balance Pts					
Order #	55 AWO8 →				

	8-10	11	12	13	14
Planned Build					
Balance on Hand	25	25	25	25	25
Release					
Lot #/Balance Pts					200 →
Order #	55 AWO8 →				

	8-17	18	19	20	21
Planned Build					
Balance on Hand	57	109	167	110	25
Release	26	58	58	58	
Lot #/Balance Pts	174	116	58		
Order #	55 AWO8 →				

	8-24	25	26	27	28
Planned Build					
Balance on Hand	25	25	25	25	25
Release					
Lot #/Balance Pts					
Order #	55 AWO8 →				

normally working ahead of schedule, with assembly operations only stopping when they ran out of material. At that point, people had a choice of going home or staying to do cleanup work.

Getting the Help of Suppliers

At Lincoln, labor cost is a small percentage of the total cost of a finished motorcycle. The major productivity payoffs are from improved quality, reduced scrap, and reduced inventory investment. To get the maximum decrease in inventory, Kawasaki needed the cooperation of their suppliers to reduce the quantities and increase the frequency of shipments.

A supplier that needed no instruction was TRICON, a subsidiary of Tokyo Seat Company, located two miles from the Lincoln plant. The three top managers of TRICON were Japanese, and they found it easy to operate the Japanese way with the Lincoln plant. Kawasaki gave them the Lincoln assembly schedules in advance and then telephoned every morning with any changes. Twice daily TRICON delivered the exact number of seats requested to the receiving department, not directly to the assembly lines as in Japan.

TRICON itself bought materials from Japan. They purchased in small quantities from American suppliers and operated with very short setup times. When the Lincoln plant got off schedule with delays followed by catch up, TRICON had to operate the same way. In turn, they passed the problem to their own suppliers, both Japanese and American.

Until 1980, Kawasaki-Lincoln typically issued blanket purchase orders covering three months and specifying shipping release dates and quantities. Their suppliers understood and accepted these terms.

By May 1981 eight suppliers, including TRICON, had agreed to what were called just-in-time purchasing agreements. These were three-month blanket orders as before, but with three major changes:

1. Shipments were to arrive at least twice a week.
2. The purchase release specified arrival dates for specified quantities to arrive at the Lincoln plant.
3. The accepted deviation from shipping quantity was reduced from $+/-10$ to $+/-1$ percent of the quantity requested.

To be classified as a just-in-time supplier, all three criteria had to be met, but the purchasing agents tried to get as many suppliers as possible to agree to one or more of the conditions.

Educating suppliers was difficult. For example, the first reaction to the request for smaller shipment sizes was usually that it was possible, but would cost more. Suppliers presumed that Kawasaki wanted others to carry their inventory for them. Getting suppliers to understand that Kawasaki would like them to cut their own setup times and costs was a very difficult sales task. Also, delivering exact quantities proved difficult.

Future Direction of the Lincoln Plant

Despite great progress, as shown in Exhibit 10, the Lincoln plant had fallen short of its goals. They had wanted to have some Kanban cards in circulation by June 1981, but the fabrication rates were not yet balanced enough with assembly rates to do it.

They had an ongoing goal to reach 26 inventory turns per year in 1982. That would be possible only if many more suppliers were converted to just-in-time agreements. Several other problems include: low-volume models with a minimum batch size on components from suppliers, start-up problems on new products, and the drop-off of old models once parts have been ordered.

Exhibit 10

Accomplishments of Kawasaki USA, May 1981

1. Reduced inventory approximately 40 percent in 18 months.
2. The amount of inventory on hand is five days for parts used in actively produced products. More inventory than that is retained, but is really obsolete.
3. The inventory goal is 26 turns per year. This requires Kawasaki USA to cut current inventory by 50 percent. Most of this can be done by attrition of the obsolete inventory.
4. Productivity has improved 20 percent in two years.
5. The ideas of just-in-time production began about March 1980, just over one year ago. Most of the improvement has occurred since then.

They wanted to use the space released by the reduction of inventory to continue plant expansion and to put as many operations as possible directly on the final assembly lines. Failing that, they wanted to cut the decoupling inventory between operations and final assembly to zero, or very near zero.

By fall 1981 Dennis Butt wanted to be alternating at least two models in final assembly on the main motorcycle line. This would be a step toward the practice in Akashi of switching models in final assembly after every five units.

Case Addendum

By 1986 Kawasaki had completed most of the work in installing a pull system in the factory, ending the need to use "pick lists" and inventory transactions in restocking material at the final assembly line. At this time mixed model production was also implemented in final assembly. Kawasaki-Lincoln now runs mixed models, usually four or five product models, sequenced by ones on the final assembly line. It took about three months to detail the positions of containers at the line to compact the line layout enough to handle mixed model assembly.

Each month the plant is rebalanced to the new final assembly schedule and the number of Kanban containers is recalculated manually. They operate a paperless factory. No paper goes to the shopfloor and no paper reports are required. Production reports are written on a board next to the line by the foreman. Shopfloor data are obtained from the boards. Other than quality information, data are not recorded on the shopfloor for analysis. Overall measurements of production, cost, and inventory are performed on a plantwide basis. Important reductions in plant overhead costs had been achieved. Currently, the plant staff includes 22 foremen, 11 process engineers, 3 production controllers, 2 accountants, and a clerical staff of 20.

CASE 10
KLEIN PRODUCTS

"Well, Alan, I think congratulations are in order," were Paul Sharman's opening comments. "It looks as though we have a commercially viable product, now that it has come through the final phase of technical testing. The market is receptive, and two of our major customers are demanding supplies as soon as possible. The prospects look good." Paul Sharman, managing director of Klein Products, was responding to the report given by the technical director, Alan Gibson, on a plastic replacement for a major metal packaging product. "It not only fits the relatively high technical profile of our business," he continued, "but also presents the chance of multiplying, by a quantum jump compared to other products, the enormous commercial opportunity of exploiting technical advantage with high volumes. It comprises a large market, much greater than any of our current segments."

Background

Klein Products is part of Toucon Industries, a large, diverse group of companies based in the United States, but with worldwide interests and sales in excess of $10 billion. Toucon's industrial holdings include electronics, furniture, office, and telecommunications equipment, food products, and packaging products, in which Klein was one of several companies within the group. In addition, it has recently expanded its interests in the finance and insurance business, particularly in North America, to the extent that the nonindustrials accounted for some 20 percent of total sales revenue.

Klein Products (KP) was purchased by Toucon Industries in the early 1980s as part of a group of companies whose principal activities were in food-related products. In group terms, KP is relatively small. However, its profit performance and return on investment record in the last five years were all above both the group average and the norms for the industry in which it operates. While many of its competitors are much larger, KP, with the financial backing of Toucon, is not disadvantaged in terms of investment support to help exploit viable commercial opportunities of a long- and a short-term nature. Furthermore, Klein's customer base has been gradually moving more and more toward large customers (with corresponding larger volumes), a fact no doubt helped by the Toucon image.

Marketing

Currently, Klein mainly sells customized packaging. In this instance, potential customers determine, often with a supplier's help, the size, shape, and color of the container they require, and the print design where applicable. With few exceptions, each product comprises a single specification in terms of the orders placed (i.e., the size, shape, color, and print are the same for each product, with only the unit quantities differing from one order to the next). To give a feel for the business, details on a representative sample of 25 products have been provided as

This case study was written by Professor T. J. Hill (London Business School) and S. H. Chambers (University of Warwick). It is intended for class discussion and not as an example of good or bad management. © AMD Publishing (U.K.).

EXHIBIT 1   Representative Sample of Products Listed by Reducing Annual Sales Revenue Based on Next Year's Forecast

Reference	Product Description	Years since Introduction	Current Year Minus 3	Current Year Minus 2	Current Year Minus 1	Current Year	Next Year's Forecast	Sales Revenue (£000s)	Contribution as Percent of Sales Revenue
1	Medium Meadow Care	2	0	1,260	5,630	11,200	13,460	555	68
2	Large Antisep	8	9,540	9,620	8,460	7,800	7,320	390	34
3	Family Disinfectant	12	3,300	3,440	2,880	3,010	3,120	321	32
4	Giant Weedblitz	2	0	420	760	830	800	177	63
5	Small Spring Blossom	5	1,250	3,300	6,680	5,210	4,570	155	43
6	Medium Body Care	7	4,200	4,650	3,910	4,240	3,630	129	45
7	Small Cream Cleaner	8	2,190	2,490	2,930	2,800	2,600	106	53
8	Family Pine Cleaner	6	400	430	480	660	950	101	48
9	Medium Standard Round	17	830	1,260	1,410	1,620	1,690	95	72
10	Family Harsh Cut	2	0	710	1,170	1,040	1,390	86	74
11	Medium Apple Leaf	1	0	0	1,250	1,570	2,010	68	64
12	Family Sterisol	0	0	0	0	770	1,280	58	34
13	Small Apple Leaf	0	0	0	0	670	1,370	49	66
14	Giant Antisep	6	210	240	230	220	240	42	46
15	Medium Siki	7	800	1,240	1,180	920	830	34	64
16	Medium Mouthwash Tablets	12	790	720	640	580	530	29	42
17	Large Disinfectant	12	700	670	610	580	640	27	38
18	Small Standard tub	17	950	920	790	830	800	23	83
19	Medium Soap	5	100	160	190	210	230	20	46
20	Large Saisco	8	310	260	270	240	250	18	36
21	Large Houseplant Food	4	60	80	110	140	150	12	45
22	Medium Sabre	0	0	0	0	180	170	10	35
23	Small Antisep	6	220	200	210	170	180	7	54
24	Medium Household Wax	1	0	0	50	40	40	3	70
25	Large Standard Antiseptic	14	15	10	15	10	10	1	46

NOTE: There are currently six other sizes of Meadow Care, with next year's forecast annual unit volumes ranging from 0.80 to 0.25 million units. These additional sizes were introduced this year and last year following the success of the medium size.

376

Exhibit 2

A Note on the Corporate Interpretation of the Phrase *Technical Competence* as Used in the Case Study

All the products made have been reviewed by the marketing and production managers, and each has been assessed for the degree of technical competence embodied in the molding and/or printing of the product. In making this assessment, the following aspects were considered.

1. The relative level of complexity of the molding or printing processes used. Low ratings were given to products molded on simple, low output machinery, which could be easily adjusted and maintained to give a satisfactory quality of output. High ratings were given to processes which involved complex adjustment, precise control, and considerable levels of knowledge and skill.
2. The degree of difficulty involved in producing the individual products. Products with complex shapes, sharp corners, very precise dimensions, or difficult plastic material (in terms of molding) increase the problems involved in achieving the required standards, and are, therefore, given higher ratings.
3. Processes developed "in-house" for specific products. These would be given high ratings of technical competence, until the technical advantage is matched by KP's competitors.

Exhibit 1. Customers with a low annual requirement sometimes choose a standard product, which the company makes and supplies from finished goods inventory (for example Products 9, 18, and 25 in Exhibit 1).

Two of the distinguishing features of KP's markets are the aspects of technical competence/price and unit volume. The technical competence and price issue concerns the degree of technical competence required at the molding and/or printing stages of production, and is explained more fully in Exhibit 2.

The company sees itself as increasingly being in the higher technical segments of its markets. However, it also recognizes that technical advantage is usually short-lived. For most products, KP can maintain a technical competence advantage for no more than two years. After this time it declines, often quite dramatically. To illustrate the relative importance of the technical competence factor this and other relevant order-winners have been provided in Exhibit 3 for the 25 representative products referred to earlier.

"In order to help better understand our markets, we have established the order-winning criteria for all our products, while also signaling qualifiers to which we need to pay particular attention," explained Art Hausemann, marketing director.

EXHIBIT 3   Weighting of Order-Winning and Qualifying Criteria for the Sample Products Given in Exhibit 1

| | | | Order-Winners and Qualifiers | | | | | |
| | | | Technical Competence | | Delivery | | | |
Product References	Year	Price	Mold	Print	Speed	On Time	Quality	Others
Market A								
	Current	50	0	40	10	QQ	Q	0
1	+2	65	0	20	20	QQ	Q	0
	+4	60	0	10	30	QQ	Q	0
	Current	60	0	20	20	QQ	Q	0
5, 6, & 15	+2	65	0	10	25	QQ	Q	0
	+4	65	0	0	35	QQ	Q	0
	Current	Q	20	50	10	Q	20	0
11 & 13	+2	20	20	40	10	Q	10	0
	+4	40	20	20	20	Q	0	0
	Current	80	0	10	0	0	10	0
22	+2	80	0	10	0	0	10	0
	+4	80	0	10	0	0	10	0
Market B								
	Current	60	10	0	25	Q	QQ	5
2, 14, & 23	+2	70	0	0	30	Q	QQ	0
	+4	70	0	0	30	Q	QQ	0
	Current	20	0	0	60	0	0	20
25	+2	20	0	0	60	0	0	20
	+4	20	0	0	60	0	0	20
Market C (unprinted)								
	Current	70	0	—	30	Q	Q	0
3, 12, & 17	+2	70	0	—	30	Q	Q	0
	+4	70	0	—	30	Q	Q	0
Market D (unprinted)								
	Current	20	70	—	0	Q	10	0
4	+2	50	40	—	5	Q	5	0
	+4	60	0	—	30	Q	Q	10
Market E								
	Current	40	0	0	40	0	10	10
7 & 8	+2	40	0	0	40	0	10	10
	+4	40	0	0	40	0	10	10
	Current	10	30	0	60	0	10	0
24	+2	30	10	0	60	0	10	0
	+4	40	0	0	60	0	10	0
Market F								
	Current	20	60	20	0	QQ	Q	0
10	+2	40	30	20	10	QQ	Q	0
	+4	60	0	20	20	QQ	Q	0

Exhibit 3 *(concluded)*

Product References	Year	Price	Technical Competence		Delivery		Quality	Others
			Mold	Print	Speed	On Time		
Market G (unprinted)								
	Current	40	0	—	40	0	0	20
9 & 18	+2	40	0	—	40	0	0	20
	+4	40	0	—	40	0	0	20
Market H								
	Current	80	0	0	20	0	0	0
16	+2	90	0	0	10	0	0	0
	+4	90	0	0	10	0	0	0
	Current	60	0	0	40	0	0	0
19, 20, & 21	+2	60	0	0	40	0	0	0
	+4	60	0	0	40	0	0	0

NOTES: 1. Order-winning weightings. Products have been grouped together by market segment, then separated, where applicable, into subsets, with the same order-winning criteria weightings. The period chosen to reflect the life cycle of KP's products is four years.

2. +2 and +4 under the column "year" mean current year + 2 years and current year + 4 years, respectively.

3. The order-winners shown here not only highlight the importance of certain criteria for different products, but also their changing nature, particularly between the factors of technical competence and price. Where there is a gradual loss of technical competence, then the weighting given to this order-winner will reduce, while the weighting given to price will increase, as illustrated in the details above.

4. In assessing the factors of technical competence and price, the company considers that where the weighting points for technical competence are greater than or similar to price, then technical competence should be considered as the relevant order-winner on the technical competence/price continuum. Where the weighting for price is significantly greater than the points attributed to technical competence, then price should be considered as the relevant order-winner on this continuum.

5. Q signifies a qualifying criterion, while QQ denotes a qualifier, which is order-losing sensitive.

The sample of products in Exhibit 3 illustrates most of the issues involved. The advantage we attempt to achieve through the factor of technical competence (and correspondingly improved margin) has different levels of endurance. The typical trend is that over time, price will become an increasingly important order-winner. How quickly this transition takes place depends on several factors, including the sales volumes involved and the distinct nature of technical competence as an order-winning criterion. Where the sales volumes are large, then the stimulus for others to compete is greater, and this will, understandably, reduce the length of time we enjoy this technically-based advantage. Also, we are now entering new segments in our markets. Let me explain by using the example of Meadow Care.[1]

Firstly, it illustrates the enormous level of success that comes from marrying technical competence and volume. This has proved difficult for us to achieve in the past, made more so by the fact that it is not possible to foresee how a segment will develop in terms of volumes, and also how long our technical

---

[1]KP manufactures and sells plastic containers to various customers. To distinguish one product from another it uses the name of the contents to describe each container: thus, "Meadow Care" refers to the container(s) in which this product will eventually be packed.

competence advantage will last. With Meadow Care, the sales quantities of the medium size have grown beyond all expectations. However, our investment in the P10 printer has proved to be an important factor in our success. Although initially the customer intended only to sell the medium size, its very success stimulated the company involved to meet the demand for other sizes. However, sales of these latter products have been relatively low.

In addition, to further enhance sales of Meadow Care, the number of print types has increased as exports have been purused. The two other suppliers of this container are both based in Continental Europe, but have neither been as fast in responding to meet the customer's needs as we have, nor in maintaining the quality levels demanded. This initiative has enabled us to increase total sales of this product. It has become clear that this type of customer-related support will increasingly become part of our overall strategy, in order to stimulate further sales volume growth.

Art Hausemann then turned the conversation toward the new product. He explained that the technical breakthrough was a first and "understandably, even a group as big as Toucon is excited." The new product will also prove to be all new business for KP. "Currently, this market is dominated by two large companies, which together account for 70 percent of total sales volumes. The advantage, however, of plastic over metal needs little explanation. The retailers see plastic as having so many plus points that they have shown themselves prepared to pay a price premium adequate to give us an acceptable return. The quantities involved are also significantly greater than anything we are in at present, with 350 million unit sales forecast for the total market this year," explained Art. He continued to say that the feature of technical competence in the new product would be quite transient (about two years) as competitors, including those manufacturing the current, metal-based product, were working on a plastic replacement. "We are aware of this," commented Art Hausemann.

> Our patents will not help, as there are many alternative design approaches that could be followed by our competitors. We also anticipate that the main supplier of the existing metal products will not yield this substantial market without a fight. What we have to do is exploit our advantage over the next 24 months. In that way, it forms an ideal part of our future marketing strategy of moving from the low volume/low technical competence toward the high volume/high technical competence market segments.

Manufacturing

The span of process within manufacturing is quite small. It comprises molding, printing, and auxiliary processes, including packing. The technical features, which manufacturing needs to provide, are in its ability to meet a product's design needs as explained in Exhibit 2.

The processes onto which products are loaded are determined at the outset, based on factors of volume and the technical demands of a product. For example, a product that requires printing comprising five colors will be routed through the five-color printer. Exhibit 4 illustrates these differences, based on the representative products used earlier. Once the contract has been received, the company designs tooling to fit a specific process. It is, therefore, difficult to subsequently load a product onto another size of process, as the tooling is specific to the chosen process type (e.g., M1). However, currently, there are several machines within each process type (e.g., in process type M3 there are 12 machines) which, for all intents and purposes, are the same in terms of loading appropriate tools (all tools designed for a process type can be loaded onto any of the machines within that type) and throughout speeds.[2] The exception is P10, where there is only one machine.

---

[2]However, within a process type, additional investment can be made to improve machine performance. For instance, on the one hand to increase throughput speed by reducing the cooling cycle or improving the take-off arrangements or, on the other hand, reducing setup times by appropriate tooling and process modifications.

EXHIBIT 4 **The Manufacturing Processes and Standard Hours for Molding and Printing the Representative Products**

Product Reference	Type of Process Used		Machine Standard Hours per 1,000 Containers		Number of Orders (current year)	Number of Production Runs (current year)	
	Molding	Printing	Molding	Printing		Molding	Printing
1	M2	P10	1.11	0.23	12	3	3
2	M3	P10	1.21	0.21	12	4	10
3	M3	—	2.45	—	6	6	—
4	M2	—	3.05	—	4	4	—
5	M2	P 9	1.23	0.25	12	3	10
6	M2	P 9	0.86	0.25	12	1	12
7	M1	P 9	0.86	0.21	6	1	2
8	M3	P 9	2.55	0.21	2	2	2
9	M1	—	2.10	—	stock	3	—
10	M3	P 3	2.88	0.27	4	4	4
11	M2	P10	0.85	0.23	12	2	6
12	M3	—	1.75	—	2	2	—
13	M1	P10	0.68	0.23	6	6	6
14	M3	P 9	4.25	0.20	2	2	2
15	M2	P10	1.35	0.23	12	4	8
16	M4	P 9	1.44	0.24	9	9	9
17	M3	—	1.30	—	4	4	—
18	M6	—	0.65	—	stock	2	—
19	M1	P 7	1.00	0.29	8	6	6
20	M1	P 6	0.95	0.30	1	1	1
21	M1	P 3	1.10	0.27	5	5	5
22	M2	P10	2.06	0.23	2	2	2
23	M6	P 2	0.71	0.24	4	4	4
24	M1	P 7	1.24	0.29	1	1	1
25	M3	P 9	1.85	0.25	stock	2	2

NOTES: 1. All molding and (some) printing processes run 24 hours per day, over five days, with weekend overtime on selected processes (for example P10).

2. While there is some variation between the length of production runs for any given product (molding and printing) generally these are similar, and should be considered so for purposes of analysis.

3. Products 1, 2, 5, 6, 11, and 15 are ordered on a scheduled basis, shown above as 12 orders per year.

4. Product 1 is completed on three machines, and Products 2 and 5 on two machines.

5. KP employs a range of molding and printing processes, not all of which are shown above because the sample of products has been based on representing volumes and order-winners within the business, rather than reflecting the range of processes used.

6. The word *stock* in the column "Number of orders" means that many orders were received for these products from many customers. The orders were supplied from finished goods inventory, as they are standard, not customized, products.

"The provision of technical competence is not a major production problem," explains Jack Jameson, manufacturing director.

As long as the technical requirements are incorporated in the early stages in the normal way, then providing the technical edge is usually a straightforward task. We support a diverse range of products, the needs of which are provided by a number of processes. Depending on where a product is in its life cycle, then the demands of each product, in terms of what manufacturing needs to provide, can be very different, as shown in Exhibit 3. One critical part of this task is providing customer support in terms of

Exhibit 5

Alternative Mold Processes and Relevant Investments for the New Product

The following is a summary of the current position.

1. Three years of research have been conducted in optimizing the product design, selecting and testing suitable materials, and in finalizing the manufacturing techniques.

2. Molds have been purchased to fit the existing, specialized molding process M8/1, and are undergoing extensive production trials. Early output was of a satisfactory quality, and final trials have proved that this process is commercially viable (see the opening remarks in the case narrative).

3. The new product is not printed. Different customers will place orders for the product for a range of order quantities. They will differentiate the container by using labels at the appropriate point in their own processes. Labels are used not only to describe the contents, but also, in many instances, to further increase product differences, for example by the use of color.

4. Letters of intent have been received (from two of the company's main customers), giving initial requirements for a total of 3 million units in two sizes, with deliveries to commence mid-next year.

5. Mold design has been initiated for an alternative higher output process M8/2, which involves similar molding technology.

6. Details have been obtained of processes M9/1 and M9/2. Used successfully elsewhere in the group for other high-volume products, this molding technology is considerably more complex and has not yet been proven capable of producing the new product.

7. Estimated prices have been received for the purchase of each type of machine and associated molds.

8. In assessing the order-winning criteria for the new product, a weighting of 70 was assigned to technical competence because of the unique combination of product design and manufacturing development associated with the product. It was recognized that the use of process M8/2 would not affect this weighting, but the use of processes M9/1 or M9/2 (which offer higher output) would further differentiate the company from competitors in terms of technical competence. These processes were assessed as having a technical competence rating of 85 for the initial period. This higher rating has been awarded to the M9/1 and M9/2 processes because it is considered that customers will perceive potential suppliers with these processes as more able to meet the higher-volume segments of these markets.

Exhibit 5
(concluded)

9. Comparison of processes

	Process Alternatives			
Feature	*M8/1*	*M8/2*	*M9/1*	*M9/2*
Annual output (millions of units) per machine	1.0	4.0	10.0	20.0
Investment per machine (£000s)	250	500	1000	1500
Investment per set of molds (£000s)	50	88	220	260
Tool change time (hours)	14	30	48	54
Availability—delivery lead time for each machine (months)	—	2	6	8

NOTES: 1. The new product is not printed (see 3 above).

2. The existing M8/1 process is currently used on other products, and has little, if any, spare capacity available.

10. As with any market of this size, the current metal product comprises several segments with a corresponding range of order quantities and different order-winners. Some segments involve quantities of a size similar to many of Klein's present products, while others are in quantities many, many times greater.

meeting schedule changes. As the number of products grows, the need to balance production run lengths and the urgent requests from customers becomes increasingly difficult to manage. Marketing have explained that they intend to move into the higher volume segments and, if it happens, we will find that a significant help in terms of managing our processes.

At the moment, our overall sales growth has caused capacity problems on certain processes, and we are having to work weekend overtime on several molding and printing processes. One in particular we need to look at is the five-color printer (P10). At the moment, we are at full stretch on this one machine, and will soon be unable to meet our delivery commitments on a regular basis. The need for additional five-color printing has been accepted: which one to purchase is the decision we need to make. Certainly, the P10 has proved to be very successful and, no doubt, was an important factor in the success of the Meadow Care business.

He then went on to discuss the new product and production implications of moving into a market with different levels of volumes. "The potential volumes are enormous," he reflected, "and the group's imagination has been caught. The debate on where to position ourselves has been in progress now for several months, a summary of which is available [see Exhibit 5]. Given the corporate interest and accepted marketing strategy, then it looks to me as though we will eventually be aiming toward the M9 machine series. The process technology will be quite something."

Opportunities of the New Product

"The new product," explained Paul Sharman, "symbolizes the nature of Klein's position in the market. The company has built up a substantial design and development capacity to enable it to create the technical competence advantages pursued by the company. In this way, it is able to provide the necessary product margin to support the business, while achieving acceptable levels of profit."

When summarizing the new product and the opportunities it presented for the business, Paul Sharman explained that the technical breakthrough they had achieved gave the company many advantages.

For one, it helps create an internal image for this company within the group. We are small in group terms, but world technology firsts help build everyone's prestige. Secondly, it will not only help us to grow overall, but will help us to reposition ourselves within our own markets. The recent news that the new product is economically viable gives us the final piece in the play.

Although it is a quantum leap on, the M9 processes must now be our next technical hurdle to overcome. For manufacturing, though, I realize that it presents a different set of problems. But that is part of the corporate game. They need to explain the options, as the investment stakes are high.

CASE 11
META PRODUCTS

"Our meeting with the group board was most rewarding," was Barry Levenger's opening remark to the executive team of Meta Products.

> Approval was given to purchase three 500-ton presses and one additional printer. The group board recognized the need to provide additional injection molding and printing capacity to support the growing market in fluid containers, and proved most supportive of our corporate strategy to exploit this market opportunity. As part of their agreement, they asked for a statement of our overall strategy and what changes, if any, we are proposing to our overall approach to meeting the needs of our markets. I explained that this was now under review and timed to coincide with the introduction of these new investments in six months time. The board accepted the timing of this revision and asked to be involved in the discussion and party to its agreement. We have already recognized this as a high priority and, therefore, need to draft ideas as soon as possible.

The meeting to which Barry Levenger referred was attended by himself, as chief executive officer, and Ted Enderby, the divisional director of Meta Products, to present the application for capital investment referred to here.

Background

Meta Products is a subsidiary of PALC Industries, a large holding company involved in a diverse range of businesses, including engineering, steel fabrication, wire-drawing, cable-making, office equipment, and packaging. As part of the packaging division, Meta Products occupies two wholly owned sites in Swindon, a large and growing industrial and commercial town in southern England. Located on the main site at Bristol Road there are three separate companies, two from the packaging division and one from the office equipment division. Recognizing the advantages of keeping apart businesses that are distinct, these three companies (of which Meta Products is one) are organized independently of one another, while enjoying some central services (such as heating) and some functions organized on a site basis. The principal unifying factor was that all three companies were responsible to the same managing director, a common feature used by the group to encourage the development of its general managers. In addition, there are the centralized functions of personnel, industrial engineering, maintenance, and a toolroom. These functions occupy central office and workshop areas. Each of the three companies had its own executive team and, with the exception of the central services described earlier, is managed as an autonomous business unit, with the exception of major capital investments, which required the approval of the group board of directors. The overhead costs associated with the centralized functions described here are allocated on an agreed basis.

In addition, there is a second site close by, situated in an industrial estate adjacent to Bristol Road. This was solely used by Meta Products as a warehouse for part-finished as well as finished goods.

This case was prepared by Professor T. J. Hill (London Business School) and S. H. Chambers (University of Warwick). It is intended for class discussion and not as an illustration of good or bad management. © AMD Publishing (U.K.).

Marketing

Meta Products makes a wide variety of (mainly customized) moldings for a number of markets. Stewart Larby, the sales and marketing manager, outlined the marketing strategy. He explained that it identifies future sales growth as taking place in the food, cosmetic, and fluid container markets.

"Current actual sales are up to forecast," he explained, "and the growth in fluid containers is proving to be greater than expected. This has resulted in longer lead times being currently quoted, even though we are, and have been, working weekend overtime. The additional machines will not only alleviate current capacity problems, but will give us the opportunity of developing this new market still further. Our markets can be broadly described as comprising six segments," Stewart continued. "Each of them is different, and the easiest way to explain these differences would be to describe each in turn."

Food Products.   Food products are customized in terms of molding and printing, and are sold to large, nationally based, food processing companies. This segment comprises only a small number of customers, but involves very high annual volumes (totaling about 25,000 standard molding hours this year) with weekly call-offs. All products (except frozen-meal packs) are printed and the variety of print designs can be as high as 20 to 25 on one item. Exhibit 1 gives details of these products, including a representative range of print varieties. Most companies, while able to give reasonably accurate weekly call-off information, tend to provide printing details only one or two days ahead of delivery requirements. As one would anticipate, all relevant aspects of quality (e.g., cleanliness, product conformance, and appearance) are most important. Each customer requires all suppliers to meet its own stringent quality assurance/control systems (which includes the requirement for an adequate quality control function within a supplier's manufacturing unit), while making rigorous checks on receipt of deliveries and undertaking random checks on suppliers at any time of the day, without previous notice.

Assembled Products.   Assembled products have two distinct characteristics. The first is that after molding they all undergo one or more additional processes before completion. For example, this involves inserting one or more components into the principal molding, joining two or more moldings together, and/or attaching a metal fitting, or applying a label, each of which requires an automatic device to complete the task. The second feature is that none of these products is printed. Within this segment, there are 14 products; Exhibit 2 provides details for a representative number of these. The products are molded on a range of machines and this year accounted for some 32,500 standard molding hours.

Industrial Products.   Meta Products has, for many years, produced a variety of customized products for manufacturing companies. As with other market segments, the mix of products changes over time, but this type of business has remained an important part of the overall business portfolio—this year, it accounted for over 45,000 standard molding hours—Exhibit 3 provides details for a representative number of products. Within this category, products are not printed, and molding quality concerns the absence of visual defects since the products do not demand exacting dimensional tolerances. However, this is not to imply that products are of low quality, but more that the product specification tends not to be difficult to achieve and maintain. Given these characteristics, it is understandable that this is a price-sensitive market, as there are many small injection molding companies able to meet the relevant customer requirements.

Fluid Containers.   Fluid container products represent a new market segment, which has arisen as a result of the successful substitution of plastic for metal as the material to be used in

Exhibit 1 Details for a Representative Sample of Food Products

Current Year

Product Code	Standard Molding Hours	Production Runs	Colors	Print Varieties	Molded in Area Number
F098	3,220	6	1	—	2
F127	5,830	4	1	3	3
F186	1,580	4	1	10	3
F201	2,700	5	1	10	3

Relevant Order-Winning and Qualifying Criteria

Product Code	Product Description	Year	Price	Delivery Speed	Delivery Reliability	Mold Quality	Print Quality	Cleanliness	Existing Supplier	Annual Standard Hours (molding)	Print Variety
F098	Frozen-meal pack	Current	30	20	Q	—	—	QQ	50	3,220	—
		+2	50	20	Q	—	—	QQ	30	3,600	—
		+4	60	30	Q	—	—	QQ	10	5,000	3
F127	Premium butter container	Current	Q	30	QQ	70	Q	QQ	—	5,830	4
		+2	20	30	QQ	50	Q	QQ	—	5,000	4
		+4	40	30	QQ	30	Q	QQ	—	2,000	4
F186	Beverage powder container	Current	60	40	Q	—	—	Q	—	1,580	10
		+2	60	40	Q	—	—	Q	—	1,200	10
		+4	60	50	Q	—	—	Q	—	800	10
F201	Luxury individual dessert	Current	Q	50	QQ	50	Q	QQ	—	2,700	10
		+2	Q	50	QQ	50	Q	QQ	—	3,000	12
		+4	Q	50	QQ	50	Q	QQ	—	3,500	12

Notes: 1. +2 and +4 in the column headed "year" mean current year plus 2 and current year plus 4, respectively.
2. Q denotes a qualifier.
3. QQ denotes an order-losing sensitive qualifier.
4. Print variety refers to the number of different print designs required by customers.
5. Dimensional accuracy is a critical feature of products F127 and F201.

EXHIBIT 2   Details for a Representative Sample of Assembled Products

| | Current Year | | | |
Product Code	Standard Molding Hours	Production Runs	Colors	Molded in Area Number
A067	1,250	4	2	4
A079	645	4	6	4
A120	460	6	8	1
A125	6,450	4	1	1 and 4
A138	920	6	1	4
A146	5,200	2	1	1 and 4

Relevant Order-Winning and Qualifying Criteria

Product Code	Product Description	Year	Price	Delivery Speed	Delivery Reliability	Molding Quality	Existing Supplier	Annual Standard Hours (molding)
A067	Labeled household item	Current	20	40	QQ	40	—	1,250
		+2	30	40	QQ	30	—	500
		+4	—	—	—	—	—	0
A079	Lid assembly	Current	100	—	—	—	—	645
		+2	100	—	—	—	—	400
		+4	100	—	—	—	—	400
A120	Box	Current	20	50	—	30	—	460
		+2	30	50	—	20	—	500
		+4	40	50	—	10	—	600
A125	Lid assembly	Current	Q	50	QQ	50	—	6,450
		+2	Q	60	QQ	40	—	6,500
		+4	Q	60	QQ	40	—	7,800
A138	Hinged base	Current	60	—	—	Q	40	920
		+2	60	—	—	Q	40	1,000
		+4	60	—	—	Q	40	1,200
A146	Audio insert	Current	—	10	Q	60	30	5,200
		+2	—	20	Q	60	20	4,000
		+4	20	30	Q	40	10	2,500

NOTES: 1. +2 and +4 in the column headed "year" mean current year plus 2 and current year plus 4, respectively.
2. Q denotes a qualifier.
3. QQ denotes an order-losing sensitive qualifier.

EXHIBIT 3   Details for a Representative Sample of Industrial Products

Current Year

Product Code	Standard Molding Hours	Production Runs	Colors	Molded in Area Number
1092	1,720	8	6	1
1104	420	3	1	1
1240	2,060	10	6	2
1362	120	2	2	2
1385	175	3	2	1

Relevant Order-Winning and Qualifying Criteria

Product Code	Product Description	Year	Price	Delivery Speed	Delivery Reliability	Molding Quality	Existing Supplier	Annual Standard Hours (molding)
1092	Car trim	Current	90	10	QQ	Q	—	1,720
		+2	80	20	QQ	Q	—	1,400
		+4	70	30	QQ	Q	—	1,000
1104	Domestic appliance clip	Current	100	—	QQ	—	—	420
		+2	100	—	QQ	—	—	600
		+4	100	—	QQ	—	—	800
1240	Car component	Current	80	20	QQ	QQ	—	2,060
		+2	90	10	QQ	Q	—	2,200
		+4	90	10	QQ	Q	—	2,600
1362	Packaging component	Current	90	—	—	10	—	120
		+2	100	—	—	—	—	130
		+4	100	—	—	—	—	140
1385	Industrial equipment component	Current	100	—	Q	Q	—	175
		+2	90	—	Q	Q	10	130
		+4	70	—	Q	Q	30	90

NOTES: 1. +2 and +4 in the column headed "year" mean current year plus 2 and current year plus 4, respectively.

2. Q denotes a qualifier.

3. QQ denotes an order-losing sensitive qualifier.

making existing fluid containers. The improvements offered by plastic and, in particular, the company's mold design allowing for a single molded unit, thus avoiding the critical problems of guaranteed sealing, has provided Meta Products with this growth opportunity. Over the last 18 months, the company has enjoyed a distinct product design advantage, which is expected to be maintained for the next two or even three years.[1] Most standard products are printed to customers' designs, and the print varieties are expected to increase to over 100 in the years to come (see Exhibit 4). All products undergo an assembly operation following printing to attach the appropriate handle. Current annual volumes exceed 30,000 molding standard hours, and this is expected to double in the next 12 months, with similar growth levels expected in subsequent years. Customers include major chemical companies (e.g., Chemex) taking customized products at one end of the spectrum, and small users taking standard products at the other.

Cosmetic Products.   Cosmetic products are customized in terms of molding and printing, and sold in different volumes, depending on the level of exclusivity embodied in the final product. To ensure that the aesthetic qualities are maintained, Meta Products' customers have developed rigorous quality control procedures, which suppliers have to follow. This includes providing an independent quality control presence on a 24-hour basis and sample checks to agreed norms. Weekly schedules are provided, which are subject to changes at relatively short notice, particularly regarding printing requirements (details are provided in Exhibit 5). Annual volumes are currently about 16,000 standard molding hours per year, which represents a 30 percent increase over last year. It is anticipated that volumes for the next two years will show similar levels of growth.

Sundry Products.   The final market category embraces a group of products with a wide range of applications. These include children's games, domestic applications, and office sundries. Products are not printed, and details for some representative products are provided as Exhibit 6. Although this category lacks a distinct marketing orientation, it has been, and still is, an important part of Meta Products' total business, accounting for almost 23,000 standard molding hours this year, a 10 percent increase on last year.

Manufacturing

The growth in sales, particularly with the introduction of the fluid container product range, has necessitated the purchase of additional processes and, for some products, regular overtime working. Explained Tim Wilcox, manufacturing manager:

> By and large, product types use the same molding and, where relevant, printing processes. The exception to this is that most of the fluid container products are relatively large. Specific molding and printing machines were, therefore, purchased to meet these size requirements and are allocated to these products on a permanent basis.
>
> With regard to other market categories, some products can be produced on the processes predominantly used by another category, but the need to exercise this option is a decision we do not frequently need to make. However, processes have been replaced or added over the years, with the result that the molding areas contain processes serving two or more market categories [see Exhibits 1 to 6]. We have already looked at the possibility of allocating certain molding machines to each product type and have

---

[1]Meta Products' design was patented two years ago, but the company recognizes that other solutions are feasible. It anticipates, therefore, that competitive alternatives will be available in the next few years, which will not infringe its own patent.

EXHIBIT 4   Details for a Representative Sample of Fluid Container Products

Current Year

Product Code	Standard Molding Hours	Production Runs	Colors	Print Varieties	Molded in Area Number
F2001	915	4	1	6	3
F2003	5,450	2	1	46	5
F2004	6,800	2	1	62	5
F2006	2,120	4	1	30	4
F2008	4,700	2	1	—	5

Relevant Order-Winning and Qualifying Criteria

Product Code	Product Description	Year	Price	Delivery Speed	Delivery Reliability	Mold Quality	Print Quality	Design	Annual Standard Hours (molding)	Print Variety
F2001	2.5-liter Vynacol	Current	Q	—	Q	30	Q	70	915	6
		+2	Q	—	Q	30	20	50	2,000	20
		+4	20	—	Q	30	20	30	3,000	25
F2003	20-liter Chemex	Current	Q	20	QQ	30	Q	70	5,450	46
		+2	40	40	QQ	20	Q	20	12,000	75
		+4	60	—	QQ	Q	Q	—	15,000	100+
F2004	5-liter Chemex	Current	Q	—	QQ	30	Q	70	6,800	62
		+2	50	—	QQ	10	Q	40	16,000	100+
		+4	60	40	QQ	Q	Q	—	20,000	100+
F2006	1-liter Agrite	Current	Q	—	Q	30	Q	70	2,120	30
		+2	40	—	Q	—	20	40	4,000	60
		+4	80	—	Q	—	20	—	1,000	100+
F2008	5-liter standard	Current	30	40	Q	—	—	30	4,700	—
		+2	60	40	Q	—	—	—	6,000	—
		+4	60	40	Q	—	—	—	7,000	—

NOTES: 1. +2 and +4 in the column headed "year" mean current year plus 2 and current year plus 4, respectively.
2. Q denotes a qualifier.
3. QQ denotes an order-losing sensitive qualifier.
4. Print variety refers to the number of different print designs required by customers.
5. F2008 is sold as an unprinted container.
6. Products F2001, F2003, and F2006 are customized products. For example, a 5-liter Chemex comprises a standard molding, which is then customized to Chemex's requirements at the printing stage. In addition, other changes (e.g., a different colored handle for the container) are also sometimes requested.

391

EXHIBIT 5 Details for a Representative Sample of Cosmetic Products

Current Year

Product Code	Standard Molding Hours	Production Runs	Colors	Print Varieties	Molded in Area Number
C068	780	4	1	3	1
C116	4,730	2	4	12	3
C210	1,200	6	1	6	3

Relevant Order-Winning and Qualifying Criteria

Product Code	Product Description	Year	Price	Delivery Speed	Delivery Reliability	Mold Quality	Print Quality	Cleanliness	Existing Supplier	Annual Standard Hours (molding)	Print Variety
C068	Facial cream tub	Current	20	—	—	80	—	Q	—	780	3
		+2	10	—	—	80	10	Q	—	700	5
		+4	Q	—	—	80	20	Q	—	700	8
C116	Supermarket moisturizer	Current	Q	30	Q	30	40	QQ	—	4,730	12
		+2	10	30	Q	30	30	QQ	—	5,000	15
		+4	20	20	Q	30	30	QQ	—	5,500	15
C210	Skin care container	Current	Q	40	Q	30	30	Q	—	1,200	6
		+2	10	30	Q	30	30	Q	—	1,600	10
		+4	30	10	Q	30	30	Q	—	1,900	10

NOTES:
1. +2 and +4 in the column headed "year" mean current year plus 2 and current year plus 4, respectively.
2. Q denotes a qualifier.
3. QQ denotes an order-losing sensitive qualifier.
4. Print variety refers to the number of different print designs required by customers.
5. Dimensional accuracy is a critical feature of these products, particularly C068.

Exhibit 6 Details for a Representative Sample of Sundry Products

Current Year

Product Code	Standard Molding Hours	Production Runs	Colors	Molded in Area Number
S025	900	5	10	2
S080	210	4	6	2
S193	155	3	3	2
S272	105	2	2	1

Relevant Order-Winning and Qualifying Criteria

Product Code	Product Description	Year	Price	Delivery Speed	Delivery Reliability	Molding Quality	Existing Supplier	Annual Standard Hours (molding)
S025	Game model	Current	50	—	—	—	50	900
		+2	75	—	—	—	25	1,000
		+4	100	—	—	—	—	1,100
S080	Office equipment item	Current	50	—	Q	50	—	210
		+2	80	—	Q	20	—	300
		+4	100	—	Q	—	—	350
S193	Household product	Current	100	—	—	Q	—	155
		+2	100	—	—	Q	—	150
		+4	100	—	—	Q	—	100
S272	Office equipment item	Current	80	20	—	—	—	105
		+2	100	—	—	—	—	125
		+4	100	—	—	—	—	130

Notes: 1. +2 and +4 in the column headed "year" mean current year plus 2 and current year plus 4, respectively.
2. Q denotes a qualifier.
3. QQ denotes an order-losing sensitive qualifier.

EXHIBIT 7   Meta Products Current Organization Chart

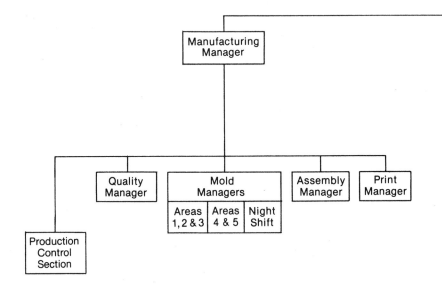

to meet the different levels of demand for the products in each market category. Following this decision, therefore, would not result in any major process difficulties or disadvantages, except that we may have to purchase the occasional molding machine somewhat earlier than would have been the case under the present molding arrangements.

On the issue of printing capacity, however, problems would arise if we were to attempt to allocate capacity to meet the specific needs of the food, fluid container, and cosmetic market categories. Such a decision would require the purchase of additional printing capacity to cover the needs of the food and cosmetic groups, as currently they share the same printing processes—the separate requirements of fluid containers has already been recognized and separate printing process capacity has been justified and allocated to these products.

However, one issue raised at the recent capital investment application meeting with the group concerned increasing the utilization level of our current molding capacity. Barry Levenger and Ted Enderby have commissioned me to report on this matter. Members of the group board had put forward the view that if we introduced continental shift work patterns, then we could increase our capacity from five days, plus current average overtime working to seven days.[2] Barry and Ted confirmed that this approach had

---

[2]Continental shifts refer to a pattern of working involving four shift teams, only three of which are involved at any one time. This provides for 24-hour coverage over seven days without involving over-

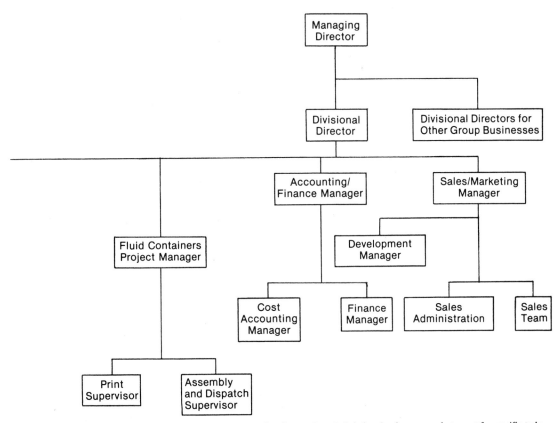

Notes: 1. The centralized site functions report directly to the managing director through their functional managers, but report for specific tasks
into Meta Products as follows:
   • Personnel to the finance manager.
   • Industrial engineering and maintenance to the manufacturing manager.
   • Toolroom to the development manager.
   2. Other relevant aspects of the organization are given in the case study narrative.

found this to be feasible, should we consider this to be a sensible move to take. If this course of action
was followed, it would still necessitate working the same level of overtime as we currently do in order
been used elsewhere in the group and had highlighted the increases in capacity which had resulted, giving details of labor costs incurred, compared to those for working a five-day week with extensive overtime. Given the large investments involved and the anticipated sales growth in the future, then it seems
to make sense. Recruiting additional people should not be a problem, and we are well able to give appropriate training where necessary. A further comment they also made was that the current shift patterns
lack uniformity. It's true, we do employ people using a number of different shift systems, some of

time working. The description "continental" comes from the fact that this shift pattern was first introduced by countries in continental Europe.

which have developed over the years, but some do reflect our needs. I do take the point that to the outsider it looks somewhat ill-planned.

He then continued to outline the present organization arrangements within the manufacturing function, which have been provided as Exhibits 7 and 8. "In order to provide the appropriate level of effort and attention to the fluid container initiative, we made special organizational arrangements," explained Tim Wilcox. "Therefore, I will first describe the manufacturing structure for all the other products, and finish by briefly outlining the current position on fluid containers." Tim then outlined the manufacturing scenario as follows:

Molding is currently located in five separate areas. Part of this separation of facilities makes sense, while the remainder has been forced upon us over the years, due to the piecemeal purchase and sale of equipment. In order to control this, it has been necessary to provide two molding managers, each looking after different areas [see Exhibit 7]. Furthermore, as molding takes place on a 24-hour basis, we need to provide for a molding manager to cover the night shift. Although the molding managers officially work from 08.00 to 17.00 hours, working a three-shift system means that problems and decisions do not stop at the end of their working day. Consequently, these molding managers cover most of the 24 hours and have established a sound communication system between them, which includes telephone conversations, revisits, starting early, or staying late, where required. Recently, we have been working much weekend overtime on several molding processes, and this is covered by a combination of managers and supervisors, all of whom would be paid for their attendance.

Where products need to be assembled, these tasks are completed in a separate area, with an assembly manager responsible for all aspects of this work. We also have an evening shift from 18.00 to 22.00 hours, which has its own supervisory structure. [See Exhibit 8.]

On the printing side, we have a mix of arrangements to meet the demands of this part of the process. Exhibit 8 shows the relevant staffing levels, which includes printer-setters on the day shift and each of the three shifts. Their role is to set up all machines, as required, to run some of these, and to monitor the other machines (run by printers) through each shift in order to maintain quality requirements and maximize throughput levels.

With regard to quality, we employ a quality manager, whose specific role is to determine sampling and other quality procedures for in-coming materials (including packing and bought-out items), molding, printing, assembly, and packing. In addition, the job involves customer liaison on quality matters, testing current materials, assessing alternative materials, and controlling the provision of necessary inspection for all hours worked. Inspectors working a three-shift pattern report on general matters to the relevant production supervisors, where the quality manager and supervisor are not on site. However, the company clearly separates the responsibility of the assurance and control of quality from that of manufacturing. In Bill Heathcote we are fortunate to have a person who is quality-oriented, appropriately qualified in terms of the materials we use (he is a chemist by training), and is well regarded by all our customers, as well as within the plant itself.

The aspect of production planning and control is organized as follows. The aspect of medium- and long-term planning falls within my own jurisdiction. The purchase of additional or replacement processes and other aspects, such as changes to shift arrangements, I retain as part of my direct responsibilities. The short-term production control activities, such as scheduling, are handled by the production control section (comprising three staff, one of whom is the section leader), who report directly to me. Their role is to schedule molding and printing processes in line with customer requirements and agreed delivery dates, and to ensure that all items necessary to run a product are available when needed. This entails coordinating materials, packaging, bought-out items, mold tool availability (for example, the toolroom checks over each mold tool before the next time it is used), and any other items necessary to complete the work. Also, this section liaises with sales administration to discuss requests by customers to alter schedules, change priorities, or to meet changes in delivery quantities.

In addition, there are several general functions [see Exhibit 8], which link into the organization in the following way. The raw materials handler, who works on days, reports to the molding manager for areas 1, 2, and 3. The warehouse supervisor reports to the assembly manager, the forklift drivers and cleaners are allocated to the two molding area groupings, while all personnel within these general functions, working on nights, report to the molding manager (night shift).

Finally, the central services of maintenance and toolroom report on an on-call basis. Unfortunately, although this does not work well, there seems little alternative. My molding and printing managers report that the urgency and necessary orientation of these staff does not match the needs in manufacturing. The managers comment that it seems almost as though manufacturing is an inconvenience. For instance, priorities in the toolroom seem directed toward making new tools and not to refurbishing and other immediate manufacturing needs. Still, the trade-off is that we do keep associated overhead costs to a minimum—it would cost far more for each business to have its self-contained facility. Maintenance would be less of an allocation problem, but this would need to be looked into in some depth.

Now, let us turn to the fluid container arrangements. Recognizing the importance of these products in terms of future company growth, and the levels of process investment involved, we approached this initiative in a different way to the one we use for the other parts of our business. The initial step was to appoint Keith Burns to be responsible for the project, and at a level higher, in organizational terms, than our current managers [see Exhibit 7]. In addition, we placed the responsibility for printing, assembly, and dispatch under his jurisdiction. At the time, we recognized the logic of also placing molding within a similar reporting format but, as the molding machines were in different areas, this was not as easy. Instead, we have given him responsibility for making the scheduling and manning decisions of the appropriate plant, which he exercises by cooperating with the relevant managers and production control. One further decision, which just evolved, was to encourage direct communication with each customer. In the early days, this shortcut the current administrative procedures, thus allowing decisions to be made in discussion with our customers, and in a way best for the business as a whole. The fact that most of the companies involved also bought other products never seemed to be a problem. As the business grew, we made no attempt to change this working relationship, and not only do we think it a satisfactory arrangement, but our customers have also found it to be a sensible and practical way of meeting their day-to-day and short-term needs.

Tim Wilcox then discussed the new molding and printing equipment, which had been sanctioned by the group. He explained that the company had recognized that the pressure on current molding space would necessitate a review of manufacturing layouts to include the industrial estate buildings adjacent to Bristol Road.

One important reason for holding onto the industrial estate facilities was to provide the opportunity to meet our anticipated future growth. The best time to do this is before the new processes are installed, so that we can use the opportunity of additional capacity provision to consider allocating processes to different parts of the business, as well as helping to alleviate the loss of production that will occur during plant relocation. Certainly, the space we have at both sites is sufficient to meet our immediate needs, while still offering the opportunity to accommodate further growth in the future. Our earlier foresight is now yielding important benefits.

The key issues we must address, therefore, do not concern the actual layout itself. There is sufficient space, when taking the two sites together, to meet our needs. The question concerns the rationale on which to base these decisions. We know it will incur costs, and these have been agreed in principle. A large capital investment allocation has already been agreed, with the full knowledge and support of the group.

Development

The development manager is responsible for the development of the company's own products and also (which is by far the biggest part of his task) agreeing on the needs of customized products. For any product, this involves all aspects of molding, printing, assembly, and packaging, as required, and embraces materials, tools, and machines.

Sales Administration

Sales administration (comprising three staff, including secretarial support) reports to the sales/marketing director and is responsible for processing customer enquiries, orders, and changes.

EXHIBIT 8   Current Shift Patterns and Manning Levels for Manufacturing and Related Functions

Location or Function	Job Title	Days 0800–1600	Three-Shifts	Evenings 1800–2200	Nights 2200–0600	12-Hour Shifts	Total Personnel
Areas 1, 2, and 3 (14 molding machines)	Molding manager	1					1
	Supervisors		1				3
	Molders		7				21
	Setters	2	1				5
Areas 4 and 5 (12 molding machines)	Molding manager	1					1
	Supervisors						0
	Molders		8				24
	Setters	1	1				4
Printing (conventional products)	Printing manager	1					1
	Supervisors	1					1
	Print-setters	1	2				7
	Printers	2			2		4
	Packers	9		6	4		19
Assembly	Assembly manager	1					1
	Supervisors			1			1
	Operators	12		6	6		24
	Setters	2					2
General functions	Night managers				1		1
	Raw material handlers	1			1		2
	Warehouse						
	Supervisors	1					1
	Staff	1			1		2
	Forklift drivers	2	2				8
	Cleaners	2					2

	Per shift		Total
Fluid containers			
Project managers	1		1
Molders	2		6
Setters	1		1
Assemblers	3		9
Packers	2		6
Assembly and dispatch supervisors	1		1
Chargehands	1		3
Printing manager	1		1
Printers		2	4
Quality assurance and inspection			
Quality managers	1		1
Supervisors	1		1
Laboratory technicians	3		3
Inspectors	2		8
Production control			
Supervisors	1		1
Staff	2		2
Maintenance and toolroom			
Mechanics	6		6
Electricians	6		6
Toolmakers	7		7

NOTES:
1. The numbers under each category are per shift. Hence in areas 1, 2, and 3 there is a supervisor on each of the three shifts, making a total of three in the far right-hand column.
2. The "three shifts" pattern is organized on a rotating basis, and comprises 0600–1400, 1400–2200, 2200–0600 hours, with a paid-for overlap, as with all interconnecting shift arrangements.
3. The "12-hour" shifts run from 0600 to 1800 and 1800 to 0600 hours with a paid-for overlap. This arrangement is of a temporary nature, but has been formalized to ensure that the printing capacity to support fluid container products is made available at all times. When additional capacity has been provided, it is intended to change this pattern of working, and this is understood by all concerned.
4. Molding managers work from 08.00 to 17.00.
5. Although maintenance and toolroom staff are centrally based, the numbers above are permanent allocations to Meta Products. However, temporary movement takes place between Meta Products and the other companies as required.

To do this, it seeks information from related functions (e.g., production control and relevant mold and print managers) and communicates it back to the customer. "Processing customer order details and clarifying the requirements of our customers is one of our prime tasks," explained Pat Dodds, who was in charge of this function.

> It is necessary then to seek a commitment from the relevant production managers, while liaising with production control on the other general (but essential) details. Once we have this agreement, then we go back to the customer and confirm details to all concerned. Customer schedule changes often cause the most difficulty, and in most instances this requires several telephone calls to the customer seeking additional detail, which the molding, printing, and/or production control function need in order to arrive at a decision. This, as you can imagine, can prove very time-consuming, but it is necessary in order to ensure that our promises can be met. Being delivery-reliable is an essential element in our business.

Future Arrangements

"Securing the group's approval to purchase the additional molding and printing processes, and the recognition of the need to consider the possibility of major structural changes involving manufacturing and other parts of the business (should they prove sensible), was the first step. What we now have to do is address the next issue, which is what makes for a sensible future arrangement. One thing is for sure, it will be costly, and will set the structure used by this business for years to come," were Barry Levenger's concluding remarks. "We are committed to getting it right, and now have the necessary opportunity. There are several options open to us. What I must ensure is that the path we follow is best for the business overall and recognizes the differing needs of our customers and the demands placed upon our business."

Case 12
Millstone Packaging

"The competitive nature of our markets is demanding on several dimensions," explained Steve Bishop, managing director of Millstone Packaging.

> Our response has, therefore, been on many fronts, and much of our sustained performance is a direct result of these actions. One aspect that is a key criterion in most of our markets is that of delivery—both speed (relating to lead times) and reliability (relating to its on-time nature). In fact, our current target on delivery reliability is 98.5 percent on all job orders.
>
> To help achieve greater control over and also reduce lead times within our total process, we have systematically invested in several areas of our prepress (i.e., preprinting) operations. This has brought improvements in many areas including quality and costs. A review of relevant aspects of our prepress activities is underway, and early insights and analyses are now available. Our task is to continue improving in this and the other aspects of our total process in order to keep ahead and maintain our good performance and sound growth record of the past few years.

Steve Bishop was commenting on the rationale and importance for completing the analysis within the prepress areas so that the necessary discussion and subsequent decisions could proceed.

Background

Millstone Packaging is a subsidiary of Kingsbury Holdings Inc., a U.S. conglomerate based in New Jersey with interests in food, tobacco, toiletries, and domestic products. Millstone was one of eight packaging companies Kingsbury recently purchased, as part of a much larger deal, from a European-based multinational. Three of the companies (including Millstone Packaging) were based in the United Kingdom. Of the other five, one was located in France and two each in Italy and Germany. Recognizing the synergy between packaging and its other subsidiaries, Kingsbury saw this move as part of its consolidation strategy within Europe.

Marketing

"As with most companies" explained Marco Angeli, marketing director of Millstone, "we are continuously reviewing our markets in order to track developments and reposition ourselves to maximize opportunities for profitable sales growth." Marco continued:

> Many of these initiatives are market segment and/or customer-oriented in that we identify specific developments or opportunities and plan accordingly. Less often we make decisions concerning much broader issues. One example of the latter was identified almost two years ago and concerned reducing our dependence on line flexographic[1] work. Developments have now enabled process flexographic processes to meet the higher demands of designs that until then could only be achieved using gravure

---

[1]Line flexographic is used for designs that only comprise solid colors and text, whereas process flexographic is used where the designs include photographic or illustrated elements.

This case study was written by Professor T. J. Hill (London Business School). It is intended for class discussion and not as an illustration of good or bad management. © ADM Publishing (U.K.).

EXHIBIT 1 Order-Winners and Qualifiers— Current Weightings and Trends

Criteria	Flexographic	
	Line	Process
Quality conformance	20 ↓	60 ↓
Delivery reliability	QQ	QQ
Delivery speed	30 ↑	30 ↑
Price	20 ↑	Q
Sales/technical support	30	10

NOTE: Q denotes a qualifying criterion; QQ, an order-losing sensitive qualifier.

processes.[2] During the last two years, we have achieved a threefold increase in sales of process flexographic work so that it now accounts for over 20 percent of total sales revenue. Process flexographic work has brought more sophisticated designs within the budget of more customers for lower-priced products, and there is no doubt that this trend will continue both in these and other similar products.

Today, meeting the design specification in process flexographic work is the key order-winner. In the future, as more companies will be able to meet these design specifications, this will decline in importance as it currently has for line flexographic work (see Exhibit 1). However, this will not happen for a few years, and our increasing ability to meet the design specification for process flexographic work will continue to be the most important factor in these markets.

Delivery performance is also an increasingly important criterion in our markets. The need to respond quickly to reducing customer lead times is already important and is generally becoming more so, while failure to deliver on time will lose business quickly. Our customers use fast-throughput, high-speed processes, and if we don't get the packaging there on time then feathers fly. Similarly, an enforced change in our customers' schedules for one of a number of reasons will trigger off the need for a relatively fast response on our part.

Marco continued then to describe the nature of the company's markets. While most (72%) of orders were for repeat items (i.e., designs for which the artwork and flexographic plates were already available), the remainder were for amendments to existing (10%) or new designs (18%) (see Exhibit 2, Note 2).

Some amended and new designs can take many months to progress. The decision to introduce such a change is typically signaled some months ahead of time. A launch date will be agreed at this time and then a series of discussions will take place, centered on a customer's decision process to agree the final design. Very often the final outcome is rushed, so by the time we get final clearance, the expected delivery date gives manufacturing little leeway. Our investment in origination over the last two years is aimed at gaining more control over the total process as well as the lead times in the organization process itself. Support for customers in this aspect of their requirements is most important in itself as well as for repeat orders.

---

[2]Lower-priced consumer products such as potato chips or potato crisps could not justify designs that could only previously be met using gravure processes. The lower costs of flexographic processes now enabled more sophisticated designs to be used on these types of products.

EXHIBIT 2 Sample of Completed Customer Orders for All Design Types

Customer	Design Type	Quantity (000s)	Customer Placement	Delivery Agreed	Delivery Actual
Browns	R	500	14 Oct.	10 Jan.	10 Jan.
Aztec	R	1,000	11 Nov.	18 Jan.	18 Jan.
Cottons	N	200	15 Jan.	6 Apr.	16 Apr.
Solent Bar	A	400	7 Oct.	23 Mar.	25 Mar.
Hartstone	A	700	6 Jan.	18 Mar.	18 Mar.
A.J. Foods	R	5,000	2 Dec.	17 Feb.	17 Feb.
Browns	N	4,660	2 Dec.	18 Mar.	18 Mar.
Mirror Foods	R	850	17 Jan.	30 Mar.	29 Mar.
Homewood	A	700	3 Feb.	27 Mar.	29 Mar.
Abbey	R	450	3 Feb.	13 Mar.	12 Mar.
F-lite	A	500	10 Jan.	20 Mar.	28 Mar.
Cottons	N	750	8 Dec.	10 Mar.	18 Mar.
Cottons	R	3,500	30 Oct.	20 Jan.	20 Jan.
Hartstone	A	1,800	8 Jan.	16 Mar.	24 Mar.
Browns	N	250	10 Dec.	8 Mar.	8 Mar.
Abbey	R	3,000	21 Nov.	10 Jan.	8 Jan.
Hartstone	N	500	17 Dec.	21 Mar.	30 Mar.
A.J. Foods	A	1,500	4 Jan.	8 Feb.	8 Feb.
A.J. Foods	N	600	29 Nov.	7 Feb.	7 Feb.
Farnells	R	800	10 Nov.	8 Jan.	8 Jan.
Alexon	A	850	14 Dec.	10 Feb.	11 Mar.
A.J. Foods	N	1,200	4 Jan.	28 Mar.	28 Mar.
Homewood	R	400	6 Jan.	25 Mar.	25 Mar.
Cowies	N	300	14 Feb.	28 Mar.	30 Mar.
Browns	A	900	10 Nov.	12 Jan.	19 Jan.
J.B. Foods	R	1,200	30 Oct.	7 Jan.	7 Jan.
Alexon	N	650	11 Nov.	1 Feb.	22 Feb.
F-lite	A	750	17 Dec.	18 Jan.	16 Feb.
A.J. Foods	N	450	6 Feb.	10 Mar.	22 Mar.
Shelleys	R	800	10 Nov.	10 Feb.	10 Feb.
Lakewood	A	300	18 Oct.	7 Jan.	16 Jan.
F-lite	N	1,500	25 Nov.	1 Mar.	14 Mar.
Farnells	A	600	7 Jan.	16 Feb.	16 Feb.
Marcos	R	200	1 Dec.	19 Mar.	19 Mar.
Richards	A	1,000	10 Oct.	12 Jan.	21 Jan.
JBK	A	900	17 Dec.	21 Jan.	21 Jan.
F-lite	R	1,200	12 Jan.	30 Mar.	30 Mar.
A.J. Foods	N	850	4 Dec.	21 Feb.	1 Mar.
Hartstone	N	600	8 Nov.	30 Mar.	18 Apr.
Abbey	R	1,000	28 Oct.	18 Dec.	18 Dec.
Shelleys	A	900	14 Dec.	29 Jan.	29 Jan.
Alexon	N	400	16 Nov.	8 Feb.	16 Feb.

NOTES: 1. R = repeat design; A = amended design; and N = new design.

2. The above sample gives 14 orders for each design type. However, of the orders processed in the first three months of this year, the actual breakdown between design types was: Repeat, 72 percent of total; amended, 10 percent, and new, 18 percent. In all other ways, however, the sample given is representative.

Manufacturing

Printing is relatively simple in operations terms, as the number of manufacturing processes through which a job passes is at most two or three. Although typically using high-volume batch processes, the nature of printing work demands highly skilled staff. One outcome of this is that the responsibility for all aspects of quality conformance, work scheduling, and setups has always been part of an operator's job.

Jim Moeller, the manufacturing director, explained that the company had systematically invested in machines in part to do with supporting sales growth and also to keep abreast of process technology developments, which included customer demands for an increased number of colors within packing designs. "In manufacturing there is pressure on a number of dimensions. Cost reduction and quality conformance have been with us for many years," explained Jim.

Customers upgrading their own processes in order to increase throughput speeds has resulted in the need for tighter packaging specifications. This has put even more pressure on quality conformance as well as contributing to the growing importance of on-time delivery. The advent of developments in process flexographic has also allowed customers to increase the features of their packaging design, a factor that has always been an important part of a customer's own product offering. Furthermore, the company has systematically invested in prepress activities such as origination and platemaking in order to increase its overall control and reduction of lead times and to strengthen ties with customers, a move that makes a lot of sense. In addition, we have achieved the substantial cost savings in all the prepress areas that the investment proposals identified.

He went on to explain that the company had also moved from rubber mats to polymer plates as the medium for print transfer. Although the actual plate costs for polymer are twice that of rubber due to material costs, the former are reusable up to five or six times whereas rubber mats could only be used once, which suited the changing mixture of the company's business to smaller, repeat orders. "Our markets are also increasingly characterized by shorter lead times," explained Jim. "Our scheduling rules call for lead times to be in the order of 10 days to allow for all manufacturing needs to be met. Given the importance of delivery reliability, breaking into schedules may put some orders at risk in terms of delivery and will undoubtedly increase costs and invariably lead to losses in machine capacity. In fact, machines are sometimes held waiting for a job to be ready to run."

Origination.   "Three years ago," explained Tom Herbert, "the company decided to invest in an origination capability."

The reasons were several. The improvements in process flexographics enabled customers to undertake pack designs that previously, because they could only be completed by gravure, could not have been justified on cost grounds. We recognized that we needed to be in at the start of these developments and build on our technical capability and the strong technical image we enjoyed in the marketplace. At that time our mix of orders for line and process work was 93 and 7 percent, respectively. Today it is 78 and 22 percent, respectively.

Similarly, three years ago we bought in all our origination work. The artwork and customer liaison was, at that time, managed within the company, but the actual artwork and negative preparation was subcontracted. From the negatives, we make plates to go onto the machines, and we have, for many years, completed this in-house. The real change has been in the preparation of artwork and the production of negatives. To be at the forefront of these changes and to offer a more complete service to our customers, we decided to undertake these tasks and have moved from a position three years ago where we bought all these services from outside to today where 82 percent of all our needs are provided in house.

Exhibit 3

Origination Department Procedures

When an order is received that requires either a new design or an amendment to an existing design, it goes to a planner within the origination department. The planner then allocates it to a buyer, taking into account existing work loads and also customer knowledge where this has relevance to the smooth running of a job. A buyer then prepares the customer brief and passes it to the studio for the artwork to be completed. Currently, there are five staff members* working in the studio, and they select the priority for completing jobs in line with customer delivery requirements. Including customer liaison, there are nine steps in the procedure before the negatives are sent to manufacturing, which then makes the plates and prints the job.

The length of time a customer takes to approve initial designs or subsequent changes varies with the customer. For planning purposes, the total lead times allowed were 21 days for an amended design and 22 and 25 days for a new design—for line and process, respectively. Many of these steps were, in fact, allocated one day in terms of overall planning yet only took a few hours. Also, 10 days were allocated to the artwork task in the studio even though the average time was only four hours. The 10 days were allocated in order that a realistic allowance would be made to include the backlog position in this part of the procedure.

The most difficult dimension in planning origination schedules was caused by customer delays in approving artwork and subsequent modifications. Customer placement dates recognized the lengthy lead times in this stage of the total procedure (see Exhibit 2). However, very often customer approvals were delayed until the point that delivery dates of the printed packaging were put at risk. Then, all efforts had to be made to ensure that the agreed deliveries were met, which often was linked to a customer's own product launch date.

Currently, the marketing/sales team was responsible for customer liaison. The customer would discuss orders of all types with the relevant sales personnel, who would be the prime contacts throughout all stages of the job. The exception was distribution. Direct discussion/confirmation of delivery details would be made with the customer by the distribution function.

---

*Of the five staff members in the studio, one is a trainee. The company has found that studio staff of the necessary experience and capability are hard to come by and can command high salaries. For these reasons it decided to also train its own staff within this area.

He went on to explain that the trend in work mix toward process flexographics would continue as the customers sought to improve their packaging designs as a way of enhancing sales of their products. The rationale for investing in origination was that it offered increased control over the new design procedures, better response times, a more integrated liaison with customers, and reduction of origination costs. The aim by next year was to complete almost all jobs

---

EXHIBIT 4   Representative Sample of the 491 Jobs in Progress in the Origination Department on March 31

Customer	Line/Process	Agreed Delivery Date	Design Type
Abbey	L	30 Jun.	N
Browns	L	15 Jul.	A
Shelleys	P	27 May	N
Hartstone	L	4 Apr.	A
Aztec	P	11 Jun.	A
Oaks	P	27 Mar.	A
A.J. Foods	L	3 Jul.	N
Aztec	L	18 Apr.	A
F-lite	L	20 Mar.	N
Texet	L	2 Aug.	A
Radcliffes	P	4 Jun.	N
Coles	P	10 Mar.	N
Texet	L	10 Jul.	A
Hartstone	L	31 Mar.	A
A.J. Foods	P	13 Apr.	A
J B. Foods	L	18 Jun.	N
Abbey	L	21 Jun.	N
Cowies	L	21 Mar.	A
JBK	P	20 May	A
Browns	L	6 Sep.	N
Alexon	P	16 Mar.	N
Crystal	L	21 Aug.	N
Oaks	P	16 Apr.	A
Marcos	L	29 Mar.	N
Solent	L	18 Jun.	A
Hartstone	P	2 Apr.	N
Crystal	L	8 May	A
Shelleys	L	10 Apr.	N
Abbey	L	2 Apr.	A
F-lite	L	4 Apr.	N
Radcliffes	P	1 May	A
Marcos	L	16 Sep.	N
Shelleys	L	30 Aug.	N

NOTES: L = line; P = process; A = amendment; and N = new.

---

in-house. A short synopsis of origination procedures is provided as Exhibit 3, and information relating to the department is given in Exhibit 4.

The Future.   "Our decision to move into origination," concluded Steve Bishop, "has given us much of what we hoped. It gets us closer to our customers and means that we can respond more quickly to changes in their needs. The investments involved were not large, but the cost advantages we have secured have yielded a good return. Overall our business is growing and this has been one contribution to our improved position. Certainly we feel we have the potential to gain more control over more of the process and at least afford ourselves the opportunity of reviewing lead times with the intention of reducing them and thereby supporting the key delivery-related criteria, which are a growing part of our markets."

CASE 13
MOOG, INC.

Moog, Inc., founded in 1951, was located in East Aurora, New York. In 1983, the company was producing electrohydraulic servovalves, actuators, and systems for use on aircraft, missiles, robots, and machine tools. These products were sold to firms such as Rockwell International, McDonnell-Douglas, Martin, Boeing, IBM, General Electric, and Lockheed. Moog manufactured customized products in its single U.S. production faculty at East Aurora. Additional manufacturing facilities to supply local industrial markets were located in England, Germany, France, Ireland, and Japan to meet export sales. The U.S. aerospace operations employed 1,950 workers. The 1983 sales were $133 million.

The aerospace business was all engineered-to-order. Since aerospace programs normally existed for several years, subsequent requirements were made-to-order. Aerospace customers tended to be large, prime contractors (e.g., Rockwell International, Grumman, Northrop). The specialized hydraulic systems produced by Moog for these customers usually had one of the longest lead times in the development cycle for aircraft and missiles. As a result, these items could have a critical impact on the contractor's ability to deliver a quality product on time.

The management at Moog felt that, to compete successfully in their markets, they must be able to:

1. *Deliver a quality product:* Moog produced items which were used in critical areas by its customers. For example, 15 actuators were used on the space shuttle to vector the engines and control the flight surfaces. A product which was either poorly designed or poorly made could have disastrous effects. It could mean not only the destruction of an expensive plane or space craft, but also loss of life. The part had to be ''right'' the first time that it was used. Failure in the field was not acceptable.

2. *Plan capacity effectively:* Effective capacity planning was important to Moog at both the aggregate and detailed levels. At the aggregate level, management was very concerned with ensuring both continuity and stability of employment. Consequently, anticipating changes in requirements enabled management to increase capacity while maintaining the current levels of quality or to decrease capacity without encountering layoffs. On the detailed level, a change in product mix could have a dramatic effect on the requirements for individual work centers.

3. *Control costs:* For some products, cost was not the only important consideration, often lower in priority than product performance, e.g., quality and design. In all circumstances, however, keeping actual costs in-line with budgets was an essential manufacturing task.

4. *Deliver products on time:* On-time delivery was the final key success factor for Moog. Many of the products made by Moog had the longest lead times in the overall development cycle. Failure to deliver on time could delay the entire project. If an

This case was edited by W. L. Berry, Visiting Professor, and represents a revised version of material reprinted with permission, the American Production and Inventory Control Society, Inc., *Shop Floor Control Principles and Practices and Case Studies,* 1987, pp. 215–46, and originally prepared by S. A. Melnyk and P. L. Carter of Michigan State University. It was written as a basis for class discussion rather than to illustrate either effective or ineffective handling of an administrative situation.

©1988 by IMEDE, Lusanne, Switzerland. Not to be used or reproduced without permission.

airplane or satellite were delayed because of a component, it would be costly for the customer and for Moog's service reputation.

Manufacturing Process

The manufacture of aerospace controls was a batch production activity. The products ranged in size from a one pound unit with 60 parts for missile fin control to a 350 pound actuator with 2,500 parts to control the space shuttle engines. Bills of material were up to seven levels deep and routings have from 5 to 150 steps, with an average of 15. There were approximately 400 end products utilizing 10,000 manufactured and 5,000 purchased components. The amount of product commonality was small in the aerospace product line. A generalized production flowchart is presented in Exhibit 1.

The fabrication lot sizes vary from 1 to 500, with most in the 5 to 100 unit range. Assembly lot sizes ran from 1 to 25 units. The manufacturing lead times were 30 to 100 weeks. Most order changes were design or process related, as opposed to quantity changes. About 2 percent of all shop orders were changed each month. The fabrication operation area was approximately three times that of the assembly and test functions. Capacity was measured by work center in the fabrication area and by department in assembly and test.

The machine shop worked three shifts, six days a week. Effective management of this work force was important to the success of Moog since it accounted for approximately 60 percent of direct costs.

The 550 workstations are grouped into 100 work centers dispersed throughout six buildings. The division used a wide variety of machines. In general, the machine capacity could be broken down as follows:

- General purpose machines .... 48 ⎫
- Special purpose machines .... 2 ⎬ percent of
- Numerical control machines (DNC)(CNC)(NC) 50 ⎭ machine capacity

The complexity and precision of the piece parts (several hundred features per part and tolerances in 10,000s of an inch) affected the production process. The key characteristics of the production process were:

- Long process routings.
- Specialized capacities.
- Significant scrap rate.

These factors were important to management because they had a significant impact on the planning process. The long routings required that planning be done well into the future as the degree of uncertainty was high. The special purpose machines required similar extensive future planning, as well as extensive current time period rebalancing (i.e., ensuring that the current work load was evenly balanced across all work centers). The significant scrap rate was a disruptive factor that could be anticipated in total, but could not be planned by part. Consequently, management had to be able to adjust priorities on the shopfloor to respond to the changing situations caused by scrap and rework, in order to ensure delivery reliability.

Production Planning

The production planning system consisted of the following modules:

- Business plan.
- Production plan.

EXHIBIT 1   Production System Chart

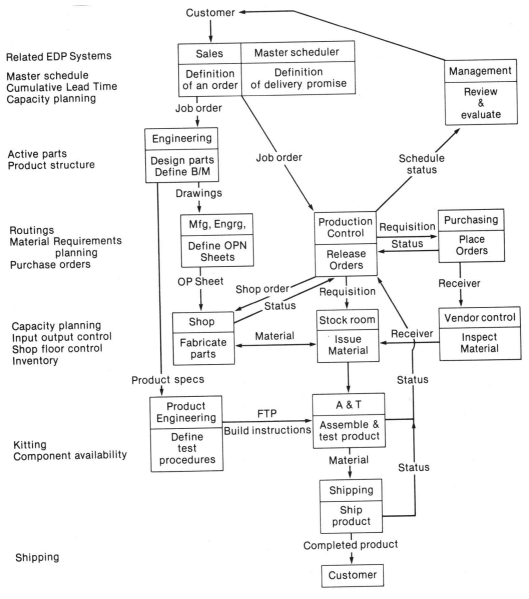

• Master schedule.

• Rough cut capacity plan.

The system was primarily a manufacturing resource planning system, as it coordinated the activities of manufacturing with those of the firm.

The production planning process began with the development of a five-year business plan. This plan was constructed annually from estimated unit sales and anticipated pricing on

EXHIBIT 2 Example Master Production Schedule

```
DATE PRINTED 03/21                                    JOB SE218GE5 REPORT NUMBER 6228A
SPACE PRODUCTS DIVISION                            SUMMARIZED MASTER SCHEDULE BY SERIES
```

MODEL	SCH	P/D	3/88	4/88	5/88	6/88	7/88	8/88	9/88	10/88	11/88	12/88
052E199	S	2	0	0	0	0	0	0	0	0	0	0
INV = 0	C	2	0	0	0	0	0	0	0	0	0	0
FLR = 0	C/D	0	0	0	0	0	0	0	0	0	0	0
0520186	S	0	0	0	0	0	0	0	0	0	0	0
INV = 0	C	0	0	0	0	0	12	0	0	0	0	0
FLR = 0	C/D	0	0	0	0	0	12-	12-	12-	12-	12-	12-
0520188	S	0	0	0	0	0	0	0	0	0	0	0
INV = 0	C	0	0	0	0	2	0	0	38	0	0	0
FLR = 0	C/D	0	0	0	0	2-	2-	2-	40-	40-	40-	40-
0520189B	S	0	0	0	0	0	0	0	0	0	0	13
INV = 0	C	0	0	0	0	0	0	0	26	0	0	13
FLR = 0	C/D	0	0	0	0	0	0	0	26-	26-	26-	13-
0520201A	S	151	0	0	0	0	0	0	7	0	0	0
INV = 0	C	0	37	38	39	37	0	0	107	0	0	0
FLR = 0	C/D	151	114	76	37	0	0	0	100-	100-	100-	100-
0520204B	S	9	0	0	0	0	0	0	7	0	0	0
INV = 0	C	9	0	0	0	0	0	0	7	0	0	0
FLR = 0	C/D	0	0	0	0	0	0	0	0	0	0	0
0520205	S	5	0	0	0	0	0	0	0	0	0	0
INV = 0	C	0	0	0	0	5	0	0	0	0	0	0
FLR = 0	C/D	5	5	5	0	0	0	0	0	0	0	0
053E144	S	0	0	0	0	0	0	0	0	0	0	0
INV = 0	C	0	0	0	0	0	0	0	2	0	0	0
FLR = 0	C/D	0	0	0	0	0	0	0	2	0	0	0
0530135K	S	0	0	0	0	0	0	3	8	8	8	8
INV = 0	C	11	12	13	12	12	11	10	18	18	19	38
FLR = 0	C/D	11-	23-	36-	48-	60-	71-	78-	88-	98-	109-	139-
0530143	S	8	6	6	6	6	8	0	0	0	0	0
INV = 0	C	8	6	10	16	0	0	0	0	0	0	6
FLR = 0	C/D	0	0	4-	14-	8-	0	0	0	0	0	6-
0530145	S	0	0	0	0	0	0	0	0	0	0	0
INV = 0	C	0	0	0	0	0	0	0	6	0	0	0
FLR = 0	C/D	0	0	0	0	0	0	0	6-	6-	6-	6-

NOTE: S = Customer Shipping Requirement, Customer Orders Only
C = Moog Completion Schedule, Customer Orders and AMPAs
C/D = Schedule Deviation: Positive: Behind Customer P.O.; Negative: Ahead of Customer P.O.

major programs. This level was used for financial planning and sizing up the basic elements of the business.

A master production schedule (an example is given as Exhibit 2) was the next segment of Moog's manufacturing planning and control system. Covering a period of 18 months or more, the master production schedule consisted of actual and anticipated orders. Anticipated orders or, more properly, advanced material procurement authorizations (AMPA) may be placed by Moog personnel in anticipation of an actual customer order. Based on prior communications with the customer, the Moog sales personnel decided whether an order would be forthcoming. Subject to manufacturing approval, the AMPA was released when the order fell within the cumulative lead time. It was intended to ensure that the customer would receive on-time delivery of the order when it was finally placed. AMPAs were also released to smooth work load peaks and valleys.

1/89	2/89	3/89	4/89	5/89	6/89	7/89	BAL
0	0	0	0	0	0	0	0
0	0	0	0	0	0	0	0
0	0	0	0	0	0	0	0
0	0	0	0	0	0	0	0
0	0	0	0	0	0	0	0
12-	12-	12-	12-	12-	12-	12-	12-
0	0	0	0	0	0	0	0
0	0	0	0	0	0	0	0
40-	40-	40-	40-	40-	40-	40-	40-
13	0	0	0	0	0	0	0
0	0	0	0	0	0	0	0
0	0	0	0	0	0	0	0
0	0	0	0	0	0	0	0
0	0	0	0	0	0	0	0
100-	100-	100-	100-	100-	100-	100-	100-
0	0	0	0	0	0	0	0
0	0	0	0	0	0	0	0
0	0	0	0	0	0	0	0
0	0	0	0	0	0	0	0
0	0	0	0	0	0	0	0
0	0	0	0	0	0	0	0
0	0	0	0	0	0	0	0
0	0	0	0	0	0	0	0
0	0	0	0	0	0	0	0
8	8	9	6	6	6	5	0
39	39	21	20	11	0	0	0
170-	201-	213-	227-	232-	226-	221-	221-
0	0	0	0	0	0	0	0
6	6	6	6	0	0	0	0
12-	18-	24-	30-	30-	30-	30-	30-
0	0	0	0	0	0	0	0
0	0	0	0	0	0	0	0
6-	6-	6-	6-	6-	6-	6-	6-

For rough cut capacity planning purposes, when the master schedule was not sufficiently filled by firm and anticipated orders, the master schedule would be supplemented withforecasted orders. These latter jobs would be utilized for planning capacities, but not for releasing material orders.

The rough cut capacity plan was developed from this "special" master schedule. The unit sales forecast was exploded by capacity planning into annual work center labor requirements, which was done twice a year.

Using the data from the rough cut capacity plan, as well as some judgment regarding inventories and new program start-ups, management would construct a production plan. The plan defined aggregate people requirements by department, as well as major equipment purchases. This information was a major building block for the annual financial plans, capital budget, and production labor targets.

forecasted orders. These latter jobs would be utilized for planning capacities, but not for releasing material orders.

The rough cut capacity plan was developed from this "special" master schedule. The unit sales forecast was exploded by capacity planning into annual work center labor requirements, which was done twice a year.

Using the data from the rough cut capacity plan, as well as some judgment regarding inventories and new program start-ups, management would construct a production plan. The plan defined aggregate people requirements by department, as well as major equipment purchases. This information was a major building block for the annual financial plans, capital budget, and production labor targets.

Detailed Planning

The detailed planning phase included order promising, material planning, and assembly scheduling. The primary step in moving from the production plan to shopfloor control was the material planning cycle. In this segment, the master production schedule was converted into a set of time-phased component requirements. The material requirements planning (MRP) system was regenerative and run weekly. (An example of the MRP planning report is given in Exhibit 3.) The output from MRP was used to:

1. Plan new order releases.
2. Reschedule existing orders.
   - Suggested reschedule for purchase orders.
   - Automatic reschedule for fabrication orders.
3. Input to capacity requirements planning (CRP).

There were several differences present between the semiannual rough cut capacity planning and the weekly capacity plan. The former incorporated forecasted orders, was not time-phased, did not utilize beginning inventory, and did not create an ending inventory. The weekly CRP used only planned and released shop orders, was time-phased, and accounted for existing inventories.

The capacity for a work center was defined as the actual, smoothed output for that work center. Anticipated changes in staffing and equipment could be incorporated. Based on this information, changes were made in the order release horizon, as well as in staff scheduling.

Shopfloor Control

The shopfloor control system was completely computerized, collecting information and communicating to the users. The primary objectives of the shopfloor control system were:

1. Presenting job priorities to shop supervisors in support of job selections.
2. Locating jobs for shop supervision.
3. Presenting order status information to production control analysts and others interested in the progress of particular orders.
4. Presenting information on work center status to shop supervision and production control.
5. Predicting normal completion dates.
6. Maintaining shop order quantities.

EXHIBIT 3   Example Material Requirements Planning Record

```
DATE 03/24     DISPLAY 4185 PART NO DISPLAY GEN DATE 3/24                    PAGE 1
PART A38179    001        FLEX SLV #1 POLICY D SHRINK FAC        .30 ORDER QTY 100
REQ. 395       M/B M PLANNER R L.T. 13 WKS            C.L.T 13 WKS NOR RUN QTY 200
```

WKS.	REQ.	SCHDL	STK	SWAN/PO	RESCHL	RES/STK	PLAN/REL

```
STARTING IN HOUSE BAL      50
********************************************************************************
SHRINK FACTOR .30
********************************************************************************
```

WKS.	REQ.	SCHDL	STK	SWAN/PO	RESCHL	RES/STK
01/18/88	3	0				50
02/08/88	2	0				50
02/22/88	2	0				50
03/07/88	1	0				50
03/14/88	1	0				50
* 03/21/88	1	0				50
03/28/88	1	0				50
04/05/88	1	0				50
04/12/88	1	0				50
04/19/88	1	0				50
04/26/88	1	0				50
05/03/88	1	0				50
05/10/88	1	17				33
05/17/88	1	0				33
05/24/88	1	0				33
05/31/88	1	0				33
06/07/88	1	4				29
06/14/88	1	38	19	604452H	14	5
06/21/88	1	0				5
06/28/88	1	0				5
07/13/88	1	0				5
07/20/88	1	76	220	656157D	168	97
07/27/88	1	0				97
08/03/88	1	78				19
08/10/88	1	0				19
08/17/88	1	0				19
08/24/88	1	0				19
08/31/88	1	0				19
09/08/88	1	78	120	656157C	91	32
09/15/88	1	0				32
09/22/88	1	0				32
09/29/88	1	2				30
10/06/88	1	40	100	661470A	76	66
10/13/88	1	0				66
10/20/88	1	0				66
10/27/88	1	0				66
11/03/88	1	40				26
11/10/88	1	0				26
11/17/88	1	0				26
11/28/88	1	0				26
12/05/88	1	0				26
12/12/88	1	22				4
12/19/88	1	0				4
01/05/89	1	0				4
01/12/89	4	0				4
02/09/89	4	0				4
03/09/89	4	0				4

NOTE: REQ   = Total Requirements
       SCHDL   = Released Orders for Production
       SWAN/PO = Open Shop Order Quantity
       RESCHL   = Projected Shop Order Quantity
       RES/STK = Projected on Hand Inventory Balance
       PLAN/REL = Planned Orders (none on this sheet)
                  Shrinkage Factor Calculators, e.g., $\frac{19}{1.3} = 14$

EXHIBIT 4   Moog Aerospace Materials Organization

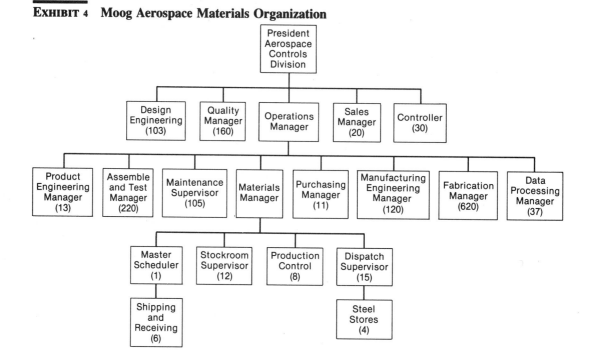

Shopfloor control was an integral part of the formal manufacturing planning system. Organizationally, shopfloor control was part of the materials organization, with the dispatch supervisor having direct formal responsibility for this system. He was also responsible for all steel stores. (The structure of the materials organization—as well as reporting relationships—is summarized in Exhibit 4.)

Aiding the dispatch supervisor were six production control analysts and eight dispatchers. The production control analysts were best described as the "bridge" between the planning system and the shopfloor. They were responsible for releasing planned orders and for changing the due dates on open orders in response to necessary date changes flagged by the MRP system. The dispatchers worked with the movement of material on the shopfloor. Their tasks included moving parts, doing item counts, and writing move tickets.

Order Review/Release

Order review/release began with the output of the MRP system, which identified all planned orders that had matured and were candidates for order release. These jobs were first assigned a unique shop work authorization number (SWAN), which was used in tracking and locating the job on the shopfloor. Next, the start quantity was adjusted for available material and for the allocation of limited components. Once the inventory availability was checked, the planned order was released.

A fabrication parts requisition (FPR) was sent to manufacturing engineering. All orders received detailed routings except model shop work and production rework. Standard hours were applied to each step for setup time per operation and run time. A drawing, an operation sheet, and stock withdrawal form were combined to form the shop traveler. This packet was then sent to steel stores or to the stockroom to release the necessary raw material or components.

Detailed Assignment

Released shop orders were assigned to work centers by the manually written move ticket. The dispatcher would refer to the operation sheet for this assignment. All shop order dates were set by MRP based on the master schedule. Changes in order due dates generated by the MRP system were *automatically* incorporated on the shopfloor. As a result, the master scheduler was in real control of order priorities.

The priority conveyed to the shop floor was a least slack time rule, using the MRP-generated due dates. A job having "+ days" priority was ahead of schedule, while one with a "− days" priority was behind schedule. The priorities were readily understood by all, and updated every day. Reports indicating progress and priority as of midnight were distributed at 7 A.M. each day.

The priorities were sequenced in the "work center daily queue list" (see Exhibit 5A). This displayed information on orders assigned to each work center, showing completed operations first, followed by operations in process, then operations available to be worked on, and lastly, a limited number of scheduled but not available operations. It showed the status of all work orders in a given work center, as well as the one to be started next.

The "work center look ahead report" (see Exhibit 5B) was often consulted by shop foremen when the current work load was low. It indicated those shop orders which had been released to the shop, were scheduled for a given work center, but were not yet available, thus revealing the incoming work load. This helped to identify and prepare for high-priority jobs, minimize setups, and smooth daily work loads.

Data Collection Monitoring.

To provide timely information, the shopfloor control system had to continually record and process updates, changes, and additions. Recording data was the responsibility of the individuals who performed the activity. (Exhibit 6A shows an example of the labor card that was completed by each employee and sent to data processing at the end of a shift.) The machinist recorded the time applied to the specific operation and whether the operation was completed.

When a job was moved from one department to another, move tickets were generated by the dispatcher who would refer to the operation sheet for routing instructions. He recorded the physical location of the job, the department and machine that would next work on the job, the next operation number, the current piece count, and the time when the job was moved (see Exhibit 6B).

Control/Feedback.

A shop order or a work center could become "out of control" when unexpected high scrap rates, master schedule changes, or a capacity bottleneck occurred. These conditions were identified within the shopfloor control system.

When a work order was needed in a shorter than normal lead time, the slack time number would become negative. Every day the production control department received a list of all negative slack time jobs in priority sequence. Dispatching personnel were responsible for bringing an "out of control" situation back under control by:

- *Operation splitting:* Running the job on multiple machines for the same operation at the same time.

EXHIBIT 5A   Work Center Daily Queue List

```
DATE PRINTED 01/24        JOB @5730F04 REPORT NUMBER 5732A
SHOP CALENDAR DAY NUMBER 951WORK CENTER DAILY QUEUE LIST

WORK CENTER 126-0930            DESCRIPTION CINCINNATI MIX
DAYS                                              DUE SCHEDULED-THIS-W/C-
E/L    SWAN    ---PART NUMBER----   DESCRIPTION  LOC  DTE OPER ST -S/U --RUN-
13-  145201A  A28784  003           FRAME        ONC  999 0070 40   7.5    3.1
 7   141358A  A28784  003           FRAME        ONC  020 0140 30   1.8   24.6
38   149623A  A28784  003           FRAME        ONC  060 0110 30  -2.2    3.3
13-  145201A  A28784  003           FRAME        ONC  999 0140 20   6.3   25.4
16   149815A  A28784  003           FRAME        ONC  040 0110 20   7.3   25.6
30   144089A  A28784  003           FRAME        ONC  040 0140 20   6.3   23.3
52   126797A  A22391  001           PROFILE      ONC  010 0120 20   3.0   14.0
52   138727A  A22391  001           PROFILE      ONC  010 0120 20   3.0   14.0
18   157677A  A28784  003           FRAME        P15  060 0070 10   7.5   34.2
WORK CENTER 126-0930  CAPACITY=  58  CRIT Q HRS=  45  TTL LOAD HRS=  194
```

EXHIBIT 5B   Work Center Look Ahead Report

```
DATE PRINTED 01/24        JOB @5715F04 REPORT NUMBER 5716A
                           SFC WORK CENTER LOOK AHEAD
W/C 120-0060 MACHINE- 0135

                                              --MOVE TICKET---  PCT -TOTAL DUE DAYS
-SWAN-- -PART NUMBER--- DESCRIPTION LOC QTY OPER    W/C      CMP HRS DS DAY  E/L
885830A  65237  002     BODY 50-414 P15  35 0060 1230320      4 389  5 710   37
889576A  72201         BODY 33      84D  40      84D          0 409  3 855   75
885830A  65237  002     BODY 50-414 P15  35 0060 1230320      4 389  5 710   37
885830A  65237  002     BODY 50-414 P15  35 0060 1230320      4 389  5 710   37
```

EXHIBIT 6A   Labor Card

COST REPORTING SECTION										PAYROLL SECTION	
Date	Employee No.	Dept.	Employee Signature				Supervisor Signature			ABSENT – PAID	
8-15	01258	120	Ralph Jones				Andy Smith			___	3 Sick
Dept.	Work Cat.	SWAN/WANT	R/N	Oper.	L/T	Mech.	Comments	W/S	References	Time Hrs. Mins.	7 Military
120	1	739495A	N	40	62	60				7:45	8 Vacation
120	9			84						:15	6 Disability
											2 Personnel
											4 Holiday
											5 Jury Duty
											0 Other___
											ABSENT - NO PAY
											1
										8-	HOURS WORKED
											Straight Time
											Overtime
											Double Time
204-01 Rev. 5/71	TOTAL TIME USED MUST EQUAL HOURS WORKED								8:00	8:00	Total Hours Worked

EXHIBIT 7A   Open Order Status Report

```
DATE PRINTED 01/24        JOB @5710F16 REPORT NUMBER 5711A
                           SFC DAILY OPEN ORDER STATUS REPORT
SHOP CALENDAR DAY 951           PART NUMBER SEQUENCE
ORDER  DAYS                      C-D             ORDR    ---MOVE TICKET---
NUMBER ER/LA --PART NUMBER-----  LOC DESCRIPTION QUAN  QUAN OPER DEPTW/C
121590A  92  A28781  002         B09 BODY 26       80    42 0120 1250600
145201A  13- A28784  003         ONC FRAME        24    24 0070 1260930
141358A   7  A28784  003         ONC FRAME        24    24 0070 1260930
149815A  16  A28784  003         ONC FRAME        24    24 0070 1260930
144089A  30  A28784  003         ONC FRAME        22    22 0070 1260930
149823A  38  A28784  003         ONC FRAME        24    24 0070 1260930
157677A  18  A28784  003         P15 FRAME        24    24 0040 1230250
145219A  27  A28798  001         C07 BLANK        84    82 0080 M210420
```

```
--COMING-FROM---  HRS- -LAST-MOVE-REPORTED-  -ORDER
OPER --W/C--- ST AWAY OPER  --W/C---  --QTY-  --QTY-
       COMPLETED         |0070 126-0343     24|   24
SSET- 6.3 SRUN-  25.4|0070 126-0343     24|   24
SSET- 7.3 SRUN-  25.6|0070 126-0343     24|   24
       AVAILABLE        |0070 126-0343     24|   24
       AVAILABLE        |0070 126-0343     24|   24
       AVAILABLE        |0070 126-0343     22|   22
       AVAILABLE        |0120 126-0343     24|   24
       AVAILABLE        |0120 126-0343     24|   24
0060 123-0250 20    12|0040 123-0210     24|   24
  CRIT Q DAYS=  0.8  TTL Q DAYS=  3.4


       WAIT ----SCH THIS W/C---- -CUM-
MODEL NO DAYS OPER  S/U  RUN TOTAL TOTAL
050-414B 26.0 0270  5.9 17.5 23.4  23.4
033-168D  4.0 0250 11.6 30.0 41.6  65.0
050-414B 26.0 0340  4.9  8.6 13.5  78.5
050-414B 26.0 0350  7.9  7.5 15.4  93.9
         TOTAL 30.3 63.6 93.9
```

EXHIBIT 6B   Move Ticket

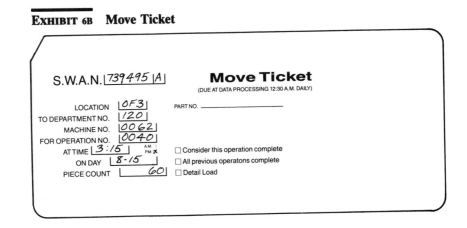

```
PCT BALNCE -START- DUE              NXT SCHEDULE WAIT
CMP HRS-DS SCH ACT DAY  MODEL-NO  OPER DEPTW/C  DAYS
 96    4  3 021 861 055  026-102B 0130 1251050   0.0
 33  453  3 906 909 999  W017-316D 0145 1230300   4.0
 35  448  3 925 883 020  W017-316D 0145 1230300   3.0
 21  535  3 947 930 040  W017-316D 0120 1261190   6.0
 33  420  3 951 896 040  W017-316D 0145 1230300   0.0
 24  511  3 967 931 060  W017-316D 0120 1230300   0.0
  0  672  3 967 946 060  W017-316D 0070 1260930   0.0
 73   20 10 965 915 994  026-219  0090 1250600  24.0
```

next operation number, the current piece count, and the time when the job was moved (see Exhibit 6B).

Control/Feedback.

A shop order or a work center could become "out of control" when unexpected high scrap rates, master schedule changes, or a capacity bottleneck occurred. These conditions were identified within the shopfloor control system.

When a work order was needed in a shorter than normal lead time, the slack time number would become negative. Every day the production control department received a list of all negative slack time jobs in priority sequence. Dispatching personnel were responsible for bringing an "out of control" situation back under control by:

- *Operation splitting:* Running the job on multiple machines for the same operation at the same time.
- *Operation overlapping:* Allowing sequential operations to occur at the same time.
- *Lot splitting:* Dividing the lot into smaller quantities, so that each remaining operation could be completed much sooner.
- *Solving the problem at a higher level:* The production control analyst could arrange to make up the schedule at a higher level part number, if slack were available at this higher level, and he could not compress the current lead times any further.

On average, only 3 to 4 percent of all shop orders would be late and require special attention.

An "out of control" work center would be identified by having high critical queue days, calculated by dividing the work center's available hours for orders with negative slack time by the historical capacity. This number appeared at the bottom of the work center daily queue list. The response to this problem was typically to work overtime until the critical queue days indicator was back down to a reasonable level. Several reports have been developed linking the planning and shopfloor control systems.

- Open order status report (Exhibit 7A above)
- Shop load status report (Exhibit 7B, p. 419)

The "open order status report" reviewed the status of all work orders for a given part number. It produced daily and contained information that was current as of the previous midnight (See Exhibit 7A). The "shop load status report" (Exhibit 7B) was printed weekly for each work center, showing both current and future loads.

Performance Evaluation/Feedback

The monthly evaluation of a dispatcher's performance concerned the prompt movement of work throughout the shop and the correct recording of information regarding the shop order. The activities of the production control analysts covered a broader range. There was a daily reporting of each analyst's shop orders specifying which were running past due. In addition, there were monthly and quarterly reviews of shipments versus the customers' schedule. There was also a monthly reporting of the value of slow-moving inventory under each analyst's control.

EXHIBIT 7B Shop Load Status Report

DATE PRINTED 12/17

JOB @5742G02 REPORT NUMBER 5742A
WEEKLY SHOP LOAD STATUS REPORT

NUMBER	DESCRIPTION	TOTAL LOAD	CURRENT PERIOD				SMOOTHER AVERAGE			
			INPUT	OUTPUT	CLOCK	O/C	INPUT	OUTPUT	CLOCK	O/C
126-0001	LABOR CHGD TO INDIRECT				630	.00			638	.00
126-0002	LABOR CHGD TO SUMRY-LOAD		300	300	304	.98	265	265	268	.98
126-0003	LABOR CHGD TO INV OPER NO				24	.00	1	1	29	.03
126-0004	LABOR CHGE TO INV MACH NO				28	.00			311	.00
126-0210	DRILL PRESS		61	61	53	1.14	21	21	43	.48
126-0300	BRIDGEPORT VERTICAL MILL	13,019	1,510	713	546	1.30	600	662	627	1.05
126-0600	BENCH STATION		16-	247	237	1.04	513	231	201	1.14
126-0910	K&T 200 SERIES	1,892							51	.49
126-0930	CINCINNATI MIX	1,133	37	37	118	.31				
126-0970	MILWAUKEE-MATIC E-B	16,784	421	1,395	1,690	.82	649	1,569	1,809	.86
126-1190	HPZ,HPMC,CPMC,MCNC									
126	DEPARTMENT TOTALS	31,843	2,314	2,753	3,630	.75	1,650	2,774	3,699	.74

419

CASE 14
NOLAN AND WARNER PLC[1]

> In conclusion, it seems agreed that we should go ahead and quote for the two new items in the VR100 product range, one of high and one of low volume demand. I support this decision, for it is essential that we increase our sales revenue to a level where the potential for making an adequate return becomes available. Our current organizational structure, the strengths which come from our position in the market, the inherent design, manufacturing capability, available plant, and process capacity provide us with the wherewithal to take on these two new items with relatively little outlay. The products are compatible with our existing range and should present few manufacturing problems.

These were John Dyson's concluding comments at the June board meeting.

Background

Nolan and Warner (N & W) was a wholly owned subsidiary of a U.K.-based automotive component supplier. As with all subsidiaries in the ATMO Group, N & W was responsible for all facets of the business, except the centralized capital funding arrangements, which operated within the group. Consequently, John Dyson, the managing director, through the group executive board, was responsible for setting N & W's corporate objectives in line with certain group-based performance criteria (for example, return on investment). The meeting described in the opening paragraph was an N & W board meeting. It was at such meetings that local company decisions were made within a set of annual corporate forecasts and activities, which had to be agreed with the ATMO Group board at the start of each year.

Although N & W's markets were in the automotive component industry, the remainder of the ATMO Group was involved in other product areas, which were based on engineering, electronics, chemicals, and construction.

Marketing

Increasing competition and excess capacity had put much pressure on to N & W's markets and sales. Exhibit 1 shows the main product ranges of its business and also the unit sales during the last six years.

Rob James, the marketing director, considered the principal marketing task in this way:

> Our main aim has been, and still is, to minimize the reduction in sales revenue in real terms, and then build on the European and U.S. demand improvements as the world economy picks up. Following the sales revenue (£s) drop five years ago, we have just about kept actual sales (£s) steady since that time. As a consequence, we have been able to minimize the revenue fall in real sales.
>
> Although the RU400 range sales have not been what the forecasts had us believe, this year (together with the known orders and forecasts for next year) shows a marked improvement over the last two years. Similarly, the VR150 and AC250 ranges are both up on the last two years' sales, and the AC200 has sold more this year than ever before. In addition, the spares market is more than holding its own, as one

---

[1]Plc means public limited company and in the United States equates to being incorporated.

This case was prepared by Professor T. J. Hill (London Business School). It is intended for class discussion and not as an illustration of good or bad management. © AMD Publishing (U.K.).

EXHIBIT 1   Annual Unit Sales by Product Range in the Last Six Years

| | Unit Sales for Year Ended December 31 | | | | | |
| | Current Year Minus | | | | | Current Year |
Product Range	5	4	3	2	1	
VR100	105,650	74,500	72,880	58,400	51,790	45,600
VR150	74,600	44,850	45,950	31,250	30,880	36,040
AC200	3,110	3,290	3,120	3,270	2,650	4,160
AC250	52,620	34,560	42,360	28,350	28,520	37,100
NT300	25,750	23,170	22,200	16,630	15,440	12,610
RU400	—	—	—	170	110	250
Total	261,730	180,370	186,510	138,070	129,390	135,760

NOTES: 1. The above are in terms of units sold and all figures have been rounded. As the unit price varies and has changed over time, it is not relevant to relate these unit volumes to the sales revenue (£s) levels given in Exhibit 2.
2. Figures for only the first eight months of the current year are available, and these have been increased on a pro rata basis.
3. Each product range above (i.e., VR, AC, NT, and RU) comprises a number of general products, each at a different stage in its own life cycle.
4. There are four main product ranges (i.e., VR, AC, NT, and RU) within which there are subranges (e.g., VR100 and VR150) with individual products within each of these.

would expect. It has been tough going over this time, and price competition has been very severe. Throughout, however, we have carefully pursued a policy of staying with all aspects of the business by attempting to meet all the demands of our customers where possible.

The two products currently being discussed represent our strategy in the past and in the foreseeable future. We have to be prepared to chase the business, especially where we think our competitors may not be willing to go. Although this takes us into some smaller-volume products, it represents good revenue and sound business. To be able to minimize the fall in real sales (£s) has meant that we have had to increase the number of product ranges with the advent of the RU400 range two years ago and also extend the number of individual products within each range during these years. This has resulted in the need for increased efforts throughout the company, from design, production engineering, to marketing and manufacturing.

Exhibit 2 reviews the balance sheets for the period and also provides the sales information referred to by Rob James as Note 3.

Manufacturing

The manufacturing processes are in three distinct production units. The first two units involve machining and other processes primarily laid out on a process or functional basis. In addition to the traditional areas, such as grinding and turning, there were also departments with processes to provide all or most of the operations necessary to manufacture similar components for the complete range of products. On the nonmachining side, the facilities include heat treatment, degreasing, and other preparatory and finishing processes. Although some of the components are bought in from outside suppliers, the policy has been, and still is, to manufacture internally wherever possible. In more recent years, the plant and process investment that has taken place has been largely to meet the requirement of new products, or for specific process improvement

EXHIBIT 2   Nolan and Warner Balance Sheet (all figures in £000s; year ended December 31)

	Current Year Minus				
	5	4	3	2	1
Total fixed assets (see Note 2)	6,963	7,751	12,860	12,589	11,727
Current assets					
Inventory (see Notes 1 and 3)	7,219	8,378	9,407	9,817	10,206
Debtors and prepayments	2,893	2,970	3,010	2,930	3,209
Cash	7	7	8	17	11
	10,119	11,355	12,425	12,764	13,426
Less current liabilities					
Creditors and accruals	4,004	4,816	3,186	3,174	2,904
Bank overdraft	2,667	5,837	5,762	8,593	8,458
	6,671	10,653	8,948	11,767	11,362
Working capital	3,448	702	3,477	997	2,064
Net assets employed	10,411	8,453	16,337	13,586	13,791
Financed by					
Intergroup capital account	7,453	7,892	12,575	10,714	13,308
Profit (loss) for the year	2,958	561	1,062	172	483
Intergroup loan	—	—	2,700	2,700	—
	10,411	8,453	16,337	13,586	13,791

NOTES: 1. The inventory values shown here are net of reserves, which averaged in this five-year period between 20–30 percent of the gross inventory value.

2. About 75 percent of the plant investment three years ago was to provide the manufacturing process capability that the company did not have at the time to enable it to make finished products. The other quarter was to help improve the process on a critical component. In turn, this improvement led to reduced manufacturing costs and a subsequent release of capacity in the related parts of the process.

3. Sales and inventory breakdown for each of the last five years are below:

Current Year Minus	Sales (£m)	Inventory (£000s)			
		Raw Materials	Work in Process	Finished Goods	Total
5	31.7	310	4,184	2,725	7,219
4	23.4	488	4,956	2,934	8,378
3	27.0	624	6,579	2,204	9,407
2	26.1	606	6,960	2,251	9,817
1	26.9	637	7,494	2,075	10,206

EXHIBIT 3   **Manufacturing Costs by Product Range**

	Percent Total Manufacturing Costs			
Product Range	*Materials*	*Labor*	*Overhead*	*Total*
VR100	40	13	47	100
VR150	39	13	48	100
AC200	33	16	51	100
AC250	42	14	44	100
NT300	35	16	49	100
RU400	43	15	42	100

NOTES: 1. Overhead recovery rates are based on direct labor hours.
2. The percentages given above are based on three products in each range, which are currently made for original equipment sales, but reflect the spread of volumes associated with the product range reviewed.
3. Original equipment (OE) sales refer to orders for products, which go onto vehicles currently in production at N & W's customer's assembly plants. When vehicles are no longer being built, the orders for products revert to sales to meet the demand for spares or service only. Where a vehicle has been made for some years, then demand for products will comprise both OE and spares or service sales.

(for example, see Note 2, Exhibit 2). The third production unit concerns subassembly, final assembly, and test. This involves subassembly and assembly lines for the higher-volume lines and bench layouts to meet low-volume requirements.

Information on some representative products in each of the three production units is given in Exhibits 3 to 5. To Mike Edwards, the production director, the manufacturing task concerned

> the introduction of new products within existing ranges and the need to reduce manufacturing costs throughout the process. Over the last year, there has also been substantial pressure to reduce inventory, in order to improve the cash-flow situation. Due to the wider product range and the need to respond quickly to customers' changes in call-offs, this has been difficult. However, reducing inventory has to be our first priority in the future and will be an essential part of our strategic review.
>
> In addition, the business is not making anywhere near the required return on investment. As a first step toward improving this, we have decided to close down our satellite plant at Banbury, some 30 miles away. This will mean moving the subassembly, assembly, and test facilities of the short-order shop[2] at Banbury into our main site but few, if any, of the operators due to the distance involved—all components for the shot-order requirements are already made on the main site.

The argument behind this move was the very necessary one to reduce costs. Spare capacity at the main factory site existed due mainly to lower unit demand and process improvements (see Exhibit 6). It was considered that closing down the Banbury site would reduce total costs, with the manufacturing requirements being absorbed by the existing capacity on the main site.

Mike Edwards continued to explain that since the mid- to late-70s there has been a stringent check on process investment. "This understandable corporate restriction has meant that, apart from the investment which has been necessary to meet new product requirements, investment has been difficult to come by. Only where high process cost savings could be achieved has any

---

[2]The short-order shop handles some low-volume products and spares and is on a separate site from the main site. The three "distinct production units" referred to earlier are all on the main site.

EXHIBIT 4   Call-offs for Components in Two of the Four Product Ranges, with Order Quantity Issues in the First Production Unit

Product Information			Monthly Average Call-offs and Typical Order Quantities			
			Current Year Minus			*Current Year*
Range	*Component*	*Issue Details*	*3*	*2*	*1*	
VR100	VR108/	Call-off	2,600	2,520	1,970	1,490
	1426	Order quantity	4,750	4,250	3,250	3,500
	VR111/	Call-off	50	—	—	—
	3278	Order quantity	255	—	—	—
	VR115/	Call-off	2,500	2,500	2,500	1,500
	1002	Order quantity	2,500	2,500	2,500	2,500
	VR116/	Call-off	800	240	140	200
	2614	Order quantity	800	800	440	400
VR150	VR151/	Call-off	—	400	1,200	900
	1214	Order quantity	—	600	1,200	1,200
	VR164/	Call-off	15	16	12	—
	1019	Order quantity	25	25	25	—
	VR170/	Call-offs	—	—	600	300
	2630	Order quantity	—	—	200	100
	VR171/	Call-offs	—	5	10	3
	2710	Order quantity	—	10	10	10
AC200	AC215	Call-off	100	70	50	25
	1816	Order quantity	100	100	100	75
AC250	AC255/	Call-off	400	300	300	400
	4914	Order quantity	400	400	400	400
	AC270/	Call-off	20	10	10	20
	5300	Order quantity	20	20	20	20

NOTES: 1. A call-off is the monthly delivery requirement to the customer.
2. The order quantity is the number of components issued to and processed through the first production unit—also known as batch size. These are not issued each month, but only as required.
3. Where order quantities exceed the call-off requirement, this implies that manufacturing produce, for instance, two months' sales at a time.

investment been forthcoming. Consequently, we are by and large running today with the processes bought some six or more years ago.''

The Future

In addition to attempting to maintain sales revenue levels and reduce process and manufacturing costs, N & W is also seriously looking at the level of organizational requirements necessary to sustain the business. The present organizational chart and personnel strengths are shown as Exhibit 7. The difficulty with this task is knowing where and how to make the savings.

EXHIBIT 5 Summaries of Typical Component Routings through the First Production Unit

Number of Machines per Category to Complete Typical Components				Process Time per Component (standard minutes)	Changeover Time (standard hours)	
A	B	C	D		Different Items	Like Items
6	5	4	5	126.6	39.0	27.5
3	7	2	2	29.2	34.5	18.0
6	4	3	4	55.5	30.0	11.0
7	5	3	3	47.4	28.0	10.0
6	4	2	3	64.5	21.5	14.0
2	2	3	2	120.1	21.0	15.0
6	4	3	1	162.1	21.5	12.5

NOTES: 1. Machine categories are:
   A. General-purpose machines.
   B. Machine dedicated to one product range (e.g., VR100).
   C. Machine dedicated to part of a product range (e.g., part of VR100 range).
   D. Machine dedicated to one operation on one component by a fixture (e.g., can only complete one operation on component VR108/1426).
2. The operations do not include in-process testing.
3. All machines are laid out by function or process.
4. The seven components shown above are representative of the range of work involved.
5. The cumulative total standard time columns mean that, for the first component, the total process time is 126.6 standard minutes per component, using 20 different machines from categories A to D inclusive, with a cumulative setup time for these 20 machines of between 27.5 to 39.0 hours.
6. Regarding changeover times: The ''like items'' relate to a product that is similar in setup terms to the product it is following and hence the changeover time is less than for a ''different item'' that is not similar.

EXHIBIT 6 Process Time Reductions and Plant Utilization Changes for One High-Volume Component on Its Route through the Second Production Unit

Aspect	Current Year Minus		Current Year
	5	2	
Total standard minutes per component	8.3	6.3	4.7
Plant utilization percentage			
Average	64	44	34
Low	14	4	3
High	89	85	82

NOTES: 1. Although the plant utilization figures given above relate to the second production unit, they are also typical of the plant utilization changes elsewhere.
2. There are a smaller number of operations (and consequently the time taken in standard minutes is significantly shorter) through which components have to go in the second production unit compared to the first production unit.

EXHIBIT 7   Nolan and Warner Organizational Chart

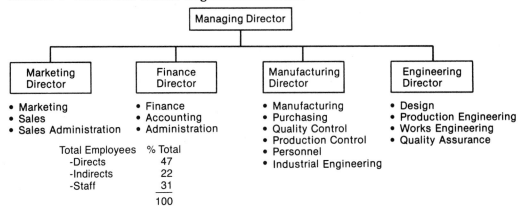

Managing Director

| Marketing Director | Finance Director | Manufacturing Director | Engineering Director |

- Marketing
- Sales
- Sales Administration

- Finance
- Accounting
- Administration

- Manufacturing
- Purchasing
- Quality Control
- Production Control
- Personnel
- Industrial Engineering

- Design
- Production Engineering
- Works Engineering
- Quality Assurance

Total Employees	% Total
-Directs	47
-Indirects	22
-Staff	31
	100

CASE 15
ONTARIO PACKAGING

It looks to me that we are agreed. The process investment proposals before us are sound in principle, providing we can increase throughput from present levels by some 40 percent, as indicated in the supporting details. I know this is no easy task, but all market segments are getting more difficult, and if we are to survive and maintain current performance levels, then this type of challenge will be illustrative of many future corporate decisions. From these initial discussions it appears that the extra volume is available, even though it places a greater emphasis on price. The new process will help, in part, to reduce costs, but higher volumes are essential if we are to maintain the group's payback requirements and protect the above-average return on investment performance we have achieved in the past.

Norm Phillips, chief executive officer of Ontario Packaging, was summing up a meeting on manufacturing investment proposals, which was intended to be the initial phase of a modernization program within the company.

Background

Ontario Packaging is part of Texet Industries, a large group of companies with diverse interests in food, cosmetics, engineering, and toys, besides a growing stake in retail holdings and other nonmanufacturing businesses. Taken over in the late 1980s, Ontario Packaging is now one of several packaging companies within the group, but the first within the province.

Having given the company time to settle down within the new corporate structure and allowed Norm Phillips to gain an understanding of the business since his transfer from within the group, some 12 months before, the executive group of Texet had recently asked the company to review its position. The review was to include an assessment of its current markets and to include any future process investment proposals it thought to be necessary, with an indication of why they should take place, and the anticipated impact on the business as a whole and on the various return-on-investment measures used within the group, in particular.

Manufacturing

Ontario Packaging produces a fairly wide range of cartons and other forms of packaging. Its manufacturing capability comprises various forms of printing, laminating, cutting, creasing, glueing, and other auxiliary processes, together with a whole range of in-house support functions.

The investment proposals under review concern replacing current laminating equipment with an up-to-date process that would provide the same capability (see Exhibit 1). The cartons that use this process account for some 30 percent of total production volumes (standard machine hours). At a cost of $2.5 million, the investment would give labor, material, and other savings to provide a payback of 6.5 years on current volumes. However, in order to meet the Texet investment payback norm of four years it would necessitate increasing current sales revenue for these cartons by some 40 percent. It is this higher level of volumes on which the investment proposals have been based.

This case study was written by Professor T. J. Hill (London Business School). It is intended for class discussion, and not as an illustration of good or bad management. © AMD Publishing (U.K.).

Details of the Investment Proposal under Review

As part of a strategy to upgrade its processes (as well as increase its process capability where appropriate) Ontario Packaging was proposing to invest in a state-of-the-art laminating process, which would replace the existing process capacity. Currently, some 30 percent of the total production volumes (standard machine hours) were laminated.

The new laminator would offer significant savings in direct labor (through reduced manning), lower material costs within the laminating process, and a reduced maintenance bill (with, however, a corresponding increase in depreciation costs).

However, in order to achieve the group payback norm of four years, the company would need to increase its sales of laminated products by about 40 percent on current levels.

While setup (or make-ready) times for the new process were similar to the existing equipment, throughput speeds were more than twice as fast. The order quantities currently processed averaged about 7 hours and ranged from 2 to 60 hours.

Current sales were split roughly half and half between those which were not price-sensitive and those where price was an order-winning criterion at some level. However, the latter orders varied in their degree of price sensitivity, with two thirds of this segment where price was given a weighting of 20 points or less.

It was recognized that the proposed increase in sales of laminated products of about 40 percent of current levels would be achieved in segments where price would increasingly be the important order-winner. The company, although recognizing that this would require significant sales effort, has identified the segments and customers that are available and consider the achievement of these higher volumes to be a realistic target within the required timescales.

NOTES: 1. Laminations consist of sheets of material (varying with individual specifications) that are glued together.
2. Due to space restrictions and to maintain the current, sensible flow of materials through the manufacturing process, the proposed new process will be installed where the existing equipment is positioned.
3. The current equipment comprises two machines and is run on a two-shift basis. It is also proposed to run the single replacement process on a two-shift basis.

Besides the basic gains accruing from increased throughput speed (a principal source of savings) and reduced material wastage, the new process would offer few additional technical advantages (setup times were marginally faster) other than those associated with the reduced performance on existing processes resulting from wear and tear with age.

While the utilization of the current process was less than 60 percent, the target set in the proposal for the new investment was 80–85 percent, based on higher volumes.

Marketing

"Ontario Packaging has, over the years, increasingly positioned itself in the higher-quality end of all its markets," explained Rod Shaw, the marketing director, who has been with the company for over 15 years. He added

> The cartons under review are no exception. While the technical features of the final carton are slightly less demanding than many of the rest of the product range, there is the same demand for high, reliable quality. While the manufacturing process currently used is able to consistently provide the quality requirements of our products, no doubt the new process will enable us to achieve these more easily.
>
> A recent marketing survey on the relative importance of different purchasing criteria to carton users revealed that in the segment which the company currently serves, providing prompt quotations and samples, together with high delivery reliability and a willingness to meet schedule changes, are critical features and ones which our company has proved to be better at providing than our competitors. This represents the view our customers expressed in the survey.
>
> While price is not an important factor in winning current orders for these products, it would increasingly be so for the new orders we would need to secure to achieve the additional volume called for by the output levels underpinning the process investment proposals being considered. However, to compensate we would be moving into higher-volume orders, which would reinforce the gains inherent in the new process in terms of the cost savings available, while obviously providing the overall volume levels associated with the whole proposal. I know we can get these additional orders, providing the price is right and we maintain all the other features of the product and necessary levels of customer service. It's a tall order, so to speak, but I know we can do it.

CASE 16
PETERSON CARTON SERVICES

"Well, Jim," concluded Gerry Townsend, "I do not understand why the downward trend in our financial performance is still continuing and particularly why last month does not show the improvement we expected." Gerry Townsend, managing director of Peterson Carton Services, was discussing the management accounts for February with Jim Redman, the financial director.

> With the increase in sales and manufacturing activity achieved since this time last year, the expected performance improvement has not materialized. In fact, the very opposite has happened. The financial position has now become very worrying. Well, by the end of next week we need to have prepared a summary of events and a review of the actions we intend to take in order to bring about the necessary improvements. So far, the group board of directors has been patient, but at next week's meeting I am sure they will demand a clear statement of why this has happened and the steps we intend to take to turn the position around. We have to know how we are going to achieve our annual budgeted profit, having made losses in the first two months of this year amounting to £46,000 and £54,000, respectively [see Exhibit 1].

Background

Peterson Carton Services (PCS) is situated in Lancaster, the county town of Lancashire in the northwest of England. Established in 1948, it was taken over in the mid-1980s by Stebro Industries Plc, a diverse group of companies involved in food processing, civil engineering, steel fabrication, general engineering, distribution, waste disposal, paper, and carton making. PCS currently employs about 200 people and processes approximately 3,000 tons of cardboard (referred to as *board* within the carton industry) a year, making it one of the top 30 carton manufacturers in the United Kingdom. The carton-making industry is highly fragmented, due principally to the costs of distribution, with some 250 companies serving the country. Most of these produce a wide range of general cartons for most market applications, with some companies also making specialty products to meet the particular needs of customers. PCS uses lithographic ("litho") printing and other traditional processes (see Exhibit 2) to make its "general" cartons (see Exhibit 3) but has also developed specialized processes to make "windowed" cartons at high speed and high quality. In addition, PCS also makes a noncarton product range of drip mats[1] for breweries and distributors of imported wines.

Three years ago, the company had brought onto its main site a smaller carton business, which it had purchased some years earlier. As part of a rationalization plan, it was anticipated that this would lead to higher profits in the longer term, due to the estimated reduction in manufacturing and overhead costs resulting from this consolidation. Although cost savings did result, lower prices for existing products brought about by higher levels of competition led to a decline in profits for that year. When in the following year sales revenue also declined

---

[1]Known in North America as *coasters,* these products are sold for distribution to hotels, taverns, and wine bars, where they are used to protect the surface of tables and bars. The shape and print details are customer-specified for each order.

This case study was written by Professor T. J. Hill (London Business School) and S. H. Chambers (University of Warwick). It is intended for class discussion and not as an example of good or bad management. © AMD Publishing (UK).

by 12 percent, the company went into a loss situation (see Exhibit 1). In order to try to identify those market segments in which there was the greatest potential for sales growth, PCS completed a major market analysis about 15 months before, with the help of a large firm of marketing strategy consultants. This exercise reviewed the potential for sales growth in each of the main segments in which PCS operated. As a result, the consultants recommended a strategy for the company to concentrate its major sales effort in the beverages, food, and "windowed products" segments, which they identified as having the greatest potential for the rapid increase in

EXHIBIT 1   Summary of Trading Results and Current Year's Budget

	Accounting Period Results and Current Year Budget							
	Current Year Minus			*Last Year*		*Current Year*		
Aspect	*4*	*3*	*2*	*January–June*	*July–December*	*January*	*February*	*Budget*
Sales revenue (£000s)	6,292	6,266	5,505	3,060	3,745	581	563	6,800
Trading profit (£000s)	283	135	(151)	76	(321)	(46)	(54)	236
Percent of sales margin	4.5	2.2	(2.7)	2.5	(8.5)	(7.9)	(9.6)	3.5
Percent of return on investment	2.8	2.5	(4.6)	1.4	(12.6)	(11.8)	(14.2)	8.0
Net working capital as percent of sales revenue	14.1	14.4	13.2	14.2	18.1	18.2	18.1	10.7

EXHIBIT 2A   Five-Color, Offset Lithographic Printing Machine

EXHIBIT 2B   A Cut and Crease Machine

Following printing, the printed sheets are passed through this machine, which cuts out the shape and creases the carton to enable it to be folded as required.

EXHIBIT 3A   Completed Cartons Waiting to Be Dispatched

NOTE: All cartons, by their very nature, are specific to a customer's needs.

EXHIBIT 3B   A Typical Carton

volume necessary to sustain the required level of recovery in sales revenue and profit. The report argued that growth in these areas would be the best way to compensate for the sales revenue decline experienced in some other market segments. The reason for the sales decline in these areas was believed to be the result of intensive competition from carton companies beginning to specialize in supplying the needs of particular industries.

Marketing

By the midpoint of last year, most of the consultant's recommendations had been actioned, and the increased understanding of the market was found to be useful in establishing sales revenue budgets for this year (Exhibit 4). As a direct result of the marketing thrust, sales revenue rose by 22 percent in the second half of last year (see Exhibit 1). Details for the main segments served by PCS are given below.

Beverages.   The long-established relationships with ARD Coffee and Tea Specialty Packers (two of PCS's main customers) are expected to be maintained. This is largely due to the company's reputation for product quality and delivery reliability, and also because of the support given by its design function to help develop new products giving greater added value (e.g., incorporating gold-leaf designs). All beverage cartons are printed in four or five colors and are normally delivered on completion.

The account with Maister Teas began with a small order first placed in May of last year for delivery in July. Since then, the business has grown. In fact, actual sales are substantially higher than the original forecasts given to the company. The potential for large sales with this customer is considerable for two reasons. First, its annual expenditure on cartons is approximately £1.5 m; second, it is moving to a position of developing a long-term relationship with a smaller number of highly competent suppliers to provide all its needs. All Maister's contracts are for high-quality, five-color products, and the company expects its suppliers to operate strict,

EXHIBIT 4 Summary of Actual Sales Revenue for Last Year and Sales Budgets for This Year (£000s)

Market Segment	Customer	Last Year's Actual	Current Year's Forecast
Beverages	Maister Tea[1]	335	610
	ARD Coffees	270	230
	Tea Specialty Packers	225	260
	Others	41	50
	Total	871	1,150
Industrial products	Agroparts[2]	178	100
	NY Equipment[2]	174	50
	Rotabearings	156	150
	F C Bruce	104	90
	Others	10	10
	Total	622	400
Food	Maister Cakes[3]	256	475
	McPhee Foods[4]	208	250
	Country Cuisine[4]	20	60
	Others	82	35
	Total	566	820
Pharmaceuticals	Pharmex	228	230
	AB Products	157	160
	HMR	103	120
	Others	40	40
	Total	528	550
Dripmats	Pride Ales[5]	309	145
	Hop Products	128	95
	Korolla Cola	31	30
	Others	42	30
	Total	510	300
Toiletries	Prince & Haywood	224	220
(non-luxury ranges)	SC Packers (Export)	187	185
	Others	75	75
	Total	486	480
Confectionery	Elizabeth Ross	181	150
	Others	105	100
	Total	286	250
Small electrical items[9]	GRA Electrical	168	100
	Domelex	62	50
	Others	50	30
	Total	280	180
Sundry[9]	Various general cartons	1,025	870
	Total	1,025	870

EXHIBIT 4   *(concluded)*

Market Segment	Customer	Last Year's Actual	Current Year's Forecast
Group[7]	Various general cartons	430	400
	Total	430	400
Windowed products[6]	Various	1,064	1,300
	Group[7, 8]	137	200
	Total	1,201	1,500
	Grand Total	6,805	6,800

NOTES: 1. The first order for Maister Tea was placed in May for delivery July of last year.

2. The sales representative serving Agroparts and NY Equipment left PCS in September last year and joined a competitor. He is known to be arranging trial orders for these customers and is offering four-week delivery for any new orders. Given the examples in the case study narrative of what has happened in these circumstances in the past, current year budget figures reflect the position which PCS forecast will result.

3. The first order for Maister Cakes was placed in July (for delivery in October last year).

4. Both McPhee Foods and Country Cuisine are introducing just-in-time (JIT) programs. This will require its suppliers to provide a weekly delivery of all their range of cartons. However, as part of this change to JIT, both customers are intending to reduce the number of suppliers they currently use.

5. Marketing has decided (with appropriate corporate approval) not to renew the annual contract, which is due for signature in the next two months. Contract work was not undertaken prior to last year.

6. The major marketing initiatives commenced this January, and are now leading to improvements in sales revenues. However, reports from the field are indicating difficulties caused by PCS's current long lead times.

7. "Group" refers to sales to companies within the carton division of Stebro Industries Plc.

8. To help boost sales in this segment PCS is encouraging other companies within the Carton Division to seek suitable work, where it could provide the subcontractor windowing capacity.

9. Many of the small electrical items/sundry accounts are under severe competitive pressure from small carton manufacturers offering short lead times.

internal, quality control procedures. Orders are generally very large, but delivery is to weekly call-offs over a three-month period. In discussions on the future, Maister's buyers have stated that they wish to further reduce their own in-house carton inventory and intend to move gradually during the current year to twice-weekly deliveries on most cartons. While sales margins are low compared to general carton work, this is normal for high-volume contracts because, with considerable overcapacity existing in the carton-making industry at this time, there is strong competition for high-volume work.

Food.   Before last year, this segment was considered to comprise general carton work, with many small to medium orders being processed for a variety of customers. The marketing strategy report, however, high-lighted the potential to acquire more regular, high-volume work in this segment. This was actively pursued last year, resulting in an early contract for McPhee Foods. In addition, the developing relationship with Maister Teas resulted in an introduction to Maister Cakes, another division of the same company from whom a first order was received in July of last year. The order characteristics of this work are very similar to those of Maister Teas. The only significant difference is that cartons for Maister Cake are physically larger. As with the tea division, orders soon increased, and sales levels for this account are expected to continue to grow in the current year. Last November, an order from Maister Cakes was delivered five working days late. This was due to a quality problem requiring sorting to remove below-standard cartons. This late delivery brought a serious complaint from Maister Cakes and a claim for compensation to cover disruption to and loss of output in their own factories.

Dripmats.   Following the marketing strategy report and corporate discussions on PCS's business as a whole, it has recently been decided to reduce the company's sales efforts in this market, in order to allow the business to develop other segments deemed to be more in line with the company's needs. Keith Bowyer, sales/marketing director, explained:

> There are several factors that make this segment unattractive. Margins are generally poor, and the total market is declining. Although contract-type business for large, nationally based brewers (e.g., Pride Ales) is ordered on an annual basis with irregular call-offs, other ("promotional") orders (accounting for about 25 percent of their business) are required relatively quickly, resulting in the need for some schedule changes to the litho print program. These promotional dripmats are very often of a five-color design and considerably more demanding in quality requirements. This necessitates slower running on the presses, and higher levels of rejects are typically experienced. In addition, because they form part of a one-off brand sales promotion, it is always critical that orders are delivered on time.
>
> Predominantly two- and four-color work, dripmats are made out of thicker and lower-quality board and use the same litho printing and die-cutting/creasing (but not glueing) processes as cartons. However, the final stripping, separating, and packing processes use specialized equipment dedicated to these products. This product range accounted for 7 percent of last year's total sales revenue, and current year budgets reflect the downward trend agreed for this segment in our strategy [see Exhibit 4]. The irregular nature of orders often leads to an imbalance in departmental workloads. This is particularly so in gluing, as dripmats do not require this process, whereas most other products do. A high level of dripmat business, therefore, results in less work for some of the subsequent sections, such as gluing.
>
> These factors have all contributed to our decision not to pursue growth in this segment, and not to defend existing accounts against competitors' price reductions.

Windowed Cartons.   There is a very large number of customers for windowed cartons, each placing irregular orders, often for small quantities. Most orders are for four- or five-color printing, generally of high-quality artwork or photographs. The function of a windowed carton is to give the eventual customer sight of the product it contains, without opening the packaging. Often quite ordinary products (e.g., car accessories) are packed in this way and are usually bought as gifts (e.g., at Christmas).

The marketing review highlighted the considerable growth potential for this product, a fact reflected in this year's budget. It is known that very few competitors possess the necessary equipment and skills to produce high-quality windowed cartons. Of particular importance is the need for a supplier to be able to work with customers in the development of suitable designs, which would enhance their products in the desired manner. This was normally achieved by a combination of sales representatives' visits, and subsequent design and prototype development by PCS's design department. Many customers use this form of packaging as a one-off marketing exercise, and hence most designs were produced once and are not subsequently re-ordered.

Other carton manufacturers within the Stebro Industries group do not possess windowing capacity. Therefore, they will sometimes use PCS as a subcontractor to provide this service, but complete all the other operations needed to make a windowed carton within their own factories. When quoting for windowing work in the group, PCS produces an estimate of the cost of this operation based on material, transport, and processing costs. The latter are calculated using the normal, hourly estimating rate for windowing machines. The carton division as a whole has recognized the potential for this product. Consequently, a similar sales effort in the other carton companies has been made and rapid growth is anticipated. Exhibit 5 lists a representative sample of orders for windowed cartons.

Other Market Segments.   The marketing strategy recognized that while "other market" business as a whole represents nearly half of PCS's sales revenue, much of this is average volume and comprises work that is of a technically undemanding nature that could be manufactured

EXHIBIT 5   A Representative Sample of Windowed Cartons Produced in the Period July to September, Last Year

Works Order Number	Customer	Invoiced Sales (£)	Actual Variable Costs (£)			Windowing Machine Hours
			Material	Processing	Delivery	
16862	Group[1]	9,320	1,306	2,795	50	124.0
16893	Panda Pottery	12,436	2,140	1,806	90	56.5
16897	Electronica	17,008	3,670	2,385	165	121.5
16912	Group	2,451	625	541	25	24.5
16935	Durham Foods	8,250	1,710	902	60	26.0
16939	Stafpots	4,241	787	447	25	19.5
16956	Group	6,895	1,651	1,668	45	74.0
16974	Giftware Enterprises	7,908	1,367	945	35	24.0
16987	AG Camm	4,266	934	759	28	9.5
17007	Photo-X	6,121	1,452	792	40	33.5
17016	Group	3,549	770	721	30	32.0
17089	Ceramica	14,733	2,748	2,368	210	51.0
17091	Essex Confectionery	12,236	2,960	2,129	185	46.0
17115	Carac Gifts	17,450	4,976	2,903	305	16.0
17144	Group	6,982	2,041	1,499	55	66.5

NOTES: 1. The term *group* refers to another company in the carton division for which a windowing subcontract service is provided by PCS, as explained in the narrative.

2. In the case of products processed for the group, material costs only include the windowing materials (PVC), adhesives and packaging used (e.g., corrugated cardboard boxes and shrinkwrap film). Processing costs normally only relate to the windowing machine, as this process also carries out any necessary gluing.

by most, if not all, carton producers. Much of this business was regular, repeat work, with only minor and infrequent design changes. Commenting on this segment, Keith Bowyer explained that it is probably retained by factors such as:

- Customers inertia (packaging may be low on a buyer's list of priorities).
- Goodwill developed by long and successful trading relationships.
- Customer's satisfaction with the service provided by PCS (comprising a combination of quick delivery when necessary, delivery reliability, and consistent product quality).
- Good personal relationships between PCS's sales representatives and the purchasing function of its customers.
- Low prices for high-volume contracts.

He continued:

Our current marketing approach recognizes that many of our customers' orders are potentially vulnerable to competition. An example of this is illustrated by the significant amount of business we lost when a salesman (specializing in handling agreements with a number of industrial customers) left our employment and joined a competitor. Unfortunately, with his knowledge of this aspect of our business, he was able to attract many orders away from us to his new company. As we supplied nothing that could be considered unique, then he was able to take many customers with him by offering a slight improvement on one or more factors, or even just offering to guarantee the same level of overall service he, and we, had provided in the past.

EXHIBIT 6   Analysis of Average Plant Utilization

Process	Machine Manning	Basic Capability		Manned Time as Percent of Available Time				
		Maximum Size	*Maximum Colors*	*Q1*	*Q2*	*Q3*	*Q4*	*Total Year*
Litho printing	L1	40	2	97	77	73	61	77
	L2	40	4	99	98	93	99	97
	L3	52	2	62	56	63	67	62
	L4	52	4	101	94	97	107	100
	L5	52	5	78	93	113	127	103
Die cutting and creasing	C1	40	—	97	85	73	84	85
	C2	40	—	52	51	42	50	49
	C3	60	—	89	81	78	99	87
	C4	60	—	91	75	81	94	85
	C5	60	—	83	83	86	98	98
Gluing	G1	—	—	67	60	84	91	76
	G2	—	—	69	58	77	81	71
	G3	—	—	56	57	46	60	55
	G4	—	—	34	29	41	40	36
	G5	—	—	59	48	55	76	60
	G6	—	—	56	52	40	45	48
	G7	—	—	56	52	36	40	49
Dripmat punching	D1	—	—	20	41	40	25	31
Windowing	W1	—	—	64	52	120	70	77
	W2	—	—	64	70	125	71	83

NOTES: 1. Manned time includes (a) all running time, including overtime, (b) all setups, and (c) short duration downtime (less than one hour), due to mechanical/electrical breakdowns, where it was not considered necessary to reallocate the operators involved.

2. Available time is taken as normal two-shift working (weekdays) and excludes shutdowns.

3. Any press can print fewer than its maximum number of colors; for example, L5 can print five-, four-, three-, two-, or one-color work. Conversely, a two-color press can print four-color work, but this would require the cartons to be passed through a second time. Neither printing fewer colors nor passing a job through the same press twice makes commercial sense and is only done as a last resort.

Our strategy is to improve our levels of service to these customers, and to defend our current business when necessary, by lowering prices. In the long term, it is intended to offset the inevitable decline in these segments by increasing sales in more profitable areas, such as windowed products—a fact that is central to the marketing review completed some 15 months ago. However, the decline in sales we experienced two years ago and the impact this had on our profit performance is a factor of which we are always mindful.

Manufacturing

Processes.   All equipment is laid out on a functional basis. For example, there is a printing area in which all printing processes are located, a die-cutting/creasing area, containing all die-cutting and creasing processes, and so on. See Exhibit 2, which shows examples of some of the plant used, and Exhibit 6, which summarizes the process capabilities and records of utilization.

EXHIBIT 7   A Representative Sample of Work Printed on L5 during Last Year

Completion Date (printing)	Works Order Number	Customer	Total Machine Time Setup and Running (hours)	Number of Colors
January	16261	ARD Coffees	46	5
January	16301	Pride Ales	27	5
February	16326	Prince & Haywood	17	5
February	16349	Tea Specialty Packers	29	5
March	16407	Agroparts	41	4
March	16514	McPhee Foods	63	5
April	16527	GRA Electrical	21	5
April	16602	S C Packers (export)	36	4
May	16640	Barking & Hollis	32	5
May	16695	Pride Ales	11	3
May	16715	S C Packers (export)	24	4
June	16756	Country Cuisine	17	5
June	16809	Hop Products	22	5
July	16846	Prince & Haywood	55	5
July	16903	Wigan Breweries	22	4
August	16954	McPhee Foods	63	5
August	17001	Group	52	5
September	17063	Maister Cakes	10	5
September	17127	Tea Specialty Packers	62	5
October	17189	Korolla Cola	28	5
October	17231	Tea Specialty Packers	83	5
November	17277	Maister Tea	35	5
November	17336	Maister Cakes	41	5
December	17392	Elizabeth Ross	32	5
December	17426	Domelex	12	5

In general, a machine can process any width of cardboard up to the maximum size stated (see Exhibit 6). But those responsible for planning orders aim to maximize the use of available machine widths by appropriate carton design layouts. Thus, for most products the 52-inch litho presses are capable of producing more cartons per sheet of cardboard than the 40-inch machines, resulting in lower processing costs and often less material waste per unit of output.[2] The cost of tooling (litho plates and die-cutting dies) increases approximately in proportion to the area covered, but this is usually more than compensated for by the lower processing costs inherent in a wider press. Any litho press can print fewer colors than its capability (e.g., a five-color litho printer can print four or fewer colors—see Exhibit 7, which gives a representative sample of orders completed on the five-color printer).

All the machines, except L5 and the windowing processes, are over 10-years old and fully depreciated. More modern equipment would offer faster running speeds, marginally quicker setups, and improved consistency of quality. However, the capital investment involved is very high.

---

[2] There is always some material waste built into sheet design, if only at the edges. This comment refers to the fact that this inherent waste would, on a 52-inch press, be spread over more carton designs than for a 40-inch press printing the same design.

**EXHIBIT 8   Overtime Premium Costs
for January to December,
Last Year**

Month	Total Overtime Premium Paid (£)
January	5,460
February	2,100
March	3,246
April	3,672
May	6,256
June	4,107
July	5,363
August	11,718
September	19,869
October	26,207
November	32,111
December	17,006

NOTES: 1. Overtime premium is the supplement paid to
employees for working overtime and ranges from
one third of their hourly rate for short periods of
weekday overtime to 100 percent of the hourly
rate for Saturday afternoons and Sundays.

2. The above figures do not include extra salaried
costs (mainly supervisors).

Because of the financial record of the company and current low market prices, replacement has been difficult for PCS to justify in the last few years.

Personnel.   The plant is operated on two shifts of 7.5 hours per shift for five days a week, with varying levels of overtime throughout the year (see Exhibit 8). Manning levels for all the main processes are agreed nationally between the relevant trade unions and employers' federations. Thus, there is an agreed manning level on a four-color printing press and another on a five-color printing press. Where an order specifies five colors, then it is more cost effective to print it on a five-color press than to have to process it twice through a four-color press. PCS, as do most other businesses, conform to these agreements, leaving only service areas (e.g., packing, materials handling, warehouse, and quality control) where manning levels are determined by agreement between local management and the relevant trade union representatives. It is in these areas that reduction in labor could be more easily achieved by investment in equipment.

Production and Materials Control.   On receipt of a customer order, the sales administration department raises a works order,[3] which is passed to the production control department. At this stage, materials are ordered (board, any special inks, and printing plates), and the order is scheduled, using a bar chart for each machine. This procedure also shows the loading for each process.

---

[3]A works order is an internal document giving details of a customer order and providing the manufacturing function with the authorization to print a particular product in line with the volumes required. It would normally be accompanied by details of design and the relevant litho printing plates.

Some excess board is always purchased to allow for both the tolerances (usually +/− 10 percent) of the manufacturer's actual supply of material, and for the uncertain material yield from the processes. Customer orders are accepted on the basis of the carton industry's "standard conditions of sale," which allow a tolerance on the quantity of cartons delivered (usually +/− 10 percent). Generally, orders are planned to produce around 10 percent more cartons than the quantity ordered. All good cartons produced can then be delivered and invoiced at the full price. All materials are usually received within three weeks of order, but this lead time can be reduced if a supplier is notified that the particular item is urgent. In addition, most specifications of board can be obtained from stockists within 24 hours, but such deliveries cost about 40 percent more than supplies direct from the manufacturers.

The principal objective of the production control function is to ensure that the capacity of all processes is allocated effectively, and supplies are obtained at the agreed level of quality and delivered on time to ensure that customers' orders are produced by the contracted date. However, many changes in these schedules have to be catered for, which are caused by factors such as:

- Special customer orders are required to be produced in less than the normal lead time.
- Customer schedule changes to quantity and/or delivery dates.
- Canceled orders.
- Machine breakdowns or manning problems.
- Quality control issues (such as faulty printing plates, inks, and board), resulting in jobs being stopped and/or taken off the process until the problem can be resolved.
- Late deliveries from suppliers.

Furthermore, the production control function is responsible for ensuring the most efficient utilization of the processes, by sequencing jobs in such a way as to minimize setup times and levels of work-in-process inventory. In addition, processes with a high level of utilization must be planned to keep levels of overtime within acceptable limits, while ensuring that order backlogs[4] do not get too long, which would result in a potential loss of orders.

During the second half of last year, many changes in these factors have apparently been brought about by the major alterations to the work mix resulting from the new strategy. Exhibit 6 summarizes changes in utilization, and Exhibit 9 is a record of the order-backlog position for all main processes.

In addition, the production control department maintains records of all material issued to production and the "good" output of cartons. As job costing is not regularly carried out by the accounting function, this information is only used by the materials planner as a guide for the purchasing and issue of board. Special analyses are sometimes carried out on new contracts to ensure that the actual material usage is in line with estimates; Exhibit 10 summarizes the data for early orders from Maister Cakes. Because the relationship between the output and input of board is shown to be within only 1 percent of the estimate, the estimating rates are considered to be satisfactory, as some improvements in material usage would normally be made as a result of producing a particular carton on a regular basis.

Quality Control.   For most customers, quality standards are established on initial production orders, usually in the presence of a customer's representative. Samples are selected that reflect

---

[4]Order backlogs (also known as *forward load*) refer to the number of orders that, at any one time, are waiting to go into the manufacturing system. Promised delivery dates to customers, therefore, have to take into account not only the process lead time (the length of time a product takes to be completed) but also the number of agreed orders ahead of it in the queue of work.

EXHIBIT 9   Order Backlog for the Principal Manufacturing Processes (in weeks)

		Last Year												Current Year	
		Q1			Q2			Q3			Q4			Q1	
Process	*Machine*	*Jan.*	*Feb.*	*Mar.*	*Apr.*	*May*	*June*	*July*	*Aug.*	*Sep.*	*Oct.*	*Nov.*	*Dec.*	*Jan.*	*Feb.*
Litho	L1	4	5	2	2	2	3	4	2	2	1	1	1	2	2
printing	L3	2	6	3	3	5	4	4	3	4	6	4	3	4	5
	L3	3	3	4	3	4	4	2	4	3	3	4	6	4	4
	L4	5	6	5	4	4	4	5	6	6	8	6	9	9	8
	L5	2	3	5	4	4	4	6	7	8	9	9	10	9	8
Die cutting	C1,2	2	2	0	1	1	1	2	1	2	1	1	2	1	1
and creasing	C3,4,5	3	2	1	1	0	1	1	1	2	3	3	3	2	2
Gluing	All	1	0	0	1	0	0	0	0	1	1	2	1	2	1
Windowing	All	5	5	4	4	5	12	10	7	4	3	2	0	2	9
Dripmat punching	—	0	0	1	1	0	0	0	0	1	0	0	0	0	0

NOTES: 1. The above information relates to the principal processes and is calculated to the nearest working week.

2. Order backlog is recorded on the last day of each month.

the extremes of acceptable quality, and subsequent production and future repeat orders are controlled to fall within these agreed parameters. Quality is maintained by the process operatives, with random inspections by patrolling quality control staff and the final inspection of random samples undertaken by the packing section.

For Maister Teas and Maister Cakes, the procedure has to be much more rigorous. Production trials are conducted (at PCS's expense) and control samples are selected and authorized off-site by Maister's quality assurance function. Generally, the acceptable limits are very close (relative to other customers' orders), and Maister also lays down strict quality control procedures, which have to be followed during production and include the frequency of patrol inspections. In addition, a specified number of cartons from each pallet of finished goods must be kept aside for subsequent inspection and referenced to the relevant pallet. When these orders are being processed, the procedures described involve some two quality inspectors on a full-time basis. Delivered goods are subject to further inspection by Maister personnel, and deviations from quality limits may result in returns to PCS of complete carton deliveries.

Finance and Accounting

The decline in performance of the company was highlighted by the "Summary of trading results" given as Exhibit 1. It was clear that two factors had contributed to the worsening position—increasing levels of working capital and decline in sales margin.

Working Capital.   At a management meeting in September 1987, it was shown that the major item of working capital was inventory, and it was agreed that this must be reduced this year by at least 40 percent. In order to achieve such a reduction, all categories of inventory would have to be cut on the following basis.

Raw Materials.   The buyer was instructed to adhere rigidly to the company policy of only purchasing for customers' orders. Inventory holdings of material for dripmats would be re-

EXHIBIT 10   An Analysis of Board Usage and Output of Cartons for All Orders from Maister Cakes during Last Year

Works Order Reference	Month Completed	Quantity of Cartons Ordered		Number of Cartons per Board (number-up)	Input—Number of Boards Issued to Production		Output—Number of Cartons Delivered	
		Number (000)	Tolerance (+/−%)		Estimate	Actual	Estimate	Actual
17063	September	150	10	12	22,000	20,050	165,000	188,850
17122		250	10	8	42,950	40,100	275,000	280,400
17181	October	200	10	12	25,800	22,950	220,000	215,600
17204		175	10	8	33,000	30,000	192,500	201,350
17212		1,000	7.5	12	95,800	99,750	1,075,000	1,053,300
17292	November	250	10	12	30,550	33,900	275,000	332,200
17336		1,500	5	12	139,000	142,500	1,575,000	1,550,950
17345		75	10	8	18,090	17,250	82,500	108,300
17372		175	10	6	38,500	38,200	192,500	190,925
17373		550	10	12	61,000	58,050	605,000	608,850
17390	December	450	10	12	50,000	50,000	495,000	508,800
17396		2,500	5	12	230,000	225,100	2,625,000	2,474,200
17411		100	10	6	25,820	26,250	110,000	120,450
17412		50	10	8	12,170	14,150	55,000	81,050
17440		1,100	7.5	8	156,400	166,000	1,182,500	160,650
				Total	981,080	984,250	9,125,000	9,065,875
				Variance Percentage	+0.32		−0.65	

NOTES: 1. Boards are normally purchased from a supplier to suit the size and specification of individual works orders. Quantities received may vary by +/− 10 percent from the ordered quantities. However, as with the final product, all quantities within this tolerance band would be paid for.

2. The number of boards issued is decided by the production control department and later adjusted by the materials controller. The production controller may plan quantities slightly greater than estimate, if he is aware that Maister has low stocks and is thus critically dependent on receiving at least the ordered quantity. The materials controller may increase the input, if the quantity of board received from the suppliers exceeds the ordered quantity (see Note 1 above).

3. The estimated output for each order exceeds the ordered quantity by a tolerance. Because of the uncertainty of quantities received from the board mills, and because of variable process material yields, the standard conditions of sale which operate throughout the carton industry allow defined maximum percentages of under- and over-production to be delivered and charged to customers.

duced, and the buffer inventory of board for regular business, such as the industrial and food segments, would be eliminated.

Work-in-Process.   Increasing levels of work in process (WIP) were attributed to unsatisfactory planning, resulting in occurrences such as:

- Interruptions to long print or die-cutting/creasing runs (e.g., Maister Teas), in order to allow the production of short-run items, where there was pressure to deliver cartons soon after receipt of raw materials and in line with customer's requirements. Output from the interrupted order would be held as WIP awaiting its later completion.
- Overloading of certain downstream processes, resulting in WIP queues.
- Failure to ensure that orders are progressed in the best sequence to minimize WIP inventory.

Apart from identifying the need to improve production scheduling procedures, the finance department proposed the introduction of a computerized planning system. This would ensure that all planning decisions resulted in a forecast level of inventory being reported. In this way, the planners would not only have a means of improving their effectiveness, but would also become more aware of the results of their decisions on inventory levels.

Finished Goods.   The main categories of finished goods inventory are:

- Overproduction (i.e., output in excess of the agreed upper-tolerance level) held in anticipation of further orders.
- Inventory held awaiting call-offs due to customers delaying deliveries.
- Cartons produced to meet the whole of an order, although actual call-offs were scheduled for delivery over an extended period.

At the end of last year, 75 percent of finished goods inventory was in the category of awaiting call-offs, where manufacturing had made the whole of an order, with specified scheduled deliveries over the following three months. From this January, planners were instructed to manufacture only for call-offs up to six weeks ahead, and this was expected to reduce finished goods inventory by approximately 30 percent.

Sales Margins.   Currently, there is no job costing system, but complete weekly records of process utilization are maintained. In addition, regular analyses are prepared, comparing actual and standard running speeds and setup times for each process. It is believed that this approach highlights critical variances from standards and provides an adequate basis for management control.

Job costings are sometimes calculated on a sample basis for new orders but are found to be extremely time-consuming. It has been calculated that to cost up to 1,000 orders each year would require additional staff and a substantial increase in overhead costs, which could not be justified at this time. On the suggestion of the group internal auditors, a one-off job costing exercise was undertaken in February, the results of which are shown in Exhibit 11.

Estimating.   Except for very regular work (contract dripmats for national brewing companies and high-volume work for Maister), an estimate is prepared for every enquiry. Two years ago, the standard estimating procedure was computerized. This has proved to be invaluable because there were nearly 6,500 enquiries processed last year, and the computerized procedure has reduced the clerical staff requirement from six down to three people.

The computer program allows the estimator to enter details of the product specification and quantities, select the process route, enter his estimate of expected material wastage, and specify delivery details. Fixed estimating data (machine throughput rates, processing costs per hour, setup times, material costs, and delivery charges) are reviewed by the accounting department every six months. The estimate provided by the computer is based on standard process running and setup times. The estimator then applies a profit margin on the basis of advice from the salesman and sales manager, while taking into account any history of prices accepted by the customer. For large enquiries and contract renewals, the management team reviews all estimates before quotations are sent to the enquirer.

EXHIBIT 11   Costings for Representative Orders: October to December, Last Year

Market/Customer	Works Order Number	Invoiced Sales (£s)[1]	Estimated Contribution[2] £s	Estimated Contribution[2] % of Order Value	Actual Costs (£s) Board	Actual Costs (£s) Other Materials	Actual Costs (£s) Processing Variable[3]	Actual Costs (£s) Delivery	Actual Costs (£s) Total
Beverages									
Maister Tea	17120	14,096	825	5.9	11,047	733	1,676	436	13,892
	17392	55,512	9,485	16.3	43,396	3,002	9,542	1,980	57,920
	17451	54,450	9,596	17.0	41,128	2,202	7,579	1,649	52,558
ARD Coffees	17186	2,836	1,203	42.7	401	188	1,025	21	1,635
	17347	30,206	3,672	12.7	17,483	2,756	5,541	1,354	27,134
	17369	15,542	6,946	45.4	3,162	2,091	3,098	245	8,596
Tea Specialty Packers	17242	4,519	2,333	52.0	646	381	1,130	29	2,186
	17301	2,374	1,002	42.2	356	286	705	25	1,372
	17405	9,799	4,889	50.5	1,496	1,585	1,808	121	5,010
Eastern Teas	17408	3,973	2,391	61.1	945	174	403	60	2,582
Industrial products									
Agroparts	17214	5,996	3,127	51.9	1,597	630	1,151	177	3,555
	17446	7,671	2,393	33.2	3,907	499	1,288	448	6,142
NY Equipment	17284	5,582	1,828	40.8	2,358	440	864	158	3,820
	17427	20,404	8,208	41.8	9,712	1,204	2,090	748	13,754
Rotabearings	17269	23,712	10,206	47.2	8,459	1,730	4,302	850	15,341
	17391	14,809	6,026	45.6	5,478	1,032	2,400	556	9,466
F C Bruce	17279	7,830	2,309	31.5	4,110	499	1,268	479	6,356
	17431	10,674	3,775	39.6	2,217	3,252	552	251	6,272
Food									
Maister Cakes	17122	15,346	1,571	10.8	11,423	1,190	2,563	677	15,853
	17212	53,366	8,164	13.9	40,062	3,963	10,224	1,712	55,961
	17440	59,971	9,541	15.4	44,606	2,953	11,994	1,838	61,391
McPhee	17190	4,403	1,641	41.8	1,728	147	1,191	123	3,189
	17320	4,766	1,299	31.0	1,888	387	1,519	125	3,919
	17448	6,397	4,053	63.4	1,205	883	2,738	249	5,075
Country Cuisine	17298	7,738	2,009	29.9	4,252	629	1,636	250	6,767
Pharmaceuticals									
Pharmex	17216	2,560	1,139	49.0	654	172	795	20	1,641
	17377	7,082	4,026	51.4	2,080	591	2,041	55	4,767
	17450	2,205	908	46.1	669	332	302	17	1,320
AB Products	17323	1,052	469	55.7	156	52	262	11	481
	17436	6,016	2,339	43.1	1,180	1,379	666	78	3,303
HMR	17356	1,728	880	58.4	227	203	469	28	927

EXHIBIT 11   *(continued)*

Market/Customer	Works Order Number	Invoiced Sales (£s)[1]	Estimated Contribution[2]		Actual Costs (£s)				
			£s	% of Order Value	Board	Other Materials	Processing Variable[3]	Delivery	Total
Dripmats									
Pride Ales	17243[4]	1,950	164	10.8	968	189	784	71	2,012
	17311[4]	2,025	259	16.6	953	72	722	67	1,814
	17400	1,885	280	18.5	838	145	397	71	1,451
	17452	3,415	590	22.4	1,368	249	354	59	2,030
Hop Products	17261	5,337	1,974	52.8	1,191	197	505	85	1,978
	17439	18,333	7,827	41.4	8,529	1,120	2,760	657	13,066
Korolla Cola	17365	5,511	1,995	42.7	2,024	246	855	95	3,220
Toiletries									
Prince & Haywood	17276	29,289	14,143	47.1	10,498	2,523	4,304	903	18,228
	17308	32,868	11,133	38.4	12,655	3,307	5,599	895	22,456
	17415	20,227	6,840	39.0	7,277	2,150	3,466	524	13,417
SC Packers (exports)	17199	10,521	5,821	46.2	3,791	837	3,394	359	8,381
	17437	3,861	1,678	48.1	1,033	354	942	79	2,408
Soap Exports	17348	8,436	4,364	49.9	2,610	445	2,656	70	5,781
Confectionery									
Elizabeth Ross	17288	2,783	1,453	58.5	370	225	449	34	1,078
	17395	3,222	1,856	60.4	456	445	664	34	1,599
Prestar	17341	6,540	4,180	60.2	1,016	686	1,370	75	3,147
Small electrical appliances									
GRA Electrical	17208	12,396	7,033	52.3	5,908	1,135	3,680	332	11,055
	17398	12,064	5,044	45.9	3,482	1,342	3,539	270	8,633
Domelex	17423	6,019	2,821	48.2	1,165	1,058	1,741	78	4,042
Exit Fans	17257	3,584	1,574	52.0	774	301	736	40	1,851
Sundry									
Jones & Straw	17193	2,646	560	20.7	1,270	330	462	90	2,152
FJ Agrichem	17278	5,762	1,656	30.7	1,639	749	1,290	250	3,928
Electronica	17370	1,875	451	21.5	996	207	325	30	1,558
London Shirts	17454	2,179	379	17.2	1,206	355	278	45	1,884
Group									
Companies in the carton division	17209	3,873	1,523	48.0	562	613	888	50	2,113
	17318	6,782	3,809	62.7	1,024	443	2,227	238	3,932
	17359	5,463	3,360	60.8	916	522	1,711	318	3,467
	17442	1,600	1,013	63.4	301	221	685	62	1,269

EXHIBIT 11   *(concluded)*

Market/Customer	Works Order Number	Invoiced Sales (£s)[1]	Estimated Contribution[2]		Actual Costs (£s)				
			£s	% of Order Value	Board	Other Materials	Processing Variable[3]	Delivery	Total
Windowed									
Panda Pottery	17246	3,672	1,912	70.7	394	741	574	18	1,724
Stafpots	17420	7,753	3,684	68.3	860	396	833	23	2,112
Electronica	17443	9,199	4,249	66.6	1,018	752	1,655	56	3,481
Windowed subcontract[5]									
Spa Cartons	17352	8,779	5,547	63.0	—	2,449	2,099	50	4,598
Stebro Packaging	17457	7,369	3,756	54.2	—	2,225	1,254	45	3,524

NOTES: 1. Invoice sales is the value of all the goods as delivered, but excludes any credit notes or returned goods.

2. Estimated contribution is the difference between the order value and the estimated variable costs of materials, processing, and delivery.

3. Processing variable costs are calculated from the machine variable (hourly) cost rates which include (a) direct labor with fringe benefits, (b) energy costs, (c) consumable materials, (d) adjustments for average downtime, and (e) repairs and maintenance materials. Typically, direct labor with fringe benefits accounts for less than 50 percent of total processing variable costs.

4. These two orders are of a contract nature, as explained in the narrative. The other two orders for Pride Ales are of the promotional type.

5. The category "windowed subcontract" refers to orders from other companies in the carton division, requiring only the "windowed" process to be completed.

CASE 17
PRECISION STEEL PLC[1]

Introduction

Although there are a few, small aspects of the report on which we could take issue, it seems to me that Bill Carey has, by and large, reflected the marketing changes we have been expressing and given some sound guidelines on where we must place our future energies. The emphasis given to increasing our share in all segments of the customized sections market and the need to continue and expand the customer-orientation strategy with Gambert Fabrique, one of our key accounts, seems to have struck a chord with us all, both in terms of past trends and our feel for these markets. What we now have is a strategic framework to give context and direction. This will help us to replace the more short-term response philosophy we have been using in our marketing decisions. Thanks, Bill, we have found your work helpful, and I am sure it will prove to be a document to which we will refer many times in the future.

Brian Finn, the chief executive of Precision Steel (PSL) was addressing the board of directors, following a meeting to discuss a recent report titled "Future Marketing Strategy Proposals," completed on behalf of the company. In addition to the board, Bill Carey (a senior executive from the strategic unit within group central services, who had been responsible for preparing the report) had also attended the final part of this meeting in order to answer any queries not addressed earlier.

Background

PSL sells high-quality steel sections in a wide range of standard steel specifications together with customer-specified material requirements. PSL is part of Harbridge Industries, a large group of companies with a wide range of interests including shipping, civil engineering, electronics, fabrication, and engineering as well as steel processing. PSL was established in 1932 to roll precision steel sections for the electric motor industry.

Although many aspects of its activities have since changed. PSL's business still principally constitutes the rerolling of steel sections, using hot and cold processes, in a variety of steel specifications, and up to a maximum section height of 250 mm. Due to falling demand and subsequent plant closures, PSL found itself, by the late 1970s (like many of its European counterparts) in a near monopoly position, as it was now the only supplier based in the United Kingdom. However, similar businesses in Europe are always keen to export to the United Kingdom, particularly to high-volume (ton) users.

PSL's Markets

PSL buys steel sections from a limited number of suppliers (principally English Billets Plc), then sells rerolled precision sections into three market segments with different characteristics.

---

[1]Plc means public limited company and in the United States equates to being incorporated.

This case was prepared by Professors T. J. Hill (London Business School) and S. H. Chambers (University of Warwick). It is intended for class discussion and not as an illustration of good or bad management. © AMD Publishing (UK).

EXHIBIT 1 **PSL's Current and Past Sales (tons) of Steel Sections for the Electric Motor Market**

	Current Year Minus				Current Year
Year	10	6	2	1	
Total sales (tons)	79,600	65,300	55,500	52,000	50,400
Average order quantity (tons)	286	205	235	220	190
Average number of sizes per order quantity	20	20	29	27	26

NOTES: 1. There are now seven different specifications (i.e. material properties) of steel raw materials (in a different range of sizes) required by this market. Each specification in all sizes is normally held in stock by PSL. Ten years ago, there were only two specifications.

2. A typical order comprises several sizes of finished precision steel sections, but usually all of the same steel specification and finishing/heat treatment requirements. The various sizes will, however, be processed in separate hot mill programs (see Exhibit 7). Therefore, although an order may be for say 200 tons, as far as manufacturing is concerned it would be similar to 20 different orders (i.e., one order per size), as similar sizes (and not one customer order) are processed through manufacturing.

3. Typical delivery lead times are 6–8 weeks from receipt of order.

These are electric motors, stockist steel sections, and customized sections, which are described below.

Electric Motors. PSL's traditional market was to provide steel sections for electric motors. While demand for this market has fallen in the last fifteen years it still accounts for almost 50 percent of PSL's revenue (£s). Steel sections are rolled, which are subsequently precision machined by the customer. This accounts for some 50,000 tons per year, and details of current and past sales are given in Exhibit 1.

Stockist Steel Sections. Sales in this market are for a range of standard sizes and shapes, all rolled from the one internationally specified steel, known by the company as PS 2000. Both home and overseas customers, therefore, ordered from a standard catalog, with items being differentiated only by size and shape.

In order to compensate for the falling sales experienced in the electric motor market, the stockist steel sections segment has been built up over the last 15 years. The annual volumes processed this year totaled 30,000 tons, and details of representative orders are given in Exhibit 2. PSL currently supplied 5 major U.K. stockists and about 50 stockists overseas. Last year, PSL had received a major contract from a French company, Gambert Fabrique (GF), which yielded orders totaling 8,000 tons in the following year. Apparently running at a substantial loss in its steel rerolling business, GF decided 10 years before to close its own rolling mill, having negotiated a contract with PSL to supply its standard steel sections, using steel PS 2000. Gambert sells a wide range of products and is a large exporter of engineering supplies and metal sections (steel, brass, and aluminum). It distributes these by a well-developed container service to its own depots and clients throughout the world.

The negotiations with Gambert resulted in agreed prices and terms for delivery by PSL to its main distribution center in Brest, an industrial port in northern France. Exhibits 3 and 4 give brief details of these agreements, as compared to other products in this segment. Last year PSL

EXHIBIT 2   PSL's Current and Past Sales of Stockist Steel Sections

Year	Current Year Minus				Current Year
	10	6	2	1	
Total sales (tons)	15,100	17,700	19,400	28,900	29,700
Average order quantity (tons)	84	95	105	130	123
Average number of sizes per order quantity	17	20	24	25	23

NOTES: 1. The steel specification for this market is PS2000 only.

2. There are 140 international standard sizes in the stockists' range.

3. Gambert Fabrique (France) orders once a month an average of 670 tons in 34 standard sizes (minimum 10 tons per size) for delivery 6–8 weeks from receipt of an order.

4. Gambert Fabrique (U.K. and Denmark) each order twice a month an average of 35 tons each in nine sizes (minimum 3 tons per size) for delivery 4–6 weeks from receipt of an order.

5. Current delivery lead times for U.K. stockists are 6–8 weeks from receipt of an order.

initiated discussions on the possibility of direct supply to some of GF's depots. John Breen, marketing director, explained the reason for this:

> The GF contract is an important part of our customer portfolio. The annual volume is substantial, characterized by relatively large orders quantities and stable schedules. But, the trade-off has been low prices. However, within a relatively short period of time, we saw the opportunity of supplying direct to GF's depots in one or more countries. The direct gains for Gambert were reduced distribution costs and for PSL an increase in price. Our first successes early last year were the United Kingdom and Denmark, with each buying about 450 tons per year. Having received permission to negotiate directly with these two parts of the Gambert organization, we were able to satisfactorily agree higher prices than for similar products, due to the fact that GF passed on distribution costs to U.K. customers (including parts of its own organization), as well as adding its own margin. We are now able, therefore, to take for ourselves some of that additional margin and still offer a favorable price for direct supply [see Exhibits 3 and 4]. Our policy is to encourage this, and the recent report on future marketing strategy highlights in this as one of the major planks on which we should build. We have now identified Brazil, Italy, and Germany as the next areas, and early soundings seem to be favorable.
>
> In addition, we propose to consolidate our relationship with Gambert by setting up direct computer links with Brest, which allow their buying office to link with our sales and production control systems. In this way we hope to lock them into a long-term dependence on PSL.

Customized Sections.   The decline in overall sales had stimulated the need to increase sales in the customized sections segment of the market. Customized sections business refers to orders that cater for the specific needs of a wide range of manufacturing businesses, including automotive components (e.g., struts), agricultural machinery, and oil rig fabrication, as well as general engineering. The growth was based on converting customers from using nonprecision, standard steel sections requiring extensive and costly machining and heat treatment, to purpose-rolled sections to meet their specifications in terms of dimensional tolerance, steel specification, and heat treatment requirements. PSL's sales force had, over the last few years, developed a broader technical knowledge in order to help increase PSL's penetration in these markets. Orders can, however, involve both standard and special steels, but size and shape will always be specified by, and therefore special to, each customer. Many customers, however, place repeat orders for the same product, often on a call-off or schedule

---
EXHIBIT 3   Some Examples of Typical Invoiced Rates per Ton (Current Prices)

Markets	Billet Size (mm)	£/Ton
Electric motor—XR7 material	70	600
	110	500
	120	465
	140	420
	190	425
	250	430
Stockist steel—PSL's U.K. stockists	70	570
	100	490
	120	475
	140	465
	170	470
	250	450
Gambert Fabrique—France	85	420
	110	340
	130	320
	150	300
	190	300
	250	300
Gambert Fabrique—United Kingdom	85	480
	110	390
	130	360
	150	350
	190	340
	250	330
Customized section—MK 200 steel	85	810
	120	680
	190	610
	210	610

NOTES: 1. All prices are corrected to ex-works equivalents.
2. MK 200 is an expensive alloy steel.

basis. Most requirements can be met by the hot rolling process,[2] and a representative sample of orders is given in Exhibit 5.

Current year's sales in this market segment totaled 20,000 tons, 85 percent of which went to U.K. companies, with the remainder sent to all parts of the world. An important element of this growth came from sales to the oil industry.

Manufacturing

Steel sections pass through a series of processes, which are now briefly described. Orders differ, and whereas all products go through the hot rolling stage, requirements from then on vary

---
[2]Hot rolling is a less expensive process than cold rolling, therefore, products are designed, where possible, to be made in a hot-rolled format.

EXHIBIT 4   Summary of Estimated Variable Cost per Ton (£) in Various Markets, for Different Tonnages per Size, Based on Current Costs

Markets	Tonnage	Input Steel Height (mm)					
		70–85	*100–110*	*120–130*	*140–150*	*170–190*	*210–250*
Electric motors	5 tons	490	411	385	350	355	360
(typical steel	10 tons	460	386	363	330	335	340
specification XR7)	20 tons	445	376	350	320	330	335
Stockist steel	5 tons	410	336	314	290	295	300
(PS2000 steel)	10 tons	380	316	298	280	285	290
	20 tons	365	306	290	275	280	285
Customized sections	5 tons	635	550	520	500	490	490
	10 tons	600	525	500	480	470	470
	20 tons	580	510	485	460	455	455

NOTE: Variable cost includes all direct labor, materials, and other direct costs (e.g., variable energy costs) and an allowance for size changes between items on a program. It also allows for average yield losses for the market category.

EXHIBIT 5   PSL's Current and Past Sales of Customized Sections

Year	Current Year Minus				Current Year
	10	*6*	*2*	*1*	
Total sales (tons)	4,200	9,600	18,200	18,600	20,400
Average order quantity (tons)	18.3	16.6	11.2	11.8	12.2
Average number of sizes per order quantity (note 2)	1.1	1.2	1.2	1.2	1.3

NOTES: 1. Steel specification, finishing process, and heat treatments are as specified by each customer. Some high-usage steel specifications are held in raw material stock at PSL either against known call-offs or in anticipation of future orders.

2. Most orders are only for one size, but a few are for up to four different sizes.

3. Call-offs or scheduled requirements (i.e., orders for a number of deliveries spread over several months) are treated in this analysis (and by the planning office and within manufacturing) as individual orders.

in accordance with the specification. Individual customer orders are cumulated, wherever possible, by input height (often referred to as billet size) in order to maximize the tonnage processed through the high-volume hot mills. The task in the production planning office, therefore, is to combine together quantities of the same billet size (irrespective of material type) and program these through the hot mills in order to minimize the numbers of major and minor changeovers (explained later) in line with customer delivery requirements. Following this initial stage through which all steel is processed, customer orders are then separated and follow the individual process requirements to completion.

Hot Rolling.   Currently, two hot rolling mills are in use. One was installed 15 years ago and the second 5 years later to replace earlier mill capacity, which had gradually been phased out.

While the basic layout for hot rolling is similar, the process capabilities are different. This difference concerns the height and length of steel sections that can be processed. Exhibit 6 gives details.

Hot Roll Finishing.   All products go through the hot roll finishing section. The processes are simple and the setup times are short. After initial cooling, the steel sections are lifted by an overhead crane into the work-in-process warehousing area. The crane is, however, limited to a maximum of a five-ton lift, which means that many order quantities are split at this stage. From this warehousing area, all products follow their own specified routing, according to the process requirements involved.

Cold Rolling.   About one third of all products are cold rolled. The orders are drawn from the work in process inventory after hot roll finishing. These processes enable higher levels of accuracy to be achieved, particularly where the product specification calls for thinner sections. They all require very long setup times and involve expensive tooling. The specialized tooling has a three-month lead time from the suppliers and, therefore, needs very careful planning. In addition, there is a disproportionate amount of tool wear at the start of a production run, until fine adjustments can be achieved.

Other Auxiliary Processes.   There are several additional processes involved, none of which have long setup or process times. They include cold roll finishing, heat treatment, cutting to precise lengths, and specified packing prior to dispatch. Not all products go through all processes.

Lead-Time Calculations

The lead times used by sales in quotations are agreed annually by the sales and production directors, being occasionally adjusted as necessary by the production planning office, if overload situations seem to be arising. The following norms were currently used as a basis for calculating lead times on which delivery promises were then made: 10 weeks were allowed for the purchase of nonstandard steel, 4 weeks for hot rolling, 1 week for standard heat treatment and finishing, and 4 weeks for cold rolling. Nonstandard finishing process lead times were calculated for each job on the basis of an assessment of the complexity involved and the degree of overall speed required by the potential customer.

In all markets where customers require quicker deliveries than the total based on the above norms, shorter lead times for customer quotations are agreed by the manager of the production planning office. This is achieved by identifying areas of process-time reduction, based on current and future loading, experience, and judgment. In all cases, delivery is quoted as "ex-works" (the standard practice for the industry) and does not, therefore, include delivery arrangements. See Exhibits 7, 8, and 9, which give details of actual deliveries in a representative period.

Standard steels are assumed by the production planning office to be available from PSL raw material stock holdings, and thus no allowance is made in sales quotations involving standard steels to cover purchase lead time.[3] The inventory holding of each size and specification of standard steel is tightly controlled by the planning manager, using simple controls, based on average usage for the last three months, current stock, and estimates of forward demand.

---

[3]Most standard steels are kept in stock as explained in the notes to Exhibit 10.

Exhibit 6

Characteristics of the Hot Rolling Mills

Mill C

- Constructed 15 years ago.
- Maximum input section height: 250 mm.
- Maximum length of output: 5,250 mm.
- Average output rate: 13.5 tons/hour (Note 1).
- Average size change time: 9 minutes within a programmed range (Note 6).

Mill D

- Constructed 10 years ago to provide efficient capacity for the high-volume electric motor sections market.
- Maximum input section height: 200 mm.
- Maximum length of output: 6,000 mm.
- Average output rate: 20.3 tons/gross hour (Note 1).
- Average size change time: 10 minutes within a programmed range (Note 6).
- Estimated cost of upgrading to provide size capability of 250 mm sections: £550,000.

NOTES: 1. The average output rates refer to the tons of processed steel averaged per hour, including any size changes made. It is known as the output rate/gross hour.
2. Output rates are not significantly affected by section width, as this is not a constraining factor.
3. Both mills are currently operated on a two-shift basis, 40 hours per shift week, 46 weeks a year.
4. Furnace shutdown, light up, and preparations for rolling each weekend cost approximately £3,000 per mill. Overnight idling of furnaces costs approximately £60/ per hour (fuel and labor).
5. Company policy is to roll minimum tonnages of five tons per size, although authorized exceptions are allowed.
6. Although size change times within a programmed range are short (between 8.5 and 10 minutes), changeovers between one range of sizes and another are much longer. Consequently, planning establishes a program which enables these short changes to take place (which amount to small adjustments in the process) before requiring a major size change to be made. These latter changes also vary in duration depending, in turn, on the extent of the changeover. If the size alteration is itself sequential (i.e., to the next size range, whether larger or smaller) then the time taken is about 1.75 hours for mill C and 2.15 hours for mill D. However, if the size range alteration is not sequential, then the changeover is increased by up to a further 1.5 times. Thus, the hot mill programs are planned to minimize downtime wherever possible, while maintaining order quantity levels within the delivery requirements of customers.

EXHIBIT 7 **A Representative Sample of Orders for U.K. Electric Motor and for the U.K. Stockist Steel Markets**

		Key Dates (week numbers)		
Works Order Number	Tons Ordered	Works Order Raised	Required and Acknowledged Delivery	Actual Delivery
Electric motor				
M864	10.0	5	12	11
M866	15.0	5	15	15
M878	8.0	5	12	12
M879	5.0	5	16	17
M880	10.0	5	12	9
M881	8.0	5	12	12
M910	6.5	6	13	16
M912	12.0	6	13	13
M913	12.0	6	13	13
M914	15.0	6	16	14
M930	8.0	7	13	14
M936	5.0	7	13	13
M937	10.0	7	13	15
M938	8.0	7	16	16
M939	8.0	7	14	13
Stockist steel				
S420	4.0	5	10	11
S426	4.0	5	10	11
S427	6.0	5	12	12
S428	5.0	5	12	11
S440	4.0	6	12	10
S441	10.0	6	12	12
S448	4.0	6	12	13
S449	4.0	6	12	11
S479	10.0	6	13	13
S480	4.0	6	13	13
S481	5.0	6	13	11
S503	5.0	7	14	14
S504	5.0	7	13	15
S505	3.0	7	13	13

NOTES: 1. A separate works order is raised for each size within a customer order.
2. Works order numbers M866, M879, M914, and M939 were also cold rolled.

Steel delivery is normally requested and acknowledged by suppliers as being 10 weeks from the order date. (See Exhibits 10 and 11 for information on the delivery performance of PSL's steel suppliers.)

Process Yields

Process yield is defined as salable output divided by the input of raw material and expressed as a percentage. The yields achieved by each different process are closely monitored

---

EXHIBIT 8   **A Representative Sample of Current Orders from Gambert Fabrique**

Delivery to/ Works Order Number	Tons Ordered	Key Dates (week numbers)		
		Works Order Raised	Required and Acknowledged Delivery	Actual Delivery
France				
S463	10.0	6	13	12
S464	25.0	6	13	13
S465	25.0	6	13	10
S466	20.0	6	13	13
S467	16.0	6	13	9
S468	28.0	6	13	12
S469	35.0	6	13	13
S470	25.0	6	11	10
S471	20.0	6	11	12
S472	20.0	6	11	11
S473	15.0	6	11	13
S474	25.0	6	11	10
S475	10.0	6	11	11
S476	20.0	6	11	13
S477	20.0	6	11	11
S478	15.0	6	11	14
United Kingdom				
S416	3.0	5	10	12
S417	5.0	5	10	13
S418	3.0	5	8	9
S419	5.0	5	8	8
S492	4.0	7	12	12
S493	4.0	7	12	11
S494	5.0	7	10	11
Denmark				
S412	4.0	5	9	13
S413	4.5	5	9	12
S414	5.0	5	9	9
S415	4.0	5	9	10
S489	5.0	7	10	10
S490	5.0	7	10	9
S491	3.0	7	10	11

NOTES: 1. A separate works order is raised for each size within a customer order.

2. Delivery promise for overseas destinations is acknowledged as the date the sections leave PSL.

EXHIBIT 9   A Representative Sample of Current U.K. Orders Received for Customized Sections (hot rolled and standard finishing)

Works Order Number	Standard Steel	Special Steel	Ordered Tons	Key Dates (week numbers)			Total Steel Input	Total Saleable Output
				Works Order Raised	Required and Acknowledged Delivery	Actual Delivery		
C026	✔		46.0	5	10	9	49.9	45.4
C052	✔		7.5	5	15	16	8.0	7.3
C053		✔	3.0	5	19	22	5.1	4.6
C057		✔	6.0	5	20	20	7.9	6.4
C061	✔		10.0	5	12	10	11.0	9.6
C082		✔	8.5	5	19	20	8.7	6.9
C092		✔	3.0	5	18	26	7.5*	2.2
C094		✔	20.5	5	20	19	23.1	19.0
C099	✔		52.0	5	11	10	58.0	53.3
C121	✔		10.0	6	10	12	11.0	10.1
C126		✔	10.0	6	22	21	13.0	11.1
C128	✔		20.0	6	9	10	22.5	20.9
C132	✔		75.0	6	12	12	83.5	77.1
C136	✔		15.0	6	8	9	15.5	15.0
C150	✔		20.0	7	18	20	22.5	19.4
C151		✔	3.0	7	21	21	4.0	3.2
C152	✔		15.0	7	12	11	17.0	15.3
C160		✔	3.0	7	24	21	4.9	4.2
C167		✔	10.0	7	26	29	22.0*	11.5
C169		✔	3.0	7	21	21	3.8	3.4
C182	✔		5.0	7	10	9	5.5	4.0
C186	✔		3.0	7	12	14	3.5	3.2
C187		✔	10.0	8	22	29	24.0*	12.5
C192		✔	12.5	8	25	23	14.0	13.4
C193	✔		3.0	8	12	12	3.5	2.6
C194		✔	3.0	8	28	28	3.7	3.1
C204		✔	3.0	8	26	32	4.2	2.5
C207		✔	16.0	8	25	24	20.3	17.3
C222		✔	4.0	8	20	22	4.0	2.6
C231	✔		10.0	8	14	12	11.0	8.9

NOTES: Works order numbers C052, C150, and C194 were also cold rolled.

*Two separate rollings were necessary to achieve the required output (all or part of the first rolling was rejected by quality control).

EXHIBIT 10 **A Representative Sample of Deliveries from English Billets Plc for Standard Steel Specification Orders**

Steel Specification	Billet Size (mm)	Tons Ordered	Week Number		
			Ordered	Required	Received
PS 2000	100	250	25	36	44
PS 2000	120	105	25	36	34
PS 2000	130	85	25	36	38
PS 2000	150	80	25	36	35
PS 2000	190	130	25	36	34
PS 2000	250	270	25	36	32
XR 6	100	45	25	36	35
XR 7	110	45	27	37	38
XR 7	120	140	27	37	41
XR 7	140	150	27	37	40
XR 7	230	105	27	37	38
SA 270	70	55	27	37	38
SA 270	85	120	27	37	37
SA 270	100	80	27	37	34
SA 275x	70	40	27	37	42
SA 275x	100	20	27	37	41
SA 275x	120	20	27	37	40
PS 2000v	230	30	27	37	43
PS 2000x	250	35	27	37	41
PS 300	70	10	29	40	40
PS 300	100	40	29	40	38
PS 2000	70	115	29	40	42
PS 2000	85	60	30	40	42
PS 2000	170	40	30	40	43
PS 2000v	100	30	30	40	42
PS 2000v	120	35	30	40	40
XR 7	70	80	30	40	39
XR 7	85	90	30	40	41
XR 7	100	40	30	40	41

NOTE: 1. English Billet Plc is PSL's principal raw material supplier.

2. A standard steel is classed as such by PSL, if it has been processed previously, irrespective of the quantity used. This distinction from special steels signals the fact that manufacturing will have processing experience of the material, which will, in turn, lead to a reduction in problems and differences associated with one-off specials. Thus, actual process lead times are more in keeping with the norms used in lead-time calculations.

3. Most (especially the high-usage) standard steels are kept in stock by PSL at levels which relate to annual usage. Orders on suppliers to replenish stocks are then made in the normal way based upon reorder levels.

EXHIBIT 11   Representative Sample of Deliveries from English Billets Plc for Special Steels Ordered for Specific Jobs

Steel Specification	Billet Size (mm)	Tons Ordered	Week Number			Received Tonnage
			Ordered	Required	Received	
5Y102	100	28	27	37	40	22.2
SD204	70	4	27	36	36	3.1
BS840	200	32	29	35	40	30.2
DX6DM	170	16	29	35	36	15.8
DN34B	85	4	29	39	36	4.2
DN36	140	32	29	35	39	31.9
Spec 2a	250	100	29	36	40	97.2
DN8	70	8	29	39	40	8.7
PS37	120	6	30	39	37	7.9
804/10	190	12	30	40	37	8.5
DL10	190	32	30	40	40	34.8
SA520	100	16	30	40	44	17.5
DL12	100	4	30	40	36	3.5
Spec 3b	250	16	30	40	38	14.9
DN8D	140	4	30	41	42	5.1
DN474	170	28	31	41	41	29.3
C2138	190	24	31	41	37	23.1
C2138	120	20	31	44	46	20.1
MK200	230	120	32	38	37	116.4
550B20	120	12	32	44	45	11.9
D142	210	4	32	42	40	3.7
820x	85	90	32	42	45	105.0
D1020	170	4	32	44	42	4.4
D1020	130	4	32	44	42	4.6
540C10	70	8	32	44	42	7.9
DN8D	210	16	33	44	45	15.5
DN36	100	4	33	44	43	4.4
SA862	100	4	33	44	43	2.8
DX6DM	210	16	33	44	40	19.6

NOTES: 1. Special steels must be ordered in multiples of 4 tons up to 40 tons because of process restrictions (ingot sizes). The effective delivery tolerance on these orders is +/− 1 ton.

2. English Billets Plc is PSL's principal raw material supplier.

every month and are reported by the market category. Losses (some of which are unpredictable) arise from oxidation (scale losses), damage in the process plant, cutting losses in the finishing section, and quality rejects (dimensional, surface finish, and metallurgical). All losses are closely monitored and investigated. They are accounted for in the estimation procedure when calculating material requirements and order pricing. Yields currently used in these calculations are based on information gathered over the last 12 months, and average 92 percent for the electric motor and stockist steel sections markets and about 85 percent for customized sections.

Exhibit 12

Customer Order Clerical Processing Procedures

- Customer orders are received by post, telex, telefax, or telephone.
- They are passed to the administrative department specializing in electric motor, stockist, or customized sections.
- They are then technically and commercially appraised by experienced sales staff.
- Works orders and acknowledgment copies are raised, typed, and duplicated.
- These are sent for final approval by both the estimating and metallurgy departments.
- Works orders are then passed to the production planning office, where orders for special steel are raised (if appropriate) and all works orders are collated in order to prepare mill programs.

Note: An analysis of a representative sample of orders is provided as Exhibit 13.

Planning Procedures

Orders are received in the sales department, where they are recorded before being passed through to the production planning office. Exhibits 12 and 13 provide information on this activity. Orders are then collated by input height (i.e., billet size) required and loaded onto the hot mills within a four-week program.[4]

This results in steel sizes being processed once in each four-week cycle, in order to maintain agreed target levels of mill utilization. The procedure, therefore, is to sequence orders so as to minimize size of section changes and so reduce cumulative setup times within a cycle. Exhibit 14 shows a typical hot mill rolling program, while Exhibit 6 gives the key data for mills C and D regarding product range, output rates, and changeover times on which these programs will be established.

After the rolling stage, each order will then be routed according to the necessary finishing process operations to be completed. Jobs in excess of five tons will have to be split down after

---

[4]Thus, works orders for the same size (by the input height) of steel (the material specification is not normally a factor to be taken into account when compiling hot mill programs) are grouped together to provide as large a quantity to be rolled as possible. However, as volumes decline, programmed quantities in the same period will decline, especially where the delivery-speed element of a market is becoming important. In these latter situations, the steel will, of course, have to be programmed into the hot mills to meet the customer delivery date, rather than to meet the programming rules used in the planning department. This would lead to lower production volumes and/or more frequent mill changes. Furthermore, when cumulative orders for the same steel size have been rolled, the individual orders are then separated to follow their own routing through the remaining processes in line with each product specification.

EXHIBIT 13 **An Analysis of Customer-Order Clerical Processing Times, Representative Period**

	Average Time Elapsed—Working Days		
Market	*1*	*2*	*3*
Electric motor	1.1	1.9	n.a.
Stockist	2.5	2.5	n.a.
Customized special steels	5.3	4.2	2.1
Customized stock steels	5.7	3.8	n.a.

NOTES: 1. This information is based on a large sample of orders which was considered to be representative.

    2. The sales administration office is responsible for the processing and interpretation of customers' orders and the provision of checked works orders for production.

    3. The first part of this procedure is completed in the sales office and involves commercial appraisal and appropriate clerical tasks. The average elapsed time to complete these tasks is shown in column 1.

    4. The second part of this procedure is completed in the metallurgy and estimating departments for technical verification of a works order. The average elapsed time to complete these tasks is shown in column 2.

    5. The final part of this procedure is completed by the production planning office, where orders for special steels are raised. Column 3 shows the delay between this office receiving order details and the time when the order is placed; n.a. = not applicable.

hot rolling, due to the crane-lifting limitations detailed earlier. The result is that delays occur in later production stages, when supervisors from these sections have to regroup part orders prior to processing, in order to avoid additional setups.

Corporate Decisions and Future Markets

Brian Finn reflected:

> Looking back over the last decade clearly illustrates an overall volume decline in some markets. But we're in no worse a position than anyone else in this industry. In fact, looking outside our business reveals that we are doing quite well. Current return on net assets is 26 percent, which is well above average for the manufacturing companies within the Harbridge group. Our problem is deciding what to do in the future to maintain the business position and profit returns we currently enjoy, and have done for the last three years.
>
> The key, we are certain, lies in getting our marketing strategy right. Bill Carey and his team's work in this matter is both opportune and supportive of our ideas. One advantage of being in a near-monopoly position is that we work closely with our customers and hence get good feedback on our performance in the light of their needs.
>
> Overall our quality seems about right. A recent analysis showed few complaints, although we have recognized the need to improve the state of cleanliness of finished products, and capital investment has been sanctioned to install the necessary processes.

**EXHIBIT 14 Rolling Program—March,
Current Year**

	Billet Size—Input Steel Height (mm)	
Date	Mill C	Mill D
March		
1	250	70
2	150	70
3	150	70
4	140	70
8	140	70
9	110	85
10	110	85
11	120	85
14	130	100
15	130	100
16	130	100
17	190	100
18	140	100
21	140	100
22	150	70
23	150	70
24	170	70
25	170	120
28	250	120
29	230	120
30	210	85
31	110	85

NOTE: Also refer to the details on Exhibit 6, which gives the
characteristics of these two mills, including product
range, throughput rates, and changeover times.

On the delivery side, we get complaints from our customers, but I'm told it's not too bad. Mike Sotheby (the director of purchasing and planning) keeps me informed of likely areas for complaint as we are very aware that this is important to future business. We regularly get reports from the U.K. Stockists and Electric Motor Manufacturers Association. This allows us to compare our delivery performance with that of our European competitors. We certainly perform as well as they do. Our records show that we achieve about 95 percent of ordered tonnage[5] delivered on time or early.

In addition, there is also a delivery-speed factor creeping into some of our markets. Companies need deliveries quickly, and if we can meet their demands then we get the business. In these markets, the customer requires delivery in less than the "standard" lead-time calculations we use. These are becoming more frequent in the customized sections market, and it is most important that we succeed in this segment, as it is an essential part of our intended expansion in this market overall.

_____

[5]Note that in all markets, PSL contracts to supply (for each size) a customer order within plus or minus 1 ton of the quantity required for each size. Also, steel suppliers to PSL work within this convention.

The final issue is that of price. While some of our markets are price-sensitive (e.g., much of the stockist steel sections and particular Gambert Fabrique), many are not.[6] This is especially so in the customized sections market. Achieving these high margins, therefore, is important to us in terms of current and future performance. This is why we see areas of high-margin businesses as an important part of our portfolio. Bill Carey has put his finger on two and they will certainly be where we will start.

---

[6]Typical invoiced prices (ex-works) are shown in Exhibit 3, and some estimates of typical variable costs in Exhibit 4.

CASE 18
RANSOM ELECTRONIC PRODUCTS

"The problem is to increase the output from our manufacturing unit in Ransom Electronic Products (REP). It seems to me that what is required is the application of basic industrial engineering to the situation in order to get better bench layouts, work flow, materials handling, and so on. And, furthermore," continued Peter Bullen, chairman of Ransom Electronic Products, "we need to act quickly." Peter Bullen was addressing the board of directors of REP, a wholly owned subsidiary of Ransom Plc.[1] The other members of the board were Jim Latham, managing director, and Tony Richards, a nonexecutive director who was an executive with the principal company, Ransom Plc. This particular agenda item had been raised at an earlier meeting in February and had been formally minuted for this meeting in July.

Background

Ransom had started business in the field of electronics about 10 years before. Part of the original arrangements had been to subcontract the manufacture of "special" items for customers to a small, local company. As the company's sales grew, Ransom put money into the local subcontractor, leading to a 49 percent share of the business.

Five years ago the company bought out the remaining 51 percent of the shares (held by the original owner), and since that time it had operated as an independent but wholly owned subsidiary. The following year this subsidiary was renamed Ransom Electronic Products and was relocated into the same premises as its parent company.

Jim Latham has been with REP since it was partly owned by Ransom Plc. When it was bought out, the original owner stayed on for a few months and then eventually left. Jim Latham seemed the natural successor to run REP, and he took up the role as managing director in June of the same year.

Organization and Staffing

REP is a small production unit with some 13 staff members in addition to Jim Latham. Of these, 10 are full-time, while the other 3 (including one clerk/typist) work on a part-time basis. The actual attendance hours in the three months ended June 30 of this year and analyzed by main activities are given as Exhibit 1, while Exhibit 2 gives an organization chart for the company.

Of the 10 full-time employees, 7 work on a subcontract basis and are supplied by Skil Lab International Plc, who specialize in providing tradesmen and other specialist labor. REP had adopted this policy primarily because it found, and is still finding, difficulty in recruiting skilled labor; secondly, it allows flexibility in labor capacity, especially in the present situation of employee protection legislation.

At present, and for some time now, REP receives all its orders from Ransom, and it is not seen, at this stage, that this pattern will change. In fact, the increase in Ransom sales has been

---

[1]Plc means public limited company and in the United States equates to being incorporated.

This case was prepared by Professor T. J. Hill (London Business School). It is intended for class discussion and not as an illustration of good or bad management. © AMD Publishing (U.K.).

EXHIBIT 1   Attendance Hours in the Three Months Ended June 30 of the Current Year, Analyzed by Main Activities

	Recorded Hours During the Month			
Employee	*April*	*May*	*June*	*Total*
Metalwork				
F. Hurst	160	128	176	464
M. Abbott	160	144	160	464
D. Inskip	174.5	150.25	167.25	492
M. Jenner	—	—	80	80
	494.5	422.25	583.25	1,500
Assembly/Wire				
J. Latham	90	112	105	307
M. Tower	92	190.75	136	418.75
P. Dyer	90	94.5	90	274.5
M. Parkes	80	84	88	252
P. Hanlan	188	187	194	569
D. Gurner	184	159.25	225.5	568.75
F. Nott	—	139	14	153
D. Gray	—	—	155.5	155.5
	724	966.5	1,008	2,698.5
Test				
J. Lees	187.5	215.5	241	644
Total	1,406	1,604.25	1,832.25	4,842.5

NOTES: 1. Source: Skill Lab International Plc invoices, pay records, and internal time sheets.
2. J. Latham's hours reflect the estimated time he spent on productive work.
3. National holidays, annual holidays, and sickness have been deducted from the recorded available hours as appropriate to give attendance hours.
4. Mary Pickard is not included in the above information (see Exhibit 2).

significant over the last two years, and this is shown in the REP sales revenue figures for the past four years as given in Exhibit 3.

Product Mix

A recent analysis of the invoiced sales for the 12 months ended June 30[2] had been completed as a check on the split between "standard" and "special" products (see Exhibits 4 and 5). This revealed that over 95 percent of the work was made up of these two types of product, with the remainder consisting of repairs, refurbishing, and factored items. As Peter Bullen said, "It's the

---

[2]The financial year ends on December 31. However, as a check on current trends, the 12-month period to June 30 has been analyzed—see Note 5 to Exhibit 3.

EXHIBIT 2   Organization Chart for Ransom Electronic Products

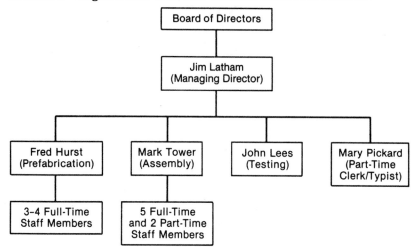

NOTE: Mary Pickard works the other part of her day for Ransom Plc.

same picture as for previous years, and I see little change in the future. We are in the 'standards market' supplying over 60 percent to Ransom from our standard catalogue.''

Performance

Sales had grown steadily in the last four years (see Exhibit 3), but in the latter part of last year and during the first six months of this year demand had risen sharply.

When a sales order was received from Ransom, the first task was to estimate the labor and material content of the work involved. For standard items, past labor estimates were used, but for specials, estimates were agreed between the planning function of Ransom and Jim Latham. The labor estimates for the work completed in the period April to June of this year, together with the March work in process already completed on sales in these months and the June work in process completed for items to be finished from July onward are given in Exhibit 6. It was considered that no work in process from any months previous to March related to April, May, and June sales.

Working Arrangements

Although REP was legally a separate company within the Ransom group it was, in principle, a small production unit almost totally captive to supplying the needs of its parent company. On the one hand, this had the advantage of providing a full order book, without any sales effort, and keeping the sales and manufacturing functions separate in terms of pressures and changes, while on the other hand, enjoying the link between sales and manufacturing experienced in a normal corporate situation.

The philosophy toward pricing also reflected this relationship in that the profit set for REP was one of making a small profit at the end of each year. It was intended that the profit for the

---

EXHIBIT 3   REP's Balance Sheet and Profit/Loss Statement for the last Five Years (£000x)

	Current Year Minus				Current Year
	4	*3*	*2*	*1*	
Fixed Assets	5.7	13.3	10.2	10.0	9.7
Current assets					
Inventory	10.2	14.5	13.6	19.7	30.1
Debtors	0.7	0.3	1.0	0.8	0.3
Cash	—	0.1	0.1	0.1	0.1
Amount due from holding company	16.7	6.8	8.0	11.9	44.8
Total	33.3	35.0	32.9	42.5	85.0
Capital and retained profits	4.7	3.6	6.6	10.7	24.3
Loan from holding company	12.0	13.2	13.2	13.2	13.2
Current liabilities					
Creditors	11.7	11.5	9.8	14.2	27.8
Bank	4.9	6.7	3.3	4.4	19.7
Total	33.3	35.0	32.9	42.5	85.0
Sales	64.3	68.2	66.6	90.3	163.8
Less cost of goods sold	25.7	39.8	44.4	50.4	79.7
Gross profit	38.6	28.4	22.2	39.9	84.1
Direct expenses					
Labor	17.9	16.1	20.9	33.4	72.7
Tools	1.7	0.9	0.9	0.6	1.6
Workshop	0.3	0.2	0.1	0.2	0.2
Depreciation	0.8	1.3	0.7	0.5	0.8
R&D	1.1	0.5	0.1	—	—
Delivery	0.2	0.1	0.1	—	—
Net profit	16.6	9.3	(0.6)	5.2	9.0

NOTES: 1. Fixed assets are net of depreciation.

2. All sales figures are net of commission.

3. All figures have been rounded.

4. The current year's figures are projected on the basis of the first six months of trading up to June 30.

5. The financial year ends on December 31. Information in this case refers to the 12-month period to June 30 as the most recent set of figures for a 12-month period.

group would be made at the sales point in the company and not shared between manufacturing and sales.

As explained earlier, there existed an important link between the project engineers of Ransom and REP. The procedure was that a salesman requested a quotation for a job. A project engineer would then discuss the requirements with the salesman and produce a drawing of the job, together with any other information relevant to manufacturing the system and equipment. Then the project engineer would discuss these requirements with Jim Latham in order to determine:

Month	Standard £s			Special £s			Repair (cum.) £s	Factor (cum.) £s	Total £s	
	Act.	Cum.	Total Cum. %	Act.	Cum.	Total Cum. %			Act.	Cum.
July	3,900	3,900	62	2,200	2,200	35	—	200	6,300	6,300
August	5,900	9,800	58	3,000	5,200	31	—	1,800	10,600	16,900
September	2,100	11,900	45	7,500	12,700	48	—	2,000	9,700	26,600
October	7,000	18,900	54	1,400	14,100	40	100	2,200	8,700	35,300
November	3,700	22,600	55	1,900	16,000	39	100	2,300	5,700	41,000
December	6,900	29,500	59	900	16,900	34	100	3,000	8,600	49,600
January	3,600	33,100	61	800	17,700	33	100	3,100	4,600	54,200
February	7,300	40,400	60	5,500	23,200	35	200	3,100	12,800	67,000
March	3,600	44,000	61	1,600	24,800	34	300	3,200	5,400	72,400
April	1,700	45,700	59	4,000	28,800	37	300	3,200	5,700	78,100
May	9,900	55,600	63	200	29,000	33	400	3,400	10,300	88,400
June	6,700	62,300	62	5,000	34,000	34	400	3,500	11,800	100,200
Total	62,300	62,300	62	34,000	34,000	34	400	3,500	100,200	100,200

NOTES: 1. All values have been rounded to the nearest £100.

2. Source: J. Latham.

3. The columns for "Repair" and "Actual" only show cumulative values. Therefore, the total actual will not add up to the analyzed values because actual sales (except for July last year) are not given for "Repair" and "Factor" (factored items) sales.

4. Act. = actual, and cum. = cumulative.

Exhibit 5

Standard Products Ordered in the 12 Months Ended June 30 of This Year

During this 12-month period, 150 orders for standard products were received from Ransom Plc. The total number of standard products requested in these 150 orders was 86, and the frequency with which each product was ordered is shown below.

Number of Standard Products	Number of Orders Received for Each Standard Product	% of Total Orders Received
56	1	65
19	2	22
8	3–5	10
2	6–10	2
1	10+	1
86	150	100

Exhibit 6

Estimated Productive Work Relating to the Period April 1 to June 30 of This Year

The details below relate to the amount of work invoiced.

Taken from relevant invoice details in the period April 1 to June 30, the figures represent the amount of work by manufacturing category, invoiced during this period. In addition, details are given on the amount of work in process carried over at March 31 and also the amount that was in the system at June 30.

Period	Metalwork	Assembly/Wire	Test
March work in process	437.50	323.00	—
April sales	149.50	250.75	12.50
May sales	401.75	867.33	52.50
June sales	164.50	558.25	231.41
June work in process	421.50	226.25	—

NOTES: 1. All figures are in hours.

2. It was considered that no work in process from months up to and including February related to the April–June sales figures above.

3. The June work-in-process figures relate to work completed in the above period, but the "value" for this work would not be seen in the form of invoiced sales until July onward, when the items, once completed, would be delivered, then invoiced in the usual way.

1. Labor estimates and, from these, labor costs for each stage in manufacturing (including test).
2. Material estimates.
3. Delivery dates.

On this basis, a quotation would be prepared for submission to the customer. Those quotations accepted by customers were passed internally from project engineering (Ransom) to purchasing (Ransom). A purchase order was prepared and sent through to Jim Latham in REP. Jim Latham would then add this purchase order to his file of outstanding orders. Each month, orders completed formed the basis of an invoice from REP to Ransom. Part-completed work would not be invoiced; however, where there was more than one item on the purchase order and one or more of these were completed, then these would be delivered and invoiced in the normal way.

Currently, there are still only two project engineers based at Ransom who have responsibility for the task described here. A problem experienced, however, was that the information link between sales (Ransom), project engineering (Ransom), and manufacturing (REP) was becoming increasingly less defined. This was due to a lack of time, more complicated specials quoted for, and the increase in marketing effort, resulting in more enquiries/quotations being required. In addition, the sales value of orders was increasing (one current quotation was five to six times larger than any currently received and processed). On the whole, this increase in sales value was

EXHIBIT 7   **Total Labor Hour Comparison between Quoted and Actual for Six Recently Completed "Large Specials"**

Order Number	Metalwork		Assembly/Wire		Test		Planning		Total	
	Quoted	*Actual*	*Quoted*	*Actual*	*Quoted*	*Actual*	*Quoted*	*Actual*	*Quoted*	*Actual*
A 6791	8	80	32	56	8	8	8	8	56	152
A 5522	3	45	50	170	5	40	5	8	63	263
A 6690	2	4	20	24	—	4	3	5	25	37
A 5495	10	120	160	150	80	150	20	20	270	440
A 4940	10	5	6	6	—	0.5	3	2	19	13.5
A 4527	1.5	4	5	24	—	4	—	2	6.5	34
Total	34.5	258	273	430	93	206.5	39	45	439.5	939.5

NOTES: 1. Source: Jim Latham and project engineering (Ransom).

2. Actual hours were estimated by Jim Latham and the staff concerned.

3. The specials analyzed were chosen on the basis of value (£s) and information availability.

4. The hours compared above are the total for the order—for the order number A6791, the quantity was 8, but all other specials were singles.

5. These specials were representative of more recent orders.

due to the fact that the specials were more complex. The more complex the order, then the more intricate was the manufacturing process, particularly at the assembly/wire stage.

It appeared that due to the pressure on project engineers described here, there had been a significant increase in the interpreting, redesigning, and development tasks of the REP staff when assembling and wiring a job. An additional factor experienced in the last six to nine months was that the customer and/or salesman were requesting modifications during the manufacturing stage. This added to the problem referred to earlier where manufacturing (REP) had to resolve these definitions, overcome problems in design, and agree to changes and modifications in the original design, in order to ensure that the specification would be met. This "defining" process was taken into account at the labor estimation stage, although it was difficult to fully appreciate what was needed until the requirements had been provided by information giving detailed design and specifications (see Exhibit 7).

At the moment, Jim Latham undertook a part "working on the manufacturing side of the product" and part management role within REP. This suited him well as he considered that he was able to keep a finger on the pulse at both ends of the organization (see Exhibit 1).

Forward Load

Sales for the 12 months to June of this year had been just over £100,000. This had represented an increase on the previous year (Exhibit 3), but the future requirement was estimated as being much higher. In order to assess the extent of the increased demand in the future months, the present outstanding orders (net of any work already completed and so falling into the category of work in process) were analyzed to extract this information. Working from his outstanding order file and from the original labor estimate agreed with project engineering (Ransom), Jim Latham compiled the information given in Exhibit 8.

The details relate only to those orders required in July and August this year. For orders required from September onward, the relevant outstanding file plus some recently confirmed sales

EXHIBIT 8   **Estimated Outstanding Work at June 30**

Purchase Order	Quantity	Item	Metalwork Each	Metalwork Total	Assembly/Wire Each	Assembly/Wire Total	Test Each	Test Total	Total Estimated Work
A6775	500	A025	—	—	0.50	250.00	.17	83.00	333.00
A8033	8	Special	30.00	240.00	160.00	1,280.00	40.00	320.00	1,840.00
A8099	1	2 VPR systems	2.00	2.00	2.00	2.00	0.50	0.50	4.50
A8035	39	126 box	2.00	78.00	3.00	117.00	0.50	19.50	214.50
A8362	1	2/3 Con 240 V	—	—	1.00	1.00	0.25	0.25	1.25
A8621	1	MTD system	60.00	60.00	—	—	—	—	60.00
A8787	12	1540	4.00	48.00	5.00	60.00	0.50	6.00	114.00
A8788	3	Specials	3.00	9.00	—	—	—	—	9.00
A8856	1	Box/2 bridge SW	10.00	10.00	30.00	30.00	2.00	2.00	42.00
A8910	1	Special	—	—	6.00	6.00	1.00	1.00	7.00
A9016	6	Unit/DC	1.00	6.00	3.00	18.00	0.50	3.00	27.00
A9016	6	Unit/mains	1.00	6.00	2.00	12.00	0.50	3.00	21.00
A9025	8	N/D system	4.00	32.00	5.00	40.00	0.50	4.00	76.00
A9055	2,000	Clips	0.08	160.00	—	—	—	—	167.00
A9001	20	127 box	2.00	40.00	—	—	—	—	40.00
A9123	12	A/6 control	5.00	60.00	40.00	480.00	1.00	12.00	552.00
A9123	50	130 control	5.00	250.00	4.00	200.00	0.50	25.00	475.00
A9123	10	Standard	2.00	20.00	1.00	10.00	0.25	2.50	32.50
A9123	6	150 standard	2.00	12.00	10.00	60.00	0.50	3.00	75.00
A9123	1	70A	—	—	3.00	3.00	0.25	0.25	3.25
A9163	1	Special	10.00	10.00	30.00	30.00	3.00	3.00	43.00
A9190	1	Special	5.00	5.00	15.00	15.00	2.00	2.00	22.00
A9198	1	Standard	—	—	2.00	2.00	0.50	0.50	2.50
A9217	2	SLO	—	—	2.00	4.00	0.50	1.00	5.00
A9218	25	Control	2.00	50.00	8.00	200.00	1.00	25.00	275.00
A9232	20	N/D	8.00	160.00	5.00	100.00	0.50	10.00	270.00
A9235	50	400 PCB	—	—	—	—	—	—	—
A9240	1	150 standard control	2.00	2.00	11.00	11.00	0.50	0.50	13.50
A9795	8	6-1A	5.00	40.00	3.00	24.00	0.25	2.00	66.00
A9263	2	Special	—	—	25.00	50.00	2.00	4.00	54.00
A9284	1	Special	8.00	8.00	—	—	—	—	8.00
A9303	3	8-123	5.00	15.00	3.00	9.00	0.25	0.75	24.75
A9330	10	306	2.00	20.00	6.00	60.00	0.50	5.00	85.00
A9355	1	Modification	—	—	2.00	2.00	0.50	0.50	2.50
A9361	6	6-20	5.00	30.00	30.00	180.00	1.00	6.00	216.00
A9280	10	Control	1.00	10.00	3.00	30.00	0.50	5.00	45.00
A9405	150	Plates	0.80	12.50	—	—	—	—	12.50
A9415	1	126D	—	—	2.00	2.00	0.25	0.25	2.25
A9418	2	Special	30.00	60.00	15.00	30.00	4.00	8.00	98.00
A9425	10	Control	2.00	20.00	3.00	30.00	0.50	5.00	55.00
A9426	1	Special	15.00	15.00	30.00	30.00	2.00	2.00	47.00
A9428	1	Modification	0.50	0.50	—	—	—	—	0.50
A9429	1	Special	—	—	4.00	4.00	1.00	1.00	5.00
A9432	1	123 control	3.00	3.00	8.00	8.00	1.00	1.00	12.00
A9443	1	10A1	5.00	5.00	3.00	3.00	0.50	0.50	8.50
A9443	2	Special	15.00	30.00	30.00	60.00	2.00	4.00	94.00
A9443	1	Box	4.00	4.00	6.00	6.00	1.00	1.00	11.00
		Total		1,540.00		3,459.00		573.00	5,572.00

EXHIBIT 9   Order and Delivery Situation on Known Significant Orders as of July 1 for the Period September This Year to March Next Year

Month Required	Total Sales Value (£s)
September	21,500
October	18,700
November	17,300
December	14,200
January	12,000
February	12,000
March	12,000

EXHIBIT 10   An Analysis of the Estimated Labor Capacity Available in the Period September This Year to March Next Year

Aspect	This Year				Next Year		
	September	October	November	December	January	February	March
Number of working days	21	22	22	16	22	20	22
Basic hours including estimated overtime	1,685	2,456	2,624	1,984	2,720	2,496	2,720
Known/estimated holidays or absenteeism	—	—	128	10	120	80	120
Net hours available	1,685	2,456	2,496	1,974	2,600	2,416	2,600

NOTES: 1. Basic hours include test.

2. Source: Jim Latham

orders (the internal paperwork for which was still in the pipeline, provided by the project manager in charge of project engineering in Ransom) were analyzed in terms of their sales invoice value; the details are given in Exhibit 9. Also, an estimate of the number of working days available in these months is given as Exhibit 10.

In addition, Exhibit 11 outlines the possible production capacity (£s) available by transferring responsibility for some manufacture to one of the existing Ransom locations in Market Drayton (Shropshire), some 120 miles away. The reason behind this proposal is that both the company and Skil Lab International are finding it very difficult to recruit skilled assembly and wiring staff who are able to cope with the requirements of the work on hand. This is increasingly the situation with regard to specials, and Jim Latham considers that the most recently quoted-for specials will add significantly to the skill levels demanded at this stage in the process. "Even the staff provided by Skil Lab," commented Jim Latham, "often require training in what, to some, is a different and higher-level range of work. The trouble is that we can then only hope that they are happy to stay with Skil Lab, and also with us."

The sharp increase in demand had led to a growing concern, and that is why this point had been tabled for the July meeting.

EXHIBIT 11   Estimated Production That Would Be Available from the Ransom Location at Market Drayton

Month	Outputs (£s)
September	600
October	—
November	1,300
December	900
January	1,300
February	1,300
March	1,300

NOTES: 1. All the space requirements at Market Drayton are available.

2. Production could not start until September of this year.

3. Initially, this production facility would take part-completed work from REP and finish it (hence £600 value in September).

4. From October, the new production unit would start the work from the beginning and this (plus the training needs required) would result in little output in this month.

5. The difficulties of recruiting, training, and retaining staff have been carefully considered and taken into account at arriving at what are considered to be realistic estimates.

6. No one at this new unit has had production experience before. Consequently, someone from REP and/or Ransom would visit the site on two days a week.

CASE 19
REMINGTON PRODUCTS, INC.

In early 1985, Walter DiGiovanni, president of Worldwide Manufacturing Operations for Remington Products, Inc., was considering the problems and opportunities associated with the production of a new electric shaver (see Exhibit 1). The so-called "traveler" shaver would give Remington a low-priced, battery-operated model (currently not in the line) and strengthen the company's ability to penetrate overseas markets, particularly in the Far East. DiGiovanni was most concerned with where and how the product was to be manufactured. He believed Remington could make the travel shaver in the company's only plant in Connecticut; however, he had also approached representatives in Hong Kong and the People's Republic of China concerning the prospect of establishing a facility in one of their respective countries. If Remington opted for either China or Hong Kong, DiGiovanni pondered how best to enter the country and wondered what effect the decision would have on the company's present marketing, personnel, and manufacturing strategies. He had to act soon, because Victor Kiam, Remington's chairman, wanted the travel shaver to be the core item in a line of travel-related appliances scheduled for introduction in the spring of 1986.

Company Background

Remington Products, Inc. was the only electric shaver manufacturer with a production facility in the United States. The first Remington electric shaver was actually introduced to the U.S. market in 1937 by Remington Rand, an established New York City–based manufacturer of typewriters and office equipment at the time. In 1955, Remington Rand merged with the Sperry Corporation, and in 1965 the shaver business was established as a separate division. During the 1950s and 1960s, Remington led the U.S. electric shaver field, but by the 1970s, increased foreign competition and poor marketing forced Remington's market share to fall significantly. In the three years from 1976 through 1978, the division consequently lost $30 million.

In March of 1979, Sperry sold Remington to Victor Kiam, who structured the acquisition as a leveraged buyout. Following the acquisition, Kiam quickly set out to improve cash flow and the company's outdated marketing practices. Within his first week, Kiam trimmed $2 million from the payroll, firing 70 executives and keeping only the key operating personnel in each functional area, including manufacturing. See Exhibits 2 and 3 for organizational charts.

Kiam, who had over 30 years of consumer products marketing experience with products as diverse as toothpaste, watches, and bras, took personal control of the marketing area and instituted three major changes. First, he focused on the company's principal product, electric shavers, and did away with unprofitable items such as curlers and hair dryers. Second, to gain advantage from the relatively low value of the U.S. dollar at the time, he reduced the prices of the shavers. Previously, Remington had been quick to match any price increase from competitors. Third, he radically increased advertising expenditures to reestablish awareness of the

This case was prepared by E. Gilhuly, N. E. Karstaedt, and V. K. Kiam III under the direction of Visiting Associate Professor Kasra Ferdows, as a basis for class discussion rather than to illustrate either effective or ineffective handling of an administrative situation. Certain data in this case have been disguised to protect proprietary information. Reprinted with permission of Stanford University Graduate School of Business, © 1986 the Board of Trustees of the Leland Stanford Junior University.

EXHIBIT 1   Remington Cordless Travel Shaver

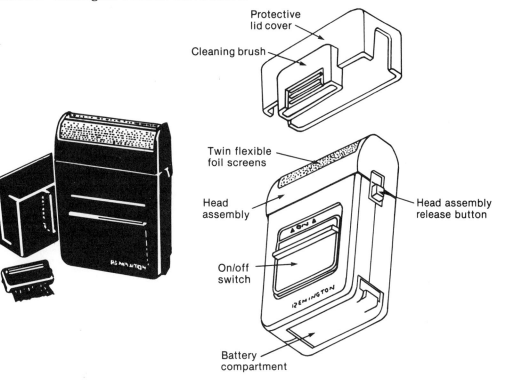

Remington name. As part of this new emphasis on advertising, Kiam starred in the company's television commercials claiming: "I was so delighted and impressed with the Remington shaver, I bought the company."

Kiam's actions had an immediate effect. In the first year Remington showed a profit of $1.5 million, and every year since then sales and profits increased. In 1979 Remington sold 1.6 million shavers generating revenues of $47 million; by 1984 Remington was selling nearly 4 million shavers with sales totaling over $130 million. Pretax profit by 1984 reached $8 million (see Exhibit 4). This dramatic increase in profitability allowed Remington to pay off the majority of the acquisition debt in less than three years.

In 1985 Remington offered eight basic men's shaver models (including a shaver for a black man's beard and a high-priced, battery model) and two ladies' models as well as a whole line of shaving accessories, including preshave, cleaning products and replacement parts. The wholesale price for each model was set relative to the competitive models, most of which had only recently been introduced (see Exhibit 5). Remington preferred to sell higher-priced shavers because they provided more gross margin dollars, which were necessary to support the company's extensive advertising expenditures, projected at $20 million for 1985. On average, advertising expense accounted for a significant portion of the wholesale price of a shaver.

In addition to the shavers, Remington had introduced a variety of other consumer electrical appliances including an air purifier, a pool alarm, and an air fragrance machine, but these had all met with limited success. Kiam was actively seeking new markets and stable new products

EXHIBIT 2   Remington Products, Inc., Corporate Staff

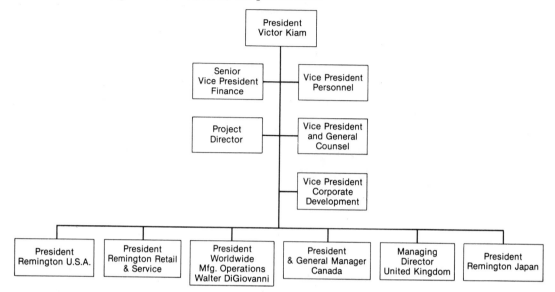

EXHIBIT 3   Remington Products, Inc., Worldwide Manufacturing Operations

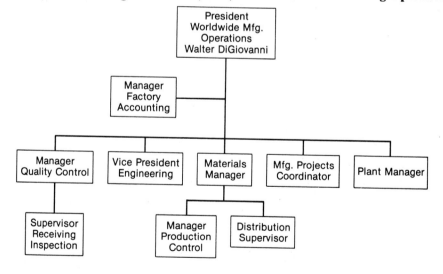

EXHIBIT 4   Remington Products, Inc., Selected Financial Data ($ millions)

	1980	1984
Sales	$47.0	$130.0
NIBT	1.5	8.0
Assets	26.0	80.0
Equity	0.5	22.0

EXHIBIT 5A   Rechargeable Models Shaver Price Grid

Model	Company	Description	5/4/83	11/14/83	5/1/84	1985	
HP-1328	Norelco	Deluxe Rotatract—alum., 9 settings, AC/DC	$52.99	$52.99	$52.99	$54.99	(1328E quick charge—special, $23.75)
3525	Braun	System 1-2-3—quick charge, silver				52.99	
3512	Braun	System 1-2-3—quick charge, black				47.25	
XLR-3000	Remington	Microscreen—AC/DC	44.98	44.98	44.98	46.98	
HP-1327D	Norelco	Rotatract—black	44.99	44.99	44.99	44.99	
3012	Braun	System 1-2-3				38.75	
HP-1337	Norelco	Rotatract—black stand, AC/DC			37.99	37.99	With stand
RR-1	Ronson	Rotary, AC/DC, 10 settings			37.99	37.99	Rebate $10.00
XLR-900	Remington	Microscreen—AC/DC	37.99	37.99	37.99	37.99	Add stand
F-40	Schick	Total Touch—AC/DC, quick charge				35.75	
F-34	Schick	Total Touch			37.99	30.00	Special, $23.75
RFD-1	Ronson	Foil, AC/DC, 52 blades			29.99	29.99	Rebate $5.00
RR-3	Ronson	Rotary, 48 blades			29.99	29.99	
SM-400	Remington	Super Mesh			28.98	$28.98	Add stand and pouch
HP-1320	Norelco	Rotary—9 settings, AC/DC				28.49	Anniversary item
RFS-1	Ronson	Single head foil, 36 blades, AC/DC				23.32	Rebate $5.00
RFS-3	Ronson	Single head foil, 36 blades				19.77	Rebate $5.00

to diversify the overall product line, because he believed the strong growth of Remington's domestic electric shaver business over the previous five years would be difficult to sustain. This was particularly true given growth projections for the domestic market and the market penetration gains already achieved. The domestic market was projected to grow at a compound annual rate of 3–5 percent for the next five years. However, Kiam believed Remington did have the potential to increase international sales and market share dramatically, especially if the U.S. dollar was to weaken.

Industry Background

By 1985, Remington was firmly established as the number two company in the U.S. electric shaver market, slightly behind the industry leader, Norelco. From 1978 to 1984 Remington's

EXHIBIT 5B   Cord Models Shaver Price Grid

Model	Company	Description	5/4/83	11/14/83	5/1/84	1985	
HP-1606	Norelco	Deluxe Rotatract Tripleheader—AC/DC	$42.99	$42.99	$42.99	$42.99	
3025	Braun	Electronic System 1-2-3				42.99	
3012	Braun	System 1-2-3				38.75	
HP-1605	Norelco	Rotatract Tripleheader—AC/DC, black	35.99	35.99	35.99	35.99	
HP-1604	Norelco	Rotatract Tripleheader—AC/DC, black			31.99	31.99	
HP-1135	Norelco	Tripleheader Rotary—AC/DC, black/chrome	28.99	28.99	28.99	discontinued, 1 free with 11	
XLR-800	Remington	Microscreen	28.98	26.48	26.48	26.48	
2101	Braun	Cord Shaver				24.99	
F-29	Schick	Deluxe Total Touch—AC/DC, silver/gold			30.99	24.00	
RR-2	Ronson	Rotary—10 settings			29.99	23.32	
F-25	Schick	Total Touch—AC/DC, chrome			25.99	21.00	
RFD-2	Ronson	Foil, AC/DC			19.99	19.77	10% DFI
RR-4	Ronson	Rotary				19.77	
F-21	Schick	Total Touch—AC/DC, black			19.79	19.25	Special, $15.24
HP-1615	Norelco	Tripleheader Rotary (repl. 1135)—AC/DC			24.99	18.99	
SM-200	Remington	Super Mesh			17.98	17.98	
PM-750	Remington	Triple Action	17.98	17.98	15.45	15.45	
RFS-2	Ronson	Foil			14.99	14.99	
F-15	Schick	Total Touch—AC, black				14.20	
HP-1622	Norelco	Speed Razor—AC/DC, (repl. 1620)				13.99	
HP-1620	Norelco	Speed Razor—2-head, black	17.99	17.99	17.99	9.00	Closeout

EXHIBIT 5C   Ladies' Models Shaver Price Grid

Model	Description	5/4/83	11/14/83	5/1/84	1985	
HP-2124	Chic Salon	$29.99	$29.99	$29.99		
HP-2132	Chic Deluxe	19.99	19.99	19.99		
HP-2131	Chic Razor	17.99	17.99	17.99		
WER-4000	Lady Remington	17.48	17.98	17.98		
WER-6000	Lady Remington Rechargeable	26.98	26.98	26.98	$26.98	
HP-2615	Satin Rechargeable (Norelco)			24.99	24.99	
LR-3	Lady Ronson Single Rotary				23.32	Rebate $5.00
HP-2612	Norelco Satin, AC/DC				19.99	
HP-2611	Norelco Satin, AC/DC				17.99	
LT-2	Lady Ronson Twin Rotary—Slot				14.99	
LS-17	Schick Lite Touch Cord			14.99	14.25	
HP-2207	Chic Battery	12.99	12.99	12.99		
HP-2602	Chic Battery			12.99		
LS-12P	Schick Lite Touch Cord			11.99	11.50	
LS-10	Schick Lite Touch Battery			9.79	9.00	
HP-2603	Norelco Chic Battery				7.99	
ELEG3	Braun Elegance 3				23.99	
ELEG2	Braun Elegance 2				21.00	

EXHIBIT 6   U.S. Market Shares—Men's and Women's Shavers

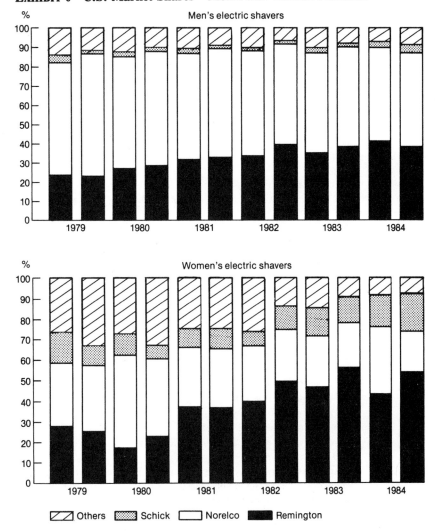

share of market in men's shavers jumped from just over 20 percent to 38 percent; in the ladies' market Remington was the market leader with a 45 percent share (see Exhibit 6). In 1984, four out of every five shavers sold were men's razors. The overall electric shaver market had grown at a compound annual rate of 6 percent over the past five years. Much of this growth was attributable to aggressive advertising designed to persuade electric shaver users that the Remington Microscreen shaver had excellent performance characteristics in shaving as close as a blade.

Remington's major competitors in the domestic market were subsidiaries or divisions of large multinational corporations, all of whom manufactured their shavers overseas (see Exhibit 7). Norelco and Schick, the two largest competitors in the U.S. market, were both owned by N. V. Phillips, a Dutch conglomerate with sales of $22 billion. Norelco had manufacturing

EXHIBIT 7   Plant Locations of Major Electric Shaver Manufacturers

Company	Factory Location
Remington	United States
N. V. Phillips (Norelco)	Holland, Austria, Japan
Braun/Eltron	Germany, Japan
Ronson	Austria (from Payerlux) Japan (from Azumi)
Sunbeam	Austria (from Payerlux)
Schick	Austria
Sanyo	Japan
Hitachi	Japan
Toshiba	Japan
Panasonic	Japan
Lowenstar (new entry)	Korea
Sears	Japan (from Azumi)
Calor	France
Payerlux	Austria

SOURCE: Remington Products, Inc.

facilities in Holland, Austria, and Japan, while Schick was produced exclusively in Phillips's Austrian facility. Braun, a West German-based subsidiary of Gillette (1984 revenues of $3 billion), had a strong position in the high-end European market and was beginning a major push into the U.S. market. Braun's manufacturing facilities were located in Germany and Japan. In addition to the European-based competitors, four Japanese companies, Hitachi, Sanyo, Toshiba, and Panasonic, had electric shaver divisions. Although these Japanese competitors had not made significant inroads in the U.S. market, they loomed as a potential threat. All these competitors could rely on the large capital base of their parents to fund advertising and R&D expenditures, whereas Remington, although the industry leader in dollars spent on advertising, relied primarily on external financing. In addition, by manufacturing overseas, these companies currently enjoyed the advantage of the strong dollar, which made their products relatively inexpensive in the U.S. market.

Significant barriers to entry existed in the U.S. market. First, brand recognition and loyalty were extremely high among electric shaver users. A competitor coming into the market consequently needed a substantial advertising budget to gain brand awareness and build a large customer base of repeat purchasers. Second, the retail trade was wary of taking on a new shaver line because of the strong relationships they already had with Remington and Norelco. Products of both companies were heavily promoted, attracting increased customer traffic into the retail outlets, which made retailers reluctant to experiment with new brands. A new competitor would have to spend heavily (through cooperative advertising or special discounts) to break into this channel. Lastly, the shavers currently available on the market were of such high quality that new models would have to compete largely on price or design features.

In the international arena, Remington was not as well positioned. Of the total world market for electric shavers (excluding small battery models), Remington had little less than 16 percent share. The company was third in world production behind Phillips and Braun (see Exhibit 8). Although overall world market growth was projected to be flat, demand in specific countries was expected to increase. These countries were Canada, United Kingdom, Japan, and the United States. The size of each of these markets differed. Also due to cultural distinctions,

EXHIBIT 8   Estimated 1985 Shipments of Electric Shavers by Manufacturer

Manufacturer	Units Shipped (millions)	Percent Total
Phillips	11.0	45.8%
Braun	5.0	20.8
Remington	3.8	15.8
Japanese (Hitachi, Panasonic, Toshiba, Sanyo)	3.0	12.5
Azumi (Ronson, Sears)	0.5	2.1
Payerlux (Ronson, Sunbeam)	0.4	1.7
Calor	0.3	1.3
Total	24.0	100%

NOTE: Excludes small battery-operated shavers.

SOURCE: Remington Products, Inc.

EXHIBIT 9   Estimated Usage of Wet and Dry Shaving in Selected Countries

Country	Dry Shaving	Wet Shaving
Sweden	90%	10%
Germany	75	25
Japan*	70	30
Austria	50	50
Switzerland	50	50
United Kingdom*	45	55
France	45	55
Canada*	40	60
Italy	33	67
Spain	33	67
United States*	30	70
Australia	25	75

NOTE: *countries where dry market is growing at significant rate.

SOURCE: Remington Products Inc.

countries varied considerably as to the percentage of men who used the "dry" electric shaving system versus the "wet blade system" (see Exhibit 9).

Approximately 20 percent of Remington's production was exported, primarily to Canada, Europe, and Australia, with some sales in the Middle East, Africa, and the Far East. The company's market share in most of these areas was not very high. The primary impediment was the strong American dollar, which had forced up the retail price of Remington's shavers in foreign currency. For example, the British pound in March 1980 was valued at $2.40; in February 1985 it hit a low of $1.03, a decline of 57 percent. As a result, Remington's retail shaver price in England doubled. Lackluster sales in Europe were also attributable to high brand loyalty and the established customer base of the two preeminent European manufacturers, Phillips and Braun.

In the Far East, and Japan in particular, Remington shavers did not sell well because the product was designed to shave a heavy Western beard and was too powerful for the more delicate Oriental whiskers. Further, even without the currency disadvantage, Remington's shavers were relatively high priced compared to the models typically purchased by Oriental customers. Approximately six million electric shavers were sold in the Japanese market in 1984, one sixth of which were of the variety produced by Remington, Norelco, and the like. The remaining five million were smaller, battery-operated models. Remington's sales in the Japanese market amounted to only 35,000 units.

U.S. Manufacturing

Remington currently produced all its electric shavers in a 235,000-square-foot facility in Bridgeport, Connecticut. Under the Sperry ownership, Remington had operated additional facilities in Scotland, France, and Singapore, but upon the change in ownership, these were closed. The Bridgeport facility was originally built as a car factory in the 1920s but had subsequently been expanded several times. In 1985 the average age of the machines in the plant was 10 years. Many of the machines and almost all tooling was designed in-house. The capacity of the Bridgeport facility depended somewhat on the product mix, but during a typical eight-hour shift up to 20,000 shavers could be produced. The plant was generally run for one eight-hour shift, five days a week. While many shavers shared certain operations, setup times for change of model on most equipment had been reduced to 30 seconds or less.

The most important components in the shaver were the cutting system (made up of the cutter and screen) and the motor. To manufacture the cutters, rolls of steel were machine stamped into rough blades, which were then flattened and sharpened in special machines. In turn these blades were fitted together to form the cutter unit and then passed through a cleaning system. Unfinished screens were purchased from suppliers and formed into a double foil in a unique, proprietary process. The thinness of the screen, just 0.002 inches, and its uniform quality were essential factors affecting the performance of the final product. In a separate area of the plant, two types of motors (linear and permanent magnetic) were manufactured using variable speed presses to punch out the necessary parts, which were then assembled on a production line. The speed and power of the motor, which caused the cutter to vibrate back and forth, were also crucial determinants of product performance. The motor in Remington's top-of-the-line shaver was the most powerful in the industry, averaging 8,800 revolutions per minute.

The cutters, screens, and motors were tested and then transferred to the assembly area in hand-carried plastic bins. A series of transport conveyors moved the parts through workstations where they were assembled along with the electric cords and plastic molding into finished products. The various processes were well balanced so that bottlenecks only occurred when a line broke down or workers ran out of materials. However, operators were in place to control the conveyors, and these operators had the benefit of a console that electronically indicated which stations were in need of material. When running smoothly, the Remington line could produce a shaver (from raw materials to finished unit) in 15 minutes.

Finished units were packaged, shrink wrapped in plastic (to prevent theft), and moved via a continuous belt conveyor from the final assembly area to the finished goods warehouse for shipment. Remington had no other warehouse facility, and all customer orders, both domestic and international, were filled directly from Bridgeport. Finished goods inventory accounted for a third of total inventory, which averaged approximately $9 million.

DiGiovanni was constantly trying to improve inventory turnover. Currently, inventory turns were 2.8x, but the company strove for 3.0x. Because of the unpredictable shifts in purchasing patterns of the retail trade, forecasting demand for shavers was extremely difficult. DiGiovanni felt it was better to have conservative forecasts because production could always be increased through longer shifts, while the carrying costs of extra inventory could, as he said, "kill you."

The carrying costs were comprised predominantly of the interest on loans used to finance the inventory as annual obsolescence costs generally amounted to under $50,000.

Because of the uncertainty in the timing of the shaver orders, Remington tried to maintain maximum flexibility with its suppliers. Approximately 20 percent of the standard cost of the shavers was contracted out, including the manufacture of the blank screens, the transformer for the motor, and all plastic molding. All shaver parts were sourced in the United States except for the screens, which were made in Germany because no American steel manufacturer would produce them. Lead times varied for different parts, ranging from days to four months. Remington's purchasing manager, Albert George, noted that suppliers were normally flexible in delaying shipments at the company's request.

Although Remington was not as automated as its major competitors, DiGiovanni was not convinced the added gains presently justified the costs of installing more sophisticated manufacturing equipment. Labor currently accounted for 12 percent to 18 percent of the average cost of a shaver.

Partially because of the low labor content, management had historically dismissed the idea of manufacturing shavers offshore (although they did use offshore sourcing for other less important products). The fact that Remington was the only U.S. manufacturer of electric shavers was used as an integral part of Remington's marketing strategy. Advertisements appealing to the strong patriotic sentiment against the flood of foreign imports stressed that Remington shavers were: "Proudly made in the U.S.A."

Quality Control

Quality control was considered the most important aspect of the manufacturing function. To help ensure quality, Remington used an acceptable quality level (AQL) system, both for its suppliers and some of its in-house production. The AQL levels for supplied parts varied, but ranged from 4.0 percent for less important parts (e.g., the plastic molding) to 0.4 percent for the most important ones (e.g., the screens). In-house, the motors and the cutting systems were 100 percent quality tested, as were all final units. For these in-house parts the reject rate varied, but as many as 5 percent of the parts inspected were reworked.

Remington had a full-time manager of quality control and employed 54 people in the quality control area (30 in fabrication and 24 elsewhere). These people made surprise inspections, updated procedural manuals, and worked with production workers to ensure that quality was maintained at all phases of the manufacturing process. DiGiovanni stressed the fact that all employees, and not just the quality control people, were responsible for quality. In addition, Remington employed an outside auditing firm to make surprise inspections to determine if the company was indeed meeting its own quality standards.

Remington was well known for the quality of its product. In 1984, *Consumer Reports* magazine cited Remington's XLR-3000 model as the top-rated electric shaver of those tested and available in the market. Kiam continually emphasized the quality of the shavers in the company's TV commercials, offering consumers their money back if the product failed to perform. Historically, less than 0.2 percent of the shavers sold were returned.

Personnel

Remington was the second largest employer in the Bridgeport area, with 1,100 total employees. Of these, 710 were in the production area. The majority of the production workers were women.

A significant contributor to Remington's success since Kiam took over was the company's personnel programs. Right from the start, Kiam instituted an incentive compensation format in which 80 percent of the hourly work force and all salaried workers were involved in some form of individual or group incentive pay program. Production workers were compensated based on piece rate system whereby workers were rewarded for each unit deemed to be of acceptable quality. The piece rate system resulted in above average compensation for most employees. For example, the average unskilled worker in the Bridgeport area earned $5.25–$5.50 an hour; at Remington, the average hourly wage for an unskilled worker was considerably higher. Remington's employee benefit programs included discretionary bonuses for outstanding performance, company picnics, and company-paid Christmas dinners.

Remington also stressed close communication between management and employees. For example, every Friday morning "coffee klatches" were held. Every employee got the opportunity to attend at least once a year, and each meeting was attended by 10 or more people. At the meetings they were told the latest news of the company, and all complaints and ideas were heard. In addition, once a quarter Kiam shut down the assembly line (at a cost of $10,000 per minute) to personally report on Remington's business. During these meetings, Kiam continually stressed that since he bought the company, Remington shavers were made in America and that he and the employees were working together to sell a U.S.-made product to the world.

Attention paid to the employees led to increased output and a contented work force. From 1981 to 1984 Remington's productivity improved 10 percent. Twice unions had attempted to organize and twice they failed. In 1984, turnover at the factory level (excluding retirements) was 7 percent, which was considerably lower than the average for the U.S. manufacturers. As a testament to the positive and productive atmosphere in the company, Remington had recently been selected for inclusion in the book, *The 100 Best Companies to Work for in America.*

The good relationship with employees allowed Remington to temporarily lay off workers when cyclical demand was at a low, because the company was confident the workers could be rehired when business once again picked up. However, during these times "bad news" rumors circulated and employee morale was typically low.

The Travel Shaver

In January 1985, Kiam decided Remington had much to gain from the introduction of a small, battery-powered shaver that would be used primarily for travel. International distributors had been requesting such a product for some time. The Japanese distributor would be particularly excited because the less powerful motor would make the shaver more appealing to Oriental customers than the currently available models. Plans called for marketing the travel shaver as a high-end, battery-operated model in Japan. It was hoped the travel shaver would sell well in the burgeoning Middle Eastern market as well. In the United States, the travel shaver would provide Remington with a low-priced shaver to compete with the flood of inexpensive models manufactured in the Far East. In fact, two companies, Schick and Sanyo, already offered electric shavers designed specifically for travel use (see Exhibit 10). Finally, the shaver would serve as the core product in a line of travel appliances that had 11 items, including an iron, a steamer, a clock, and a flashlight. Kiam planned to introduce the line in the spring of 1986 in time for the summer travel demand.

As with all new products, representatives from research and development, engineering, and manufacturing met to lay out the design and manufacturing process for the travel shaver. Members of the marketing department were asked to provide forecasts of expected demand for the product. They predicted the initial demand for the product would be 50,000 units, but, if successful, over time could reach 800,000 units per year in the United States alone. Kiam noted the "softness" of this projection and was also uncertain of the potential demand in each of the foreign markets.

EXHIBIT 10   Estimated 1986 Prices for Travel Shaver Models Sold in the United States

Company	Model	Dealers' Price, Including Discount	Suggested Retail	Catalog Retail
Schick	F1000	$16.35	$28.99	$20.00
Schick	F2000	18.25	34.99	23.00
Sanyo	73LANE	18.00	24.00	21.00
Remington (proposed)	TL-2001	14.99	20.99	16.99

Manufacturing Alternatives

DiGiovanni reflected on Remington's manufacturing operations and contemplated the possible recommendations he might make to Kiam later that week. He first turned his attention to developing a list of plausible options. After some time he had boiled the possibilities down to four:

1. Manufacture the travel shaver in the Bridgeport facility.
2. Form a joint venture to produce the travel shaver in Hong Kong.
3. Work directly with the Chinese government to establish a new facility in China.
4. Negotiate an agreement with a third party in conjunction with the Chinese government to produce the travel shaver in China or Hong Kong.

Regardless of which alternative was selected, DiGiovanni expected Remington would have to invest $100,000 in tooling to produce the travel shaver. Under any alternative Remington intended to keep control over the proprietary technology associated with the manufacture of the foil and cutters. Lastly, under any scenario, production would likely follow an assembly line format similar to the one currently employed in Bridgeport.

DiGiovanni was aware that Remington had the capacity to produce the shavers in the Bridgeport plant. He was also confident the product introduction would go smoothly from a manufacturing standpoint if undertaken at Bridgeport. All parts would be supplied by U.S. manufacturers except for the screens and the battery motors (which would come from Japan). Retaining all production in the United States also lessened potential problems associated with losing the proprietary technology. DiGiovanni noted that any foreign manufacturer could develop a cutting system that could still compete with Remington's among less discriminating consumers, but it would take time. Lastly, Remington would not have to bear the costs involved in shipping the travel shaver from the Far East. DiGiovanni projected a shipment would take 30 days by boat and that, therefore, Remington would need to maintain an adequate inventory of finished goods to meet the expected fluctuation in retail demand.

There were a number of arguments against manufacturing the travel shaver at the existing facility, not the least of which was the projected cost differential when compared to either Hong Kong or China (see Exhibit 11). However, DiGiovanni noted only 15 percent of the cost of the travel shaver would be allocated to labor if it were manufactured in Bridgeport. Another negative was that Remington would carry the entire cost of added inventory that manufacture of the shaver entailed.

Representatives of Charlie Inc., a manufacturing firm based in Hong Kong, had asked Remington to consider manufacturing a shaver product in Hong Kong. Charlie was run by Ho Fat Tung, a native of Hong Kong with a Ph.D. in engineering from McGill University. Over the past

---

EXHIBIT 11   Estimated Manufacturing Costs[1] ($/unit)

Costs	Bridgeport	Hong Kong	China
Material and direct labor			
Foil assembly[2]	1.54	0.98	0.75
Cutter assembly[2]	1.21	0.87	0.78
Other parts and final assembly	4.95	3.02	2.53
Total materials and labor	7.70	4.87	3.88
Overhead	1.60	1.15[3]	1.18[3]
Total costs	9.30	6.02	5.06

NOTES: 1. The costs are estimated by Remington and do not necessarily apply if the plant is managed by Charlie.

2. Foil and cutter parts would be shipped to Hong Kong or China through Bridgeport.

3. Includes transportation cost to United States. Salaries and expenses of expatriate managers paid by Remington for management of the plant in Hong Kong or China are not included.

20 years Remington had developed a good relationship with Charlie. Many of the nonshaver electrical appliances that Remington sold, including the air purifiers, fragrance machines, and popcorn makers, had been manufactured by Charlie. Production runs of these products exceeded 100,000 units. Over the years, DiGiovanni had gained confidence in Charlie's ability to execute a product start-up and to deliver a product that conformed to specifications. In addition, Hong Kong's established industrial, financial, and educational infrastructure as well as its transportation and communication networks were also viewed as arguments in favor of the Hong Kong alternative.

If Remington chose this alternative, the company would require Charlie to send samples from every production lot to Bridgeport for inspection of quality. If the samples did not meet the company's standards, Remington rejected the entire lot. All foreign suppliers had to meet the quality specifications set by the company.

China had also actively pursued Remington as a potential manufacturer because Kiam already did business with the government through a jewelry business that he currently controlled, and because Remington's law firm, Surrey & Morse, also represented China's embassy in America. The Chinese very much wanted American manufacturers to have facilities in China, not only to employ local workers but especially to provide the government with products for export to earn foreign currency.

Relative to Hong Kong, the People's Republic of China presented Remington with a riskier option. Over the last three years, DiGiovanni had made several trips to China to inspect facilities and to discuss products that could be potentially manufactured there. DiGiovanni was unsure whether the travel shaver was such a product, and he felt some trepidation beginning in China with a new product introduction. To begin with, DiGiovanni was not sure how well he would be able to control quality in a facility in China. Further, the China Light Industry, the government entity that was Remington's most likely joint venture partner, had informed DiGiovanni that any factory in Canton (the location chosen as the most attractive from Remington's viewpoint) would be required to shut down one day each week because of a shortage of electrical power. Perhaps the most onerous aspect of this problem was that power failures were not uncommon. By 1987, though, a new nuclear power plant was expected to be completed, alleviating this problem. Besides the potential quality control and power shortage problems, there were other concerns that DiGiovanni had, including difficulties in transferring the equipment to China, increased training time needed for workers (up to a month in China versus 10 days in the United States), the potential drain on management time, and the lack of developed infrastructure. Management estimated the investment in the plant, excluding the tooling, to be between $400,000 and $500,000.

Despite his fears, DiGiovanni believed Remington had much to gain from a manufacturing presence in China. First, in certain areas of the country, people wanted and could afford to purchase consumer grooming products. In Canton, for example, it was reported the average person spent $8 a month on his/her hair. Although Canton had a population of only 11 million, the potential size of the Chinese market (one billion plus people) was enormous. Second, before Mao Tse Tung came to power, Remington had been a well-recognized name in China. By manufacturing and selling products in the country, Remington could reestablish brand awareness. Third, a number of existing battery manufacturers existed in China. The presence of these manufacturers was attractive for two reasons: It provided a ready source of cheap batteries, and it increased China's desire to attract manufacturers of battery-operated appliances. Fourth, all the other components of the travel shaver could be sourced in China. The same Japanese company that would supply Remington with the motor if the shaver were manufactured in Bridgeport already had a facility in China. Finally, China had agreed to barter goods with American manufacturers, and DiGiovanni felt Remington could make a good profit reselling these Chinese barter goods in the United States.

Ho Fat Tung had suggested a second alternative to his original proposal. This alternative entailed allowing Charlie to produce shavers for Remington in one of Charlie's existing facilities in China. The existing factory had been used for the production of heating elements in hair dryers. It was approximately 15,000 square feet with an abutting 5,000-square-foot warehouse. DiGiovanni realized that Charlie's experience and familiarity with Chinese customs, coupled with their proximity to China, made Charlie an attractive intermediary if Remington chose to enter China. It also occurred to DiGiovanni that a joint venture with Charlie would make it possible to transfer much of the risk associated with entering China to Charlie.

Having begun the necessary decision-making process, DiGiovanni made an analysis of the investment costs of the manufacturing alternatives for the travel shaver (see Exhibit 12). He felt the most effective way to proceed would be to formulate a more comprehensive list of the relevant issues to be addressed in selecting the best option. With this in mind he went back to work.

EXHIBIT 12   Investment by Remington ($ 000)

| | | Hong Kong | | China | |
| | | Managed by Remington | Managed by Charlie | Managed by Remington | Managed by Charlie |
Investment	Bridgeport				
Tooling	100	100	100	100	100
Facilities	50	400	—	400	—
Inventories	2,657[1]	1,720[2]	556[3]	1,446[4]	467[4]

NOTES: 1. Assuming annual U.S. sales of 800,000 units, 2.8 times inventory turnover: (800,000/2.8) × $9.30 (from Exhibit 11) = $2,657.00. The number was expected to be substantially reduced as a result of the company's current inventory reduction program.

2. Assuming U.S. sales of 800,000, 2.8 times inventory turnover (taking into account the 18-week pipeline between the Far East and the United States), and evaluating inventories at estimated Hong Kong cost (Exhibit 11).

3. Same as Note 2, plus also assuming that Charlie would own two thirds of the pipeline inventory.

4. Same as Notes 2 and 3, except for evaluating inventories at Chinese costs (from Exhibit 11).

CASE 20
SHIRE PRODUCTS

Over the last eight years we have recognized the need to link the marketing and manufacturing functions as an important factor in improving our competitive performance. Certainly, the level of coordination between these major parts of the business has been substantial in itself and very rewarding in terms of our overall corporate results. We have consistently been in the top three performers in the group and last year saw us at number one for the first time. Part of this has been secured by our developments in manufacturing. We have become attentive to the needs of our different markets and this has formed an important part of our total corporate support for customers. We are now reviewing some of the key elements of infrastructure to check how well we are achieving business fit in all that we do. The details before us are yet another part of this reviewing mechanism. Jim Meadows, managing director of Shire Products, was addressing a board of director's meeting to discuss some of the performance measures and other reviews currently used in the business.

Background

Shire Products is a wholly owned subsidiary of Belcordia, a French conglomerate comprising engineering, electronics, textiles, building materials, and packaging. Based in Toronto, Canada, Shire Products supplied a range of Canadian and U.S.-based companies.

Marketing

The company sells plastic bottles and containers to a range of companies in a variety of industries such as food, toiletries, chemicals, agriculture, and household products. In most instances the products are customized; that is, a bottle, normally in terms of specification and print, is made only for the one customer. Some products are standard in that customers purchase a given bottle size and then either have it specifically printed or attach a label to it during their own filling and packing operations. In all instances, however, the products are relatively high volume and orders are received over a long period of time.

"Some time ago," explained Rob Castle, "we undertook an in-depth review of our markets and have, on a regular basis, reviewed them ever since. The latest update [given in Exhibit 1] shows the characteristics of our overall business based on a representative sample of products. With current sales revenue forecasts at $55 million, we are continuing to show sustainable growth at required levels of profit." He then continued to explain that each different market the company serves has its own order-winners and qualifiers. A brief summary of the meaning of each is given in Exhibit 2.

Rob continued,

we anticipate that the volumes of most products we are currently selling will tend to increase in years to come [see Exhibit 1]. In reality, some of these products will be superseded by new product designs, and as often is the case, we anticipate that we will continue to provide each follow-on design. Also, we do realize that we will lose some of our existing business as we know some is under a lot of competitive

This case study was written by Professor T. J. Hill (London Business School) and S. H. Chambers (University of Warwick). It is intended for class discussion and not as an example of good or bad management. © AMD Publishing (U.K.).

EXHIBIT 1   Market Analysis Based on Representative Products

Product Codes	Seasonality Factor	Order-Winners and Qualifiers									Annual Sales ($ millions)	
		Price	Delivery Speed	Delivery Reliability	Technical Competence	Quality Conformance	Ramp-up Capability	Product Design	Product Development Support	Existing Preferred Supplier	Current Year	Current Year +4
Unit A												
A0040	High	QQ		QQ		QQ	80			20	6.7	7.7
A0110	High	QQ		QQ	60	QQ	20			20	5.0	5.6
Unit B												
B2011	Zero	Q	50	Q		Q				50	2.4	2.6
B1046	Medium		30	QQ		Q	20	30		20	2.8	3.2
B3010	Zero			Q				100			3.0	3.3
B1650	High	Q	30	QQ			35	15		20	0.9	1.1
Unit C												
C6600	Medium	30		Q		50				20	1.1	1.1
C4505	Medium	10	30	Q		40	30				0.7	1.0
C7100	Zero	100	Q	Q		Q					2.4	2.4
C1000	Zero	80	QQ	Q	20	QQ					0.2	0.3
C6100	Zero	50			20					30	0.5	0.6
Unit D												
D1500	Zero	Q		QQ	Q	Q		50	50		3.7	4.0
D1750	Zero	Q	25	QQ	50	Q			25		0.4	0.5
D4600	Zero	Q		QQ	40			30		30	0.9	1.2
D7400	Zero	80		Q		Q				20	1.2	1.2
D8150	Zero	Q		Q		Q				100	1.3	1.3

NOTE: Q indicates a qualifier; QQ an order-losing sensitive qualifier.

Exhibit 2

The Order-Winners and Qualifiers Relating to the Company's Markets

- *Price*—This being an order-winner means that the profit margins on the products in question are relatively low, thereby requiring cost reduction to be a priority task. Price being a qualifier signals that the company achieves relatively high profit margins and must strive to ensure that they keep price at a point where the customer considers it acceptable.
- *Delivery speed*—Customer lead times are shorter than the total lead time within the company.
- *Delivery reliability*—Delivering a customer's order on the due date agreed.
- *Technical competence*—Resolving the difficult technical demands of one or more aspects of a product or process when making it. This being an order-winner means that the company's ability to resolve technical problems is a factor in securing that part of a customer's business.
- *Quality conformance*—Making a product to specification.
- *Ramp-up capability*—Having manufacturing capability to significantly increase the total output of a given product in a short period of time (normally days). It would be linked to the seasonality factor within a market.
- *Product design*—The design perspective of the technical competence factor referred to earlier.
- *Product development support*—Concerns design support for a customer both during and after product development.
- *Existing/preferred supplier*—This criterion is linked to the fact that customers often prefer not to move sourcing arrangements once the technical proving and mold/machine fit has been established. Even where tooling is wholly owned by the customer (and this is not always the case), there is a reluctance to invest the time and effort to reestablish a fresh source of supply. The exception is where the demand for products is of a high-volume nature. In these circumstances, products are often second sourced, so a customer is more willing to consider changing suppliers.

pressure. The figures [in Exhibit 1] provide a realistic overview of the future, even though the mix will certainly change and not all anticipated increases will line up with our forecasts.

Manufacturing

As explained earlier, most products made by Shire Products are customized. A small quantity, both in number and revenue, are standard products sold to more than one customer. The prin-

EXHIBIT 3   Outline of the Manufacturing Process

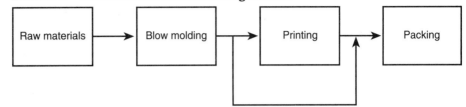

cipal manufacturing process for all products is blow molding (see Exhibit 3). Many are then printed, with the remainder being sold as plain bottles/containers that would then be labeled in the customers' own manufacturing process at the point of filling. The final step is packing, which may be of a loose nature (referred to as *jumble packed,* in that a given number of bottles/containers are loosely packed in a large container) or upright packed, which requires the containers to be stacked in a given pattern and upright.

> Over the last few years, we have forged important links with the rest of the business. This has enabled the company to debate and agree the characteristics of our different markets and then to determine the response that manufacturing, as well as other functions, needs to take to best support the business. Two years ago we decided to reflect the differences in our markets by moving to focused units based on the order-winners as perceived at the time [see Exhibit 2]. We now have four of these [Exhibit 1]. By regularly reviewing how we win orders, we can monitor changes and ensure that our manufacturing developments and investments are consistent with market requirements. For example, a recent review has highlighted the investment needed to move Product D7400 from Unit D to Unit C, and we are also monitoring Products D1750 and C4505 as possible future candidates for moving to Unit B.

Other developments have included merging the responsibility for quality control into a machine operator's job and also moving to a four-shift continental pattern[1] of working in Unit A to facilitate meeting the ramp-up requirements for these customers. The other three units work 24 hours per day over five days. In times where ramp-up is not required, then the machine operators from Unit A would, over the weekend period, be employed in one of the other three units undertaking work to meet relevant customer demands. "In this way," explained Ron Wilcox, "we are always fully manned in Unit A over seven days during the many consecutive months of high demand. Before these arrangements there were times when the machine operators would be asked to work overtime every weekend for a period of up to four to five consecutive months, and, understandably, they were not always prepared to meet our needs due to the cumulative effects of working seven days per week."

As is typical elsewhere, the manufacturing function in Shire Products records and reviews a whole range of activities on a regular and frequent basis. Detailed here are the more important ways in which this is undertaken. The aspects selected concern the reports received, the meetings held, and a sample of the annual assessments completed for all personnel on a group basis. Details are given in Exhibits 4 to 9, and a brief explanation of selected aspects is provided in the following sections.

---

[1] A four-shift continental pattern of working is an arrangement whereby four groups of operators and support staff are employed, with any three of these working at one time and the fourth resting. This arrangement allows all seven days per week over 24 hours to be covered without overtime working.

EXHIBIT 4   Summary of Performance Reports Received by the Manufacturing Director

Report Title	Source and Frequency	Principal Contents
Industrial engineering	Industrial engineer, weekly	• Output rates (bottles/hour) • Material as a percent of sales value • Actual versus planned output percent • Total output $s and bottles
Unit A	Unit A manager, weekly	• Number of machines used • Effective performance percent • Efficiency percent • Rejects percent • Actual versus planned unit output percent • Downtime hours analysis, percent • Packer effective performance • Overtime as a percent of basic pay
Unit B	Unit B manager, weekly	• As for Unit A
Unit C	Unit C manager, weekly	• As for Unit A
Unit D	Unit D manager, weekly	• As for Unit A
Distribution	Distribution manager, weekly	• Number of pallets despatched • Pallets per warehouse man hour • Overtime as a percent of basic pay
Toolroom	Toolroom supervisor, weekly	• Overtime-actual versus planned hours • Downtime analysis (tool problems) • List of new molds received
Tool development	Tooling engineer, weekly	• Drawing office overtime hours • Machine hours used for tool development/proving • Hours lost due to technical problems (by unit)
Weekly operating statement	Accounts department, weekly	• Weekly output value ($s) • Raw material as a percent of sales • Direct labor as a percent of sales • Trading profit as a percent of sales • Overtime cost as a percent of sales • Variances against budgets by category
Unit A	Unit A manager, monthly	• Effective performance percent • Efficiency percent • Utilization analysis (hours percent) • Reject percent • Scrap percent • Output variance ($s) • Percent returned by customer • Complaints analysis • Description of problems and plans
Unit B	Unit B manager, monthly	• As for Unit A
Unit C	Unit C manager, monthly	• As for Unit A
Unit D	Unit D manager, monthly	• As for Unit A

NOTES: 1. The industrial engineering report relates to all four units.

2. Effective performance $= \dfrac{\text{standard hours produced}}{\text{actual hours worked}} \times 100.$

3. Efficiency $= \dfrac{\text{actual standard hours produced}}{\text{budgeted standard hours}} \times 100.$

4. The weekly operating statement provides the data above for each unit and as a summary.

Reports

In order to help manage a diverse set of tasks, manufacturing collects data and compiles reports on a frequent and regular basis. A summary of the performance-related reports received by Ron Wilcox is given as Exhibit 4.

Meetings

Once a month there is a board meeting at which the functional directors review and discuss the previous month's sales and profit results. To link in with this, functional heads also undertake regular reviews of key activities in line with particular board meeting items and requests from the managing director or other directors. The systematic review of the function's activities is an integral part of managing and controlling different facets of the business.

Manufacturing holds several ad hoc meetings and is represented in meetings held by other functions. The two main meetings, however, are the daily unit managers' meeting and the weekly production meeting. Typical minutes for both are provided in Exhibit 5.

Unit Managers' Daily Meetings.   These relatively short (about 30 minutes) daily meetings involve the relevant unit manager, production supervisors, and a maintenance supervisor. No formal minutes of these meetings are kept, but details of what is typically included are provided in Exhibit 5.

Weekly Production Meetings.   The weekly production meeting is called by the manufacturing director for 10.00 hours each Monday. The permanent members of this meeting are the four unit managers and those managers responsible for maintenance, distribution, production planning and control, and engineering/product development. The quality assurance and purchasing managers attend on an ad hoc basis. Lasting up to three hours, all aspects of manufacturing and other relevant issues are discussed. As the manufacturing director explained, "It not only serves as a review of what is going on and what has been achieved, but it is an excellent vehicle for communication, improving coordination, and exchanging ideas."

Annual Assessments

Annual assessments are an integral part of the group's policies and are undertaken down to the level of supervisor. The period of review is over 12 months, and assessments are usually undertaken by mid-February of the following year. Selected assessments are given in Exhibits 6, 7, 8, and 9.

Concluding Remarks

"Our performance over the last five or six years is most encouraging," reflected Jim Meadows. "Many of the important parts of our corporate strategy are in place, and the outcome has been a direct contribution to the overall and sustained improvement we have achieved. Regular reviews keep us strategically alert and other important developments are in hand. We are now also looking at refining other parts of the activities, and one important aspect is contained in the analyses present here. Not only will any improvements bring benefits in their own right but will also, we have found, add substantially to the overall support for the business."

Exhibit 5

Typical Details/Minutes for the Daily Unit Managers' and Weekly Production Meetings

Unit Managers' Daily Meetings

No formal minutes are recorded for these meetings. Below is a summary of the format typically followed by all unit managers.

Shift Performances.   The performance of each shift is provided on the following aspects. This is given as a separate sheet for each day, which is then summarized as an average for each unit's weekly report (see Exhibit 4).

- Number of machines used.
- Effective performance percent (for blow molding, printing, and packing where relevant).
- Efficiency percent (for blow molding, printing, and packing where relevant).
- Rejects percent.
- Actual versus planned output percent.
- Downtime hours analysis percent.

Tasks and Problems.   A review of the tasks and problems that were addressed the previous day and a discussion and listing of the tasks and problems to be completed that day and in the near future. The latter would entail relevant details of the task or problem, identifying materials and staff requirements.

General Issues.   Basically a mechanism for general communication, particularly regarding interfunctional developments.

Weekly Production Meetings

The minutes of a particular weekly production meeting follow.

Minutes of Weekly Production Meeting on February 8

Present:	Ron Wilcox,	manufacturing director
	Paul Smith,	engineering manager
	Al Holmes,	toolroom manager
	Jay West,	Unit A manager
	Ray Hatton,	Unit B manager
	Ian Watts,	Unit C manager
	Peter Kennings,	Unit D manager
	Chris Johnson,	quality manager
	Jim Brody,	distribution manager

Exhibit 5
(continued)

	Action
1. Distribution	
a. Storage space—J. B. to investigate additional external storage to cope with anticipated temporary increase in finished goods.	J. B.
2. Unit A	
a. Recruitment—Production performance adversely affected by shortage of electricians. R. W. to see if maintenance supervisor needs help to speed up selection procedure.	S. W.
b. Toolroom—Inadequate notice has been given for tool preparation. The planner to investigate establishing short-term forecasts. R. W. to be advised of action taken.	A. H.

   c. Performance—Unit A consolidated performance figures for last week were:
- Effective performance, 91%.
- Efficiency, 95%.
- Average machine utilization, 76% (budget 82%).
- Unit output, 94% of planned volume.
- Material yield, 93% (budget 94.5%).
- Overtime, 6% over budget.

The reasons for the poor performance were discussed. J. W. confirmed that this week's figures were running better than budget, which should restore the overall performance for the month back to budget.	J. W.

3. Unit B

a. New shampoo containers (Project Rainbow)—Problems with establishing surface finish standards for new colors in this range. R. H. to liaise with sales to solve this problem. Advise R. W. of progress.	R. H.
b. Print loading—The potential contract for 20 million containers per year could put a strain on print capacity. R. H. to liaise with the planning manager and report on the capacity implications.	

   c. Performance—Unit B consolidated performance figures for last week were:
- Effective performance, 98%.
- Efficiency, 101%.
- Average machine utilization, 81% (budget 82.5%).
- Unit output, 101% of planned volume.
- Material yield, 96.3% (budget 95%).
- Overtime, 5% over budget.

R. W. congratulated R. H. on a generally good set of figures; however, overtime costs should be closely watched.	R. H.

4. Unit C } (Details similar to those of Units A and B
5. Unit D } were provided but have been omitted here.)

Exhibit 5
(concluded)

6. **Annual Staff Appraisals**
   These should be completed by the end of this week and given to   All
   Anne (R. W.'s secretary).
7. **Resin Supplies**
   A report that trials would begin soon using new supplies of PET   All
   raw materials, which give a substantial saving through group purchasing arrangements: probably amounting to about 2.0% reduction in costs of PET materials throughout the group. The different
   physical properties of the material and new logistics arrangement
   with the suppliers will require effort from everyone to ensure that
   the trials are successful.

Exhibit 6

Annual Assessment

Name: Ron Wilcox
Job Title: Manufacturing Director
Job Tenure: Five years
Appraiser: Jim Meadows
Date: January 20

OVERALL PERFORMANCE RATING	CHECK ONE ONLY
The overall rating is an evaluation of the employee's performance in the total job throughout the review process. With this in mind, take into account: • Key performance objectives. • Achievement of personal improvement objective. • Any additional achievements. • Factors clearly outside the employee's control impacting results for which the employee was unable to compensate.	☑ Performance excellent ☐ Successful performance ☐ Employee moving toward successful performance and is perceived as being capable of achieving successful performance within an acceptable period of time ☐ Unsuccessful performance

Rating Comments

Ron has done an excellent job to keep his department's costs down. Made a major contribution to profit where, despite sales being down by 10%, we achieved above budget profit.

Restructured print department with resultant savings.

High Unit A demand at a time when we did a lot of reorganization. Quality improved and we kept this major customer (25% of our total sales revenue) supplied.

Last Year's Objectives and Results—R. D. Wilcox

		Achieved		
Objectives	*Results*	*Yes*	*No*	*Comment*
Cost Control Decrease direct labor cost as a percentage of value added to 18.2%	Previous year the figure was 20.2%. Current year reduced to 19.8%. Depends on prices, and for some major products the company agreed price reductions to get larger share of business	✔		

Exhibit 6
(continued)

Last Year's Objectives and Results—R. D. Wilcox *(continued)*

Objectives	Results	Achieved Yes	No	Comment
Weight of waste material discarded to be reduced to 5.0% or less of total processed **Note:** this is dependent upon production run lengths	Previous year this was 5.5%, and we reduced to 5.2% last year. Shorter run lengths were required, plus product mix changes and no weekend running of PVC machines caused figure to be higher. Therefore, not totally under his control		✔	
Ensure that effective performance increased in each operating unit as follows: Unit Standard hours/ Actual hours worked A 90% B 87% C 84% D 90%	Only problem was Unit B, where sales volume was well below forecasts		✔	
Install one automatic palletiser in Unit A	Achieved on time	✔		
Extend the use of autodeflashing equipment to other Unit D machines; two completed in August and three completed in October	Four working. Decision taken by board to delay installing the last one	✔		
Develop machine monitoring system for Unit C, which integrates with planning system by May. Extend machine monitoring system to Unit D by third quarter and Unit A by fourth quarter	Fully achieved	✔		
Setup reduction. Implement quick screen change proposals across all print machines by June to reduce setup cost by up to 50%	Implemented	✔		
Quality				
Reduce the number of bottles held for further QC checks to 1.7% (or less) of production	Achieved. Now at 1.5%	✔		
Reduce customer returns to 0.8% (or less) of production	Reduced to .69%	✔		
Training and Development of Personnel				
Recruit industrial engineer/project engineer to assist with cost control project	Used an outside consultant. New person joined November 1	✔		
Industrial Relations				
Obtain trade union acceptance of planned machine operator/QC job merge and implement new assessment scheme by May	Implemented on schedule	✔		

Exhibit 6
(continued)

Next Year's Objectives—R. D. Wilcox

Key Result Area	Objectives	Achieved Yes	No	Comments
Cost control	1. Weight of waste material generated to be less than 4.5%.			
	2. Reduce direct labor percentage from 19.8% to 18.5%.			
	3. Phased installation of three autodeflashers. All three to be running by the end of May.			
	4. Fixed costs to be controlled within budget.			
Customer service	1. Improve tool change performance to meet market needs. Work with outside consultant. Recommendations to be implemented by September 30.			
	2. Recommend and install two secondhand PET machines to meet increased demand. Machines to be in operation by June 30.			
Quality	1. Internal held work to be reduced from 1.5% to 1.3% of sales.			
	2. Customer returns to be reduced from .69% to .6% of sales.			
	3. Commence TQM introduction to a programme yet to be agreed.			
Industrial relations	1. Complete pay negotiations within or better than budget.			
Training	1. Training of personnel to successfully operate machine monitoring equipment.			
	2. Set unit managers clear targets and objectives and measure on a quarterly basis.			

Planning for Future Success—R. D. Wilcox

Strengths
Consider and identify significant abilities, skills, or knowledge evident in the employee's performance
- Knowledge of manufacturing and all the implications
- Good grasp of industrial relations
- Knows the blow molding industry
- Motivates his team and focuses them on key result areas

Areas for Improvement
Define areas of performance where the employee can be more successful in the future
- Needs to face up to people who are not performing rather than defending them
- Presentation skills need improving
- Apt to make his point then switch off from further discussion

Ongoing Coaching/Training Actions
Specifically, what coaching and training actions are planned?
- The cost control project will give him refined productivity

Achievement Measure
How will the programs be measured?

- Report due end of June

Exhibit 6
(concluded)

Planning for Future Success—R. D. Wilcox (*continued*)

Responsibility	**Timing**
Who, in addition to the employee, is responsible for making it happen?	*When will progress be reviewed?*
• Managing director	• Ongoing

Employee Comments (to be completed by the employee)

A very complementary assessment.

Signature ...*Ron Wilcox*.....................

Signing acknowledges that the contents of the appraisal have been discussed with you, not necessarily that you agree.

Appraiser Comments

He has had a good year and done an excellent job in implementing a lot of new ideas and procedures. He has reacted well to cope with a considerable amount of work, particularly in the industrial relations area. Ron's contribution to our cost reduction program is particularly valued.

Signature ...*Jim Meadows*...........

Appraiser's Manager's Comments

Signature ....

Exhibit 7

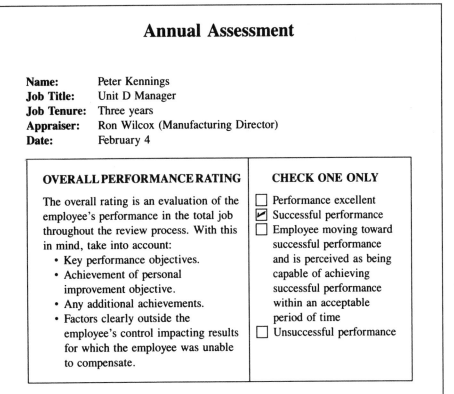

Annual Assessment

Name: Peter Kennings
Job Title: Unit D Manager
Job Tenure: Three years
Appraiser: Ron Wilcox (Manufacturing Director)
Date: February 4

OVERALL PERFORMANCE RATING	CHECK ONE ONLY
The overall rating is an evaluation of the employee's performance in the total job throughout the review process. With this in mind, take into account: • Key performance objectives. • Achievement of personal improvement objective. • Any additional achievements. • Factors clearly outside the employee's control impacting results for which the employee was unable to compensate.	☐ Performance excellent ☑ Successful performance ☐ Employee moving toward successful performance and is perceived as being capable of achieving successful performance within an acceptable period of time ☐ Unsuccessful performance

Rating Comments

Peter has worked hard at the areas for improvement highlighted in his current assessment—well done.

Contributions outside of Key Results

Machine performances have been improved and this is reflected in the level of utilization, which was increased from 51.8% to 62.6% (2nd half of current year = 67.7%).

Successfully completed a quality audit program and now conducts quality audits on a regular basis.

The grinding bay and print department were restructured during the year reducing manning and improving productivity.

Exhibit 7
(*continued*)

Last Year's Objectives and Results—P. Kennings

Objectives	Results	Achieved		Comments
		Yes	*No*	
Average effective performance to exceed 90%	Actual average in the period 88%		✔	
Material rejects to be reduced to less than 2% of the total processed	Actual was 4.4%. Represented a 0.7% reduction from previous period—Peter explained that machine wear on several key machines had contributed to this higher than targeted figure. Also, average production run lengths were lower thus increasing material wastage on changeovers		✔	
Labor efficiency to exceed budget	Achieved. The installation of three collating tables helped to boost actual labor performance	✔		
Tool changeovers—80% to be completed during an eight-hour shift	Tool change leadership changed during the year under review. Monthly meetings improved level of coordination. However, 80% target not achieved. Target considered unrealistic given the increasing number of tool changes		✔	
Meet following budgeted quality performances:				
• Customer returns <0.5% of sales	• Actual returns of 0.97%, down from previous year's performance of 1.8%		✔	
• Production held <1.5% of total	• Actual production held of 3.02%		✔	
Install modification to all six 6148 machines by April of current year	Completed by end February. Showed improved actual performance of 0.07% after installation	✔		
Resite packing conveyor by June of current year	Packing conveyor resited on time	✔		
Complete job merge between operators and quality inspectors with necessary training	All completed to schedule	✔		
Introduce new quality control procedures by September of current year	New procedures introduced to schedule	✔		

Exhibit 7
(*continued*)

Next Year's Objectives—P. Kennings

		Achieved		
Key Result Area	*Objectives*	*Yes*	*No*	*Comments*
Cost Control	1. Material rejects to be reduced to less than 2.5% of total processed.			
	2. Direct labor cost as a percentage of added value to average less than 21.47% blow molding, 52.7% print.			
	3. Fixed costs to be controlled within budget.			
	4. Deflash equipment to be fitted and operational on Machine 168 by end of March this year.			
	5. Machine monitoring system to be utilized by supervisor and machine operators to control quantity and quality of production. Machine personnel to receive feedback on the performance of their own machines.			
	6. Install productivity measures by June. Report to be issued by June 30, stating targets to be achieved by end of year.			
Quality	1. Internal held work to be reduced from 3.02% to 2.5%.			
	2. Customer returns to be reduced from 0.97% to 0.75%.			
Training	1. Production supervisors and machine operators to be trained in the operation of new machine monitoring system. Peter is to ensure that we achieve maximum productivity increases using this new technology.			
	2. Assessment scheme to be used to highlight operator training requirements. Peter to ensure that adequate training is given to improve factory performance.			

Planning for Future Success—P. Kennings

Strengths
Consider and identify significant abilities, skills, or knowledge evident in the employee's performance
• Peter is very good at analyzing a situation and can be relied upon to present a considered view for immediate implementation

Areas for Improvement
Define areas of performance where the employee can be more successful in the future
• Peter should concentrate on achieving his next year's objectives. He has the right personal qualities to be successful in these aims

Ongoing Coaching/Training Actions
Specifically, what coaching and training actions are planned?
• Last year Peter completed a diploma program in management studies and this, together with the short courses arranged, is considered sufficient at present

Achievement Measure
How will the programs be measured?

Exhibit 7
(*concluded*)

Planning for Future Success—P. Kennings (*continued*)

Responsibility	**Timing**
Who, in addition to the employee, is responsible for making it happen?	*When will progress be reviewed?*
	• Production performance to be measured monthly and reviewed quarterly

Employee Comments (to be completed by the employee)

In general I agree with the comments in this appraisal. I am keen to achieve next year's objectives and recognize the need for further training and development, both for myself and my staff.

Signature ....*Peter Kennings*.........

Signing acknowledges that the contents of the appraisal have been discussed with you, not necessarily that you agree.

Appraiser Comments

Peter works hard and should do well. He must, however, prioritize his work to ensure that his unit gives good service and helps us to achieve our demanding profit targets.

Signature ..*Ron Wilcox*.......................

Appraiser's Manager's Comments

A good year. Well done!

Signature ...*Jim Meadows*...........

Exhibit 8

Annual Assessment

Name: Joe Watts
Job Title: Maintenance Supervisor (all units)
Job Tenure: 2.5 years

A. Indicate any major achievements during the period	**Comments**

1. During the period under review, with reduced labor levels due to increased labor turnover, Joe has coped extremely well.
2. Has exercised a tight control on his department's overtime costs.
3. Holds regular meetings with department chargehands thereby improving communications. In addition, holds a monthly briefing meeting with his departmental personnel.
4. Joe spent a considerable amount of his own time preparing and teaching a practical training program.
5. Joe has played a major part in installing machine monitoring throughout all units. He has also been involved in installing the planned maintenance system.

B. Any comments on last year's performance and on the person being assessed

While all major objectives have been achieved, it is the opinion of the unit managers that more direct contact on the factory floor would be of considerable benefit. It would also expose Joe to problems that often require hands-on experience.

Joe has once again shown enthusiasm for the many projects carried out throughout last year in all units. The installation of a workshop computer has enabled the department to be more involved, therefore helping improve overall efficiency.

There is also some evidence that scheduled maintenance is reducing purchasing costs of spare parts.

C. Next year's objectives

1. Complete a machine overhaul on one M20 machine, with the minimum of disruption to production requirements.
2. Complete overhaul of machines 616 and 804 as per the last overhaul of machine 680.

Exhibit 8
(*concluded*)

	Comments

C. Next year's objectives (*continued*)

3. Ensure maintenance department's involvement in Unit A's expansion of four machines to ensure minimum installation time. Essential support for key customers.
4. Continue to use new planned maintenance system to highlight problem areas and indicate accurate individual machine costs.
5. Seek to improve methods to reduce downtime costs by investigating problem areas and implementing solutions.

D. Overall performance rating

(In assessing rating, achievements during the year, personal characteristics, leadership qualities, and administrative ability should be taken into consideration.)

	Unsatisfactory performance	F	......
80–87%	New man gaining experience or less than adequate performance	E	......
88–95%	Adequate but less than fully acceptable	D	✔...
96–104%	Fully acceptable	C	......
105–112%	Superior sustained performance or recognition of experience	B	......
113–120%	Exceptionally high performance	A	......

Estimated speed through normal range: 5–7 years (when applicable).

E. Potential

(If and when recommended for promotion, limitations, personal qualities, etc.)

Stay in present position

F. Personal development

(To include short- and long-term training.)

Signed ..*C. Smith*........... Appointment .... Date ..*Feb. 9*..

Jobholder's signature ......*J. W. Watts*................................. Date ..*Feb. 9*...

Exhibit 9

Annual Assessment

Name: David Burton
Job Title: Shift Supervisor, Unit C
Job Tenure: Six years

	Comments
A. Indicate any major achievements during the period	

1. Frequently proposes new production methods to reduce costs, and if these are within his scope, he will implement them.
2. Holds regular training sessions with shift personnel (e.g., SPC and machine monitoring).
3. Has become very competent in controlling all machine groups.
4. Has made good progress in reducing cost of scrap on his shift.
5. Achieved best productivity level of the three shifts in Unit C.

B. Any comments on last year's performance to also include the person being assessed

1. Last year's training in industrial engineering is now helping David to identify further areas for automation and cost reduction.
2. David is keen to learn and motivated to apply his knowledge in the development of the unit.

C. Next year's objectives

1. Implement machine monitoring, ensuring that good production is recorded at two hourly intervals, checking that reject levels are below set targets and corrective action is taken and recorded as and when needed.
2. Factory efficiency to exceed 90%.
3. Material wastage (purging/sweepings) to be less than 2% (last year = 4.1%).
4. Quality control standards to be raised and customer returns/complaints to be reduced.
5. At regular intervals (weekly), audit quality process sheets and check that all completed pallets that leave the shopfloor have operators' identification number.
6. Labor productivity to be within stated standards.

Exhibit 9
(concluded)

	Comments
D. Overall performance rating	

(In assessing rating, achievements during the year, personal characteristics, leadership qualities, and administrative ability should be taken into consideration.)

	Unsatisfactory performance	F	......
80–87%	New man gaining experience or less than adequate performance	E	......
88–95%	Adequate but less than fully acceptable	D	......
96–104%	Fully acceptable	C	✔.
105–112%	Superior sustained performance or recognition of experience	B	......
113–120%	Exceptionally high performance	A	......

Estimated speed through normal range: 10 years (when applicable).

E. Potential

(If and when recommended for promotion, limitations, personal qualities, etc.)

Stay in present position

F. Personal development

(To include short- and long-term training.)

Further SPC training

Signed ...*d. Watts*......... Appointment ....   Date ....

Jobholder's signature ....*P. Burton*..   Date ....

CASE 21
TAMA ELECTRONICS INC.

Our decision to rearrange manufacturing in line with the strategic review completed four years ago has been a major factor in the improved performance of our business. Before this change the facilities had been organized using functional/process layout principles. Even at the level of output we were recording at that time, this approach had created a high level of complexity in terms of the problems of control, high inventory, and business orientation. If we had continued to use this manufacturing approach the level of complexity that would have been created by now (particularly following our significant growth in sales) would have been difficult to imagine. One advantage we have gained at a level far above that we anticipated is the high degree of involvement demonstrated by all our employees. In fact, they have developed a proactive attitude to bringing about improvements, as illustrated by the recent suggestion put forward by the manufacturing units. They have suggested that they should present their views on the type of payment system that would best suit their individual units. However, although I have no wish to dampen the enthusiasm underpinning these initiatives (and there is some logic in rewarding each unit in line with it own efforts), I feel it opportune to review the existing focus decisions to ensure that they are consistent with the current needs of the business. When this is complete, I will then feel that we will be more able to address the payment system review initiative mentioned earlier.

Gary Wilson, vice president, manufacturing, of Tama electronics, was summarizing an agenda item of an executive meeting entitled "Manufacturing Strategy Developments."

Background

Tama Electronics is part of Colbeck Industries Inc., a large conglomerate involving a wide range of manufacturing and service businesses. Established eight years ago, Tama Electronics (TE) was a purpose-built factory, which formed part of the group's response to the expanding field of electronics. As with all parts of Colbeck Industries, TE is run as an autonomous company. As such, it presents strategic reviews for group endorsement and is required to seek corporate approval for proposals involving major capital expenditure.

TE supplies fully assembled printed circuit boards (see Exhibit 1) and, over the years, has gained a reputation for high-quality performance and an excellent record of delivery reliability. The company only supplies to U.S.-based companies involved in a range of industries, including televisions, domestic appliances, and vending machines.

Stimulated by the corporate culture within the group, TE was very aware of the need to develop marketing and manufacturing strategies that were consistent with its business needs. As part of this, a major review of manufacturing was undertaken four years ago, which led to a reorganization of manufacturing into different units, as referred to earlier.

Corporate Overview

Paul Hart (president of Tama Electronics) explained,

This case study was written by Professor T. J. Hill (London Business School) and S. H. Chambers (University of Warwick). It is intended for class discussion and not as an example of good or bad management. © AMD Publishing (U.K.).

EXHIBIT 1   Basic Manufacturing Stages of a Typical Product

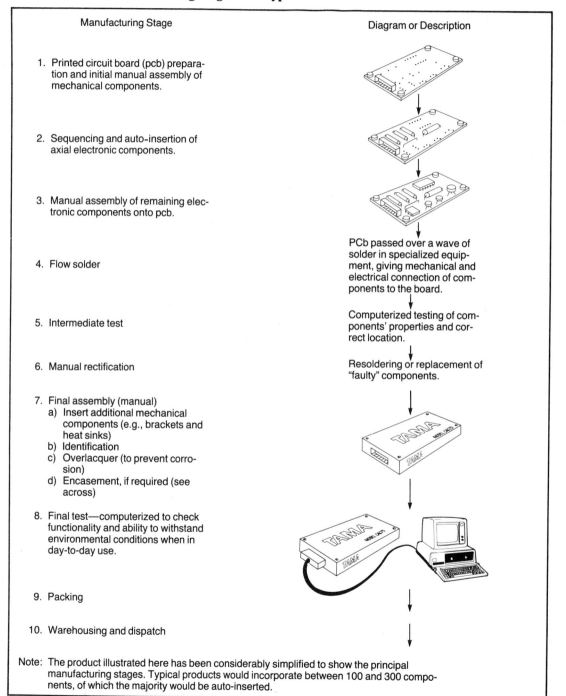

Manufacturing Stage

Diagram or Description

1. Printed circuit board (pcb) preparation and initial manual assembly of mechanical components.

2. Sequencing and auto-insertion of axial electronic components.

3. Manual assembly of remaining electronic components onto pcb.

PCb passed over a wave of solder in specialized equipment, giving mechanical and electrical connection of components to the board.

4. Flow solder

Computerized testing of components' properties and correct location.

5. Intermediate test

6. Manual rectification

Resoldering or replacement of "faulty" components.

7. Final assembly (manual)
   a) Insert additional mechanical components (e.g., brackets and heat sinks)
   b) Identification
   c) Overlacquer (to prevent corrosion)
   d) Encasement, if required (see across)

8. Final test—computerized to check functionality and ability to withstand environmental conditions when in day-to-day use.

9. Packing

10. Warehousing and dispatch

Note: The product illustrated here has been considerably simplified to show the principal manufacturing stages. Typical products would incorporate between 100 and 300 components, of which the majority would be auto-inserted.

One important corporate objective is to maintain the present level of RONA,[1] which is well above the average for this manufacturing sector. We do not wish to diversify nor to supply other market segments. Other parts of the group are serving these segments and, while not wanting to create additional competition, we also intend to stay where we are well known, our reputation is established, and where our skills and know-how lie. To enable us to continue to grow, the group has agreed on the necessary levels of capital expenditure, in terms of floor space and equipment. With regard to the latter, we have given particular emphasis to computerized test equipment, as this is where the bias of capital expenditure lies. This is not only to provide adequate capacity, but also to provide essential reports on test failures as a necessary feedback to design, manufacturing, and component sourcing.

Paul then continued to explain that the working capital to sales percentage would gradually be improved as the levels of component and work-in-process inventory are reduced.

"Future plans," he remarked, "look for a 10 percent actual growth over the next three years, which will need to come from an increase in market share. Our markets vary, however, and we need to provide relevant support if we are to succeed. For example, some require a high level of design and technical support and we have developed the necessary capability in computer-aided design." He concluded that throughout the organization, the need to link markets to manufacturing, design, and other capabilities is well recognized as a critical feature of strategic developments.

Marketing

"TE sells three distinct markets" was Steve Maskovic's (vice president, marketing) opening comment (see Exhibit 2). "Over the years we have been increasing our sales revenue in all markets through a combination of replacement and additional applications. The easiest way to explain these differences is to provide a short overview of each one in turn." The sections that follow summarize Steve's explanation of the different markets.

Television, Radio, and Video Products.   This market is characterized by high-volume products, where customers use several suppliers engendering high levels of competition. One common development with this market is the movement toward just-in-time supply agreements.[2] As a consequence, delivery reliability is becoming even more important and an essential characteristic of supplier performance. It is recognized that one way to increase market share is to continue to achieve total delivery reliability where competitors' performance on this dimension becomes suspect.

Domestic Appliance Products.   Compared to the previous market, this market segment has a wider range of volumes and product types. The result is that for some high-volume products the level of price competition is very high, whereas with others it is less so. One characteristic of this market is that some customers are seeking a high level of design change and the relevant technical support from suppliers to achieve this. In addition, and somewhat related to the characteristics of design change, there is a higher level of schedule change also required for certain products. The future in this segment is seen to be one of moderate growth but, as at present, when product designs have been agreed, then typically the characteristic of this market is for high volume demand.

---

[1]RONA is the abbreviation for return on net assets, which comprises net profit as a percentage of net assets (total assets less current liabilities).

[2]Just-in-time (JIT) supply refers to the requirement by customers that suppliers deliver regularly (sometimes daily or even twice daily) in line with a given schedule in order to reduce inventory levels and associated production and inventory control costs.

EXHIBIT 2   An Assessment of the Order-Winning Criteria for the Three Markets Using a Number of Representative Products

Market	Product Reference	Current Year				In Two Year's Time			
		Price	Delivery Speed	Quality	Other	Price	Delivery Speed	Quality	Other
Television, radio, and video products	AT 79		25		75				100
	130		25		75				100
	131	100					25		75
	157	100				100			
	161	30	50		20				100
	261	50	50			80	20		
Domestic appliance products	T 04				100				100
	14	100					20		80
	15				100				100
	24	60		40		80		20	
	SS 63				100				100
	101	100				100			
	127		40	40	20	100			
	MC 07	40	60			50	50		
	21	40	60			50	50		
Vending machine products	CAC 21	60		40		60		40	
	43	60		40		60		40	
	52	20		70	10	30		60	10
	SS 46				100				100
	126		40	40	20	50	25	25	
	VLC 8	40	20		40	40		20	40
	11	80	20			80	20		
	16	20			80	50			50
	17				100	20			80
	DC 39	20		20	60	30		30	40
	52	30		20	50	40		30	30
	79	10	60		30	30	50		20
	T 32	40	60			60	40		

NOTES: 1. Product references:
    AT Amplifier/tuner
    T Timer
    SS Switching system
    MC Motor control
    CAC Coin acceptance circuit
    VLC Vending logic circuit
    DC Display control
2. "Others" refers to nonmanufacturing criteria; for example, design, technical support, and being an existing supplier.
3. Delivery reliability is an order-losing sensitive qualifier for all OEM items.

EXHIBIT 3   Actual and Forecast Sales for a Number of Representative Products

	Annual Sales (units)			
	Current Year Minus		Current	Current Year
Product Reference	4	2	Year	+2
AT261	0	0	34,500	120,000
CAC52	0	0	1,150	10,000
DC79	0	0	2,530	5,500
SS126	0	0	9,200	32,000
SS127	0	0	13,800	40,000
T32	0	0	35,880	75,000
VLC17	0	0	920	12,000
AT131	46,500	86,100	167,900	2,500
AT157	6,450	76,230	81,420	90,000
MC07	0	16,780	23,460	25,000
MC21	0	0	35,650	48,000
SS101	0	72,150	80,500	95,000
T14	35,620	260,570	255,300	3,000
T24	0	0	56,580	180,000
CAC21	7,380	8,100	8,050	8,000
CAC43	2,730	15,710	16,560	17,000
DC39	0	5,215	8,280	8,000
DC52	0	0	13,110	15,000
VLC8	915	1,840	1,840	2,000
VLC11	0	1,060	18,860	20,000
VLC16	0	0	1,610	5,000
AT79	1,040	880	690	500
AT130	16,730	18,070	2,760	2,000
AT161	26,200	30,900	4,830	3,000
SS46	15,550	13,760	1,150	1,000
SS63	12,600	36,400	3,590	3,500
T04	136,490	1,090	460	400
T15	45,250	45,900	2,990	3,500

Vending Machine Products.   Volume in this market has shown the highest level of growth in recent years, which, in part, is a result of the increased range of applications. Most products are dual sourced, but TE's ability to give design support often results in the company becoming the main supplier. Maintaining this position over time is a result of providing a high level of quality and achieving reliable deliveries.

In order to assess our markets, we have provided the order-winners relating to a number of products that represent these different segments [see Exhibit 1]. As one would expect, products are at various stages in their own life cycles [see Exhibit 3], and the difference between an original equipment (OE) and spares product[3] has been reflected in this analysis, a fact also shown in the order-winners for both types

---

[3]Original equipment (OE) refers to PCB supplies to customers who are currently making original equipment (e.g., new television sets or vending machines) as opposed to orders constituting a supply of spares.

of products. One factor we also must bear in mind is that our delivery performance in supplying orders for spares has an impact upon future orders for OE products. Unfortunately, in recent months we have tended to deliver spares orders late on several occasions.

Manufacturing

"Before we reviewed our approach to manufacturing," explained Gary Wilson, "we arranged facilities on the basis of process layout, a classic approach in batch manufacturing." As explained earlier, however, this led to a relatively high level of complexity in terms of the requirements for production control, capacity planning, inventory control, and other aspects of production. In addition, TE had problems with employee motivation, especially regarding their lack of identification with the business and plans for growth. As a result of the strategy review, TE changed its approach to one based upon smaller manufacturing units, each focused to different aspects of our business. These units were each provided with their own relevant support functions and, as a result, had responsibility for many aspects of the total production task, including day-to-day scheduling, changeovers, maintenance, and quality control. The operatives were given a broader set of responsibilities, and TE successfully introduced statistical process control[4] to great effect.

The different units have identified around the aspect of the business for which they were made responsible. A healthy competition has evolved with each unit apparently wishing to outperform the others. In addition, these units identify strongly with the initial products allocated to them, and see them as "their products." Certainly, when suggestions have been made to reallocate products, strong resistance has developed, such that it has been more sensible not to jeopardize the significant gains that have resulted from employee involvement. Similarly, when new products have been allocated following the initial production phase, one argument always taken into account is to try to balance demand across the units to minimize the transfer of people from one unit to another. As Gary Wilson explained, "People management is undoubtedly a critical factor in the achievements we have made so far, and we have no wish to slow down the momentum."

The units established four years before principally concern the assembly, test, and packing of printed circuit boards (PCBs). Each unit shares the more expensive processes (e.g., flow solder, component sequencing, autoinsertion, and any expensive testing equipment, which are centrally grouped on a process basis), but otherwise are fully equipped. Also, each unit had its own managerial and supervisory structure, and includes production and industrial engineering, maintenance, and production control personnel, together with the responsibility for quality, job training, and even involvement in recruitment.

Of the four units, one is termed the "pilot line" and is responsible for the development and introduction of products. A second was set up to handle low-volume spares requirements, while a third was made responsible for all vending machine products. A fourth unit handles the rest (see Exhibit 4).

"Because of the types of tasks involved, the 'pilot line' unit was given the most skilled operators, due to the development nature of the task, which often involves using product drawings and discussing specification changes," continued Gary Wilson.

The spares unit also needs a high level of skilled labor, but often we find difficulty in resourcing both these units. Certainly, in the last year, we have experienced some capacity difficulties in this unit, which

---

[4]Statistical process control involves the use of control charts (normally completed by the operator) to monitor the process and initiate corrective action as the need arises. Thus, it focuses directly on the process and tunes it as required.

EXHIBIT 4   Details Relating to Representative Products and Manufacturing Units

Manufacturing Unit	Product Reference	Market Reference	Labor Standard (minutes/PCB)	Average Weekly Output (PCBs)	Average Number of Direct Operatives in Unit	Total Number of Different Products Made in Unit
1—Pilot line	AT261	A	21.0	750		
	CAC52	C	15.4	25		
	DC79	C	3.9	55		
	SS126	C	10.6	200	32	22
	SS127	B	12.3	300		
	T32	C	7.2	780		
	VLC17	C	46.1	20		
2—Others	AT131	A	16.4	3,650		
	AT157	A	17.9	1,770		
	MC07	B	3.7	510		14
	MC21	B	3.2	775		
	SS101	B	8.1	1,750	116	
	T14	B	5.9	5,550		
	T24	B	8.0	1,230		
3—Vending machines	CAC21	C	26.6	175		
	CAC43	C	21.7	360		
	DC39	C	4.6	180	60	20
	DC52	C	6.1	285		
	VLC8	C	39.8	40		
	VLC11	C	62.0	410		
	VLC16	C	51.8	35		
4—Spares	AT79	A	14.3			
	AT130	A	22.1			
	AT161	A	46.2			
	SS46	C	9.9	(Note 4)	24	46
	SS63	B	13.6			
	T04	B	4.0			
	T15	B	6.7			

NOTES: 1. Product references:
   AT Amplifier/tuner
   CAC Coin acceptance circuit
   DC Display control
   SS Switching system
   T Timer
   VLC Vending logic circuit
   MC Motor control
2. Market references:
   A = TV, video, radio
   B = Domestic appliances
   C = Vending machines
3. The factory is operated 46 weeks per year.
4. Spares demand is so variable that averages are not meaningful and are not included.

has affected our record of delivery reliability. The other two units require less skilled labor. Their job concerns assembling a range of quantities for different products. To do this, we installed mixed mode lines, which allow the assembly of several products [see Exhibit 4].

On the issue of payment system development, it is necessary to appreciate the background events. To facilitate the original changes in working practices, part of the agreement necessary to gain employee support was to provide a guaranteed bonus payment at the average level recorded at that time. The employees' wish to review the current method of remuneration is a desire for the payment system to reflect the changes in structure and responsibility, which have taken place. We accept that this is a legitimate request and agree, in principle, the need to consider more suitable alternatives. To be frank, we must be ready to respond to the employees' initiative, as considerable interest has been generated and expectations have been raised.

Current Performance and Future Needs

"Although we have made considerable improvements in the past few years," explained Paul Hart.

> Future business is going to be even more difficult to acquire. Relevant order-winners are under even more pressure. We need to reduce costs in the high-volume segments, give technical support where necessary, and provide delivery speed for other products. Furthermore, customer complaints about unreliable delivery of spares and some other products have increased in the last six to nine months. This, without a doubt, will harm future business unless we bring about the necessary improvements. One underlying factor in all this is our manufacturing strategy, and we must ensure that this is kept finely tuned in line with the different market requirements. Certainly, it has been important in our past success, and will continue to be a major factor in the future.

CASE 22
THE GREAT NUCLEAR FIZZLE AT OLD B & W

Everything went wrong when the venerable boilermakers turned to building pressure vessels for atomic reactors. The whole electric-power industry felt the consequences.

The long-awaited transition for the U.S. electric-power industry into the nuclear age has been slowed by a number of factors, including technological difficulties and public resistance. But a specific and unexpected cause for delay has been one company's crucial failure to deliver a single vital component of nuclear power plants. The failure, basically, was a management failure, and on a scale that would be cause for concern even in a fly-by-night newcomer to the nuclear industry. The company, however, was no newcomer. It was proud old Babcock & Wilcox Co., a pioneer of the steam generating business, whose boilers were used in one of the first central power plants ever built (in Philadelphia, in 1881). Babcock & Wilcox had an impressive $648 million in sales last year, making it 157th on *Fortune*'s list of 500 largest industrials, and it has been engaged in nuclear work in a major way for 15 years, producing, among other things, atomic power systems for Navy submarines.

Moreover, the corporation is one of only five that are engaged in building nuclear power plants in the United States. With consumption of electricity growing by nearly 10 percent a year, the utilities are counting heavily on the new nuclear stations to avoid brownouts and power failures in the years ahead. Poor performance at Babcock & Wilcox is thus one of those problems that could send ripples through the whole economy.

All of B & W's troubles involve a single product: nuclear pressure vessels. These are the huge steel pots—some are more than 70-feet long and weigh more than 700 tons—that contain atomic reactions. They must meet rigid specifications set by the Atomic Energy Commission, and B & W built a $25 million plant at Mount Vernon, Indiana, just to fabricate them. Cockily sure that the Mount Vernon plant would operate as planned, B & W sold its entire projected output of pressure vessels for years ahead. But nothing seemed to go right at Mount Vernon. Plagued by labor shortages and malfunctioning machines, the plant produced just three pressure vessels in its first three years of operation. Late 1968, after the production snarl reached horrendous proportions, a vice president responsible for the Mount Vernon operation committed suicide in a bizarre fashion.

Last May, B & W was forced to make a humiliating disclosure. Every one of the 28 nuclear pressure vessels then in the Mount Vernon Works was behind schedule, by as much as 17 months. For the utility industry, the news from B & W meant intolerable delays in bringing 28 badly needed nuclear plants into service, with all the added expense and problems that would be entailed. Philadelphia Electric Co. estimated that it would have to spend an extra $50,000 a day just to provide from other sources, such as high-cost gas turbines, the power that it had counted on getting from its delayed nuclear units.

Creating Its Own competition

With so much at stake, B & W's customers could not well afford to be patient. Twenty-one of the pressure vessels tied up in Mount Vernon Works were there on subcontracts from the two

This article was written by H. B. Meyers and published in *Fortune*, November 1969. It is reprinted with permission by the publishers © 1969 Time Inc. All rights reserved.

giants of the nuclear industry, General Electric and Westinghouse Electric. Both companies swiftly took the almost unprecedented step of forcing B & W to turn most of their partially completed vessels over to other manufacturers. When B & W, in an ill-conceived gambit, tried to hang onto two of the transferred vessels, Westinghouse took the case to court and won. In all, 14 G.E. and Westinghouse vessels—perhaps $40 million worth—were taken out of B & W's shops. Some of the firms that got the business had never made a pressure vessel before for use in a U.S. reactor; B & W had managed to create hungry new competitors in its own line of work. Only four G.E. and three Westinghouse vessels remain at Mount Vernon.

The company itself has barely begun to pay the high price of failure. Its earnings last year were still a robust $2.04 a share. In the first six months of this year, losses associated with nuclear work pushed earnings down to 22 cents a share—not even enough to cover the 34-cent quarterly dividend. From a 1969 high of 40.5 last January, Babcock & Wilcox stock has sagged into the low 20s. At that price, the stock is hovering around book value.

The man in the middle of all these troubles is President George G. Zipf (pronounced Ziff), 49, a low-key executive who started with B & W in 1942 as a metallurgical engineer. But the man who bears the main onus of responsibility is Zipf's predecessor, Chairman Morris Neilson, 65, who chose Zipf for his present job a year ago, and handed him his present problems.

In Trouble down by the Ohio

"All areas of the company were profitable in 1968 with the exception of automatic energy," President George P. Zipf told Babcock & Wilcox stockholders, after taking over as chief executive officer from Chairman Morris Neilson in September 1968. Up to then, losses on nuclear work had never seemed particularly troublesome. They were regarded simply as the price of B & W's ticket into the automatic age—and B & W had been getting into, and prospering in, new technologies for a hundred years.

But one segment of its nuclear venture has driven B & W into deep trouble. The plant that it built along the Ohio River at Mount Vernon, Indiana, to produce huge steel pressure vessels for atomic reactors, failed to function as expected, with all kinds of dire results. One especially unhappy result was that B & W had to give up some partially completed pressure vessels to competitors.

Bad Boy from Blair, Nebraska

Neilson is a flamboyant leader, a big bluff man with bright blue eyes and a full head of gray-blond hair, who has a gift for salty language. More than one secretary quit "Doc" Neilson's employ because of his profanity, and more than one executive suffered a colorful tongue-lashing in the chairman's office.

Neilson got his nickname by virtue of being a doctor's son in Blair, Nebraska, where he was known as "Young Doc." That was as close to earning an academic degree as Neilson came. As a boy, he himself has said, he was "incorrigible" and was kicked out of school "for being a bad influence on the rest of the students." He then enrolled in a Lincoln, Nebraska, high school and worked part-time as an embalmer. "I got into trouble in Lincoln, too," Neilson told an interviewer a few years ago. "One night, I came home with my nose over and under my eye. I'd been in a fight and got hit with a pair of pliers. I woke up my old man and he looked at my nose, and said, 'You're going to look like a goddamn syphilitic the rest of your life.' My old man used to tell me that there were two steps ahead of me—first reform school and then the pen."

Instead, Young Doc became a steeplejack and ironworker and in 1924 joined the corporation he was later to head. "I came to B & W by accident," Neilson has recalled. "I was working at American Bridge as an ironmonger on a job in Chicago, and another fellow and I got drunk. We got on the train and got off at Des Moines. We were walking past this construction job, and a fellow slid down a column and said, 'You looking for work?' We figured we were.'' It was a B & W job, erecting boilers for central station power plants, and from the start Doc Neilson felt at home in the two-fisted company. ''Those construction workers were goddamn rough people. They were hard drinkers, fighters, and lived by their wits.''

By the time World War II came along, Neilson was superintendent of marine erection. He supervised the installation of B & W boilers in 4,100 Navy and merchant-marine ships during the war. Later he headed the entire boiler division, including manufacturing, and in 1957 became president and chief executive officer.

When Neilson took charge of B & W the company was already deeply involved in nuclear work. Neilson's predecessor, Alfred Iddles, had recognized early that B & W would have to prepare for the day when the atom would challenge fossil fuels as a source of energy for central generating plants. Under Iddles, B & W attracted an outstanding stable of nuclear scientists and engineers and, in 1956, set up an extensive research facility at Lynchburg, Virginia. One of B & W's first important nuclear jobs was to build Consolidated Edison's Indian Point Plant. Another project was the reactor for the nuclear ship Savannah. B & W lost money on these jobs, but it gained experience needed to secure a corporate toehold in the nuclear era.

Nuclear losses continued under Neilson, but he improved B & W's overall profitability dramatically. Iddles had run the company as a loose-knit grouping of semiautonomous subsidiaries. Neilson centralized and systematized management. Every executive's areas of responsibility and authority were carefully spelled out in manuals that defined company policies and aims in all sectors of the business. Although sales stayed near or below the 1958 figure of $366 million until 1963—this was a low period in the utility buying cycle—earnings climbed year by year. Profits went from $13 million in 1958 to $22 million in 1963. At that point, sales also began to go up, rising 71 percent in the next five years. Profits peaked in 1967 at $33 million, at $2.69 a share (compared to $1.05 a share in Neilson's first full year).

In view of his critics, who have lately become numerous, the seeds of B & W's present problems were planted in the years of Neilson's rich harvests. It can be seen, in retrospect, that he may have been too successful in keeping B & W lean. His determination to keep down the fat sometimes ''had the effect of cutting into good red meat'' says a former B & W executive. Experienced managers found themselves stretched too thin to cover all their areas of responsibility. Worse, they did not always feel that their authority matched their responsibility, (i.e., men in the field were held responsible for results they did not have the power to bring about).

The most biting criticism of Neilson's regime comes from men charged with nuclear assignments. In their eyes, Neilson's lack of formal education proved a serious handicap. Explains one former B & W executive: ''Neilson created an atmosphere in which engineers and technical people just didn't feel at home. Their ideas were not treated with respect. They felt that top management didn't understand technical problems, and didn't trust those who could understand them.''

A Touch of Corporate Arrogance

From the start, B & W had foreseen a long wait before its nuclear work became profitable. Developing the necessary skills and technologies to compete in the nuclear industry has proved to be a slow and expensive process for every company that has tried it, including G.E. and Westinghouse. But what B & W had not expected was to lose money on its Mount Vernon Works. When the plant was planned in the early 1960s, Neilson appeared to believe that he had found a niche in the nuclear industry that offered a quick return. A nuclear pressure vessel, though huge and manufactured to demanding technical standards, is essentially just the kind of heavy steel unit that B & W was accustomed to fabricating with ease.

While the Mount Vernon plant was under construction, U.S. utilities went on a nuclear-plant buying spree, starting in 1965. At the time, the surge in orders seemed like a lucky break for B & W. The Mount Vernon plant was designed to produce one completed pressure vessel a month, once it was in full operation, and there had been considerable doubt during the planning stages "if we'd ever get enough work to fill the place," a former B & W executive recalls. Orders for pressure vessels poured in, faster than anyone had predicted, and the Mount Vernon plant soon got loaded up with work. It is now clear that management made too little provision for the time it would take to get the new plant operating at full capacity. Says one B & W customer: "I think you have to say that corporate arrogance was involved."

The first delays at Mount Vernon were caused by suppliers falling far behind schedule in providing vital equipment. A linear accelerator, used to detect welding flaws, was not delivered until August 1966, 11 months late. Even worse, a highly automated, tape-controlled machine center—the heart of the plant as originally conceived—arrived a full year behind schedule, in September 1967.

The Lure of Unspoiled Labor

By then, the plant had been operating on a makeshift basis for almost two years. And it had already become apparent that B & W's century of demonstrated competence in the fabrication of heavy steel products had not protected the company from grievous error. A principal one was the site itself—a cornfield near the little farm town of Mount Vernon (population: 6,200) in southwestern Indiana. The location had been chosen mainly because of its position on the Ohio River, safely above any known flood level, and yet reliably accessible for deep-water barges. This was an important advantage because nuclear pressure vessels are so immense that they can best be transported by water. B & W had owned the land for a number of years, and had set up a small plant there for making boiler parts.

What Mount Vernon did not have was a pool of skilled labor. This was a serious drawback because the AEC, for safety reasons, sets rigid standards for machine work and welding on nuclear projects. Late last year, a company memorandum reviewing the Mount Vernon fiasco observed: "Production workers required a new level of knowledge, intelligence, and judgment to operate the machinery, perform operations, and maintain the very high quality standards." At the outset, however, B & W took an optimistic view of its prospects—choosing, according to that 1968 memorandum, to regard Mount Vernon as "an unspoiled labor market." Presumably, the company expected to find a more tractable group of workers there than it had at Barberton, Ohio, where B & W's power generator division had had its headquarters and principal manufacturing facilities for many years.

The company planned to overcome the obvious shortcomings of Mount Vernon's labor pool in two ways. First, through automation—using that sophisticated machining center—and second, through a massive training program that would entice farmers away from their cornfields and quickly turn them into skilled welders and machinists. In one year, B & W spent $1 million just to train welders. But almost as fast as men reached the levels of skill required, they left B & W for jobs elsewhere. On September 30, 1968, only 514 of the 1,060 hourly employees hired in the preceding three years were still working for B & W; in other words, the company had hired three men for each one it trained. "Turnover of the Mount Vernon workforce has been a particularly frustrating problem, and a major reason B & W has been unable to bring its full manufacturing capabilities to bear on the situation," the 1968 memorandum concluded. Some potential workers proved to be untrainable, others had a "general negative attitude" toward heavy industry, and "some were not able to adjust, and therefore returned to their farms."

"It Drove Us out of Our Minds"

Workers who remained with B & W did not prove to be as unspoiled as the company had hoped. Even before the pressure vessel plant opened, it was organized by the Boilermakers Union (which also represents B & W workers at Barberton) amid charges of unfair labor practices against the management. The plant was closed by labor disputes on several occasions. The most serious occurred when the three-year contract expired in 1967, while equipment was still being installed. The Boilermakers went on strike over wages and work rules, and the plant was down for 40 days—unnecessarily long, in the view of President Thomas Ayers of Chicago's Commonwealth Edison, who had pressure vessels tied up at Mount Vernon.

From the standpoint of production, Neilson won a victory that amounted to overkill. Under the new contract, wages remained too low to stem the flow of workers away from B & W or to attract qualified workers from other areas. The B & W memo cites the "noncompetitiveness of our wage scale" as a reason for the high turnover rate in the Mount Vernon work force. Even for experienced workers, welding two pieces of eight-inch steel together is a demanding task, particularly in nuclear work, in which each weld is examined by X ray. When an imperfection is found, the weld must be "mined out" and done over again. In most plants, less than 10 percent of the welds must be reworked, and a rework of less than 1 percent is sometimes achieved. But at Mount Vernon 70 percent or more of the welds were rejected on being inspected. "It drove us out of our damned minds," recalls Ayers. "So costly! So time-consuming!" Ayers and other B & W customers say that they urged the company to increase the supervisory force—which regularly worked one and a half to two shifts daily—so that a closer watch could be kept on the welds as they were built up.

In addition to its problems, B & W ran into unexpected trouble with equipment. The linear accelerator for X-raying welds was installed in mid-1966 but did not go into full operation until a year later. The tape-controlled machining center was even more of a headache, and began functioning as planned only a few months ago. In this center, huge vessel segments are positioned on optically aligned ways, and then moved a distance of 250 feet, while a series of precise machining operations are performed simultaneously, controlled by computer-prepared tape. The concept was a good one, since nuclear pressure vessels are custom jobs, each tailored to a customer's specifications. But "debugging" of the machinery proved unexpectedly difficult. One problem was that the plant was not air-conditioned, and temperature changes threw off the many delicate adjustments that had to be made. In addition, an earthquake—fairly rare in Indiana—shook up the plant last year and it took nearly a week to reset the machine tools. Other start-up difficulties were simply incomprehensible. For example, a vital boring mill was put out of operation for several weeks when a tool broke. There was no spare on hand.

Death in a Dry Bathtub

The man directly responsible for the Mount Vernon plant was John Paul Craven, vice president in charge of the power generation division at Barberton. As head of B & W's largest division, Craven was number three man in the company, and was paid $87,000 a year. At one time, there was speculation in the company that Craven might someday become president. A gentle, upright bachelor of 60, Craven was tall and distinguished looking. An engineer by training, he had been with B & W all his working life, and he had no interests outside his job. For a while, Craven had raised roses as a hobby, but after he was made vice president he gave up roses in order to devote himself more fully to B & W. "His work was his whole life," says an old friend.

As the bottleneck at Mount Vernon grew worse, Craven came to feel that neither his customers nor corporate headquarters in New York fully appreciated the difficulties of Mount

Vernon's advanced machine tools. Nor did he believe that he was given the authority, the budget, or the personnel that he needed to fulfill the plant's commitments. Says another of Craven's old friends: "Paul couldn't bear to sit in Barberton and have all the shots called from New York—and then be expected to take responsibility for not producing."

In September 1968, before the seriousness of the pressure-vessel crisis at Mount Vernon became generally known, Neilson stepped aside as chief executive in favor of George Zipf. For a man destined for the top at B & W, Zipf had an unusual background. All of his predecessors had been identified with boilers, but Zipf came from B & W's tubular-products division at Beaver Falls, Pennsylvania, near Pittsburgh. This division, whose work is more akin to steel manufacturing than boilermaking, produces tubing for B & W's own use and for sale to other industrial customers; it accounts for roughly 30 percent of B & W's total sales, and more than half its profits. When he transferred to New York as executive vice president in 1966, Zipf had been at Beaver Falls for 20 years, ever since graduating from Lehigh University. He was a stranger to the problems of the power generation division, and to that division's big corporate customers.

Less than a month after taking over as chief executive from Neilson, Zipf scheduled a meeting at the Mount Vernon plant with Craven and Austin Fragomen, vice president for manufacturing. The meeting was set for a Monday morning. During the preceding weekend Craven told friends that for the first time in his life he thought his job was getting beyond him. Sometime on the Sunday afternoon or evening before his scheduled meeting with Zipf, Craven took off his clothes and climbed into a dry bathtub in his $250-a-month apartment at Akron's luxurious Carlton House. Then he slashed his ankles, cut his throat, and stabbed himself in the heart with the serrated eight-inch blade of a butcher's knife.

After Craven's death, George Zipf took personal charge of the power generation division, and of the Mount Vernon works in particular. Before long, both Austin Fragomen and the Mount Vernon plant manager, Norman Wagner, resigned. That left Zipf free to put a whole new team to work on the company's pressure-vessel debacle.

The Chairman Sells Some Stock

Beginning in 1967, both GE and Westinghouse, along with many of the utilities that were the ultimate customers for B & W pressure vessels, repeatedly expressed worry over the Mount Vernon plant's faltering operations. In the fall of 1968, B & W pacified GE to some extent by setting up a temporary welding shop on barges anchored at Madison, Indiana, where expert welders from Louisville, Kentucky, labor pool could be obtained. But for the most part, B & W brushed aside its customers' worries with assurances that things at Mount Vernon were not really as bad as they seemed. Even after Craven's death, the B & W management continued to maintain that its optimistic scheduling, with some minor changes, would prove to be realistic.

Some utility executives who met with Zipf to express their concern left with the conviction that he did not appreciate just how serious the pressure-vessel delays had become. On some occasions, he seemed to regard his callers as bothersome intruders. "He just sat there like a damned Budha," reported one customer after such a meeting.

Faced with such frustrations, GE and Westinghouse began to consider the drastic step of pulling some of their delayed pressure vessels out of the overloaded Mount Vernon shops. Both companies assigned teams to scout for other manufacturers that might be able to take over B & W vessels and complete them. There were not many potential candidates. Up to then, B & W and Combustion Engineering, Inc. had pretty much divided the U.S. pressure-vessel business between them. Combustion Engineering had managed to keep close to schedule on its deliveries, and had been expanding its Chattanooga machine shops. It had unused capacity. In addition, Chicago Bridge & Iron Co., which had previously done only on-site fabrication, was setting up a pressure-vessel plant in Memphis. (On-site fabrication is a more expensive method of constructing pressure vessels, used only when it is extremely difficult to transport the massive units to a site intact.) The GE and Westinghouse teams also looked abroad for companies that might be able to take over some of the work.

In April, while B & W's biggest customers were searching for other suppliers, Doc Neilson—who was retiring on May 1 as an officer of the company, but keeping the title of chairman—quietly sold 15,000 of his 20,000 shares of B & W stock. The price at the time was about $33 a share. A couple of weeks later B & W stockholders got their first official hint of serious trouble ahead. George Zipf revealed at the annual meeting that he expected earnings to drop by 20 to 30 percent in 1969 because of the company's losses on nuclear business. (The actual decline, of course, has since proved to be much greater than Zipf predicted.) Before long, the price of B & W's stock sank into the 20s.

Quick Trip to Court

On May 14, less than a month after the annual meeting, B & W sent out telegrams brusquely letting customers know that the situation at Mount Vernon was even worse than they had suspected. Zipf and his new team had completed a gloomy reevaluation of the plant's capabilities, and B & W was adding 2 to 12 months to earlier delivery schedules, some of which had already been stretched past the dates called for in B & W's original contracts.

On receiving this news, both GE and Westinghouse sought B & W's cooperation in transferring vessels to the other shops that they had scouted out. B & W agreed to subcontract some of its work to these plants. But an unexpected difficulty soon arose. Westinghouse had determined that Rotterdam Dockyard Co., a major shipbuilding and steel fabricating firm in the Netherlands could take two vessels and improve on the B & W schedule—provided that the vessels were transferred promptly. Westinghouse located space on a ship that would be calling at New Orleans on the desired date and, by paying a premium, was able to arrange for the ship to cancel calls at other ports and proceed directly to the Netherlands. B & W agreed to put the two pressure vessels on barges and start them on their way to New Orleans, while it negotiated a subcontract with Rotterdam dockyard. But negotiations broke down when B & W and Rotterdam could not come to terms. To the horror of Westinghouse officials, B & W ordered the barges back to Mount Vernon.

Westinghouse then decided to pay B & W for the work it had already done, and take over the vessels itself. But speed was required. If the barges did not continue down the river while these new arrangements were made they would miss the ship to Rotterdam. Now Westinghouse found itself at a strange impasse—it could not reach anyone at B & W who could rescind the order for the barges to return to Mount Vernon. Neilson was "not available." Zipf was "out of the country." Frustrated in its efforts to reach top management and work out an amicable settlement, Westinghouse reluctantly went into U.S. district court in Pittsburgh, and won a temporary restraining order to prevent B & W from taking the vessels back to Mount Vernon.

During the hearing, Federal Judge Wallace S. Gourley had a revealing exchange with John T. Black, B & W's manager for commercial nuclear components.

> *Judge Gourley:* On this contract for $2,542,000, what would you say that you expect to make on this?
> *Black:* This specific contract?
> *Judge Gourley:* Yes.
> *Black:* I don't expect to make a profit.
> *Judge Gourley:* You don't expect to make a profit?

Black: No, sir.

Judge Gourley: I don't know why you would want the material to work on. You are not in business to lose money for your stockholders.

Black: We do not expect to make it.

Judge Gourley: In other words, on this contract (for) $2,542,000, you don't expect to make a penny profit for your corporation, if you went ahead and finished it?

Black: No, sir.

Judge Gourley: How much on this other one (for) $2,304,789. What profit could you be reasonably expected to make on this contract, if you finished it?

Black: I would think that one probably (is) in the same condition.

Judge Gourley: If you went ahead and finished this, you wouldn't make a cent?

Black: I think on direct cost, we would cover our direct cost to labor and shop expenses.

Judge Gourley: I meant after everything, would you or would you not make any money on this?

Black: No.

Judge Gourley: I wouldn't think your stockholders would want you to finish. I certainly wouldn't.

Back on the Track

After Westinghouse won possession of the two pressure vessels and sent them off to Rotterdam, B & W raised no further objections to transferring work out of its shop. Indeed, it actively cooperated with its customers to get the job done. Westinghouse sent five vessels to Combustion Engineering's Chattanooga shops and two to a French firm, Societe des Forges et Ateliers du Creusot. General Electric turned three vessels over to Chicago Bridge & Iron and had B & W send two others to Japan's Ishikawajima-Harima Heavy Industries. In every case, these firms are expected to equal or better the delivery dates set in May by B & W.

With the load at Mount Vernon lightened, prospects look better for the 14 pressure vessels that remain there, including 7 for nuclear plants that B & W itself is building. For example, the Sacramento Municipal Utility District has been notified that the vessel for its Rancho Seco nuclear plant, a B & W project, will be only a couple of months late, instead of the year that seemed likely in May. That means that the vessel for Sacramento is essentially on schedule again, since the delays now expected are no more than could be accounted for by the labor disputes and earthquake that Mount Vernon suffered.

To his utility customers, George Zipf remains very much a man on trial. But now that their pressure vessels are moving along again, some utility executives are convinced that he has quietly managed to put B & W back on the track. One move that has met their approval was the appointment in September of an experienced Westinghouse man as vice president in charge of the power generation division—John Paul Craven's old job. Bringing in an outsider at such a level is something new for B & W, and one B & W customer believes that he knows what it means: "I think George Zipf is really in command now." If this is so, he will have a lot to do to restore the honored old name of Babcock & Wilcox to its former luster.

Technical Note

Nuclear equipment, as stated earlier, is manufactured in a job-shop environment, while most of the fossil equipment is manufactured in a flow-shop environment. In fossil manufacturing operations, the work stations are usually arranged in proper sequence to allow materials to enter one end of the shop, and flow sequentially to completion. The normal work mix means that some work be performed at each work station, but seldom requires the product to pass over any of the work stations more than once. All jobs follow, essentially, the same path from one work station to another. Consequentially, it is relatively easy to "line-up" or "load" each shop with a high degree of certainty as to work content, schedule requirements, and completion capabilities. Over the years, certain rules of thumb were developed, which allowed relatively accurate manufacturing planning decisions to be made for fossil manufacturing operations.

A shipping unit for a large fossil-fired boiler, such as used in power plants, differs greatly from a shipping unit for a nuclear plant. Fossil boilers are shipped as a large number of parts, which are assembled, erected at the job site. Nuclear equipment is mostly shop assembled, whereby a small number of large, assembled components are shipped to the site for installation. Complex planning is, therefore, required for the nuclear shop operations, which produce all detail parts fabricated into various levels of subassembled, and finally into large components.

Source: E. D. Thomas and D. P. Covelski. "Planning Nuclear Equipment Manufacturing." *Interfaces* 9, no. 3 (May 1975), pp. 18–29.

CASE 23
TYNDALL FURNITURE COMPANY (A)

Greg Procter, vice president of marketing for the Tyndall Furniture Company, knew that the single most important marketing decision a company made was the selection of products and markets to serve. He was acutely aware of the need to focus his firm's resources because sales growth in the most recent period had slowed significantly. Profits also were below the industry average. Further complicating the task he faced were the dramatic changes going on in the industry. He was most concerned about the increasing competition at the retail level. A major problem was the recent popularity of galleries in the retail store. He had to decide just where he would marshal his energies, both on products and on markets.

Company Background

Established in 1898 by Henry H. Tyndall, the company remained a family-owned business until 1963 when it was bought out by Berkron Industries Inc., a large conglomerate with interest in textiles, chemicals, food, clothing, retailing, and, more recently, financial services. Although predominantly based in North America, Berkron also had interest in Australasia and Europe.

Although the company had in the past been an above-average profit earner within the furniture industry as a whole, in recent years its performance had declined (Exhibit 1)—a fact that led to the appointment of Matt Culley as chief executive officer two years before. As with most markets, the furniture industry was becoming increasingly more competitive and witnessing significant changes in both products and market outlets (Exhibit 2).

Sales of the company had shown significant growth in recent years but slowed dramatically in the most recently completed year (Exhibit 2). Productivity increases and judicious cost cutting, combined with some advantageous product mix changes, kept net profits growing. Unfortunately, profitability as measured by net profit percentage and return on total assets was still below the industry average. It was felt that the increasingly competitive nature of the industry was largely responsible for this below-average performance.

The company made traditional furniture for the kitchen, dining room, and bedroom (referred to as case goods in the industry) in three plants, all located in the Grand Rapids, Michigan, area. Much of the furniture was made from solid wood and was designed for long wear and usefulness.

Industry Trends

The furniture industry was undergoing significant change. Most notably, a rash of acquisitions had resulted in dramatic increase in concentration. In fact, the top 10 producers in the industry were growing at three times that of the industry. These were all firms that were staying very focused in their acquisition activities, unlike Berkron, which was a classic conglomerate with a diverse set of holdings. These large competitors were becoming increasingly difficult to deal

---

This case was prepared by Professors W. L. Berry (Ohio State University), T. J. Hill (London Business School), J. E. Klompmaker (University of North Carolina), and W. G. Morrissey (North Carolina State University) as a basis for class discussion rather than to illustrate either effective or ineffective handling of an administrative situation.
© Professor W. L. Berry, Professor J. E. Klompmaker, Professor W. G. Morrissey, or AMD Publishing (U.K.).
Inquiries in the U.S.A. to Zip Publishing, 1634 N. High Street, Columbus, Ohio 43201.

EXHIBIT 1   Furniture Industry Comparisons

Companies	Current Year Minus				Current Year
	4	3	2	1	
Tyndall					
Sales	100.0%	100.0%	100.0%	100.0%	100.0%
Cost of goods sold	79.1	78.3	78.3	79.2	78.1
Net profit before tax	4.8	3.7	4.4	3.5	4.2
Return on total assets	5.4	5.1	6.5	6.0	7.1
Return on investment	—	8.6	9.0	9.4	10.5
Sales growth	—	10.1	13.7	13.3	4.1
Average all case goods companies					
Sales	100.0%	100.0%	100.0%	—	—
Cost of goods sold	75.9	75.2	76.7	n.a.	n.a.
Net profit before tax	7.7	7.4	7.3	n.a.	n.a.
Return on total assets	n.a.	n.a.	7.0	n.a.	n.a.
Average all furniture companies					
Sales	100.0%	100.0%	100.0%	—	—
Cost of goods sold	75.6	74.6	75.1	n.a.	n.a.
Net profit before tax	7.6	8.3	8.4	n.a.	n.a.
Return on total assets	8.2	8.7	8.9	n.a.	n.a.

NOTE: n.a. signifies that the particular industry information is not available.

with at the retail level. They were able to command large amounts of floor space in the retail sales environment, thus leaving little for the smaller producers to fight over.

Added to the problem of industry consolidation was the trend toward galleries in the retail stores (Exhibit 3). Galleries are areas in retail stores devoted entirely to the product offering of a single manufacturer. Areas can be as small as 1,000 square feet or as large as 10,000. Typically, the furniture is displayed in a setting similar to that found in a home—with a room full of furniture, accessories, pictures, and so on. This is in marked contrast to the traditional practice of displaying chairs in one area, couches in another, tables in another, and so forth. Retailers welcome the opportunity to turn over merchandising to the manufacturer and appreciate the greater floor appeal created by the more professional display. On the other hand, they give up control of a significant amount of selling space. It also limits the number of manufacturers with which they can do business.

Furniture Buyers

Furniture is most often viewed as a discretionary purchase, thus it is one of the first items in a family's budget that gets cut as the economy worsens. It is also still viewed primarily as a female-dominated decision even in the less traditional, more modern households. Although the industry often worries over the small portion of the typical household's budget devoted to furniture purchases, three out of five respondents to a survey by *Better Homes and Gardens* said they planned to buy some home furnishings in the next two years. Upholstery was mentioned by 59 percent and case goods by 41 percent. The average expenditure for case goods in the past year was $1,071. Traditional styles were favored by 34 percent of the respondents, with country favored by 31 percent.

EXHIBIT 2   Tyndall Sales Analysis

Market Types	Current Year Minus		Current Year
	2	1	
Small chains			
Sales	$ 1,188,189	$ 1,468,848	$ 1,389,077
Outlets	14	14	14
Small independents			
Sales	$19,417,109	$20,005,636	$18,162,589
Outlets	577	594	601
Large independents			
Sales	$ 1,504,000	$ 1,841,000	$ 1,742,000
Outlets	5	5	5
Galleries			
Sales	$ 7,655,279	$ 8,534,630	$10,307,532
Outlets	48	50	50
Mom and pops			
Sales	$ 6,813,000	$ 4,288,000	$ 4,921,200
Outlets	1,365	1,126	883
Mass merchandiser			
Sales	$ 5,576,000	$ 5,285,000	$ 6,242,400
Outlets	1	1	1
Total sales	$42,153,577	$41,423,114	$42,764,798
Total outlets	2,010	1,790	1,554

Consumers said they visited 2.3 types of outlets before buying, with general furniture stores the most popular (62 percent). Department stores were visited by 31 percent and stores with brand-name furniture by 31 percent. Brand-name furniture galleries were mentioned by 24 percent. A store's reputation and service were the most frequently mentioned reasons for shopping a particular store (cited by 68 percent). Price was a reason for 63 percent of the respondents.

Comfort (79 percent), construction (74 percent), durability (61 percent), and styling/design (56 percent) played the biggest role in the consumer's decision to buy a particular piece of furniture. Price was mentioned by 54 percent.

Tyndall's customer profile matched much of that of the industry as a whole, but it also varied in some significant respects. Tyndall's customer could be typified as blue-collar, in the 35–55 age range, with an increasing level of discretionary income (Exhibit 4). As with other furniture manufacturers, the key decision maker is female. Tyndall's customers also tended to buy furniture in sets or collections rather than individual pieces from different lines.

Competition

Tyndall faced a variety of manufacturers, particularly in the kitchen and dining room furniture markets. These competitors included:

- S. Bent
- Dinaire
- Virginia House
- Tell City
- Universal
- Kincaid
- Cochrane
- Temple Stuart

EXHIBIT 3   Furniture Gallery Survey

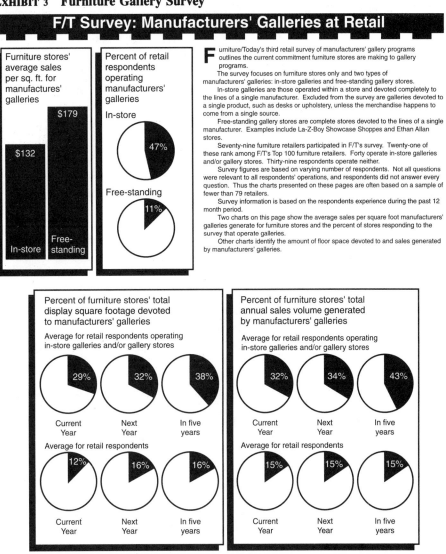

The firms' market share of 0.7 percent has not suffered in competing with other large manufacturers. In this market, the price/value relationship is extremely important (Exhibit 4). Because the customer is looking for durability and wear with a style that will not go out of date, the initial purchase price is offset against the product's ability to provide years of service. Tyndall enjoys a dominance in this price and quality relationship relative to its major competitors. Through improvements in its manufacturing, the company is working on creating a technological and quality advantage. For example, the company is reducing its raw lumber costs by investing in an automated rough mill, and improving the furniture's surface finish by investing in the latest sanding technology.

Exhibit 4

Market Analysis

- One Lexington table and chair set represents 25 percent of sales, while six Lexington table and chair sets represent 65 percent of sales volume.
- Fifty-five dealers operate galleries with 20 new galleries per year is the planned growth.
- The price/quality relationship is very important in Tyndall's markets. Tyndall currently enjoys a dominance in price and quality relative to its competitors.
- Tyndall's sales are to 1,800 active dealer accounts with 400 key accounts.
- Sales to dealer inventories represent 95 percent of dollar sales and 80 percent of unit sales.
- The distribution of dollar sales by customer type is:
  small independents, 42 percent.
  galleries, 24 percent.
  Mass merchandiser, 15 percent.
  Mom and pops, 12 percent.
  Large independents, 4 percent.
  Small chains, 3 percent.
- Consumers of Tyndall's furniture include:
  a. An increasing population of people in the 35–55 age range who have increasing discretionary income.
  b. 75 percent of Tyndall's customers are blue-collar workers, who are hard working and want high-quality, long-lasting, and traditional furniture.
- The "ideal" customer lead time is four weeks from the receipt of the customer's order on the most popular items.

Marketing Strategy

Products. Tyndall produced five major collections of furniture in oak and cherry woods (Exhibit 5). Bedroom furniture was seen as a major growth area, while dining room furniture's growth was restricted by capacity constraints on chair construction. While the typical style lasted for a 12-year period, sales over the period varied with time. The first three to five years of a product's life saw dramatic growth. This was followed by seven to nine years of modest growth. However, once decline set in, the drop-off in sales was sharp. This made product design and new product introductions critical. Over the last 11 years, Tyndall had introduced six completely new furniture groupings.

Target Markets. Galleries were becoming an increasingly important fact of life (Exhibit 6), for a number of reasons. Small dealers were disappearing due to consolidation in the industry and the increasing price of entry. Also, manufacturers were finding it increasingly difficult to

Exhibit 5

Product Line and Design Summary

- Tyndall is building an image as a full-service manufacturer of furniture.
- Tyndall focuses on solid-wood kitchen furniture in the upper portion of the medium-price range.
- Tyndall manufactures five major collections of furniture:
    1. Lexington II: Kitchen, dining room, and bedroom furniture in oak.
    2. Monroe: Kitchen, dining room, and bedroom furniture in oak.
    3. Philadelphia: Bedroom furniture in oak.
    4. Maddison: Dining room and bedroom furniture in cherry.
    5. Scandanavian: Line in oak.
- Bedroom is a new high-growth area for the firm.
- Dining room furniture is a non-growth area because of the lack of capacity for chairs.
- The Tyndall look is a "safe" design that has been around and has been successful in the industry.
- Six furniture groupings have been introduced by the firm in the last 11 years:
    1. Lexington dining room and kitchen group (11 years ago).
    2. Monroe dining room and kitchen group (eight years ago).
    3. Philadelphia bedroom group (four years ago).
    4. Maddison dining room and bedroom group (three years ago).
    5. Lexington bedroom group (one year ago).
    6. Scandinavian group (past year).
- The typical product life cycle for Tyndall's products is about 12 years.
- Growth will come from product diversification.
- Must avoid saturating a particular line.

---

serve a large number of small dealers. The retail market was also becoming more competitive due to the smaller portion of the typical consumer's budget being used to buy furniture.

For now, galleries, mass merchandisers, and large independents seemed to offer the best growth opportunities, along with product diversification.

Geographically, Tyndall showed particular strength in the Midwest and the Northeast. Minnesota and North and South Dakota were particularly good markets for Tyndall's traditionally styled furniture. The Southwest, Far West, Northwest, and the Rocky Mountain states were not particularly strong markets.

Pricing.   Pricing of furniture varied across customers. For example, sales discounts on furniture sold by Tyndall varied from 9 percent on products sold to mom-and-pop retailers to 28 percent on products sold to the one mass merchandiser Tyndall currently served (Exhibit 7). Fortunately, discounters did not play much of a role in Tyndall's market or these discounts may have been even larger.

Exhibit 6

Market Trends

- A rapidly increasing number of furniture gallery outlets.
- The total number of dealers in the customer base is decreasing.
- Small dealers are concerned about manufacturers limiting their distribution of furniture.
- A reduction in the number of dealers sold to in the gallery communities.
- The furniture market includes an increasing number of 35–55 year olds who have increasing discretionary income, but the percentage of consumer discretionary income actually spent on furniture is decreasing.
- The investment barrier for becoming a dealer is increasing.
- Manufacturers have less tolerance for small customers.
- Small dealers can't get some furniture lines.
- The big dealers are getting larger.
- The big chains are implementing acquisition programs.
- Increasingly, the big dealers are coming to Tyndall's markets.
- The successful dealers tend to dominate their sales territories, and they tend to be "determined" marketers with large advertising budgets.

EXHIBIT 7 Customer-Order Data

Customer Type	Average Sales Discount	Estimated Average Customer Lead Time (days)	Average Number of End-Product Items Shipped	Average Dollars Sales per Year per Customer
Galleries	21%	35	52	$ 206,151
Mom and pops	9	110	29	5,573
Small independents	17	35	41	30,221
Large independents	26	52	39	348,400
Small chains	22	44	43	99,220
Mass merchandiser	28	30	8	6,242,400

Profitability.   Because prices varied and because the product mix purchased differed from one customer type to another, average contributions also varied (Exhibit 8). Mom-and-pop stores yielded an average contribution per unit of $70.80 while small chains only yielded $31.09 per unit. There also was considerable variation in profitability across product types. Chairs contributed $24.11 per unit on average while tables contributed $125.42.

EXHIBIT 8   Average Contribution to Fixed Costs and Profit

	Contribution per Unit
Product type	
Chairs	$ 24.11
Tables	125.42
Case goods	98.17
Customer type	
Galleries	$ 39.77
Mom and pops	70.80
Small independents	52.79
Large independents	32.31
Small chains	31.09
Mass merchandiser	35.47

Sales force.   Tyndall did no exporting nor did it do much, if any, contract sales.[1] Thirty manufacturers' representatives handled the sales of Tyndall's products to its dealers, and most handled Tyndall's lines exclusively. Greg Procter was responsible for their activities and performance. He also was charged with the oversight of the production of sales literature, furniture industry journal advertising, and furniture market participation.

Procter felt that a Tyndall dealer ought to have a strong financial position, be able to display the full line, be willing to place a minimum order of $3,000, and do a minimum of $3,000 per year of business with Tyndall. Otherwise, Procter felt that the effort to serve and maintain a relationship with a dealer could not be justified.

---

[1]Sales to contractors, hotels, restaurants, and so forth.

CASE 24
TYNDALL FURNITURE COMPANY (B)

Don Rutkowski (vice president, manufacturing) was just finishing his presentation of a proposal to invest in a new rough mill at the company's component plant in Grand Rapids, Michigan (see Exhibit 1). He concluded,

> It is most important that we come to a decision in the near future. As the issues involved have been discussed for some time now, the proposed investment is not something that's new to us all. However, in order to capitalize on the advantages that having a modernized rough mill will provide, an important consideration is to phase its introduction in line with marketing's plans for a new product range linked to the High Point Furniture Fair this time next year. Getting the timing right is often, as we all know, as important as the investment itself.

Company Background

Established in 1898 by Henry H. Tyndall, the company remained a family-owned business until 1963, when it was bought out by Berkron Industries Inc., a large conglomerate with interests in textiles, chemicals, food, clothing, retailing, and, more recently, financial services. Although predominantly based in North America, Berkron also had interests in Australasia and Europe.

Although in the past the company had been an above-average profit earner within the furniture industry as a whole, in recent years its performance had declined (see Exhibit 2), a fact that led to the appointment of Matt Culley as chief executive officer two years before. As with most markets, the furniture industry was both becoming increasingly more competitive and witnessing significant changes in both products and market outlets (see Exhibit 3).

Product Strategy

"Part of our decline," explained Greg Procter (vice president, marketing), "has been the failure in the past to offer an adequate product range. Understandably, our customers have been demanding a fuller product line as a key feature in boosting overall sales. Our principal furniture designs," he continued, "are Colonial and Early American, and within these 'looks' we use primarily oak and cherry woods." In order to enhance the styles they sell, many of the items are made of solid wood and, even where they use laminates, the products all look the part—good and solid. One advantage of this has been that Tyndall enjoys relatively stable designs. In fact, their designs typically sell for 10 to 12 and even 15 years. This compares to the furniture industry as a whole where designs sell over a much shorter product life cycle. Within these two sectors Tyndall's primary market focus in on kitchen and dining room furniture in the upper portion of the medium-price range. In order to avoid saturating a particular line, they have in recent years

This case was prepared by Professors W. L. Berry (Ohio State University), T. J. Hill (London Business School), J. E. Klompmaker (University of North Carolina), and W. G. Morrissey (North Carolina State University) as a basis for class discussion rather than to illustrate either effective or ineffective handling of a business situation. © Professor W. L. Berry, Professor J. E. Klompmaker, Professor W. G. Morrissey, or AMD Publishing (U.K.). Inquiries in the U.S.A. to Zip Publishing, 1634 N. High Street, Columbus, Ohio 43201.

Exhibit 1

TO: Tyndall Furniture Company Board of Directors
FROM: Don Rutkowski, Vice President of Manufacturing
SUBJECT: Proposed Rough Mill for the Tyndall Components Plant

We propose to purchase an Oliver rough mill to replace the current manual cross-cutting operation at the components plant. This mill would convert kiln-dried raw lumber into semifinished dimension stock for further processing in the fine mill, utilizing advanced computer-controlled machining and material handling systems. The new equipment would also include a Taylor edge-gluing system to increase the output of laminated dimension stock components for the chair, table, and miscellaneous case goods assembly plants.

The overall impact of this proposal would be to increase the rough mill capacity to 230 percent of the current capacity in terms of net board feet per day. All of this capacity increase will be used to decrease our dependence on outside suppliers for edge-glued dimension stock components. The purchase of edge-glued dimension stock components will decrease from the current level of 85 percent to 15 percent of the total requirements for these items. The overall production output of the other components produced by the components plant will not be significantly affected by this proposal.

The new equipment will increase the capacity of the rough mill and provide important cost savings in direct labor and material to enhance our competitive position in price-sensitive markets. Specific benefits include:

- Annual direct labor and dimension stock material savings of $1 million.
- Material cost savings by purchasing lower-grade raw lumber.
- Direct labor savings due to improved productivity (obtained by a 130 percent increase in output with only a 10 percent increase in direct labor) and reduced setup time because families of parts can now be run on the molding and tenoner machines.
- Reduced manufacturing lead times from four months to six weeks due to manufacturing instead of purchasing long lead-time dimension stock components.*
- Improved product quality in chair-seat glued joints and other panel stock.
- Reduced work-in-process inventory, finished component inventory, and component part shortages because of a more even flow of dimension stock material through the components plant. (Vendors currently tend to deliver material in large batches, which produces an undesirable mix of products that does not fit well with the manufacturing schedule, creating unnecessary levels of inventory.)

The investment cost of the new production process is $4.2 million. This includes the cost of extending the components plant building, the rough mill and edge-gluing equipment, the additional dry kiln capacity required, and the installation and training costs. If approved at the board of directors meeting at the end of this week, this equipment could be installed and in operation within a six-month period.

*Dimension stock is wood components ready for fine mill operations.

EXHIBIT 2   **Furniture Industry Comparisons**

	Current Year Minus:				Current Year
	4	*3*	*2*	*1*	
Tyndall (%)					
Sales	100.0	100.0	100.0	100.0	100.0
Cost of goods sold	79.1	78.3	78.3	79.2	78.1
Net profit before tax	4.8	3.7	4.4	3.5	4.2
Return of total assets	5.4	5.1	6.5	6.0	7.1
Average all case goods companies (%)					
Sales	100.0	100.0	100.0	—	—
Cost of goods sold	75.9	75.2	76.7	n/a	n/a
Net profit before tax	7.7	7.4	7.3	n/a	n/a
Return on total assets	n/a	n/a	7.0	n/a	n/a
Average all furniture companies (%)					
Sales	100.0	100.0	100.0	—	—
Cost of goods sold	75.6	74.6	75.1	n/a	n/a
Net profit before tax	7.6	8.3	8.4	n/a	n/a
Return on total assets	8.2	8.7	8.9	n/a	n/a

NOTE: n/a signifies that the particular industry information is not available.

---

been increasing efforts in bedroom and upholstered product segments, recognizing that growth will also come from product diversification. In the last five years, they have introduced the equivalent of a new group[1] of products each year, three of which were bedroom lines.

Keeping marketing initiatives in line with manufacturing capabilities and capacity has been, however, an important and necessary consideration. "It is," explained Greg, "essential for the overall success of the business to take into account the available spare capacity within the different parts of manufacturing as one factor in new product range decisions." While they could easily sell more kitchen furniture than they currently make, they have a problem in chair capacity that restricts overall sales. This factor has also made dining room furniture a nongrowth area. On the other hand, Tyndall now sees bedroom furniture as the new high-growth area for the firm, as they have more than adequate capacity in existing case good facilities to meet a significant increase in sales of these products. In that way, the company will best be able to improve overall company performance by increasing the utilization of existing investments in process capacity.

Marketing Strategy

Greg went on to explain that the retail outlets for furniture sales had undergone changes in recent years (see Exhibit 4) and that recognizing these was important if the company wished to maintain its market share, let alone grow. He then continued to outline the marketing strategy being developed as having the following important features.

First, the company needs to continually review its product range. We must build on the good-quality image developed over the years by continuing to push hard in those segments in which our products

---

[1]A group refers to a collection of products that go into one room in a home.

EXHIBIT 3   Tyndall Sales Analysis

	Current Year Minus:		Current Year
	2	1	
Small chain:			
$ Sales	$1,188,189	$1,468,848	$1,389,077
Number of outlets	14	14	14
Small independents:			
$ Sales	$19,417,109	$20,005,636	$18,162,589
Number of outlets	577	594	601
Large independents:			
$ Sales	$1,504,000	$1,841,000	$1,742,000
Number of outlets	5	5	5
Galleries:			
$ Sales	$7,655,279	$8,534,630	$10,307,532
Number of outlets	48	50	50
Mom and pops:			
$ Sales	$6,813,000	$4,288,000	$4,921,200
Number of outlets	1365	1126	883
Mass merchandiser:			
$ Sales	$5,576,000	$5,285,000	$6,242,400
Number of outlets	1	1	1
Total sales $	$42,153,577	$41,423,114	$42,764,798
Total outlets	2010	1790	1554

---

already have a good position and in which we currently do well. In addition, we have recognized the need to consider other products that will help us develop new markets, both as a way to grow overall sales and to meet our customers' expectations with regard to our image as a full-service manufacturer.[2]

The second major feature is then to remain alert to the changes taking place in each of our segments. With regard to this last point, the large dealers are getting larger due to their successful acquisition programs. In addition, we also recognize the increasing use of furniture galleries as an important means of getting our furniture in front of the general public. It has been necessary, therefore, to ensure that we have an adequate presence in this segment as the total number of galleries eventually available will be limited. Fortunately, we saw this ahead of time and were early into the development. We intend to continue this initiative. Currently, we support 50 furniture galleries, and we intend to double that number in the next three years. In some ways, galleries provide two sets of advantages—on the one hand, the total segment sales are large, giving to us a homogeneous marketing thrust; while on the other, as each individual outlet is small, we do not experience the same level of customer pressure as we do with other large outlets. For this reason, we are giving considerable support to this segment, a fact that certainly is encouraging us to continue to expand our product range, thus maximizing the level of product exposure to the public. Add the galleries initiative to our small independent market segment, and the combined sales represents two thirds of our total sales.

We sell another 15 percent through a mass merchandiser, which takes the overall to 81 percent of total sales. Our policy, therefore, has been to try to keep a balance. Certainly we have deliberately limited sales to the mass merchandiser outlet as a policy of not putting too many eggs in this one basket.

---

[2]A full-service manufacturer is a company that produces a wide range of furniture products including case and upholstered furniture.

EXHIBIT 4   Furniture Gallery Survey

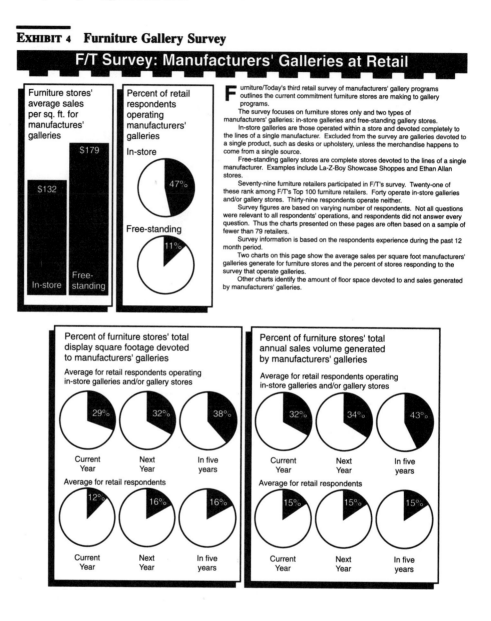

F/T Survey: Manufacturers' Galleries at Retail

Furniture stores' average sales per sq. ft. for manufactures' galleries

$179

$132

In-store

Free-standing

Percent of retail respondents operating manufacturers' galleries

In-store

47%

Free-standing

11%

Furniture/Today's third retail survey of manufacturers' gallery programs outlines the current commitment furniture stores are making to gallery programs.

The survey focuses on furniture stores only and two types of manufacturers' galleries: in-store galleries and free-standing gallery stores.

In-store galleries are those operated within a store and devoted completely to the lines of a single manufacturer. Excluded from the survey are galleries devoted to a single product, such as desks or upholstery, unless the merchandise happens to come from a single source.

Free-standing gallery stores are complete stores devoted to the lines of a single manufacturer. Examples include La-Z-Boy Showcase Shoppes and Ethan Allan stores.

Seventy-nine furniture retailers participated in F/T's survey. Twenty-one of these rank among F/T's Top 100 furniture retailers. Forty operate in-store galleries and/or gallery stores. Thirty-nine respondents operate neither.

Survey figures are based on varying number of respondents. Not all questions were relevant to all respondents' operations, and respondents did not answer every question. Thus the charts presented on these pages are often based on a sample of fewer than 79 retailers.

Survey information is based on the respondents experience during the past 12 month period.

Two charts on this page show the average sales per square foot manufacturers' galleries generate for furniture stores and the percent of stores responding to the survey that operate galleries.

Other charts identify the amount of floor space devoted to and sales generated by manufacturers' galleries.

Percent of furniture stores' total display square footage devoted to manufacturers' galleries

Average for retail respondents operating in-store galleries and/or gallery stores

29% Current Year   32% Next Year   38% In five years

Average for retail respondents

12% Current Year   16% Next Year   16% In five years

Percent of furniture stores' total annual sales volume generated by manufacturers' galleries

Average for retail respondents operating in-store galleries and/or gallery stores

32% Current Year   34% Next Year   43% In five years

Average for retail respondents

15% Current Year   15% Next Year   15% In five years

In addition, we are also pushing sales with small chains and large independents in order to create a more balanced portfolio within our segments. We know that mom and pops are declining and see little prospect in this segment for the future. These perspectives need to be reflected in the amount of effort and resource we are putting behind each segment. Keeping a watch on the various segments will give us the necessary balance we require while ensuring the necessary sales growth we need.

Our strategy has been aimed at contributing to the need to reverse the company's profit decline over recent years. By securing our future market outlets and expanding the product range offerings, we feel that this will not only safeguard the future but also make best use of manufacturing's capabilities and capacity in the short term.

Manufacturing

The company has a number of plants in the Grand Rapids area. The component plant includes drying kilns, which take "green" lumber and dry it before processing. The wood first goes through the rough mill and then the fine mill, and these components are then sent to the chair and case plants against agreed schedules. In addition, both the chair and case plants at Grand Rapids make some of the components they need while others are purchased from outside. The next stages are subassembly and assembly before a final product is finished and packed. Exhibits 5A and 5B gives details of the various stages in manufacturing.

"Most of our products go through the main production lines," explained Don Rutkowski, "although some are handled (in part) in an off-line mode because of the low volumes involved. Over the years we have continuously improvised and improved our processes in order to reduce process times. This has enabled us not only to reduce direct labor costs but also to increase effective capacity. Whenever possible, we have attempted to increase throughput while ensuring that quality levels have been maintained."

The various types of products that comprise a furniture group within one of the furniture styles are made in Tyndall's own production plant. As implied by its name, the chair plant makes all the chair designs called for in any of the numerous groups within each furniture style. Currently, this totals over 60 chair types. All the other items that go into a furniture group are made in the case plant (see Exhibit 5A). Although, as explained earlier, some component parts are brought in from outside, there are very few instances when an actual furniture product is purchased complete, "It is imperative that we retain control over our quality," explained Don, "a factor that underlines the proposal to invest in the new rough mill facility." (See Exhibit 1.) Finished items are then collated to meet outstanding customers' orders or otherwise go into inventory to support future sales.

The three plants (i.e., component, chair, and case) primarily work on a single, eight-hour shift, with overtime as required. At certain times in the year the different plants do work a second shift. However, within the furniture industry there is a strong and well-established argument against double-shift working, especially with regard to maintaining high quality levels. "In order to meet demand, it is imperative that we keep the processes well scheduled to avoid delays elsewhere," explained Don. "The only capacity problems we have concern the chair plant, particularly in the seating and finishing processes." He continued by explaining that overtime is worked at most times of the year, which helps keep good schedules and reduce waiting time in the plant.

EXHIBIT 5A

Process Flow Chart

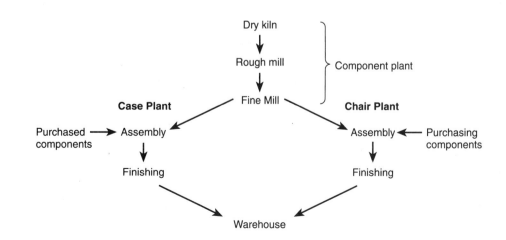

Manufacturing Process Description

Dry Kiln

Green lumber must be dried to 6–8 percent for use in furniture. This is accomplished through a combination of air drying and drying at elevated temperatures with forced air circulation in a dry kiln. The kiln-drying process can take from one to eight weeks, depending on such factors as species, thickness, and initial moisture content. To cope with the mix required, a number of kilns are typically installed.

Rough Mill

The function of the rough mill is to convert rough lumber into blank parts that are free of defects and ready for detail machining. The defects are removed in the rough mill in the process of cutting up the boards. Depending on the parts specifications, the defect-free boards are then either edge-glued into wide panels or machined in the molder into appropriate shapes. The processing of the lumber is performed on equipment that is normally connected by conveyors so that there is a continuous flow of the work in process. The rough mill process generates about 40 percent waste based on the board feet of lumber brought in, and so it is an important cost-control center in the whole manufacturing process.

Fine Mill

Parts are processed into final shapes and dimensions in the fine mill using a wide variety of types of machines. The operations performed include turning, shaping, routing, sawing, bending, boring, and a variety of sanding steps, with some of these operations being performed in combination on special equipment. The company has been quite creative in linking various machines together with special conveyors so that parts like chair turnings, bent chair-back bows, chair seats, and drawer sides and backs can be economically processed in large production runs. The trade-off in these process developments has been long setup times for low processing times and decreased work in process. This type of equipment has been utilized most extensively in the chair plant. The machinery in the case plant is arranged so that tables, panels, and solid-wood rails follow their own flow paths. This provides for easier control of the flow of these parts from operation to operation. Materials handling is by skids that are moved by "jack boys" using hydraulic lift jacks.

Assembly

Parts are accumulated until all of the necessary parts to complete an item are on hand. The final assembly is carried out in a variety of hand and mechanical operations that are grouped for tables, cases, and chairs in separate sections of the

Exhibit 5B
(concluded)

plant. Wherever possible, these operations have been arranged on conveyors so the flow is easily controlled and paced. Various fitting and hand-sanding operations are performed along these conveyors so that when the assembled items reach the finishing room they are ready for the finishing process.

Finishing

Tables and cases are finished on a palletized conveyor with the pallets driven through the finishing steps in a continuous flow. Chairs are placed on an overhead conveyor. The various spray booths and ovens are sized for the speed at which the conveyor is designed to operate so that there is time to perform the various spraying operations and dry the different finish coats.

"The relatively long life cycle for our typical products and the stability of our product designs generate greater total volumes over the life of a product and underpin our process improvement strategy. We are making an increasingly wide range of products," he commented, "and the range of shopfloor order quantities varies significantly. However, we feel we are up to the task in all aspects of the job." He then highlighted the good product designs that the company had consistently provided and the excellent image it currently enjoyed in the marketplace in terms of the quality of its products. "Some species of wood," commented Don, "are more difficult to process than others (for example, cherry is more demanding than oak), and this leads to a higher reject level in the process. However, we have a good quality-control system, which helps maintain the high standards necessary in the segments in which we compete."

Exhibits 6–9 show data on representative current products, and Exhibit 10 reports order-winning and qualifying criteria.

Manufacturing Strategy

Don Rutkowski then outlined the rationale behind the principal investments and improvements that manufacturing had successfully introduced over the last few years. "We have been trying to pursue a number of improvements within manufacturing to be better able to support our products in the marketplace," he explained.

Although there are numerous examples of small but important improvements in all the plants, we have been pursuing two principal activities whenever they made sense. One has been to automate processes, such as the table leg turning system, in order to reduce direct labor costs, increase output levels, maintain a more consistent level of quality, and enable us to gain a greater control over scheduling. The second initiative has been to link a number of processes together within a series so that a product goes through two or more operations before it comes out of the process. An example of this is our multiple-head boring machine. In addition to the gains similar to those secured by automation, these initiatives also have reduced work-in-process inventory in the particular part of the process involved. Of course, and it almost goes without saying, we have also increased capacity by these investments, a factor high in our priorities.

EXHIBIT 6   Representative Current Products[1]

Item Number	Description (year of introduction[2])	ABC Code[3]	Current Year Annual Sales (units)	Production Line	Production (units/eight-hour shift)[4]
B2089	Table, Maddison cherry dining room group (3)	B	635	Table	133
B2126	Chair, Maddison cherry dining room group (3)	B	1,826	Chair	675
B2241	Chest, Maddison cherry dining room group (3)	C	70	Case	190
C2313	Dresser, Tyler cherry bedroom group (3)	B	365	Case	145
B2474	Headboard, Maddison cherry dining room group (3)	C	183	Case	130
A1073	Table, Monroe oak kitchen group (8)	C	155	Table	126
A1085	Table, Monroe oak kitchen group (8)	A	543	Table	222
A1106	Chair, Monroe oak kitchen group (8)	AA	10,841	Chair	1,400
A1024	Table, Lexington oak kitchen group (11)	A	2,156	Table	281
A1145	Chair, Lexington oak kitchen group (11)	B	758	Chair	30
A1126	Chair, Lexington oak kitchen group (11)	AA	33,170	Chair	1,100
C2201	Chest, Lexington oak bedroom group (1)	A	729	Case	300
C1221	Chest, Lexington oak bedroom group (1)	B	214	Case	160
C1424	Headboard, Lexington oak bedroom group (1)	C	15	Case	165
C1544	Footboard, Lexington oak bedroom group (1)	C	10	Case	175
C1457	Headboard, Philadelphia oak bedroom group (4)	C	3	Case	90
C1567	Footboard, Philadelphia oak bedroom group (4)	C	1	Case	115

NOTES: 1. The products selected here are representative of the wide range of products in terms of ABC code, related annual units produced, production line, and year of introduction.

2. The figure following description denotes the number of years since this item was introduced. So, item B2089 was introduced three years ago.

3. ABC code: The code letters in this column are the company's designation relating to the number of units produced each year as shown below.

AA = Very high-volume items selected by management.

A = Remainder of items.

B = Chairs, 401–2,000 units/year; cases, 201–1,000 units/year; tables, and pedestals, 201–800 units/year.

C = Chairs, 0–400 units/year; all others, 0–200 units/year.

4. Low-volume items are frequently made off-line with varying labor levels being allocated. This accounts for the low production rate in some instances (eg A1145).

5. Tables are assembled and finished in the case plant.

Corporate Overview

"As a company," reflected Matt Culley, "we have been attempting to reverse the decline in profits experienced over the last 10 years. We recognize that the source of the problem lies both in marketing and manufacturing. What we make and where we sell it is a prerequisite for success. Couple the recent and proposed process investments and we should have the plant in better shape. Certainly we are looking to the substantial improvements provided by the proposed rough mill to lead the way to better profits."

EXHIBIT 7 Current Year's Data for Representative Current Products

Item Number	Wholesale List Price	Average Selling Price	Unit Variable Cost	Defects per 1,000 Units Shipped	Average Inventory (units)	Average Sales Order Backlog (units)
B2089	$419	$384	$267	74	349	69
B2126	100	96	60	18	735	179
B2241	356	357	178	140	12	21
C2313	494	485	378	11	20	53
B2474	219	202	126	283	65	36
A1073	418	384	138	19	23	11
A1085	272	198	113	8	29	345
A1106	66	51	23	0	73	1,806
A1024	209	144	87	15	459	824
A1145	119	102	69	0	30	114
A1126	99	74	43	2	1,078	11,132
C2201	159	159	130	0	476	370
C1221	359	346	210	0	66	100
C1424	279	239	135	0	29	1
C1544	190	170	98	0	38	2
C1457	303	250	119	0	29	1
C1567	192	158	105	0	31	1

NOTES: 1. All figures have been rounded to the nearest whole number.

2. Average number of defects per 1,000 units *shipped to customers.*

EXHIBIT 8 Customer-Order Data

Customer Type	Average Sales Discount	Contribution to Fixed Costs and Profit/Unit	Average Lead Time (Days)*	Average Defects/ 1000 Units Shipped	Average Assembly Line Hours/Unit	Estimated No. of End Products Items Shipped to Each Customer Type	Average Sales $/Year/Customer
Galleries	21%	$39.77	35	11	.0153	52	206,151
Mom and pop	9	70.80	110	7	.0188	29	5,573
Small independents	17	52.79	35	11	.0206	41	30,221
Large independents	26	32.31	52	2	.0114	39	348,400
Small chains	22	31.09	44	10	.0126	43	99,220
Mass merchandisers	28	35.47	30	7	.0110	8	6,242,400

*All customers tend to want delivery of products as soon as possible. The lead times given in this column are the average delivery times which the company provides for all products and hence reflects company preference and customer leverage.

Exhibit 9   Current Year's Manufacturing Data

Production Line	Sales Discount Percentage	Defects per 1,000 Units Shipped	Lead Time (days)[1]	Contribution to Fixed Costs and Expenses per Unit	Chair Plant Capacity Utilization Percent Run Time	Percent Setup Time	Percent of Items Stocked in Finished Goods Inventory
Case goods	2	41	8	$ 74.51			
Chairs	24	2	44	30.53			
Tables	22	24	15	80.67			
ABC categories[2]							
AA	25	2	47	30.26	23%	5%	6%
A	25	10	24	55.48	20	4	18
B	6	22	23	61.40	36	4	29
C	7	148	2	153.99	7	1	47
					86	14	100

NOTES: 1. Lead times are the average days taken to deliver items within each product type or category. They reflect the fact that some products are held in finished goods inventory while others have order-backlog requirements.

2. See footnote 3 of Exhibit 3.

EXHIBIT 10   Order-Winning and Qualifying Criteria

	Small Chain			Large Independent			Small Independent			Mass Merchandiser			Gallery			Mom and Pop		
	C	2	5	C	2	5	C	2	5	C	2	5	C	2	5	C	2	5
Lexington/Philadelphia—Bedroom, High–Medium Volume (items C2201, C1221)																		
Quality conformance	60	60	55	60	55	50	60	60	60	60	60		60	50	55	60	50	50
Price	QQ	QQ	35	QQ	35	40	QQ	QQ	20	30	30		20	30	35	QQ	10	10
After-sales service	10	10	10	10	10	10	10	10	20	5	5		20	20	10			
Delivery reliability	QQ	QQ	QQ	QQ	QQ	QQ	QQ	QQ	Q	5	5		QQ	QQ	QQ			
Design	30	30	Q	30	Q	Q	30	30	Q	Q	Q		Q	Q	Q			
Design changes																		
New products																		
Customer relations	Q	Q	Q	Q	Q	Q	Q	Q		QQ	QQ		Q	Q	Q	40	40	40
Lexington/Philadelphia—Bedroom, Low Volume (items C1424, C1544, C1457, C1567)																		
Quality conformance							40	40	40				50	50	50	40	40	40
Price							Q	Q	Q				10	10	10	Q	Q	Q
After-sales service							Q	Q	Q				5	5	5	Q	Q	Q
Delivery reliability							Q	Q	Q				QQ	QQ	QQ	Q	Q	Q
Design							60	60	60				35	35	35	60	60	60
Design changes																		
New products																		
Customer relations																		
Tyler Cherry—Bedroom, High Volume (items C2313, B2474)																		
Quality conformance	40	40	40				50	50	50				50	50	50	55	55	55
Price	15	20	25				20	25	35				20	25	35	Q	10	15
After-sales service	10	10	10				10	10	10				10	10	10	10	10	10
Delivery reliability	Q	Q	Q				QQ	QQ	QQ				QQ	QQ	QQ	Q	Q	Q
Design	35	30	25				20	15	5				20	15	5	35	25	20
Design changes																		
New products																		
Customer relations	Q	Q	Q					Q	Q				Q	Q	Q		Q	Q
Maddison Cherry—Dining Room, High–Medium Volume (items B2089, B2126)																		
Quality conformance		50	50				50	50	50				50	50	50	55	55	55
Price		25	30				20	25	30				20	25	30	Q	10	20
After-sales service		10	10				10	10	10				10	10	10	10	10	10
Delivery reliability		QQ	QQ				QQ	QQ	QQ				Q	QQ	QQ	Q		
Design		15	10				20	15	10				20	15	10	35	25	15
Design changes																		
New products																		
Customer relations		QQ	QQ				QQ	QQ	QQ				Q	QQ	QQ	Q	QQ	QQ

EXHIBIT 10 *(concluded)*

	Small Chain			Large Independent			Small Independent			Mass Merchandiser			Gallery			Mom and Pop		
	C	2	5	C	2	5	C	2	5	C	2	5	C	2	5	C	2	5
Maddison/Tyler Cherry—Bed/Dining Room, Low Volume (item B2241)																		
Quality conformance				40	40	40							50	50	50	40	40	40
Price				Q	Q	Q							10	10	10	Q	Q	Q
After-sales service				Q	Q	Q							5	5	5	Q	Q	Q
Delivery reliability				Q	Q	Q							QQ	QQ	QQ	Q	Q	Q
Design				60	60	60							35	35	35	60	60	60
Design changes																		
New products																		
Customer relations													Q	Q	Q	Q	Q	Q
Monroe/Lexington Oak—Chairs/Case Goods/Tables, High Volume (items A1106, A1126)																		
Quality conformance	50	50	40	50	50	40	60			60	60	60	50	50	50	50	50	50
Price	40	40	50	40	40	50	20			20	30	30	30	40	40	10	10	10
After-sales service	10	10	10	10	10	10	20			20	10	10	20	10	10			
Delivery reliability	QQ	QQ	QQ	QQ	QQ	QQ	Q			QQ	QQ	QQ	QQ	QQ	QQ			
Design	Q	Q	Q	Q	Q	Q	Q			Q	Q	Q	Q	Q	Q			
Design changes																		
New products																		
Customer relations	Q	Q	Q	Q	Q	Q				QQ	QQ	QQ	Q	Q	Q	40	40	40
Monroe/Lexington Oak—Kitchen, Medium Volume (item A1085)																		
Quality conformance	55	50	45	55	50	45	60	55	50				50	45	40	50	50	50
Price	35	40	45	35	40	45	20	30	40				30	35	40	10	20	30
After-sales service	10	10	10	10	10	10	20	15	10				20	20	20		Q	Q
Delivery reliability	QQ	QQ	QQ	QQ	QQ	QQ	Q	Q	Q				QQ	QQ	QQ		QQ	QQ
Design	Q	Q	Q	Q	Q	Q	Q	QQ	QQ				Q	Q	Q			
Design changes																		
New products																		
Customer relations	Q	QQ	QQ	Q	QQ	QQ		Q	QQ				Q	QQ	QQ	40	30	20
Monroe/Lexington Oak—Kitchen/Dining Room, Low Volume (item A1073)																		
Quality conformance	60	60	60	60	60	60	60	60	60				50	50	50	30	30	30
Price	Q	Q	Q	Q	Q	Q	Q	Q	Q				10	10	10	Q	Q	Q
After-sales service	10	10	10	10	10	10	10	10	10				10	10	10	Q	Q	Q
Delivery reliability	Q	Q	Q	Q	Q	Q	Q	Q	Q				Q	Q	Q			
Design	30	30	30	30	30	30	30	30	30				30	30	30	30	30	30
Design changes																		
New products																		
Customer relations	Q	Q	Q	Q	Q								Q	Q	Q	40	40	40

NOTES: 1. C = current year; 2 = in two years; 5 = in five years

2. Q denotes a qualifier. QQ denotes an order-losing sensitive qualifier.

3. Blanks indicate that these products are not (or will not be) sold to the particular type of customer.

CASE 25
TYNDALL FURNITURE COMPANY (C)

"The proposal for the new shopfloor control system has been in your hands for a week now, and I would like to schedule a meeting to discuss it tomorrow morning at nine. We have all had high hopes that this would help us to improve delivery performance and productivity. Now is the time to review it and see if we feel this is the system for us." Don Rutkowski, vice president of manufacturing, was just concluding a meeting with his plant managers and key staff people. A great deal of work had gone into the preparation of the proposal, and management was enthusiastic about it.

Company Background

Established in 1898 by Henry H. Tyndall, the company remained a family-owned business until 1963, when it was bought by a large conglomerate, Berkron Industries, Inc. The Tyndall Furniture Company had grown conservatively in its production of dining room and bedroom furniture in primarily Early American designs. The company wanted to grow at a faster rate to take advantage of some market opportunities and to increase its profitability, which was lagging that of the industry (see Exhibit 1 in Case 23). One of the expansion moves currently underway involved the acquisition of a nearby plant producing fully upholstered furniture, which is a new product category to Tyndall. Adding fully upholstered furniture to its line would open new opportunities in living room furniture while increasing the company's appeal to dealers as a full-product-line supplier.

Marketing and Product Strategy

"Sales in our market segments have been shifting somewhat over the past several years (see Exhibit 2 in Case 23). We intend to double our in-store galleries while continuing our retreat from the mom and pop segment," stated Greg Procter, vice president of marketing.

> The mass merchandiser is obviously an important customer, but we do not want to become too dependent on a single customer, so we have tended to limit our sales with him. At the same time we need to stay sensitive to developments in our other market segments and remain flexible enough to respond to these changes while achieving a 10 percent annual growth rate in total sales.
>
> Our past product strategy has been part of our current problem in achieving more growth. We have been short of dining room chair capacity while having some surplus case capacity. This recently prompted us to bring out more bedroom groups, taking advantage of this case capacity. It is nearly impossible to closely control our sales in each category, and it is apparent that at some point we will have to increase our production capacity in order to service our customers. In the meantime, we have kept our delivery service commitments to key dealers by giving them first priority on available-to-ship products. See Exhibit 10 in Case 24 for a review of the order winners in the company's different methods.

This case was prepared by Professors W. L. Berry (Ohio State University), T. J. Hill (London Business School), J. C. Klompmaker (University of North Carolina), and W. G. Morrissey (North Carolina State University) as a basis for class discussion rather than to illustrate either effective or ineffective handling of an administrative situation. © Professor W. L. Berry, Professor J. E. Klompmaker, Professor W. G. Morrissey, or AMD Publishing (U.K.). Inquiries in the U.S.A. to Zip Publishing, 1634 N. High Street, Columbus, Ohio 43201.

Manufacturing

The company has a number of plants in the Grand Rapids area. The component plant, which is some distance outside of Grand Rapids, includes the dry kilns that take green lumber and dry it before processing. The rough mill removes all defects from the lumber to produce "blanks," which then are processed into finished parts in the machining and sanding departments of the component plant. Some blanks are obtained from outside suppliers. The component plant supplies parts to the case plant. It is scheduled to start supplying parts to the case plant and to the fully upholstered plant in the near future. The chair plant machines all of its own parts on separate facilities. See Exhibit 5B in Case 24 for an outline of the manufacturing process.

Rutkowski, in discussing the machining of fully upholstered parts, stated, "There is sufficient kiln capacity. Our equipment and people are more than adequate to machine these parts. Fully upholstered parts are made from lower-grade lumber, require less machining, and are not sanded so they will not materially add to our work load. The dowel joints used in upholstered furniture construction do not require the more complex machining of the products in our current product line. The typical upholstery plant has rather rudimentary equipment compared to the sophisticated machinery we have so we should have no trouble."

The plants primarily work on a single, eight-hour shift, with overtime as required. At certain times in the year the plants do work a second shift. However, within the furniture industry there is a reluctance to work a double shift because of quality and supervision problems.

"The relatively long life cycle for our typical products and the stability of our product designs generate greater total volumes over the life of a product and underpin our process improvement strategy. However, we are making an increasingly wide range of products," Rutkowski commented, "and the range of production order quantities varies significantly. We do feel we are up to the task in all aspects of the job." Rutkowski then highlighted the good product designs that the company had consistently provided and the excellent image it currently enjoys in the marketplace in terms of the quality of its products.

"Greg Procter has expressed his concerns about maintaining reliable deliveries in the face of capacity problems." Rutkowski was obviously concerned as he made these comments: "Currently I estimate that we are running at 100 percent of our chair capacity while the table and case lines are at 90 and 80 percent levels each (Exhibit 1). We are going to have to do some careful analysis of this situation in view of some of the changes that are taking place. It takes two years to build and bring new capacity on-line."

Manufacturing Planning and Control (MPC) System

The current MPC system began with master production scheduling being done by Jack Joyner in the marketing division. Joyner described his procedures, "We usually schedule about twice a month. Our priority is to load AA- and A-class items into production first. These are classifications that were set up when we had a consultant design the system for us [Exhibit 2]. B- and C-class items are loaded as capacity is available. A list of the items and quantities is sent to Louise in the case plant and Donna in the chair plant. They actually schedule the date of production of these items and return the schedules to me. They request any change in order sequence or quantity they feel would benefit manufacturing efficiency."

Louise and Donna prepared the schedules based on the standard hours required of critical work centers. With the assistance of several clerks, they operated a simple manual shopfloor control system that allowed them to load and monitor critical operation performance rather closely. Donna stated, "I often ask Jack for changes in the quantities of individual chair orders for class AA and A items so they are made in smaller runs. This allows us to work in the smaller

---

EXHIBIT 1   Current Year's Manufacturing Data

Production Line	Customer Lead Time (days)	Production Contribution	Units	Current Year's Sales $	Percent of Total
Chairs	44	$30.53	277,400	$22,194,800	51.9%
Tables	15	80.67	29,699	5,345,700	12.5
Cases	8	74.51	41,148	15,224,300	35.6
				$42,764,800	100.0%

ABC Categories	Customer Lead Time (days)	Contribution	Percent Items in Finished Goods Inventory
AA	47	$ 30.26	6
A	24	55.48	18
B	23	61.40	29
C	2	153.99	47
			100%

NOTE: See footnote 3 of Exhibit 3, Case 24 for explanation of ABC categories.

B and C item orders that would otherwise never get made. Our chair production facilities are not geared for small runs, but the customers cannot wait forever for these items.''

Louise had somewhat more difficulty than Donna in that parts were supplied from the components plant that was not on the same site. She overcame this problem by means of a daily conference call between herself and the foremen and production control staff of the two plants. By means of this call she was able to impart any priorities and to anticipate when needed parts would be delivered. While dependent on the knowledge of the individuals involved, the system had proven to be simple and effective. Louise was more enthusiastic about the new shopfloor control system than Donna, who felt it would be hard to make it easier or more effective than the present system. Donna was determined to keep an open mind even though she had her doubts.

As finished case goods were packed they were placed into a large warehouse. Using the information on the inventory in the warehouse (Exhibit 3) and production schedules, customer orders were lined up for shipment, with first priority going to the mass merchandiser, galleries, and key customers. In this manner reliable, short delivery cycles to critical customers had been maintained. It had become increasingly difficult over the past two years to keep this working well as chair capacity in particular became strained.

The proposed changes in the MPC system related to shopfloor controls. It was felt that a modern, computerized system would eliminate the manual work and provide information in a real time mode. A consultant had been selected, and it was his proposal that Rutkowski had just received. An outline summary of the proposal's main points is shown in Exhibit 4. The cost of the software and training was quoted at $300,000 and would require nine months to implement.

Exhibit 2

Plant Loading and Scheduling Rules

Order Point

	Order Point Calculation	
ABC Class	Chairs/Cases Lead Time = 16	Tables/Pedestals Lead Time = 13
AA	$D \times LT + SS$	$D \times LT + SS$
A	$D (LT - 7)$	$D (LT - 7)$
B	$D (LT - 13)$	0
C	0 for 10 weeks	0 for 13 weeks

- D = forecasted weekly demand for an item; LT = lead time in weeks; and SS = safety stock quantity.
- Order when available to sell < order point.
- Available to sell = inventory + on order − backlog.
- Reviewed quarterly.

Order Quantity

Order quantity = $52D$/number of cuttings per year, where the number of cuttings per year for AA = 8, A = 4, B = 2, and C = 1. (Reviewed quarterly.)

Master Production Scheduling

- AA and A items are loaded first.
- Schedules are created by loading forward to individual items' daily capacities and with an allowance for setup time on critical operations.
- Schedules are created irregularly every one to four weeks.

EXHIBIT 3   Representative Item Inventory Status

Item Number	ABC Code	Production Line	Weekly Demand	Gross Inventory	Weeks of Inventory	Allocated Inventory	Scheduled Production	Order Backlog	Weeks of Backlog	Available to Sell
7344	A	Case	17	264	15.5	13	99	238	14.0	112
6306	A	Case	24	32	1.3	32	341	183	7.6	158
3461	A	Chair	24	151	6.3	151	500	484	20.2	16
6212	A	Chair	112	928	8.3	284	3,500	655	5.8	3,489
1247	A	Chair	26	0	0.0	0	599	483	18.6	116
6011	A	Table	22	1,050	47.7	9	440	761	34.6	720
4151	A	Table	15	0	0.0	0	350	224	14.9	126
6036	A	Table	36	130	3.6	24	2,304	1,491	41.4	919
4264	AA	Chair	43	−11	−0.3	33	0	487	11.3	−531
6261	AA	Chair	883	0	0.0	0	15,500	11,781	13.3	3,719
6186	AA	Table	19	15	0.8	3	342	129	6.8	225
4197	AA	Table	22	130	5.9	26	196	121	5.5	179
3306	B	Case	6	58	9.7	51	0	10	1.7	−3
6313	B	Case	13	66	5.1	2	100	100	7.7	64
4337	B	Case	9	71	7.9	21	248	37	4.1	261
4310	B	Case	9	14	1.6	1	306	106	11.8	213
6324	B	Case	3	65	21.7	3	100	31	10.3	131
7355	B	Case	4	88	22.0	2	0	36	9.0	50
1310	B	Case	5	79	15.8	5	139	69	13.8	144
1600	B	Chair	6	76	12.7	0	0	61	10.2	15
6296	B	Chair	12	64	5.3	26	0	55	4.6	−17
1085	B	Table	2	131	65.5	0	0	22	11.0	109
6138	B	Table	2	23	11.5	0	50	23	11.5	50
4158	B	Table	10	0	0.0	0	198	113	11.3	85
4129	B	Table	3	22	7.3	0	100	17	5.7	105
1337	C	Case	1	76	76.0	0	0	8	8.0	68
7322	C	Case	3	81	27.0	0	0	32	10.7	49
6378	C	Case	1	0	0.0	0	30	3	3.0	27
7352	C	Case	2	0	0.0	0	40	11	5.5	29
1341	C	Case	2	5	2.5	1	39	12	6.0	31
6344	C	Case	2	123	61.5	0	0	25	12.5	98
1324	C	Case	1	31	31.0	1	100	13	13.0	117
6511	C	Chair	6	2	0.3	2	200	71	11.8	129
6256	C	Chair	1	79	79.0	0	399	34	34.0	444
6274	C	Chair	1	553	553.0	1	0	59	59.0	493
4270	C	Chair	4	133	33.3	0	0	60	15.0	73
4351	C	Chair	1	5	5.0	2	0	15	15.0	−12
2191	C	Table	14	0	0.0	0	250	187	13.4	63
1097	C	Table	2	90	45.0	2	0	21	10.5	67
2136	C	Table	1	16	16.0	0	49	20	20.0	45
1185	C	Table	1	61	61.0	0	0	21	21.0	40
4133	C	Table	4	3	0.8	0	54	70	17.5	−13

Exhibit 4A

Proposed Shopfloor Control Activities

Master Scheduling	*Case Plant*	*Component Plant*

Data Base Development and Maintenance

Master Scheduling	*Case Plant*	*Component Plant*
	Complete master route sheets	Complete master route sheets
	Specific routings	Specific routings
	Standards	Standards
	Attrition levels	Attrition levels
	Common set-ups	Common set-ups
	Maintain overstock data	Maintain overstock data
Determine standard cutting rotation	Determine standard assembly line-up	
	Maintain data	Maintain data

Master Scheduling and Production Planning

Master Scheduling	*Case Plant*	*Component Plant*
Receive cuttings from sales		
Develop tentative and firm daily assembly schedules	Receive proposed daily assembly schedules	
	Study line-up impact	
Produce cutting impact formats	Receive cutting impact formats	Receive cutting impact formats
	Study impact on work centers	Study impact on work centers
Negotiate changes in assembly schedule	Negotiate changes in assembly schedule	Negotiate changes in assembly schedule
	Make/buy decisions	Make/buy decisions
Input final schedule to computer for plant floor control and purchasing processing		

Plant Floor Control

Master Scheduling	*Case Plant*	*Component Plant*
	Produce and distribute route sheets and drawings	Product and distribute route sheets and drawings
	Daily work center schedules	Daily work center schedules
	Work center impact	Lumber requirements projection
	Process report-back tickets	Process report-back tickets
	Produce and distribute update production reports	Produce and distribute update production reports
	Track inter/inter plant parts' progress	Track inter/inter plant parts' progress
	Morning meeting on status of production	Morning meeting on status of production

Exhibit 4A
(*concluded*)

Master Scheduling	Case Plant	Component Plant
Track assembly readiness status Track assembled items' progress	Track assembly readiness status Track assembled items, progress	
	Produce and distribute daily management reports	Produce and distribute daily management reports
Resources Management		
	Produce and study • Labor use analysis • Equipment use analysis • Attrition variance report	Produce and study • Labor use analysis • Equipment use analysis • Attrition variance report
Residual Data Utilization		
	Produce parts' cost analysis	Produce parts' cost analysis

Summary of Reports—1

PROJECT SCOPE

Master Scheduling	*Plant Floor Control*	*Resources Management*	*Integration*
• Cutting impact analysis	• Priority scheduling • Machine loading	• Labor • Equipment • Materials	• Inventory control • Purchasing • Costing/pricing

COMMUNICATIONS FORMATS

Master Scheduling

CP-1 Assembly schedule
CP-2 Cutting impact summary
CP-3 Work center status projection
CP-4 Visanalysis—4/6 weeks.

Plant Floor Control
CP-5   Routine sheet—drawing on reverse

CP-6   Daily work center schedule
CP-7   Lumber need forecast
CP-8   Daily work center load status and forecast A–B

MF-1   Production control report-back ticket

CP-9   (Optional—computerized report-back)
CP-10   Parts progress analysis (optional)
CP-11   Report-back ticket analysis
CP-12   Daily work center off-schedule report
CP-13   Daily assembly readiness report (by exception)
CP-14   Assembly item progress control (optional)
CP-15   Daily work center status summary
CP-16   Daily management report (by exception)

CS-1   Individual parts status
CS-2   Parts off-schedule
CS-3   Parts status by case
CS-4   Work center status analysis

Resources Management
CP-17 Labor utilization—department and
      individual
   a. Weekly report
   b. History—department/individual
   c. Graph
   d. Management summary

CP-18 Work center utilization/performance
   a. Weekly report
   b. History
   c. Graph
   d. Management summary

CP-19 Materials utilization
   a. Attrition variance report
   b. Parts attrition history
   c. Management summary
Screens (on-line)
CP-20 Cost data—part/item buildup
   a. Set-up: standard/actual variance
   b. Run: standard/actual variance
   c. Materials utilization

Exhibit 4B
(*concluded*)

Production Planning
   CP-1   Assembly schedule
   CP-2   Cutting impact summary
   CP-3   Work center status projection and/or
   CP-4   Visanalysis
   CP-16 Daily management report
         Ref: CS-1   Individual parts status (on-line)
               CS-2   Parts off-schedule by case (on-line)
               CS-3   Parts status by case (on-line)
               CS-4   Work center status analysis (on-line)

Senior Management—Executive

Production Scheduling Manager
   CP-1   Assembly schedule
   CP-16 Daily management report
Case Goods Production Manager
  Production Planning:
    CP-1   Assembly schedule
    CP-2   Cutting impact summary
    CP-3   Work center status projection and/or
    CP-4   Visanalysis
  Production Management:
    CP-16 Daily management report
          Ref: CP-15   Daily work center status summary
                CP-13   Daily assembly readiness report (by exception)
                CS-2   Parts off-schedule by case (on-line)
                CS-3   Parts status by case (on-line)
                CS-4   Work Center Status Analysis (On-Line)
  Resources Management
    CP-17 Labor utilization/performance summary
    CP-18 Work center utilization/performance summary
    CP-19 Materials utilization summary (attrition variance)
    CP-20 Cost analysis (standard/actual variance)
Vice President, Manufacturing
   CP-16 Daily management report
         Ref: All other communications as needed

NOTE: CP = computer printout; MF = manual form; and CS = computer screen.

Exhibit 4C

Summary of Reports—2

PLANTS

Production Planning
  Plant manager—area managers/superintendent:
        CP-1   Assembly schedule
        CP-3   Work center status projection and/or
        CP-4   Visanalysis
Plant Floor Control
  Worker:
        CP-5   Route sheet/drawing
        CP-6   Daily work center schedule
        MR-1   Production control report-back ticket
        CP-12   Daily work center off-schedule report
  Supervisor:
        CP-6   Daily work center schedule
        CP-8   Daily work center status & forecast
        CP-12   Daily work center off-schedule report
                Ref: CP-4   Visanalysis
                       CP-15   Daily work center status analysis
  Parts processing manager (superintendant/plant manager):
        CP-15   Daily work center status summary
        CP-12   Daily work center off-schedule report
                Ref: CP-16   Daily management report
                       CP-1   Assembly schedule
                       CP-13   Daily assembly readiness report (by exception) and/or
                       CP-10   Parts progress analysis (optional)
  Plant Manager
        CP-16   Daily management report
                Ref: CP-15   Daily work center status summary
                       CP-12   Daily work center off-schedule report
                       CP-13   Daily assembly readiness report (by exception)
                       CP-1   Assembly schedule
Plants 30–15
        CP-13   Daily assembly readiness report (by exception) and/or
        CP-10   Parts progress analysis (optional)
        CP-12   Daily work center off-schedule report
        CP-11   Report-back ticket analysis
        CP-16   Daily management report
Plant 10
        CP-1   Assembly schedule
        CP-13   Daily assembly readiness report (by exception) and/or
        CP-10   Parts progress analysis
        CP-12   Daily work center off-schedule report
        CP-14   Assembly item progress

Exhibit 4C
(concluded)

Control (optional)
    CP-11   Report-back ticket analysis
    CP-16   Daily management report
Rough mill special report—Plants 30–15
    CP-7   Lumber need forecast (optional)
General reference
    Plant manager
    Area manager (superintendent)
    Supervisor
    Worker
    Production control centers:
        CS-1   Individual parts status (on-line)
        CS-2   Parts off-schedule by case (on-line)
        CS-3   Parts status by case (on-line)
        CS-4   Work center status analysis (on-line)
Resources Management
    Plant manager
    Area manager
    Foreman
    Worker
    Production control centers:
        CP-17   Labor utilization/performance
        CP-18   Work center utilization/performance
        CP-19   Materials utilization (attrition variance)
    Costing
        CP-20   Cost data/analysis (standard/actual variance)

NOTE: CP = computer printout; MF = manual form, and CS = computer screen.

CASE 26
WINKLER, A. G.

"Our marketing initiatives are designed to help us achieve our objective of increasing sales volume by 25 percent (in DM) over the next three years," remarked Kurt Schuring, marketing director at Winkler, in his strategy presentation to the firm's supervisory board. "Presently we have a major market share in the fiber container business and our objective is to increase this by 35 percent, while holding our current contribution margin of 25 percent.

"We think that we can convince several of our current customers to reduce their self-manufacture of fiber containers in order to provide for this sales growth," he continued. "We should be able to meet their business needs through three marketing initiatives: the just-in-time delivery program, new product developments, and our competitive pricing policy. Furthermore, we believe that these initiatives will enable us to gain market share from our competitors."

Marketing Strategy

Winkler is a manufacturer of packaging materials for the electronics, office products, houseware, and food industries. The company head office is in Berlin, with manufacturing operations in Hamburg and Stuttgart (see Exhibit 1.)

One product line produced by Winkler is the fiber container used for packaging snack food products. This includes nuts, potato chips, candies, and a wide variety of bakery items. The containers are produced in small, medium, large, and extra-large sizes. They come with metal ends and have attractive, multicolored printed designs on the labels to meet the specifications of customers. Nuts and potato chips represent about half of the total product purchased by consumers, and the large-size container represents about 80 percent of the total market.

A major portion of Winkler's fiber container sales are made directly to large food companies with branded products. Last year, over half of Winkler's fiber containers were sold to five processing company accounts, Basler, Reckmann, Morick, Hansert, and Niemann. Winkler is a single-source supplier to all of these firms with the exception of Basler, which produces 75 percent of its own fiber container requirements. The remaining sales are to grocery chain accounts, such as Kaufhof and Helco, and to food processors, such as Hess, who sell to the grocery chains. In this portion of the market, Winkler has just under a 50 percent share of total fiber container sales.

Fiber container production at Winkler takes place at two plants: Stuttgart and Hamburg. Actual sales for last year and forecast sales for three years hence for these two plants are shown in Exhibit 2. Four market segments are apparent in the fiber container market served by each of the plants. At Hamburg, most of the sales are made to four large customers, who place differing requirements on manufacturing. For example, Morick is highly sensitive to product quality and delivery reliability. Because of Winkler's superior past performance on these criteria, Morick has placed all of its fiber container business with the company. Information on all of the order-winning and qualifying criteria for these segments is shown in Exhibit 3.

This case was prepared by Professors W. L. Berry (Ohio State University) and J. E. Klompmaker (University of North Carolina) as a basis for class discussion rather than to illustrate either effective or ineffective handling of an administrative business situation. © Professor W. L. Berry or Professor J. E. Klompmaker. Inquiries to Zip Publishing, 1634 N. High Street, Columbus, Ohio 43201.

EXHIBIT 2   Unit Sales by Market Segment (000s)

Segment	Last Year's Actual	Forecast in Three Years
Stuttgart		
Price	137,556	171,500
Small volume	68,966	82,100
Hansert	117,000	120,000
Large volume	150,480	370,000
Hamburg		
Holstein	4,096	4,000
Hess	41,455	46,600
Eisenbeis	18,000	18,000
Morick	49,400	57,000

NOTE: Sales to Basler are part of the large-volume market at Stuttgart and last year accounted for 107,180,000 units. The forecast in 3 years is for 300 million unit sales.

Likewise, the customers served by the Stuttgart plant can be grouped into four segments based on their buying behavior. The order-winning and qualifying criteria for these segments also are shown in Exhibit 3. Summary statistics concerning the characteristics of these segments are shown in Exhibits 4 and 5. These statistics have been developed from the customer-order sample shown in Exhibits 6 and 7.

Competitors

The overall market for fiber containers is trending downward by 1 percent per year (in units) because of the increasing consumer preference for other packaging forms. Products such as packaged nuts are, however, providing some incremental growth in the market offseting some of the decline in other products. Last year the total market for fiber containers was two billion units, with Winkler gaining the largest market share. Winkler has five major competitors. These companies and their market shares are: Baumgarten (20%), Basler (20%), Kunz (5%), Niehoff (2%), and Hess (1%).

Baumgarten is a major competitor in the European packaging industry, with over 100 plants worldwide. Its principal sales are to the brewing, soft drink, food, drug, and paint industries. Although it is a financially strong company, it is believed that the firm's container development and manufacturing expertise is relatively weak.

Baumgarten recently acquired a major portion of its fiber container capacity through the purchase of Kummer. This operation competes with Winkler in selling private label brands to food processors. It is too early to tell just what Baumgarten's strategy will be in the fiber container market. It is possible that the company might (1) sell the fiber container operation to Winkler, (2) elect to stay in the fiber container market in order to broaden its product offering, or (3) invest to develop and introduce a second generation fiber container in order to gain market share.

Basler self-manufactures three quarters of its fiber containers. Its line of snack food products includes Sport Frites and a variety of other snack items. The company has no external sales of fiber containers and is believed to have little capability for fiber container development. It also has lower manufacturing speeds than Winkler. Currently, Basler purchases all of its metal ends from Winkler and uses Winkler as a second source for containers.

EXHIBIT 3   Order-Winning Criteria and Qualifiers

Hamburg Plant	Holstein Current	Holstein In Three Years	Hess Current	Hess In Three Years	Eisenbeis Current	Eisenbeis In Three Years	Morick Current	Morick In Three Years
Price	20	20	10	10	60	40/80*	10	10
Quality conformance	Q	Q	QQ	QQ	QQ	QQ/QQ	40	40
Delivery speed			90	90	40	60/20*		
Delivery reliability	Q	Q			Q	Q/Q	30	30
Technical/sales support	Q	Q					20	20
Relationships	80	80						
National distribution							Q	Q

*Major competitor (Baumgarten) leaves market/remains in market.

Stuttgart Plant Price Segment	Engel Current	Engel In Three Years	Eisenbeis Current	Eisenbeis In Three Years	Niemann Current	Niemann In Three Years
Price	98	98	100	100	100	100
Quality conformance	QQ	QQ	QQ	QQ	QQ	QQ
Delivery speed	1	1				
Relationships	1	1				

Stuttgart Plant Small-Volume Segment	Hess Current	Hess In Three Years	Grummes Current	Grummes In Three Years	Kaufhof Current	Kaufhof In Three Years
Price	50	30	50	50	50	50
Quality conformance	QQ	QQ	QQ	QQ	QQ	QQ
Delivery speed	50	70	20	20	30	30
Technical/sales support					10	10
Relationships			30	30	10	10

Stuttgart Plant Beecham's Segment	Penner Current	Penner In Three Years
Price	Q	25
Quality conformance	33	17
Delivery reliability	33	17
Technical/sales support		25
Relationships	33	15

Stuttgart Plant Large-Volume Segment	Basler Current	Basler In Three Years	Pluss Current	Pluss In Three Years
Quality conformance	QQ	QQ	QQ	QQ
Lack of internal capacity	100			
Available winkler capacity	Q			
Non-competitor in packing	Q			
Technical development		100	50	50
Relationships			50	50

**EXHIBIT 4	Summary Statistics by Market Segment: Hamburg**

	Holstein	Hess	Eisenbeis	Morick
Average invoice price (DM)	166.61	94.12	112.04	123.12
Average net price (DM)	165.24	85.72	111.33	122.19
Average price discount (DM)	1.37	8.38	.71	.93
Average production order quantity	61,576	21,020	36,130	77,144
Plant productivity (units/line hour)	22,374	18,568	19,785	25,809
Delivery lead time (days)	1.0	3.9	2.5	6.0

Hess self-manufacturers about 40 percent of the fiber containers it uses for its snack food. Its primary sales are private label brands sold to grocery chains.

Competition also comes from alternative packaging for snack foods. Plastic containers, folding cartons, and a quick-opening carton produced by Fethke all represent competitive packaging forms. The quick-opening carton currently represents about 0.3 percent of the fiber container market.

Recent Marketing Initiatives

In order to achieve the company's objective of increasing market share in fiber containers, Schuring has implemented three marketing initiatives.

Just-in-Time Delivery Program.	In response to pressures from Hess to reduce delivery time and to increase flexibility to make production schedule changes, Schuring announced the JIT delivery program to provide for a quick turnaround on customer orders. He noted, "In order to provide better service to our customers, we have agreed to produce and ship product within a 24- to 36-hour period after order receipt."

The production and quick delivery of small quantities enables food processors such as Hess to respond much more quickly to the demands of the grocery chains. Recently, Hess invested heavily in new processes to shorten their manufacturing cycle so that JIT deliveries can be made to their customers. Furthermore, Hess is a major customer in several other product lines at Winkler. As a result, Hess has requested that Winkler become a JIT supplier to them.

Customers such as Hess represent an important part of the fiber container sales volume at both the Hamburg and the Stuttgart plants (Exhibit 2). According to Schuring, "These customers represent a critical and growing part of our business. We believe that we have an opportunity to take customers such as Hess out of the self-manufacture of their fiber containers."

New Product Introductions.	"We will grow our market share in the fiber container business by means of a differentiation strategy via the implementation of new packaging innovations to meet customer requirements," Schuring emphasized. "Winkler has been a leader in the development of new products for the packaging industry over the years. Within the fiber container market segment, this has meant the development of new designs for containers and labels and the use of new materials. Developments such as plastic bottoms, quick-opening features, improved labeling, new materials for board stock, and improved graphics have enabled the company to provide distinctive packaging for its customers. It also has enabled Winkler to receive improved prices and margins.

EXHIBIT 5 **Summary Statistics by Market Segment: Stuttgart**

	Price	*Small Volume*	*Hansert*	*Large Volume*
Average invoice price (DM)	100.37	95.69	105.61	105.39
Average net price (DM)	99.74	90.54	105.36	104.11
Average price discount (DM)	.63	5.15	.25	1.30
Average production order quantity	156,681	52,240	442,499	258,610
Plant productivity (units/line hour)	22,936	15,933	27,025	24,477
Delivery lead time (days)	5.8	6.4	6.1	6.1

"We hope to convert Basler out of self-manufacturing by introducing a packaging innovation involving the use of fiber containers with paper instead of metal ends," Schuring continued. "The company currently is losing market share to Niemann, and Basler's new managing director has mandated that differentiation in the market place be achieved. New technical developments in packaging provide one possibility. This marketing initiative will require a 1,025,210 DM investment in process development to produce the paper ends. Without this investment Basler may transfer its volume to another vendor such as Baumgarten or make greater use of the quick-opening carton offered by Fethke."

Competitive Pricing. "We have pursued an aggressive pricing program for sometime now," Schuring indicated. "The fiber container segment is a mature market marked by increasing price competition. Pricing is especially critical now with Baumgarten reevaluating its business strategy in the fiber container market. The current price levels and their impact on profitability could clearly affect Baumgarten's decision to pursue this market.

"We expect manufacturing to support this marketing initiative by pursuing a low-cost manufacturing strategy," Schuring said. "This pricing sheet for a Hess order [Exhibit 5] is an example of how we develop our prices from cost data. We take into account all of the manufacturing costs, including direct material costs, pallet and packaging costs, variable manufacturing costs, and changeover costs. The productivity figure of 24,499 is used for all large size containers. We also consider customer discounts, rebates and transportation costs where they are relevant in arriving at a price that provides an acceptable margin."

Manufacturing

In order to support our customers, we have organized manufacturing on a geographic basis, locating our plants in close proximity to customers," noted Karl Bessemer, the manufacturing director for Winkler. "Stuttgart is a good example of this strategy. A major portion of the fiber containers produced at this plant are shipped to companies in southern Germany and Switzerland. As in our other plants, Stuttgart has its own sales, order entry, and customer service functions."

The Stuttgart plant is typical of the manufacturing operations at all of Winkler's fiber container plants. As shown in Exhibit 9, this plant has three processing lines designed to produce fiber containers in a particular size range. Each customer order requires a changeover since the label, paper liners, and metal ends differ. However, changeover times can be substantially reduced by running a group of orders for the same size container together. The total time to process an order can vary from as little as one hour to several shifts, depending on the quantity ordered.

EXHIBIT 6A Hamburg Customer-Order Data

Order Number	Size	Product Type	Strip Color	Liner Type	End Type	Label Type	Customer	Date Order Received	Shipping Date	Shipping Address	Freight Charge (DM) per M	Freight Paid (DM) per M
075-8816	Large	X	White	1	A	Paper	Holstein	2/19	2/20	Dortmund, Germany	4.57	4.57
074-4626	Extra-large	Y	White	2	B	Paper	Hess	n.a.	n.a.	Brandenburg, Germany	0.00	0.00
065-6659	Large	Y	White	2	B	Paper	Hess	2/4	2/6	Brandenburg, Germany	0.00	0.00
061-9520	Extra-large	Y	White	2	B	Paper	Hess	n.a.	n.a.	Brandenburg, Germany	0.00	0.00
052-3277	Extra-large	Y	White	2	B	Paper	Hess	n.a.	n.a.	Brandenburg, Germany	0.00	0.00
074-2307	Large	X	White	1	A	Paper	Hess	2/4	2/11	Brandenburg, Germany	0.00	0.00
047-4178	Extra-large	Y	White	2	B	Customer	Hess	8/14	8/17	Brandenburg, Germany	0.00	0.00
060-9942	Large	Y	White	2	B	Paper	Hess	2/19	2/22	Brandenburg, Germany	0.00	0.00
039-5824	Large	Y	White	2	B	Customer	Hess	2/2	2/8	Brandenburg, Germany	0.00	0.00
047-5569	Extra-large	Y	White	2	B	Paper	Hess	8/14	8/17	Brandenburg, Germany	0.00	0.00
053-0143	Extra-large	Y	White	2	B	Customer	Hess	n.a.	n.a.	Brandenburg, Germany	0.00	0.00
072-7169	Large	Y	White	2	B	Paper	Hess	2/12	2/20	Brandenburg, Germany	0.00	0.00
062-8930	Large	X	White	1	A	Paper	Hess	2/1	2/4	Brandenburg, Germany	0.00	0.00
056-5720	Large	Y	White	2	B	Paper	Hess	2/5	2/12	Brandenburg, Germany	0.00	0.00
062-8930	Large	X	White	3	A	Paper	Hess	8/1	8/7	Brandenburg, Germany	0.00	0.00
070-3233	Large	X	White	4	A	Foil	Eisenbeis	2/6	2/8	Potsdam, Germany	5.94	5.94
072-1268	Large	X	White	3	A	Paper	Eisenbeis	8/14	8/17	Arnhem, Netherlands	0.00	0.00
065-2902	Large	X	White	1	A	Paper	Morick	2/11	2/19	Potsdam, Germany	5.94	5.94
072-2178	Large	X	White	1	A	Paper	Morick	2/6	2/7	Potsdam, Germany	5.94	5.94
056-5793	Large	X	White	3	A	Paper	Morick	8/8	8/13	Potsdam, Germany	6.17	6.17
075-1001	Large	X	White	1	A	Paper	Morick	2/7	2/14	Potsdam, Germany	5.94	5.94
074-8169	Large	X	White	1	A	Paper	Morick	2/21	2/28	Potsdam, Germany	5.94	5.94
075-2178	Large	X	Yellow	1	A	Paper	Morick	1/30	2/5	Potsdam, Germany	5.94	5.94
075-3722	Large	X	White	1	A	Paper	Morick	1/30	2/5	Potsdam, Germany	5.94	5.94
075-5917	Large	X	White	1	A	Paper	Morick	1/30	2/6	Potsdam, Germany	5.94	5.94
062-9047	Large	X	White	3	A	Paper	Morick	8/8	8/13	Potsdam, Germany	6.17	6.17
075-3802	Large	X	White	1	A	Paper	Morick	2/21	2/27	Potsdam, Germany	5.94	5.94
056-5793	Large	X	White	3	A	Paper	Morick	8/1	8/7	Potsdam, Germany	6.17	6.17
056-5793	Extra-large	X	White	1	A	Paper	Morick	2/12	2/21	Potsdam, Germany	5.94	5.94
072-2178	Large	X	Yellow	1	A	Paper	Morick	2/26	3/1	Potsdam, Germany	5.94	5.94
074-8169	Large	X	White	1	A	Paper	Morick	2/6	2/14	Potsdam, Germany	5.94	5.94

EXHIBIT 6B   Hamburg Customer-Order Data

Order Number	Customer	Machine Number	Setup Type	Good Production Quantity	Scrap Percentage	Total Time per Order	Total Variable COST per M	List Price per M	Net Price per M	Contribution per Order	Contribution per Line Hour	Rebates per M	Discounts per M
075-8816	Holstein	2	B	61,576	4.59%	2.75	96.08	166.61	165.24	4,564	1,658	0.00	1.37
074-4626	Hess	3	A	1,790	9.50	0.13	76.21	126.67	118.69	86	691	7.85	0.13
065-6659	Hess	2	A	2,864	4.75	0.20	56.66	88.00	80.09	72	366	7.85	0.06
061-9520	Hess	3	A	4,296	4.91	0.29	64.67	126.67	118.75	253	859	7.85	0.06
052-3277	Hess	3	B	5,012	60.81	0.34	81.28	135.02	127.03	551	1,614	7.85	0.14
074-2307	Hess	2	A	8,950	8.38	0.59	75.45	105.08	94.48	201	342	10.52	0.08
047-4178	Hess	3	B	10,740	9.45	0.69	45.81	92.46	82.93	462	666	9.42	0.11
060-9942	Hess	2	A	14,320	7.19	0.90	52.61	88.31	80.32	444	495	7.85	0.14
039-5824	Hess	4	B	18,258	20.76	1.11	38.51	79.87	70.27	776	700	9.42	0.17
047-5569	Hess	3	B	21,122	8.89	1.25	76.05	92.32	84.37	298	239	7.85	0.09
053-0143	Hess	3	A	26,492	9.50	1.50	49.09	92.46	82.96	1,033	686	9.42	0.08
072-7169	Hess	2	A	32,936	7.21	1.78	59.24	71.39	63.32	188	107	7.85	0.22
062-8930	Hess	2	A	38,306	4.42	1.99	62.50	99.93	91.70	1,203	603	7.85	0.38
056-5720	Hess	2	A	45,824	1.89	2.26	55.75	89.57	81.61	1,220	539	7.85	0.11
062-8930	Hess	2	A	63,366	2.58	2.80	59.05	105.08	97.09	2,539	906	7.85	0.14
070-3233	Eisenbeis	2	A	18,975	5.40	1.14	93.84	136.01	136.01	867	757	0.00	0.42
072-1268	Eisenbeis	2	B	53,284	1.93	2.51	70.98	103.49	102.69	1,757	700	0.00	0.80
065-2902	Morick	2	A	11,456	9.51	0.74	75.44	123.67	122.68	630	856	0.00	0.99
072-2178	Morick	2	A	17,184	31.77	1.05	74.14	124.19	123.20	1,319	1,254	0.00	0.99
056-5793	Morick	2	A	25,712	1.12	1.47	73.62	123.45	123.14	1,291	878	0.00	0.31
075-1001	Morick	2	A	45,466	16.83	2.25	75.52	123.67	122.68	2,785	1,236	0.00	0.99
074-8169	Morick	2	A	57,280	7.19	2.63	75.99	123.67	122.70	3,000	1,141	0.00	0.97
075-2178	Morick	2	A	68,373	3.33	2.93	75.88	124.19	123.21	3,396	1,157	0.00	0.97
075-3722	Morick	2	A	74,464	7.21	3.09	73.48	123.21	122.27	4,066	1,317	0.00	0.94
075-5917	Morick	2	A	81,266	18.87	3.24	75.38	123.21	122.24	5,092	1,570	0.00	0.97
062-9047	Morick	4	A	95,586	2.67	3.54	79.19	118.35	117.73	3,895	1,101	0.00	0.61
075-3802	Morick	2	A	97,376	10.85	3.57	76.57	123.21	122.29	5,300	1,484	0.00	0.93
056-5793	Morick	2	A	103,462	4.89	3.69	70.85	123.45	122.48	5,839	1,584	0.00	0.97
056-5793	Morick	2	A	107,400	0.84	3.75	85.58	123.21	122.22	3,945	1,050	0.00	0.99
072-2178	Morick	2	A	114,560	3.69	3.87	74.84	124.19	123.20	5,848	1,510	0.00	0.99
074-8169	Morick	2	A	180,432	0.96	6.01	76.05	122.70	122.70	8,465	1,407	0.00	0.97

EXHIBIT 7A Stuttgart Customer-Order Data

Market Segment	Order Number	Size	Product Type	Strip Color	Liner Type	End Type	Label Type	Customer	Date Order Received	Actual Shipping Data	Shipping Address	Freight Charge per M	Freight Paid per M
1	073-2327	Large	X	Plain	5	C	Paper	Niemann	8/8	8/8	Rottweil, Germany	4.00	3.52
1	163131	Large	Y	Plain	2	B	Paper	Engel	2/13	2/15	St. Gallen, Switzerland	0.00	0.00
1	074-0559	Large	X	Plain	5	C	Paper	Engel	7/26	8/30	St. Gallen, Switzerland	0.00	0.00
1	074-0568	Large	Y	Plain	2	B	Paper	Engel	8/22	8/24	St. Gallen, Switzerland	0.00	0.00
1	62724	Large	X	Plain	5	C	Paper	Engel	2/6	2/8	St. Gallen, Switzerland	0.00	0.00
1	066227	Large	Y	Plain	2	B	Paper	Engel	2/24	2/28	Basel, Switzerland	0.80	0.46
1	071-3320	Large	X	Plain	5	C	Paper	Eisenbeis	8/20	8/23	Bern, Switzerland	0.00	0.00
1	15124	Large	Y	Plain	2	B	Paper	Engel	2/6	2/8	St. Gallen, Switzerland	0.00	0.00
1	066213	Large	Y	Plain	2	B	Paper	Engel	2/20	2/22	Grummes, Switzerland	9.56	9.00
2	129219	Small	Y	Plain	2	B	Paper	Kaufhof	2/18	2/25	Regensburg, Germany	0.93	0.61
2	071-4481	Large	X	Plain	5	C	Paper	Telemann	8/17	8/24	Bamberg, Germany	1.60	4.18
2	WAYNE4	Large	X	Plain	5	C	Paper	Telemann	2/5	2/12	Bamberg, Germany	1.85	4.32
2	184214	Large	Y	Plain	2	B	Paper	Wimleitner	2/11	2/18	Munich, Germany	1.71	1.21
2	061-4963	Large	X	Plain	5	C	Paper	Telemann	8/17	8/24	Bamberg, Germany	1.60	4.18
2	412219	Large	X	Plain	5	C	Paper	Kaufhof	2/18	2/25	Regensburg, Germany	1.71	1.21
2	611219	Large	X	Plain	5	C	Paper	Kaufhof	2/13	2/20	Regensburg, Germany	1.71	1.21
2	058-2337	Large	X	Plain	5	C	Paper	Baumgarten	8/7	8/14	Regensburg, Germany	1.63	1.16
2	066-7102	Large	X	Plain	5	C	Paper	Kaufhof	8/14	8/14	Regensburg, Germany	1.63	1.16
2	074-8935	Large	X	Plain	5	C	Paper	Akli	8/20	8/27	Karlsruhe, Germany	1.98	1.88
2	071-2492	Large	X	Plain	5	C	Paper	Kaufhof	8/4	8/6	Regensburg, Germany	1.63	1.16
2	072-6628	Small	Y	None	2	D	Paper	Hess	8/10	8/17	Brandenburg, Germany	5.18	0.00
2	075-1010	Large	Y	Plain	2	B	Paper	Gummes	8/17	8/24	St. Gallen, Switzerland	0.00	0.00
2	074-5171	Large	Y	Plain	2	E	Paper	Karstadt	8/1	8/8	Wiesbaden, Germany	1.63	1.16
2	068-6341	Large	Y	None	2	F	Paper	Kaufhof	8/14	8/21	Regensburg, Germany	1.63	1.16

2	069-1905	Large	Y	Plain	2	E	Paper	Telemann	8/14	8/23	Bamberg, Germany	1.60	4.18
3	13224	Large	X	Plain	5	C	Paper	Hertie	1/29	2/5	Hertie, Austria	1.81	0.46
3	641227	Large	X	Plain	5	C	Paper	Penner	2/21	2/28	Zurich, Switzerland	2.51	2.17
3	645227	Large	X	266	5	C	Paper	Penner	2/21	2/28	Zurich, Switzerland	2.51	2.17
3	646227	Large	X	375	5	C	Paper	Penner	2/21	2/28	Zurich, Switzerland	2.51	2.17
3	644227	Large	X	485c	5	C	Paper	Penner	2/21	2/28	Zurich, Switzerland	2.51	2.17
3	074-8034	Large	X	Plain	5	B	Paper	Penner	8/17	8/20	Zurich, Switzerland	2.40	2.09
3	067-9590	Extra-large	Y	16	2	B	Paper	Basler	7/25	8/1	Worms, Germany	2.21	1.81
3	14225	Large	Y	Plain	2	C	Paper	Penner	1/31	2/6	Zurich, Switzerland	2.51	2.17
3	074-8034	Large	X	Plain	5	B	Paper	Penner	8/3	8/7	Zurich, Switzerland	2.40	2.09
3	23728	Large	Y	165c	2	B	Paper	Penner	2/7	2/12	Zurich, Switzerland	2.51	2.17
3	05427	Large	Y	135c	2	B	Paper	Penner	2/7	2/12	Zurich, Switzerland	2.51	2.17
3	074-3627	Large	Y	135c	2	B	Paper	Penner	8/2	8/10	Zurich, Switzerland	2.40	2.09
3	070-8764	Large	X	Plain	5	C	Paper	Hansert	8/9	8/15	Zurich, Switzerland	2.40	1.52
3	481215	Large	Y	Plain	2	B	Paper	Penner	2/14	2/22	Zurich, Switzerland	2.51	0.25
3	088221	Large	X	Plain	5	C	Paper	Werner	2/20	2/25	Achen, Germany	0.00	1.44
4	386213	Medium	Y	Plain	2	B	Paper	Basler	2/18	2/25	Worms, Germany	1.88	1.30
4	341213	Medium	X	Plain	5	C	Paper	Besler	2/18	2/25	Worms, Germany	1.88	1.30
4	15726	Small	Y	Plain	2	G	Paper	Basler	2/4	2/11	Worms, Germany	1.02	0.74
4	060-2002	Medium	Y	Plain	2	B	Paper	Basler	8/9	8/16	Mannheim, Germany	0.89	1.13
4	651213	Small	Y	6	2	G	Paper	Basler	8/9	8/16	Mannheim, Germany	0.89	0.64
4	074-2959	Large	Y	Plain	3	B	Paper	Werner	8/8	8/13	Achen, Germany	0.00	1.40
4	474226	Large	X	None	5	H	Paper	Basler	2/20	2/27	Worms, Germany	1.88	1.44
4	639130	Medium	Y	10	2	B	Paper	Basler	2/5	2/12	Worms, Germany	1.88	1.30
4	336213	Large	Y	Plain	3	B	Paper	Werner	2/13	2/19	Achen, Germany	0.00	1.44
4	44728	Large	Y	Plain	3	B	Paper	Werner	2/7	2/11	Achen, Germany	0.00	1.44
4	341131	Medium	X	Plain	5	C	Paper	Basler	1/28	2/4	Worms, Germany	1.88	1.30
4	060-7301	Medium	X	Plain	5	C	Paper	Basler	8/17	8/20	Worms, Germany	1.81	1.40
4	053-3756	Extra-large	X	P16	5	C	Paper	Basler	7/25	8/2	Worms, Germany	2.21	1.81
4	053-7075	Medium	Y	J10	2	B	Paper	Basler	8/9	8/16	Mannheim, Germany	1.63	1.13

EXHIBIT 7B   Stuttgart Customer Order Data

Market Segment	Order Number	Machine Number	Good Production Quantity	Scrap Percentage	Total Time Order	Total Variable Cost per M	Gross Price per M	Net Price per M	Contribution per order	Contribution per line hour	Rebates per M	Discounts per M
1	073-2327	2	40,812	2.42%	2.67	74.79	100.81	100.54	1,111	416	0.00	0.00
1	163131	1	74,822	1.52	3.92	68.26	93.45	93.45	1,947	497	0.00	0.74
1	074-0559	2	77,328	0.93	3.92	75.33	102.99	102.16	2,113	539	0.00	0.83
1	074-0568	2	115,992	0.70	5.12	64.59	92.94	92.21	3,242	633	0.00	0.74
1	62724	2	147,048	1.40	6.92	77.23	108.86	108.86	4,787	692	0.00	0.88
1	066227	2	153,045	0.73	6.42	64.84	96.21	95.80	4,798	747	0.00	0.75
1	071-3320	1	179,770	1.15	7.87	86.74	109.05	108.16	3,955	503	0.00	0.89
1	15124	2	235,384	0.69	8.72	64.43	92.43	91.70	6,496	745	0.00	0.72
1	066213	1	385,924	0.47	15.92	64.75	104.97	104.78	15,545	976	0.00	0.75
2	129219	3	6,303	54.21	1.68	80.81	76.93	74.14	42	25	2.36	0.75
2	071-4481	1	12,172	10.25	1.83	93.21	109.92	102.33	150	82	3.93	1.08
2	WAYNE4	2	12,536	10.88	1.86	98.77	125.58	117.56	292	157	4.32	1.24
2	184214	1	15,931	1.63	1.92	64.67	88.67	85.69	344	179	2.62	0.86
2	061-4963	1	18,884	0.93	2.02	87.48	112.87	105.25	340	168	3.93	1.11
2	412219	2	25,239	1.83	2.33	69.58	99.27	95.66	678	291	3.14	0.97
2	611219	2	25,418	0.13	2.33	80.67	113.95	110.20	749	321	3.14	1.11
2	058-2337	2	25,776	2.11	2.22	65.99	90.34	87.24	569	256	2.67	0.89
2	066-7102	2	25,776	2.15	2.27	81.07	107.15	103.43	598	264	3.14	1.05
2	074-8935	1	28,640	1.36	2.42	47.45	98.71	95.20	1,395	575	2.62	0.97
2	071-2492	2	51,552	2.17	3.17	76.79	96.41	92.80	862	272	3.14	0.94
2	072-6628	3	56,154	8.92	4.61	50.43	88.19	74.23	1,524	345	7.85	0.93
2	075-1010	1	87,710	3.36	4.42	50.16	72.93	69.54	1,809	409	2.67	0.72
2	074-5171	2	115,992	1.58	5.42	55.20	83.32	79.44	2,883	532	3.53	0.82
2	068-6341	1	144,274	3.44	6.79	51.64	80.45	76.99	3,876	571	3.14	0.79
2	069-1905	1	183,475	0.96	7.17	55.01	86.37	79.02	4,463	622	3.93	0.85

3	13224	2	22,106	2.96	2.17	72.74	94.61	95.03	520	240	0.00	0.93
3	641227	1	47,614	1.13	3.17	85.72	115.32	1143.75	1,414	446	0.00	0.91
3	645227	1	94,333	0.50	4.17	86.98	123.21	122.57	3,381	811	0.00	0.99
3	646227	1	94,512	0.40	4.42	87.29	123.06	122.41	3,335	754	0.00	0.99
3	644227	2	95,228	2.28	4.67	83.01	111.66	111.12	2,815	603	0.00	0.88
3	074-8034	1	133,534	2.17	6.82	72.25	101.69	101.23	4,054	594	0.00	0.77
3	067-9590	1	176,762	1.11	9.37	80.90	117.42	116.86	6,479	691	0.00	0.97
3	14225	2	212,652	0.34	7.92	69.54	100.13	99.71	6,441	813	0.00	0.00
3	074-8034	1 & 2	272,438	1.01	10.92	71.03	101.69	101.22	8,383	768	0.00	0.79
3	23728	1	346,544	1.03	13.17	74.56	100.18	99.76	8,915	677	0.00	0.77
3	05427	2	367,286	1.23	13.17	66.44	96.04	95.66	10,990	834	0.00	0.72
3	074-3627	1 & 2	896,790	1.14	31.72	63.32	93.60	93.21	27,386	863	0.00	0.71
3	070-8764	1	1,525,080	1.61	50.12	73.07	103.70	103.79	48,396	966	0.00	0.79
3	481215	1	1,910,109	0.53	67.42	65.91	96.19	97.72	61,231	908	0.00	0.74
4	088221	2	9,666	5.52	1.73	93.24	111.82	107.76	169	98	1.73	0.88
4	386213	2	10,382	6.92	2.17	90.21	108.13	107.84	221	102	0.00	0.86
4	341213	3	17,810	1.61	2.08	84.21	112.47	112.16	515	248	0.00	0.89
4	15726	2	33,807	1.59	2.38	58.03	89.85	89.44	1,092	459	0.00	0.69
4	060-2002	1	53,700	0.34	3.95	68.37	77.24	76.43	434	110	0.00	0.58
4	651213	1	79,476	0.75	3.82	82.25	108.02	108.82	2,141	561	0.00	0.82
4	074-2959	1	111,412	0.91	4.92	71.48	106.04	102.08	3,496	711	1.73	0.83
4	474226	2	126,356	5.08	6.81	84.03	98.27	97.81	2,064	303	0.00	0.89
4	639130	2	219,454	0.95	8.28	61.64	104.58	104.33	9,507	1,148	0.00	0.83
4	336213	1 & 2	247,378	1.56	9.17	72.24	110.28	106.24	8,538	931	1.73	0.86
4	44728	2	259,013	2.99	11.67	74.51	110.28	106.24	8,728	748	1.73	0.86
4	341131	1	293,202	1.03	10.60	74.15	111.00	110.70	10,908	1,029	0.00	0.88
4	060-7301	2	490,460	1.84	17.58	67.54	101.78	101.39	17,196	978	0.00	0.80
4	053-3756	1	543,444	1.49	23.72	93.26	136.65	135.91	23,779	1,002	0.00	1.15
4	053-7075	2	1,382,596	6.46	49.60	61.14	94.58	94.33	51,868	1,046	0.00	0.75

Exhibit 8

Winkler Product Cost

Manufacturing Location: Hamburg
Design Bill 111-212
Product Number 4005
Cab Description: Hess Large size-X type Container

Element	Standard Units/M	Scrap Factor	Total Units/M		Cost/M Containers/Ends	
Liner	.3020	.0450	.3155	MSF	7.58	
Board-1st ply	.3060	.0450	.3218	MSF	6.47	
Label	1.000	.0380	1.038	M	17.63	
Adhesive	3.2000	.0450	3.344	LB	1.52	
Seamed end	1.0000	.0110	1.011	M	20.41	
Seamed end frt	1.0000	.0110	1.011	M	.67	
Pull tab tape	1.2270	.0200	1.2515	LB	1.43	
Hot melt	.1660	.0200	.1693	LB	.41	
					56.25	Total material

Element	Container/Ends Ctn/Bag/Plt	Cost per Ct/Bg/Plt	Cost Incr.	Scrap Factor/M	Cost/M Containers/Ends	
Short pallets	3,240	.0000	.0000	.0000	1.51	
					1.51	Total shipping

Element	Var. Cost /Mach. Hr.	Cost Incr.	Thed. CPH	Eff. Fact.	Net CPH	Cost/M Containers	
Container Line	246.54	.0000	27,000	.9074	24,499	10.06	Hamburg: Large size

Element	Cost C.O. Hr.	Cost Incr.	Run Size(M)	Hours/ C.O	Cost/M Containers	
Changeover	.0000	.0000	370	5.40	.63	
					10.69	Total converting
					68.31	Total container costs

Sales Price
  Containers: 101.28 DM
  End: .02
  Other: .00
Gross Sales: 101.30
Sales discount (1%) 1.02
Frt - Bill to cust.: .00
  Pay to carrier: .00
Freight Absorbed: .00
Other deductions: 11.20 average rebate
Net sales: 89.08 DM/M
Total variable cost: 68.30/M
Contribution: 20.78M
Contribution: 23.32%

Exhibit 9   Stuttgart Plant Layout

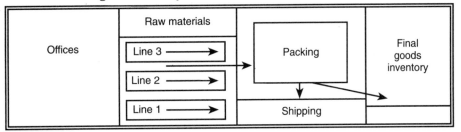

NOTES: Line 1 runs large and extra-large containers. Line 2 runs medium and large containers. Line 3 runs small and large containers.

Each line performs several operations. The labels and paper liner materials are received separately on large reels. The first operation involves unwinding these materials and merging them into a continuous ribbon from which individual containers are cut. Next, this continuous ribbon is wound in a spiral fashion around a long cylindrical mandrel to form a continuous tube of material at high speed. In the third step, a single pass of the gang saw cuts the tube into 12 individual containers, which are then transported by conveyor to the fourth operation where a metal end is sealed on one end of the container. Finally, the containers are transported by conveyor to the packing area where they are mechanically packed at high speed into pallet-sized boxes for either direct shipment or storage.

Because of the size of the pallet boxes and the wide variation in label design, there is very little finished goods inventory. As a result the lines are scheduled on a make-to-order basis. Some label and paper liner material is, however, carried in inventory since the suppliers encourage large orders through a pricing policy that provides substantial discounts for large orders.

The metal ends are produced in Bonn and supplied to both the Hamburg and Stuttgart plants. The production of metal ends involves adding a protective coating on the steel strip on a continuous production basis and stamping the metal ends from coils of steel strip on a high-speed press. As there are several sizes and types of metal ends, some inventory is carried by the company for these items also.

Recent Manufacturing Initiatives

Investments in fiber container manufacturing at Winkler primarily have been to support the low-cost manufacturing objective. Most of the cost reduction initiatives have been concerned with reducing downtime, increasing productivity and efficiency, increasing line speeds, and reducing overhead and operating costs (direct labor and material). Examples of these investments for the Stuttgart and Hamburg plants are shown in Exhibits 10 and 11.

Stuttgart.   Rebuilding the sealing and cutting chambers on the container-making lines at Stuttgart resulted in a 33 percent increase in line speed. Another project involved replacing the two stage stamping presses with single stage presses in the metal-end plant. This resulted in doubling output (in terms of containers per hour), but also increased the setup time from 3 to 12 hours.

Two other projects were undertaken to reduce customer-order lead time. One involved instilling the necessary parts on lines two and three to increase their flexibility, permitting a

EXHIBIT 10 Recent Manufacturing Initiatives: Stuttgart

	Low-Cost Manufacturing				Delivery Speed				
	Reduced Down-time	Increased Productivity and Efficiency	Increased Line Speed and Output	Reduced Overhead and Operating Cost	Reduced Setup Time	Reduced Inventory and Customer Lead Time	Increased Product Range	Improved Employee Skills	Improved Quality
Containers									
Rebuilt sealing and cutting chamber		****							
Installed new palletizer and shrink wrap			****	****					
Installed the required parts to run medium size on line 2							****		
Installed the required parts to run large size on line 3 with small size							****		
Installed on line data collection system									****
Implemented TQS training and QIT teams				****				****	****
Metal ends									
Replaced two stage presses with single stage presses (increased setup time)			****	****					
Increased compounding capacity on 200 multi stage die			****						
Installed computer-based maintenance program				****					

EXHIBIT 11 Recent Manufacturing Initiatives: Hamburg

	Low-Cost Manufacturing				Delivery Speed			
	Reduced Downtime	Increased Productivity and Efficiency	Increased Line Speed and Output	Reduced Overhead and Operating Cost	Reduced Setup Time	Reduced Inventory and Customer Lead Time	Improved Employee Skills	Improved Quality
Process consolidation (dropped two CPC lines)	****	****		****				
GKN unit installed on line 4	****	****						
Conversion of 100 line (4) to 200 line. Moved small size to Stuttgart. Dedicated line 4 to large size. Eliminated last CPC line	****		****	****	****			
Packing system upgraded	****		****					
New maintenance software installed	****							
New controllers installed	****		****	****				
Process control data monitoring system installed				****				****
Bar coding system installed						****		
Sealer unit rebuilt	****							
Winding roll converted to positive discharge	****							****
Operator/staff training program							****	

EXHIBIT 12   Hamburg Plant Layout

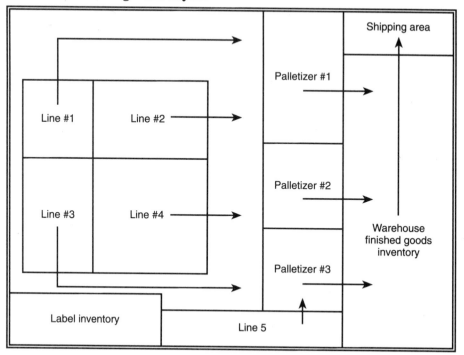

NOTE: Lines 1, 3, and 5 run all sizes of fiber containers. Lines 2 and 4 run only large-sized containers.

broader range of product sizes to be run. The other was the creation of quality improvement teams trained at Stuttgart to improve product yields and reduce scrap.

Hamburg.   Recently, line four at Hamburg (see Exhibit 12) was upgraded by converting the line from a 100 design to a 200 design. This increased the output by 20 percent (in terms of containers per hour), provided a major reduction in process downtime, and a significant improvement in efficiency. In addition, this line and line two were dedicated to the production of large-size containers, thereby eliminating much of the cost associated with changing from one size container to another. The impact of this project on changeover time is shown in the analysis presented in Exhibit 13.

Proposed Process Investments.   "We have a number of process improvement projects in which we could invest," Bessemer noted (see Exhibit 14). "However, given our capital budget and staff limitations in engineering and manufacturing because of our emphasis on maintaining low overhead costs, we need to choose our projects carefully. As we have discussed the firm's marketing strategy in our recent supervisory board meeting, we will be discussing our manufacturing strategy at the next board meeting; and I need to prepare process investment recommendations."

EXHIBIT 13   Changeover Time Analysis

Market Segments	Average Total Time per Order	Average Changeover Time per Order	Percent Changeover Time to Total Time per Order
Stuttgart Plant			
Large volume	10.6	.86	8.1%
Hansert	16.4	.68	4.1
Small volume	3.3	.73	22.1
Price	6.8	.65	9.6
Hamburg plant			
Holstein	2.8	.14	5.0%
Hess	1.1	.06	5.5
Eisenbeis	1.8	.07	3.9
Morick	3.0	.17	5.7

NOTE: Time measured in hours.

Concluding Remarks

In reviewing the firm's marketing initiatives Schuring presented at the recent board meeting, the managing director, Jurgen Schmidt, commented, "It is critical that we pursue the JIT delivery program. When one considers our entire business, Hess is a major customer that is very important to us. Furthermore, many companies have recognized the importance of supporting a JIT delivery program for their customers. Clearly, numerous firms are moving to time-based competition. It is important that we take the lead on this initiative as this could be very important in achieving our sales and profit objectives."

EXHIBIT 14 Proposed Process Improvement Projects

Project	Productivity Improvement			Setup Time Reduction			Improved Quality	Cost Reduction
	Small Runs	Large Containers	Run Time	Height Change	Angle Change	Label Changeover		
Modified tension device	****							
New plant gauging method	****							
A.D.M. labeling method	****							
Conco palletizer		****				****		****
Modified saw design			****					
Matching winder type to product type			****				****	
Self-cleaning cutting blade			****				****	
Hardened cutting mandrels			****				****	
Improved trimmers and adhesive coaters			****					
Equipment modifications for faster changeovers				****				
Automatic adjustments				****				
KGM winder improvements				****				
Motorized knife holder				****				
Computer controlled mandrel adjustments					****			
Process control								
Container cleaning work							****	****
Materials Improvements							****	****

Index